Women's Rights in the United States

Women's Rights in the United States

A COMPREHENSIVE ENCYCLOPEDIA
OF ISSUES, EVENTS, AND PEOPLE

Volume 1: Moral Reform and the Woman Question (1776–1870)

Tiffany K. Wayne, Editor
Lois Banner, Advising Editor

ABC-CLIO

Santa Barbara, California • Denver, Colorado • Oxford, England

Library of Congress Cataloging-in-Publication Data

Women's rights in the United States : a comprehensive encyclopedia of issues, events, and people / Tiffany K. Wayne, editor, Lois Banner, advising editor
volumes cm
Includes bibliographical references and index.
ISBN 978-1-61069-214-4 (hardback : alk. paper : 4 vol. set) — ISBN 978-1-61069-215-1 (ebook)
1. Women's rights—United States—History—Encyclopedias.   2. Feminism—United States—History—Encyclopedias.   I. Wayne, Tiffany K., 1968–   II. Banner, Lois W.
HQ1236.5.U6W677   2015
323.3'40973—dc23   2014006603

ISBN: 978-1-61069-214-4
EISBN: 978-1-61069-215-1

19 18 17 16 15   1 2 3 4 5

This book is also available on the World Wide Web as an eBook.
Visit www.abc-clio.com for details.

ABC-CLIO, LLC
130 Cremona Drive, P.O. Box 1911
Santa Barbara, California 93116-1911

This book is printed on acid-free paper ∞

Manufactured in the United States of America

Contents

List of Entries

List of Primary Documents

List of Entries by Topic

People

Adams, Abigail (1744–1818)

Alcott, Louisa May (1832–1888)

Anneke, Mathilde Franziska (1817–1884)

Bagley, Sarah (1806–1883?)

Barton, Clara (1821–1912)

Beecher, Catharine (1800–1878)

Blackwell, Elizabeth (1821–1910)

Bloomer, Amelia Jenks (1818–1894)

Cary, Mary Ann Shadd (1823–1893)

Child, Lydia Maria (1802–1880)

Dall, Caroline Healey (1822–1912)

Davis, Paulina Kellogg Wright (1813–1876)

Dix, Dorothea (1802–1887)

Douglass, Frederick (1818–1895)

Edmonds, Sarah Emma (1841–1898)

Evans, Augusta Jane (1835–1909)

Farnham, Eliza (1815–1864)

Fern, Fanny [Sarah Payson Willis] (1811–1872)

Foote, Julia A.J. (1823–1900)

Foster, Abby Kelley (1810–1887)

Fuller, Margaret (1810–1850)

Garrison, William Lloyd (1805–1879)

Gibbons, Abigail Hopper (1801–1893)

Griffing, Josephine White (1814–1872)

Grimké, Charlotte L. Forten (1837–1914)

Grimké, Sarah Moore (1792–1873)

Grimké Weld, Angelina (1805–1879)

Hale, Sarah Josepha (1788–1879)

Hasbrouck, Lydia Sayer (1827–1910)

Higginson, Thomas Wentworth (1823–1911)

Howe, Julia Ward (1819–1910)

Jacobs, Harriet (1813–1897)

Kemble, Fanny (1809–1893)

Lee, "Mother" Ann (1736–1784)

Lee, Jarena (1783–?)

Livermore, Mary (1820–1905)

Martineau, Harriet (1802–1876)

May, Abigail Williams (1829–1888)

May, Samuel Joseph (1797–1871)

Meriwether, Elizabeth Avery (1824–1916)

Mitchell, Maria (1818–1889)

Mott, Lucretia (1793–1880)

Mullaney, Kate (1845–1906)

Murray, Judith Sargent (1751–1820)

Nichols, Clarina Howard (1810–1885)

Nichols, Mary Gove (1810–1884)

Peabody, Elizabeth (1804–1894)

Phillips, Wendell (1811–1884)

Pillsbury, Parker (1809–1898)

Pleasant, Mary Ellen (1814–1904)

Remond, Sarah Parker (1826–1894)

Restell, Madame [Anna Trow Lohman] (1812–1878)

Ropes, Hannah (1809–1863)

Rose, Ernestine (1810–1892)

Sampson, Deborah (1760–1827)

Schuyler, Louisa Lee (1837–1926)

Seton, Elizabeth (1774–1821)

Smith, Gerrit (1797–1874)

Southworth, E.D.E.N. (1819–1899)

Stewart, Maria W. (1803–1879)

Stone, Lucy (1818–1893)

Stowe, Harriet Beecher (1811–1896)

Swisshelm, Jane Grey (1815–1884)

Taylor, Susie Baker King (1848–1912)

Tilton, Theodore (1835–1907)

Towne, Laura Matilda (1825–1901)

Truth, Sojourner (1797–1883)

Tubman, Harriet (1822–1913)

Van Lew, Elizabeth (1818–1900)

Publications

Preface to Volumes 1–4

The history of women's issues and women's rights is essential to any understanding of the social and political history of the United States. The struggle for gender and sexual equality intersects with other civil rights and social movements throughout U.S. history and provides historical context for many current and ongoing debates and issues, such as reproductive freedom, political participation, pay equity, family welfare, violence against women, and LGBTQ civil rights.

Women's Rights in the United States: A Comprehensive Encyclopedia of Issues, Events, and People places these struggles within a broader and deeper historical context by looking at a range of activists, events, and organizations working on issues of inclusion, opportunity, and equality over a longer period of time. The encyclopedia also places women's rights movements alongside other related historical movements such as civil rights movements for racial equality, labor movements, and the gay and lesbian rights movements.

The four volumes of *Women's Rights in the United States* are organized according to broad chronological eras that cover the scope of U.S. history. Although there is some overlap and conversation between and across the volumes, the chronological divisions correspond to periods that are particularly relevant to understanding the key issues and themes of the women's rights struggle:

Volume 1: Moral Reform and the Woman Question (1776–1870)

Volume 2: Suffrage and a New Wave of Women's Activism (1870–1950)

Volume 3: Civil Rights and Modern Feminism (1950–1990)

Volume 4: Third-Wave and Global Feminisms (1990–Present)

Each volume includes materials that are relevant for students and researchers in the social and political sciences at both the high school and college levels, as well as general readers interested in women's history in the United States. In Volume 1 readers will discover how 19th-century women's rights arguments emerged out of the antislavery movement. Volume 2 reveals that, in the early 20th century, winning the vote was not the end of the women's movement for many suffrage activists who continued to debate women's roles in politics and who were active in the peace and labor movements. In Volume 3 the African American Civil Rights movement of the 1950s and 1960s inspired a new generation of women's liberation activists and a 1965 U.S. Supreme Court case allowing married persons to use contraception (*Griswold v. Connecticut*) established a right to privacy that paved the way to the court's decision regarding abortion in *Roe v. Wade* just a few years later. Volume 4 moves into the 21st century and reveals the current and ongoing issues related to women's civil and political equality, feminism and images of women in contemporary media and culture, reproductive rights, and LGBTQ issues.

About This Book

More than 300 scholars, teachers, and professional writers contributed to *Women's Rights in the United States: A Comprehensive Encyclopedia of Issues, Events, and People*. Each volume includes alphabetically arranged biographical and topical entries, including individuals who worked for (and sometimes against) women's rights, or who made important contributions to issues crucial to gender equality; significant events and organizations; publications, films, and other mass media by, for, and about women; and legislation and court cases relevant to the cause of women's rights.

The combined volumes include 650 entries with See Also cross-references to other entries and primary documents within and across volumes. Most entries include references for Further Reading, including books, articles, websites, and videos. Each volume provides a chronologically arranged collection of Primary Documents, many not easily available in other sources, including longer excerpts for more thorough reading and research. Each primary source document is prefaced with a short introduction explaining the relevance and historical context of the document. There are a total of 127 primary documents in this work.

Other special features include a detailed Chronology of women's rights issues and milestones, located in Volume 1. Each volume includes an Index to the entire set, and a General Bibliography for further research is found in Volume 4. Finally, a list of the 305 contributors and their affiliations is found at the end of Volume 4.

Acknowledgments

The first round of thanks goes to the contributors for sharing their knowledge and commitment to recording women's history. I am grateful for the connections and friendships I have made in working on a project of this scope in the company of so many fine scholars and writers. Special thanks to my good friends and colleagues Lee Ritscher and Emily Moberg Robinson for help with editing, formatting, and researching the bibliographies.

I would like to thank the editors at ABC-CLIO who entrusted me with this project, especially Kim Kennedy White, who helped me develop the format and scope and locate early sources. The editorial and content expertise of Stephen Gutierrez and Anne Thompson saved me many hours and many errors. Thanks to Anne, in particular, for patiently seeing me through the neverending details in shaping the individual entries and bringing the project to completion. I have worked with both Kim and Anne on several projects now and it is an honor to work with publishing professionals who are committed to producing high-quality materials.

Thanks are also due to Advising Editor Lois Banner, professor emerita of history and gender studies at the University of Southern California, for her early advice on the scope and coverage for *Women's Rights in the United States: A Comprehensive Encyclopedia of Issues, Events, and People.*

To my family—David, Miles, and Lillian—for always asking the right questions, always listening with interest to the stories that emerg from the history, and always supporting all of my endeavors.

Tiffany K. Wayne

Chronology: Women's Rights in the United States, 1776–Present

---

1776   Abigail Adams writes to her husband, John Adams, one of the founders and signers of the Declaration of Independence to "remember the ladies" while writing their document. They do not heed her call, and the Declaration specifies that "all men are created equal."

1821   The first school for girls, the Troy Female Seminary in New York, is founded by Emma Hart Willard.

1829   Fanny Wright becomes the first woman in the United States to address an audience of both sexes when she lectures on free love and the abolition of marriage.

1833   Oberlin College in Ohio becomes the first coeducational college in the United States. It awards its first academic degrees to women in 1841. Several well-known suffragists, including Lucy Stone, are alumnae.

1836   Angelina Grimké writes *An Appeal to the Christian Women of the South,* published by the American Anti-Slavery Society, urging Southern women to speak out against slavery.

1837   Sarah Grimké is the first to compare slavery to the treatment of women.

Mount Holyoke College in Massachusetts, the first four-year college exclusively for women, is established. The founding of Vassar follows in 1861 and Wellesley and Smith Colleges in 1875.

1838   Sarah Grimké publishes *Letters on the Equality of the Sexes,* the earliest women's rights arguments published in the United States.

The Congregational Church of Massachusetts issues a "Pastoral Letter" denouncing the public speaking efforts of the Grimké sisters.

1839   The first Married Women's Property Act is passed in Mississippi, and the trend will continue into the 1870s. Such laws gave married women control over the property they brought into marriage or were deeded during the marriage.

1841   Amelia Bloomer founds *The Lily,* the first journal published by and for women.

1845   Margaret Fuller publishes *Women in the Nineteenth Century,* a foundational text for the American women's movement.

1848   The first women's rights convention is held in Seneca Falls, New York. Organized by Elizabeth Cady Stanton, and Lucretia Mott, the convention presents a Declaration of Sentiments, calling for equal treatment for women and the right to vote.

1849   Harriet Tubman escapes from slavery and leads many slaves to freedom by the Underground Railroad over the next 10 years.

1850   The first National Women's Rights Convention is held in Worcester, Massachusetts.

Lucretia Mott publishes her speech, "Discourse on Woman," about the inequalities of women.

Amelia Jenks Bloomer promotes the dress reform movement by wearing the "bloomers costume." Suffragists later abandoned the bloomers for fear that it detracted attention from taking women's rights issues seriously.

1851   Sojourner Truth delivers her "Aren't I a Woman?" speech at the women's rights convention in Akron, Ohio.

1852   Harriet Beecher Stowe's *Uncle Tom's Cabin* is published and quickly becomes a bestseller.

1853   Antoinette Brown becomes the first ordained woman minister in the United States.

1855   Prominent reformer Lucy Stone retains her maiden name after marriage to Henry Blackwell and the couple rejects traditional vows.

1860   New York amends its Married Women's Property Act to allow married women to be the owners of their earnings.

1862   The Morrill Bill makes bigamy a federal crime. The legislation is directed at Mormon polygamists who often skirt the law because Utah does not record marriages.

1865   The American Civil War ends and the Thirteenth Amendment to the U.S. Constitution ends racial slavery in the United States.

1866   Susan B. Anthony and Elizabeth Cady Stanton form the American Equal Rights Association, an organization dedicated to the goal of universal suffrage.

1867   Kansas holds one of the first state referendums on suffrage.

1868   Stanton and Anthony begin publishing *The Revolution.*

The Fourteenth Amendment to the U.S. Constitution is ratified, stipulating that "all persons" born or naturalized in the United States should have equal protection under the law, allowing legal rights previously denied to slaves and African Americans, but continues to refer to citizens as males.

1869   Disagreement among the women's rights movement supporters splits them into two factions. Elizabeth Cady Stanton and Susan B. Anthony form the National Woman Suffrage Association to secure a federal amendment for voting rights. Lucy Stone, Henry Blackwell, and Julia Ward Howe form the American Woman Suffrage Association to push for state-by-state recognition of woman's right to vote and to continue support for black civil rights.

The Wyoming Territory passes the first woman suffrage bill.

1870   The Fifteenth Amendment to the U.S. Constitution is ratified, extending voting privileges to African American men but omitting any reference to woman suffrage.

Lucy Stone founds *The Woman's Journal* to compete with *The Revolution.*

1871   Paulina Kellogg Wright Davis publishes *A History of the National Woman's Rights Movement.*

1872   Victoria Woodhull is the first woman to run for president of the United States.

Susan B. Anthony is arrested for attempting to vote for Ulysses S. Grant in the presidential election.

Sojourner Truth demands a ballot at a polling booth in Battle Creek, Michigan, but is turned away.

1873	The Federal Comstock Act is passed, specifically defining birth control information as obscene and illegal to obtain or disseminate.
1874	The Woman's Christian Temperance Union is founded by Annie Wittenmyer. Under the leadership of Frances Willard, who becomes president of the WCTU in 1879, the organization is a key force in the fight for woman's suffrage.
1878	The Anthony Amendment, that would give women the right to vote, is introduced in Congress.
1879	Massachusetts allows women to vote in school elections.
1881	Julia Ward Howe founds the Association for the Advancement of Women to foster educational and professional opportunities.
1889	Hull House is founded by Jane Addams to provide programs for workers and immigrants in Chicago, inspiring the spread of a national settlement house movement.
1890	The National Woman Suffrage Association and the American Woman Suffrage Association merge to form the National American Woman Suffrage Association (NAWSA).
1891	Ida B. Wells starts her nationwide anti-lynching campaign following the murders of African American businessmen in Memphis, Tennessee.
1892	Olympia Brown forms the Federal Suffrage Association to push for a constitutional amendment.
	Charlotte Perkins Gilman publishes *The Yellow Wallpaper*, a story of one women's descent into madness under the pressures of marriage and domesticity.
1893	Colorado approves a bill to allow women to vote.
1895	Matilda Joslyn Gage aids Elizabeth Cady Stanton in writing *The Woman's*

	Bible, a gender-reversed interpretation of scripture.
1896	The National Association of Colored Women is formed in Washington, DC, by former slave Harriet Tubman and reformers Ida B. Wells-Barnett, Mary Church Terrell, Margaret Murray Washington, Fanny Jackson Coppin, Frances Ellen Watkins Harper, and Charlotte Forten Grimké.
1900	The International Ladies' Garment Workers' Union is founded in New York City in 1900 and becomes one of the largest unions in the United States.
	Susan B. Anthony resigns as president of NAWSA, naming Carrie Chapman Catt as her successor.
1902	The last volume of the *History of Woman Suffrage* is published.
1903	The National Women's Trade Union League is formed to improve working conditions for women.
1904	Mary Bethune opens Daytona Normal and Industrial Institute for Negro Girls in Florida.
1907	Harriot Stanton Blatch organizes the Equality League of Self-Supporting Women, comprising more than 20,000 factory, laundry, and garment workers on New York City's lower East Side.
	Congress passes the Expatriation Act, an immigration law providing that an American woman who marries a foreigner takes her husband's nationality and so loses her U.S. citizenship.
1908	Ida Husted Harper publishes her multi-volume *Life of Susan B. Anthony.*
1910	Major suffrage parades are organized in both New York City and Washington, DC, and are continued periodically until 1913.
1911	The U.S. Supreme Court rules in *Thompson v. Thompson* that a wife may not sue her husband for physical injuries he inflicts on her.

1912   Theodore Roosevelt's Progressive Party becomes the first national political party to adopt a woman suffrage plank.

1913   Jane Addams publishes the satiric "If Men Were Seeking the Franchise."

Alice Paul and Lucy Burns initiate the Congressional Union to work for a federal suffrage amendment.

Inez Milholland Boissevain leads a parade of over 8,000 suffragists through the streets of Washington, DC, on the eve of Woodrow Wilson's inauguration.

Members of the Congressional Union form the "Silent Sentinels" and picket in front of the White House. Many are jailed for "obstructing traffic."

1916   Carrie Chapman Catt unveils her "Winning Plan" to reenergize the members of NAWSA.

Margaret Sanger opens the first birth control clinic in Brooklyn, New York.

Jeanette Rankin of Montana becomes the first woman elected to Congress as a member of the House of Representatives.

The National Woman's Party is founded.

1918   President Woodrow Wilson announces his support of a woman's suffrage amendment.

1920   The Nineteenth Amendment to the U.S. Constitution is ratified, granting American women the right to vote.

The Women's Bureau of the Department of Labor is formed.

1921   Margaret Sanger founds the American Birth Control League, eventually renamed the Planned Parenthood Federation of America (1942).

1922   Congress passes the Cable Act, which changes immigration law to allow an American woman who marries a foreigner to retain her American citizenship if she remains in the United States and makes it easier for foreign wives of American men to become naturalized citizens.

1923   The Equal Rights Amendment is proposed by the National Woman's Party to eliminate gender-based discrimination. The amendment has never been ratified.

1931   Jane Addams becomes the second American and first woman nominated for a Nobel Peace Prize.

1932   Hattie Wyatt Caraway of Arkansas is the first woman elected to the U.S. Senate.

1935   Mary McLeod Bethune organizes the National Council of Negro Women.

1941   President Franklin Roosevelt signs the first executive order prohibiting government contractors from engaging in employment discrimination.

1946   The United Nations establishes a Commission on the Status of Women.

1948   The Universal Declaration of Human Rights, created in part by Eleanor Roosevelt, is accepted by the United Nations.

South Carolina becomes the last state to lift its ban on divorce.

The American Bar Association recommends adopting no-fault divorce.

In *Goesaert v. Cleary,* the U.S. Supreme Court upholds a Michigan law denying any woman from working in a bar unless she is "the wife or daughter of the owner."

1950   Margaret Sanger raises $150,000 for a reproductive scientist, Gregory Pincus, to develop a universal contraceptive. The oral contraceptive pill will be released to the American market in 1960.

1955   Civil rights activist Rosa Parks refuses to give up her seat on a bus to a white man and is arrested in Montgomery, Alabama.

**1955
(cont.)** The Daughters of Bilitis, the first lesbian organization, is founded.

1961 President John F. Kennedy appoints Eleanor Roosevelt to head the President's Commission on the Status of Women.

President John Kennedy establishes the President's Committee on Equal Employment Opportunity, which becomes the Equal Employment Opportunity Commission (EEOC).

Bella Abzug founds Women's Strike for Peace to fight for a nuclear test ban treaty.

Esther Peterson is appointed head of Women's Bureau in Department of Labor.

1963 Betty Friedan publishes *The Feminine Mystique* that incites the second wave of feminism.

Congress passes the Equal Pay Act, making it illegal to pay a woman less than a man for the same job.

1964 The Civil Rights Act establishes the EEOC to investigate complaints of employment discrimination.

Fannie Lou Hamer becomes a delegate to the Democratic Convention, representing the Mississippi Freedom Democratic Party.

1965 Helen Gurley Brown takes over *Cosmopolitan* magazine and changes the demographics to appeal to single women.

In *Griswold v. Connecticut,* the U.S. Supreme Court establishes the right to privacy, allowing married couples to obtain birth control information. Single people will not gain the same right until 1972.

1966 The National Organization for Women (NOW) is founded by Betty Friedan and others, eventually becoming the largest women's rights association in the country.

1967 President Lyndon B. Johnson expands Executive Order 11375 that provides affirmative action based on gender.

Pauli Murray aids the American Civil Liberties Union in revising policy on gender discrimination.

1968 The EEOC rules that separating help wanted advertisements by gender is illegal.

Feminists protest the Miss America Pageant as degrading to women.

1969 California institutes a "no fault" divorce law. Within four years, another 36 states adopt similar laws.

Redstockings, a "consciousness-raising" group, is formed in New York City.

1970 Kate Millett publishes *Sexual Politics,* a critique of patriarchy as socially conditioned.

Alix Kates Shulman publishes "A Marriage Agreement," an essay that advocates that marriage should be the shared responsibility of both sexes.

Germaine Greer publishes *The Female Eunuch.*

Lesbians protest against NOW due, in large part, to Betty Friedan's labeling them the "lavender menace" and implying their issues were contrary to the movement goals.

1971 Gloria Steinem launches *Ms.* magazine.

Gloria Steinem, Bella Abzug, and Shirley Chisholm found the National Women's Political Caucus to encourage women to seek public office.

NOW "acknowledges the oppression of lesbians as a legitimate concern of feminism."

1972 The Equal Rights Amendment (first introduced by Alice Paul in 1923) is passed by Congress due to the efforts of U.S. Representative Martha Griffiths.

1972 (cont.) Shirley Chisholm announces her candidacy for president of the United States.

Birth control is made legally available to single women.

Phyllis Chesler publishes *Women and Madness,* broadening the field of feminist psychology.

Title IX of the Education Amendment prohibits discrimination in schools based on gender, which increases women's participation in athletic programs.

1973 *Roe v. Wade* establishes the trimester framework for guaranteeing a woman's right to a safe, legal abortion.

Our Bodies, Ourselves is published by the Boston Women's Health Collective, launching the women's health movement. .

1974 Phyllis Chesler cofounds the National Women's Health Network to offer accurate and unbiased information on women's health care.

1975 The U.S. Supreme Court rules in *Weinberger v. Wiesenfeld* that men do not necessarily have primary responsibility to provide for a family—women, too, can be the primary breadwinners.

1976 The first marital rape law is passed in Nebraska, making it illegal for a husband to rape his wife.

Shere Hite publishes *The Hite Report: A Nationwide Study on Female Sexuality.*

President Jimmy Carter creates the National Advisory Committee on Women.

Craig v. Boren establishes a "heightened scrutiny" standard for measuring the constitutionality of sex-based classification. The court rules that an Oklahoma statute allowing women to purchase beer at 18 years old but limiting men until they are 21 violates the male's constitutional rights.

1977 A National Women's Conference is held in Houston, Texas.

1978 The Pregnancy Discrimination Act bans hiring and firing discrimination based on pregnancy.

The first "test-tube baby," Louise Brown, is born.

1979 Susan Brownmiller founds Women against Pornography.

1980 Audre Lorde publishes the *Cancer Journals,* the first work to address the viewpoint of a lesbian of color and cofounds the Kitchen Table Women of Color Press.

bell hooks initiates a support group for African American women, Sisters of the Yam.

1981 Sandra Day O'Connor becomes the first woman justice on the U.S. Supreme Court.

In *Rostker v. Goldberg* the court upholds the male-only registration for the draft.

The court rules in *Michael M. v. Superior Court of Sonoma County* that only men can be criminally liable for statutory rape.

1982 The Equal Rights Amendment fails ratification by the states.

The court rules in *Mississippi University for Women v. Hogan* that the purpose of a policy restricting men from admission to a nursing program is to "exclude members of one gender because they are presumed to suffer from an inherent handicap or to be innately inferior."

1983 Catharine MacKinnon and Andrea Dworkin are hired to draft a city ordinance making pornography a civil rights violation.

1984 The term "glass ceiling" is coined to describe the lack of advancement of women in the workplace.

Geraldine Ferraro is the first woman candidate for vice president of the United States.

The New York Court of Appeals, the state's highest court, overturns the marital rape exception, ending the final component of coverture whereby husbands had a right to their wives' bodies.

1985   Wilma Mankiller is elected as principal chief of the Cherokee Nation.

1986   The Court decides *Meritor Savings Bank v. Vinson,* which defines sexual harassment law and establishes two distinct categories of harassment: quid pro quo and hostile work environment.

1988   In *North Carolina v. Norman,* "battered woman syndrome" is first used as a defense for killing an abusive spouse.

1990   Camille Paglia publishes *Sexual Persona* and criticizes feminists as perpetual victims and man-haters.

Naomi Wolf publishes *The Beauty Myth: How Images of Beauty are Used Against Women.*

1991   The court in *United Auto Workers v. Johnson Controls* gives women the right to equal employment opportunities without regard to childbearing capacity.

The confirmation hearings for the nomination of Clarence Thomas to the U.S. Supreme Court are televised after allegations surface that he has harassed one of his employees, Anita Hill. Thomas is confirmed despite the controversy and Hill's explicit testimony.

1992   The American Association of University Women publishes research on how schools shortchange girls.

Susan Faludi publishes *Backlash: The Undeclared War Against American Women,* showing the media's negative portrayal of women.

A Congressional resolution names March as Women's History Month.

1993   Congress passes the Family and Medical Leave Act.

Ruth Bader Ginsburg becomes the second woman appointed to the U.S. Supreme Court.

The Hawaii Supreme Court finds that refusing to let same-sex couples marry constitutes impermissible sex discrimination under the state's constitution.

1994   The Violence Against Women Act tightens penalties for sex offenders and funds services for victims of rape and domestic violence.

Mary Daly publishes a feminist version of the dictionary.

Katie Roiphe publishes *The Morning After: Fear, Sex and Feminism,* implying that women should be held responsible for their actions instead of crying date rape.

1995   The United Nations Fourth World Conference on Women is held in Beijing. First Lady Hillary Rodham Clinton delivers the keynote address, outlining an international agenda for women's human rights.

1996   The U.S. Supreme Court rules that all-male military schools must admit women or lose public funding.

1997   Madeline Albright is sworn into office as United States Secretary of State.

1998   The U.S. Supreme Court rules on a series of cases that outline the definition of and liability for sexual harassment n the workplace and in schools.

In *Miller v. Albright,* the court upholds a federal law automatically granting U.S. citizenship to a child born of an American mother but denying citizenship to a child born of an American father unless the father proves paternity.

1999   The U.S. Supreme Court rules that a woman can sue for damages due to sex discrimination.

2000   The Food and Drug Administration approves RU-486, the so-called abortion pill that terminates early pregnancy without surgery.

2001   The Fetal Protection Act makes the killing or harming of a fetus a federal crime. Twenty-four states immediately pass laws following the federal law.

2002   California becomes the first state to offer paid family leave to care for either a new child or an ailing relative.

2003 The U.S. Supreme Court overturns a 1986 precedent that allowed states to criminalize sodomy, holding instead that gays have a right to sexual privacy.

The Massachusetts Supreme Court holds that barring same-sex couples from marrying lacks a rational basis and is unconstitutional under the Massachusetts state constitution.

President George W. Bush signs the Partial-Birth Abortion Ban Act, the first act to ban a specific type of abortion procedure; the ban is later upheld by the U.S. Supreme Court.

2004 A Washington state lower court, echoing Massachusetts, finds that the ban on same-sex marriage fails to satisfy the state constitutional rational relationship test.

The U.S. Senate rejects a proposed Federal Marriage Amendment to the U.S. Constitution that would define marriage as between one man and one woman.

Missouri voters approve a constitutional amendment at the state level defining marriage as between one man and one woman, with other states holding similar referenda in November 2004.

2007 Nancy Pelosi is the first woman to serve as the Speaker of the U.S. House of Representatives.

2008 Hillary Clinton loses the Democratic nomination for president of the United States to candidate Barack Obama.

Sarah Palin is the first woman to be listed on the national Republican Party ticket when she is named as the vice-presidential running mate of candidate John McCain.

Connecticut and California legalize same-sex marriage.

2009 President Obama signs into law the Lily Ledbetter Fair Pay Restoration Act in which pay discrimination victims can file complaints against their employers.

Iowa and Vermont legalize same-sex marriage.

2010 President Obama signs healthcare reform legislation. The Affordable Care Act (ACA) prevents healthcare insurance plans from charging women more than men, covers maternity care, and eliminates preexisting conditions, among other coverages.

Nebraska passes a ban on abortions after 20 weeks of pregnancy.

New Hampshire legalizes same-sex marriage.

2011 New York legalizes same-sex marriage.

2012 Washington, D.C., Washington state, and Maine legalize same-sex marriage.

2013 Twenty-three states enact laws prohibiting health insurance coverage of abortion.

Maryland, Delaware, Minnesota, Rhode Island, and New Jersey legalize same-sex marriage.

In *Hollingsworth v. Perry*, the U.S. Supreme Court rules that Proposition 8, an anti–same-sex marriage initiative in California, is unconstitutional.

In *United States v. Windsor*, the U.S. Supreme Court rules that defining marriage as a heterosexual union in the federal Defense of Marriage Act (DOMA) is unconstitutional.

2014 In *Burwell v. Hobby Lobby*, the U.S. Supreme Court allows a corporation to claim exemption from providing federally mandated contraception coverage to female employees based on religious objections of the company's owners. Justice Ruth Bader Ginsburg writes a scathing dissent criticizing the "blind spot" of the conservative male justices when it comes to women's rights.

Transgender actress Laverne Cox is featured on the cover of *TIME* magazine with the story, "The Transgender Tipping Point: America's Next Civil Rights Frontier."

The number of states that have legalized same-sex marriage reaches 32.

Introduction to Volume 1

Volume 1: Moral Reform and the Woman Question (1776–1870)

The period between the American Revolution and the Civil War brought great changes not only to the nation as a whole but also to women. During the 19th century the United States shifted from an agricultural society to an industrial one. Simultaneously, religious ferment and reform stirred the land. The period closed with a brutal, destructive civil war, which freed all slaves but enfranchised only the men. The documents presented here examine the effect of the tumultuous events of this period on women's rights.

Early feminists challenged the prevailing ideology of "separate spheres"—that is, roles and functions—for men and women based on sexual differences. They presented a radical counterimage to that ideology; instead of acknowledging biological difference as the sole determinant of gender roles, early feminist activists focused on the characteristics that were common to both men and women. Traditional forces of society objected to, fought against, and felt threatened by the campaign for women's rights.

In the postrevolutionary period, Americans instrumental in establishing the republic were concerned about whether it would succeed. What factors, what conditions of society, and what behavior, they asked, would ensure that the American republican experiment would endure? The answer was an active, well-educated citizenry that was willing to defend the country. But, they reasoned, men could not do it alone: they required the assistance of women. Early proponents of women's education believed that if women remained within the traditional framework established by religion and common law, their talents would enhance the civic virtues needed by males in a republic. Thus, while some traditionalists argued that society benefited when women adhered to their pure and pious nature, in the 1770s educators, such as Benjamin Rush, advised a concerned public that

women's contribution, as their husbands' helpmates and as mothers who trained their sons and daughters to serve the republic, required special "female" education. That the education of girls and boys be distinct was not unusual, for it reflected the long-held view that the nature of males and females differed, and that this difference, when nurtured through specialized training, would enhance society. The new feature here is the significance Rush attached to the instrumental role played by postrevolutionary American women. Indeed, before the Revolution mothers educated their sons only until the age of seven, when their fathers or tutors assumed their instruction, while in England servants supplemented a wife's or mother's work. Uniquely, an American republican mother with the kind of education proposed by Rush was deemed competent to continue educating her son for citizenship even after he reached the age of seven, and she could, in addition, tend to her husband's affairs.

We find another role assigned to women of the new republic by Alexander Hamilton, the first Secretary of the Treasury, who believed that working-class American women, like their English counterparts, could contribute to a new manufacturing economy by working outside the home, in factories, which would allow the republic to compete favorably with Europe. Thus, in each of these ways women's talents were considered valuable to the new country's prosperity.

The development of commerce and industry drew more and more men to jobs outside the home, while women remained there. The "ideology of separate spheres" seemed to confirm reality and served to promote women's domestic autonomy, a status unknown when their husbands were at home to rule the household. Did this separate domestic status have an effect on women's rights? Perhaps in an intangible social sense, but not legally during these early republican years, for most married women had limited civil and property rights, and were still expected to exhibit the characteristics of passivity, purity, and docility.

Nevertheless, historical perspective reveals the emergence of a counter-ideology that began to undermine the construct of the republican-antebellum gendered world. The most important of these undermining elements was the increase in educational opportunities for women, welcomed by many but rejected by others for fear that women would acquire masculine characteristics. In the end, only a few women had the opportunity for formal, private education, while the majority of the white, northern female population had to wait until the mid-19th century to receive an adequate education.

Arguments in favor of the education of women were also advanced by Catharine Beecher, who took the conservative position that when you educate a woman you educate a family and that an educated woman offers her husband effective companionship which enhances the marital relationship. A middle ground was presented by educators Emma Willard and Mary Lyon, who claimed that educated women could fill the country's need for teachers, a profession that would allow them to express their natural, nurturing qualities and provide the unmarried with an income. The most radical proposed that women should be educated no differently from men, because they shared the same *human* qualities. At variance in the extreme with the republican, antebellum gendered world order, this 19th century human rights perspective rejected sexual differences as determinative in all areas except those of physical strength and woman's fulfillment of her duties as wife and mother, and maintained that females should be granted equal opportunities and equal rights with males. And when some women succeeded in male professions, as did, for example, Elizabeth Blackwell in medicine and Antoinette Brown Blackwell in the ministry, their peers, proud of their accomplishments, held them up as role models and as evidence of women's capacity to perform equally with men.

The Quakers continued to advocate equal education. Their participation in antislavery organizations also served to undermine the system of separate spheres. Nothing could demonstrate this better than the activities of two Quaker-educated sisters, Angelina and Sarah Grimké, whose public protest against slavery led the Massachusetts Congregational Church to censure their behavior, claiming that their public addresses were injurious to female character. The religious establishment's position was upheld and expanded by those who maintained that any activity outside the female sphere was to be regarded as dangerous to the well-being of society. Subtle methods of persuasion, including that of instilling guilt, were applied to keep women docile and subordinate. No doubt this helped to silence many, but not the sisters Grimké, who remained adamant in their belief in human rights while simultaneously becoming increasingly aware of how the oppression of women was analogous to that of the slave. Other women responded similarly. Antislavery activity influenced the women's rights beliefs of Elizabeth Cady Stanton who, along with Quaker Lucretia Mott, organized a historic meeting for women at Seneca Falls in 1848. Using the format of the Declaration of Independence, the women created a Declaration of Rights and Sentiments that echoed the language of the Enlightenment by proclaiming that the inequality of women was in opposition to the intention of the Creator, for "all men and women are created equal."

After Seneca Falls, feminists organized national women's rights conventions, at which they demanded the right to suffrage, equality as human beings, equal education, reform in the common law, and much more. In addition, feminists petitioned political conventions held in Ohio and in Massachusetts, demanding the right to vote. They poured their ideas, beliefs, hopes, and sentiments into petitions, their only officially recognized political tool. They used them to declare their entitlement to suffrage, to press for passage of married women's property rights, and to express their opposition to the extension of slavery. In their petitions, speeches, and writings, these activists rejected society's characterizations of women as weak, submissive, and lacking in intellect. And through these activities they demonstrated the unfairness of excluding them from the public arena and forbidding them to control their own property on the basis of traits arbitrarily assigned to their sex.

The issue of temperance agitated and consequently activated more women than any other, for it underscored their helplessness against alcohol, emphasized their lack of control over husbands who were under its sway, and demonstrated society's double standard, which required purity of them but permitted men liberty of behavior. The effects of intemperance were a primary motivation for Elizabeth Cady Stanton to recommend to the New York State legislators that the divorce laws be liberalized. The temperance movement also helped white middle-class women to empathize with their black female slave sisters. Some feminists protested against the subjugation of married women by exchanging marriage vows that reflected principles of equality.

The women's rights movement developed in the workplace as well. At the Lowell factories in Massachusetts, women workers jeopardized their wages and even their jobs when they went out on strike to protest wage cuts and excessively long hours. Women also formed unions to protest substandard working conditions and to fight for their rights as workers. However, many were discouraged from joining male unions.

Despite these elements of "subversion," the ideology of separate spheres for men and women remained largely undamaged through the mid-19th century, entrenched in the power establishment of government and culture. Most women overwhelmingly accepted its propaganda, believing that marriage and motherhood should define their lives. Few had the leisure or education to study the issues presented by the feminists. In addition, the continuing strength of the patriarchal—common law tradition remained. Despite evidence of physical and sexual abuse, women seeking divorce were hardly ever granted one, and the courts still allowed the husband the sole choice of domicile. The continuing vitality of the separate sphere ideology was evident when, at the end of the Civil War, the call for woman suffrage was denied when the vote was extended to black men.

What, then, can we say about how this period affected the rights of women? In substantive legal areas, the rights they gained were meager. But a significant barrier to patriarchy was broken with passage of the married women's property acts, which ended the legal myth of the unity of husband and wife. (Many men endorsed this legislation for their own personal economic gain. And judicial interpretation of these laws largely confirmed the common law interpretation of property ownership.) Further legislation kept chipping away at the common law, and despite some regression during the time of the Civil War, in the areas of property rights, divorce law, and child custody, women were somewhat better off than they had been in the early part of the 19th century. Most important, feminists brought a new perspective to the image of women. No longer were they restricted to the domestic sphere, for feminists emphasized and demonstrated that women could contribute to the outside world as well as to the home. This counterimage of women continued to inspire the feminists of the late 19th and early 20th centuries.

Further Reading

Bartlett, Elizabeth Ann. *Liberty, Equality, Sorority: The Origins and Interpretation of American Feminist Thought: Frances Wright, Sarah Grimké, and Margaret Fuller.* Brooklyn, NY: Carlson Publishing, 1994.

Douglas, Ann. *The Feminization of American Culture.* New York: Alfred A. Knopf, 1977.

DuBois, Ellen Carol. *Feminism and Suffrage: The Emergence of an Independent Women's Movement in America, 1848–1869.* Ithaca, NY: Cornell University Press, 1999.

Ginzberg, Lori. *Women and the Work of Benevolence: Morality, Politics, and Class in the Nineteenth Century.* New Haven, CT: Yale University Press, 1992.

Gundersen, Joan R. *To Be Useful to the World: Women in Revolutionary America, 1740–1790.* New York: Twayne Publishers, 1996.

Hoffert, Sylvia. *When Hens Crow: The Woman's Rights Movement in Antebellum America.* Bloomington: Indiana University Press, 1995.

Hoffman, Ronald, and Peter J. Albert, eds. *Women in the Age of the American Revolution.* Charlottesville: University Press of Virginia, 1989.

Jeffrey, Julie Roy. *The Great Silent Army of Abolitionism: Ordinary Women in the Antislavery Movement.* Chapel Hill: University of North Carolina Press, 1998.

Kierner, Cynthia A. *Beyond the Household: Women's Place in the Early South, 1700–1835.* Ithaca, NY: Cornell University Press, 1998.

McMillen, Sally G. *Seneca Falls and the Origins of the Women's Rights Movement.* New York: Oxford University Press, 2008.

Nash, Margaret A. *Women's Education in the United States, 1780–1840.* New York: Palgrave Macmillan, 2005.

Norton, Mary Beth. *Founding Mothers and Fathers: Gendered Power and the Forming of American Society.* New York: Knopf, 1996.

Ryan, Mary. *Women in Public: Between Banners and Ballots, 1825–1880.* Baltimore, MD: Johns Hopkins University Press, 1990.

Yellin, Jean, and John Van Horne, eds. *The Abolitionist Sisterhood: Women's Political Culture in Antebellum America.* Ithaca, NY: Cornell University Press, 1994.

Zagarri, Rosemarie. *Revolutionary Backlash: Women and Politics in the Early American Republic.* Philadelphia: University of Pennsylvania Press, 2007.

A

Abolitionism and the Antislavery Movement

Antebellum moral reform causes brought women increasingly into the public realm as speakers and lecturers on a range of topics, combining a spiritual imperative toward individual and social progress with secular or political concerns. The first female lecturers were 19th-century reformers who, like female preachers, justified their presence at the podium or on the stage in spiritual terms. In the early 1830s, women such as Maria Stewart, a free black believed to be the first American woman to lecture in public, and sisters Sarah Grimké and Angelina Grimké (Weld), white women raised in the South who came to the North to become prominent abolitionists, emphasized that God had called them in their special duty as women to speak out on the wrongs of slavery.

Maria Stewart emerged as part of the same tradition explaining the proliferation of black female preachers in the early 19th century, but her lectures included a broader, more explicitly political message. Like black women preachers of the era, Stewart explained to an audience in Boston in 1832 how she felt called by God to speak out as a woman against slavery and oppression in all forms: "Methinks I heard a spiritual interrogation—'Who shall go forward, and take off the reproach that is cast upon the people of color? Shall it be a woman?'— And my heart made this reply—'If it is thy will, be it even so, Lord Jesus!'" Stewart addressed black women specifically to rise up from "beneath a load of iron pots and kettles" and take on a larger public role for the sake of the entire race: "O, ye daughters of Africa, awake! Awake! Arise! No longer sleep nor slumber, but distinguish yourselves. Show forth to the world that ye are endowed with noble and exalted faculties."

Sarah and Angelina Grimké came from a South Carolina white slave-holding family and moved north after converting to Quakerism. Like Stewart, the sisters also couched their arguments for an expanded public role for women in terms of God's mandate for Christian women to reach out and help their enslaved "sisters." Angelina Grimké's "An Appeal to the Women of the Nominally Free States" (1837) reminded Northern women that their duty was not to their families alone, but that they "have high

and holy duties to perform in the work of emancipation—duties to themselves, to the suffering slave, to the slaveholder, to the church, to their country, and to the world at large, and, above all to their God." Grimké connected the plight of all women with that of the female slave, urging white Northern women into the antislavery cause by reminding them that, under slavery, women were prevented from fulfilling their roles as wives and mothers. As long as slavery existed within the United States, this was "a country where women are degraded and brutalized, and where their exposed persons bleed under the lash . . . torn from their husbands, and forcibly plundered of their virtue and their offspring. . . . They are our countrywomen—they are our sisters."

The Grimké sisters sparked controversy as much over the fact that they were women speaking in public as over their antislavery message. In order to work against slavery, they ultimately had to campaign for women's right to speak publicly and did so by continuing to argue that women, in particular, had a moral duty to change society. The controversy and criticism surrounding the Grimkés inspired other women to demand their own right to engage in public reform work. In 1837, the same year that Angelina Grimké's "Appeal" was published, the Antislavery Convention of American Women met in New York and resolved "that it is the duty of woman, and the province of woman, to plead her cause of the oppressed in our land and to do all that she can by her voice, and her pen, and her purse, and the influence of her example, to overthrow the horrible system of American slavery."

The abolitionist movement continued to grow throughout the 1840s and 1850s along with the other political events and sectional crises that were leading the United States to Civil War. But abolitionism was also part of a larger network of women's reform activities in the first decades of the 19th century. The abolitionists themselves were individuals largely concentrated in the Northeast, who were often simultaneously involved in multiple reform causes and organizations. Abolitionism shared with other reforms the desire to end social wrongs, the idea of middle-class benevolence in aiding the oppressed and downtrodden, and the spiritual imperative to allow each individual to reach his or her potential as the route to a perfected society.

White women had to fight for their right to speak publicly, but black women, in their public activism, had to confront the forces that sought to keep them quiet both as women and as African Americans. Whereas white women tried to identify with the black female slave in order to articulate their own sense of oppression, free black women struggled to claim their identity as "women" in the first place by pointing out that ideas about "true womanhood," or about women's domestic and moral roles, often did not apply to black women. Sojourner Truth, a former slave from New York, was a well-known speaker throughout the 1850s who articulated the dual oppression of black women. Truth not only spoke at women's rights conventions organized by white women reformers, but she also pointed out that for black women, suffrage alone would do little to change their lives as long as racism existed. At a speech before an 1851 women's rights convention in Akron, Ohio, Truth highlighted the false idea of completely separate gender roles by emphasizing that black women, especially, often worked as hard as men, and therefore they ought to have the same rights as men:

> I have as much muscle as any man, and can do as much work as any man. I have plowed and reaped and husked and chopped and mowed, and can any man do more than that? I have heard much about the sexes being equal; I can carry as much as any man, and eat as much too, if I can get it. I am as strong as any man that is now.

Whether white or black, women's involvement in the antislavery movement transformed women's own sense of themselves and of their public roles. Through their work in the antislavery movement, women learned how to be political activists, how to organize, and how to pursue new strategies beyond just "moral suasion," such as gathering petitions, lobbying legislatures, writing for and editing newspapers, organizing conventions, and delivering public speeches. Angelina Grimké went from justifying her right and duty to speak in public to becoming the first woman to testify before a government committee. Beginning in the 1830s, women established and led local and state level antislavery societies, lectured at conventions, and published antislavery tracts. Lydia Maria Child was a well-established author of books and magazines for children and homemakers before she moved into reform work with the 1833 publication of *An Appeal in Favor of That Class of Americans Called Africans*. In 1841 she took over as editor of the New York-based newspaper, the *National Anti-Slavery Standard*.

Abby Kelley Foster was a Quaker who worked with radical abolitionist William Lloyd Garrison and launched a public speaking career, which she insisted on continuing even after marriage and motherhood. Of course, many women who did not become famous or whose names have not been recorded in the history books were politicized by and contributed to the strength of the antislavery cause through their work in local societies, fundraising, subscribing to antislavery newspapers, and attending abolitionist lectures.

Female reformers brought their special roles and duties as women, and as mothers, to the antislavery movement. Articles in abolitionist newspapers as well as the narratives of former slaves themselves, and, most famously, Harriet Beecher Stowe's *Uncle Tom's Cabin* (published in 1852), all made special appeal to the hearts of Northern women readers as mothers and as keepers of the home. From the poor Eliza escaping in fear as she crossed the icy river with her children in tow, to the heart-wrenching accounts of the physical abuse and deaths of slave children, Stowe's novel highlighted the effect of slavery on families, both black and white, and on women and children in particular. And perhaps the most compelling theme of Harriet Jacobs's 1861 autobiography, *Incidents in the Life of a Slave Girl*, was the fact that Jacobs herself was a mother, separated for years from her own children, unable to protect them from slavery. Because of slavery's destruction of the family and its blatant physical abuse of women and of children, antislavery activists clearly urged that abolitionism was a cause all women, black and white, should see as their own. As one lecturer urged, "every woman in the community should raise her voice against the sin, that crying evil that is degrading her sex."

Many women did begin to raise their voices. The 1820s and 1830s saw a proliferation of women's auxiliary antislavery societies in support of the national organizations led by men, but by 1840 there was a split within the abolitionist ranks over women as members of associations, as officeholders, and as public speakers for the cause. William Lloyd Garrison, the founder of the radical abolitionist newspaper, *The Liberator*, often took revolutionary positions such as supporting full civil and political rights for black citizens and attacking the U.S. government and churches for allowing slavery to continue, and he was among those who supported the right of women to speak out against slavery and to participate in the movement on equal terms. Quaker reformer Lucretia Mott helped found the Philadelphia Female Anti-Slavery Society in 1833 and was one of the delegates, along with Garrison, to the international World

Anti-Slavery Convention in London in 1840. Also among the delegates was the newly married Elizabeth Cady Stanton. To their surprise, the first debates were not about slavery, but about the female delegates at the convention who, ultimately, were not allowed to speak. Stanton reported in a letter from London to Angelina and Sarah Grimké that, "as the female delegates were not received and were not permitted to take their seats as delegates, [William Lloyd Garrison] refused to take his, consequently his voice was not heard throughout the meeting." Over the next several days of the convention, Elizabeth Cady Stanton and Lucretia Mott decided that more attention needed to be focused on the plight of "oppressed woman." It was not until 1848, however, that they finally met in Seneca Falls, New York, to discuss the rights, or lack of rights, of American women.

Building upon the previous decades of work in the antislavery movement and on a generation of women trained as activists and leaders, by the 1850s, women's rights had emerged as an identifiable movement separate from the issues and organizations of abolitionism. Although many of the same women lent their voices and energies to both causes, there were reasons explaining the need for a separate movement at this time. First, as revealed in the controversies over the Grimkés and over the female convention delegates, not all abolitionists supported women as public reform speakers and some women activists needed a forum from which to address this issue. Second, the abolitionist movement was focused on a single goal—ending slavery—while women's rights activists sought to address a variety of issues affecting women's lives, especially during the radical decade of the 1850s. The association between the two movements, however, meant that Southern white women were not involved in creating the early women's rights movement, a trend that continued to be a problem for the suffrage movement even after the Civil War.

Tiffany K. Wayne

See Also: Cary, Mary Ann Shadd; Child, Lydia Maria; Dix, Dorothea; Education of Women (before the Civil War); Fifteenth Amendment; Foster, Abby Kelley; Fourteenth Amendment; Garrison, William Lloyd; Grimké, Sarah Moore; Grimké Weld, Angelina; Jacobs, Harriet; *The Liberator*; Moral Reform; Mott, Lucretia; Quakers; Stewart, Maria W.; Stowe, Harriet Beecher; Temperance Movement; Truth, Sojourner; United States Sanitary Commission; Stanton, Elizabeth Cady (Vol. 2)

Primary Documents: 1851, "Aren't I a Woman?"; 1852, *Uncle Tom's Cabin*; 1861, *Incidents in the Life of a Slave Girl*

Further Reading

Dixon, Chris. *Perfecting the Family: Antislavery Marriages in Nineteenth-Century America.* Amherst: University of Massachusetts Press, 1997.

Hansen, Debra Gold. *Strained Sisterhood: Gender and Class in the Boston Female Anti-Slavery Society.* Amherst: University of Massachusetts Press, 1993.

Jeffrey, Julie Roy. *The Great Silent Army of Abolitionism: Ordinary Women in the Antislavery Movement.* Chapel Hill: University of North Carolina Press, 1998.

Newman, Richard S. *The Transformation of American Abolitionism: Fighting Slavery in the Early Republic.* Chapel Hill: University of North Carolina Press, 2002.

Salerno, Beth A. *Sister Societies: Women's Antislavery Societies in Antebellum America.* DeKalb: Northern Illinois University Press, 2005.

Venet, Wendy Hamand. *Neither Ballots nor Bullets: Women Abolitionists and the Civil War.* Charlottesville: University Press of Virginia, 1991.

Yee, Shirley. *Black Women Abolitionists: A Study in Activism, 1828–1860.* Knoxville: University of Tennessee Press, 1992.

Yellin, Jean Fagan. *Women and Sisters: The Antislavery Feminists in American Culture.* New Haven, CT: Yale University Press, 1989.

Yellin, Jean, and John Van Horne, eds. *The Abolitionist Sisterhood: Women's Political Culture in Antebellum America.* Ithaca, NY: Cornell University Press, 1994.

Abortion (17th and 18th Centuries)

Induced abortion has been practiced from ancient times, and the women of colonial America knew of various methods to end an unwanted pregnancy. Although not unheard of, abortions in colonial America were almost never performed by use of instruments or attempts to manually remove the fetus from the womb. The use of herbs was the most common technique for inducing a miscarriage.

Prior to any effective means of contraception, unwanted pregnancies were regular occurrences for both single and married women alike. Social stigmatization was obviously much higher for an unmarried woman, who could either quickly marry her lover or bring him to court to demand financial support for the child. Both were common practices, with as many as one-third of brides being pregnant in early 18th-century America. If a woman was unwilling or unable to marry her lover, she might have sought means to terminate her pregnancy through abortion.

Throughout most of the colonial period there were no explicit laws regarding abortion. Because colonial law borrowed heavily from England, it is worth examining the more fully developed laws of England regarding abortion. There were no sanctions against the deliberate termination of a pregnancy before the fetus had "quickened"—when a woman could first feel the fetus moving inside her. Quickening usually happened by the fourth month of pregnancy. Such feelings were the only concrete proof a woman was pregnant, as other medical explanations could account for lack of menstruation. Because "blocked menstruation" was believed to be a sign of a dangerous medical condition, an attempt to remove a menstrual blockage was considered morally acceptable. Even if the blockage was later discovered to have been a pregnancy, there was no stigma or legal ramifications for clearing the blockage, as long as quickening had not occurred. Contemporaries did not believe that a fetus was a living child until it had quickened, and knowingly terminating an early pregnancy was not legally banned.

British jurist Edward Coke (1552–1632) formulated much of the English common law tradition. Regarding abortion, he denied that it was possible for anyone to be accused of murder for ending a pregnancy, though any action taken against a child that has been born alive is clearly murder. He cited cases in which a pregnant woman was physically assaulted and lost a pregnancy as a result. Such cases could not be considered murder, since it was not conclusive that the woman would have successfully produced a living child.

Perhaps the best documentation of women's attempts to thwart the progression of a pregnancy can be found in medical books and herbals. Such texts contain repeated references to herbs that can be used to release "blocked menses" or serve as "menstrual stimulators." The most common herbs cited for such uses were pennyroyal, willow, and juniper leaves. Although rarely identified specifically as techniques to end a pregnancy, it is likely that midwives and physicians fully understood that blocked menstruation was usually the result of pregnancy. In some instances, the texts specifically identified which herbs should never be given to a pregnant woman, for they were known to bring on early labor. Vigorous exercises, such as horseback riding or jumping rope, were also suggested to induce menstruation or "remove a dead fetus."

It is difficult to determine how effective these techniques were, since successfully terminated pregnancies were unlikely to be documented in the historical record. Only in cases where the woman died or brought a malformed child into the world was there reason to note the attempted abortion. Historian Cornelia Hughes Dayton documents a case from 1742, in which Sarah Grosvenor attempted several times to abort her pregnancy through the ingestion of herbs. After merely becoming sick, she resorted to a "physick" who used tools to induce a surgical abortion. Sarah sickened and died. The abortionist and Sarah's lover stood trial for Sarah's murder, but not that of the infant. Both were eventually acquitted. This is the only documented case in colonial America in which a surgical abortion was attempted, although there are occasional references to assault and punching in an attempt to terminate a pregnancy.

The use of herbs was problematic for women, because the dosage had to be precise. Although herbs such as pennyroyal could induce a miscarriage, too little merely sickened the woman, and too much could be toxic. Side effects from these herbs could cause liver damage, breathing difficulties, or convulsions. Herbs such as juniper leaves, pennyroyal, and rue were usually brewed into a strong tea that was orally ingested. In some cases women might have inserted the leaves into the vagina to induce a miscarriage. Although occasionally successful, it is unlikely that herbal techniques were very effective. Had herbal remedies been effective, there would have been no need to pursue the dangerous and chilling surgical techniques resorted to in later generations.

Despite the wide availability of herbs and texts that provided instruction on the termination of pregnancy, there were moral and ethical problems raised by the practice. Many herbals warn against tampering with the sanctity of life. William Buchan's 1769 text *Domestic Medicine* provided detailed instructions on how to cure menstrual irregularities and precautions that must be used by pregnant women. He acknowledges that these techniques can be used to wickedly procure an abortion and begs a woman considering such an act to "stop her murderous hand" by contemplating the child whom she might one day learn to cherish. Many herbals and medical texts carried such heartfelt exhortations, although they are absent from others. Thus, the writers of these texts knew that in instructing women which herbs to avoid during pregnancy, they had little control over how that information would be applied.

Perhaps the first attempt to prosecute someone for procuring an abortion occurred in 1650, when Captain William Mitchell attempted to force his 21-year-old bond servant, Susan Warren, to abort the child he had fathered. He forced her to drink a noxious potion, which made her break out in boils and lose her hair but did not terminate the pregnancy. When she gave birth to a stillborn child shortly afterward, a Maryland grand jury indicted Captain Mitchell for having tried to force an abortion on Susan Warren. It was ultimately decided that the death of the child could not be conclusively traced to Mitchell, though he was fined 5,000 pounds of tobacco for fornication. Susan Warren was flogged for fornication but released from further indenture to Captain Mitchell.

Over time the moral prohibitions against abortion gathered momentum. Most failed, but in 1821, Connecticut became the first American state to pass a law against the deliberate termination of a pregnancy after quickening. This law would become the model for other states, which enacted numerous laws against abortion over the next 20 years.

Dorothy A. Mays

See Also: Birth Control (17th and 18th Centuries); Infanticide; Legal Status of Women (18th Century)

Further Reading

Dayton, Cornelia Hughes. "Taking the Trade: Abortion and Gender Relations in an Eighteenth Century New England Village." *William and Mary Quarterly* 48 (1991): 19–49.

Klepp, Susan E. "Lost, Hidden, Obstructed, and Repressed: Contraceptive and Abortive Technology in the Early Delaware Valley." In *Early American Technology: Making and Doing Things from the Colonial Era to 1850,* ed. Judith A. McGaw. Chapel Hill: University of North Carolina Press, 1994.

Olasky, Marvin. *Abortion Rites: A Social History of Abortion in America.* Washington, DC Regnery, 1995.

Riddle, John M. *Eve's Herbs: A History of Contraception and Abortion in the West.* Cambridge, MA: Harvard University Press, 1997.

Tone, Andrea, ed. *Controlling Reproduction: An American History.* Wilmington, DE: Scholarly Resources, 1997.

Adams, Abigail (1744–1818)

Abigail Adams has become probably the most widely and intimately known woman of the Revolutionary era for three reasons. The first foundation of her fame is her visibility as the wife of John Adams, who was both a leader of the Revolution and second president of the United States. This has placed her in a select group of early presidential wives (not yet called First Ladies), along with Martha Washington and Dolley Madison. Abigail's position as John Adams's wife gave her access

Abigail Smith Adams, from a portrait by artist Gilbert Stuart, about 1800. (Library of Congress)

to several prominent persons, particularly Thomas Jefferson, who recorded their favorable impressions of her. Second, nearly 65 years after the Declaration of Independence, the correspondence that she exchanged with her husband as well as letters written to her sisters and to a few close friends, notably Mercy Otis Warren and Jefferson, began to appear in print. These intimate letters, never intended for publication, portray her as a lively and intelligent woman who made her own sacrifices to achieve her country's freedom. Finally, with the gradual development of feminism in American life, Adams has been anointed, on the basis of a few of her letters, as a powerful voice for women's rights in an age that afforded women little independence of thought and action.

Abigail Smith was born on November 22, 1744, in Weymouth, Massachusetts. She was the second child of the Reverend William Smith, pastor of the town's first parish church, and Elizabeth Quincy, a member of the most prominent family in neighboring Braintree (now Quincy). Abigail was somewhat sickly as a child and, like nearly all women of her day, was educated entirely at home. In her case, however, home was full of books containing history, theology, and literature in English and several works in French, Latin, and Greek. She did not study the ancient classics, but she read widely in European history, as well as Shakespeare and the English poets, especially Alexander Pope and James Thompson, whom she quoted frequently in her letters. At some point, perhaps shortly before her marriage, her brother-in-law, Richard Cranch, also taught her some French.

On October 25, 1764, Abigail Smith married John Adams of neighboring Braintree after a three-year courtship that is charmingly described in a handful of surviving letters exchanged between the two. Her parents may have disapproved of their daughter's marriage to a lawyer, a profession that was still struggling for full respectability in post-Puritan New England, but she was determined in her choice of a husband. She continued her self-education in her new husband's growing library and raised four children, Abigail (b. 1765), John Quincy (b. 1767, later sixth president of the United States), Charles (b. 1770), and Thomas Boylston (b. 1772).

The Adamses lived alternately in Braintree and Boston until the Revolution. In the next decade (1774–1784), Adams stayed in Braintree with her daughter and younger sons while John spent most of his time first in Congress and, after 1778, in France and Holland, to which he took John Quincy. Adams joined her husband in Europe in 1784, returned with him to America in 1788, and lived mostly in Braintree (renamed Quincy in 1792) for the rest of her life, with extensive stays in New York and Philadelphia and one brief visit to the new executive mansion in Washington, DC, while John served as vice president and president. Even in the 1790s, however, Adams often remained in Quincy in rather poor health while her husband was in the nation's capital.

These long separations were emotionally hard on both Adamses and especially on Abigail, who during the Revolutionary War had to run both her household and small farm for years with little assistance, tasks she performed with dedication and skill, while also educating her children. This experience was one she shared with tens of thousands of other women, a few richer but most poorer than herself, while their husbands, fathers, brothers, and sons were off at war. And at age 39 Adams, who had never left Massachusetts, crossed the ocean, of which she was terrified, to join her husband and manage two substantial houses in Paris and London. Used to having just one or two servant girls, she now supervised staffs of eight to ten, considered the minimum that anyone in John Adams's diplomatic posts could keep in a respectable home.

These same long, painful separations made Abigail's reputation. Between their first courtship letter in 1762

and President Adams's last letter home to Quincy in 1800, Abigail and John Adams exchanged more than 1,000 letters, one of the largest, and incomparably the finest, correspondences of any presidential couple in American history. The quality of this exchange owes much to the exciting times and places in which they lived and much to John's lively pen, but it owes most to Abigail, who was as fine a letter writer as any American of her century. Her range of interests was broad, her reporting on America's home front—the farms and villages away from the congresses and battles—was superb, and she had a talent for expressing, in a few short passages, the vital truths of Revolutionary politics that no writer has ever exceeded.

Adams's claim to fame as an early American feminist—a label and concept that would have astonished her—are solid but must be seen in context. When in her most famous letter (March 30, 1776) she urged her husband in Congress to "remember the ladies" as he and his colleagues framed laws for the new nation just taking shape, she was not, as some have imagined, advocating suffrage for women. Instead, she had her eye on the central legal and cultural problem for most women of her day: the nearly absolute power that husbands had over their wives' persons, time, and property. It was, in short, equality within marriage that concerned Adams. Her husband, however, while probably genuinely sympathetic to her view, was embarrassed by her exhortation. Congress had no power to give women any rights within marriage, and if they had enjoyed such power, John Adams would not have had the courage, or foolhardiness, to propose such rights in 1776. The simple legal justice within marriage that Abigail sought—let alone the right to vote—lay far in the future for most American women.

And Abigail herself played a fairly traditional role within marriage. She and John did discuss such matters as land purchases, a matter that most wives would have thought beyond their sphere, but John probably listened to her advice on this matter because she had proven herself to be so sensible in household management and so generally intelligent. In raising her children, Adams was the classic "republican mother," exhorting her three boys to virtue, self-sacrifice, and public service and urging her daughter to prepare for becoming a mother who could raise virtuous and achieving sons. And she was a spirited advocate for the full recognition of John Adams's political and intellectual achievements, whether in Massachusetts or Philadelphia.

Adams's long life was not without bitter disappointments. Her alcoholic son Charles died in 1800, thoroughly estranged from his father. Beginning in the 1790s, she became even more deeply estranged by partisan politics from her old friend Thomas Jefferson than was her husband, who was eventually reconciled to Jefferson and resumed a rich correspondence with him. And her daughter Abigail, after playing the dutiful wife to an unworthy husband for more than two decades, came home to Quincy to die of cancer in 1813. Adams's own health was often poor from the 1790s onward, but she lived until shortly before her 74th birthday, dying on October 28, 1818, survived by her 83-year-old husband and two sons, including John Quincy Adams, then America's secretary of state.

Richard Alan Ryerson

See Also: The American Revolution; Republican Motherhood

Further Reading

Barker-Benfield, G. J. *Abigail and John Adams: The Americanization of Sensibility.* Chicago: University of Chicago Press, 2010.

Ellis, Joseph J. *First Family: Abigail and John Adams.* New York: Alfred A. Knopf, 2010.

Gelles, Edith B. *Portia: The World of Abigail Adams.* Bloomington: Indiana University Press, 1991.

Gelles, Edith B. *Abigail Adams: A Writing Life.* London: Routledge, 2002.

Holton, Woody. *Abigail Adams: A Life.* New York: Free Press, 2009.

Advocate and Family Guardian

The *Advocate* magazine was one of the foremost messengers in the crusade for moral reform from the mid-19th to the mid-20th centuries. The *Advocate of Moral Reform* was originally the publication of the New York Female Moral Reform Society, a women's organization which later became the American Female Moral Reform Society, with the renamed *Advocate and Family Guardian* as its national organ. The magazine had two specific missions: to convert prostitutes and to broadcast the occasions of seduction. It did not blame women for prostitution. Rather, it laid a full measure of responsibility on men and it also educated children against becoming either victims or future perpetrators of lewd behavior.

The eight-page publication disseminated these messages as the *Advocate of Moral Reform* when it superseded *McDowall's Journal* in 1835. It changed its name to the *Advocate of Moral Reform and Family Guardian*

in 1847 and, in 1849, to the *Advocate and Family Guardian,* which it remained until ceasing publication in 1941.

A group of women banded together to follow the example of missionary John McDowall, who had issued a controversial report in 1832 on the need for reform of New York society. In the journal he started a year later, McDowall outlined his strategy for reform as one of prevention, "persuading the virtuous to maintain their integrity, and [to] pluck from ruin as many of the degraded as possible." He cited his journal's mission:

> The principal design of the Journal is to expose public immorality, to elicit public sentiment, and to devise and carry into effect the means of preventing licentiousness and vice.
>
> It is desirable, for the public good, that a copy of each number should be placed in every family in the land.

Through his writings, McDowall documented the evils of the city. The women sought further inspiration in the revivals of theologian and reformer Charles Grandison Finney and formed their own society, the New York Female Moral Reform Society, on May 12, 1834. Through this society they endeavored to carry on the mission McDowall had defined. In the fall of 1834, the society voted to purchase McDowall's *Journal* and "transform it into a national women's paper with an exclusively female staff." The journal was named the *Advocate of Moral Reform* and was begun at the start of the year.

Impassioned by their cause of reforming society's morals, these women expanded their influence beyond their domestic sphere. Editors allowed many women's voices to be heard. Readers submitted accounts of seduction, which they could share nowhere else. Editors made efforts to check information before printing it, as is evidenced by a note that ran as an apology for delaying one submission. "The facts were of such a character, that the Executive Committee deemed it best, at the time, to defer their publication till further information was received." The story was about a woman who was raped while traveling alone by coach. The note also contained this caution: "Let those of the weaker sex who may read it, be admonished never to travel alone in a public conveyance, till a renovated state of society is apparent."

The *Advocate* boldly spoke out about matters ministers hesitated to address, and often with a decidedly feminist perspective. In an account of a woman acquitted of stabbing a man to death, the *Advocate* came out on the side of the woman, not advocating killing, it explained, but glad that the man was recognized as a seducer. As radical as such a perspective was, the society did not "openly espouse" women's rights. Still, more than a decade earlier than the 1848 Seneca Falls convention—an event traditionally recognized as the beginning of the U.S. women's rights movement—the Female Moral Reform Society was advocating that women should enlarge their sphere of influence.

However, the *Advocate* presented contradictory tendencies. While it exposed the double standard of sexual morality, it also portrayed the 19th-century ideal of "true womanhood." A core of educated, morally righteous women, the editors recognized the vast number of ignorant people to be the cause of much of what was wrong in society. For instance, in addition to the "partial silence on the pulpit," wrong training in childhood was shown to be one of the primary causes of crime. The journal gave much space to addressing what was to be done about the destitute. Women were to expand their familial roles by educating destitute children. The society housed victims, later adding to the masthead of the *Advocate,* "Home for the Friendless."

Most of the target audience were mothers, who were held responsible for the formation of the moral character of their children. Pages were filled with cautionary tales, such as the analysis of a news item sent in by a reader. A man had just been imprisoned for molesting children on their way home from school. The reader pointed out that in the case of two of the girls molested, the crime was not known until their mothers noticed they had contracted a disease and began asking questions. The court nearly set the man free because the children did not cry out at the time of the offense. Keeping silent on improper but crucial matters was seen as the culprit. Editors most often spoke directly to women, but some pieces were thought to be of particular interest to children, such as memoirs of saintly children who had died or wretched victims of unfortunate circumstances.

The editorial staff was all female, and it was important that readers knew that the journal was "edited entirely by a lady."

Perhaps spawned by the women's recognition that they were disrupting an economic livelihood when they discouraged prostitution, these Protestant, mainly middle-class women became interested in women's economy and soon began addressing female labor on the pages of the *Advocate:* "Females must be better paid for their labor . . . A great deal of light work that is performed by men might be given to females." The publication took a stance that the sewing machine was evil, because it deprived women who hand-sewed at home of employment. In 1859, the society developed a sewing machine

fund through which they could supply the "most worthy with sewing machines." They bought sewing machines from manufacturers and sold them to the independent seamstresses, receiving installment payments of three dollars to five dollars a month. After one year, the fund had distributed 42 sewing machines, and most of the money had been repaid.

Circulation increased fairly steadily, a trend that persisted throughout the Civil War, although the high price of paper forced some thinner issues during that time. There was a slight decline in circulation in the postwar years. Even though as many as half of the issues printed of the *Advocate* were circulated without cost, much of the profit from the *Advocate* and the other tracts that the society published went toward the society's home for the destitute. The society also housed victimized women in a House of Industry where women were offered employment training, such as typesetting and printing. By June 1859, the publisher's box ran the line "Printed at the Home of Industry." By 1861 the paper was entirely produced by women.

Although the society initially addressed its influence to the domestic sphere, it expanded to address affairs of state. Of particular note was the push for legislation against the men who seduced women, as opposed to merely sanctioning the women involved. Problems of the nation were personalized, as the family was used as a natural stepping-stone to the nation and even the world.

In the 1860s, the publication reflected the strife of the Civil War. Its society lost members with "the decided stand taken by the majority for the Union side." The *Advocate* commented that America was a "nation of mourners," since many family circles had been broken, in great part because of lives given to the country. These rents in the social fabric of the nation were seen as the great evil of the Civil War, and, thus, the reuniting of the nation was the great triumph.

During the depression of the 1870s, a women's shelter was opened; with other institutions closing over the following decade, the society accepted the overflow. Affluent summer homes were donated; funds were started to house homeless children; and the society bought buildings and playgrounds. In 1902, the society moved into a new home, and in 1929 construction was completed on a building that would serve as a dormitory for older boys and a recreation facility for all the children. During World War I, despite a lack of charitable gifts and an increase in the price of commodities, the society remained solvent.

Increasingly, the mission of the society shifted from reforming women to housing children, providing a home for them until they graduated from high school and were ready to support themselves. The society eventually became the Woodycrest Youth Service. With the changing of the times and the recentering of its mission, the society ceased publication of the *Advocate* in 1941.

Therese L. Lueck

See Also: Moral Reform

Further Reading

Hewitt, Nancy A. *Women's Activism and Social Change: Rochester, New York, 1822–1872.* Ithaca, NY: Cornell University Press, 1984.

Ryan, Mary. *Cradle of the Middle Class: The Family in Oneida County, New York, 1790–1865.* New York: Cambridge University Press, 1981.

Whiteaker, Larry. *Seduction, Prostitution, and Moral Reform in New York, 1830–1860.* New York: Garland, 1997.

Alcott, Louisa May (1832–1888)

Louisa May Alcott, best known as the author of the novel *Little Women* (1868), was born in Germantown, Pennsylvania, on November 29, 1832. She was the second of four daughters of Abigail "Abba" May, daughter of a prominent family of social reformers, and the controversial educator and philosopher Amos Bronson Alcott.

Bronson Alcott's idealistic endeavors gave him notoriety but kept the family in chronic poverty with frequent relocations. In 1834, Bronson moved his family from Germantown to Boston to found the innovative Temple School. After it failed, the Alcotts moved to Concord, Massachusetts, home of three notable literary families—the Emersons, Thoreaus, and Hawthornes— who became their lifelong friends and greatly influenced the developing Louisa. Despite their poverty, Louisa enjoyed living in Concord, taking nature walks with her teacher Henry David Thoreau, and writing and acting in plays with her sisters Anna (b. 1831), Elizabeth (b. 1835, called Lizzie or Beth), and Abigail May (b. 1840, called May); Louisa May Alcott later immortalized the four sisters as Meg, Jo, Beth, and Amy of *Little Women*.

Louisa May Alcott read widely and eagerly. She also demonstrated an early gift for writing, completing her first poem, "To the First Robin," in 1842. She had some formal schooling; for instance, in 1840, Anna and Louisa attended Henry and John Thoreau's liberal Concord Academy. Bronson Alcott oversaw the academic and moral education of his "model children" as he waited for Victorian society to accept his progressive ideas.

Louisa May Alcott, Civil War nurse and author, is best known for her 1868 novel, *Little Women*, a story of four New England sisters based on her own family life. (Library of Congress)

In 1843, Bronson Alcott established a vegetarian utopian community in Massachusetts named Fruitlands, where he hoped to foster Transcendentalism. When the community failed after eight months, Bronson left his family to rely on charity and Abba's strong leadership while he embarked on unsuccessful speaking tours.

The Alcotts moved to Boston in 1848 where Abba supported the family by doing social work. Supplementing the family income, Louisa was a companion, seamstress, domestic servant, and teacher. Louisa was exceptionally close to her mother, a relationship that was often a burden given Abba's intense needs and frequent illnesses. To Abba's delight and Bronson's disdain, Louisa was filled with drive, independence, and financial ambition, and soon found her vocation in writing. In 1849, she wrote her first novel *The Inheritance,* never published in her lifetime. Her first publication, the poem "Sunlight," appeared in *Peterson's Magazine* in 1851 under the pseudonym Flora Fairfield; soon followed her first story, "Rival Painters," in *Olive Branch* (1852). The year 1854 marked her first published collection, *Flower Fables,* a compilation of fairy tales written for Ralph Waldo Emerson's daughter Ellen. In the 1850s and 1860s, Alcott wrote for prestigious literary magazines, including *The Saturday Evening Gazette* and *The Atlantic Monthly*. Over the next 30 years, she actively published juvenile novels and short stories including fast-paced Gothic tales written anonymously or pseudonymously.

The 1850s brought personal and economic hardship to the Alcotts. Louisa's sister Elizabeth succumbed to scarlet fever, suffering greatly and dying in 1858 in Orchard House at Concord; Louisa fictionally translated Lizzie's death into the most poignant episode of *Little Women*. Soon after, Anna became engaged and married John Bridge Pratt in 1860. Then came the Civil War (1861–1865), a pivotal event in Louisa May Alcott's writing career and health. In December 1862, Alcott enlisted as a nurse to aid the war effort, contracting typhoid in January 1863. As a result of the mercury-based calomel treatment, she lost her hair and her good health. Returning to Concord, she turned life into literature, basing *Hospital Sketches* (1863) on letters written home while serving at the Union Hotel Hospital in Georgetown. While the memoir was a major step professionally, Alcott forever suffered the effects of the treatment for typhoid that gradually poisoned her body.

While living in Boston and Concord, Alcott continued her writing career. Unknown to her family and distinguished friends, in 1863 she launched a secret writing career to augment the family income: beginning with "Pauline's Passion and Punishment," she wrote thrillers for "penny dreadfuls" such as *Frank Leslie's Illustrated Newspaper* and *Flag of Our Union*. Her first novel for adults, *Moods* (1865), a tale of thwarted love, received mixed reviews. In 1867, she became editor of *Merry's Museum*, a magazine for children. With the publication of *Little Women* (1868), an immediate best seller, Alcott earned international acclaim and financial security for her family. Ironically, Alcott won fame for a book that she perceived as an artistic regression. She despairingly called herself "a literary nursery-maid who provides moral pap for the young." Alcott continued writing stories and seven subsequent juvenile novels (some of which appeared serially prior to book publication). *An Old-Fashioned Girl* (1870), *Eight Cousins* (1875), *Rose in Bloom* (1876), and particularly the two sequels to *Little Women—Little Men* (1871) and *Jo's Boys* (1886)—enjoyed a wide readership in America and abroad.

In real life, Louisa May Alcott did not follow the traditional path of her juvenile fictional heroines. She never doted on children as her fans presumed. An ardent abolitionist, she championed reform in dress, diet, child labor, prisons, and gender roles. She reveled in her spinsterhood and grew active in women's suffrage, contributing regularly for the feminist periodical, *Woman's Journal*. Despite her efforts to be dutiful and conquer sin—ideals she presents in her best-loved juvenile books—in her adult fiction, including *Work: A Story of Experience* (1873), she defended a woman's right to work rather than marry. Moreover, Louisa's success as a juvenile fiction writer made travel possible, and she twice toured Europe – in 1865, and again in 1870 with her sister, May.

From her writing, she supported her family, including Anna and her two sons following Pratt's death in 1870. Louisa's financial savvy and literary success seem all the more remarkable given that from 1863, she was plagued with ill health and addicted to opium for sleep and pain control. She also experienced more significant loss in the late 1870s. Abba died in 1877, and Louisa grew closer to her father, especially when May married the Swiss banker Ernest Nieriker in Paris in 1878. She experienced further grief when May, while launching her art career, died late in 1879, shortly after giving birth to Lulu, named after Louisa.

In the 1880s, Louisa May Alcott raised Lulu and cared for her aging father, who suffered a paralytic stroke in 1882. Her own health declining, she sought homeopathy and mind-cure treatments while completing *Jo's Boys* and three volumes of stories entitled *Lulu's Library*, dedicated to her niece. From 1887 until her death in 1888, Alcott lived in Dr. Rhoda Lawrence's convalescent home in Roxbury, Massachusetts. Having transferred her energies to her father following Abba's death and reached a better understanding with Bronson once she achieved the success that eluded him, Louisa seems to have relinquished her will to live while visiting Bronson at his deathbed on March 1, 1888. Louisa died on March 6, 1888, two days after her father's death, and a joint funeral was held. Anna Alcott Pratt continued to live in Concord, caring for her sister's estate and for Lulu, who returned to Europe in 1893 to live with Nieriker.

Catherine J. Golden

See Also: Slavery and the Civil War

Further Reading

LaPlante, Eve. *Marmee & Louisa: The Untold Story of Louisa May Alcott and Her Mother.* New York: Free Press, 2012.

Matteson, John. *Eden's Outcasts: The Story of Louisa May Alcott and Her Father.* New York: W.W. Norton, 2007.

Reisen, Harriet. *Louisa May Alcott: The Woman Behind Little Women.* New York: Henry Holt, 2010.

Sizer, Lyde Cullen. *The Political Work of Northern Women Writers and the Civil War, 1850–1872.* Chapel Hill: University of North Carolina Press, 2000.

The American Revolution

In evaluating the impact of the American Revolution upon women and of women upon the American Revolution, it is worth considering a question posed by the early 20th-century historian Carl Becker: How revolutionary was the American Revolution? Answering this query in regard to women requires a consideration of issues of class, place, and race. Generally speaking, the economic and political status of women, regardless of class, race, or place, was not greatly altered by the Revolution. Nevertheless, women's contributions to the Revolutionary struggle were more significant than Betsy Ross stitching the flag, Abigail Adams admonishing her husband John Adams to remember the ladies, the slave Phillis Wheatley publishing poems that praised emancipation, and Deborah Sampson Gannett posing as a man in order to participate in combat as a Patriot. Although they were excluded from formal participation in the political debates of the Revolutionary era, women contributed labor, intelligence, and courage that was crucial to the triumph of the Patriot cause. Contemporary recognition of the essential role played by women in the struggle for independence is evident in the cult of the republican woman that arose during and after the war and that enhanced the educational opportunities and status of white middle- and upper-class women in the post-Revolutionary period.

To properly evaluate the impact of the Revolution upon women, it is first necessary to examine whether life in 18th-century colonial America constituted a golden age for women as some scholars have suggested. In support of this view, historians point to the increased value of women due to their scarcity for marriage as well as the importance of females laboring alongside men in the fields, thus providing women, so this argument goes, with a rough degree of equality under difficult frontier conditions common in much of colonial America. Primitive frontier conditions, however, were not necessarily chosen or welcomed by women. Rather, they were perceived as a necessary temporary expedient in the transition to a more settled lifestyle. The lives of women in the 18th-century British colonies were burdened by work. With more than 90 percent of colonial families involved in farming, a woman was responsible for raising children, preparing nearly all the family's food, sometimes working beside her husband in the fields to produce that food, maintaining the home, and using her sewing skills to make the family's clothing. Only fairly affluent women, who could afford indentured servants or slaves, were able to escape the hardships of physical labor in colonial America.

Nor did the imbalance of women to men provide a protected status for women. In order for women to take full advantage of their childbearing years, colonial society encouraged them to marry early, usually in their late teens. In 18th-century America, there were approximately 14 live births for every 1,000 persons. A young woman might thus expect to bear 8 to 9 children, spending most of her adult life pregnant, nursing, and caring for children.

The colonial frontier experience also did little to alter the political status of women. British, Dutch, and German settlers immigrating to the colonies carried with them the patriarchal notion of family in which women, no matter how valuable their labors in the home and fields, were expected to be subordinate to their husbands. Thomas Jefferson instructed his just-married daughter to obey her husband, insisting that her happiness depended upon her pleasing him above all other concerns. Accordingly, colonial women were excluded from active participation in politics, and women who challenged the patriarchal order, such as Anne Hutchison in the Massachusetts Bay Colony, were severely censured.

Since every woman in early America was expected to assume the roles of wife, mother, and homemaker—and only those roles—there was little emphasis placed upon educating young women, even in affluent families. Higher education was considered too intellectually challenging, while teaching the more refined domestic arts to young women in private homes was one of the few professions deemed appropriate for middle-class young women. It is estimated that on the eve of the Revolution, fewer than half of white females in the colonies were literate, while the white male literacy rate may have approached 80 percent. The patriarchal political order was supported by the colonial religious establishment, which asserted that women were to be obedient to their husbands and practice the virtues of piety and humility. The one major exception to this rule was in the Quaker community, where women were accorded some degree of equality in religious participation, although generally not in economic pursuits.

On an economic level, women might work alongside their husbands, both in the fields and in urban shops, but married women forfeited their property rights to their spouses. Due to this fact, arranged marriages were not uncommon among the colonial landed gentry. The only way a woman could achieve and maintain financial independence was to become a widow or to never marry, and this was effective only for women who were born into families of means or who had married men of means. Divorce, while possible, was rarely granted. And to remain a widow—especially a young widow—after the death of a spouse or, even more, to remain single by choice was rare, for matrimony was the accepted and expected status for both men and women. Also, as some scholars have suggested in examining the witchcraft trials of the 17th-century in Massachusetts, property-owning unmarried women could be perceived as threats to the orderly transfer of male property rights.

The protection of property rights, however, was not a vital concern for all women in colonial America. Many were too poor to own or enjoy property, either as wives or on their own. And perhaps one-third of colonial households included servants, of whom roughly one-third were women. There is also considerable evidence that female servants, in addition to having no property and little security, were often subject to sexual abuse from their male masters.

The general material condition of women in early America began to improve with the growing urbanization and commercialization of the colonial economy, beginning early in the 18th century. This trend toward a market economy and widespread consumerism first significantly affected women in the northern colonies. The southern colonies, of course, were not immune to these changes, but for the region's many African American women, this economic growth simply enhanced the prospects for racial slavery and the sexual exploitation that often accompanied it. For many widowed white women in both the northern and southern colonies, however, an expanding economy resulted in greater commercial opportunities, with widowed women successfully running such businesses as inns, taverns, and dry goods stores. For example, one of the most prominent businesswomen in colonial and Revolutionary Virginia was Clementina Rind, who, following the death of her husband in 1773, assumed the editorship of the *Virginia Gazette.* Most white women on the eve of the Revolution, however, continued to maintain their traditional roles as wives, mothers, and homemakers.

The events of the Revolution itself could at times both affect and engage the interests of colonial women. While the course of public political debate was defined by masculine voices, women were not unaware of the political discourse of Revolutionary America. Literate women enjoyed access to political tracts of the period, while many less educated women were exposed to the economic deprivations and boycotts of the day. Although denied formal participation in the political process, many women of every social class must have engaged their husbands in dialogue regarding the impact of Revolutionary activities and choices upon their domestic lives. Political and military decisions taken by husbands had tremendous economic repercussions for their wives and children. While men were away from home engaged in political meetings or serving on the battlefield, it was up to women to educate and provide for their children and to protect and manage their family farm or business. The burden fell heavily upon women whether their husbands were enlisted in the Patriot or Loyalist causes. Backing the losing Loyalist side meant that many women suffered ridicule, physical abuse, the loss of a home, and economic deprivation, all based on the political choices made by their husbands.

Women contributed greatly to the ultimate Patriot victory in the war. In the port cities of the Northeast, women, sometimes referred to as "daughters of liberty," were part of the urban crowds whose protests against British mercantile policy sometimes turned violent. In October 1774, 51 women in Edenton, North Carolina, drafted a resolution declaring their allegiance to the Patriot cause and promising to do all in their power to ensure its triumph. During the war, the Ladies Association of Philadelphia directed a campaign to raise financial support for American troops, gathering approximately $300,000 in a matter of weeks. But most women made their contributions to the cause within the domestic sphere. During the 1760s and early 1770s, colonial protestors advocated the use of boycotts of British goods as a weapon against British policies. Much of the economic burden of these boycotts fell upon women, who had to alter their families' patterns of consumption. Support for the boycotts also depended upon women sitting at their looms and spinning wheels, providing homespun clothes for themselves and their families. During the war, many women made the sacrifice of widowhood as their husbands perished on the battlefield.

Women's contributions to the Patriot triumph, then, were immense. There were few calls, however, for the establishment of gender equality in the political realm. Some women, of course, were noted for their outspokenness. Hannah Lee Corbin, whose private life was considered somewhat scandalous following the death of her husband, complained in 1778 to her politically powerful brother, Richard Henry Lee, that she was being taxed without representation. She believed that widows, at least, deserved the right to vote. Her brother, while agreeing in principle, took no action.

Perhaps the best-known political statement by a woman of the Revolution is Abigail Adams's 1776 letter to her husband John, requesting that he and his colleagues "remember the ladies" when Congress framed the laws of the new republican nation. An intelligent and competent woman who maintained the family's affairs for years while her husband was in Congress and later on diplomatic assignment in Europe, Abigail, nonetheless, did not intend to challenge traditional gender roles. Rather than demanding equal suffrage, she was arguing for an equality of legal status within the domestic sphere of marriage in which women primarily operated.

If the natural rights doctrine of the Declaration of Independence was not proclaimed for women, many colonial Americans recognized the incompatibility of slavery with Jefferson's notion that all men were created equal. Thus, many black men and women expressed the hope that the Revolutionary ideology of the colonists might culminate in the abolition of slavery. The legacy of the Revolution did lead to the outlawing of slavery, by constitution, law, or court ruling, in several northern states. But when the Revolution ended, most African Americans in the United States remained securely in bondage. Approximately 5,000 male slaves did earn their freedom by fighting for the Patriot cause, and British offers of freedom were seen as promising for both enslaved men and women. Yet when the British lost the war, they abandoned many of the black men and women who had flocked to their side in pursuit of emancipation.

At its conclusion, the Revolution failed to alter the condition of most enslaved women, the legal status of most married free women, or the level of political participation of all women. But in New Jersey, unmarried women who met the required property qualification were allowed to vote for a quarter century following independence. Despite such limited structural change, however, there were clearly gendered elements to the rhetoric and impact of the Revolution. As the clash between the colonies and Britain intensified in the 1760s, the perception of the mother country was altered from that of a nurturing female to that of a tyrannical force with more masculine qualities. Thus, John Adams likened Great Britain to Shakespeare's Lady Macbeth, while Thomas Paine called King George III the "royal brute of Britain." While the British were increasingly portrayed with negative masculine characteristics, American liberty was depicted in a more passive feminine fashion. In many graphics produced before the Revolution, liberty was also presented as a chaste, vulnerable, fragile female figure who needed protection from the rapacious British.

During the Revolutionary War, this gendered reading of the conflict did not translate into a more positive status or esteem for women. Liberty required protection, and this could only come through the aggressive fighting abilities of the male citizen-soldier. Republicanism was identified as virtue with the physical courage and self-sacrifice of men who served as soldiers in the Revolutionary cause. Women were relegated to the more passive role of supporting this male republicanism, in which citizenship was based largely upon military service.

This more militaristic masculine definition of citizenship fell into disfavor following the Revolutionary War, when Americans felt the need to develop a less combative ideology of republicanism to ensure peace, stability, and social order. Millennial expectations of social perfection were replaced by more practical concerns. The Federalist Papers and the Constitution made it clear that not all men were needed to serve the state. Instead, the greater common good could be achieved through individuals competitively pursuing their self-interests. Virtue was, accordingly, defined less as a collective public trait than a private one. This meant that virtue was increasingly relegated to the sphere of friendship and family, where women enjoyed greater influence.

The traditional patriarchal conception of marriage was also gradually undermined by an emerging republican ideology of equality on the domestic front. Men and women were increasingly urged to marry based on an affectionate friendship. The relationship between husband and wife was extolled as voluntary and based upon a degree of equality within the domestic sphere, an appropriate metaphor for the relationship among citizens of a republic. This was the type of equality that Abigail Adams appeared to have had in mind.

The ideology of the republican woman insisted that married women and mothers were essential to the survival of the American experiment in republican government. Woman's civic duty lay in the civilizing influence that she might bestow upon her husband and sons. The future of the nation, therefore, was in the hands of its "republican mothers." To ensure that women were prepared to handle such a charge and serve as intellectual helpmates to their husbands, the post-Revolutionary era witnessed a new emphasis on the education of women. During the 1780s and 1790s, schools and academies for young women were established to ensure the proper education for republican motherhood. Typical of the mission of these schools was the ceremony that marked the founding of the Philadelphia Young Ladies Academy, at whose dedication Benjamin Rush spoke. Rush asserted that education would prepare women to serve as intelligent companions for their husbands and as mothers who would guide their sons in republican virtues and values.

The concept of republican motherhood enhanced the status of women while providing an ideological justification for excluding women from participation in public life. Republican motherhood was thus a double-edged sword. Furthermore, the social status and greater educational opportunities accorded republican motherhood were largely reserved for white women of the middle and upper classes. For both women of color and poorer white women, the Revolution brought little immediate change to the masculine order of political and economic domination. For most women, the American Revolution was hardly a revolutionary experience. The Revolutionary era, nevertheless, did undermine social constraints, providing most women with greater freedom in the choosing of husbands. Also, the expanded educational opportunities of the postwar era, while bestowed upon white women of the upper and middle classes, did provide a foundation upon which women's reform movements of the later 19th century could challenge slavery and male bastions of power.

Ron Briley

See Also: Adams, Abigail; Boycotts; Education of Women (before the Civil War); Molly Pitcher Legend; Murray, Judith Sargent; Republican Motherhood; Sampson, Deborah; Ward, Nancy; Warren, Mercy Otis; Wheatley, Phillis; Young Ladies' Academy of Philadelphia

Primary Document: 1804, Paul Revere Defends Deborah Sampson Gannett, a Female Soldier

Further Reading

Berkin, Carol R. *First Generations: Women in Colonial America.* New York: Hill and Wang, 1996.

Gundersen, Joan R. *To Be Useful to the World: Women in Revolutionary America, 1740–1790.* New York: Twayne Publishers, 1996.

Hoffman, Ronald, and Peter J. Albert, eds. *Women in the Age of the American Revolution.* Charlottesville: University of Virginia Press, 1989.

Kerber, Linda K. *Women of the Republic: Intellect and Ideology in Revolutionary America.* Chapel Hill: University of North Carolina Press, 1980.

Mayer, Holly A. *Belonging to the Army: Camp Followers and Community during the American Revolution.* Columbia: University of South Carolina Press, 1996.

Norton, Mary Beth. *Founding Mothers and Fathers: Gendered Power and the Forming of American Society.* New York: Knopf, 1996.

Zagarri, Rosemarie. *Revolutionary Backlash: Women and Politics in the Early American Republic.* Philadelphia: University of Pennsylvania Press, 2007.

Anneke, Mathilde Franziska (1817–1884)

The feminist Mathilde Anneke was one of the first women in Germany to write as a professional. Forced to flee after taking part in the revolutionary upheavals there in 1848, she was called one of the "three Amazons of the German Revolution" by socialist feminist Clara Zetkin. Although Anneke never really settled into her adopted home of Milwaukee, Wisconsin, remaining among a tight-knit community of German exiles, she played an important role in the U.S. antislavery and suffrage campaigns.

Born in Westphalia, Anneke came from a middle-class, Roman Catholic family of 12 children. She was married off at 17 to a French wine merchant much older than herself but left her husband soon after and in 1846 fought a custody battle to bring up her small daughter, struggling to support them both by her writing. For a while, Anneke lived a quiet and pious life as a devout Catholic, writing religious poetry, publishing a book of prayers, and translating the work of others. In 1844 she published the play *Oithono,* which was staged in Münster. In 1846–1847, to express sympathy for Louise Aston, another woman married young who had fought a battle for divorce, Anneke wrote the pamphlet "Woman in Conflict with Social Conditions." Her second marriage to Prussian officer, radical, and freethinker Fritz Anneke in 1847 brought her into a whole new world of revolutionary ideas through his work as editor of the workers' daily *The New Cologne Newspaper* and their activities in Rhenish political circles. When her husband was imprisoned for his links with communist agitators, Anneke, who had renounced her religion and become a freethinker, took over editing the paper from September 1848. After it was suppressed in December 1848, she launched her own *Women's Newspaper,* which in its sole issue discussed the separation of German schools from the control of the church.

During 1848–1849 the Annekes took part in the resistance to the Prussians in the Rhenish Palatinate, with Mathilde riding alongside her husband and serving as his orderly and messenger. Her account was later published in German in Newark in 1853 (*Memoirs of a Woman from the Campaigns in Baden and the Palatinate*). But Prussian successes and the fall of Rastatt in July 1849 forced the couple to flee to the United States via Switzerland as part of a group of "forty-eighters" (as the German exiles were known).

They settled in Milwaukee, Wisconsin, where Anneke became an active supporter of the abolitionist cause. In 1846–1847 she had written on the subjection of women in her pamphlet "Woman in Conflict with Social Conditions," and in 1852 she established the *German Woman's Newspaper,* which advocated women's emancipation, the first German-language journal in the United States to be run by a woman. Despite the hostile reception it received, Anneke kept the paper going for another two and a half years by giving lectures. In 1853 she met and became good friends with Susan B. Anthony and Elizabeth Cady Stanton, the leaders of the U.S. women's movement, and with their encouragement founded a suffrage association in Wisconsin. From 1869 Anneke regularly attended conventions of the National Woman Suffrage Association, where she was admired as an eloquent speaker. In 1858 tragedy struck the family when three of the Annekes' six children died in a smallpox epidemic.

In 1860 Anneke joined her husband in Europe, where he had gone to work as a newspaper correspondent. When he returned to the United States in support of the Unionists in the Civil War, Anneke, by then used to living an independent life, remained in German-speaking Switzerland with their children, supporting them through her journalism. She wrote in support of the Union cause, producing antislavery stories such as "The Slave Auction" (1862) and underlining the particularly cruel double enslavement of black women. She returned to the United States at the end of the Civil War in 1865 and turned her attention to women's education and training, believing them to be essential if women were to achieve equality with men both in society and in the professions. She opened the Milwaukee Tochter Institut, a German-language girls' school (also known as Madam Anneke's German-French-English Academy), acted as its administrator, and also taught there while raising funds to keep the school going by giving lectures and selling articles to the *Illinois State Times.*

Helen Rappaport

See Also: Anthony, Susan B. (Vol. 2); Stanton, Elizabeth Cady (Vol. 2)

Further Reading

Cocalis, Susan L., and Kay Goodman, eds. *Beyond the Eternal Feminine: Critical Essays on Women and German Literature.* Stuttgart: Akademischer Verlag Hans-Dieter Heinz, 1982.

McFadden, Margaret. *Golden Cables of Sympathy: The Transatlantic Sources of Nineteenth-Century Feminism.* Lexington: University of Kentucky Press, 1999.

Piepke, Susan L. *Mathilde Franziska Anneke: The Works of a German–American Activist.* New York: Peter Lang Publishing, Inc., 2006.

B

Bagley, Sarah (1806–1883?)

Sarah Bagley was president of the Lowell Female Labor Reform Association (LFLRA) and a writer for the *Lowell Offering*, exerting influence as a labor leader beyond her local area. Bagley was born in Candia, New Hampshire. Little is known of her life before she arrived in Lowell, Massachusetts, in 1836, although she obtained enough formal education to become a highly articulate writer and speaker.

In 1836, Lowell was considered the ideal factory city and was a popular tourist destination, as well as a thriving industrial concern. Bagley originally took part in Improvement Circles, designed to enrich the educational and cultural lives of mill workers, and she wrote for the *Lowell Offering,* a paper sponsored by the Boston Associates, the consortium that owned Lowell's textile mills. Conditions in Lowell worsened even before Bagley arrived, however, with a short walkout occurring in 1834. The Panic of 1837 caused more wage cuts, speed-ups in the factory, and high turnover rates. Another wage cut and strike in 1840 apparently radicalized Bagley. She became an advocate of the theories of Charles Fourier, a French utopian advocate of cooperative production and communal living.

In December 1844, Bagley became the cofounder and first president of the LFLRA, widely hailed as America's first union of factory women. Within six months it had over 500 members, and Bagley left her mill job to expand the association's reach to other cities. Eventually Female Labor Reform groups met in Waltham and Fall River, Massachusetts; Dover, Nashua, and Manchester, New Hampshire; and across western Pennsylvania. Central to the LFLRA platform was the call for a 10-hour work day. Bagley immersed herself in the 10-hour struggle and testified before a Massachusetts legislative committee on behalf of the cause in 1845. She also affiliated the LFLRA with the New England Working Men's Association and served as the editor of its newspaper, *The Voice of Industry.* Her attacks on the *Lowell Offering* hastened that paper's demise, and her organization the Industrial Reform Lyceum, brought a steady stream of radical speakers to Lowell.

Despite Bagley's tireless efforts, the 10-hour plea was rejected by the Massachusetts legislature and a call for a general strike on July 4, 1846, fizzled. *The Voice of Industry* foundered and Bagley resigned after a dispute with a sexist editor. In 1846, Bagley became the first female telegraph operator in the city of Lowell, a trade she also plied in Springfield, Massachusetts, in 1847, before returning to Lowell as a millhand. She later moved to Philadelphia and became a Quaker. Sometime in the 1850s she married James Durno, an Albany, New York homeopathic doctor and patent medicine manufacturer. They moved to Brooklyn Heights, New York, where Durno died in 1872. Bagley disappears from the historical record after 1883.

Robert E. Weir

See Also: Labor Unions (19th Century); *The Lowell Offering*; Lowell Textile Mills

Primary Document: 1845, Testimony of Female Factory Workers before Massachusetts State Legislature

Further Reading

Dublin, Thomas. *Women at Work: The Transformation of Work and Community in Lowell, Massachusetts, 1826–1860.* New York: Columbia University Press, 1979.

Foner, Philip. *Women and the American Labor Movement: From the First Trade Unions to the Present.* New York: Free Press, 1982.

Murphy, Teresa. *Ten Hours' Labor: Religion, Reform, and Gender in Early New England.* Ithaca, NY: Cornell University Press, 1992.

Selden, Bernice. *The Mill Girls: Lucy Larcom, Harriet Hanson Robinson, Sarah Bagley.* New York: Atheneum, 1983.

Barton, Clara (1821–1912)

Clara Barton, the "Angel of the Battlefield," was to the American Civil War what Florence Nightingale, the "Lady with the Lamp," was to the Crimean War. As humanitarians and nurses, both of them improved standards of care among the sick and wounded and contributed to the establishment of women's nursing. Like Nightingale, Barton never married and developed her own brand of ruthless and energetic efficiency. Her determination would result in the founding of the American Red Cross in 1881; her insistence on her own unchallenged control would, however, lead to her ouster from the organization in 1904.

Clara Barton, Civil War nurse, humanitarian, and founder of the American Red Cross. (National Archives)

Born in Oxford, Massachusetts, the last of five children, Barton grew hearing stories from her father about his days fighting in the Indian wars and his love of the army. After nursing her sick brother for two years, Barton took up teaching, first in local schools and then, in 1850, at the Liberal Institute in Clinton, New York. In 1852 she founded one of the first American free public schools in Bordentown, New Jersey. After commending Barton on her success, the authorities promptly appointed a man above her to take charge. Barton resigned in protest in 1854. She had for years suffered intermittently from bouts of depression, during which she would lose her voice, and she decided to move south to a warmer climate in the hope that this would help. Settling in Washington, D.C., in a bold move she entered the male preserve of the civil service. Barton was probably the first officially appointed woman to take up a clerical job there, copying documents in the Patent Office. She interrupted her appointment to return to Massachusetts from 1857 to 1860.

When the Civil War broke out in April 1861, Barton befriended casualties from the Sixth Massachusetts Regiment quartered in Washington and called for donations and supplies from their families back in her home state. The response was huge, and Barton took a mule train and wagon to distribute the supplies, which included brandy, tobacco, and sewing kits. But Barton quickly realized that small acts of charity such as hers would not be enough to alleviate the large-scale suffering of Union troops and that she had to take her work to the front lines. Her experience of the aftermath of the Second Battle of Bull Run in August 1862—in which 3,000 men were wounded and during which she helped hold down the operating table under artillery fire—galvanized her to bypass the bureaucracy and dilatoriness of official military channels and organize her own medical supplies and food for the wounded, who, at Bull Run, she had described as covering "acres."

Barton was appalled by the unnecessary loss of life among wounded men who were not receiving medical attention quickly enough. With groups of volunteers, she traveled to the scenes of fighting by mule train to nurse the wounded and provide much-needed succor, such as hot soup and coffee. At Antietam in September 1862, her clothes drenched in blood, Barton attended the wounded in the thick of fire, at one point nearly being killed herself when a wounded man she was tending was hit by a bullet. It was not just on the battlefield that men suffered, however, as Barton witnessed the inadequacy of army hospitals. In 1864 Barton was given an official appointment as head nurse of the Army of the James, running corps hospitals in Virginia. Meanwhile, the official Union appointee, Dorothea Dix, had been acting as overall superintendent of women nurses for the Sanitary Commission since 1861, but Barton resisted any suggestion that she should join her nursing team, determined to act independently.

After the war, Barton exposed the sufferings of those who had died or nearly starved to death in prison camps, such as the Andersonville Prison in Georgia. This Confederate camp housed 33,000 Union prisoners by war's end, and 13,000 died there, to be buried in mass graves. Beginning in 1865, with the sanction of President Abraham Lincoln, Barton worked to trace and identify killed, wounded, and missing Union troops, funding her own office for the purpose in Annapolis, Maryland, and supporting it on the lecture circuit for two years. She received letters from many thousands of families anxious to trace their missing men, in return writing something like 22,000 letters herself and supervising the laying out of a proper cemetery for those who had died at Andersonville. Barton continued her attempts to trace missing soldiers until 1869, by which time she had spent $1,750 of her own income in responding to a flood of over 63,000 letters inquiring about missing soldiers.

After the end of a two-year tour in which she gave 300 public lectures on her experiences of the war, Barton went to Europe on a rest cure in 1869 but soon was drawn into new activities when she discovered the work of the International Committee of the Red Cross, founded in 1864. She volunteered her services and helped organize relief and military hospitals in Strasbourg, Metz, and Paris during the Franco-Prussian War of 1870–1871, distributing supplies raised by donations in the United States.

Barton returned to the United States in 1873, spent the next five years campaigning for a national organization of medical aid, and again toured with lectures on medical issues. In 1877 she was asked to establish the American Association of the Red Cross, which after its incorporation in 1881 elected Barton president. Subsequently, Barton crusaded for the United States to support the Geneva Convention on the humane treatment of prisoners of war, which it signed in 1882. Believing in the "wise benevolence" of preparing in peacetime not only for the exigencies of war but also for natural disasters, she urged the American Red Cross to set up relief programs for such emergencies as floods in Ohio and Mississippi in 1884, a hurricane on the Sea Islands off South Carolina in 1893, and a tidal wave in Galveston, Texas, in 1900. At the age of 77, still unwilling to delegate her humanitarian work to others, Barton traveled to Cuba in 1898 to work as a nurse during the Spanish-American War and organized Red Cross medical supplies and relief to Cuban civilians, traveling by her now familiar mode of mule train.

By the end of the century, Barton was struggling to keep the American Red Cross afloat as funds ran low. The U.S. Congress insisted on less centralized control by Barton after objections raised by board member Mabel Boardman had led to an investigation of the organization's business management. Barton resigned in 1904 and returned to her home in Glen Echo, Maryland, where she lived a life of semi-reclusion and wrote *A Story of the Red Cross* (1904) and *Story of My Childhood* (1907). Having always endorsed the women's rights movement in the United States, Barton had become an important figure, making personal appearances at landmark events such as the first convention of the National Woman Suffrage Association, held in Washington, D.C., in January 1869. In 1902 she attended the first international woman suffrage conference. Like her contemporary Florence Nightingale, she received many honors and lived a long life—into her nineties—despite the rigors of her long years of campaigning.

A Clara Barton National Historic Site was established by the National Park Service in 1975 at Barton's home at Glen Echo, Maryland, the original headquarters of the American Red Cross, from where she had distributed relief supplies.

Helen Rappaport

See Also: Dix, Dorothea; Slavery and the Civil War; United States Sanitary Commission; National Woman Suffrage Association (Vol. 2)

Further Reading

Burton, David H. *Clara Barton: In the Service of Humanity.* Westport, CT: Greenwood Press, 1995.

Jones, Marian Moser. *The American Red Cross from Clara Barton to the New Deal.* Baltimore, MD: Johns Hopkins University Press, 2012.

Oates, Stephen B. *A Woman of Valor: Clara Barton and the Civil War.* New York: Free Press, 1994.

Pryor, Elizabeth Brown. *Clara Barton: Professional Angel.* Philadelphia: University of Pennsylvania Press, 1987.

Bathsheba Spooner Case (1778)

Although there was no doubt as to the guilt of Bathsheba Spooner (ca. 1746–1778), her controversial death sentence raised serious questions regarding the execution of women in Massachusetts.

Bathsheba Spooner was the privileged daughter of Brigadier General Timothy Ruggles. She was profoundly unhappy in her marriage to Joshua Spooner, a man to whom she confessed "an utter aversion." In March 1777, Bathsheba took an ailing continental soldier into her home. Probably suffering from influenza, Ezra Ross was nursed back to health by Bathsheba. He rejoined the army, but visited the Spooner house on two more occasions in the coming year. At some point the two embarked on a romantic relationship, and Bathsheba became pregnant. Knowing she could not pass the child off as belonging to her husband, Joshua, she panicked and began plotting his murder. She enlisted the aid of her lover and two additional soldiers, promising them money and alcohol in exchange for the murder.

On the night of March 1, 1778, Joshua Spooner was beaten to death and dumped headfirst down his own well. All three soldiers were apprehended the following day, confessed to the crime, and named Bathsheba as the instigator. The four conspirators were tried, found guilty, and sentenced to hang.

Bathsheba Spooner begged for a delay of execution until her child could be born. Condemned women who were known to be pregnant were always permitted to carry a child to term, both in England and America.

Spooner was examined by a panel of 12 women, all of whom signed a statement declaring she was not pregnant. Spooner appealed their finding, asserting that she knew herself to be approximately four months pregnant. She wrote in a letter to the Council of Massachusetts that her child was "innocent of the faults of her who bears it, and has, I beg leave to say, a right to the existence which God has begun to give it."

A second physical examination of Bathsheba took place less than three weeks later, at which several of the examining matrons switched their opinions, claiming they believed the condemned to be quick with child. Two of the examiners were adamant in their conviction that Bathsheba was not with child, and authorities chose to proceed with the execution.

The insistence upon a speedy hanging for Bathsheba raises questions as to the motives of the authorities. Bathsheba's father was the notorious Brigadier General Timothy Ruggles, whose powerful loyalist support for the British made his name anathema in Massachusetts. It is possible that the intolerance shown to Bathsheba was prompted in part owing to political vengeance. The legal validity of her execution was further tarnished by the council member who authorized the final warrant for execution, John Avery Jr., the murder victim's stepbrother. The failure of Avery to recuse himself from this case added another layer of unseemly bias to the execution.

Although Bathsheba never formally confessed to the crime, on the scaffold she acknowledged that she "died justly." Following the execution an autopsy was performed per Bathsheba's request. The perfectly formed five-month-old male fetus proved the state had caused the death of a child in their haste to carry out the execution of a notoriously unpopular woman. Bathsheba roused the wrath of her community for her adultery, the murder of her husband, and stubborn loyalist sympathies. They retaliated against her by refusing to allow her a few additional weeks to prove the existence of her pregnancy. The horror of executing a pregnant woman so upset the community that the execution of females was called into question. Although there were two additional women executed in Massachusetts before female execution was outlawed, never again would a woman claiming pregnancy be summarily executed in the American colonies.

Dorothy A. Mays

See Also: Abortion (17th and 18th Centuries)

Further Reading

Naish, Camille. *Death Comes to the Maiden: Sex and Execution, 1431–1933.* New York: Routledge, 2013 [1991].

Navas, Deborah. *Murdered by His Wife.* Amherst: University of Massachusetts Press, 1999.

Beecher, Catharine (1800–1878)

The American educational and domestic reformer Catharine Beecher came from a family of campaigning evangelicals and was the elder sister of abolitionist and writer Harriet Beecher Stowe. A staunch advocate of women's separate sphere of work, which she emphasized as at all times being in the service of God, she was an opponent of the women's suffrage movement. Beecher believed that to invest political power in women would cause them to turn their backs on their duties within the home, where she saw their role as teacher-missionaries engaged in the moral regeneration of society.

Born in East Hampton, New York, Catherine Esther Beecher was the eldest of 13 children of congregational preacher Lyman Beecher. She was educated at home in her mother Roxana's private school and subsequently at a private school in Litchfield, Connecticut. But at the

Catharine Beecher, proponent of women's education and author of the widely read *A Treatise on Domestic Economy* (1842). (Cirker, Hayward and Blanche Cirker, eds., *Dictionary of American Portraits*, 1967)

age of 16, Beecher became a surrogate mother to her siblings when their own mother died. In 1821 she took up a teaching post at a girls' school in New London. She was briefly engaged to a Yale mathematics professor, Alexander Fisher, and went into a deep depression when he was lost at sea in 1823. She never married, instead accepting this loss as a sign from God that she should devote her life to the cause of women's education. In 1824 she founded a school for young ladies with her sister May, which later became the Hartford Female Seminary, a few years after another educational pioneer, Emma Willard, opened her own similar establishment, the Troy Seminary.

Beecher also began writing the first of numerous essays on women's education as well as textbooks for schools, such as "Female Education" in 1827 and the 1829 pamphlet, "Suggestions Respecting Improvements in Education." In it, she advocated not only the intellectual advancement of women but also the moral training that would guide them in their leadership of the regeneration of society through the professions of nursing and teaching. Her strong support for temperance and women's role in the movement was colored by her belief, as with teaching, that women occupied a higher moral ground than men.

In 1832 Beecher moved to Cincinnati with her father when he took up a post as president of the Lane Theological Seminary there. She opened another school, the Western Female Institute, which she ran until 1837, when financial difficulties and her ill health forced her to give up her position. Believing that a whole new generation of women teachers was urgently needed in the new frontier towns of the West, Beecher preempted the later exhortation of Horace Greeley by urging not young men but young women to "go west." In her 1835 *Essay on the Education of Female Teachers,* Beecher estimated that 30,000 teachers were needed and that women were the ideal candidates because they would accept lower wages. Throughout the 1840s, Beecher worked energetically to encourage more women to go into the teaching profession, selecting and appointing likely candidates through her membership in the Ladies' Society for Improving Education in the West and the Board of National Popular Education, which enlisted 500 women from New England to take up the teaching challenge in the West. Her founding in 1852 of the American Woman's Educational Association was instrumental in the establishment of colleges to train women teachers in Wisconsin, Iowa, and Illinois. Sadly, these ventures were short-lived.

In 1837 Beecher returned to the East Coast. In 1841 she did for American homemakers what the celebrated Mrs. Beeton would do in England by writing a housewife's bible, in which she lauded the vocational domestic skills of women. *A Treatise on Domestic Economy, for the Use of Young Ladies at Home and at School* would be the first American manual to approach the subject of household management from a scientific as well as a domestic point of view. It proved so popular that it was regularly reprinted over the next 15 years and provided Beecher with a welcome income. Another later revision of this work, undertaken with her sister Harriet Beecher Stowe, was published as *The American Woman's Home: or, Principles of Domestic Science* (1869) and laid down further ground rules for the running of an efficient and hygienic home.

Beecher's writings were considerable, including "An Essay on Slavery and Abolitionism with Reference to the Duty of American Women to Their Country" (1837), which emphasized women's pacifism and decried their involvement in combative campaigning. In her 1846 pamphlet, "The Evils Suffered by American Women and American Children," and the 1851 work, *The True Remedy for the Wrongs of Woman,* Beecher further argued against the lack of fresh air and exercise afforded to women and the subjection to tight corseting that caused them physical and mental damage. As an early advocate of calisthenics—a gentle form of gymnastics that had originated in Germany—she encouraged the adoption of healthy and regular exercise in her 1857 work, *Physiology and Calisthenics for Schools and Families.*

By 1871 Beecher had been obliged to compromise on her opposition to equal pay for women (she had originally justified lower pay for women as a necessity if they were to gain more work), but in *Woman Suffrage and Woman's Profession* (1871) she continued to argue for women's primary dedication to domestic roles as wives and mothers. Although Beecher's insistence on this limiting role alienated her from many feminists and suffragists, notably illustrated in her 1837 debate with Angelina Grimké over women's entry into public life (Grimké had made public speeches against slavery), she did at least prompt women to enter the less controversial movement for moral reform.

In 1874 Beecher published her autobiography, *Educational Reminiscences.* She also tackled religious and moral issues in an opus of over 30 published works, including *Elements of Mental and Moral Philosophy* (1831), *Letters on the Difficulties of Religion* (1836), and *Common Sense Applied to Religion* (1857). Despite her frail health and recurring mental and physical crises, Beecher thrived on hard work and lived to the age of 78.

Helen Rappaport

See Also: Education of Women (before the Civil War); Grimké, Sarah Moore; Grimké Weld, Angelina; Stowe, Harriet Beecher; Willard, Emma Hart

Primary Documents: 1841, *A Treatise on Domestic Economy*; 1869, "Why Women Should Not Seek the Vote" (Vol. 2)

Further Reading

Boydston, J., et al., eds. *The Limits of Sisterhood: The Beecher Sisters on Women's Rights and Woman's Sphere.* Chapel Hill: University of North Carolina Press, 1988.

Sklar, Katharine. *Catharine Beecher: A Study in American Domesticity.* New Haven, CT: Yale University Press, 1976.

Tonkovich, Nicole. *Domesticity with a Difference: The Nonfiction of Catharine Beecher, Sarah J. Hale, Fanny Fern, and Margaret Fuller.* Jackson: University Press of Mississippi, 1997.

White, Barbara A. *The Beecher Sisters.* New Haven, CT: Yale University Press, 2003.

Birth Control (17th and 18th Centuries)

References to techniques for limiting family size are rare in colonial America. Folk wisdom was inherited from Europe, where a few techniques doubtlessly traveled with the immigrants to the New World. Demographers have traced a steady decline in American family size from the 17th century through the late 19th century. Although external factors such as war or the older age of brides at time of marriage might have influenced these declining rates, even studies that took these factors into account indicate that certain segments of the population seemed to have been able to reduce the number of their pregnancies.

Families in colonial America were large, typically averaging six to eight children. The number and spacing of childbirths among women who married young compared against those who delayed marriage until after the age of 25 reveals an interesting pattern. Both groups clustered their births toward the beginning of marriage, but the younger wives finished bearing their children at a much earlier age than the older wives. On average, the younger set bore their last child at age 37, whereas the older wives continued to bear children another four years. Given that both sets of women would still have been premenopausal, historians have concluded that women who had achieved the desired number of children were practicing some form of family limitation.

The primary technique used for discouraging conception was breastfeeding. Most women in colonial America breastfed their children and only turned to wet nurses should they be physically unable to nurse their own children. Among mothers who did not breastfeed their children, 20 percent would regain fertility within one month following childbirth. By the third month almost 80 percent of nonnursing mothers are capable of conception. Conversely, a nursing mother might not resume normal menstrual periods for almost a year. This drastic reduction in fertility was obvious to women, and nursing might have been deliberately prolonged by women choosing to delay conception.

Despite the effect nursing had on reducing a woman's fertility, it was not a guaranteed method of birth control. Abstinence was the only certain way to prevent conception, and this was widely used by women determined to prevent pregnancies.

Less reliable forms of birth control were known to exist, including crude condoms, made from animal intestine. Dating as far back as the 16th century, condoms were primarily intended to discourage the spread of venereal disease. Because the animal membranes were prone to tearing and slipping off during intercourse, they were an unreliable method of contraception until the vulcanization of rubber in the 1840s made a viable product. The expense and limited availability of condoms made them off-limits to any but the wealthy. Coitus interruptus, or male withdrawal before ejaculation, was also used. Abstinence, condoms, and withdrawal all depended on the willingness of the male and did not provide women with reproductive control.

Women were known to resort to barrier devices in an attempt to discourage conception. Crude pessaries, made of sponges and soaked in solutions such as lemon juice or honey, could be used in an attempt to block conception. Such devices lacked reliability, but were not completely ineffective. Douching, while not unknown, is rarely mentioned in colonial medical books as a technique for contraception.

Some herbal medicine books made reference to teas and medicinal brews that were intended to prevent conception. Some of these herbs, such as juniper, angelica, and pennyroyal, were known to provoke menstruation. Although in rare cases these herbs could be used as abortifacients, they were useless for preventing conception. Until the invention of the hormonal birth control pill in the 20th century, there was no known form of oral contraception.

Superstition was also rampant in an era before full understanding of human anatomy. Folklore claimed that a woman who touched emeralds or sapphires would have temporary protection against conception. Drinking the tea of fruitless trees was said to render a woman sterile. Stranger beliefs, such as the suspension of hare's dung wrapped in a mule's hide over a bed, might have been perversely effective because they doubtlessly discouraged romantic encounters. Other folk beliefs relied on a woman tossing seeds into a river or turning the wheel of a grain mill backward at the midnight hour. Although such beliefs were based on superstition and were doubtlessly sneered at by many contemporaries as sheer nonsense, the frequency and persistence of rituals to prevent contraception can be seen as an indicator of the desire of women to control their reproductive lives.

We know less about techniques for preventing conception among Native Americans. Anthropological studies have revealed some Cherokee women chewed on the roots of certain plants to prevent conception, although there is no evidence that such a technique would have been effective. The lack of written records regarding contraception among Native Americans cannot be construed as evidence they did not have use of techniques, just that the historical record does not mention them.

Social acceptance of the use of contraception varied depending on geography and religion. In the late 17th century, Cotton Mather, a New England Puritan, expressed concern that women were prolonging breast-feeding as a way of delaying conception. Women who nursed babies past the first year might be looked on with disfavor, because such an action might be interpreted as detrimental to the colonial desire for large families. This concern over the use of contraceptive means was rooted in suspicion of sexuality. For a woman to willingly make use of contraceptives, she was interfering with God's plan for procreation in order to satisfy sexual desires. Although many colonial religions, including Catholicism and the Puritan sects, condoned healthy sexuality in marriage, the use of contraceptives implied wanton sexuality divorced from procreation. Suspicion of attempts to interfere with conception can also be detected in medical texts, which warn of the harmful effect of coitus interruptus.

Despite the suspicion of women who attempted to postpone or prevent conception, many women advised their daughters of the benefits of long periods of breast-feeding as a means of protecting their own health. The persistence of superstitious beliefs, however irrational, also reveals a deeply rooted desire to control fertility. The declining rates of childbirth, beginning in the 18th century and plummeting by the 19th century, reveal that fertility control was widespread.

Dorothy A. Mays

See Also: Abortion (17th and 18th Centuries); Infanticide

Further Reading

Gordon, Linda. *Woman's Body, Woman's Right: A Social History of Birth Control in America.* New York: Grossman Publishers, 1976.

Klepp, Susan E. "Lost, Hidden, Obstructed, and Repressed: Contraceptive and Abortive Technology in the Early Delaware Valley." In *Early American Technology: Making and Doing Things from the Colonial Era to 1850*, edited by Judith A. McGaw. Chapel Hill: University of North Carolina Press, 1994.

Riddle, John M. *Eve's Herbs: A History of Contraception and Abortion in the West.* Cambridge, MA: Harvard University Press, 1997.

Blackwell, Elizabeth (1821–1910)

In pursuit of a medical career, Elizabeth Blackwell was rejected by 29 medical schools. She established the first medical training school for women in the United States. She also promoted the cause of women's medical education in Britain, wrote on the importance of sex education, and campaigned against vivisection and the Contagious Diseases Acts, the latter passed in the United Kingdom in the 1860s. She believed that women, with their maternal instincts of care and self-sacrifice, were the natural opponents of cruelty and injustice.

Blackwell was born in Bristol, England, one of nine children, whose father, Samuel, a well-known local dissenter and lay preacher, was in sugar refining. After the family business was destroyed by fire in 1832, the Blackwells emigrated to New York, where they became involved in the abolitionist cause, helping runaway slaves on the Underground Railroad. After suffering financial losses during the economic depression of 1837, the family moved to Cincinnati in 1838, but Samuel Blackwell died soon after, and Elizabeth taught music before opening a school for girls with her sisters, Anna and Marian, in order to help support the family. Blackwell also continued to work in the abolitionist movement, at various times being active in the Abolitionist Vigilance Committee, the Anti-Slavery Working Society, the Ladies Anti-Slavery Society, and the New York Anti-Slavery Society.

Everything changed for Blackwell in 1845, when she visited Mary Donaldson, a sick friend suffering from uterine cancer. Donaldson admitted to her that she would certainly have turned to medical help sooner if women doctors had been available to her. Blackwell set her sights on training as a doctor, but the study of medicine was at that time impossible for women. She began writing letters to medical academies while teaching music in North Carolina. There she boarded with a doctor's family, and her landlord, John Dickson, allowed her to begin self-study using his books. Blackwell moved to Philadelphia, where she took private anatomy lessons while applying to more than a dozen medical schools. She was finally allowed to enter Geneva Medical School in New York state in 1847, after the question of her admittance was put to a vote by the male students. They condescendingly agreed to give her admittance their "entire approval," convinced she would never stay the course.

Blackwell completed her studies, handicapped by subjection to a constant barrage of hostility, belittlement, and isolation. Considered immoral for pursuing medical studies, she had great difficulty in finding a boardinghouse to take her and, during the two years she spent at Geneva, was ostracized by the female population, who resolutely refused to pay her visits or even speak to her. Undaunted, Blackwell set her sights on a career in women's surgery, having gained valuable clinical experience working in the women's syphilis ward at the Blockley almshouses in Philadelphia during the summer of 1848.

A gathering of 20,000 people witnessed Blackwell's graduation in January 1849, for which she wrote a thesis on ship fever that was published in the *Buffalo Medical Journal.* Although she became an American citizen in April, it still proved impossible for her to obtain hospital experience in the United States, and she was forced to go to Paris. There, however, she was only allowed practical training as a student midwife at the La Maternité lying-in hospital, where she had to endure a spartan life in communal dormitories with other trainees and work 14-hour days. It was here, too, that Blackwell first encountered the abuse of women patients in the charity wards for the poor by doctors who subjected them to painful and degrading examinations and medical procedures. She viewed the forced removal of women's ovaries in the treatment of menstrual problems as particularly inhumane. Like Anna Kingsford, who also studied at La Charité and was appalled at practices she saw there, Blackwell linked the abuse of women by medical science with that of the vivisectionists on helpless animals.

While she was in Paris, a tragedy overtook Blackwell's ambitions to be a surgeon: while treating a baby with purulent ophthalmia, she accidentally infected her own eyes. She lost the sight in one eye (which was later removed, leaving her permanently disfigured); the vision in her other eye was also severely impaired. Finally accepting that she would never be able to undertake surgery, Blackwell decided instead to go into general practice. She traveled to England and undertook further training in the autumn of 1850, this time under the eminent surgeon Dr. James Paget at St. Bartholomew's Hospital in London. Perversely, the hospital ruled that she was not allowed to treat female diseases. During her time in England, Blackwell made lifelong friends of feminist activists Barbara Leigh Smith (later Barbara Bodichon) and other radical women in the Langham Place Circle.

Blackwell returned to New York in August 1851, but despite her excellent credentials, no one would employ her as a doctor. She set up a private practice in March 1852, but had so few patients that she was soon in financial difficulties. She undertook a series of public lectures, published in 1852 as *The Laws of Life, with Special Reference to the Physical Education of Girls.* The book attracted the attention of some Quaker women, who became her patients, and the income enabled Blackwell to open a small clinic in 1853 and to buy a house in a decent district, where she took in several of her brothers and sisters, and a medical partner, German immigrant Marie Zakrzewska. Although Blackwell had long since decided never to marry, in 1856 she adopted a seven-year-old orphan named Kitty Barry.

The demand for Blackwell's clinic was such that she moved to bigger premises in a poor area on the East River and she initiated fund-raising to open a hospital. Blackwell's New York Infirmary for Women and Children opened on Bleecker Street in Greenwich Village on May 12, 1857, with Blackwell and Zakrzewska joined by Elizabeth's younger sister, Emily. After suffering the same rejections and setbacks of her older sister, Emily Blackwell had finally qualified as a doctor at Western Reserve University in 1854. The hospital became an important venue where women doctors could gain essential experience in clinical medicine, even offering home visits to the poor; soon more staff were needed and more money had to be raised.

Elizabeth Blackwell returned to England to encourage Englishwomen to enter medical training. She met Florence Nightingale in the summer of 1858 and again in January 1859, but disagreeing with Nightingale's view that women should confine themselves to nursing,

Blackwell refused to take charge of a training school for nurses that Nightingale was establishing at St. Thomas's Hospital. While in England, Blackwell gave lectures on "Medicine as a Profession for the Ladies" in London, Manchester, Birmingham, and Liverpool. She was also formally enrolled on the British medical register, having already practiced in Britain before the passing of the 1858 Medical Act. In 1860 she and her sister Emily co-wrote one of the first important books to promote her case, *Medicine as a Profession for Women.*

Blackwell returned to the United States, determined to establish her own medical school for women, the outbreak of the Civil War in April 1861 put her plans on hold. Blackwell helped organize women nurses to go to the front and founded the Women's Central Association for Relief, which later became the U.S. Sanitary Commission, the official body that would train and send out nurses to the Union troops under the leadership of Dorothea Dix.

Blackwell's New York Infirmary finally opened its own Women's Medical College in 1868, which offered the most rigorous medical training yet available to women. Elizabeth was professor of hygiene for 30 years (until the school closed in 1899), and her sister Emily served as the college's dean and professor of obstetrics and diseases of women. Emily Blackwell proved an efficient administrator and devoted the next 40 years of her life to the infirmary's efficient management, overseeing the training of 350 women doctors during the medical college's lifetime and becoming one of the first women in the United States to undertake complex surgical procedures.

Elizabeth Blackwell devoted her time to giving lectures and spreading her message on hygiene as well as setting up a program of public sanitary inspection. In 1869 she returned to England with her adopted daughter Kitty and set up a private practice in London. There, in 1874, she cofounded the London School of Medicine for Women with Sophia Jex-Blake and was appointed chair of gynecology there and at Elizabeth Garrett Blackwell's New Hospital for Women and Children. Blackwell was also active in numerous organizations, such as the National Anti-Vivisection Society, and cofounded the National Health Society of London in 1871.

Blackwell became increasingly drawn into issues of moral reform, believing as she did in the moral superiority of women. She became a member of the Social Purity Alliance, the National Vigilance Association, and the Council of National Vigilance, and worked with Josephine Butler for repeal of the Contagious Diseases Acts to combat state-regulated prostitution. In *Counsel to Parents on the Moral Education of Their Children*

(1879), she supported sex education and called for an end to double standards in sexual morality, which demanded that women remain pure, although setting no such standard of sexual behavior for men. However, in the 1880s she would oppose the use of contraceptives, seeing them as encouragement for men to increase the sexual demands they made on their wives.

Blackwell also offered her tireless energy to the campaign for women to become Poor Law Guardians; she was active in antivaccination and antivivisection campaigns and took an interest in spiritualism, rabies treatment, and psychology. She participated in local politics in Hastings and cooperative farming in the nearby Kent countryside. After meeting Charles Kingsley, the English clergyman and novelist, she converted to Christian socialism, a movement closely allied to the Workers' Education Association, and supported the concept of workers' cooperatives and the welfare state. Many of Blackwell's ideas on these themes were outlined in her 1902 book, *Essays in Medical Sociology.*

Blackwell finally retired in 1894 and wrote her autobiography, *Pioneer Work in Opening the Medical Profession to Women.* In 1907 a bad fall severely confined her, and she died of a stroke in 1910. She was buried in Kilmun, Scotland.

Helen Rappaport

See Also: Butler, Josephine; Dix, Dorothea; United States Sanitary Commission; Zakrzewska, Marie; Blackwell, Henry Brown (Vol. 2); Gage, Matilda Joslyn (Vol. 2)

Primary Document: 1867, Support for Female Physicians

Further Reading

Blake, Catriona. *The Charge of the Parasols: Women's Entry to the Medical Profession.* London: Women's Press, 1990.

Bonner, Thomas Neville. *To the Ends of the Earth: Women's Search for Education in Medicine.* Cambridge, MA: Harvard University Press, 1992.

Morantz-Sanchez, Regina. *Sympathy and Science: Women Physicians in American Medicine.* New York: Oxford University Press, 1985.

Walsh, Mary Roth. *"Doctors Wanted: No Women Need Apply": Sexual Barriers in the Medical Profession, 1835–1975.* New Haven, CT: Yale University Press, 1977.

Bloomer, Amelia Jenks (1818–1894)

A perceptive social critic, Amelia Jenks Bloomer was the owner and editor of *The Lily,* a temperance and women's rights newspaper. Although she became an accomplished journalist, she is best remembered as a dress reformer who popularized more comfortable and functional clothing for women, including the pants worn under a shorter skirt that became known as "bloomers" in her honor.

Amelia Jenks was born in Homer, New York, on May 27, 1818, the daughter of Ananias Jenks, a clothier, and Lucy Webb. Because her family included six children and was not wealthy, Amelia received only two years of formal education. At 17, she taught briefly in Clyde, New York, before becoming the governess and tutor for the children of Oren Chamberlain in 1837.

While employed by Chamberlain, Amelia met Dexter Bloomer, a law student from Seneca Falls, New York, who owned the *Seneca County Courier,* a weekly newspaper. The couple married in April 1840, notably omitting the word *obey* from their wedding vows. They had no children of their own but adopted two. After the

The "Bloomer" costume, named after editor and dress reformer Amelia Bloomer, became popular among women's rights activists in the 1850s. (Library of Congress)

marriage and the move to Seneca Falls, Bloomer encouraged his new wife to write. In spite of her lack of education, she took his advice and began to add her views to his newspaper on the social and political topics of the day under the pseudonym of "Gloriana."

In 1840, as many of the women of her day, Amelia entered temperance work and expanded her writing opportunities by contributing to the temperance paper, the *Water Bucket.* She served as an officer in the Ladies Temperance Society. Since she lived in Seneca Falls and was acquainted with Elizabeth Cady Stanton, Bloomer attended the first women's rights convention in 1848, although she did not sign the Declaration of Sentiments.

During the following year, her temperance group decided there was a need for a new paper that would appeal specifically to their women members. As a writer who was married to a journalist, Amelia Bloomer was the natural choice to initiate such an endeavor. *The Lily* was the first journal published exclusively by and for women; in addition, it was the only publication in the United States to be owned, operated, and edited by a woman. Initially, the paper was used as a tool for temperance reform but slowly it began to evolve toward issues wrapped more around social justice. The tone of the pieces changed rapidly, however, when Bloomer's friend, Stanton, under the pen name, "Sunflower," began contributing columns. Within a few months, *The Lily* had reinvented itself as the primary news instrument of the women's rights movement and featured articles ranging in topic from recipes to morals to activism. Even the masthead that read "devoted to the interests of women" was later altered to advocate women's emancipation.

Dexter Bloomer was politically active in the region and for his part as a campaign worker, he was appointed postmaster of Seneca Falls. Although it was not customary for women to hold such posts, Bloomer appointed Amelia as his deputy. They used the spare room next to the post office to hold women's meetings. Through her paper, Amelia Bloomer met most of the activists of the day, including Susan B. Anthony, who was then involved only in abolitionist and temperance work. One day, while Anthony was visiting Bloomer, the two encountered a group talking on the street. Since she knew each of the women, Amelia introduced Anthony to Elizabeth Cady Stanton, an auspicious encounter that would solidify much of the progress toward women's rights over the following decades.

In 1850, the state legislature in Tennessee publicly determined that women had no souls, thus, they had no right to own property. Bloomer was up in arms and used her journalistic skill to mount an attack. Realizing that Stanton had been correct all along, Bloomer transformed her personal views and *The Lily*'s editorial stance, proudly wearing the title of the first woman's suffrage journal in the United States. The paper began promoting marriage reform laws, higher education for women, and the vote.

Although she did not create it nor was she was the first to put on the costume, Amelia Bloomer's national notoriety came in 1851 when she began dressing for comfort rather than style. The attire, designed by Elizabeth Smith Miller, the daughter of Stanton's cousin, Gerrit Smith, and first worn by activist Fanny Wright, consisted of Turkish pantaloons worn under a skirt that came above the knee. Despite the fact that the garment was denounced by the church, Bloomer continued to defend the look in person and in print. Her articles were picked up by the *New York Tribune* and widely published. Because she was associated with the defense of the clothing style, the outfit became known as "The Bloomer Costume," which was eventually shortened to "bloomers." The fashion was adopted by many of the forward-thinking women of the era, including Stanton, but eventually abandoned because it was diverting attention away from the movement.

In 1852, Bloomer traveled to a temperance meeting in Rochester, New York, with 1,800 others in attendance. She was elected secretary of the group and Stanton was elected president. It was her first venture into public speaking but by the next year, she was making continuous presentations for both temperance and women's rights.

When her husband purchased another paper, the *Western Home Visitor,* the couple moved to Mount Vernon, New York, to manage it. By that time, *The Lily* had a paid circulation of over 6,000 and enabled Bloomer to hire a professional typesetter, a woman. In 1855, they relocated once again to Council Bluffs, Iowa. Both publications were liquidated in order to finance the move with Mary Birdsall taking over *The Lily.* Their home became a stopover for the parade of suffragists moving their campaigns to the West. Amelia Bloomer joined the Iowa Woman's State Suffrage Society, campaigned in both Iowa and Nebraska, became vice president in 1870, and petitioned the Iowa state assembly for state suffrage.

After furnishing the chapter on Iowa for Volume III of the *History of Woman Suffrage* (1887), the opus edited by Stanton and Anthony, Bloomer suffered partial paralysis of her vocal chords. She died on December 30, 1894, of heart failure. Her grave marker in Council Bluffs states

simply that she wished to be remembered as "a pioneer in woman's enfranchisement."

Joyce D. Duncan

See Also: Dress Reform; *The Lily*; Anthony, Susan B. (Vol. 2); Cady, Elizabeth Stanton (Vol. 2)

Further Reading

Coon, Anne C., ed. *Hear Me Patiently: The Reform Speeches of Amelia Jenks Bloomer.* Westport, CT: Greenwood Press, 1994.

Cunningham, Patricia A. *Reforming Women's Fashion, 1850–1920: Politics, Health, and Art.* Kent, OH: Kent State University Press, 2003.

Fischer, Gayle V. *Pantaloons and Power: A Nineteenth Century Dress Reform in the United States.* Kent, OH: Kent State University Press, 2001.

Russo, Ann, and Cheris Kramarae. *The Radical Women's Press of the 1850s.* New York: Routledge, 1991.

Boycotts

Without a vote or the ability to serve in public office, women in early America had limited ability to influence community decisions or behavior. One of the few ways to make their wishes heard was with their purchasing power—and their ability to withhold it. During the American Revolution, women's ability to organize and enforce boycotts was an effective means of lending support to the Revolutionary cause.

The colonies depended on Britain for the importation of manufactured goods and luxury items. In protest of the modest taxes that were levied on these goods, many communities vowed to boycott imported goods. Tea was the most obvious casualty of the boycotts. The sale of tea was highly profitable for the British, but hardly essential to daily survival of the Americans. Tea was thus an easy item to target for boycotts. Consumption of tea dropped from 900,000 pounds per year in 1769 to 327,000 pounds following the outbreak of the war. Boycotting tea became a public statement of support for the war. Women opted for substitutes such as "Liberty Tea," made of brewing lemon balm, rosehips, peppermint, and raspberry. Some women engaged in public demonstrations, such as when a group of women in Wilmington, North Carolina, burned their tea during a solemn procession.

Aside from the Boston Tea Party, the most famous boycott was referred to as the "Edenton Ladies' Tea Party," organized by a group of women from Edenton,

North Carolina. The town had only 600 inhabitants, but 51 ladies signed a declaration in support of their husbands who were preparing to fight the British. Although they nowhere mention the word *tea,* the declaration quickly became associated with the widespread tea boycotts. The Edenton declaration was published widely in colonial newspapers, where it was praised as an example of feminine support and resolve. When news of the Edenton Ladies' Tea Party reached England, it was greeted with ridicule. It received satirical treatment in cartoons and political essays.

Tea was the most prominent, but not the only, luxury item that was boycotted. Imported fabric, brandy, and sugar all came under censure. Women were urged to increase their production of homespun fabric rather than buy imported cotton or silk. In order for the boycotts of imported goods to have any effect on British policy, leaders of the Revolution knew they needed the cooperation of women. Articles appeared in newspapers throughout the colonies urging women to support the boycott efforts.

Although boycotts served as a means for women to assert their political will, boycotts could also contain an element of coercion. In 1774 a group of ladies in Charleston announced they would be visiting households "to obtain the assent of every Mistress of a Family" in town so they could promise to reject the "baneful Herb." People who chose to purchase tea or silks might find a rock thrown through their windows. Merchants who chose to sell such goods risked a tar and feathering or watching their shop go up in flames. Many of the shopkeepers who refused to cooperate with the boycotts were women. With smaller supplies of locally produced inventories and a smaller financial base to cushion the economic downturn, many women shopkeepers were unable to afford a boycott and were often blacklisted as a result.

Dorothy A. Mays

See Also: The American Revolution

Further Reading

Gundersen, Joan R. *To Be Useful to the World: Women in Revolutionary America, 1740–1790.* New York: Twayne, 1996.

Kierner, Cynthia A. *Beyond the Household: Women's Place in the Early South, 1700–1835.* Ithaca, NY: Cornell University Press, 1998.

Norton, Mary Beth. *Liberty's Daughters: The Revolutionary Experience of American Women, 1750–1800.* Boston, MA: Little, Brown, 1980.

Bread Riots

During the American Civil War, Southern women planned and executed urban food riots in a number of Southern states, including Georgia, Louisiana, Virginia, Tennessee, Alabama, and North Carolina. Most disturbances were well-planned reactions focused on the dramatic escalation in the prices, combined with a growing scarcity in the markets, of household commodities such as flour, sugar, coffee, butter, and bacon. In many cases, these food shortages resulted from the activities of Confederate impressment agents who, under the provisions of the Impressment Act of March 1862, traveled throughout the South, negotiating agreements with local farmers to sell their produce to the Confederate army at fixed prices. In anticipation of the impressment agents' arrival, farmers frequently withheld their goods from market, thus increasing scarcity and driving up the prices of the commodities available for sale to private citizens.

The largest Civil War food riot, which took place in Richmond, Virginia, on April 2, 1863, typified most

Southern women involved in bread riots during the Civil War, as depicted in *Frank Leslie's Illustrated Newspaper* on May 23, 1863. (Library of Congress)

wartime Southern food riots. In this riot in the Confederacy's capital, a crowd estimated at nearly 500 women, accompanied by adolescent boys and a few men, broke open the doors of Richmond's Main Street and Cary Street merchants. They seized coffee, candles, shoes, flour, bacon, and sides of beef. Although a number of the women were armed with guns or axes, which they apparently brandished in the faces of resisting merchants, no fatalities occurred. The riot ended after a short time when the city's Public Guard, which had been summoned at the request of Virginia Governor John Letcher, trained loaded rifles on the rioters. The crowd dispersed quickly, with many women carrying their seized bacon and flour home to share with family and neighbors. More than two-thirds of the 68 people arrested in the riot were women. During the next few months, Richmond's municipal courts were filled with trials resulting from the arrests of female rioters. Many of those found guilty of misdemeanor charges for their role in the bread riot were required to pay fines. A few women who were identified as the leaders of the Richmond bread riot were convicted of felonies and sentenced to prison terms of five years or more.

Most Richmond newspaper accounts characterized the rioting women as prostitutes or vagrants. However, many involved in the Richmond disturbance, as well as in the bread riots occurring elsewhere in the Confederacy, were working-class women with husbands and sons in the Confederate army. Other participants worked in the ammunition laboratories and in sewing factories manufacturing percussion caps and uniforms for Confederate soldiers. These working-class women experienced more acutely the personal and economic privations of the Civil War than did their more affluent Southern sisters. Consequently, through the bread riots, they demanded that their government fulfill its responsibility to protect and feed them.

Southern politicians attempted to respond to this dilemma by developing social welfare initiatives aimed at assisting needy Confederate families. In urban communities, they created free markets, which appear to be prototypes for 20th-century food banks. Farmers contributed their excess produce, which was then sold at reduced prices to families meeting specific criteria. To qualify as free market recipients, women had to be the mothers or legally married wives of soldiers, either conscripts or volunteers, who were currently serving in the Confederate army. The families of substitute soldiers were excluded because these men typically received financial compensation for their military service from the families of the wealthy men they replaced. Common law wives and the children born of these unions were also not entitled to relief because these relationships did not meet the criteria for respectability. In North Carolina, eligible recipients received coupons that could be redeemed for food, a precursor to food stamps and Independence cards. In rural areas, county relief agents worked with home visitors, who were often married middle- and upper-class women from the community and who interviewed the families in their homes to determine their eligibility. The most ambitious statewide relief programs, which can be accurately characterized as precursors to the social welfare initiatives of the Progressive Era and perhaps even the New Deal, were implemented in Georgia and North Carolina.

E. Susan Barber

See Also: Slavery and the Civil War; "Woman Order"

Primary Document: 1862, A Northern Newspaper Supports Butler's Woman Order

Further Reading

Barber, E. Susan. "Cartridge Makers and Myrmidon Viragos: White Working-Class Women in Confederate Richmond." In *Negotiating Boundaries of Southern Womanhood: Dealing with the Powers that Be,* edited by Janet Coryell. Columbia: University of Missouri Press, 2000.

Faust, Drew Gilpin. *Mothers of Invention: Women of the Slaveholding South in the American Civil War.* Chapel Hill: University of North Carolina Press, 1996.

C

Cary, Mary Ann Shadd (1823–1893)

One of the first to resettle escaped American slaves in Canada was Mary Shadd Cary, a free black from Delaware. A combative and hardworking woman, she founded the *Provincial Freeman* to promote this work and advocated the full integration of immigrants into Canadian society.

Mary Ann Shadd grew up in Wilmington, Delaware. One of 13 children of a freed slave and notable abolitionist, she inherited her father's forthrightness in promoting a sense of pride in their own worth among blacks. She attended a Quaker school for the children of free blacks in Westchester, Pennsylvania, and, at the age of 16, back in Wilmington, established her own school for black children. She spent the next 11 years teaching there and in New York, New Jersey, and Pennsylvania.

In 1849 she published a pamphlet, "Hints to the Colored People of the North," extolling the virtues of hard work among black people and cautioning them against seeking to imitate the profligacy of whites. Shadd moved to Windsor, Ontario, in 1851 to avoid the possibility of being enslaved under the Fugitive Slave Act, passed by the U.S. Congress the previous year. Arriving in Canada, she used funding from the American Mission Association (AMA) to set up a school for the children of free black emigrants and those of escaped slaves coming into Canada on the Underground Railroad from the United States.

After publishing her call to free blacks to emigrate from the United States to Canada in "A Plea for Emigration: Or, Notes of Canada West, in Its Moral, Social and Political Aspect . . . for the Information of Colored Emigrants" in 1852, Shadd also founded a nonsectarian black newspaper, the *Provincial Freeman* (1853–1859), in which she published antislavery editorials, highlighted women's work in safeguarding the welfare of escaped slaves, and advocated the integration of blacks into Canadian society. These activities brought her into conflict with other male activists who, more reliant on donations from patrons and well-wishers, sought to settle black emigrants in their own separate communities. A very public controversy erupted between segregationists and integrationists, which ended with the AMA, rattled by Cary's outspokenness, withdrawing its financial support for her school. Despite these developments, Cary continued to condemn black separatism, while some African Americans chose to live in special settlements.

Shadd returned to the United States to raise funds to keep her school and newspaper going through lecturing, and she returned to Toronto, Canada in early 1854 to bring the paper out more frequently. The publication struggled on through numerous financial crises for another five years, moving again to Chatham. Mary Ann Shadd married Thomas F. Cary in 1856 and had two children, but her husband died in 1860. Despite her loss, she was buoyed up by hopes of an end to slavery after meeting radical abolitionist John Brown in Canada in 1858. During the years 1859–1864, Shadd Cary went back to running her own school in Chatham. Anxious to play her part after the American Civil War broke out in 1861, she returned to the United States in 1863 to encourage black recruitment in the Union Army in Indiana, Michigan, Pennsylvania, and Ohio. After the war was over, Cary decided to stay in the United States to take up much-needed work in the resettlement and education of its emancipated slaves.

She studied for a teaching qualification and in 1868 returned to teaching, first in Detroit and then in several public schools in Washington, D.C., during 1872–1874 serving as principal of a grammar school. In 1869 when she was 46, she decided to take up the law, studying until 1871 at Howard University; it was not until 1883 that she finally received her law degree. In the meantime, she had become engaged in activism for women's suffrage and promoting better education facilities for blacks. It is not known whether she ever practiced as a lawyer.

Helen Rappaport

See Also: Abolitionism and the Antislavery Movement; Elizabeth Freeman Case; Slavery and the Civil War; Stewart, Maria W.

Further Reading

Bearden, Jim, and Linda Jean Butler. *Shadd: The Life and Times of Mary Shadd Cary.* Toronto: NC Press, 1977.

Rhodes, Jane. *Mary Ann Shadd Cary: The Black Press and Protest in the Nineteenth Century.* Bloomington: Indiana University Press, 1998.

Sadleir, Rosemary. *Leading the War: Black Women in Canada.* Toronto: Umbrella Press, 1994.

Child, Lydia Maria (1802–1880)

Writer, editor, abolitionist, and social reformer, Lydia Maria Child was one of the premier 19th-century literary figures whose political and social activism helped to shape northern antebellum politics and to establish women's rightful role in public discourse.

Lydia Maria Francis was born in Medford, Massachusetts, on February 11, 1802, to Susannah Rand and David Convers Francis, and exhibited an early brilliance as a child. As was typical of the period, she was sent to a preparatory school that prepared young girls

Lydia Maria Child was a novelist, abolitionist, and supporter of women's rights. She wrote an early antislavery book, *An Appeal in Favor of That Class of Americans Called Africans* (1833). (Library of Congress)

for domestic life. Her older brother Convers, however, shared his books and lessons with her, nurturing her desire for intellectual advancement. Upon the death of her mother in 1814, Lydia was sent to live with her older sister, Mary Francis Preston, then living in Norridgewock, Maine. Lydia would later serve as a teacher in a local school in Gardiner, Maine, allowing her to earn her own income and pursue her passion for education.

Returning to Massachusetts in 1822, Lydia joined brother Convers Francis's Watertown household. A Unitarian minister, Convers participated in the intellectual and literary movement of Transcendentalism. It was through Transcendentalist meetings in the Francis home that Lydia Francis met American literary, philosophical, and political figures and theorists such as John Greenleaf Whittier, Theodore Parker, and Ralph Waldo Emerson. Her own literary ambitions were revealed with the publication of her first novel, *Hobomok,* in 1824. Its highly controversial plot involving the marriage of a white woman to a Native American man challenged racial assumptions and called for racial tolerance. The boldness of her work earned her considerable attention, launching her into Boston's highly elite literary circle and she began a prolific writing career that would last five more decades. Another novel, *The Rebels,* quickly followed a collection of short stories about New England. By 1826, she was editing and publishing a bimonthly educational magazine for children called *Juvenile Miscellany,* the first of its kind in the country.

In 1828, Lydia Francis met and married David Lee Child, a lawyer, writer, and antislavery activist. Following her marriage, Child's work focused almost exclusively on women's lives and domestic concerns. In 1828, she published *The Frugal Housewife,* a guidebook on domestic duties. It was reprinted over 30 times, including several foreign editions, becoming one of the most enduring and popular books on household economy during the mid-19th century. The book celebrated women's contributions to the home, but it did so within the gendered conventions of the day. Child followed this achievement with *The Mother's Book* and *The Little Girl's Own Book,* both successful works that rode the wave of popularity of female advice literature and the growing commodification of a separate female sphere. With no children of her own, she continued to pursue writing on a full-time basis. Writing almost exclusively for women, she published a series of compositions called "The Ladies' Family Library" and then broadened her work into three volumes of biographical sketches, published between 1832 and 1833, which earned her accolades from the prestigious *North American Review*. It was her next book, however, that not only created an uproar among the nation's literary, political, and cultural elite, but also launched Child into a political career that would help shape and define public discourse on the subject of slavery and abolition for the next three decades.

Published in 1833, *An Appeal in Favor of That Class of Americans Called Africans* demanded immediate emancipation of the country's slaves, a shocking and daring call for action seen as radical and dangerous, particularly coming from a woman. Child interwove the history of slavery and the slave trade with arguments against the colonization of free blacks back to Africa, demands for racial equality, and an exposé of racial discrimination in the North. *An Appeal* was the product of Child's own expanding consciousness and years of research and correspondence with William Lloyd Garrison, Boston's foremost abolitionist and editor of *The Liberator*. In spite of heavy criticism, the book became standard reading for abolitionists throughout the North. Child wrote several more books on the subject, though none had as great an influence as *An Appeal*. She joined the Boston Female Anti-Slavery Society in 1834, beginning years of cooperative activism with other women abolitionists from New England, New York, and Pennsylvania.

Child and her husband remained committed to abolitionism and destruction of the slave system. They moved to an experimental community in Northampton, Massachusetts, in 1838, where they farmed sugar beets. Lydia Child continued to write, becoming a regular contributor to the abolitionist annual, *The Liberty Bell*. In 1841, after a divisive controversy over the appointment of women as officers in the American Anti-Slavery Society split that organization, Child became editor of its publication, the *National Anti-Slavery Standard*.

Her years at the *Standard* were challenging ones for Child. Her personal problems included a difficult marriage, complicated by Lydia's living in New York with abolitionist Isaac Hopper while David fruitlessly tried to keep the farm going in Massachusetts. Professionally, Child struggled to maintain a moderate editorial position in a highly fractured national abolition movement. Criticized from all factions of the movement for being either too radical or not radical enough, Child ultimately abandoned participation in any antislavery society. Her weekly personal ruminations—called "Letters from New York," reflections on daily life in New York City that she used to critique the worst of American culture and to suggest paths to greater spiritual awareness—were immensely popular, helping to push readership to new highs.

Frustrated and embattled, Child stepped down as editor of the *Standard* in 1843. Still estranged from her husband, who by now was deeply in debt and facing bankruptcy, Child published an edited collection of "Letters from New York," as well as a collection of children's stories. In 1849, she left New York, reunited with her husband, and settled in Wayland, Massachusetts to care for her aging father.

The rising tensions over the issue of slavery during the 1850s drew Child back into the public discourse over abolition. John Brown's raid and his subsequent trial brought Child back into the public view when she began a vigorous correspondence with Virginia Governor Henry Wise and his wife over their denouncement of the antislavery movement. Published by *The New York Tribune,* the letters were reprinted in pamphlet form by the American Anti-Slavery Society, selling over 300,000 copies and sparking renewed interest in the movement. Taking advantage of this momentum, Child published more antislavery essays during 1860 as the nation prepared for sectional conflict. The following year, Child wrote the introduction to and helped publish Harriet Ann Jacobs' autobiography, *Incidents in the Life of a Slave Girl,* a highly significant slave narrative that highlighted the particular plight of enslaved women. Critical of President Abraham Lincoln's early stance on emancipation and his refusal to allow the recruitment of black soldiers, Child continued to use her influence to promote the cause of the newly liberated slave, including education and the redistribution of confiscated Southern lands. She used her own funds to publish and distribute *The Freedman's Book,* an educational reader for newly freed blacks featuring historical and contemporary essays for and by African Americans.

After the war, she was highly critical of President Andrew Johnson's Reconstruction policies. In the postwar years Child continued writing articles advocating a variety of reform movements, including equal rights, African American suffrage, Indian rights, land redistribution, labor reform, and civil service reform. An advocate of woman suffrage, Child shied away from any associations with national or local suffrage organizations.

Her husband David died in 1874. Lydia Child remained close to William Lloyd Garrison, Wendell Phillips, Thomas Wentworth Higginson, Lucretia Mott, and other activists from her antislavery days. She died October 20, 1880.

Kate Clifford Larson

See Also: Abolitionism and the Antislavery Movement; Garrison, William Lloyd; Jacobs, Harriet; Mott, Lucretia; Reconstruction; Slavery and the Civil War

Further Reading

Karcher, Carolyn L. *The First Woman in the Republic: A Cultural Biography of Lydia Maria Child.* Durham, NC: Duke University Press, 1994.

Mills, Bruce. *Cultural Reformations: Lydia Maria Child and the Literature of Reform.* Athens: University of Georgia Press, 1994.

Salerno, Beth A. *Sister Societies: Women's Antislavery Societies in Antebellum America.* DeKalb: Northern Illinois University Press, 2005.

Sizer, Lyde Cullen, ed. *The Political Work of Northern Women Writers and the Civil War, 1850–1872.* Chapel Hill: University of North Carolina Press, 2000.

The Constitution and Women

Delegates to the Constitutional Convention in 1789 did not specifically discuss women's rights (at least, not as distinct from the rights of other persons), and no delegate appears to have suggested that women might one day occupy public offices. Thus, the original U.S. Constitution contains no specific mention of women or women's rights. In contrast to the Declaration of Independence, however (with its words "all men are created equal"—words that are usually understood to include all persons), the language of the Constitution is largely gender-neutral, with the term "person" or "persons" used instead of "man" or "men." However, the Constitution occasionally used the male pronoun "he" to refer to the president.

The term "sex" was used at the Convention to designate both men and women in a resolution that Pennsylvania's James Wilson first offered on June 11. In describing how he thought the House of Representatives should be equitably apportioned, Wilson, in a motion that South Carolina's Charles Cotesworth Pinckney seconded, proposed that this representation be made

> in proportion to the whole number of white & other free Citizens & inhabitants of every age sex & condition including those bound to servitude for a term of years and three fifths of all other persons not comprehended in the foregoing description, except Indians not paying taxes, in each State.

The Committee of the Whole voted to accept this motion by a 9–2 vote. The Convention eventually forwarded it to the Committee of Style and Arrangement. This committee, in turn, compressed the language into its ultimate form, which referred to "the whole number of free persons, including those bound to servitude for a term of years, and excluding Indians not taxed, three fifths of all other persons."

Jan Lewis, a close scholar of the subject, has observed, however, that whereas the delegates had previously voted both to delete the word "white" as superfluous and to replace the word "servitude" for "service," they had adopted no such change in the language regarding "sex." Lewis thus concludes that the committee's change was intended to be merely a stylistic one that did not change Wilson's original inclusion of women in the polity. She further concludes that the Constitution did intend to include women. Indeed, she argues that the acceptance of Wilson's motion represented the first occasion in what any government had considered basing representation "upon inhabitants rather than taxpayers or adult men." She further observes, however, that the Founders chiefly anticipated that women's citizenship would be in the civil rather than in the political realm.

Similarly, Rosemarie Zagarri has concluded that early Americans often applied an individualistic Lockean view of rights to men and the view often associated with the Scottish Enlightenment (tying rights to duties, often of a domestic nature) to women. She further observes that Mary Wollstonecraft's *A Vindication of the Rights of Woman,* which pushed thinking about women closer to the Lockean view, was not published until 1792.

Much to the chagrin of 19th-century women's rights activists like Susan B. Anthony and Elizabeth Cady Stanton, who worked for the emancipation of American blacks and who often tied this cause to their own desire for suffrage, the word "male" finally entered the Constitution not with the Founding Fathers, but with the authors of the Fourteenth Amendment (ratified in 1868), who intended to penalize states that denied the right to vote to "male" inhabitants. With the Fourteenth and Fifteenth Amendments (the latter ratified in 1870 and prohibiting discrimination in voting on the basis of race), the U.S. Constitution neither extended the nor denied the right to vote to women; instead, it allowed that the qualifications to vote in national elections would be the same as they were in state elections. At the time, no state had granted women the right to vote except New Jersey, where those with property were permitted to vote from 1776 to 1807. The U.S. Constitution did not prohibit discrimination in voting on the basis of sex until the ratification of the Nineteenth Amendment in 1920, which finally declared that "the right of citizens of the United States to vote shall not be denied or abridged by the United States or by any State on account of sex."

The Framers of the Constitution undoubtedly anticipated that most issues involving the rights of women would be addressed at the state rather than the national level. Under the common law, such matters would largely have fallen into the area of domestic law, which was at the time almost solely supervised by state courts. Today the equal protection clause of the Fourteenth Amendment is the primary legal mechanism used to protect women's rights in federal courts. Although an Equal Rights Amendment failed at the national level, many states have adopted their own equal rights amendments.

John R. Vile

See Also: Fifteenth Amendment; Fourteenth Amendment; Republican Motherhood; Wollstonecraft, Mary; Anthony, Susan B. (Vol. 2); Equal Rights Amendment (ERA) (Vol. 3); Nineteenth Amendment (Vol. 2)

Primary Document: 1774, "An Occasional Letter on the Female Sex"

Further Reading

Baker, Jean. H. *Women and the U.S. Constitution, 1776–1920.* Washington, DC: American Historical Association, 2008.

Goldwin, Robert A. *Why Blacks, Women, and Jews Are Not Mentioned in the Constitution, and Other Unorthodox Views.* Washington, DC: AEI Press, 1990.

Lewis, Jan. "'Of Every Age Sex & Condition': The Representation of Women in the Constitution." In *What Did the Constitution Mean to Early Americans?,* edited by Edward Countryman. Boston: Bedford/St. Martin's, 1999.

Schwarzenbach, Sibyl A., and Particia Smith, eds. *Women and the United States Constitution: History, Interpretation, and Practice.* New York: Columbia University Press, 2003.

Vile, John R. *Encyclopedia of Constitutional Amendments, Proposed Amendments, and Amending Issues, 1789–2002.* 2nd ed. Santa Barbara, CA: ABC-CLIO, 2003.

West, Thomas G. *Vindicating the Founders: Race, Sex, Class, and Justice in the Origins of America.* Lanham, MD: Rowman and Littlefield Publishers, 1997.

Zagarri, Rosemarie. *Revolutionary Backlash: Women and Politics in the Early American Republic.* Philadelphia: University of Pennsylvania Press, 2007.

Coverture

Coverture is defined as the legal status of a woman following marriage that sublimated her legal identity under the authority of her husband. Most early American law was imported from English common law, which severely restricted women's legal status following their marriage. Under English law, an *unmarried* adult woman was entitled to almost all the legal rights of a man. She could sue and be sued, make contracts, write a will, buy and sell property, and operate a business in her own name. Such legal privileges were lost to her upon marriage, when her legal identity became folded into that of her husband.

Sir William Blackstone's *Commentaries on the Laws of England* (1765) provided a clear reflection of the legal implications of coverture:

> By marriage, the husband and wife are one person in law; that is, the very being or legal existence of the woman is suspended during the marriage, or at least is incorporated and consolidated into that of the husband; under whose wing, protection, and cover, she performs everything.

All property a woman brought into marriage, including real estate, clothing, furniture, or money, became the property of her husband. If the woman was employed outside the home, her wages belonged to her husband. Because a woman was not free to enter contracts under her own name, she could not buy or sell property, establish a business, or write a will. Because she could not enter into a lease or purchase a home, should she choose to live separately from her husband, she could not legally do so without his assistance.

The law of coverture, while it relegated the wife to the legal status of a child, worked well if the husband respected his wife and consulted her on important decisions. If the husband provided for his wife and sought her consent before making decisions and the pair were able to come to amicable agreements, coverture was not likely to be a burden to most colonial women. The difficulty lay in that the law of coverture assumed all women to have a loving and considerate husband. There were no provisions for women who were in an unhappy marriage. If a man frittered away money, neglected to provide for his family, or deserted his wife, there was little a woman could do to prevent such actions or provide for her own economic well-being.

The only major protection women were provided by the law of coverture was that a husband could not sell real estate his wife brought into the marriage without his wife's consent. This was a legacy from the laws of England, where the importance of land to an aristocratic lineage needed protection from wastrel husbands. Colonial statutes recognized that a wife's consent to sell property could be coerced. The law required for a wife to be questioned by a judge outside the presence of her husband, in order to determine if she concurred with the proposed sale of property. This procedure was notorious for being neglected, but if a woman strenuously objected, she had the ability to render the transaction null if there was no proof she consented to the sale of the land. Even with this protection, it was acknowledged that a private interview with the wife was not a foolproof means to prevent coercion. Judges concluded that if a woman agreed to the sale of property in a private meeting with a judge, she must be taken at her word.

In an effort to protect a woman's property and well-being, a number of legal techniques were developed to skirt coverture. A concerned father might set up a trust for his daughter, which insisted that funds be paid directly to the daughter without interference from her husband. Prenuptial agreements might also set property aside for the exclusive use of the wife. Despite the autonomy conferred by such legal arrangements, the beneficiary still depended on the generosity and goodwill of others to ensure that the legal protections were enforced.

Women who were deserted by their husbands lived in an especially difficult position. Because of the difficulty of obtaining a divorce, many men in unhappy marriages simply abandoned the home, leaving their wives to fend for themselves. Likewise, the wives of mariners and soldiers might go years without seeing their husbands. Their husbands might have been lost at sea, but having a missing man declared dead was a long and difficult process. These women could petition to be allowed to enter into contracts and keep the proceeds of any earnings, but were not able to sell or dispose of their husband's property. They needed the assistance of a court administrator to dispose of a husband's goods, should it be determined that he was unlikely to ever return.

The law as it was structured clearly put women in a subordinate position, and women who married an abusive or neglectful husband had few options. However, in practice, many of the laws of coverture were ignored. Studies of businesswomen in New York and Virginia reveal that many married women maintained thriving businesses, entered into contracts, and initiated lawsuits, all contrary to the law of coverture. Likewise, women were routinely able to obtain credit at the marketplace unless their husbands had specifically warned a merchant he would not honor the agreement. It appears that few objections were raised in relation to these activities. In rare instances, some Anglo-American women were able to obtain the legal status of *feme sole* trader, which allowed them the ability to conduct business without their husband's supervision. This status was usually granted to women who had been abandoned by their husbands or whose husbands spent extended periods of time away from home.

A unique exception to the laws of coverture existed in the Dutch colonies of New Netherlands until the 1660s. According to Dutch tradition, women could select an *usus* marriage, in which she retained her legal identity, maiden name, and ability to conduct business affairs independent of her husband. Alternatively, she could opt for a *manus* marriage, which was remarkably similar to the laws of coverture. Women of the Dutch colonies were able to make this choice for themselves until the colony came under the control of England in 1664.

Mississippi was the first state to begin reforming the law of coverture when the state code was modified in 1839. Coverture was not fully abandoned throughout the United States until the 1880s.

Dorothy A. Mays

See Also: Divorce (before the Civil War); *Feme Sole* and *Feme Sole* Trader Status; Legal Status of Women (18th Century); New York Married Women's Property Acts

Primary Document: 1848–1849, New York Married Women's Property Acts

Further Reading

Dayton, Cornelia Hughes. *Women before the Bar: Gender, Law, and Society in Connecticut, 1639–1789.* Chapel Hill: University of North Carolina Press, 1995.

Gundersen, Joan R. *To Be Useful to the World: Women in Revolutionary America, 1740–1790.* New York: Twayne, 1996.

Salmon, Marylynn. *Women and the Law of Property in Early America.* Chapel Hill: University of North Carolina Press, 1986.

D

Dall, Caroline Healey (1822–1912)

Caroline Dall was a reformer and prolific writer who, beginning in the 1840s and through the 1890s, published on the questions of women's suffrage, labor and equal pay, education, and health. She regularly attended women's rights conventions and her voluminous letters and journals reveal connections with all the leading writers, activists, lecturers, and reformers of her time.

Caroline Wells Healey was the first of eight children born to Unitarian parents in Boston in 1822. Her father was a successful merchant and banker. Caroline was well educated and introduced to reform work as a young child. In 1844, she married Charles Appleton Dall, a Unitarian minister who later left her behind with their two children to pursue missionary work in Calcultta, India. Her husband's long absence from the United States—and her need to earn a living to support herself and her children—surely contributed to her ability to pursue a very long and active reform and writing career.

In 1841, a young Caroline Healey was invited by Transcendentalist and reformer Elizabeth Palmer Peabody to attend Margaret Fuller's famous series of "conversations" for women. Dall attended and recorded the spring series of conversations, which she later published as *Margaret and Her Friends* (1895), one of the few transcripts made of Fuller's talks. By the time this work was published in 1895, Dall was among Fuller's devotees who were working to secure Fuller's place in 19th-century intellectual history.

An admirer of Ralph Waldo Emerson as well, Dall was attracted to Transcendentalist ideas about self-culture and intellectual expression, ideas that were radical when applied to women. This perspective influenced her work as a feminist author, editor, and activist, in particular as coeditor (with Paulina Wright Davis) of *The Una* (1853–1855), a newspaper dedicated to women's rights and intellectual culture. While Dall argued for women's right to the vote, to education and entrance into the professions, and to equal pay and property rights, she believed that women had to fight a greater cultural battle in developing themselves as individuals. This self-development, she believed, would be the foundation that made political and legal rights possible. She developed this argument more fully in her treatise on women's education and vocation, *The College, the Market, and the Court* (1867).

Dall was particularly interested in women's history and literary traditions. Besides the numerous articles she authored and selected for *The Una,* she also published a women's history text, *Historical Pictures Retouched* (1860), and a biography of a contemporary, *Life of Dr. Marie Zakrzewska* (1860). Caroline Dall wrote one of the first histories of the Transcendentalist movement of which she had been a part, *Transcendentalism in New England* (1897). In this history she argued that Transcendentalism, and in particular the work of Margaret Fuller, inspired much of the women's rights agitation of the 19th century.

Dall was also a theologian and guest preacher active in the Unitarian church. She published several tracts on religious topics. She was one of the cofounders of the American Social Science Association. In her later years Dall moved to Washington, D.C., where she died of pneumonia in 1912.

Tiffany K. Wayne

See Also: Davis, Paulina Kellogg Wright; Education of Women (before the Civil War); Fuller, Margaret; Peabody, Elizabeth; *The Una*; Zakrzewska, Marie

Further Reading

Deese, Helen. *Daughter of Boston: The Extraordinary Diary of a Nineteenth-Century Woman, Caroline Healey Dall.* Boston, MA: Beacon Press, 2006.

Wayne, Tiffany K. *Woman Thinking: Feminism and Transcendentalism in 19th-Century America.* Lanham, MD: Lexington Books, 2005.

Davis, Paulina Kellogg Wright (1813–1876)

Paulina S. Kellogg Wright Davis played an essential role in the development of the 19th-century American women's rights movement. Her most significant contributions were organizing and chairing the earliest national women's rights conventions, publishing the first newspaper dedicated exclusively to women's rights, and lecturing on anatomy and physiology.

Paulina Kellogg Wright Davis, health reformer and leader of the 19th-century women's rights movement. (Library of Congress)

Born in what has been called the "burned-over district" of western New York State (because of the intensity of religious revival that had swept over the area), Paulina Kellogg participated in revival meetings and joined the Presbyterian Church in 1823. Shortly thereafter, according to Elizabeth Cady Stanton, she was "roused to thought on woman's position by a [church] discussion as to whether women should be permitted to speak and pray in promiscuous assemblies."

As a young adult in Utica, New York, she became a leader in reform as a founding member of the Female Anti-Slavery Society, the Female Moral Reform Society, and the Martha Washington Temperance Union. In 1835, she and her first husband, Francis Wright, a merchant of wealth and position, organized the first antislavery convention to be held in Utica.

Paulina Kellogg Wright and Ernestine Rose were the first women to support the New York Married Woman's Property Bill, a measure designed to enable married women to retain inherited property in their own name. During the winter of 1836–1837, Wright collected 30 signatures on a petition in support of the proposed legislation, while Rose collected five signatures on a similar petition in another part of the state.

Wright's first experience in speaking to mixed audiences occurred in the early 1840s when she presided over a joint convention of the Martha Washington Temperance Union and the Washingtonians. Although Wright wrote of her desire to lecture on slavery, women's rights, and physiology, she deferred such activity, citing responsibility for her husband who was ill. After her husband's death in January 1845, however, she studied anatomy and physiology and spent the next four years travelling widely as a lecturer.

Wright helped to make lecturing a respectable and lucrative profession for women and to open the medical profession to women, and she supplied important information to women regarding their bodies and their health. She studied anatomy and physiology on her own. When barriers obstructed her formal education, she persuaded guards to lock her into libraries and classrooms overnight so that she could study and work with the skeletons and manikins. She also convinced professors to give her private lessons very early in the morning because she was prohibited from taking classes with male students at the regularly scheduled times. She had a thorough knowledge of her materials as well as life-sized color plates and the first *modelle du femme* in this country to illustrate her talks about female anatomy. Although she was generally well received at her lectures, she told of women who dropped their veils, fled the room, or fainted. Although she was financially secure, she said that one of her goals in lecturing was to open more professions to women, including lecturing and medicine, in part for economic reasons. Many women who attended her classes later attended medical school and became physicians.

Despite the demands placed on her by her second marriage in April 1849 to Thomas Davis and the subsequent adoption of two daughters, Wright Davis continued to lecture. The subjects of her lectures, which were attended by as many as 400 people, included "The Muscular System," "The Structure of the Eye," "The Nervous System," "Reproduction: The Origins of Life," "Pregnancy and the Changes It Causes," and "Diseases and Displacements of the Uterus." According to the minutes of the Providence Physiological Society, which she helped found in 1850, these topics were discussed very explicitly. "Mrs. Davis touched upon several points requiring moral courage with the prevailing ideal of delicacy," noted the secretary.

Without the efforts of Paulina Kellogg Wright Davis, the yearly national women's rights conventions held throughout the 1850s might never have occurred. She was one of a group of women who met at the 1850 antislavery convention in Boston and decided to issue a call for a women's rights convention. She is credited with organizing the first national women's rights convention held in Worcester in 1850 as well as taking primary responsibility for organizing the next two national conventions held at Worcester in 1851 and Syracuse in 1852. She presided over the two Worcester conventions and delivered addresses at all three. In addition, she participated in the founding of the American Equal Suffrage Association (1866), the New England Woman Suffrage Association, and, with Elizabeth Buffum Chace, was a founder and first president of the Rhode Island Woman Suffrage Association.

She organized and presided over the second-decade celebration in 1870, which marked the 20-year anniversary of the first national women's rights convention at Worcester, Massachusetts. There she delivered the opening address on the history of the movement, which was later published along with the proceedings of the convention. Wright Davis was one of the strong supporters of the Washington, D.C., conventions because they enabled the attendees to lobby Congress, and she financially insured the presence of a full-time lobbyist and organizer in the capital for a time.

Following discussion at the 1852 national convention of the need for a periodical devoted solely to women's rights, she worked with Elizabeth Oakes Smith to start a paper. When that venture failed, she decided to publish and edit a paper herself. *The Una* debuted in February 1853, and was published and edited by Wright Davis until the end of 1854. One goal of the paper was "to endeavor to preserve a correct history, not only of this specific movement, but of the lives of those engaged in it." For the length of its existence, *The Una* extensively covered national and regional conventions, and despite the demise of the paper, she accomplished her goal of maintaining a correct history of the movement. The history of the women's rights movement that she presented to the 1870 convention became the basis for the first volume of the *History of Woman Suffrage.*

Because of ill health and family obligations, Wright Davis was unable to continue assuming sole responsibility for *The Una.* In December 1854, a new publisher moved the paper to Boston, and Caroline Healey Dall became coeditor; publication ceased a year later. At the time *The Revolution,* published by Susan B. Anthony

and edited by Elizabeth Cady Stanton and Parker Pillsbury, began having serious financial problems, Wright Davis became corresponding editor (1869–1870) and provided financial assistance to ensure that women reformers would continue to have a voice. In 1870, with Kate Stanton of Rhode Island, she attempted publication of another reform paper, the *New World,* which apparently continued for about a year, but there is little information about it. In addition to her work on these papers, she wrote for the *Water-Cure Journal,* the *Liberty Bell, The Liberator,* the *New York Tribune, The Woman's Advocate,* and *McDowell's Journal.*

Wright Davis's basic philosophy was one of equality in human rights, based on natural rights. In her addresses to both the first and second national conventions, she spoke not of women's rights but of human rights. In 1850, she noted:

Nature does not teach that men and women are unequal, but only that they are unlike. . . . I ask only freedom for the natural unfolding of [woman's] powers, the conditions most favorable for her possibilities of growth, and then, I ask that she shall fill the place that she can attain to.

She clarified further in 1851: "I have said Human Rights, not Woman's Rights, for the relations, wants, duties, and rights of the sexes center upon the same great truth, and are logically, as they are practically, inseparable."

Her adherence to principle is exemplified by her split with the New England Woman Suffrage Association (NEWSA), forerunner of the AWSA, over the Fifteenth Amendment to the Constitution. NEWSA supported the amendment, which would grant suffrage to all male citizens, including African American men. She also resigned from the Rhode Island Woman Suffrage Association over their support of the Fifteenth Amendment.

Wright Davis once again chose principle over expediency when she was confronted over a resolution she presented at the 1871 NWSA Convention: "Resolved: That the evils, sufferings and disabilities of the women, as well as of men, are social still more than they are political, and that a statement of woman's rights which ignores the right of self-ownership as the first of all rights is insufficient." She clarified this point, explaining that by advocating self-ownership she was referring to a married woman's right to reject compulsory sexual relations and compulsory maternity. Nonetheless, in the pages of the *New York Tribune,* editor Horace Greeley continued to challenge her either to repudiate this position or accept the label of "free-lover." She responded with a tactic characteristic of her discourse and redefined free love:

> Love is an emotion of the heart, founded upon respect, esteem, admiration, and devotion. . . . I propose to stand upon this line and fight it out, rescuing the words from the base prostitution, and showing that only to the corrupt can corruption be made out of those resolutions.

In a speech on that same subject in 1852 to the third national women's rights convention, she argued that "correction of [marriage's] abuses is the starting point of all other reforms."

Despite more than two decades of organizing, reporting on, chairing, attending, and financing conventions, Paulina Kellogg Wright Davis disliked conventions and doubted their efficacy in furthering the cause. She believed that writing, lecturing, and interpersonal contact were more useful in obtaining support for the movement and it was through these methods that she helped open the fields of medicine and lecturing to women, enhanced women's property rights, and chronicled as well as advanced the movement for the rights of women.

Lynne Derbyshire

See Also: Dall, Caroline Healey; Nichols, Mary Gove; *The Una*; Free Love Movement (Vol. 2)

Primary Document: 1867, Support for Female Physicians

Further Reading

Clymer, John F. *This High and Holy Moment: The First National Woman's Rights Convention, Worcester, 1850.* Fort Worth, TX: Harcourt Brace, 1999.

Morantz-Sanchez, Regina. *Sympathy and Science: Women Physicians in American Medicine.* New York: Oxford University Press, 1985.

Tonn, Mari Boor. "*The Una*, 1853–1855: The Premiere of the Woman's Rights Press." In *A Voice of Their Own: The Woman Suffrage Press, 1840–1910,* edited by Martha Solomon. Tuscaloosa: University of Alabama Press, 1991.

Wayne, Tiffany K. *Woman Thinking: Feminism and Transcendentalism in Nineteenth-Century America.* Lanham, MD: Lexington Books, 2005.

Divorce (before the Civil War)

Rates of divorce were extremely low in the early colonial period, with many communities having a divorce filed only every few years. By the 1740s rates began to increase, with some communities having multiple divorce cases filed annually.

Like other laws in colonial America, rules regulating divorce and separation were inherited from England. English divorce was governed by the Church of England, which regarded a valid marriage as indissoluble. The religious dissidents who settled in New England had little respect for the laws of the Church of England. The Puritans of the northern colonies viewed marriage as a civil contract, rather than a spiritual sacrament. As such, it could be dissolved for breaches such as adultery, desertion, cruelty, or incorrigible enmity between the spouses. These actions constituted a breaking of the marriage covenant, and thus the offended party could look to a civil court for relief.

There were two types of divorce available, *divortium a vinculo,* or true divorce, was the most complete severing of ties. It allowed both parties the ability to remarry, but was only granted in cases in which the marriage was judged null from the outset. Massachusetts and Connecticut had the most liberal divorce laws of the colonies and extended the grounds for complete divorce to include adultery, abuse, and desertion. Absolute divorces were not permitted in the southern colonies until after the American Revolution. In the years following the war, each of the states liberalized the conditions under which an absolute divorce could be granted. Only South Carolina refused to permit absolute divorce until 1868.

Divortium a mensa et thoro, or separation from bed and board, was more common. All the legal obligations of marriage were maintained with the exception of cohabitation. It did not allow for the remarriage of either party. If the wife was found to be the innocent party, she was generally provided with ongoing financial support.

Reasons for Divorce

Adultery: Adultery was generally the claim most likely to result in a successful divorce application. To obtain a divorce on grounds of adultery, the adulterous act had to be testified to by two eyewitnesses or a confession of the guilty spouse. Alternatively, a male petitioner could prove adultery if his wife bore a child during a period when the husband was on an extended absence. Divorces were almost always granted if the wife was found guilty of adultery. Very few women even attempted to file for divorce based on an adulterous husband, and those who did were rarely granted one. A double standard clearly existed, in which sexual infidelity was not to be tolerated in a wife, but condoned when committed by a husband. Some of this double standard can be accounted for by the reluctance of the law to force a man to leave his estate to a child who might not be his own. Divorcing an adulterous wife was therefore considered a man's right to protect his bloodline and inheritance.

Cruelty: An 18th-century euphemism for physical abuse, cruelty by itself was rarely accepted as grounds for divorce. A successful appeal on grounds of cruelty had to prove the woman feared grave bodily harm or death. Occasional or slight acts of physical violence were not substantial enough to warrant a divorce. If the cruelty escalated to the point where a wife could prove she feared for life or limb, the courts were willing to intercede on her behalf and force the husband to provide for her maintenance in a separate household. Thus, divorce from bed and board could be obtained, but an absolute divorce, with privileges of remarriage, were less common if abuse was the only charge.

Marital rape was not regarded as a crime or grounds for divorce. Alcohol abuse was frequently cited by both husbands and wives seeking divorce. Unless the problem of drinking was associated with infidelity or extreme physical violence, it was not considered a factor in divorce petitions.

Women who were the target of severe abuse and had failed to obtain a divorce might simply leave their marriage. When Charity Barr left her husband, the enraged Mr. Barr took out an advertisement in the paper claiming his wife had deserted him for no reason. Mrs. Barr replied with an advertisement of her own, claiming repeated beatings and being "sometimes almost strangled by him, at other times thrown to the floor and stamped on, [with him] swearing he would murder her" (*Pennsylvania Gazette,* August 10, 1785). Mrs. Barr was fortunate in her ability to leave, because women who left their homes had no right to financial support from their husbands.

Desertion: Some unhappy spouses simply left home, leaving their partner abandoned yet unable to remarry while the marriage was still valid. Depending on the colony, a period between three and seven years had to expire before an abandoned spouse could file this claim. Colonies with a heavy seafaring population also permitted the "absent and presumed dead" category. Because divorce law tended to be punitive, meaning the guilty party received an unfavorable financial settlement, a spouse who had been unfaithful might have perceived desertion a more desirable option.

Women who were deserted by husbands were placed in an odd sort of limbo. Because married women had the *feme covert* status, meaning they had little legal identity, they were unable to sue, engage in or enforce contracts, or own a business. A woman who had been abandoned by her husband would almost certainly need the support of her family for her basic support.

Child Custody

There is a surprising lack of documentation regarding women's attempts to gain custody of their children after a divorce. During the 18th century, custody was almost systematically granted to the father, with little regard for the child's best interests. There was little sentimentality about children, who were viewed as economic assets under the direction and guidance of their father. It is possible that women who felt strongly about raising their children simply did not seek divorces, knowing they would almost certainly lose contact with the children. By the late 18th century, courts began to consider the best interests of the child when assigning custody.

The American Revolution spurred a liberalization of divorce policies in most of the new states. The fight against the tyranny of the king was translated into women's struggle to be free of tyrannical husbands. Yet there was still the presumption everywhere that one spouse had to be at fault for a divorce to be obtained.

In some New England and Middle Atlantic states grounds for divorce were expanded. In Pennsylvania a statute was passed in 1785 that allowed for divorce on grounds of inability to perform marital duties, adultery, bigamy, and desertion. In 1815 the law was amended to include cruelty on the part of the husband and, later, the wife as well. Rhode Island was the first to incorporate an omnibus clause that granted discretion to judges to decide whether other grounds for divorce were present.

In the western territories and states, divorces became even easier to obtain. Generally these divorce statutes included adultery, desertion, and cruelty as grounds and sometimes added an omnibus clause. The southern states showed the greatest change with their newfound willingness to grant divorce rather than only separation. The exception was South Carolina, which would not budge on its no-divorce policy. In both Virginia and Maryland, divorce statutes listing grounds seemed to have been spurred by the specter of interracial sex, that is, cases in which wives of white men had borne children with slave fathers. In 1827 a divorce bill was passed in Virginia that allowed courts to give a divorce on grounds of impotency, idiocy, and bigamy and legal separations on the basis of adultery, cruelty, and fear of bodily danger. In 1841 desertion was added to the grounds for separation.

In the 19th century, women's rights reformers began to argue not only for married women's property rights, but for mother's rights in custody cases and for more lenient divorce laws so that women could escape unhappy marriages. Women were more often those who sued for divorce and men were more often found at fault. By 1849 most northeastern states had added cruelty and drunkenness to the bedrock grounds of adultery and desertion. In 1851, California passed a divorce statute that included a compendium of causes that reflected the legal thinking of the time. Causes included impotence, adultery, desertion, cruelty, fraud, failure to support, habitual intemperance, and conviction of a felony. Some states added verbal abuse to their list of grounds for divorce and "cruelty" was increasingly interpreted by courts to include both physical and emotional cruelty.

The seeming leniency with which divorce was being treated precipitated a divorce crisis in the 1850s. Horace Greeley of the *New York Tribune* published a series of articles linking divorce to the corruption of U.S. civilization in 1852 and 1853. The debate became more strident as attempts were made to liberalize New York's divorce law in 1860. Greeley made an all-out attack on that effort and arguably won the debate, since the divorce laws in New York remained unchanged.

Reliable statistics from the Civil War are scarce, but it is reasonable to conclude that during the war divorce fell, owing to other exigencies of life. After the war, the number of divorces appears to have risen to new levels. Absence during war, changed expectations, and physical impairment led to increased divorce. In 1868, South Carolina placed a divorce clause into the state constitution that was followed two years later by a statute allowing divorce for the first time in that state on the grounds of adultery, desertion, and cruelty. The liberalization was short-lived, as the state went back to its no-divorce policy 10 years later and held to that policy until 1949.

Dorothy A. Mays and Bonnie L. Ford

See Also: Legal Status of Women (18th Century); New York Married Women's Property Acts; Nichols, Mary Gove; Wright, Frances; Divorce (Civil War to WWII) (Vol. 2); Domestic Violence (pre-1970) (Vol. 2); Stanton, Elizabeth Cady (Vol. 2)

Primary Documents: 1839, Mississippi Married Women's Property Act; 1845, *Shaw v. Shaw*; 1848–1849, New York Married Women's Property Acts; 1861, Address on Behalf of the New York Divorce Bill

Further Reading

Basch, Norma. *Framing American Divorce: From the Revolutionary Generation to the Victorians.* Berkeley: University of California Press, 1999.

Chused, Richard H. *Private Acts in Public Places: A Social History of Divorce in the Formative Era of American Family Law.* Philadelphia: University of Pennsylvania Press, 1994.

Cott, Nancy F. *Public Vows: A History of Marriage and the Nation.* Cambridge, MA: Harvard University Press, 2000.

Dayton, Cornelia Hughes. *Women before the Bar: Gender, Law, and Society in Connecticut, 1639–1789.* Chapel Hill: University of North Carolina Press, 1995.

Griswold, Robert L. *Family and Divorce in California, 1850–1890: Victorian Illusions and Everyday Realities.* Albany: State University of New York Press, 1982.

Riley, Glenda. *Divorce: An American Tradition.* New York: Oxford University Press, 1991.

Salmon, Marylynn. *Women and the Law of Property in Early America.* Chapel Hill: University of North Carolina Press, 1986.

Smith, Merril D. *Breaking the Bonds: Marital Discord in Pennsylvania, 1730–1830.* New York: New York University Press, 1991.

Dix, Dorothea (1802–1887)

A lone and persistent female voice for reform of the mental health system in the United States, Dorothea Dix argued for such care to be removed from its traditional dependence on acts of private charity and for provisions to be made available at the federal level. During the Civil War, Dix faced the hostility of the male medical establishment when she oversaw the nurses of the Union Army's Sanitary Commission. Like her British counterpart Florence Nightingale, she had an iron will and an extraordinarily thick skin, and she was not afraid of confronting and alienating people by being tough—so much so that she was nicknamed "Dragon Dix."

Born Dorothea Lynde Dix in Hampden, Maine, the daughter of a farmer who was also an itinerant Methodist lay preacher, Dix was consigned to looking after her younger siblings. She suffered neglect as a child as a result of her mother's ill health and her father's alcoholism and was eventually sent to live with her wealthy grandmother and then her great-aunt in Boston. At 15 years of age, she began teaching at her own dame

Dorothea Dix was world-renowned for her work on behalf of the mentally ill and for her services as a nurse during the Civil War. (Library of Congress)

school for girls in Worcester, Massachusetts, while continuing to educate herself by reading books from her Harvard-educated grandfather's library. In 1821 she broke off her engagement to her second cousin, Edward Bangs, and opened a school for young ladies at her grandparents' home in Boston. By 1836, when she had to nurse her sick grandmother, Dix began suffering recurring bouts of ill health that turned out to be tuberculosis and gave up her school. For a while, she concentrated on writing moral tales for children, a Unitarian hymn-book, and a science textbook, *Conversations on Common Things* (1824), while living the confined life of a semi-invalid. Having been ordered to rest by her doctor, she traveled to England and for 18 months stayed in Liverpool with the family of the Unitarian reformer William Rathbone (later the grandfather of British feminist Eleanor Rathbone), who introduced her to other English social reformers.

She returned to the United States and in March 1841 began teaching a Sunday school class for women inmates of the House of Correction at East Cambridge.

She was horrified by the filthy, damp, dark, and cold conditions endured by the women, many of whom were not criminals but insane, having been confined in prison for want of an alternative institution in which to house them. On questioning such inhumane treatment, Dix was told that the insane had no awareness of cold or the squalor of their surroundings and that since they would never recover or be cured, there was little point in making life more comfortable for them. Dix was appalled at their maltreatment and the indiscriminate use of corporal punishment: the insane were often kept in cages or fetters and chains and also suffered sexual abuse by their jailers. With a small legacy from her grandmother, Dix spent the next 18 months visiting insane asylums, brothels, workhouses, and jails in Massachusetts and saw firsthand how widespread was the practice of keeping the mentally ill cooped up alongside common criminals. She prepared a report of her findings, the "Memorial to the Legislature of Massachusetts," which she submitted in 1843. In it she argued that the insane should be separated from criminals. As result of her report, the Massachusetts legislature initiated improvements at the state insane asylum in Worcester.

From 1843 to 1845, Dix traveled 10,000 miles from Rhode Island through New York, Pennsylvania, Kentucky, Maryland, Ohio, Illinois, Mississippi, Alabama, Tennessee, and North Carolina, inspecting prisons, almshouses, and mental asylums. In 1844, while in New Jersey, she lobbied for the construction of a proper mental asylum; funds were raised to construct the New Jersey State Lunatic Asylum in Trenton. It was only one of 32 mental asylums and 15 schools for the feebleminded established in 15 states as a result of Dix's efforts, at the end of which she published her detailed observations in *Remarks on Prisons and Prison Discipline in the United States* (1845).

Dix marched on Washington in 1848 to launch a campaign at the federal level. She presented her request for "Grant of Land for the Relief and Support of the Indigent Curable and Incurable Insane in the United States," in which she appealed to the U.S. government for a grant of 5 million acres of public lands to provide tax revenues that would help support the indigent curable and incurable insane. Dix advocated the construction of new asylums, the reorganization of existing ones, and the retraining of their warders in more humane methods. She suggested the introduction of educational programs and the segregation of prisoners in separate groups according to the severity of their crimes. President Franklin Pierce vetoed Dix's bill in 1854, insisting that the care of the insane was the responsibility of public philanthropy. It would not be until 1933 that Franklin D. Roosevelt's Federal Emergency Relief Administration would grant government funds for direct services.

Dix went on another convalescent trip to Europe in 1854, during which she appealed to the pope to intercede on behalf of the insane. She visited jails and asylums in Scotland and the Channel Islands before traveling from Sweden in the north to Turkey in the south and east from Belgium across to Russia, everywhere lobbying officials to reform their prisons and insane asylums. Once again back in the United States in 1856, Dix resumed her investigations of insane asylums but eventually found another cause when the Civil War broke out in April 1861.

She volunteered herself to the Union Army as a nurse and in June was appointed superintendent of women nurses in charge of the military hospitals in the north (later known as the Army Nursing Corps of the Sanitary Commission). Working for no pay for the next five years, she applied her customary energy to converting public buildings into hospitals and imposing a strict regime, but her administration antagonized many. She dismissed any romantic notions her women volunteers might have about becoming ministering angels on the battlefield and refused to accept nuns or women under 30. As for their mode of dress, "All nurses are required to be very plain-looking women. Their dresses must be brown or black, with no bows, no curls, no jewelry and no hoop skirts." With the imposition of such strict regulations, it is not surprising that Dix's reputation went before her, for the equally indomitable Clara Barton—the more celebrated nursing pioneer of the Civil War—declined the offer of joining her nursing corps, thus avoiding an inevitable clash of personalities.

At the end of the Civil War, Dix returned to her interest in mental health reform in 1867 and also helped societies promoting charitable work for orphans; disaster victims; and the deaf, dumb, and blind. In 1881 she retired, having seen the number of mental asylums in the United States grow from 13 in 1841 to 123. She took up residence in guest quarters at the New Jersey State Lunatic Asylum in Trenton, her "firstborn child," as she called the first mental hospital built as a result of her crusading, no doubt content that she had fulfilled the objective laid out in a letter written to Lydia Maria Child on December 31, 1844: "In a world where there is so much to be done, I felt strongly impressed that there must be something for me to do."

Helen Rappaport

See Also: Abolitionism and the Antislavery Movement; Barton, Clara; Child, Lydia Maria; Education of Women (before the Civil War); United States Sanitary Commission

Further Reading

Brown, Thomas J. *Dorothea Dix: New England Reformer.* Cambridge, MA: Harvard University Press, 1997.

Dix, Dorothea L. *Asylum, Prison, and Poorhouse: The Writings and Reform Work of Dorothea Dix in Illinois,* edited by David L. Lightener. Carbondale: Southern Illinois University Press, 1999.

Gollaher, David. *A Voice for the Mad: The Life of Dorothea Dix.* New York: Free Press, 1995.

Hersteck, Amy Pualson. *Dorothea Dix: Crusader for the Mentally Ill.* Berkeley Heights, NJ: Enslow, 2001.

Douglass, Frederick (1818–1895)

Runaway slave Frederick Douglass was an instrumental part of the abolitionist movement. He became an agent and lecturer for the American Anti-Slavery Society in 1841 and later published his autobiography to aid in the fight against slavery. Consistent with the egalitarian impulse of abolitionism, Douglass also advocated for the rights of women throughout his life.

The son of Harriet, a black slave, and an unknown white father, he was born Frederick Augustus Washington Bailey (or Baily) at Holme Hill Farm in Talbot County, Maryland. Separated from his mother at an early age, he lived with his grandmother Betsey on a plantation until the age of eight, when he was sent to work for the Hugh Auld family in Baltimore. Defying state law, Auld's wife, Sophia, acquiesced to Douglass's request and taught him to read. From 1836 to 1838, Douglass worked in the Baltimore shipyards as a caulker, where he met Anna Murray, a free woman of color, who worked as a domestic. He and Murray married after he escaped to New York City in 1838. After hearing him speak at a meeting of the Bristol Anti-Slavery Society in 1841, William Lloyd Garrison arranged for Douglass to become an agent and lecturer for the American Anti-Slavery Society. Anna Douglass supported her husband's travels and their five children by working in a shoe factory.

In addition to the lecture circuit, Frederick Douglass was also a familiar figure at abolitionist conventions. In 1845, the Anti-Slavery Society assisted in the publication of the first of Douglass's three autobiographies: *The Narrative of the Life of Frederick Douglass: An American Slave.* The book's popularity forced Douglass to spend the next two years in England to avoid recapture. In the interim, American abolitionists raised money for his eventual emancipation.

Although abolitionists generally agreed on the principal goal of ending the practice of slavery, the movement exhibited deep philosophical divisions. Primary among them was the issue of gender equality. While both Garrison and Douglass believed that women's voices should be heard, the exclusion of women from decision making by the Anti-Slavery Society leadership precipitated the growth of same-sex antislavery societies. Douglass, however, became well known for his outspoken stance on women's rights. Although he and Garrison were in agreement on the role of women in the abolitionist movement, they parted ways in December 1847 when Douglass decided to publish his own antislavery newspaper, *The North Star*, along with Martin R. Delany and black Boston historian William C. Nell. After 1851, the newspaper became known as *Frederick Douglass' Paper*.

Drawn in part by his friendship with abolitionist Amy Post, Frederick and Anna Douglass moved their family to Rochester, New York, in 1847. Already known as a haven for abolitionism, the women of Rochester were active in antislavery societies and Douglass was in close proximity to the leaders in the fight for women's rights, including Susan B. Anthony, Lucretia Mott, and Elizabeth Cady Stanton.

Douglass's personal relationships with white women, however, raised the ire of both white and black communities. One of his financial supporters was Julia Griffiths, whom he had met in England. Griffiths was one of six founders of the Rochester Ladies' Anti-Slavery and Sewing Society, which held annual festivals or bazaars that raised money for the movement through the sale of items and sponsorship of lectures by activities. The efforts not only kept *The North Star* afloat, but they also supported individual fugitives and a school for freedmen in Kansas. In 1848, Douglass brought Griffiths to Rochester as a live-in tutor for his children and wife. Citizens of Rochester objected vociferously when Griffiths began to serve as his office and business manager and personal companion.

Douglass participated in the first women's rights convention haled in in Seneca Falls, New York in 1848 and signed the Declaration of Sentiments. Elizabeth Cady Stanton afterward credited Douglass's efforts for the passage of the resolution calling for women's suffrage by the convention. In the July 1848 issue of *The North Star*, Douglass published an editorial entitled "The Rights of Women." In 1853, Douglass endorsed "The Just And Equal Rights of Women," a call and resolutions for the state women's rights convention held in Rochester, and he was a featured speaker at the meeting.

During the antebellum period, Douglass was a close friend of Susan B. Anthony and her family. Between 1865 and 1870, however, Douglass split from many women's rights activists over the issue of the passage of the Fourteenth and Fifteenth Amendments. Douglass aligned himself with abolitionists who believed that it was more important to gain the rights of African American males than the rights of women. As an advisor to President Abraham Lincoln, Douglass protested the discrimination against black enlisted troops and fought for the adoption of constitutional amendments that guaranteed voting rights and other civil liberties for blacks. In 1866, he clashed with women's rights leaders at the convention of the Equal Rights Association over their insistence that the vote not be extended to black men unless it was also given to all women. For their part, Anthony and Stanton refused to support the Fifteenth Amendment because it excluded women. After the amendment was ratified in 1870, Douglass immediately called for an amendment giving women the right to vote, writing an editorial supporting women's suffrage entitled "Women and The Ballot." In 1878, he attended the 30th anniversary celebration of the first Women's Rights Convention, held by the National Woman Suffrage Association (NWSA) in Rochester. He also attended the 1881 NWSA meeting held in Washington, D.C. In 1888, Anthony introduced Douglass to the audience of the International Council of Women as a women's rights pioneer.

Douglass continued to form personal attachments to white women throughout his life. After the pressure of an interracial relationship with Douglass caused Julia Griffiths to return to England, Douglass met Ottilie Assing, a German journalist, when she traveled to Rochester in 1856 to interview him. An abolitionist herself, Assing entered into a liaison with Douglass that lasted for 26 years. In 1884, two years after the death of his wife Anna, Frederick Douglass married Helen Pitts, a white woman from New York who was his secretary. Pitts was a graduate of Mount Holyoke Seminary and the daughter of Gideon Pitts Jr., an abolitionist colleague and friend of Douglass. Prior to her marriage, Helen had worked on a radical feminist publication called the *Alpha*. Stanton defended Douglass and Pitts against their detractors.

Relocating to Washington, D.C., during the 1870s, Douglass not only worked with his sons to publish the weekly *New National Era,* but also entered government service. The newspaper chronicled the political progress of the Republican Party and its new black constituency. In 1872, the Equal Rights Party, on a ticket headed by Victoria Woodhull, nominated him for the vice presidency of the United States. Douglass became District of Columbia Recorder of Deeds (1881–1886) and then director of United States diplomatic relations with Haiti (1889–1891). In Washington, Douglass, John Mercer Langston, and others contributed to the growth of a cadre of black intellectuals that included women such as Frances Ellen Watkins Harper, Maria Stewart, and Charlotte Forten Grimké.

In 1893, articulating a vision of America as a "composite" nation of many peoples and cultures, Douglass assisted Ida B. Wells in her sustained campaign against lynching. Douglass seems to have valued Wells's focus on women's rights and social justice during the 1880s and 1890s. In reaction to the exclusion of blacks from the 1893 Chicago World's Fair, Wells and Douglass collaborated on a pamphlet entitled "Reasons Why the Colored American is Not in the World's Colombian Exposition," which documented the progress of blacks since their arrival in America. He encouraged Wells to hire detectives to investigate a lynching in Paris, Texas, and to subsequently share her findings on a European speaking tour. He also wrote an introduction to *A Red Record,* her 1895 statistical report on lynching since the passage of the Emancipation Proclamation.

The day of Douglass's death, February 20, 1895, he had attended a meeting of the National Council of Women in Washington, D.C. During that meeting, he was recognized for his lifelong commitment to women's rights and given a standing ovation by the audience. At his funeral, Susan B. Anthony delivered a eulogy written by Elizabeth Cady Stanton.

Jayne R. Beilke

See Also: Abolitionism and the Antislavery Movement; Fifteenth Amendment; Freedmen's Bureau; Garrison, William Lloyd; Grimké, Charlotte L. Forten; Seneca Falls Convention; Slavery and the Civil War; Suffrage in Early America; Anthony, Susan B. (Vol. 2); National Woman Suffrage Association (Vol. 2); Stanton, Elizabeth Cady (Vol. 2); Wells-Barnett, Ida B. (Vol. 2)

Primary Document: 1848, Declaration of Sentiments

Further Reading

Diedrich, Maria. *Love Across Color Lines: Ottilie Assing and Frederick Douglass.* New York: Hill and Wang, 1999.

Foner, Philip S., ed. *Frederick Douglass on Women's Rights.* Westport, CT: Greenwood Press, 1976.

McMillen, Sally G. *Seneca Falls and the Origins of the Women's Rights Movement.* New York: Oxford University Press, 2008.

Oakes, James. *The Radical and the Republican: Frederick Douglass, Abraham Lincoln, and the Triumph of Antislavery Politics.* New York: W.W. Norton & Company, Inc. 2007.

Dress Reform

Dress reform in the anteblleum era (1820–1860) was spurred on by a number of motives. Dress was seen by many reformers as the stumbling block between women and their greatest potential as individuals. The popular fashions of the period were cumbersome and were seen to support the submissiveness of women in society. The greatest proponents of this movement—women such as Amelia Bloomer, Elizabeth Cady Stanton, Lydia Sayer Hasbrouck, and others—saw dress at the center of the growing dependency of American women. But dress reform was an issue that was embraced for a number of other reasons. Health reformers, for example, were typically more concerned about the physical damage that fashionable women's dress might cause than its political or psychological burdens.

Among those concerns high on the list of health reformers was the custom of lacing corsets tightly to achieve a narrower waist. Those against the custom included physicians such as Dr. William Alcott, as well as women who were also active in other forms of activism such as the Beecher sisters, Harriet Beecher Stowe and Catharine Beecher. Dr. Alcott explained that "corsets impeded full expansion of the lungs in breathing, thus causing weakening of the lungs, shortness of breath, and poor circulation." He also "likened tight lacing to the Chinese practice of foot binding well known for its crippling effects." The Beecher sisters included a list of ailments caused by tight-lacing in their arguments against it, including "curvature of the spine, displacement of the internal organs, weakening of the diaphragm, 'palpatations of the heart,' and consumption." Women's footwear also found a place on the list of health reformers. Small, thin-soled shoes were cited for the pain they caused. The fashion for wearing a too-small shoe gained popularity as an expression of society's notion of the petite female stereotype. Of particular note was the blame they placed on the practice of constructing shoes that were straight, as opposed to those designed to fit only the right or left foot, a practice that was applied to men's and children's shoes as well as women's.

English writer Frances Trollope, in her wry observations of the *Domestic Manners of the Americans* (1832), notably commented on their habit of dressing out of the needs of fashion instead of suitably for the season. This complaint was shared by the health reformers. One reformer, Florence Hartley, claimed "many a fair head has been laid in a coffin, a victim to consumption, from rashly venturing out of a heated ball room, flushed and excited, with only a light protection against the keen night air." Fashionable skirts were also blamed for adding to women's ill-health and the spread of disease. Long trains, when worn outside, were faulted with catching and carrying unsanitary street debris.

When discussing 19th century reform dress, the "Bloomer costume" comes to mind most readily. This ensemble was composed of a knee-length sacque or loose tunic dress worn over loose trousers, which were bound at the ankles. Despite its reform nature, the costume did nod toward fashionable attire. While it could be worn without stays, the Bloomer costume was worn with a number of petticoats to recreate the fashionably full skirt of the period.

This ensemble was not, in fact, introduced to America by Amelia Bloomer. Instead, women's rights activist Elizabeth Cady Stanton is far more responsible for introducing this reform dress to American women. She, in turn, was first exposed to it by her cousin Elizabeth Smith Miller in 1851. The costume was first published as a sketch in June 1852 by Amelia Bloomer (a friend of Stanton's and fellow reformer) in her paper, *The Lily*, after she had worn the costume for some time. Although she would eventually print a pattern for the "Turkish costume" or "the shorts" (as some women referred to the costume) in response to requests, it soon became known as "Bloomers" for Amelia Bloomer's role in publicizing it.

The Bloomer costume was reviled by many men and women of the time, as well as by many who would come after. Take Elizabeth McClellan's commentary on the costume for example: "Early in the decade [1850s] a novel and hideous costume was devised by Mrs. Bloomer, editor of a temperance journal in the United States, who went about the country giving lectures in 1851–1852, on woman suffrage, and advertised the new dress henceforth known as the 'Bloomer costume.' By way of manifesting the independence of her sex she advised the women to adopt a part at least of the customary costume of the men."

The fashion press of the period was one of the Bloomer costume's greatest detractors, however. In *Godey's Lady's Book* in January 1852, the magazine gave itself a proverbial pat on the back for turning its nose up at the Bloomer costume: "The 'Rome Courier' says, 'We have been much gratified that Mr. Godey has given no encouragement to the bloomer folly.' We were right. Even those who paraded our streets at night have given it up. The thing is dead."

The Bloomer costume eventually found more success overseas, although in time the Bloomer's most ardent supporters gave up the style in the later 1850s as they felt the negative press it received was injurious to their cause. By the end of the 1860s, the fashion had disappeared.

When it was worn, the Bloomer costume was often most successfully adopted by those in isolated circumstances, such as pioneer women. Many times it was worn for purposes far removed from the reform motivations that inspired it. Other more subtle alterations to dress on the prairie might also be seen as echoing those of the reform movement. However, it is more likely that they occurred out of necessity in performing physical labor than political motivation.

The dress reform movement that had begun in the 1850s continued into the next decade, but never became a major factor in changes in women's fashions. If anything, the hoop skirt fashions of the Civil War period of the 1860s were even more ornamental and more restrictive, and corsets remained standard for several more decades. There were several women who continued to wear the Bloomer costume, but they often received public humiliation when they appeared in public in bifurcated garments. Satirists, husbands, ministers, and many women reacted very emotionally to garments that seemed to obscure, even to a minute degree, the traditional separation of roles and appearances between the sexes. In fact, one of the main thrusts of detractors from reform dress was that the style unsexed women or made them more like men.

This association, in particular, led many women, who on a rational level thoroughly accepted the principles of the Bloomer style, to forgo actually adopting it. Members of the suffragist movement tended to distance themselves from it as well because of the controversy surrounding the types of women who adopted the reform dress.

One group did wear a costume closely resembling the Bloomer style. Female members of the Oneida Community, which occupied a communal living space in New York State for nearly 20 years in the late 1840s through the late 1870s, are shown in numerous photographs wearing simple dresses with long, full sleeves, high necklines, and bell-shaped skirts without hoops that stop below the knee. Under these dresses are straight-leg pants that appear to be made of the same fabric as the dresses. The Oneida Community attempted to be self-sufficient, which meant that all members had to work and be productive. Apparently they decided that their adopted style of dress helped facilitate that productivity. Given that community members were ostracized and ridiculed by most of the rest of society for their unusual beliefs and practices (such as male continence as the preferred method of birth control and the practice of complex marriages), any additional negative publicity they might receive because of their dress styles was likely of very little consequence to them.

Aside from its wholesale adoption by females at the Oneida Community, the major usefulness of the Bloomer costume was in the arena of private life. At least some women adapted the concept for work or exercise, both of which they expected to practice removed from public view.

Some religious groups specified acceptable dress for their community members. In the Midwest, the Icarians shunned uniqueness or differences from each other by their manner of dress. Other religious groups, such as the Quakers and Amish, wore plain clothing, simply cut and untrimmed, as a statement of their beliefs and to set them apart from their more worldly neighbors.

Although there is some disagreement as to the extent to which tight lacing of corsets negatively impacted feminine health, most authorities agree that much of the lore surrounding ultra-tight lacing is myth. Corsets were sold by waist measurement, and surviving corsets can certainly be measured, but the measurements do not indicate how closely the two halves were drawn together by the laces. Conceivably the back sections could have spread by several inches. Certainly during pregnancy they would have had to spread to accommodate the increasing stomach girth, as few women could afford to buy corsets specifically designed for maternity wear.

The dress reform movement offered an alternative to corsets that was designed to provide a more healthful garment while still preserving some of the staid posture society dictated for the virtuous woman. The emancipation waist was a closely fitted underbodice very similar to a closely fitted corset cover. The waist was proposed in the 1870s, when corsets were particularly long, high, and tight. Its main feature was that buttons along its lower edge allowed the weight of the skirt and petticoats to be borne by the waist and entire upper body rather than pulling directly on the woman's waist. Like many of the attempts to reform dress for rational or health reasons, the emancipation waist was not particularly successful.

Some women, no doubt, did carry lacing to an extreme that was injurious to their health, but evidence does not support the notion that this was ever anything more than a small minority, possibly with fetishistic or obsessive connotations. For most women, the corset was simply an accepted item of apparel they would not consider themselves dressed without, just as today women view wearing brassieres as essential.

Fashion would eventually change and allow much greater freedom of movement, less restriction of lungs and waist, and a more healthful effect on women's bodies in general. These changes evolved gradually as women became involved in increased physical activity and as larger numbers of women entered into the workforce and thus needed functional clothing.

Michelle Webb Fandrich and Jill Condra

See Also: Bloomer, Amelia Jenks; Hasbrouck, Lydia Sayer; *The Lily*; Nichols, Mary Gove; *The Sybil*; Walker, Mary Edwards; Stanton, Elizabeth Cady (Vol. 2)

Primary Document: 1851, "Reflections on Woman's Dress"

Further Reading

Cunningham, Patricia A. *Reforming Women's Fashion, 1850–1920: Politics, Health, and Art*. Kent, OH: Kent State University Press, 2003.

Fischer, Gayle V. *Pantaloons and Power: A Nineteenth-Century Dress Reform in the United States*. Kent, OH: Kent State University Press, 2001.

Kidwell, Claudia Brush, and Valerie Steele. *Men and Women Dressing the Part*. Washington, DC: The Smithsonian Institution, 1989.

Mattingly, Carol. *Appropriate[ing] Dress: Women's Rhetorical Style in Nineteenth-Century America*. Carbondale: Southern Illinois University Press, 2002.

Severa, Joan. *Dressed for the Photographer: Ordinary Americans & Fashion, 1840–1900*. Kent, OH: Kent State University Press, 1995.

Steele, Valerie. *The Corset: A Cultural History*. New Haven, CT: Yale University Press, 2001.

E

Edmonds, Sarah Emma (1841–1898)

Few expected New Brunswicker Sarah Emma Edmonds to emerge as the Civil War's most famous female soldier, spy, and nurse.

Born in 1841 as the fifth daughter of Isaac and Elisabeth Edmonds, Sarah's disapproving father compounded the rural drudgery, isolation, and severity that characterized her early life. Despite her ability to hunt, fish, and work hard, her father continued to punish Sarah for not being a boy. Sarah hoped that the birth of her brother would soften her father's emotions toward her and make her life easier. Relief turned to despair when her brother displayed signs of epilepsy and her father's anger toward her intensified. In 1856, Isaac betrothed Sarah to a much older and, in her opinion, unacceptable man. Rather than marry him, Sarah fled to a family friend in Moncton, New Brunswick, and worked as a salesgirl in a hat shop before making her way to Flint, Michigan, where she survived by posing as a man and working as a door-to-door bible salesman.

With the outbreak of the Civil War in 1861, Sarah volunteered for service under the name Franklin Thompson and was mustered into the Second Michigan Volunteer Regiment as a nurse. She served in the hospitals and on the battlefields of Bull Run and Antietam, among others, and several times she donned the disguise of a slave to spy behind Confederate lines. Disguised as a slave, Sarah/Franklin could listen to and observe Confederate plans unnoticed. In March 1862, she discovered that the Confederates planned to bluff the Union at Yorktown, Virginia. Instead of cannons, the Confederates crafted Quaker guns, that is, logs painted to look like cannons and designed to exaggerate the size of the force the Union would meet. Sarah/Franklin relayed the information to the Union command, perhaps contributing to the Union victory in April 1862.

In the spring of 1863, Sarah contracted malaria and chose to abandon the Second Michigan Volunteer Regiment rather than seek medical help that might reveal her identity as a woman. She planned to recover in Cairo, Illinois, and return to service, but she discovered that the Union army had listed Frank Thompson as a deserter. Instead of returning to her regiment, she published a highly fictionalized version of her life in 1864. *Nurse and Spy in the Union Army* detailed Sarah Edmonds's adventures during the war, but excluded the details relating to her time disguised as Franklin Thompson. Edmonds donated all the proceeds from the book to various charities, including the United States Sanitary Commission. For the remainder of the Civil War, Sarah Edmonds worked for the Commission as a nurse and Franklin Thompson remained, in the eyes of his comrades and the United States government, a deserter.

Sarah Edmonds returned to Canada after the Civil War and married fellow Canadian Linus Seeyle in 1867. The two raised a family while frequently moving between Illinois, Michigan, Ohio, and Kansas. Over the course of these years, Franklin Thompson's status as a deserter bothered Edmonds. In 1884, she revealed the truth to her military comrades at a reunion. Although surprised by the revelation, they supported her quest to clear Franklin's name. Many veterans offered up affidavits that Edmonds used to petition the federal government for an honorable discharge and a pension. On July 7, 1886, President Grover Cleveland granted both of her requests. Sarah Edmonds received a $12-a-month veteran's pension for the rest of her life. She spent her remaining years in La Porte, Texas.

She died on September 5, 1898, of malaria, the very disease that led her to desert her military post during the Civil War. On Memorial Day in 1901, Edmonds's military comrades reburied her with full military honors in the Grand Army of the Republic cemetery in Houston, making her the organization's only female member. In 1988, the United States Military Intelligence Hall of Fame inducted Sarah Edmonds into their organization. Four years later, the Michigan Women's Hall of Fame followed suit. Both recognized Sarah Edmonds's contributions to the United States generally and specifically to the Union military effort.

Cheryl A. Wells

See Also: United States Sanitary Commission; Wakeman, Sarah Rosetta

Sarah Emma Edmonds disguised herself as a man and enlisted with the Union Army during the Civil War. She later revealed her true identity and received a veteran's pension for her service. (Kean Collection/Archive Photos/Getty Images)

Further Reading

Blanton, Deanna, and Lauren M. Cook. *They Fought Like Demons: Women Soldiers in the Civil War.* New York: Vintage, 2002.

Gansler, Laura Leedy. *The Mysterious Private Thompson: The Double Life of Sarah Emma Edmonds, Civil War Soldier.* New York: Free Press, 2005.

Hoy, Claire. *Canadians in the Civil War.* Toronto: McArthur & Company, 2004.

Leonard, Elizabeth D. *All the Daring of the Soldier: Women of the Civil War Armies.* New York: W. W. Norton & Company, 1999.

Stevens, Bryna. *Frank Thompson: Her Civil War Story.* Toronto: Maxwell MacMillian Canada, 1992.

Education of Women (before the Civil War)

After the American Revolution, the traditional role of women as mothers was central to the educational goals of the new nation, as mothers were the first and primary educators of young children. In the 19th century, however, women took on new educational roles as students themselves and as schoolteachers. At the turn of the 19th century, the spread of public or common schools made it possible for more girls to attend school for the first time. As more girls entered school, the demand for women's continued education beyond the lower grades sparked the founding of the first all-female seminaries and then colleges in the first half of the 19th century.

Promoters of women's education, however, continued to emphasize that education should be in service to women's primary roles in the home. As reformer Catharine Beecher explained in her 1841 *A Treatise on Domestic Economy for the Use of Young Ladies at Home and at School,* "The proper education of a man decides the welfare of an individual; but educate a woman, and the interests of a whole family are secured." Still, the 19th century saw women's roles shift from being the educated mothers of future citizens, to schoolteaching as a predominantly female occupation, to women's presence in the highest levels of university and professional education and administration.

Beginning in the 1790s, a new emphasis was placed on education to impart newly formed American cultural and political values to the next generation. Women had always been responsible for the moral and religious training of children in the home, but although they were denied their own rights at citizens in the creation of a new nation, women's roles as mothers took on new political meaning and their education became the subject of national debate. In 1790, Judith Sargent Murray, a prolific magazine essayist and New England intellectual, published an article, "On the Equality of the Sexes," in which she challenged the belief that there were inherent or natural intellectual differences between men and women. If there were such differences, Murray argued, it was only because of women's lack of education, and that woman, "an intellectual being," needed greater "ideas, than those which are suggested by the mechanism of a pudding, or the sewing of the seams of a garment." Murray was an early voice for a woman's right to an education as self-development, introducing what would become one of the main issues of the 19th-century women's rights movement.

The idea of "republican motherhood," that is, emphasizing women's role in educating children as future citizens, opened up the debate and the educational opportunities for white women, as the importance of education for women could no longer be denied. Thomas Jefferson planned the studies of his own daughters according to the expectation that they would eventually fulfill adult roles as planter's wives. He explained that girls needed "a solid education which would enable them to become mothers to educate their own daughters & even to direct the course for sons should their fathers be lost or incapable or inattentive." To this end, their daily schedule included French lessons, music, drawing, and reading literature and political theory, as well as instruction by their mother in housekeeping and needlework. Although Jefferson's daughters, like most young women of the late 18th and early 19th century, were educated at home, the new emphasis on the importance of women's education justified more formal training, and many "ladies' academies" were founded in the 1780s, 1790s, and early 1800s.

Ladies' Academies

Whereas boys needed education as career training, early 19th-century parents like Jefferson wanted to prepare their daughters for their future roles as wives and mothers. Young ladies' academies or seminaries offered high-school equivalent educations, but this training and legacy inspired the next generation to establish the first women's colleges with the goal of providing a more rigorous academic curriculum, similar or equal to that offered in men's colleges. Increasingly, middle- and upper-class parents sent their daughters as well as sons to school, expecting both academics and social training.

Many Northern women born at the turn of the 19th century attended seminaries and went on to become the first generation of female teachers, writers, and reformers. For white middle-class women born in the 1810s and 1820s and beyond, educational options increased greatly. Seminaries gradually expanded their curriculum and women's colleges were established to match the more rigorous academics of men's colleges.

Beneficiaries of such educations took a central role in expanding the justifications and the opportunities for women's education by founding their own schools. Tutored primarily at home, Emma Hart Willard became a teacher at age 15, and, even after her marriage, ran a boarding school in her home. She sought to continue her own education by studying the college textbooks of her nephew and resolved that women should have access to the same information and knowledge. Willard sought public acceptance and funding for her educational plan, and to that end, in 1818 self-published "An Address to the Public, Particularly to Members of the Legislature of New York, Proposing a Plan for Improving Female Education." The state legislature rejected her proposal, but when the merchant city of Troy offered free land for her to build a school, Willard moved her family there and founded her school in 1821.

The ripple effect of a Troy education was felt throughout the coming decades as graduates of Willard's school went on to found and teach at other institutions. Mary Lyon, a student at Troy, established Mount Holyoke in Massachusetts in 1837, which, in turn, became the model for other schools and for an expanded curriculum for women. Many Troy graduates went on to become teachers in New England and beyond. Graduate Urania Sheldon became head of the Utica Female Academy in New York. Troy women also created schools and spread their influence farther south, such as Caroline Livy, who established an academy in Rome, Georgia, and Almira Lincoln Phelps, whose Patapsco Female Institute in Maryland, a border state, was attended by many Southern women.

Although historians seem to pay the most attention to the important role of these early female seminaries and academies in the Northeast, by 1860 the South had actually established more women's colleges than the North. All Southern states except Florida had at least one women's college before the Civil War, and most states had several. In North Carolina, there were more women's colleges than men's, and the women's schools established between 1830 and 1860 throughout the South were committed from their beginnings to offering female students a rigorous education comparable to men's. Before Radcliffe College became the model for a women's adjunct to Harvard University much later in the century, the Alabama Female Institute had arranged by the 1830s for students to take courses at the all-male University of Alabama. The Georgia Female College, now known as Wesleyan University, was established in 1836 and is considered to be the first full-course women's college. In the early 1840s, the college advertised that "the object of the founders of the College was to give our daughters as good a disciplinary education as was offered by the best colleges for our sons."

Others were inspired by the model of female academies and colleges to found schools to meet their own community needs and goals. The Cherokee people had pursued a strategy of assimilation into white society in the first half of the 19th century and many had achieved a certain economic and educational level. This strategy did not, however, shield them from involuntary removal from the Southeast by the U.S. government in the 1830s. The Cherokee Female Seminary was opened in 1851 and run by educated and middle-class mixed-blood tribal members. The school prided itself on offering a "white" education well into the 20th century and students compared their school with white seminaries in the Northeast. As a student named Edith explained in the student paper, the *Cherokee Rose Buds* in 1854, "the taste, refinement, and progress of civilization" now shown by the Cherokee people was because of such educational advancements.

Education Reformers

The spread of female academies and seminaries had a society-wide impact on women's roles. By 1840 female literacy in New England had reached nearly 100 percent, compared to around 50 percent at the time of the American Revolution. However, even some of the most vocal proponents of women's education, such as Sarah Josepha Hale, whose own daughters attended Emma Willard's Troy Female Seminary, believed that "we should solicit education as a favor, not exact it as a right." As more women received an education, they were subsequently more likely to reach outside their "sphere" of influence, to marry later, or to forego marriage and motherhood altogether in favor of public careers as teachers or reformers. A study of Mount Holyoke College during its early years found that the median age of marriage for graduates was 26, compared to 21 among the population at large, and that as many as 19 percent of graduates never married at all.

Early female academies and colleges created the first generation of formally educated young women, women with expanded expectations about their duties not only to their families, but to society at large. This was reflected in Mount Holyoke's stated mission in 1839 of educating women for the "great task of renovating the world." The era of radical social and political reform also resulted in the founding of the first coeducational (both men and women) and first interracial classes offered at Oberlin College in Ohio beginning in 1833. Although this was a new opportunity for white women and for African Americans, the college maintained a separate curriculum for men and women. A "Female Department" employed women teachers and administrators (most of whom were trained at female seminaries and academies on the East Coast) to oversee a more literary, less rigorous, course of study for early women students. Even after the program was expanded to provide equal undergraduate educations for men and women, women were prevented from entering graduate and professional study programs. Still, by 1860, Oberlin College had produced more than 300 women graduates with bachelor's degrees, inspiring other institutions to either go coeducational or to establish women's full-course colleges.

By the 1850s, gaining access to education and to the professions were major issues for the emerging women's rights movement. After the Civil War, educational reformers and women's rights activists had moved beyond arguing for women's need for an education in order to fulfill their roles as mothers and teachers, and explicitly connected the issues of education to women's pursuit of a vocation, or profession. In her 1867 text, *The College, the Market, and the Court; or, Woman's Relation to Education, Labor, and Law,* Caroline Dall argued that it was not enough for reformers to focus on women's presence in "facilities of school education," when women were systematically excluded from entering the professions and putting those educations to any practical use. In an 1849 essay titled "Reforms," Dall had outlined women's need for "a finished education" and "a livelihood" as two main issues of the emerging women's right movement. Dall was a student of theology and history and had hoped to become a minister, but even in her liberal Christian church, women were not allowed to be regular preachers.

White Women as Teachers

Schoolteaching became one of the few employments open for young women with education, and many of the 19th century's most prominent reformers and writers began their careers as teachers or private tutors. The effect of educating more girls and young women at seminaries and colleges, and simultaneously limiting or closing off their access to other professions, was that a pool of educated, eager, and available young teachers was created just as the number of students attending school necessitated their services. Although the male schoolteacher was most common in the first half of the century, by the 1860s, teaching had become fully recognized as a female profession. In Massachusetts, for example, where the common school movement spread to provide schools in even remote rural locations and female seminaries dotted the landscape, as many as one-quarter of native-born white women worked as teachers before the Civil War. Their presence in the profession continued to increase so that, by the 1870s, nearly three-quarters of the teachers in New England were women.

Some reformers continued to argue that education could support, rather than undermine, women's traditional roles. Reformer Catharine Beecher's greatest influence was, somewhat paradoxically, as promoter of both women's education and domesticity. She founded the Hartford Female Seminary in 1823 and went on to write numerous articles, and the full-length *A Treatise on Domestic Economy* (1841), on women's proper roles as wives and mothers. Beecher argued that the fulfillment of those roles began with a proper education and that American women had a duty to receive an education so that they could become responsible teachers of the young, whether as mothers or as schoolteachers. She focused not only on women's role as mothers, but also advocated teaching as a "true and noble" profession for single women and encouraged women to leave factory work and pursue teaching instead. As she wrote to a friend in 1830, at a time when the female schoolteacher was not yet the norm, "To enlighten the understanding and to gain the affections is a teacher's business . . . is not *woman* best fitted to accomplish these important objects?"

Even as more women became available as teachers, and even as some reformers were emphasizing teaching as an extension of women's maternal role, school districts were sometimes reluctant to hire a woman for what was perceived as a man's job, especially where most of the students were boys. In this case, it was not the intellectual but the physical differences between men and women that were emphasized. It was believed that male teachers could hold better discipline over male students; as one superintendent explained, a woman should not be a teacher "for the same reason that she cannot so well manage a vicious horse or other animal, as a man might do."

Even if they were hired, women teachers faced extreme pay discrimination, even for the same jobs. In Connecticut in the mid-1830s, male teachers received a salary of $14.50 per month, compared to the $5.75 per month received by their female colleagues. Civil War nurse and founder of the American Red Cross Clara Barton had begun her career as a teacher. Barton was not against women volunteering their services without pay, but as a schoolteacher, she declared that "I may sometimes be willing to teach for nothing, but if paid at all, I shall never do a man's work for less than a man's pay."

Many women bypassed the common schools and founded their own schools for girls or taught privately in their homes. Either way, women forced their way into the profession and by 1870, the tables had turned and a child's teacher was just as (or more) likely to be female than male. By that date, women made up more than half of the nearly 200,000 schoolteachers in the United States. Even male officials had eventually been won over by the argument that women were, in fact, better suited as teachers as they were "the natural guardians of the young," as explained by Governor William Seward of New York. Thus, by the end of the century,

schoolteaching came to be dominated by women, with the same justification that it was suited to their particular natures and roles as with other occupations, such as textile mill work, social reform work and, later, nursing. Women initially encountered opposition to pursuing any occupation that took them out of the home, but each of these eventually came to be seen as primarily "women's work."

Black Women as Students and Teachers

A more democratic vision of education meant that not only women, but the poor, immigrants, and African Americans all eventually benefited from the spread of educational options in the early 19th century, although in an uneven manner. By the 1850s, nearly 75 percent of white children in the North attended some school, compared to less than one-third of white children in the South. The spread of the common school movement was hampered in the South, in part, because of the wide geographical distance between communities and plantations, and many white children continued to be tutored at home. In the black community, access to education was a different kind of struggle, as the education of blacks was strictly forbidden in the South before the Civil War, and racism in the North posed a barrier to the education of even free black children. Both black and white women reformers and teachers fought to expand educational opportunities for black children as well as adults throughout the 19th century.

In the pre-Civil War South, slaves were prevented by custom and by law from acquiring the basic tools of literacy, much less receiving a full education. Former slave Hannah Crasson remembered how reading or even possessing books was a serious offense on her white master's plantation: "The white folks did not allow us to have nothing to do with books. You better not be found trying to learn to read. Our marster was harder down on that than anything else. You better not be catched with a book." Ellen Betts, a former slave from Louisiana, shared a similar experience about her master's attitude toward slave learning: "If Marse catch a paper in your hand he sure whip you . . . Marse don't allow no bright niggers around. If they act bright he sure sell them quick. He always say: 'Book learning don't raise no good sugarcane.'" In this case, Betts's master made clear that education interfered with the economic productivity of his plantation, whether it be in terms of slaves spending time reading, or, more likely, the fear that literacy and knowledge could lead to resistance and even attempted escapes. A white woman, Margaret Douglass, was found guilty by a Virginia court of teaching a young slave girl "to read the Bible," defined by the court as "one of the vilest crimes that ever disgraced society."

The first schools for free African Americans in the North were established in the 1790s. Former slave Catherine Ferguson opened her School for the Poor in New York in 1793 and had both black and white students. Schools founded by black educators and reformers were more likely to be interracial as well as to teach boys and girls together, so that black women did not have their own separate academies to the same extent as white women of the same generations did. Only large cities were able to establish and maintain separate black schools. Segregation and inferior resources led some middle-class black families in cities to educate their children at home or open their own private schools. In Cincinnati, Ohio, the public schools did not admit black students, but in 1832 black and white abolitionists worked together to establish a school where white women taught classes attended by black children and adult women.

A young, free black woman named Sarah Harris was emboldened to apply to a white school in Canterbury, Connecticut, in the early 1830s. The teacher, Prudence Crandall, was a white antislavery Quaker who recalled that Harris was "a colored girl of respectability" who clearly stated her case: "'Miss Crandall, I want to get a little more learning, enough if possible to teach colored children, and if you will admit me to your school, I shall be under the greatest obligation to you.'" Sarah continued politely, however, that she would "not insist on the favor." Sarah Harris's family had ties to the abolitionist community, and she had already attended an integrated public school with some of the white girls who had gone on to Crandall's academy.

Crandall admitted Harris to the school, but after receiving threats from a local women's group, and perhaps sensing a greater social point to be made, Crandall went further and specifically recruited more black students by placing an ad in the radical abolitionist paper, *The Liberator,* for a school "for young Ladies and little Misses of color." The larger community, however, was not ready for such change in black women's educational or social roles. The *Norwich Republican* newspaper charged that Crandall was attempting "to foist upon the community a new species of gentility, in the shape of sable belles . . . to cook up a palatable morsel for our white bachelors. . . . In a word, they hope to force the two races to amalgamate." The entire town rose up against the school and eventually the harassment, the attacks on the school building, and fear for the safety of the students forced the school to close in 1834. The original black student, Sarah Harris, did ultimately realize her goal of securing an education and becoming a teacher.

As with middle-class white women, teaching became one of the most significant employments of free black women in the North before the Civil War. Black women as teachers was a challenge to the idea that African Americans in general were not capable of education. Because of such beliefs, free black women had to struggle not only for their own education, but in deciding to become teachers, they committed themselves to the struggle for the education of the entire race. Despite racism and segregation in the North and the outright prohibition against educating blacks in the South, committed women created opportunities to teach black children.

In slaveholding areas, teachers took great risks in running schools, sometimes doing so secretly. Catharine Deveaux hid her school for the children of friends and neighbors in Savannah, Georgia, from the white community for 27 years. Between 1828 and 1831, Ann Marie Becroft ran a school for black girls in Washington, D.C., that was sponsored by the Catholic Church before becoming a nun herself, the Catholic Church being one of the primary providers of education for poor, immigrant, and black children.

The commitment of black teachers to educating the race continued through the century, for even after freedom was secured with the end of the Civil War, the education of African American children remained a struggle against racism and poverty well past the end of the 19th century. Because slaves were not allowed to read or write, most freedpeople at the close of the Civil War were illiterate. Education was one of the first goals for the newly freed people and one pursued vigorously by former slaves. Both black and white women assisted in this effort in the last decades of the century by working as teachers in Southern schools for black children, their efforts resulting in nearly 9,000 teachers being sent to the South and some 600,000 African Americans enrolled in schools by 1870. Black women trained in Northern schools who went south to teach during the war usually followed alongside or not far behind Union troops, and, therefore, even before the war had ended, there were numerous schools established throughout the Southern states.

Although many Northern white women came south during the Civil War and Reconstruction periods, many blacks preferred that teachers be recruited from within their own community. Former slave Harriet Jacobs, best known for the 1861 publication of her autobiography detailing her own escape from slavery, *Incidents in the Life of a Slave Girl,* spent time working in Union camps to help slave refugees with medical care, raising money for clothing and supplies, and reporting to Northern abolitionist papers on conditions in Southern camps. At one freedmen's school, Jacobs was involved in insisting that black teachers be hired. She explained that she did not "object to white teachers but I think it has a good effect upon these people to convince them their own race can do something for their elevation. It inspires them with confidence to help each other."

One of the most famous and well-recorded wartime educational and social experiments was the Port Royal Experiment in the South Carolina Sea Islands, where Southern slaveholders fled their homes and deserted their plantations in 1862. In an effort to save the crops and to employ the thousands of former slaves who remained, the federal government took over the area, and, among other projects, recruited Northern teachers to establish schools for black children and adults. Among the first to arrive was Charlotte Forten, a free black from Philadelphia who already held the distinction of being the first black teacher of white children in Salem, Massachusetts, where she had also been active in the antislavery movement.

Forten and two other Philadelphians, white teachers Laura Towne and Ellen Murray, taught a full academic course to nearly 100 children on the Sea Islands during the day, and basic literacy skills to working adults in the evenings. Forten remembered that the children "listened very attentively," and she felt her presence there provided more than just academics, believing "it is well that they sh'ld know what one of their color c'ld do for his race. I long to inspire them with courage and ambition (of a noble sort), and high purpose." She sought to inspire them with lessons in black history but, undoubtedly, it was Forten's very presence that modeled the "courage and ambition (of a noble sort)" she desired for her students. Charlotte Forten published several essays titled "Life on the Sea Islands" in the *Atlantic Monthly* in 1864, telling of her success and further promoting the idea that freedpeople needed and were capable of education.

Black teachers became pillars of the community, not only because of their work in the classroom, but also because they were educated members of the community who could serve as mentors and advisors for freedpeople trying to build new lives. There was a downside, however, to being a visible and successful member of the community, for in providing a service that many

Southern whites felt blacks were not entitled to, teachers and their schools were sometimes subject to intimidation and violence. This was in addition to the difficult working conditions, decrepit buildings, lack of textbooks, and low pay. The special need and calling of African American teachers, however, was addressed in Fanny Jackson Coppin's 1879 address to a graduating class of future teachers: "You can do much to alleviate the condition of our people. Do not be discouraged. The very places where you are needed most are those where you will get least pay. Do not resign a position in the South which pays you $12 a month as a teacher for one in Pennsylvania which pays $50."

Tiffany K. Wayne

See Also: Beecher, Catharine; Dall, Caroline Healey; Murray, Judith Sargent; Oberlin College; Reconstruction; Republican Motherhood; Slavery and the Civil War; Willard, Emma Hart; Wollstonecraft, Mary; Young Ladies' Academy of Philadelphia; Education of Women (after the Civil War) (Vol. 2)

Primary Documents: 1787, "Thoughts upon Female Education"; 1790, "On the Equality of the Sexes"; 1819, "A Plan for Improving Female Education"; 1841, *A Treatise on Domestic Economy*; 1856–1857, Writings on Women's Education

Further Reading

Farnham, Christie Anne. *The Education of the Southern Belle: Higher Education and Student Socialization in the Antebellum South.* New York: New York University Press, 1994.

Kaufman, Polly Welts. *Women Teachers on the Frontier.* New Haven, CT: Yale University Press, 1984.

Mihesuah, Devon. *Cultivating the Rosebuds: The Education of Women at the Cherokee Female Seminary, 1851–1909.* Urbana: University of Illinois Press, 1993.

Nash, Margaret A. *Women's Education in the United States, 1780–1840.* New York: Palgrave Macmillan, 2005.

Scott, Anne Firor. "The Ever-Widening Circle: The Diffusion of Feminist Values from the Troy Female Seminary, 1822–1872." In *Making the Invisible Woman Visible.* Urbana: University of Illinois Press, 1984.

Solomon, Barbara. *In the Company of Educated Women: A History of Women and Higher Education in America.* New Haven, CT: Yale University Press, 1985.

Strane, Susan. *A Whole-Souled Woman: Prudence Crandall and the Education of Black Women.* New York: W. W. Norton, 1990.

Tolley, Kimberley. *The Science Education of American Girls: A Historical Perspective.* New York: Routledge, 2003.

Elizabeth Freeman Case (1781)

Elizabeth Freeman (ca. 1742–1829), also known as "Mumbet," was one of the first slaves to successfully sue for her freedom in colonial America. She was born to first-generation African slaves sometime in the early 1740s, and grew up in the household of Peter Hogeboom. She did not have a last name growing up and was usually referred to as Mumbet, or simply Bett. When her owner died in 1758, Elizabeth and her sister, Lizzie, were transferred to the household of Mr. Hogeboom's youngest daughter, Hannah Ashley of Sheffield, Massachusetts.

Hannah Ashley was a woman of short temper. When she attempted to discipline Elizabeth's sister with a heated shovel, Elizabeth intervened and received the blow herself. She bore the scar on her arm for the rest of her life and later said it was this incident that triggered her desire to seek freedom. She ran away from the Ashley household immediately after the event and never returned.

In 1781 Elizabeth sought shelter and legal help from a promising young attorney, Theodore Sedgwick. While a slave in the Ashley household, Elizabeth had overheard the conversations of Colonel Ashley and fellow revolutionaries, in which they discussed a proposed bill of rights and the idea that all people were born free and equal. Since such rhetoric did not exclude slaves, Elizabeth was prepared to sue for her freedom. Theodore Sedgwick was not only willing to take her case, but he granted her refuge in his home until the case could be heard. Elizabeth became a paid servant in the Sedgwick home, where she became well known for her skills as a nurse and a caring nanny for the Sedgwick children.

Elizabeth's suit was joined with another escaped slave from the Ashley's household named Brom, and the case was subsequently known as *Brom and Bett v. Ashley*. The jury found in favor of the escaped slaves, claiming they had been illegally held in bondage, and ordered Colonel Ashley to pay 30 shillings in compensation. The colonel vowed to appeal the decision, but shortly after the *Brom and Bett* case, the Supreme Court of Massachusetts ruled that slavery was unconstitutional in Massachusetts, and Ashley decided to drop his appeal.

Elizabeth elected the surname "Freeman" following her successful suit. She continued to work as a paid housekeeper and nurse for the Sedgwicks for several decades and became a beloved figure in the Sedgwick home. Mrs. Sedgwick suffered bouts of severe depression that bordered on insanity. During the bad spells, Elizabeth was the only person able to comfort the distraught woman. In her old age Elizabeth retired to a small home she purchased with her own savings. Little is known of Elizabeth's personal life. It is believed she married at a young age, but her husband was killed in the Revolutionary War. She had at least one daughter and several grandchildren.

Elizabeth Freeman was buried in the Sedgwick family burial ground. The respect the Sedgwick family held for Elizabeth is apparent from her gravestone epitaph:

Elizabeth Freeman, known by the name of MUMBET died Dec. 28, 1829. Her supposed age was 85 years. She was born a slave and remained a slave nearly thirty years. She could neither read nor write, yet in her own sphere she had no superior or equal. She neither wasted time nor property. She never violated a trust, nor failed to perform a duty. In every situation of domestic trial, she was the most efficient helper, and the tenderest friend. Good mother fare well.

Dorothy A. Mays

Further Reading

Adams, Catherine, and Elizabeth H. Pleck. *Love of Freedom: Black Women in Colonial and Revolutionary New England.* New York: Oxford University Press, 2010.

Wilds, Mary. *Mumbet: The Life and Times of Elizabeth Freeman: The True Story of a Slave Who Won Her Freedom.* Greensboro, NC: Avisson Publishers, Inc., 1999.

Evans, Augusta Jane (1835–1909)

Augusta Jane Evans Wilson was one of the 19th-century South's most popular female authors.

Born in Columbus, Georgia, on May 8, 1835, Evans spent most of her childhood and preteen years in San Antonio, Texas, which provided her with the inspiration for her first novel, *Inez: A Tale of the Alamo.* In 1849 Evans moved with her family to Mobile, Alabama, where she lived until her death on May 9, 1909. Her works with their dates of publication are as follows: *Inez: A Tale of the Alamo* (1856); *Beulah* (1859); *Macaria; or, Altars of Sacrifice* (1864); *St. Elmo. Or, Saved at Last* (1866); *Vashti; or, Until Death Us Do Part* (1869); *Infelice* (1875); *At the Mercy of Tiberius* (1887); *A Speckled Bird* (1902); and *Devota* (1907).

While many literary critics and reviewers panned her work along with that of many other domestic novelists, some consistently praised Evans's work in reviews and editorials for her adherence to traditional sentimental values. Readers responded to her novels with enthusiasm. Though most of her works have been forgotten today, two of her books, *Beulah* and *St. Elmo,* were national bestsellers of their time. Indeed, Evans's publishers were so sure of her popularity after the publication of *St. Elmo* that they sent her an advance of $25,000 for any novel she had to submit, sight unseen. Evans's works provoked loyal fans to name or rename homes, towns, steamboats, hotels, and pets as well as countless children in honor of her heroes and heroines. Eudora Welty may have even been one such loyal fan. In *The Ponder Heart* (1954), Welty named the heroine who owned the Beulah Hotel, Edna Earle Ponder, after the main character, Edna Earle, in Evans's novel, *St. Elmo.*

Despite the best-selling status of *Beulah* and *St. Elmo* and the generally prolific nature of her authorship, Evans is best-known for her third novel, *Macaria.* She wrote the novel on scraps of paper while she kept watch over Confederate soldiers' bedsides at Camp Beulah, a makeshift Civil War hospital near her home. Because it was published during the war and appeared initially only in the South, *Macaria* did not sell enough copies to warrant bestseller status. Even so, this war-themed novel contributed significantly to Evans's reputation as one of the leading literary women of the 19th-century South.

One of only several books published in the South during the war, *Macaria* was arguably the most popular book in the Confederacy. Published on crude brown wrapping paper in 1863 by the Richmond firm of West and Johnson, more than 20,000 copies eventually circulated throughout the South during the war. Filled with celebrations of the Southern way of life, tributes to the heroism of Southerners, the glorification of Confederate politics and victories, and criticisms of the demagogic North, *Macaria* delighted Southern men and women. While many Northern fans lauded it for its typically sentimental virtues, others did not receive *Macaria* as graciously. Northern General G. H. Thomas considered it so damaging to Northern morale that he banned it among his troops. Thereafter, if one of his soldiers was found with the novel, it was confiscated and immediately burned.

The novel was so popular in the South, however, that it generated several romantic war legends. One such tale was based on a passage of the novel in which the hero survived because an enemy bullet hit the ambrotype of his lady love that he carried in his pocket. Similarly, the legend holds that a volume of *Macaria* had saved a

Confederate soldier's life when a Yankee bullet struck it as he carried it over his heart. *Macaria* was a call to arms for Southern women. It gave them a portrait of exemplary feminine wartime behavior in the character of Irene Huntingdon, a beautiful and intelligent young woman born into a life of wealth and privilege, who gave everything up to serve the Confederacy when her beloved, Russell Aubrey, died in battle. *Macaria* remained a continual favorite among Southerners for many decades after the war, being reprinted numerous times between 1867 and 1903. In the later editions, *Macaria* was altered to remove the most vitriolic denunciations of the North and some of the more obscure analogies, gaining it greater acceptance among Northern readers.

Although none of Evans's novels are purely autobiographical, *Macaria* perhaps comes closest with its nontraditional ending in which the heroine chooses to remain single because her true love dies in the war. In 1861, three years prior to the publication of *Macaria,* Evans had been engaged to James Reed Spaulding, a Northern journalist whom she had met several years earlier. She ended this engagement when the war erupted because she believed their opposing political positions— he was as pro-Northern as she was pro-Southern— would impede any chance for a happy marriage. While writing *Macaria* in the midst of the war and after the end of this engagement, Evans noted in letters to several friends that she had sacrificed love and her chance at matrimony for the Confederacy. The combination of the rising death toll among Southern men and her ever-increasing age must have made her chances for true love and marriage seem increasingly slim. Despite all this, in 1868 Evans did marry, finding a spouse in Colonel Lorenzo Madison Wilson, a Confederate veteran several years her senior. They had been married over 20 years when he died in 1891.

A number of scholars have labeled *Macaria* a protofeminist novel, interpreting Evans's decision to keep her heroine Irene single as a feminist act. Others disagree, arguing that Evans's overall portrayal of women's proper place and duties in *Macaria* and in all her other works was consistently traditional. Never in any of her novels or in her own life did Evans advocate the overthrow of the traditional gender roles of the patriarchal system. Rather, she recognized the validity of 19th-century gender prescriptions. Second, any variation from this theme in *Macaria* was less a symptom of her own change in beliefs and more the result of the historical context of the war. In a region in which tens of thousands of young men would die before the war's end, these scholars argue, Evans empathized with the many

Southern women who would face the dilemma of manlessness. For these scholars, Evans's *Macaria* is a traditional work of domestic fiction that recognized a grim future for the postwar South, asserting that, when marriage is impossible as it was for many Southern women during and after the war—and as it seemed for Evans herself—women could still find happiness, fulfillment, usefulness, and perhaps even glory in their lives as single women.

Jennifer Lynn Gross

See Also: Slavery and the Civil War

Further Reading

Faust, Drew Gilpin. *Mothers of Invention: Women of the Slaveholding South in the American Civil War.* Chapel Hill: University of North Carolina Press, 1996.

Fidler, William Perry. *Augusta Evans Wilson, 1835–1909.* Tuscaloosa: University of Alabama Press, 1951.

Jones, Ann Goodwyn. *Tomorrow Is Another Day: The Woman Writer in the South, 1859–1936.* Baton Rouge: Louisiana State University Press, 1981.

Sexton, Rebecca Grant. *A Southern Woman of Letters: The Correspondence of Augusta Jane Evans Wilson.* Charleston: University of South Carolina Press, 2002.

F

Farnham, Eliza (1815–1864)

In the 1840s, the American freethinker and prison reformer Eliza Farnham was the first woman to head a state prison, following in that great tradition of female Quaker prison reformers established by Elizabeth Fry. As the author of *Woman and Her Era* (1864), she also acquired a reputation as an eccentric feminist figure. Together with early feminist writers such as Lydia Maria Child and Catharine Beecher and the Grimké sisters, she propagated the idea that women's moral superiority better equipped them to reform society.

Her Quaker mother died five years after Eliza Wood Burhans was born in Rensselaerville, New York, and the young Eliza was sent to live with relatives at Maple Springs, enduring a strict regime under her ill-tempered aunt until in 1830 she went to live with an uncle. After attending Quaker boarding school for a year, she transferred to the Albany Female Academy but soon after fell ill with overwork. In 1836 Farnham married a lawyer and pioneer settler, Thomas Jefferson Farnham, and moved out west to Illinois, later describing her life in this frontier area in *Life in Prairie Land* (1846).

Returning to New York in 1840 without her husband (who had gone to California), Farnham published an essay on women's role in the magazine *Brother Jonathan,* in which she argued that women should take greater care in their responsibilities as wives and mothers to set a moral example for society. In 1844, inspired by the work of the English prison reformer Elizabeth Fry, she succeeded in persuading the all-male Quaker board of Sing Sing prison in Ossining, New York, to appoint her matron of its adjacent women's prison, Mount Pleasant. Her introduction of methods of prisoner rehabilitation and incentives for good behavior during her administration there was a considerable success. In January 1846, Farnham made concessions to the old and much-hated "silent system" prohibiting prisoners from talking to each other, by allowing conversation at certain times daily. She instituted numerous changes that improved the quality of life of the inmates, set up a nursery for prisoners' children, gave them lessons, obtained donations of books from friends and well-wishers (including Margaret Fuller, who also advocated prison reform

and visted Sing Sing), and even introduced curtains and flowers to enliven the drab surroundings. A piano was brought into the prison, the women were encouraged to sing and read, and the younger ones were provided with dolls.

By 1846 Farnham had become interested in the fashionable practice of phrenology, which linked character traits with the shape of the skull, and she edited the U.S. edition of the *Rationale of Crime* by the English phrenologist Marmaduke B. Sampson. Two years later, continuing official male antipathy to Farnham's innovations at Sing Sing resulted in Farnham's dismissal early in 1848, after the prison's administration had changed. Farnham later took up other prison work, making a critique of the conditions at San Quentin prison and working for a year as matron of the Female Department of Stockton Insane Asylum, when she was in California from 1861 to 1862.

Farnham moved to Boston in the late 1840s after leaving Sing Sing and worked at Samuel Gridley Howe's pioneering Perkins Institution for the blind, where she taught Laura Bridgman, the first deaf, dumb, and blind girl in the United States to be educated using new techniques by Howe. After her husband's death in California in 1848, she traveled there to settle his estate, taking the sea route via South America and eventually arriving after several months in late 1849. Having bought a farm in Santa Cruz County, she wrote down her impressions of life in the land of the Gold Rush, *California, In-doors and Out* (1856). While in California, Farnham remarried, but the relationship foundered after four years, and the couple divorced in 1856.

After returning to New York, Farnham took up the private study of medicine from 1856 through 1858 and published her autobiography, *My Early Days,* in 1859. She set up a society to help poor women resettle out west and accompanied several groups of female migrants to California. Although she opposed women's suffrage and their involvement in politics, she gave a speech at the national women's rights convention held in New York in 1858, in which she endorsed the abolition of slavery. In 1863, as a member of the National Women's Loyal League, she collected signatures for a petition to Congress on abolition. She volunteered as a nurse at Gettysburg, but died of tuberculosis in 1864, the year in which she published her best-known work, the two-volume *Woman and Her Era,* a radical, mystical view of women's biological and moral superiority and leadership qualities.

In this work, Farnham echoed the sentiments expressed earlier in Margaret Fuller's *Woman in the Nineteenth Century* (1845), including drawing on a wide range of cultural and historical sources in asserting women's moral and spiritual superiority over men. Both Farnham and Fuller believed that the time had come for women to extend their intellectual capabilities and their civilizing influence beyond the domestic sphere. In exalted, religious tones, Farnham invested the procreative role of women with a messianic quality: "Life is exalted in proportion to its Organic and Functional Complexity; Woman's Organism is more complex and her totality of Function larger than those of any other being inhabiting our earth. Therefore her position in the scale of Life is the most exalted—the Sovereign one." Her mystical arguments, based on a vision of the Virgin Mary as the spiritual redeemer of humanity alongside Christ, failed to have any impact, however, partly due no doubt to their complex technical structure and Farnham's highly rarefied style. Farnham's intellectual legacy would lie in giving added impetus to the "new abolitionism" movement of the second half of the 19th century, which sought to bring an end to prostitution through the reform of men's immorality, and the social purity movement, which sought to eliminate the sexual double standard. Farnham's further thoughts on the roles of men and women can be found in her autobiographical fiction, *Eliza Woodson, or, The Early Days of One of the World's Workers* (1859), and in the posthumously published, *The Ideal Attained* (1865).

Helen Rappaport

See Also: Beecher, Catharine; Child, Lydia Maria; Fuller, Margaret; Gibbons, Abigail Hopper; Grimké, Sarah Moore; Grimké Weld, Angelina; Lowell, Josephine Shaw; National Women's Loyal League; Quakers

Further Reading

Freedman, Estelle. *Their Sisters' Keepers: Women's Prison Reform in America, 1830–1930.* Ann Arbor: University of Michigan Press, 1980.

Levy, JoAnn. *Unsettling the West: Eliza Farnham and Georgiana Bruce Kirby in Frontier California.* Berkeley, CA: Heyday Books, 2004.

Lewis, W. David. *From Newgate to Dannemora: The Rise of the Penitentiary in New York, 1796–1848.* Ithaca, NY: Cornell University Press, 2009 [1965].

Feme Sole and *Feme Sole* Trader Status

Feme sole is the legal status that granted women legal identity independent of a male relative. According to the laws of coverture that existed in the American colonies, once a woman entered a marriage, she and her husband were one person in the eyes of the law, and that one person was the husband. A married woman could not enter into contracts, make a will, or buy or sell property without the consent of her husband. No such restrictions applied to men.

In early America, adult single women were not under any such paternalistic legal form. After attaining the age of majority, usually 21, a single woman had an independent legal identity, meaning she was free to own and operate a business, obtain employment, retain the wages she earned, and purchase property. In short, she had all the legal rights a man had, with the exception that she could not vote. Such a status was known as *feme sole,* or "woman alone."

There is little in the historical record to indicate that women in early America shunned marriage because it meant abandoning *feme sole* status. The world of a spinster was dismal and presented few opportunities for a satisfying life. Women with serious concerns about losing legal control over their property could initiate a prenuptial agreement, also known as a marriage settlement. These legal agreements preserved a limited amount of control for a woman over the property she brought into the marriage. The rarity of prenuptial agreements, whether from ignorance or disinterest, is an indicator that the loss of *feme sole* status was rarely in the forefront of a young bride's mind. If a woman became widowed, her status as *feme covert* was immediately switched back to *feme sole.*

Feme sole trader is the legal status that granted married women the ability to conduct business independent of their husband's permission. Under limited and unusual circumstances, a married woman could obtain a legal identity independent of her husband. Because of the difficulty in obtaining a divorce in early America, rates of marital desertion were high. An abandoned wife needed a means to support herself, and if she lacked the ability to enter contracts, many people would refuse to do business with her. Any transaction executed by the wife, such as sums paid for the purchase or rental of a home, purchase of goods, or sale of property, could all be rendered null and void if the absent husband emerged and objected. Likewise, a dishonest woman could claim coverture laws relieved her of the obligation to pay debts contracted outside of the presence of her husband. Because entering into any legal transaction with a married woman acting independently of her husband was risky, careful merchants and landlords often refused to deal with an abandoned wife.

Feme sole trader status was created to restore limited legal identity to wives who found themselves without a husband. The women had to publicly announce her intentions of adopting this status, and in some colonies she needed to register with officials as a *feme sole* trader. She thereafter was entitled to all the privileges and responsibilities of entering into contracts, buying and selling property, and operating a business. This status could also be conferred upon a woman whose husband was absent for years at a time, such as if he were a mariner or a soldier.

Dorothy A. Mays

See Also: Coverture; Divorce (before the Civil War); Legal Status of Women (18th Century); New York Married Women's Property Acts; Widowhood

Further Reading

Berkin, Carol. *First Generations: Women in Colonial America.* New York: Hill and Wang, 1996.

Dayton, Cornelia Hughes. *Women before the Bar: Gender, Law, and Society in Connecticut, 1639–1789.* Chapel Hill: University of North Carolina Press, 1995.

Gundersen, Joan R. *To Be Useful to the World: Women in Revolutionary America, 1740–1790.* New York: Twayne, 1996.

Salmon, Marylynn. *Women and the Law of Property in Early America.* Chapel Hill: University of North Carolina Press, 1986.

Sturtz, Linda L. *Within Her Power: Propertied Women in Colonial Virginia.* New York: Routledge, 2002.

Wulf, Karin. *Not All Wives: Women of Colonial Philadelphia.* Ithaca, NY: Cornell University Press, 2000.

Fern, Fanny [Sarah Payson Willis] (1811–1872)

Fanny Fern was one of the most popular and widely read authors of the antebellum and postwar period. Her opinions and commentary significantly influenced public opinion, especially Northern women's attitudes, both before and during the Civil War.

Fanny Fern was born Sarah Payson Willis on July 9, 1811. Willis's marital history—she was widowed and then divorced before a lasting third marriage to James Parton in 1856—and many of her decisions about her life and her work were considered by many as unacceptable choices for a woman of the middle class. However,

Fanny Fern was a popular writer best known for her novel, *Ruth Hall* (1854). (Library of Congress)

as the writer Fanny Fern she was highly successful. Her ability to combine her often iconoclastic opinions with the dominant sentimentalism of the period enabled her to reach and influence women and men. Fern established herself as an independent and audacious voice on women's issues and current events in her widely reprinted newspaper columns, which were gathered together in *Fern Leaves from Fanny's Portfolio* (1853), *Fresh Leaves* (1857), *Folly as It Flies* (1870), *Ginger-Snaps* (1870), and *Caper Sauce* (1872), as well as in her novels, *Ruth Hall* (1854) and *Rose Clark* (1856).

Before, during, and after the Civil War, Fern found her audience through her regular columns written for the *New York Ledger* and often reprinted in other papers, giving her a national audience. The *Ledger*'s publisher, Robert Bonner, wanted the paper's writers to avoid taking any particular political positions, and Fern made some attempts to comply. At the same time, she was determined to express her ideas about and her critique of the society in which she lived. Fern came to her ideas about women and the war from a foundation of deep religious beliefs. She was an independent thinker who rejected much of the dominant theological thought of her time as it was expressed by male ministers. Instead, she developed what she called maternalist Christianity. She saw in Christ's love a model of women's love for their children, which she then extended to society as a whole. She saw a need for women to demand that material help and care be given to the poor, that economic opportunities become available for women, and that injustice be challenged, wherever it occurred.

As tensions increased in the country, Fern made her abolitionist sympathies clear in a number of *Ledger* columns, although she seldom discussed specific events. Her style varied. Sometimes she used satire; at other times her work exemplified the sentimental style of mid-century women writers. After the war began, she began to write more directly about the war, including columns that argued for enlistment and that expressed contempt for Northern men who would not support the Union cause or who tried to avoid conscription. A sincere abolitionist, Fern wrote admiringly about the colored troops and was clear that her support for the war was based on an understanding of the evil of slavery. She was friendly with Harriet Jacobs and opened her house to Jacobs's daughter, Laura, during 1856–1858. Fern's conversations with Jacobs undoubtedly contributed to her understanding of the issues facing African American women, but Fern did not use their friendship directly in her work.

Fern's columns also explored how the war affected women. The inequities of women's economic condition during and after the war were a deep concern. She argued that the economic conditions of the war would affect poor and working-class women more than any other group. She declared that women, as both consumers and workers, in both the North and the South, were involved not just in the Civil War, but in an ongoing conflict in which their antagonists were business owners and industrialists. She recognized, too, the loneliness, fear, and physical dangers that the war brought to women left without the protection of their fathers, husbands, and sons. At the same time, she had hopes that the war would offer new possibilities for women and that in the aftermath of the war women would have greater scope, including suffrage. She supported the U.S. Sanitary Commission, especially the work of women with the commission, as a model of what women could do.

Fern wrote three books for children, and in *The New Story Book for Children* (1864) she included a chapter on John Brown. This highly favorable biography was a further indication of her abolitionist attitudes and was well received by Northern abolitionist parents. Fanny Fern died on October 10, 1872.

JoAnn E. Castagna

See Also: Abolitionism and the Antislavery Movement; Jacobs, Harriet Ann; National Women's Loyal League; Slavery and the Civil War; United States Sanitary Commission

Further Reading

Sizer, Lyde Cullen. *The Political Work of Northern Women Writers and the Civil War, 1850–1872.* Chapel Hill: University of North Carolina Press, 2000.

Tonkovich, Nicole. *Domesticity with a Difference: The Nonfiction of Catharine Beecher, Sarah J. Hale, Fanny Fern, and Margaret Fuller.* Jackson: University Press of Mississippi, 1997.

Walker, Nancy A. *Fanny Fern.* New York: Twayne Publishers, 1993.

Warren, Joyce W. *Fanny Fern: An Independent Woman.* New Brunswick, NJ: Rutgers University Press, 1994.

Fifteenth Amendment (1870)

Conflicts over the Fifteenth Amendment resulted in a 21-year split (1869–1890) in the 19th century woman suffrage movement. After the 1868 presidential election and the end of slavery, Congress continued to focus on several unfinished Reconstruction issues. The Fourteenth Amendment had granted black men citizenship, but not voting privileges. As a condition of readmission into the Union, former Confederate states gave black men the vote, but Congress feared they would eventually be disenfranchised by Southern states where Democrats had regained control. Thus, Congress began drafting an amendment to enfranchise black men. Seeing an opportunity to enfranchise women, Elizabeth Cady Stanton and Susan B. Anthony circulated petitions for an amendment that would grant women voting rights.

Members of Congress introduced many versions of the Fifteenth Amendment. Some, like Congressmen George W. Julian and Samuel Pomeroy, were open to the idea of universal suffrage. Julian introduced an amendment to grant voting rights to all citizens without regard to race, color, or sex, and Pomeroy's bill enfranchised black men and women, but Congress did not debate these bills. Most opposed including woman suffrage in the amendment, fearing that the issue would jeopardize the enfranchisement of black men. Thus the amendment did not include woman suffrage.

To ensure that Congress and the states would vote in favor of the amendment, Senator Henry Wilson of Massachusetts asked abolitionist Abby Kelley Foster to campaign in favor of the Fifteenth Amendment. She agreed.

She held fundraisers for the campaign and sent copies of the *Standard,* the journal of the American Anti-Slavery Society, to each member of Congress and state legislators. On February 26, 1869, Congress passed the Fifteenth Amendment, prohibiting states from denying voters the ballot on the grounds of race, color, or previous condition of servitude. Outraged, Elizabeth Cady Stanton published several anti-Fifteenth Amendment articles in *The Revolution,* a feminist newspaper headed by Stanton and Anthony.

By contrast, members of the New England Woman Suffrage Association supported the Fifteenth Amendment. The association also favored woman suffrage but was willing to delay women's enfranchisement until black suffrage was achieved. Unlike Stanton and Anthony, the women of the New England association carefully avoided sparking any debates about black suffrage and the Fifteenth Amendment, choosing instead to petition state legislatures on the issue of women's enfranchisement and to lobby for legislation enfranchising women who lived in the District of Columbia and the territories of the United States.

The approach of the New England association did not sit well with Anthony and Stanton, who saw Reconstruction as a chance for change. They feared that, once the debates over citizenship and voting for black men had been concluded, it would be years before the issue of woman suffrage would be revisited by Congress. The New England association viewed the passage of the Fifteenth Amendment as a progression in the securing of democratic rights for women, thus making it less difficult to pass woman suffrage. By contrast, Stanton believed that the inclusion of the Fifteenth Amendment in the U.S. Constitution would render women politically powerless, making it much more difficult to enfranchise women.

Working against the passage of the amendment, Stanton and Anthony used racist and elitist arguments. Stanton, for instance, suggested that it was unacceptable for Chinese immigrants and former slaves to make laws governing educated middle- and upper-class women. Anthony spoke in favor of limiting the franchise to those who were educated and intelligent.

In addition to their anti–Fifteenth Amendment campaign, Anthony and Stanton convinced Congressman Julian to draft a woman suffrage amendment to the Constitution. He introduced this amendment, the Sixteenth Amendment, on March 15, 1869. Recalling their success in the passage of the Thirteenth Amendment, Stanton and Anthony circulated petitions favoring the passage of the amendment. They also toured several

Western states, organized new suffrage associations, and identified many new allies for the cause of woman suffrage.

At the May 1869 meeting of the American Equal Rights Association, the debates were fierce, and some of the delegates turned against Anthony and Stanton. Frederick Douglass chastised Anthony and Stanton for the use of racist arguments against the Fifteenth Amendment, and he introduced a resolution to support the Fifteenth Amendment. Anthony objected to Douglass's comments and introduced an anti–Fifteenth Amendment resolution and another favoring educated suffrage. Lucy Stone rose and objected to Anthony's anti–Fifteenth Amendment resolution, speaking in favor of the amendment. In the end, the association defeated Anthony's anti–Fifteenth Amendment resolution in favor of Douglass's resolution to support the Fifteenth Amendment.

Anthony and Stanton concluded that women needed a separate organization run entirely by women, and they formed the National Woman Suffrage Association. The association favored the passage of a Sixteenth Amendment to the Constitution to enfranchise women, and it opposed the Fifteenth Amendment. In November 1869, Lucy Stone and other abolitionists formed the American Woman Suffrage Association. Unlike the National Woman Suffrage Association, which hoped to secure women's enfranchisement through an amendment to the U.S. Constitution, the American Woman Suffrage Association chose to secure women's enfranchisement through state campaigns.

On March 30, 1870, the Fifteenth Amendment was ratified and equal rights for black men had been secured in the U.S. Constitution.

Jennifer Ross-Nazzal

See Also: Abolitionism and the Antislavery Movement; Douglass, Frederick; Fifteenth Amendment; Foster, Abby Kelley; Fourteenth Amendment; National Woman Suffrage Association; Phillips, Wendell; Reconstruction; Stone, Lucy; American Equal Rights Association (Vol. 2); American Woman Suffrage Association (Vol. 2); Anthony, Susan B. (Vol. 2); Stanton, Elizabeth Cady (Vol. 2)

Further Reading

DuBois, Ellen Carol. *Feminism and Suffrage: The Emergence of an Independent Women's Movement in America 1848–1869.* Ithaca, NY: Cornell University Press, 1978.

Dudden, Faye E. *Fighting Chance: The Struggle over Woman Suffrage and Black Suffrage in Reconstruction America.* New York: Oxford University Press, 2011.

Kerr, Andrea Moore. "White Women's Rights, Black Men's Wrongs, Free Love, Blackmail, and the Formation of the American Woman Suffrage Association." In *One Woman, One Vote: Rediscovering the Woman Suffrage Movement*, edited by Marjorie Spruill Wheeler, 61–80. Troutdale, OR: NewSage Press, 1995.

Sterling, Dorothy. *Ahead of Her Time: Abby Kelley and the Politics of Antislavery*. New York: W. W. Norton & Company, 1991.

Foote, Julia A. J. (1823–1900)

Julia A. J. Foote was born in Schenectady, New York, four years before that state abolished slavery in 1827. Her father was born free, but kidnapped and sold into slavery. Her mother was born a slave, and her stories of abuse had a profound impact on her daughter. Eventually Julia's father managed to buy his freedom as well as the freedom of his wife and first child. Foote was the fourth of eight children.

Julia's father, the only literate member of her family, taught her the alphabet using the family Bible. When she was 10, Julia was hired as a domestic servant by a nearby white family, the Primes. The young girl initially regarded Mrs. Prime as a surrogate mother until her mistress falsely accused her of stealing food and whipped her with a rawhide despite her protestations of innocence. Julia remained with this family for two years and received her only extended formal education at a country school. She was greatly affected by the execution of her schoolteacher, John van Paten, for the murder of his fiancée's best friend. She later became an opponent of capital punishment.

She returned to her parents in Albany to care for her younger siblings, and at age 15 she was converted and joined the African Methodist Episcopal Zion Church. At age 18 Julia married a sailor, George Foote—her maiden name is unknown—and moved with him to Boston. By her early twenties Foote had received sanctification (a belief that she was free of sin and able to achieve spiritual perfection) and a call to preach. Both her mother and husband vehemently opposed her public preaching. Her mother told Foote she would rather hear of her daughter's death than her exposure at the pulpit. Her husband threatened to commit her to an insane asylum. Foote persisted in her ministry, and her husband returned to sea. Having no children, the couple lived separate lives until his death in the mid-1850s.

Foote traveled as a preacher from 1845 to the mid-1850s, covering territory ranging from Canada to Ohio. Troubles with her throat forced her into temporary retirement until the late 1860s. When her health improved she returned to the circuit, participating in the religious awakening that swept the Midwest after the Civil War. In 1879, her spiritual autobiography, *A Brand Plucked from the Fire,* was published and the book was reprinted in 1886. In 1894 she became the first woman deacon of the A.M.E. Zion Church and later its second woman elder. She died on November 22, 1900.

Julia Foote's *A Brand Plucked from the Fire* borrowed from two distinct genres: the fiery rhetoric and politics of the African American slave narrative (Frederick Douglass, Harriet Jacobs, Olaudah Equiano) and the introspection and evangelism of American spiritual narratives (Michael Wigglesworth, Mary Rowlandson, Elizabeth Hudson, Ann Moore). Foote attacked America for its racism and harsh treatment of African Americans in the chapters "An Undeserved Whipping" and "Indignities on Account of Color." However, Foote was primarily interested in defending her call to preach and encouraging other women who have a vocation (see chapters "My Call to Preach" and "A Word to My Christian Sisters"). Foote made her goal clear in her Preface: "My object has been to testify more extensively to the sufficiency of the blood of Jesus Christ to save all from sin."

Little attention is given in Foote's biography to her siblings or her marriage. Instead, Foote retained her focus on the events and people who influenced her development as a preacher. The title for her work comes from Zechariah 3:2. Thematically, this spiritual autobiography was chiefly concerned with persecution and salvation. As a woman writer, furthermore, Foote imbued her text with themes of woman's place in a patriarchal society and the pursuit of identity. Her travels as a minister supplied a questing motif to the text.

Foote's autobiography has received a fair amount of critical attention. It is most often paired with other spiritual narratives by 19th-century African American women, particularly *The Life and Experience of Jarena Lee* (1836) and *Memoirs of the Life, Religious Experience, Ministerial Travels, and Labours of Mrs. Zilpha Elaw* (1846).

Ann Beebe

See Also: Lee, Jarena

Further Reading

Andrews, William, ed. *Sisters of the Spirit: Three Black Women's Autobiographies of the Nineteenth Century.* Bloomington: Indiana University Press, 1986.

Fleischner, Jennifer. *Mastering Slavery: Memory, Family, and Identity in Women's Slave Narratives.* New York: New York University Press, 1996.

Haywood, Chanta. *Prophesying Daughters: Black Women Preachers of the Word, 1823–1913.* Columbia: University of Missouri Press, 2003.

Moody, Joycelyn. *Sentimental Confessions: Spiritual Narratives of Nineteenth-Century African American Women.* Athens: University of Georgia Press, 2001.

Foster, Abby Kelley (1810–1887)

A pioneer abolitionist, freethinker, and feminist who with quiet modesty dressed and lived according to Quaker tenets, Abby Kelley Foster believed that women, like slaves, were denied their equal rights. Foster not only passionately defended her beliefs in public, frequently encountering virulent antagonism, but also fought against chauvinism within the abolitionist movement itself. She embraced a range of social issues from dress reform to temperance, seeing all her humanitarian concerns as being "bound up in one great bundle."

Abigail Kelley grew up on a farm in Worcester, Massachusetts, and became a teacher in the early 1830s. During this time, she was inspired by the writings of the abolitionist William Lloyd Garrison, published in his journal the *Liberator,* and took up work for the abolitionist cause, at first as secretary of the Lynn Female Anti-Slavery Society. By the end of 1838, she had given up her teaching post at the Quaker school at Lynn, after attending the Boston Peace Convention that September when she joined a Quaker organization, the New England Non-Resistance Society. As a vehicle for pacifist ideals, the society attracted numerous other women members, including Lucretia Mott, Lydia Maria Child, and the Grimké sisters. Kelley was also active in the American Anti-Slavery Society (AASS), a national organization established by William Lloyd Garrison in 1833. Along with Garrison, she argued persuasively for women to be given equal status in the society, which agreed in 1839 that they should be allowed to lecture for it.

Immediately, and much to her widowed mother's dismay, Kelley embarked on a vigorous lecture tour at a time when simply the sight of a woman lecturing to mixed-sex audiences was considered scandalous by many. Until 1860, she traveled extensively in New England, Pennsylvania, Michigan, Indiana, and Ohio, lecturing on both antislavery and women's rights. By the end of her travels, she had earned a degree of fame, if not notoriety, achieved by few women of her time, and like other prominent female abolitionists, such as Sarah and Angelina Grimké, she found herself having to face ridicule for her public appearances, despite the care she had taken to have a chaperone at all times. However, Kelley's anticlericalism and the attacks she made on evangelicals in New York state and Ohio for supporting slavery frequently resulted in her being blocked from speaking in certain churches, for example, the Presbyterian church in Seneca Falls, New York. Nevertheless, Kelley steadily enlisted new women supporters wherever she went, including Lucy Stone and Susan B. Anthony, the latter becoming a regular on the abolitionist lecture circuit with Kelley during 1857–1861. In 1841, however, Kelley reluctantly resigned from her own church, the Society of Friends, because of its continuing criticism of the antislavery activities of some members and its refusal to allow her to use its meeting houses for her lectures.

Garrison, meanwhile, had placed great confidence in Kelley's administrative skills, appointing her to the business committee of the American Anti-Slavery Society in May 1840 and an official AASS delegate to the World Anti-Slavery Convention in London that summer. But opposition persisted among the male membership to Kelley's having a hand in running the society's finances, and some conservative and clerical male members left in protest. Eventually, a profound division developed over the role of women in the society, which ended with the formation of a splinter group, the American and Foreign Anti-Slavery Society.

In 1845, after a long engagement, Abby Kelley married fellow abolitionist Stephen Symonds Foster, who was equally radical in his advocacy of social justice and would support her later work for women's rights. In their marriage they respected each other as equal partners, with Stephen taking turns with Abby to go out lecturing, while the other looked after their farm and children.

In 1850, when the newly introduced Fugitive Slave Act demanded the return of escaped slaves, Abby Kelley Foster upheld the right of slaves to resist oppression and urged abolitionists in Ohio (a well-known stop on the Underground Railroad) to defy the law and help them escape to the North. In October 1850, after helping plan a women's rights convention held at Worcester, Massachusetts, Foster turned increasingly to lecturing on women's rights and suffrage, urging young women to become financially self-supporting.

By the time the Civil War broke out in 1861, Foster was worn out and did not contribute to the war effort.

Despite being an ardent suffragist, she supported those petitioning for the Fifteenth Amendment, which in 1870 eliminated race as a criterion in having the right to vote. Foster was greatly saddened by the profound split in the suffrage movement in 1869 caused by the earlier decision by some activists to support suffrage for black men ahead of that for women, and she responded to the call of Stone's moderate group to establish an American Woman Suffrage Association. During the 1870s, Foster campaigned for temperance and in 1880 attended the 30th-anniversary celebrations of the Worcester women's rights convention of 1850 as one of its keynote speakers. On that occasion, she denounced the moves by some suffragists to settle for partial suffrage at state level—for example, in the case of school board elections, for which women in Massachusetts were now allowed to be nominated—being of the opinion that "half a vote" was worse than none at all.

Foster and her husband refused to pay their taxes between 1874 and 1878, arguing that since she had no right to vote, she should not therefore be liable for taxation, thus echoing the calls for "no taxation without representation" that had been the slogan of the American Revolution. As a result, the Fosters' farm in Connecticut was sold by the authorities. But the couple's supporters, who backed their symbolic gesture, later secured the return of the deeds. The Fosters subsequently called a convention on taxation without representation and continued refusing to pay their taxes until 1880, when they finally settled with the revenue authorities.

Foster spent her remaining years as an invalid, retaining her absolute moral integrity to the end. Perhaps the finest tribute to her work can be found in a letter written to her in July 1859 by William Lloyd Garrison, who commented: "Of all the women who have appeared upon the historic stage, I have always regarded you as peerless—the moral Joan of Arc of the world."

Helen Rappaport

See Also: Abolitionism and the Antislavery Movement; Child, Lydia Maria; Dress Reform; Garrison, William Lloyd; Grimké, Sarah Moore; Grimké Weld, Angelina; Mott, Lucretia; Quakers; Stone, Lucy; Temperance Movement; Underground Railroad; American Woman Suffrage Association (Vol. 2); Anthony, Susan B. (Vol. 2)

Further Reading

Bacon, Margaret Hope. *I Speak for My Slave Sister: The Life of Abby Kelley Foster.* New York: Thomas Y. Crowell, 1976.

Bacon, Margaret Hope. *Mothers of Feminism: The Story of Quaker Women in America.* San Francisco, CA: Harper and Row, 1986.

Jeffrey, Julie Roy. *The Great Silent Army of Abolitionism: Ordinary Women in the Antislavery Movement.* Chapel Hill: University of North Carolina Press, 1998.

Sterling, Dorothy. *Ahead of Her Time: Abby Kelley and the Politics of Antislavery.* New York: W. W. Norton, 1991.

Fourteenth Amendment (1868)

Directly following the Civil War, three amendments were passed that severely constrained state power: the Thirteenth prohibited slavery, the Fifteenth protected the right to vote, and the Fourteenth protected due process and equal protection of the laws. Although women were active in attempting to have gender explicitly included in the protections afforded freed slaves in these amendments, they were unsuccessful. One clause in particular in the Fourteenth Amendment gave women hope that they would be given the same citizenship as black Americans, as well as the same benefits such citizenship would provide: "All persons born or naturalized in the United States are citizens of the United States and of the state wherein they reside." Early on, however, the U.S. Supreme Court decided that although women were indeed citizens of the national government, citizenship rights did not include the right to vote or practice a profession. Instead, it was legal for states to restrict women in various endeavors.

But women's rights would expand with another clause in this amendment. Equal protection of the law, or the Equal Protection Clause, reads: "Nor shall any state . . . deny to any person within its jurisdiction the equal protection of the law." Today, interpretations of the Fifth Amendment and various state constitutional provisions also guarantee equal protection of the law, but women have used the Fourteenth Amendment to push many issues through the courts. Since 1971 the Supreme Court has extensively applied this clause in challenges to sex-based laws and government practices.

The limitation to this clause is that the amendment, and therefore equal protection of the law, addresses the conduct only of state and federal government. Private parties (e.g., individuals, groups, corporations) cannot violate it and are presumably free to violate it. In race discrimination cases "government conduct" has been interpreted widely and now encompasses the actions of public schools and universities as well as various governmental entities. But definitions of the word "equality" in gender discrimination cases have not been so broad.

The Supreme Court has ruled that the word "equality" does not require that people of different genders be treated in the same way. Instead, in gender discrimination cases, the Fourteenth Amendment has been interpreted to mean that women be placed in more equal positions, as well as that like cases be treated alike. There are instances, then, in which women can be treated differently from their male counterparts, unlike race cases, in which people of different races must be treated the same.

In determining how to examine whether laws are not equal in race and gender discrimination cases, the Supreme Court has formulated three standards of review. These contrasting equal protection standards now used in discrimination cases range on a continuum from lenient to stern; the most lenient is the "rational basis standard," and at the stern end is the "strict scrutiny standard." The vast majority of laws are reviewed under the lenient, rational basis standard and are rarely declared discriminatory. Essentially, courts will presume the validity of a state statute if there is any rational basis for it; this test requires that the purpose of a law must be constitutionally legitimate and the means selected to achieve this purpose must be rationally related to accomplishing this end. Only when a law is suspected of discriminating against a traditionally disadvantaged group (e.g., race) is the strict scrutiny standard used. A law subject to the strict scrutiny test must serve a compelling government interest, and the specific provisions of the statute must be "strictly tailored" to the achievement of the compelling purpose, with no less invasive means available. Very rarely are laws *not* declared discriminatory when this standard is used.

Since the 1950s, women have attempted to persuade the courts that gender discrimination is analogous to race discrimination and should be held to the same strict scrutiny standard. The Supreme Court has consistently relegated sex discrimination to the lower rational basis standard. But by the 1970s the court became much more critical in gender discrimination cases of both the importance of a discriminatory law's purpose and the means by which the statute proposed to accomplish this purpose. In 1976 (*Craig v. Boren*) the court articulated an "intermediate" level of review for sex-based discrimination claims; sex-based laws must now meet a higher standard than rational basis but a lower standard than strict scrutiny. In this intermediate category the law must be substantially related to the achievement of an important governmental objective. Equal protection challenges focus only on whether a benefit or a burden is imposed equally on both men and women; the courts do not address the content of the law, that is, that the law does not treat equally men and women who are similarly situated.

Ashlyn K. Kuersten

See Also: Abolitionism and the Antislavery Movement; The Constitution and Women; Douglass, Frederick; Fifteenth Amendment; Stone, Lucy; Anthony, Susan B. (Vol. 2); Civil Rights Act of 1964 (Vol. 3); *Craig v. Boren* (Vol. 3); Equal Rights Amendment (Vol. 3); *Frontiero v. Richardson* (Vol. 3); *Geduldig v. Aiello* (Vol. 3); Ginsburg, Ruth Bader (Vol. 3); Stanton, Elizabeth Cady (Vol. 2)

Further Reading

DuBois, Ellen Carol. *Feminism and Suffrage: The Emergence of an Independent Women's Movement in America 1848–1869*. Ithaca, NY: Cornell University Press, 1978.

Foner, Eric. *Reconstruction: America's Unfinished Revolution, 1863–1877*. New York: Harper & Row, 1988.

Griffith, Elisabeth. *In Her Own Right: The Life of Elizabeth Cady Stanton*. New York: Oxford University Press, 1984.

Stetson, Dorothy McBride. *Women's Rights in the USA: Policy Debates and Gender Roles*. New York: Garland Press, 1997.

Freedmen's Bureau

Established by U.S. Congress in March 1865, the Bureau of Refugees, Freedmen and Abandoned Lands, or Freedmen's Bureau, was intended to help formerly enslaved black men and women in their transition to freedom.

Charged with providing rations, distributing lands, mediating labor contracts, establishing schools, promoting education, and securing civil rights for freed blacks, the Freedmen's Bureau had an almost impossible task. Aside from its restricted resources and limited lifespan, the Freedmen's Bureau faced opposition from Southern whites, Democrats in Congress, and President Andrew Johnson. The Freedmen's Bureau also relied heavily on the goodwill of Southerners to treat freedmen as their equals. By the time of its final disbandment in 1872 due to sustained opposition, the Bureau still left many of its goals unaccomplished.

Major General Oliver Otis Howard, a pious and dedicated soldier, served as the Bureau's commissioner for its entire existence. At the close of the Civil War, thousands of refugees, blacks and whites, needed medicine, food, clothing, and aid. Freedmen's Bureau officers distributed needed supplies and helped many individuals find their way home. Bureau agents also offered temporary shelter for blacks who needed a place to rest while they tracked down their lost family members, scattered by the antebellum slave trade and the war.

The bureau's most crucial test involved the conflict between Southern whites and blacks over the issues of land and labor. Many former slaves saw the ownership of their own farms as the pinnacle of true freedom. Following the war, the Freedmen's Bureau controlled vast amounts of land confiscated from rebellious Southerners. Despite the fact that many freedmen had already settled on some newly distributed lands, President Andrew Johnson, a staunch opponent of the Freedmen's Bureau, brought an end to the program by pardoning former Confederates, ordering that their seized lands be returned to them, and evicting freedmen, a reversal of one of the Bureau's primary principles.

The Bureau was under great pressure to get African Americans working again because one of its main fears was that continued aid would create a class of dependent freedmen. The Freedmen's Bureau pressed black men and women to sign labor contracts with landowning whites. Bureau agents did not entirely recognize the fact that Southern whites resented having to pay their former slaves and that many freedmen did not wish to work in any capacity for their former masters. Despite the fact that many blacks were forced into signing contracts to work on white-owned lands, freedmen were often given the chance to choose their employers and Bureau agents aided them in negotiating fair contracts.

Freedmen's Bureau agents tried to get blacks of both sexes and all ages back to work. Many black husbands attempted to shield their wives and children from labor, saying that freedwomen should, like white women, tend to the home and that their children should attend school. Control over one's family was, after all, one of the freedoms that had been denied to slaves. For their part, freedwomen, some of whom were single parents, took whatever opportunities they could to provide for their children. Many black women found it difficult to gain employment not only because of their sex but also because they had to find a way to take care of their children. Bureau agents sometimes stepped in and attempted to get wayward husbands to take responsibility for their wives and families.

The Freedmen's Bureau's greatest achievement came in the realm of education. Even before the bureau began to support freedmen's schools, many blacks had organized schools for themselves in churches and private homes. Freedmen of all ages understood the necessity of education and filled up classrooms all over the South. In conjunction with Northern aid societies such as the American Missionary Association (AMA), the Freedmen's Bureau helped acquire land and supply building materials for thousands of new schools. The AMA and organizations like it helped recruit Northern teachers to come South.

Many of those who answered the call to teach were young, educated, middle-class white women from New England. While the Freedmen's Bureau donated funds for construction and resources, the AMA helped pay the salaries of these Northern teachers. Teachers believed that slavery had degraded blacks and sought to instill the virtues of responsibility and discipline, corresponding with the Bureau's policy of getting freedmen to work on their own. Southern whites often shunned these schools, not allowing their own children to be educated alongside freed blacks. Other than local schools, the Freedmen's Bureau also helped create institutions of higher learning such as Howard University, the Hampton Institute, and Fisk University. When the Bureau was finally disbanded, it had established thousands of schools throughout the South.

Freedmen's Bureau agents also served the vital function of being blacks' advocates in the Southern courts, helping with labor contract negotiations, advising freedmen on legal matters, and defending blacks' civil rights, including the right to impartial justice. Even as the state statutes were altered, Southern courts remained prejudiced against blacks. Due to its limited resources and temporary mandate, however, the Bureau ultimately could not guarantee justice for freedmen in local courts.

While blacks saw the Freedmen's Bureau as their ally, Southern whites viewed it as a symbol of Northern oppression and learned to associate it with the Confederacy's defeat. Black men and women came to the agents with personal and domestic problems but also lodged complaints against whites who defrauded or threatened them. Determined to halt black advancement and curb the influence of the Freedmen's Bureau influence, Southerners used various means to thwart the agents' activities. Northern schoolteachers, also seen as representatives of a triumphant North, were harassed and terrorized by local whites. Paramilitary groups burned down black schools and interfered with the Bureau's operations. Without troops to uphold federal policy, it became very difficult to maintain Bureau operations in hostile communities.

On the national level, Southerners had allies in Congress and the White House. Democrats and President Andrew Johnson warred against the Freedmen's Bureau from the very start of its operations. When former Confederates attempted to reestablish limits on black freedoms with the notorious black codes, the Republican-controlled Congress moved to extend the life of the Freedmen's Bureau for an additional year and also proposed the Civil Rights bill. President Johnson, arguing that the Freedmen's Bureau represented federal patronage that favored one group of citizens over another and citing fiscal limitations, vetoed the two bills. Republicans passed the measures over Johnson's veto and also sought to guarantee freedmen's civil rights by successfully including the Fourteenth and Fifteenth Amendments to the U.S. Constitution.

By the late 1860s, support for the Freedmen's Bureau waned, many Northerners believing that the task of getting blacks back to work and securing blacks' civil rights had been accomplished. The Freedmen's Bureau remained partially functional after 1868 and permanently closed its offices in 1872. Overall, the Freedmen's Bureau had a mixed record that highlighted some of the ideological limitations and failures of Reconstruction.

Kanisorn Wongsrichanalai

See Also: Fifteenth Amendment; Fourteenth Amendment; Griffing, Josephine White; Grimké, Charlotte L. Forten; Reconstruction; Slavery and the Civil War

Further Reading

Cimbala, Paul A., and Randall M. Miller, eds. *The Freedmen's Bureau and Reconstruction: Reconsiderations.* New York: Fordham University Press, 1999.

Edwards, Laura F. Edwards. *Gendered Strife and Confusion: The Political Culture of Reconstruction.* Urbana: University of Illinois Press, 1997.

Farmer-Kaiser, Mary. *Freedwomen and the Freedmen's Bureau: Race, Gender, and Public Policy in the Age of Reconstruction.* New York: Fordham University Press, 2010.

Faulkner, Carol. *Women's Radical Reconstruction: The Freedmen's Aid Movement.* Philadelphia: University of Pennsylvania Press, 2003.

Jones, Jacqueline. *Soldiers of Light and Love: Northern Teachers and Georgia Blacks, 1865–1873.* Chapel Hill: University of North Carolina Press, 1980.

Fuller, Margaret (1810–1850)

In 1845 the American feminist writer and journalist Margaret Fuller, an imposing and idiosyncratic intellectual figure in literary circles in New England, published an

Margaret Fuller was one of the leading thinkers of the Transcendentalist movement and a pioneer in advocating women's rights in the first half of the 19th century. (Library of Congress)

important early contribution to the history of American feminism. Her discussions of women's roles and their need for an independent life in *Woman in the Nineteenth Century* added impetus to the call in 1848 for the first women's rights convention in Seneca Falls, New York.

Born in Cambridgeport, Massachusetts, Sarah Margaret Fuller was educated by her demanding and domineering lawyer father. A strict Calvinist, he kept her on a treadmill of self-improvement and intense study. She was soon set apart from her peers as an extraordinary, precocious child who studied Greek, Latin, and Italian and read classics and Shakespeare from a young age. When Fuller was sent to a local school at the age of 14, she was ostracized for her strangeness. Painfully aware of her "otherness," she later ruefully observed of her early years: "My book life and lonely habits had given a cold aloofness to my whole expression and veiled my manner with a *hauteur* which turned all hearts away."

During the 1820s, word spread in Harvard intellectual society about her prodigious talents, but in 1833 Fuller moved back to the countryside on her father's retirement, and when he died in 1835 she was obliged to teach to help support her family. She accepted a post from the Transcendentalist Bronson Alcott, the father of the writer Louisa May Alcott, at his progressive Temple School in Boston (1836–1837). There Fuller became friendly with the educational reformer Elizabeth Palmer Peabody and in 1837 left to set up a school of her own similar to Alcott's, the Greene School, in Providence.

During this time, Fuller continued with her own private study, turning to German literature—translating Johann Eckermann's *Conversations with Goethe* (1839)—and philosophy, in particular the work of Immanuel Kant. On moving to Jamaica Plain near Boston in 1839, Fuller became friendly with the essayist and poet Ralph Waldo Emerson, who invited her to join discussions of the German and French philosophers with members of a small, select group of Transcendentalist intellectuals who gravitated around Emerson in Concord, Massachusetts. These included Bronson Alcott and Henry David Thoreau, with Elizabeth Palmer Peabody the only other woman invited to join. Fuller soon had a reputation for being a formidable debater.

During the period 1839–1844, in an attempt to encourage women to educate themselves and learn to debate and speak in public, Fuller convened a series of "conversations" for women on sexual equality and women's rights. Cultural subjects such as philosophy, mythology, education, and art were also discussed. Taking place at Elizabeth Peabody's bookshop on Boston's West Street, Fuller's gatherings were soon unkindly nicknamed the "Babel of talkers" by Thoreau, and even Peabody herself described them as often degenerating from "conversations" into audiences at which "Queen Margaret" (as Peabody later referred to Fuller) held forth with great eloquence to an awestruck audience on subjects such as "The Great Lawsuit—Man versus Men. Woman versus Women." This essay was published by Fuller, along with several others, in the Transcendentalist quarterly journal *The Dial,* which she founded with Emerson in 1840 and which she co-edited over the next several years.

Having garnered a considerable reputation as an intellectual, in 1844 Fuller published her first book, *Summer on the Lakes in 1843,* recording a trip she had made to Chicago and her impressions of pioneering out west. She moved to New York in 1844, where for the first time she witnessed the life of the poor in the city's tenement buildings. She took up journalism, writing on charitable work in the city, including the creation of a Women's Prison Association, and began her own analysis of the economic and social ills that beset the United States. She also became a book reviewer and before long was considered a major literary critic of her day, publishing in the *New York Tribune* from 1844 to 1846.

In 1845 Fuller produced an exposition of her feminist ideas in *Woman in the Nineteenth Century and Kindred Papers Relating to the Sphere, Condition and Duties of Woman.* Despite a certain lack of unity in its subject matter and arguments, its arcane references, and the mystical and religious overtones of its literary language, the book is a penetrating study of the far-reaching consequences of women's traditional submissiveness and their unquestioning acceptance of their own inequality. Emphasizing women's need for inner growth, Fuller urged them not to be inhibited by their physical weakness. They should embark on their own self-discovery and self-liberation on the basis of their accepted difference from—but not inequality with—men. Thus, Fuller encouraged her readers to act independently of men, instead of being led by them and continuing to accept their view of the world. It was only then, in her view, that women would be able to unite in what she saw as their sacred duty and a great spiritual and moral crusade—collective social action to help other underprivileged and oppressed women such as prostitutes, seamstresses, and poor laundry women. In urging women to reject traditional sexual stereotyping and secure their free access to the professions and employment, Fuller famously advocated, "Let them be Sea-Captains if they will." For her, women's self-liberation was all part of the greater cosmic purpose of human existence, in which the complementary natures of men and women should work in harmony toward the achievement of their divine purpose on Earth.

In 1846, the year that she published *Papers on Literature and Art,* Fuller became the first American woman to be appointed a foreign correspondent when Horace Greeley, proprietor of the *New York Tribune,* gave her a front-page column, to which she contributed regular letters during a trip to Europe. In London Fuller was feted as an intellectual celebrity and became friends with Harriet Martineau, as well as meeting the poet William Wordsworth and the historian Thomas Carlyle. In her reports home, however, she registered her shock at the poverty and deprivation she encountered in London and in the industrial north. Traveling on to Paris, Fuller met the lioness of French literature, George Sand, and her lover Frédéric Chopin. With revolutionary activity boiling all over Europe, she traveled to Rome in 1847, where she interviewed the Italian nationalist leader Giuseppe Mazzini after his return to Italy in 1848.

In Italy, Fuller met one of Mazzini's followers, Giovanni Angelo, the Marchese Ossoli. She had a son by him, Angelo, in 1848 and married him in secret in the summer of 1849, after living with him for two years. With Ossoli, Fuller joined republicans fighting in the

Italian war of liberation against the papal government. At the siege of Rome by the French in February 1849, she nursed the wounded in the makeshift Fate Bene Fratelli hospital. But the couple was forced to flee to Florence when the republic collapsed. There, for a while, Fuller became friendly with the English poet Elizabeth Barrett Browning and settled down to write what she considered her magnum opus, a history of the Italian Revolution of 1848–1849. In 1850, because of financial difficulties and continuing police harassment for their participation in the revolution, the Ossolis decided to sail for the United States. But Margaret, her husband, and baby son were all drowned and the manuscript of her Italian history lost, when the ship on which they sailed from Leghorn was wrecked at Fire Island, in sight of the coast of New York.

Two collections of Fuller's writings were published shortly after her death, as *At Home and Abroad* (1856) and *Life Without and Life Within* (1860). The poet and reformer Julia Ward Howe edited *Love-Letters of Margaret Fuller, 1845–1846* in 1903, and Fuller devotee and attendee of the conversations, Caroline Healey Dall, published an account of the early conversations as well as a history of Transcendentalism that emphasized Fuller's place in the movement. But it was a posthumous *Memoirs of Margaret Fuller Ossoli* of 1852, selectively edited by Emerson and others (and including rewrites of Fuller's own original words), that laid the foundation for the later distortion of Fuller's personality and career. It is said that the character of the doomed suicide Zenobia in Nathaniel Hawthorne's novel *The Blithedale Romance* was based on Fuller, as were, allegedly, the eponymous heroine of Oliver Wendell Holmes's *Elsie Venner,* Verbena Tarrant in Henry James's *The Bostonians,* and Miranda in James Russell Lowell's poetry collection, *A Fable for Critics,* a collective belittlement of Fuller's extraordinary intellect by her erstwhile male admirers.

Helen Rappaport

See Also: Dall, Caroline Healey; Howe, Julia Ward; Martineau, Harriet; Peabody, Elizabeth Palmer; *Woman in the Nineteenth Century*

Further Reading

Bartlett, Elizabeth Ann. *Liberty, Equality, Sorority: The Origins and Interpretation of American Feminist Thought: Frances Wright, Sarah Grimké, and Margaret Fuller.* Brooklyn, NY: Carlson Publishing, 1994.

Capper, Charles. *Margaret Fuller: An American Romantic Life, vol. 1, The Private Years.* New York: Oxford University Press, 1992.

Capper, Charles. *Margaret Fuller: An American Romantic Life, vol. 2, The Public Years.* New York: Oxford University Press, 2007.

Matteson, John. *The Lives of Margaret Fuller: A Biography.* New York: W. W. Norton, 2012.

Reynolds, Larry J., and Susan B. Smith, eds. *"These Sad but Glorious Days": Dispatches from Europe 1846–1850.* New Haven, CT: Yale University Press, 1991.

Tonkovich, Nicole. *Domesticity with a Difference: The Nonfiction of Catharine Beecher, Sarah J. Hale, Fanny Fern, and Margaret Fuller.* Jackson: University Press of Mississippi, 1997.

G

Garrison, William Lloyd (1805–1879)

As one of the nation's foremost radical abolitionists, William Lloyd Garrison first became involved in antislavery activism in the 1820s. By 1830, his confrontational, inflammatory rhetoric, which exposed the evils of slavery and demanded immediate emancipation, had earned him a reputation as an extremist and a fanatic. Garrison's fire-breathing oratory soon became his trademark, a style that inspired and rallied antislavery sympathizers to the cause while alienating many others. When Samuel Joseph May criticized him for an overly acrimonious speech, Garrison explained, "Brother May, I have need to be all on fire, for I have mountains of ice about me to melt." In January 1831, Garrison founded and became publisher and editor of *The Liberator,* one of the most influential antislavery periodicals. A champion of many social reforms, Garrison was most active as leader and principal activist of the American Anti-Slavery Society (AASS), the New England Anti-Slavery Society (NEASS), and the Massachusetts Anti-Slavery Society (MASS).

Garrison proved a powerful role model, and his white-hot, no-holds-barred verbosity was a style that many other abolitionist orators emulated. Susan B. Anthony's admiration of Garrison stemmed from his support and promotion of women's rights. He had not only urged women to be actively involved in the abolitionist movement from its earliest days but had also demanded that female activists in the AASS, the NEASS, and the MASS be given the same rights, privileges, and authority as male members. He attended and supported women's rights conventions throughout the 1850s and after the Civil War, and staunchly supported equal opportunities for women in all areas of political and social life.

There is no question that throughout the 1850s, Susan B. Anthony and many of her feminist-abolitionist colleagues idolized Garrison—frequently deferring to him and his opinions. Since he had been instrumental in engineering the path that enabled them to participate fully in abolitionist reform, many women Garrisonians were undoubtedly influenced by their awareness of the debt they owed him.

In 1860, however, Garrison and Wendell Phillips's strong, negative reaction to Anthony's efforts to help a woman escape the cruel, abusive tyranny of her husband and brothers proved the harbinger of an abrupt change in her relationships with her male mentors. When the woman's husband and her male relatives, all prominent politicians, threatened to sue Anthony and bring charges against her, both Garrison and Phillips immediately penned letters of reprimand, ordering Anthony to tell them the whereabouts of the woman and her child. Anthony refused. Although she understood that they were concerned about the effect the negative publicity about her would have on the abolitionist movement, she was appalled that Garrison and Phillips, who had devoted their lives to helping enslaved African Americans, refused to support her efforts to save an enslaved woman.

Garrison was affronted when Anthony declined to do as he indicated. He cornered her at a meeting and demanded, "Don't you know the law of Massachusetts gives the father the entire guardianship and control of the children?" Anthony grabbed the opportunity to make Garrison understand what he had been ignoring in his effort to protect the movement's reputation. "Yes, I know it," she replied, "and does not the law of the United States give the slaveholder the ownership of the slave? And don't you break it every time you help a slave to Canada?" Garrison admitted that he did. She then added, "You would die before you would deliver a slave to his master, and I will die before I will give up that child to its father." Garrison, however, was not persuaded by the analogy.

The entire incident distressed Anthony because, as she wrote, "Only to think that in this great trial I should be hounded by the two men whom I adore and reverence above all others." But beyond her shock at her beloved colleagues' treatment of her, the event, like Garrison and Phillips's unexpected rejection of Elizabeth Cady Stanton's resolution on divorce in 1860, highlighted the gaps in the two men's support for women's rights. As much as she had come to rely on their undivided advocacy of all women's rights concerns, their lack of support in this instance gave her one of the first indications that their sympathy and understanding were not limitless and that their past wholehearted support in no way guaranteed approval of all her future activism.

Although Garrison was not directly involved in the calamitous events of 1865–1870, when Wendell Phillips

73

and most male abolitionists abandoned the cause of woman suffrage to enhance the possibility of achieving political rights for African American males, Garrison's support of Phillips's position angered and frustrated Anthony and Stanton. Then, in a letter to Anthony in January 1868, Garrison castigated her and Stanton for their association with the Democrat George Francis Train, questioning their judgment in a manner that Anthony and Stanton found insulting and condescending.

The final blow occurred in October 1869, when Stanton, determined to assert a woman's right to direct her own movement, lambasted Garrison for being "despotic in spirit and purpose" in an editorial in *The Revolution*. A month later, it came as no surprise to Anthony or Stanton when Garrison backed Lucy Stone and Henry Blackwell in the formation of the American Woman Suffrage Association (AWSA), an organization intended to rival Anthony and Stanton's National Woman Suffrage Association (NWSA), established in May 1869.

By 1870, Anthony and Garrison occupied completely opposite camps, with much bitterness on both sides. Garrison's letter to abolitionist Theodore Tilton in April 1870 conveyed that he was still overwrought about the Anthony–Stanton issue. He confided to Tilton that he could not work with the two suffragists who were so "untruthful, unscrupulous, and selfishly ambitious." Garrison never seemed to fathom how his attempts to strong-arm Anthony and Stanton cost him the fond devotion and fealty he had once valued. Long accustomed to his leadership position, Garrison became resentful and truculent when his attempts to shape, control, and execute veto power within the women's rights movement were rejected.

Although Stanton and Garrison never resolved their estrangement, Anthony did not give up on her relationship with him. During the 1870s she corresponded with him on occasion. In 1878, when she asked him to write a letter in favor of the Sixteenth Amendment suffrage campaign, he refused, explaining her strategic errors and why the campaign would surely fail. Yet the relationship continued because Anthony was able to accept Garrison's limitations while continuing to value his past contributions to society, to abolitionism, and to her own development as a social activist and orator.

Judith E. Harper

See Also: Abolitionism and the Antislavery Movement; Douglass, Frederick; *The Liberator*; May, Samuel Joseph; Phillips, Wendell; *The Revolution*; Slavery and the Civil War; Stone, Lucy; Anthony, Susan B. (Vol. 2); Blackwell, Henry Brown (Vol. 2); Stanton, Elizabeth Cady (Vol. 2)

Primary Document: 1861, Address on Behalf of the New York Divorce Bill

Further Reading

Kraditor, Aileen S. *Means and Ends in American Abolitionism: Garrison and His Critics on Strategy and Tactics, 1864–1850.* New York: Random House, 1969.

Mayer, Henry. *All on Fire: William Lloyd Garrison and the Abolition of Slavery.* New York: St. Martin's Griffin, 1998.

Stewart, James Brewer. *William Lloyd Garrison and the Challenge of Emancipation.* Arlington Heights, IL: Harlan Davidson, 1992.

Stewart, James Brewer. *Holy Warriors: The Abolitionists and American Slavery.* New York: Hill and Wang, 1997.

The Genius of Liberty

The Genius of Liberty, a monthly journal edited and published by Elizabeth A. Aldrich in Cincinnati, Ohio, was created in October 1851 to appeal to "the general interests of woman; to whatever will improve her physical, mental, moral, social, and industrial condition."

The daughter of a local physician, Aldrich had the financial resources to launch *The Genius of Liberty* out of her own pocket, and she continued the venture through a total of 26 monthly issues, from October 1851 to November 1853. *The Genius of Liberty* was professionally typeset and printed by the *Cincinnati Gazette*, a local daily newspaper, and sold at a subscription rate of one dollar per year. By the end of its first year, it was successful enough to expand the original four-page format to eight pages. Although Aldrich included outside material—poetry, sermons, excerpts from exchange papers, and reports from regular correspondents—most of the writing in *The Genius of Liberty* was her own. Aldrich focused on the legal and cultural barriers that denied women full participation in the realms of education, professional training, property ownership, salaries, legal protection, and access to business opportunities. Aldrich spelled out in an early issue that "[Women] want a mental, moral and business field *equal* to their capacities, and equal to their rights which spring from their capacities."

Aldrich saw absolutely no conflict between woman's self-development and her family responsibilities: "The old dominions of woman—the kitchen and the parlour—she does not wish to give up . . . but she desires the government and labor of them improved, and the boundaries of her territory so much enlarged as to give free scope to her mental and physical abilities."

Possibly because of her familiarity with her father's medical library, Aldrich had a deep interest in women's health and published many commonsense articles on diet, exercise, and preventive medicine. She deplored the elaborate and restrictive Victorian dress: "How unnatural, ungraceful, and antiphysiological those garments are which make the human form a double cone with a common apex" and promoted instead "a natural healthy costume." *The Genius of Liberty* also favored vigorous exercise for women as a remedy for overcoming helplessness in women: "Women's principal difficulty is not the opposition of the other sex, but the weakness and imbecility of herself."

Above all, Aldrich championed equal education for women, not only to broaden their minds and qualify them for the professions but to free them from "that *degrading dependence,* so fruitful a source of female misery." To this end, *The Genius of Liberty* regularly published news of women's colleges in the United States, tracked the deliberations of state boards of education, and promoted the German model of primary school education, an eight-year curriculum much favored in midwestern cities like Cincinnati that had large German populations.

The Genius of Liberty also reported the progress of women in "profitable and honorable" businesses. The development of women writers and editors was a favorite cause: "Every woman that can wield a pen should write and those who cannot should aid those who can." Aldrich devoted most of the February 1853 issue to an annotated list of occupations denied by law and custom to women. She included medicine, the apothecary trade, art, accounting, banking, the administration of church and social service agencies, retailing, and the ministry. She contrasted them with the "pecuniary avocations," such as needlework, laundering, boarding, and schoolteaching—those jobs women could perform, but at bare survival wages, so low that "no woman can pursue them and accumulate an independence."

Along with progress in the world of work, *The Genius of Liberty* published news of state and national women's conferences. Aldrich traveled to New York to report on the 1852 national women's rights conference in Syracuse, at which Lucretia Mott, Susan B. Anthony, Lucy Stone, and other activists were gathered. Aldrich wrote: "Our sex everywhere should take courage by these brilliant luminaries; fling away the customary ideas of female inferiority, and feel, claim, and assert the mental equality of the sexes."

The Genius of Liberty claimed to be nonpolitical, but Aldrich was quick to chastise members of the U.S. Senate who killed an antislavery amendment, and she made sure readers knew the names of the supporters of the antislavery clause in the House. She proposed "the education of free men and women of color . . . in the departments of science, literature and art" and also advocated education for poor whites in the South.

Like most editors of small papers, Aldrich frequently had to remind readers to pay their subscriptions. Several times she was forced to solicit outright donations, reminding readers that *The Genius of Liberty* was "the only paper in the State devoted to the interests of women, and we believe, the only female paper in the Western valley." Many donors responded, but even these did not save the paper in the end. Abruptly and without notice, *The Genius of Liberty* published its last issue in November 1853.

Jean E. Dye

See Also: Dress Reform; *The Lily; The Sibyl; The Una*

Further Reading

Aronson, Amy Beth. *Taking Liberties: Early American Women's Magazines and Their Readers*. Westport, CT: Praeger Press, 2002.

Russo, Ann, and Cheris Kramarae. *The Radical Women's Press of the 1850s*. New York: Routledge, 1991.

Gibbons, Abigail Hopper (1801–1893)

The American abolitionist, Civil War nurse, and prison reformer Abigail Gibbons became head of the Female Department of the Prison Association of New York in 1845. In this capacity, she worked toward the social rehabilitation of women prisoners and for the reeducation of their keepers into adopting more humane methods of treatment. In so doing, she was instrumental in the creation of a women's prison system, run by women, that shifted its attitude from moral condemnation and punishment to a more compassionate concern for prisoners' welfare, during and after their term of sentence.

Gibbons's father, Isaac Tatem Hopper, was a Quaker abolitionist and prison reformer who believed in women's equality with men. He was a vigorous supporter of abolitionism and made his home a stop on the Underground Railroad, which assisted runaway slaves in getting north to Canada. Gibbons grew up in Philadelphia and was educated in Quaker schools. After moving to New York, where she ran a Quaker school from 1830, she met and married a Quaker businessman and later banker, James Gibbons, in 1833. After two years in Philadelphia, the couple returned to New York, where, as leading members of the Manhattan Anti-Slavery Society, they raised funds among sympathizers. Their home became renowned as a stop on the Underground Railroad and a meeting place of abolitionists, including Lydia Maria Child and Sarah Moore Grimké. In 1842 both her father and husband were disowned by the New York Yearly Meeting of the Quakers for their militancy over abolitionism, and she resigned her membership in protest, although she retained her Hicksite Quaker beliefs for the rest of her life.

In New York, Gibbons became involved in welfare work among the poor in the city's tenements and slums. She became a prison visitor, working with her father after he founded the Prison Association of New York in December 1844. Early the following year, the association established a Female Department, with Gibbons appointed to lead a team of female volunteer workers. In 1845, the Female Department founded a halfway house to aid former women prisoners in their voluntary rehabilitation after their discharge from prison. The women who lived there took in work as laundresses and needlewomen to help pay for their keep and were assisted in finding jobs in domestic service. Known as the Home for Discharged Female Convicts, it was probably the first institution of its kind in the world.

In 1853 Gibbons's Female Department was given its autonomy and renamed the Women's Prison Association (WPA). Along with another prison reformer, Josephine Shaw Lowell, she felt women prisoners would be better served if they were not held, segregated, within men's prisons, and she advocated the establishment of separate women's reformatories run by women. Gibbons also retained her interests in education, in 1859 setting up a German Industrial School for the welfare of homeless German immigrant children and remaining its director until 1871.

When the Civil War broke out in 1861, Gibbons volunteered her services to the U.S. Sanitary Commission. After training at David's Island Hospital in New York, she went to Washington, D.C., with her daughter Sarah and niece Maria Hopper. Gibbons organized the distribution of supplies donated by the New York Relief Agency and went on to set up two field hospitals at Strasburg and Falls Church, Virginia. Sent to nurse in Maryland, she encountered the Sanitary Commission's superintendent of nurses, Dorothea Dix. Gibbons secured the post as matron at Hammond General Hospital, where she took full advantage of her position to ensure that wounded "contrabands" (runaway slaves who had volunteered for the Union Army) who arrived for treatment retained their liberty. Like Dix, Gibbons was outspoken in her criticism of the brutal medical methods of U.S. Army doctors and the mismanagement of supplies by its male administrators.

When the war ended, Gibbons established the Labor and Aid Society to help in the rehabilitation of war veterans and the relief of their families, but it failed to take off. She returned to her work for the WPA in New York and the many other reformist activities she had embraced in the 1850s—improvements in the care of the mentally ill and conditions in mental asylums, temperance, and the abolishment of the death penalty. She also worked for blind and disabled children in the local poorhouse at West Farms (later the Randall's Island Children's Asylum). She founded the New York Diet Kitchen Association in 1873 to offer nutritious meals to children, the sick, and the poor and joined the moral campaign of the New York Committee for the Prevention of State Regulation of Vice, serving as its president.

In 1877 Gibbons became president of the WPA and in 1890, after many years of lobbying, she saw the introduction of women matrons to manage the women held in police custody. In 1892, at age 91, Gibbons gave evidence before the New York legislature that resulted in the passage of a bill shortly before her death establishing a reformatory for women and girls to serve New York and Westchester.

The spirit of Gibbons's pioneering work on behalf of women prisoners is continued today by the Women's Prison Association in institutions such as the Hopper Home and its Alternative to Incarceration Program in New York, which enables women offenders to remain in the community with their children. The Transitional Services Unit offers counseling and training in parenting skills, as well as rehabilitation programs designed to help women released from prison avoid reoffending.

Helen Rappaport

See Also: Child, Lydia Maria; Dix, Dorothea; Farnham, Eliza; Grimké, Sarah Moore; Grimké Weld, Angelina; Quakers; United States Sanitary Commission; Lowell, Josephine Shaw (Vol. 2)

Further Reading

Bacon, Margaret Hope. *Mothers of Feminism: The Story of Quaker Women in America.* San Francisco, CA: Harper and Row, 1986.

Bacon, Margaret Hope. *Abby Hopper Gibbons: Prison Reformer and Social Activist.* Albany: State University of New York Press, 2000.

Freedman, Estelle B. *Their Sisters' Keepers: Women's Prison Reform in America, 1830–1930.* Ann Arbor: University of Michigan, 1981.

Ginzberg, Lori D. *Women and the Work of Benevolence: Morality, Politics, and Class in the Nineteenth-Century United States.* New Haven, CT: Yale University Press, 1990.

Godey's Lady's Book

Few women's magazines or editors have been so heralded as *Godey's Lady's Book* and its editor, Sarah Josepha Hale. The magazine's ability to attract the nation's top literary names and its almost 70-year successful run were enough to guarantee *Godey's* place in history. Under the firm direction of Sarah Hale, *Godey's* defined middle-class women's roles during much of the 19th century.

Godey's Lady's Book and Hale's association with the magazine resulted from an 1837 merger of two journals: the *Ladies' Magazine* and the *Lady's Book.* The former

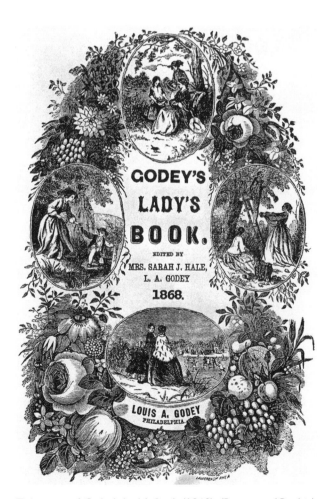

Title page of *Godey's Lady's Book* (1868). (Bettmann/Corbis)

began in 1828 in Boston when Sarah Hale, a reasonably well-known New Hampshire author, was offered a job by the Reverend John L. Blake to edit a new magazine. The *Lady's Book* was begun by Louis Godey in Philadelphia in 1830. Godey's purchase of the *Ladies' Magazine* was one step in the expansion of his publishing interests.

Sarah Josepha Hale never intended to become a magazine editor. Her husband died in 1822, two days after the Hales' ninth wedding anniversary, leaving Sarah Hale with five children to support. To provide for her family, she reluctantly opened a millinery shop with her sister-in-law, Hannah Hale. Writing was a side venture, but it quickly became her lifework. In 1823, she published a book of poems. This was quickly followed by poetry and prose submissions to a variety of magazines, including *The American Monthly Magazine,* the *U.S. Literary Gazette, The Minerva,* and *The Boston Spectator.* The latter publication published the majority of Hale's poetry and prose throughout the 1820s.

Although her poetry and prose caught the attention of editors in Boston and New York, Hale's first novel, *Northwood,* a story of the North and South, gained her real fame and her first editing job. Shortly after her novel's publication, Hale received a letter from the Reverend John L. Blake asking her to move to Boston from her New Hampshire home and take up the editorship of a new women's magazine. Hale began editing the *Ladies' Magazine* in 1828. The magazine was almost entirely literary, offering poems, short stories, biographical sketches, some fashion plates, and sheet music. The *Ladies' Magazine* lasted for nine years, then was purchased by Louis Godey in 1837.

Godey's purchase of the *Ladies' Magazine* and his continuation of Sarah Hale as editor did wonders for his own publication. *Godey's Lady's Book* became the most popular women's magazine of the mid-1800s under Hale. Most of the nation's leading authors and poets wrote for the journal before the Civil War, including literary women such as Harriet Beecher Stowe, Eliza Leslie, Ann Stephens (who later edited Godey's competitor, *Peterson's Magazine*), Caroline M. S. Kirkland, and Hannah F. Gould. Godey and Hale also published the leading male writers of the time, including Ralph Waldo Emerson, Nathaniel Hawthorne, Henry Wadsworth Longfellow, and Edgar Allan Poe.

Hale's real mission was to encourage and publish as many quality women writers as possible. She recalled that none of the books she read while growing up were written by women. "The wish to promote the reputation of my own sex and of my country was among the earliest mental emotions I can recollect," Hale once remarked. Godey's and Hale's selection of authors reflected more than their good taste in poetry and prose. It also represented a sound business practice. Both Godey and Hale attracted a wide circulation for their publication by promising never to publish any fiction that was less than moral and pure.

The two decades before the Civil War proved to be *Godey's* golden years. Circulation increased from 25,000 to 150,000, largely on the strength of the magazine's literature and poetry. Two years after Hale's arrival, Godey announced that his magazine had more subscribers than all three of his competitors' magazines combined.

Godey's and Hale's content requirements resulted in a total editorial blackout of war news during the Civil War. While the conflict raged, the magazine provided its usual staple of sugary poetry, stories of gallant men and beautiful women, engravings, and music. The lack of war coverage was not surprising, as both editors viewed war news as vulgar and not of interest to women. Ten years earlier, in January 1850, Harriet Beecher Stowe had attacked *Godey's* in *The Independent* for not crusading against slavery.

Louis Godey had a clear understanding of what the middle-class Victorian woman wanted in a magazine, including fashion plates, literature, decorative engravings, craft patterns, and sheet music. Hale, however, resented the inclusion of fashion plates and had earlier waged an unsuccessful battle against including fashion news in the *Ladies' Magazine* during the first three years of its publication, eventually giving in to reader demand in 1831. Hale published fashion plates and news but announced: "There is no part of our duty as editor of a ladies' journal which we feel so reluctant to perform, as to quote, or exhibit the fashions of dress." Her readers got their fashions but also received harsh words from Hale's pen about the foolishness of outright adoption of European fashions, which she saw as frivolous and extravagant.

Through her editorials, Hale defined and promoted a role for middle-class women in American society. Hale's ideal woman served her family. From her domain in the home, a woman could be a helper to her husband, a guide to her children, and, perhaps most important, the moral center of the family. Hale held up Queen Victoria as a role model of femininity, morality, and intellect. She urged the queen to encourage education for women, claiming it was "the best means of improving the moral conditions of society." From the magazine's outset, Hale consistently crusaded for education

for women. Women, Hale believed, had to be educated if they were to be fit companions for their husbands and competent homemakers. She believed that women, if educated, could pursue some professions outside the home, particularly teaching, missionary work, and medicine. These fields were suited for women, Hale said, because they lent themselves to women's highly moral talents.

Godey's began its decline after the Civil War. The journal's chief competitor, *Peterson's Magazine,* increased its expenditures and published even more fashions and literature than did *Godey's.* Hale and Godey stopped editing the magazine in 1877. The journal's new editors kept the same sentimental, Victorian content, despite literature's shift toward realism. The inability of *Godey's Lady's Book* to continue to reflect the times led to its demise in 1898.

Mary M. Cronin

See Also: Hale, Sarah Josepha; Stowe, Harriet Beecher

Further Reading

Bradley, Patricia. *Women and the Press: The Struggle for Equality.* Evanston, IL: Northwestern University Press, 2005.

Lehuu, Isabelle. *Carnival on the Page: Popular Print Media in Antebellum America.* Chapel Hill: University of North Carolina Press, 2000.

Okker, Patricia. *Our Sister Editors: Sarah J. Hale and the Tradition of Nineteenth-Century American Women Editors.* Athens: University of Georgia Press, 1995.

Rose, Anne C. *Voices of the Marketplace: American Thought and Culture, 1830–1860.* New York: Rowman & Littlefield Publishers, 2004.

Griffing, Josephine White (1814–1872)

Abolitionist, lecturer, women's rights activist, and freedmen's aid reformer, Josephine Griffing participated in the Western Anti-Slavery Society, the National Women's Loyal League, and the National Freedmen's Relief Association of Washington, D.C.

Born on December 18, 1814, in Hebron, Connecticut, Josephine was the daughter of farmer Joseph White and Sophia Waldo. Her father had also served in the state legislature. Little is documented of her childhood. She married Charles Stockman Spooner Griffing on September 16, 1835; they soon moved to Litchfield, Ohio, and became active in the Western Anti-Slavery Society, affiliated with the Garrisonian wing of abolitionism. Josephine Griffing gave birth to five children, although two died in childhood.

During the 1850s Griffing offered her home to slaves using the Underground Railroad. As a paid agent for the Western Anti-Slavery Society, she lectured and sang abolitionist songs at several antislavery meetings and contributed to the *Anti-Slavery Bugle,* published in Salem, Ohio. Griffing also used this newspaper to present her views on women's rights, joining and later serving as president of the Ohio Woman's Rights Association. Griffing's efforts increased with the commencement of the Civil War. She joined the National Women's Loyal League in 1863 and spearheaded an antislavery petition drive. As a paid lecturing agent, she traveled to Ohio, Indiana, Illinois, Michigan, and Wisconsin to secure signatures for petitions.

In September 1864, in a letter to President Abraham Lincoln, she addressed issues of newly emancipated freedmen, whose loss of bondage meant that they needed training and employment for sustenance. She also recommended unlimited asylum for freedmen, and cooperation between the churches and other relief organizations. Having foresight not exhibited by other abolitionists, Griffing went to Washington, D.C., in 1864 to become the general agent of the National Freedmen's Relief Association of the District of Columbia. Here she managed a vocational school for seamstresses.

Griffing promoted creation of the Bureau of Refugees, Freedmen, and Abandoned Lands, commonly known as the Freedmen's Bureau, and was hired in 1865 as the assistant to the Assistant Commissioner for Washington, D.C. She made many public appeals, much to the chagrin of the Bureau and was dismissed later that year. Even after her departure, she worked to secure free transportation of former slaves to the North by contacting the presidents of the Baltimore and Ohio and Pennsylvania Railroads.

Rehired by the Freedmen's Bureau as an employment agent in 1867, Griffing located jobs for former slaves. In 1868 she convinced the Bureau to adapt the U.S. Sanitary Commission building as a tenement for the poor. When the Freedmen's Bureau ceased in 1869, Griffing continued her work with the National Freedmen's Relief Association, helping especially the elderly and disabled. She was credited with assisting 7,000 freedmen in their quest for new jobs and homes in the North. During her final years, Griffing was elected a vice president of the American Equal Rights Association in 1866, and addressed the Senate Judiciary Committee in 1871.

Josephine Griffing died on February 18, 1872, likely of tuberculosis.

Ralph Hartsock

See Also: Abolitionism and the Antislavery Movement; Freedmen's Bureau; Garrison, William Lloyd; National Women's Loyal League; Slavery and the Civil War; Underground Railroad

Further Reading

Faulkner, Carol. *Women's Radical Reconstruction: The Freedmen's Aid Movement.* Philadelphia: University of Pennsylvania Press, 2004.

Robertson, Stacey M. *Hearts Beating for Liberty: Women Abolitionists in the Old Northwest.* Chapel Hill: University of North Carolina Press, 2010.

Grimké, Charlotte L. Forten (1837–1914)

Abolitionist, educator, civil rights activist, and poet, Charlotte Forten Grimké kept detailed journals of her time as a teacher to the freedpeople in Port Royal. Her attention to detail, her keen commentaries, and rare insights offer an important perspective of 19th-century African American life during the Civil War and Reconstruction eras.

The daughter of Mary Woods and Robert Forten, prominent antislavery activists and a leading African American family of Philadelphia, Charlotte Forten was born on August 17, 1837. After her mother died in 1840, Forten became very close to three of her aunts: Sarah and Harriet Forten Purvis, and Margaretta Forten. Their antislavery politics would define her life. Precocious and bright, Charlotte received tutoring at home, and later, when she expressed a desire to become a teacher, she was sent to Salem, Massachusetts, to study in integrated educational institutions, including Higginson Grammar School and Salem Normal School. She boarded with the renowned Remond family, which afforded her many opportunities to mingle with New England's abolitionist vanguard.

Continuing a long family tradition of antislavery and civil rights activism, Forten joined the Salem Female Anti-Slavery Society, one of the oldest in the country. In June 1854, the trial of Anthony Burns, a fugitive slave, was held in nearby Boston. His conviction and return to slavery sparked mass protest and mob action. This event deeply troubled Forten, and she dedicated herself more deeply to fighting for immediate emancipation and the cause of the enslaved.

During this time, she met William Lloyd Garrison, editor of *The Liberator,* and, with his encouragement, she published several works in his newspaper and, later, in the *National Anti-Slavery Standard* and the *Anglo-African* magazine. While poetry dominated much of her writing, she also wrote essays. Antislavery themes were common, but she also wrote on a variety of topics, including love, morality, religion, temperance, education, and politics. Forten completed her studies, and in 1856 began teaching at the Epes Grammar School, becoming Salem's first African American public school teacher. Tuberculosis forced her to resign after two years, and she returned to Philadelphia. She continued to write, however, maintaining a strong presence in local and national abolitionist politics.

With the onset of the Civil War, Forten hoped to contribute her services to the Union cause. When the Boston Education Commission called for volunteers for its Port Royal Experiment in South Carolina in early 1862, Forten applied. They were slow to approve her application, however, so she turned to the newly forming Pennsylvania Freedmen's Relief Association, which was just beginning to organize and eager to send its own teachers to the war zone. Forten would be the first African American teacher assigned to the Port Royal district, and, for many of her students and their parents, she would be the first free, well-educated African American they would meet.

Forten arrived in the late fall of 1862 and devoted two years to teaching the newly freed slaves of the local Sea Islands. With two friends, Laura Towne and Ellen Murray, Forten set up a school in a local Baptist church on St. Helena Island. She published several essays in *The Atlantic Monthly* about her work and observations of the local people. While many Northerners and some abolitionists doubted the abilities, both intellectually and physically, of the newly freed people of the South, Forten provided a convincing portrait of an eager and fully capable people, striving, through education and training initiatives, to make the transition into a free society.

She also recorded many of her thoughts and experiences in journals that reveal the daily joys and struggles Forten faced teaching her students, her keen interpretations of life in the community, and her observations of the bravery and deportment of the increasing number of black troops stationed in the district. She became quite close to several of their commanding officers, and she recorded both the excitement over their victories and the tremendous pain of their losses.

She described with great excitement her meeting with Harriet Tubman, the famous Underground Railroad conductor who was then serving Union forces in the district as a spy and scout, nurse, and cook. Forten was also there at the reading of the Emancipation Proclamation on January 1, 1863, at Camp Saxton near Beaufort, South Carolina.

Her father, Robert, had become frustrated by the persistent racism in America and moved his family from Philadelphia to Ontario, Canada, in 1855, then to England. The Civil War and the Emancipation Proclamation brought him back to the United States, and, at the age of 51, he joined the Forty-third United States Colored Troops. Promoted to sergeant, he had been assigned to recruit black soldiers in Maryland when he caught typhoid fever and died. After the war, Charlotte recruited teachers for posts in the South under the auspices of Boston's Freedmen's Relief Association. She taught briefly at the Sumner High School in the nation's capitol, then served as a clerk in the United States Treasury Department during the 1870s.

On December 19, 1878, Charlotte Forten married Francis Grimké, the son of a formerly enslaved woman, Nancy Weston, and her master, Henry Grimké, and nephew to Henry's famous abolitionist sisters, Sarah and Angelina Grimké. Frank, as he was known, studied at Lincoln University and Princeton Theological Seminary and later took a position as pastor at the Fifteenth Street Presbyterian Church in Washington, D.C., in 1877. He became a prominent African American civil rights activist and a vocal critic of Booker T. Washington.

The death of their infant daughter, Theodora, in 1880, devastated Charlotte and Frank Grimké. They moved to Jacksonville, Florida, when Frank accepted a pastorship. Charlotte Forten Grimké published little after her marriage, but she remained a dedicated minister's wife and activist. Persistent illness significantly restricted her activities the last 20 years of her life. She died on July 23, 1914.

Kate Clifford Larson

See Also: Abolitionism and the Antislavery Movement; Education of Women (before the Civil War); Freedmen's Bureau; Garrison, William Lloyd; Grimké, Sarah Moore; Grimké Weld, Angelina; Reconstruction; Remond, Sarah Parker; Slavery and the Civil War; Towne, Laura Matilda; Tubman, Harriet

Further Reading

Perry, Mark. *Lift Up Thy Voice: The Grimké Family's Journey from Slaveholders to Civil Rights Activists.* New York: Viking Penguin, 2001.

Rose, Willie Lee. *Rehearsal for Reconstruction: The Port Royal Experiment.* Athens: University of Georgia Press, 1999 [1964].

Stevenson, Brenda, ed. *The Journals of Charlotte Forten Grimké.* New York: Oxford University Press, 1988.

Grimké, Sarah Moore (1792–1873)

Sarah Grimké is considered one of the first women in the United States to campaign directly and openly for women's rights. Beginning as an activist for the emancipation of slaves, she was among the first to note the similarity between her condition as a woman and the condition of the enslaved people for whom she was advocating.

Sarah Grimké was born in Charleston, South Carolina, on November 26, 1792. Her father, Judge John Faucheraud Grimké, was a Revolutionary War hero, state senator and, eventually, judge on the South Carolina

In the 1830s, Sarah Grimké and her sister, Angelina Grimké, were among the earliest reformers to link the antislavery and women's rights causes. (Library of Congress)

Supreme Court. Her mother, Mary Smith, sprang from southern aristocracy and gave birth to 14 children. The family owned not only a home in Charleston but a plantation in nearby Beaufort that was operated by hundreds of slaves. As a small child, Sarah witnessed a horsewhipping of one of the slaves and each of the Grimké children was assigned a slave child of the same approximate age who was required to serve them. After befriending her assigned servant, Sarah secretly spent her evenings by lamplight teaching the young slave, Kitty, to read, knowledge that was forbidden by the culture and the law. When her father uncovered what she was doing, he told Sarah that she had committed crimes against the state and could be sent to prison. Shortly after his discovery, Kitty became ill and died. Sarah adamantly refused to allow her family to find another companion for her. When Sarah was 13, her last sibling, the 14th child, was born. Sarah asked to be named the new baby's godmother. Her wish was granted and Sarah raised the newborn, Angelina, as her own, spending the rest of her life in her sister's company.

Because of their wealth, the Grimké children were taught by tutors who came to the plantation. Her father, however, took one child, her brother Thomas, under his wing to further his training in law. Sarah was allowed to attend the sessions, learned to debate along with her brother, and studied Thomas's lessons in the evenings when no one noticed. She was secretly preparing for college but when her parents discovered her goals, she was forbidden to read and encouraged to study sewing and music instead. When Thomas was admitted to law school at Yale, Sarah was left behind. Feeling cheated, the young woman appealed to her father who remarked that she would have made the greatest jurist in the country, if only she had been born a boy.

In 1818, when Sarah was 26, her father became seriously ill and moved to Philadelphia in search of a specialist. Sarah was selected to be his traveling companion. The young woman was given the freedom to wander about the city and for the first time she witnessed life without slavery. She also discovered the Quaker religion. After almost a year of various doctors and no cure, Sarah and her father left Philadelphia for the Atlantic coast, but Judge Grimké died en route in New Jersey.

Sarah returned to Charleston, turned down two proposals of marriage and, less than a month after her return, packed her belongings and, in spite of her family's protest, moved permanently to Philadelphia. She joined the Quaker Society of Friends, lodging with one of their families, and volunteered with area charities and prisons.

In the evenings she studied theology, desperately seeking answers to the injustice she saw in the world. Several years later, Angelina followed, having been converted to Quakerism by her sister.

In 1834, the sisters joined the Female Anti-Slavery Society founded by Lucretia Mott. Revealing much of what she had witnessed on the family plantation concerning slavery, Angelina wrote a letter to William Lloyd Garrison, editor of the radical abolitionist newspaper, *The Liberator.* After the letter was published, the lives of the sisters changed; they were reprimanded by the Quakers, embraced by the abolitionists, and placed under threat of arrest if they returned to the South. Angelina was asked to become a speaker for the American Anti-Slavery Society with Sarah as her manager. Eventually, under the tutelage of Theodore Weld, editor of the *Emancipator,* both sisters began speaking in private homes about the horrors of slavery. Sarah, however, accepted the task reluctantly, rationalizing the calling as her Christian duty. They were among the first women to speak publicly in the United States and the only white Southern women to become abolitionist speakers.

Rebuffed again by the Philadelphia Society of Friends, the Grimké sisters relocated to Providence, Rhode Island, among a more liberal group. In 1836, they penned a series of antislavery pamphlets and books. Angelina wrote *An Appeal to the Christian Women of the South* (1836) and Sarah produced *An Epistle to the Clergy of the South* (1836), followed by *An Address to Free Colored Americans* (1837). When *An Appeal* was mailed out to interested parties, it was confiscated and burned in a South Carolina post office. Publication of their work gained more attention and in 1837, Sarah and Angelina began a 23-week tour throughout the Northeast, including New York, Pennsylvania, Rhode Island, and Massachusetts. The sisters paid for the tour themselves and visited 67 cities in the region. Although many were inspired by their antislavery sentiment, others were shocked that women had the audacity to speak in public. From those who favored their message, the sisters collected over 10,000 signatures, calling for immediate emancipation of the slaves; in 1838, Angelina became the first woman ever to appear before the Massachusetts legislature to present their petition.

By the end of 1837, the focus of their presentations was twofold, slavery and women's rights. Sarah Grimké compared the existence of two systems of oppression, one for blacks and one for women. She was the first to define slavery as having no legal recourse, no access to education, no independent income, and no control over basic lifestyle decisions. She argued, furthermore, that white women were denied these same freedoms that were denied to enslaved African Americans.

As a consequence of her views, Quakers closed their meeting houses to the sisters, their posters were ripped down, and they suffered constant verbal abuse and threats of violence. Under attack from the public and the pulpit, Sarah Grimké fought back, scheduling meetings in barns or wherever else she could gather a crowd, and growing more convinced that her position was correct and her defense of it was the right thing to do.

Ten years before the first women's rights convention was held in Seneca Falls, New York, Sarah Grimké published *Letters on the Equality of the Sexes* (1838), the first women's rights book by an American. The treatise offered her theory on the link between slavery and the subjugation of women and forecast many of the beliefs of the modern women's movement. She called for immediate emancipation of both blacks and women, defiance, and, if necessary, revolution. Shortly after publication of the work, the Grimké sisters were denounced by the Congregational Clergy of New England. The Reverend Nehemiah Adams issued a "Pastoral Letter" to be read from pulpits throughout the region, calling Sarah "unnatural," noting that she had brought "shame and dishonor" to her gender and forbidding church members to attend her speeches. Sarah responded with a series of articles in the *Boston Spectator* comparing the attitude of the church to the witch trials in early American history and countering their arguments point by point.

In 1838, Angelina married her former speaking coach, Theodore Weld. Weld encouraged Angelina to avoid emphasizing women's rights in order to concentrate on antislavery but Sarah continued to accept speaking engagements on both topics. To counteract what he considered a split in attention to the issues, Weld attacked Sarah's ability to present herself well in front of a group. Between her undermined self-confidence and the ironic prejudice from the Anti-Slavery Society over her double allegiances, she resigned from the speaker's podium and moved in with her sister and her husband. For a while, the three operated a school in Eagleswood, New Jersey, and Sarah published a translated biography of Joan of Arc to offer inspiration to other women. They agreed to board two freed slaves whom they discovered were sons of one of their brothers, fathered on the South Carolina plantation. One of the young men, Archibald Grimké, became the first black student to graduate from Harvard Law School; while the other, Francis, attended the Princeton Theological Seminary and later married teacher and reformer Charlotte Forten.

Reprinting collected newspaper editorials from Southern papers, Sarah Grimké, Angelina Grimké Weld, and Theodore Weld produced *American Slavery as It Is: Testimony of 1000 Witnesses* in 1839. Considered the most important antislavery document then published, the work sold over a hundred thousand copies and became the basis for *Uncle Tom's Cabin,* written in 1852, by Harriet Beecher Stowe. Although she continued to pursue her own writing, Sarah Grimké also became an agent for John Stuart Mill's *The Subjection of Women* (1869), his treatise revealing that the life of women under the law was worse than that of slaves in some countries. Sarah sold the copies from door to door and donated the money to a woman suffrage journal.

After the Civil War, Sarah Grimké and the Welds moved to Hyde Park, a section of Boston, where they opened a coeducational school. On March 7, 1870, when she was 79 years old, Grimké led a procession through a blizzard to the local polling place. She argued that since the Fourteenth Amendment, passed in 1868, granted the equal rights to all citizens, she, as a citizen, should be able to vote as well. Although she was not allowed to enter her ballot, and although she and the other 43 women were attacked in route, she was not arrested because of her age. She continued to campaign for equal rights until her death on December 23, 1873.

Joyce D. Duncan

See Also: Abolitionism and the Antislavery Movement; Garrison, William Lloyd; Grimké, Charlotte L. Forten; Grimké Weld, Angelina; *Letters on the Equality of the Sexes*; *The Liberator*; Mott, Lucretia; Quakers; Slavery and the Civil War

Primary Documents: 1837, Massachusetts Churches Respond to Grimké Sisters Speaking in Public; 1838, *Letters on the Equality of the Sexes*

Further Reading

Bartlett, Elizabeth Ann. *Liberty, Equality, Sorority: The Origins and Interpretation of American Feminist Thought: Frances Wright, Sarah Grimké, and Margaret Fuller.* Brooklyn, NY: Carlson Publishing, 1994.

Lerner, Gerda. *The Feminist Thought of Sarah Grimké.* New York: Oxford University Press, 1998.

Lerner, Gerda. *The Grimké Sisters from South Carolina: Pioneers for Women's Rights and Abolition.* New York: Oxford University Press, 1998.

Perry, Mark. *Lift Up Thy Voice: The Grimké Family's Journey from Slaveholders to Civil Rights Activists.* New York: Viking Penguin, 2001.

Grimké Weld, Angelina (1805–1879)

Angelina Grimké Weld was one of the first women public speakers in the United States. Although her public career spanned less than a decade, her status as a female orator and her contribution to abolitionism and women's rights are widely acknowledged. She was the daughter of John Grimké, a wealthy South Carolina judge and plantation owner, and the younger sister of abolitionist and women's rights advocate Sarah Grimké. Although Angelina had little formal education, the Grimké family encouraged intellectual pursuits; the children had access to the family library, read widely, and engaged in discussions of law, politics, philosophy, and history. Angelina Grimké continued to educate herself throughout her life.

At a young age, Angelina Grimké became convinced that slavery was evil, a belief that put her at odds with her family and the southern society in which she lived. She was also unusually religious for a young woman of her time. Born into an Episcopalian family, she was converted in the revivalistic wave of the early 19th century and became a Presbyterian. She followed her sister Sarah Grimké into the Quaker faith but was excommunicated for marrying outside the church. Later in life, she held no formal church membership but continued to devote much time to reading and interpreting the Bible.

When Judge Grimké fell ill and needed medical treatment, Sarah Grimké accompanied her father to Philadelphia. She later decided to settle permanently in the North and encouraged her younger sister to join here there. Angelina Grimké left the South in 1829 at the age of 24. She eagerly absorbed the abolitionist teachings popular in Quaker circles. Her private convictions became public knowledge when a letter she wrote to William Lloyd Garrison was published in his anti-slavery journal, *The Liberator.* The letter attracted the attention of many in the abolitionist movement. Among the readers was Theodore Weld, the abolitionist orator, who invited Grimké to become one of his antislavery agents.

Although she was horrified at the publicity generated by the appearance of her letter, Grimké felt she must do whatever she could to aid the abolitionist efforts. Thus, the two Grimké sisters began writing and speaking of their firsthand experiences with the system of slavery and recruiting women to the work of abolitionism. Together they lectured throughout New England in 1837 and early 1838. During this period, the sisters also wrote prolifically on both abolitionism and woman's role in social reform. Angelina Grimké authored *Appeal to the Christian Women of the South* (1836), a tract that laid out her challenge to southern women. This was followed by *Appeal to the Women of the Nominally Free States* (1837), Grimké's address to the Anti-Slavery Convention of American Women. Meanwhile, Catharine Ward Beecher published a series of letters opposing the sisters' public performances as an unsuitable activity for women. Angelina Grimké responded to Beecher in *Letters to Catharine E. Beecher* (1838). Both sisters began to formulate ideas for a tract on women's rights, but Sarah Grimké completed and published *Letters on the Equality of the Sexes* (1838).

In her *Appeal to Women of the Nominally Free States,* Angelina Grimké argued that slaves are human beings and women are human beings. Therefore, both should immediately be accorded all the rights and privileges guaranteed by the Creator and the state. She refused to base her appeal for women's rights on the commonly accepted idea that woman's moral character and moral duty were different than man's. She wrote:

> We have hitherto addressed you more as moral and responsible beings, than in the distinctive character of women; we have appealed to you on the broad ground of *human rights* and human responsibilities, rather than on that of your peculiar duties as women. . . . *All moral beings have essentially the same rights and the same duties,* whether they be male or female. This is a truth the world has yet to learn.

She wrote that she considered women's rights part of the "great doctrine of human rights," and thus a natural and necessary extension of the abolitionist cause. She felt that "it must be discussed whether there is such a thing as *male and female virtue and male and female duties* etc. My opinion is that there *are none* and that this false idea has driven the plowshare of ruin over the whole field of morality."

Although Frances Wright and Maria Stewart preceded her to the public platform, Angelina Grimké was a groundbreaker in women's oratory who inspired others to follow her example. Abby Kelley Foster and Lucy Stone, among others, found in her the impetus for their own public careers. Her character was above reproach by the standards of the time, her appearance and demeanor were "ladylike" enough to deflect the sort of criticism leveled at Wright, while the cause for which she served, the abolition of slavery, was an issue of national concern, raising her above accusations of selfish publicity seeking. Having recruited Grimké, Theodore Weld trained her as one of his 70 antislavery agents, the only woman among the group. Her firsthand experience

as a southern eyewitness to the system of slavery enhanced her credibility as an abolitionist speaker with northern audiences.

Grimké and her sister began their public careers in 1837, meeting informally with women in homes but soon lecturing to audiences of women engaged in social reform. In a tour of Massachusetts, supported by the Boston Female Anti-Slavery Society, they found much encouragement from both male and female abolitionists. Their first formal public lecture was delivered before a meeting of that organization. As the sisters' fame grew, men began filtering into their audiences, and they soon found themselves lecturing to mixed groups. Writing to her friend, Jane Smith, in 1837, Grimké told of her reaction on finding a man in the audience: "so there he sat and somehow I did not feel his presence at all embarrassing and went on just as tho' he was not there." In Lynn, Massachusetts, the sisters addressed their first "promiscuous" audience of about 1,000 men and women and also encountered similarly mixed audiences at Salem and Amesbury. At the latter location, they engaged in a well-attended public debate with two young men who had recently visited the South. The Grimkés reportedly "demolished" their opponents. At Lowell their audience was estimated at 1,500 persons of both sexes, including a large number of mill girls.

Angelina Grimké married Theodore Weld in 1838, a few days before her last public lecture. Weld was a major force in the evangelical branch of the abolitionist movement and Grimké's mentor in her public activities. He encouraged the sisters to lecture, tutored them in abolitionist principles, and trained them in the art of public speaking. Weld was not opposed to women's rights but firmly believed the issue should not be intruded into the abolitionist cause. As their convictions on the subject grew, however, the sisters found it difficult to confine their public remarks to abolitionism. They believed abolitionism and women's rights were fundamentally related, being based on the same moral and political principles.

Her disagreement with Weld certainly was one reason for Grimké Weld's retirement from public lecturing following her marriage, although there are no indications that she intended her silence to be permanent. Initially, marriage provided her an excuse to rest and recover from an extremely arduous travel schedule. The sisters (the newlyweds had invited Sarah Grimké to live with them) plunged enthusiastically into a domestic routine. The Welds' first child was born in 1839, soon followed by three others. Grimké Weld's health remained fragile, which was another reason she did not return to public lecturing. In addition, the Welds were deeply disturbed by the factions that had arisen among abolitionists and withdrew rather than take sides on a number of issues. Although she collaborated with her husband on *American Slavery As It Is* shortly after her marriage, Grimké Weld did not lecture or write extensively after 1838. However, her correspondence indicates that she remained committed to both the abolition of slavery and women's rights. Angelina Grimké Weld died in 1879 at the age of 74.

Phyllis M. Japp

See Also: Abolitionism and the Antislavery Movement; Beecher, Catharine; Garrison, William Lloyd; Grimké, Sarah Moore; *Letters on the Equality of the Sexes*; Quakers; Slavery and the Civil War

Primary Documents: 1836, Letter to Catharine Beecher; 1837, Massachusetts Churches Respond to Grimké Sisters Speaking in Public

Further Reading

Abzug, Robert H. *Passionate Liberator: Theodore Dwight Weld and the Dilemma of Reform.* New York: Oxford University Press, 1980.

Browne, Stephen Howard. *Angelina Grimké: Rhetoric, Identity, and the Radical Imagination.* East Lansing: Michigan State University Press, 1999.

Ginzburg, Lori D. *Women and the Work of Benevolence: Morality, Politics, and Class in the Nineteenth-Century United States.* New Haven, CT: Yale University Press, 1990.

Lerner, Gerda. *The Grimké Sisters from South Carolina: Pioneers for Women's Rights and Abolition.* New York: Oxford University Press, 1998.

Yellin, Jean Fagan. *Women & Sisters: The Antislavery Feminists in American Culture.* New Haven, CT: Yale University Press, 1989.

Hale, Sarah Josepha (1788–1879)

Sarah Josepha was born on October 24, 1788, the third child of Gordon and Martha Whittlesey Buell. That was the year George Washington assumed the presidency of the new United States. Sarah was educated at home, in Newport, New Hampshire, with her older brothers Charles and Horatio. When Horatio went off to Dartmouth, he shared his notes and texts with Sarah, thus affording her more education than most women of her time. She conducted a dame school for six years until her marriage to David Hale in 1813.

An ambitious lawyer and a Freemason, Hale encouraged Sarah to continue her studies and to write. Several of her poems were published by *The New Hampshire Spectator,* Newport's weekly newspaper. Sarah Hale bore five children during her happy nine-year marriage. David died suddenly, in 1822, and Sarah tried the millinery trade to support herself and her children while continuing to write stories and poems. David's Freemason lodge paid for the publication of Sarah Hale's first book of poems, *The Genius of Oblivion and Other Original Poems* (1823). Although not a critical success, the book sold well, allowing Hale to write full-time. *The Atlantic Monthly, The Literary Gazette,* and *The Spectator and Ladies' Album* published her poems and stories. She submitted winning entries to several poetry contests. In 1826, *The Spectator and Ladies' Album* published 17 of Hale's poems, two short stories, and one literary review. Four other poems appeared in the fashionable gift book, *The Memorial,* in 1827. Hale's novel, *Northwood,* was published that same year to enthusiastic reviews launching her national literary career.

John Lauris Blake invited her to edit his new publication, *The Ladies' Magazine.* Although she tried editing the journal from Newport, she had to move to Boston to continue her work. Hale envisioned a magazine containing only well-written, original materials. She particularly encouraged women authors to submit their writings. Desire for originality forced Hale to write many of the stories and poems for the first issues of the magazine herself. Later contributors included Lydia Sigourney, Elmira Hunt, and Sarah Whitman.

Hale's magazine encouraged the education of women, published American authors writing about American scenes and themes, and promoted the good works of its readers. *The Ladies' Magazine* supported the Perkins School, the first school for the blind; organized a mammoth fair that raised the funds to complete the Bunker Hill Monument; founded the Seaman's Aid Society; and promoted a school for the children of poor working women.

In 1830, Marshall Lowell, a composer and a friend of Hale's, asked her to write verses for children, which he then set to music, thus making them easy to learn and remember. *Poems for Our Children* (1830) were metrically regular poems with a different moral message as the theme of each one. "Mary Had a Little Lamb" was one of these poems.

Although Hale supported poor women who had to work, she publicly espoused the notion that men and women belonged in separate spheres of influence and that women, the morally purer of the two sexes, would be polluted by entering into the public sphere that men inhabited. In the February 1832 issue of *The Ladies' Magazine,* she opined, "I consider every attempt to induce women to think they have a right to participate in the public duties of government as injurious to their best interests and derogatory to their character. Our empire is purer, more excellent and spiritual." She reiterated this theme in the encyclopedic *Woman's Record; or Sketches of All Distinguished Women from "The Beginning" till A.D. 1850* (published in 1853 with revised editions in 1855 and 1876).

Louis Godey's *Lady's Book* and *The Ladies' Magazine* merged in 1836. Hale and Godey made the new magazine, which kept the name *Lady's Book,* the most influential and most widely circulated periodical of its era. The magazine's hand-tinted fashion plates and sentimental poems and stories raised the number of subscribers to 150,000 just prior to the Civil War. In 1841 Hale moved to Philadelphia to be close to the publisher of *Godey's Lady's Book.*

During the 1840s and 1850s, Hale championed daily bathing; psychologically sound childrearing practices; playgrounds for city children; the career of the first female doctor, Elizabeth Blackwell; healthful clothing

Sarah Josepha Hale was the highly influential editor of *Godey's Lady's Book*, the most popular magazine of the 19th century. (Library of Congress)

styles for women; and the rehabilitation of Washington's home at Mt. Vernon, which became a national monument. She advised Matthew Vassar on the creation of Vassar College and lobbied the college's trustees to hire female faculty members. In 1863, Hale encouraged President Lincoln to declare the third Thursday of November to be a day of national thanksgiving.

When arguments concerning slavery rent the Union, Hale published *Northwood* (1852), reminding abolitionists in her introduction that "the master is their brother as well as the servant." Her novel *Liberia* (1853) makes the case for educating slaves before their liberation and subsequent repatriation in Liberia. Both novels dealt with the differences in life and industry between the northern and southern states and the question of slavery. She supported education and liberation of slaves and their repatriation in Africa.

Hale supported Godey's policy that forbid political or religious issues from appearing in the pages of their magazine. Believing that women at home wielded moral suasion, which would help to end the war, she elided

her conservative social ideology and editorially neutral position in the wartime pages of the *Lady's Book*. She promoted the moral education of children, which she believed was a mother's most important task. Her etiquette, homemaking, and recipe books also demonstrate her interest in making women's work at home more scientific and more praiseworthy. In December 1877, Hale retired from *Godey's Lady's Book*.

Contemporary scholarship questions whether Hale was a proto-feminist, through the example of her own life, or a negative influence due to her conviction that separate spheres for the sexes were divinely ordained. While early biographers argued that Hale was the consummate feminist, later feminist biographers agree that Hale's ideology marked her as an adherent of Victorian womanhood that sought to keep women out of the public realms of politics, commerce, and ideas. Hale's strong antisuffrage rhetoric is also seen as evidence of her valorization of an ideology that limited, rather than liberated, her loyal female readers.

Aleta Cane

See Also: Bloomer, Amelia Jenks; Davis, Paulina Kellogg Wright; Education of Women (before the Civil War); *Godey's Lady's Book*

Primary Document: 1856–1857, Writings on Women's Education

Further Reading

Douglas, Ann. *The Feminization of American Culture.* New York: Alfred A. Knopf, 1977.

Okker, Patricia. *Our Sister Editors: Sarah J. Hale and the Tradition of Nineteenth Century American Women Editors.* Athens: University of Georgia Press, 1995.

Rogers, Sherbrooke. *Sarah Josepha Hale: A New England Pioneer 1788–1879.* Grantham, NH: Tompson and Rutter, 1985.

Tonkovich, Nicole. *Domesticity with a Difference: The Nonfiction of Catharine Beecher, Sarah J. Hale, Fanny Fern, and Margaret Fuller.* Jackson: University Press of Mississippi, 1997.

Hasbrouck, Lydia Sayer (1827–1910)

Lydia Sayer Hasbrouck is not often acknowledged in histories of the 19th-century women's rights movement, but her work as a physician, health reformer, dress reformer, and editor of the newspaper, *The Sybil*, advanced the cause alongside her more well-known colleagues.

Lydia Sayer was born in Warwick, New York, in 1827. Her father was a wealthy farmer and apple brandy distiller. She was formally educated beyond the high school level, attending New York Central College, one of the few colleges that admitted both women and African Americans before the Civil War. She had been denied admission to another school, Seward Seminary, a decision she believed was due to her wearing the new reform costume of a knee-length skirt and baggy trousers underneath. Like several other politically active New York women, such as Amelia Jenks Bloomer and Elizabeth Cady Stanton, Sayer began wearing the new costume in 1849. Sayer later resented the fact that the introduction of the reform dress was so quickly credited to Amelia Bloomer and thereafter referred to as the "bloomers" costume.

Interested in a medical career, in the 1850s she took courses at the Hygeio-Therapeutic College in New York City, where she was trained in and subsequently practiced hydropathy, or the water-cure treatment. She befriended other female doctors, such as Mary Edwards Walker (who later received a Medal of Honor for her service during the Civil War), and Sayer embarked on a lecturing tour through several eastern cities before returning to Middletown, New York, in 1856 to begin editing and publication of a dress reform and women's rights newspaper, *The Sibyl: A Review of the Tastes, Errors and Fashions of Society.* The newspaper was a joint project with John Whitbeck Hasbrouck, publisher of the local *Whig Press.* Lydia Sayer and John Hasbrouck were married in July 1856, the same month that the first issue of *The Sibyl* appeared. Lydia Hasbrouck reportedly wore the reform costume in all white for her wedding ceremony.

Lydia Sayer Hasbrouck edited *The Sibyl* until 1864. The paper primarily focused on the issue of dress reform (and she herself continued to wear the bloomer costume long after other women's rights activists had given up the issue), but *The Sibyl* was also a forum for other reform issues such as women's education, health reform, temperance, and women's suffrage. Hasbrouck served as president of the National Dress Reform Association in 1863–1864. After the demise of *The Sibyl,* Hasbrouck continued to work with her husband on editing and publishing political newspapers and, in 1880, she was one of the first women elected to public office in New York when she was elected to the local board of education in Middletown. She died in 1910.

Tiffany K. Wayne

See Also: Bloomer, Amelia Jenks; Dress Reform; *The Sibyl*; Walker, Mary Edwards; Stanton, Elizabeth Cady (Vol. 2)

Further Reading

Cunningham, Patricia A. *Reforming Women's Fashion, 1850–1920: Politics, Health, and Art.* Kent, OH: Kent State University Press, 2003.

Fischer, Gayle V. *Pantaloons and Power: Nineteenth-Century Dress Reform in the Untied States.* Kent, OH: Kent State University Press, 2001.

Mattingly, Carol. *Appropriate[ing] Dress: Women's Rhetorical Style Women's in Nineteenth-Century America.* Carbondale: Southern Illinois University Press, 2002.

Higginson, Thomas Wentworth (1823–1911)

Unitarian minister, radical abolitionist, social reformer, orator, and writer, Thomas Wentworth Higginson was the consummate 19th-century intellectual whose ideas and theories compelled him to a life of militant social activism. In the years following his graduation from Harvard College in 1841, Higginson was intrigued by the possibility of study at Harvard's Divinity School yet doubted his vocation for the ministry. Through his increasing involvement in several social reform movements, including temperance, antislavery, and women's rights, he discovered his immense attraction to the social activism of liberal Unitarian clergymen Theodore Parker and William Henry Channing. Thus inspired, he enrolled in Harvard Divinity School to prepare for a ministry in which he would exhort his congregants to follow him in missions of committed social reform. He was also a correspondent with and friend of Emily Dickinson. After her death, he promoted and edited Dickinson's poetry.

Higginson served as pastor of the First Religious Society in Newburyport, Massachusetts, from 1847 to 1849 and as minister of the Free Church in Worcester, Massachusetts, from 1851 to 1861. In 1850, he made an unsuccessful bid for Congress as a Free Soil Party candidate but eventually withdrew from that party's politics because of a deeper personal commitment to the principles of disunionism, believing that dissolution of the Union was the only way to extract slavery permanently from the lives and consciousness of Northerners.

In 1851, Higginson conceived a plan to free the fugitive slave Thomas Sims, who was incarcerated in Boston, and although the plot failed and Sims was returned to slavery, the incident confirmed for Higginson the necessity of concerted militant action against a government responsible for upholding the evil institution of slaveholding. In 1854, Higginson and several other abolitionists devised a plan to free the fugitive Anthony Burns. This attempt also failed and resulted in Higginson's arrest and a facial wound. Higginson found that the more he engaged in "forcible resistance," the more convinced he became of its necessity and the more he sought its opportunities.

Following the passage of the Kansas–Nebraska Act, also in 1854, Higginson became the New England agent for the Massachusetts Kansas Committee, the militant branch of the New England Emigrant Aid Society, an organization that actively supported the settlement of free-state emigrants in Kansas. In that capacity, Higginson made two trips to Kansas and also purchased arms and ammunition to help free-state settlers defend their settlements against attacks by proslavery forces.

In 1857, Higginson became one of the group of six abolitionists, all members of the Massachusetts Kansas Committee, who collaborated to provide John Brown with funds to stop proslavery forces in Kansas and who helped subsidize John Brown's raid on Harpers Ferry. The "secret six"—which besides Higginson included Samuel Gridley Howe, Theodore Parker, Frank Sanborn, Gerrit Smith, and George Luther Stearns—provided funding, arms, and other supplies Brown required to execute his plan. Higginson fervently believed that participation in an insurrection would prepare enslaved African Americans to assume independent lives in a democratic society. Higginson also favored Brown's plan because he was convinced of the need to destroy the belief among Northerners that all slaves were docile and submissive.

After the raid's failure and Brown's capture, Higginson's colleagues panicked and frantically destroyed evidence of their involvement. Higginson neither destroyed his records nor denied his role but instead dedicated himself to raising money for Brown's defense and developing a plot to free Brown from captivity. Although these efforts were unsuccessful, Higginson was more disturbed by the failure of Brown's raid to trigger a massive slave insurrection that would break Southern slaveowners. From this point on, Higginson realized that only unified action by Northern whites could destroy slavery.

Higginson welcomed the outbreak of hostilities that began the American Civil War. In November 1861, the governor of Massachusetts authorized him to raise a regiment, which he filled by August 1862. In November 1862, Higginson eagerly accepted an appointment as colonel of the first all-black regiment in the Union army, the First South Carolina Volunteers, which was composed entirely of freed slaves. He enthusiastically trained the recruits, then sought skirmishes with the enemy as a means of giving his men the opportunity to exercise, display, and prove their valor. In 1864, persistent ill health brought on by a leg wound and malaria forced Higginson to resign his post and return to civilian life.

Although Higginson became briefly involved in supporting radical reconstruction after the war, including full citizenship and enfranchisement for freedmen, he soon recognized that his decades of radical militancy had passed. He wrote to Ralph Waldo Emerson of his new longing to be "an artist . . . lured by the joy of expression itself." By 1867, Higginson had devoted himself to writing, prolifically producing essays, literary criticism, fiction, and the memoir *Army Life in a Black Regiment* (1870). He remained an ardent supporter of women's rights and woman suffrage, and with fellow former abolitionists Lucy Stone and Henry Blackwell, he edited *The Woman's Journal* from 1870 to 1884. In 1884 he published an early biography of Transcendentalist and feminist Margaret Fuller Ossoli.

Judith E. Harper

See Also: Abolitionism and the Antislavery Movement; Fuller, Margaret; Slavery and the Civil War; Stone, Lucy; Blackwell, Henry Brown (Vol. 2); *The Woman's Journal* (Vol. 2)

Further Reading

Edelstein, Tilden G. *Strange Enthusiasm: A Life of Thomas Wentworth Higginson.* New Haven, CT: Yale University Press, 1968.

Meyer, Howard N., ed. *The Magnificent Activist: The Writings of Thomas Wentworth Higginson (1823–1911).* Cambridge: Da Capo Press, 2000.

Renehan, Edward J., Jr. *The Secret Six: The True Tale of the Men Who Conspired with John Brown.* New York: Crown, 1995.

Smith, John David, ed. *Black Soldiers in Blue: African American Troops in the Civil War Era.* Chapel Hill: University of North Carolina Press, 2002.

Wineapple, Brenda. *White Heat: The Friendship of Emily Dickinson and Thomas Wentworth Higginson.* New York: Alfred A. Knopf, 2009.

Howe, Julia Ward (1819–1910)

The abolitionist, women's rights campaigner, and advocate of prison reform Julia Ward Howe was also one of the leaders of the women's international peace

Julia Ward Howe was a prominent reformer in the abolitionist and women's rights movement, but is perhaps best known as the author of "The Battle Hymn of the Republic," one of the great rallying songs of the Civil War era. (Miller, Francis Trevelyan and Robert Sampson Lanier. *The Photographic History of the Civil War*, 1911)

movement. As a woman of deep religious faith and author of "The Battle Hymn of the Republic," she also supported women's religious ordination and was an unofficial lay preacher.

The daughter of a wealthy banker, Julia Ward was educated by governesses and at private schools until she was 16, studying Latin, Greek, French, German, and Italian and the social graces of singing and piano playing. Romantic and impressionable, she read the novels of George Sand, Honoré de Balzac, and the German Romantic poet Johann Wolfgang von Goethe. She reached marriageable age beautiful, wealthy, and accomplished but disappointed her guardians (her mother and father were dead) by marrying a man 20 years her senior, Samuel Gridley Howe, a reformer, teacher, and director of the New England Asylum for the Blind.

Julia Ward Howe spent most of her life in south Boston after enjoying a honeymoon in Europe and meeting

Charles Dickens, Thomas Carlyle, and William Wordsworth in London. On the voyage home, she met Florence Nightingale and was so impressed that she named her second child after her. Isolated at home with, eventually, five children, Howe began writing plays and poetry and continued with her self-study of languages and philosophy. The family home, meanwhile, had become a meeting place for local abolitionists, but her husband refused Howe any active role in the movement. In 1853 he briefly allowed her to help edit his antislavery journal, *The Commonwealth;* mindful of his reservations about her work and his dismissive attitude toward her literary gifts, she published her first volume of poetry, *Passion Flowers,* anonymously in 1854. In 20 years of marriage, Samuel Howe never acknowledged any of Julia's many accomplishments, a fact that led to their increasing alienation until his death in 1876.

During the Civil War, the Howes visited Washington, D.C., where after the Battle of Bull Run, Julia witnessed Union troops being reviewed by General George McClellan at a camp near the Potomac River in November 1861. It was here that she heard soldiers singing "John Brown's Body," the popular wartime song set to a traditional folk song. Howe's husband had been a supporter of John Brown, and Julia, as a poet, wanted to honor his memory. She did so in song, inspired by her religious feelings to write what she felt were more appropriate, respectful lyrics to fit the haunting melody she had heard the soldiers singing. The "Battle Hymn of the Republic" was written by her in her room at the Willard Hotel in Washington, and published in February 1862 in the *Atlantic Monthly.* She may have only been paid four or five dollars for it, but the song's enduring popularity in the United States ensured Howe's subsequent fame when she was in her forties.

At the end of the Civil War and after the emancipation of the slaves, Howe turned her attentions to the growing women's rights campaign. After the death of her son in 1868, she attempted to dissipate her grief by throwing herself into religious and philosophical study—of Immanuel Kant, Johann Fichte, G. W. F. Hegel, and Baruch Spinoza—and giving public lectures on social ethics, in the 1870s addressing such bodies as the Boston Radical Club and the Concord School of Philosophy. With Lucy Stone, she founded the New England Women's Club in 1868, initially a loose network of study clubs in which women could take literacy classes and which also offered community libraries, playgrounds, and child care facilities and lobbied for women's education and strengthening of their rights over their property and children. The society also donated funds to run holiday schools for children and provided bursaries for students of academic promise. Howe's work for women's clubs, as president of the society almost uninterruptedly from 1871 to 1910, would also involve her in the establishment of the Association for the Advancement of Women and the General Federation of Women's Clubs, which would eventually boast 2 million members.

After the split in the women's suffrage movement in 1869, Howe, already president of the moderate New England Woman Suffrage Association (1868–1877, 1893–1910), became a founder with Lucy Stone of the American Woman Suffrage Association and for 20 years edited *The Woman's Journal*. During 1870–1878 and 1891–1893, she was also president of the Massachusetts Woman Suffrage Association. In 1878 she attended the first international women's rights congress held in Paris, France.

As an ardent pacifist, Julia Ward Howe was one of the first women in the United States to elaborate on the idea of an international network of peace activists. In 1870 she published an "Appeal to Womanhood throughout the World," exhorting women to come together and hold a conference to set up international cooperation and peace mediation to avert future wars. Horrified by the carnage of the Franco-Prussian War in Europe (1870–1871), she lent further support to the idea of an international women's peace movement as president of the U.S. branch of Marie Goegg's International Association of Women from 1871. She visited England in 1872 in hopes of organizing a women's peace conference there, but when this failed to materialize, Howe had to accept the difficulty for women of coming together from many countries for such a conference. She suggested instead the founding of a Woman's Peace Party in the United States, supported by national branches and the inauguration of June 2nd as a women's international peace day; it was not until 1915, however, after Howe's death, that a Woman's Peace Party was established in the United States and the International Committee of Women for Permanent Peace was established in The Hague. Howe's international sympathies and interests were also reflected in her 1891 foundation of the American Friends of Russian Freedom and her presidency, from 1894, of the United Friends of Armenia.

Howe was a devout Unitarian and believed in women's ability and right to be ordained as ministers. She became an unofficial lay minister, giving sermons wherever the opportunity arose, mainly in Unitarian and Universalist churches, beginning in 1870. In 1873 she initiated the first of annual private conventions of women preachers at her home, providing such women with an opportunity to be mutually self-supporting.

Howe continued writing into her old age, in 1895 producing a work of social criticism (*Is Polite Society Polite?*) in which she criticized contemporary cultural values. She promoted the work of her feminist precursor Margaret Fuller, writing a biography, *Margaret Fuller* (1883), and editing *The Love-Letters of Margaret Fuller, 1845–1846* (1903). Howe's own *Reminiscences, 1819–1899* appeared in 1900. She was awarded three honorary doctorates, and in 1908 she was the first woman elected to the American Academy of Arts and Letters. Howe was also one of the first to address women's capacity for academic study, in her *Sex and Education* (1874), in which she argued for coeducation.

By the time she died at the age of 91, Julia Ward Howe was revered as the "Dearest Old Lady in America," and the images of her in old age, sitting demurely in her lace cap, testify to that perception of her. At her memorial service in 1910, the voices of 4,000 mourners were raised in singing "The Battle Hymn of the Republic." Although the public affection for the woman who wrote the unofficial national anthem of the United States endured, the memory of her work in support of many social issues receded into the background.

Helen Rappaport

See Also: Abolitionism and the Antislavery Movement; Fuller, Margaret; Stone, Lucy; American Woman Suffrage Association (Vol. 2); Education of Women (after the Civil War) (Vol. 2); *The Woman's Journal* (Vol. 2); Woman's Peace Party (Vol. 2)

Further Reading

Clifford, Deborah. *Mine Eyes Have Seen the Glory: A Biography of Julia Ward Howe*. Boston: Little, Brown, 1979.

Grant, Mary H. *Private Woman, Public Person: An Account of the Life of Julia Ward Howe from 1819 to 1868*. Brooklyn, NY: Carlson Publishing, 1994.

Williams, Gary J. *The Hungry Heart: The Literary Emergence of Julia Ward Howe*. Amherst: University of Massachusetts Press, 1999.

Ziegler, Valarie H. *Diva Julia: The Public Romance and Private Agony of Julia Ward Howe*. Harrisburg, PA: Trinity Press/Continuum Publishing, 2003.

Infanticide

Single women who gave birth to an illegitimate child in early America faced appalling consequences. Such women were often publicly shamed through whippings or time in the stocks. Living in small communities where there was little place to hide from a checkered past, the woman's reputation was ruined for life. Her odds of marriage dropped, and unless she had the support of a well-to-do and sympathetic family, she was likely to face a life of extreme poverty and isolation.

Early Americans had little means for controlling pregnancy. There was no reliable form of contraception other than breastfeeding, which was obviously not an option for young, single women. Methods of abortion were primitive and generally ineffective, leaving unmarried pregnant women with few choices but to carry the baby to term. Paralyzed with fear and unwilling to face the bleak repercussions of bearing a bastard, some women hid their pregnancies as long as possible. Although many women's pregnancies were discovered and means for supporting the child were found, some were successful in carrying and delivering their children in secret. At this point they had only three options. Some fell upon the mercy of their employer, parents, or lover in looking for assistance. Some abandoned the infant in a place where it was likely to be discovered and cared for. Others concealed the birth through infanticide, usually by abandoning the child in the woods or drowning it.

When the body of a dead newborn was found, it was almost impossible to determine if it had been born dead, died of natural means, or had been killed through violence or neglect. A 1624 English law resolved this problem by declaring that any woman who concealed a birth would be assumed to have given birth to a live child unless she could conclusively prove otherwise. The law assumed that women who hid their pregnancies and gave birth in private were anxious to hide their sin from the community and were likely to have hostile intentions toward the infant. Women who concealed the birth of a child who subsequently died were to be sentenced to death. Most American colonies adopted the English law, and several women were hanged after the bodies of their newborn infants had been discovered.

Most women charged with infanticide were poor, single women. Many of them were indentured servants, who knew they would have one to three years added to their term of service if they gave birth to a child. Free women who were employed knew they were likely to lose their job, as a nursing mother was unlikely to keep apace with a normal workload. Few people wanted to be associated with a woman of dissolute character, and mistresses were likely to dismiss any servant girl who was guilty of fornication. Most women would have seen firsthand how unmarried mothers became social outcasts in their communities and knew their likelihood of ever marrying would plummet if they had a child. Pregnant single women could even be driven out of town as an undesirable. This was especially likely to happen if the town officials believed she lacked means of supporting herself and there was no family to either take her in or defend her. The severe social pressures that discouraged single motherhood might have been exacerbated by hormonal depressions and mood swings.

In the rare instances that a well-to-do defendant was charged with killing her newborn, juries were more likely to accept her version of events. Anne Tayloe was a wealthy planter's widow in 1714 when rumors began circulating she had given birth to a child, killed it, and buried it in her yard. There was strong evidence of her guilt, including the body of the child and eyewitness testimony from a servant and a slave who had seen Anne burying an object in the yard. Tayloe flatly denied having been pregnant, and she was ultimately released despite the strong evidence against her. Despite her economic status and legal good fortune, Tayloe's reputation never recovered, and she was subsequently brought to court for immoral behavior.

Infanticide was a woman's crime. Men were rarely charged, even when the paternity of the infant was known. In some cases an accused woman claimed the father of the child participated in the concealment or murder of the infant. In 1786, the bodies of twin babies were discovered in the Pennsylvania woods. Twenty-seven-year-old tavern maid Elizabeth Wilson was quickly identified as the mother, but pointed to the infants' father as the murderer. Wilson claimed that the father had stomped the children to death when she threatened to take him to court for child support. Wilson was hanged, but her lover was never apprehended or brought to trial. Many people were uncomfortable for sentencing Wilson to death when it appeared she was prepared to raise the children. There was sympathy for a woman who might have feared her lover's brutality could turn against her if she reported him.

In part because of the Elizabeth Wilson case, there was a shift in the attitudes toward concealed births in the late 1780s. Concealing a birth was viewed as a lack of judgment that should be punished in jail, not on the gallows. The burden of proof shifted, and the state had to prove the child had been born alive, rather than the mother proving it was born dead. A woman could help her case if she could prove she intended to care for the child, usually by having infant clothes and bedding prepared prior to delivery of the child. Following the American Revolution the role of mothers became romanticized, and it was difficult for juries to believe a woman would choose to harm her own child. Juries became more willing to accept a woman's story, so long as she expressed remorse and love for her infant.

Judging from the number of reports and the details relating to cases of abandoned or killed infants, it appears that people were fascinated with this topic. Babies found in wells, ponds, or abandoned in the woods were noted in local newspapers. If the mother had not yet been determined, the articles provided enough details of the infant's location and approximate date of birth in hopes of soliciting people with information. The confessions of young women after their convictions were often printed and distributed in town as a means of warning others of the folly young girls could be led into. Other stories focused on abandoned babies. It is clear some of these infants were cared for, wrapped carefully in clothing and left on doorsteps where they were sure to be found soon. One baby found in 1807 Philadelphia was "sewed up in a double blanket with a straw pillow under its head and a sugar teat in its mouth."

The cases of slave women who killed their children must be treated separately. There are a handful of cases in which slave women killed their children in the face of despair over their condition. In 1787 Spanish Florida, the slave woman Juana was informed she was to be sold to a new owner in Cuba, but her two children (five-year-old Juan and two-year-old Isabel) would remain in Florida. Juana drowned her children rather than see them be raised alone in a harsh environment, then attempted to flee. She was apprehended and found guilty of murder. Despite the horror of her crime, she was not sentenced to execution in accordance with homicide law, but rather received a severe flogging and sale to a new master. There was clearly a recognition that Juana acted not from attempt to cover her own illicit behavior, but rather out of despair. In 1856, Margaret Garner, an enslaved woman in Kentucky who attempted to flee with her husband and children to freedom in Ohio, murdered one of her children when they were confronted near Cincinnati by slave hunters and U.S. marshals, intent on returning them all to slavery. This event inspired part of the plot of Toni Morrison's 1987 Pulitzer Prize winning novel, *Beloved,* as well as the 2005 opera, *Margaret Garner.*

Dorothy A. Mays

See Also: Abortion (17th and 18th Centuries); Birth Control (17th and 18th Centuries); Legal Status of Women (18th Century); Slavery and the Civil War

Further Reading

Dayton, Cornelia Hughes. *Women before the Bar: Gender, Law, and Society in Connecticut, 1639–1789.* Chapel Hill: University of North Carolina Press, 1995.

Hine, Darlene Clark, and Kathleen Thompson. *A Shining Thread of Hope: The History of Black Women in America.* New York: Broadway Books, 1998.

Hoffer, Peter C., and N.E.H. Hull. *Murdering Mothers: Infanticide in England and New England, 1558–1803.* New York: New York University Press, 1981.

Hull, N.E.H. *Female Felons: Women and Serious Crime in Colonial Massachusetts.* Urbana: University of Illinois Press, 1987.

Smith, Merril D. "Unnatural Mothers: Infanticide, Motherhood, and Class in the Mid-Atlantic, 1730–1830." In *Over the Threshold: Intimate Violence in Early America,* edited by Christine Daniels and Michael V. Kennedy. New York: Routledge, 1999.

Weisenburger, Steven. *Modern Medea: A Family Story of Slavery and Child-Murder from the Old South.* New York: Hill and Wang, 1998.

Interracial Marriage and Sex (17th and 18th Centuries)

From the outset of the European colonization of America, there was close contact between Europeans, Native Americans, and Africans. Because the overwhelming majority of people coming from Europe and Africa were males, the skewed sex ratio created pressure to form unions with Indian women. Such a pattern was exceptionally strong in Latin America, where almost no Spanish women immigrated to the colonies. There was far less interracial mixing in North America, but it occurred with regularity until the sex ratio came into balance in the 18th century. The exception to this pattern was in the New England colonies, where Puritans encouraged immigration in family groups. A normal sex ratio, as well as a reluctance to intermingle with non-Christians, resulted in little sexual mingling among Europeans and Indians or African slaves. New England settlers were able to transplant their traditions to America with ease, unlike people in settlements in the middle and southern colonies. There, the unbalanced sex ratio, lack of family structure, and frontier conditions created an environment in which European men were willing to shed restrictive social norms.

One notable feature of interracial marriage and sex in North America was that it did not result in widespread acculturation and assimilation, as it did in Latin America. This might be because the sex ratio in the British colonies came into balance relatively quickly, which never occurred in the Spanish colonies.

During the earliest phases of settlement, both French and English authorities endorsed marriage between white men and Native American women. Recognizing the opportunity to improve relations with the Indians, the French government even offered dowries to settlers who married Indian women. French fur traders were especially eager to take Native wives. Sexual attraction and the need for human companionship, of course, played a role. Usually traveling alone deep into the American wilderness, European traders benefited in numerous ways from healthy relations with the Indians, including ensuring basic survival and securing access to hunting grounds. Native women likewise benefited from affiliation with a European. When a European trader married into an Indian community, he increased the prestige of the tribe. Access to trade and friendly relations with European settlements also benefited the entire tribe. Consequently, the woman married to the trader might assume increased authority and prestige within her tribe. The fur traders' wives rarely joined European communities, although they might learn French or English, possibly convert to Christianity, and interact with other Europeans at Jesuit missions. Native women often served as cultural mediators between Indian and European communities, although many women who married European men still clearly retained their native identity, language, dress, and customs.

Perhaps the most famous Indian-white marriage was that between Pocahontas and John Rolfe in 1614. Although it is likely that both partners had affection for one another, it was clearly a marriage motivated by political expediency. Requiring the permission of both the deputy governor of Virginia and the Indian king Powhatan, both sides wished to see an expansion of trade and a reduction in conflict between the settlers and Indians. During Pocahontas's lifetime these objectives were achieved, although they did not long survive her death.

The primary motivations for interracial mixing between Native Americans and English colonists were sex, military alliance, and trade. All of these objectives could be accomplished without marriage. Indian communities did not condemn women for premarital sexual relations, and alliances could be cemented without the formal bonds of marriage. Children born to such unions almost always remained within the Indian culture. Such children were fully embraced by Indians, but were tainted in the eyes of Europeans.

Few white women entered relationships with Native American men. The major exception was when women were captured and adopted into Indian communities. If a girl was captured while an adolescent or younger, there was a good chance that she would elect to remain with her new family, even when offered the opportunity to return to European civilization. Speculation about this curious phenomenon was rampant. Mary Jemison, taken captive in 1758, stated that by the time she was offered the opportunity to return she had a number of Indian children she did not believe would be warmly embraced by the English colonists. Other women reported they had formed loving ties to their new families and husbands. Some historians speculate that women might have found Indian culture, free of European restrictions, a more meaningful and untroubled way of life.

One of the few cases in which a white woman freely chose to marry an Indian occurred in 1740, when Molly Barber, the daughter of well-to-do Connecticut parents, eloped with James Chaugham, a Narraganset Indian. The couple fled to the rural area of Barkhamsted, where they created a small, mixed-race community known as "the Lighthouse." Stagecoach drivers dubbed the community the Lighthouse because the cracks in the inhabitant's cabin walls emitted firelight, guiding coaches along their way. For over a century, families of blacks, Indians, and whites found refuge at the Lighthouse.

After the European sex ratio came into a healthy balance in the 18th century due to increased emigration and natural increase among the colonists, unions with Indian women were stigmatized. Still envious of the excellent relations between the French and the Indians, American colonial authorities made a few halfhearted attempts to encourage English-Indian marriages. In 1784 Patrick Henry proposed a bill that would offer tax relief, free education, and a financial bonus to white men who married Indian women. This and similar bills were defeated, but they document the government's attempt to encourage marriage along such lines. Despite the wishes of the government, society was growing increasingly suspicious of interracial mingling, and both North Carolina and Virginia ultimately passed legislation outlawing Indian-European marriage.

Relations between Africans and Europeans were complex in early America. Most Africans were slaves imported into the southern colonies, where the unbalanced sex ratio resulted in sexual liaisons between slave owners and black women. Even after the sex ratio among Europeans came into balance, sexual contact between white men and black women continued unabated. Such liaisons rarely resulted in marriage, and little attempt was made to regulate these relationships.

During the earliest period of colonization, Africans brought to the colonies did not remain enslaved for the duration of their lives. Like white indentured servants, these Africans eventually earned their freedom after a predetermined number of years. The small community of free blacks occasionally chose to intermarry with whites, usually fellow indentured servants. Complications with such marriages arose after slavery became a lifelong condition. When a white woman chose to marry a black slave, the status of the children and the wife were ambiguous. In 1661, Maryland passed a law clearly intended to wipe out such ambiguities and discourage interracial marriage. Any white woman who married a slave was to become enslaved for the duration of her husband's life. Any children born to the marriage would be permanently enslaved. This law backfired when it became apparent that white masters were coercing their female indentured servants to marry slaves, so they might gain economic advantage by acquiring an additional slave, plus future child slaves. The law was modified in 1681 so that if a master consented to the union, the woman and her children would retain their free status.

Although there were social stigmas associated with black–white marriages, the flurry of laws prohibiting interracial marriage make it clear that such unions were occurring with enough frequency to call for legal constraint. Marriage between blacks and whites was outlawed in Virginia (1691), Massachusetts (1705), and Maryland (1715). Delaware, Pennsylvania, North Carolina, South Carolina, and Georgia all passed legislation that gradually prohibited interracial marriage in the 18th century.

Despite the infrequency of marriages between blacks and whites, the fact that there were numerous mulatto children indicated that sexual relations between the races had not ceased. Further laws were passed to punish interracial sexual activity. Any white woman who bore a mulatto child was fined, and in many cases the child would be bound out into a life of servitude until he or she reached the age of 30. Although treated more leniently, white men who fathered children of black slaves were also occasionally fined, and the children of such unions clearly remained slaves their entire lives. Curiously, the laws against interracial sex punished only the white partner. This was possibly an acknowledgment that slaves often had little choice in the relationship.

The greatest condemnation for interracial alliances was directed toward white women who willingly had relations with a black man. There was overwhelming concern with preserving the whiteness of the European race. White women who produced mulatto children were clearly a threat, whereas black women who did likewise were not viewed as endangering white racial purity.

Rules in the French colonies provided more protection for black women. The *Code Noir,* first passed in 1685, required that a man who fathered a child with a willing black woman should be punished with a fine of 2,000 pounds of sugar. If he was not married to another, he was required to marry the woman, and she and her children would be set free. A revision of the *Code Noir* in 1724 outlawed interracial marriages, although acceptance of biracial relationships remained far greater in French colonies than in British areas. Frenchmen often openly took black or mulatto mistresses and housed them in separate quarters. Such relationships were not condoned, but were tolerated.

There was substantial intermingling between Native Americans and Africans or African Americans in early America. Slaves who escaped often fled to the wilderness where they found refuge within Indian tribes. Such escaped slaves were almost always black men, because women were far more reluctant to flee and leave children and family behind.

Sex ratios in 18th-century Native communities tended to be badly skewed, with an overabundance of women. Colonial wars took such a heavy toll on the male Indian population that some Native communities had 50 percent more women than men. Because there was a preference for importing male slaves from Africa, the sex ratio in the black population was the inverse of the Indian imbalance. There were mutual advantages for Indian women who married black men. In most Indian communities, women performed all the agricultural work, food preparation, and other chores. Slave men had no such tradition, and their willingness to undertake manual labor might have been welcome among Indian women.

There is evidence that some Native women even purchased black male slaves before setting them free and marrying them.

There were many advantages for black men who married into an Indian community. Usually landless and penniless, they gained access to land and other resources. Native Americans were usually willing to fully accept newcomers regardless of their race. Former slaves therefore found a welcoming refuge from an otherwise predominantly hostile world. Although most mixed marriages involved black men and Indian women, there are a handful of known cases of black women who married Indian men.

Black–Indian marriages increased as white settlements expanded. As whites gradually appropriated Indian land, dispossessed Indians often migrated to towns and port cities where they found employment. They were generally compelled to live in segregated areas, where they shared the same taverns, jobs, and neighborhoods as members of the free black community.

In the northern colonies there were no cultural or legal impediments to interracial marriage between blacks and Indians. Conversely, settlers in southern colonies were deeply suspicious of fraternization between blacks and Indians. Acutely conscious of their numerical weakness, whites feared that if Indians joined forces with blacks they would have the power to overwhelm white settlers. Various methods were deliberately employed to foment hostility between slaves and Indians. Black men were rewarded for taking part in Indian wars. Indians were rewarded with substantial bounties for the return of runaway slaves. Despite these efforts, a large number of slaves succeeded in escaping and living productive lives in Indian communities.

Dorothy A. Mays

See Also: Interracial Marriage and Sex (19th Century); Legal Status of Women (18th Century)

Further Reading

Clinton, Catherine, and Michele Gillespie, eds. *The Devil's Lane: Sex and Race in the Early South.* New York: Oxford University Press, 1997.

Fischer, Kirsten. *Suspect Relations: Sex, Race, and Resistance in Colonial North Carolina.* Ithaca, NY: Cornell University Press, 2002.

Godbeer, Richard. *Sexual Revolution in Early America.* Baltimore, MD: Johns Hopkins University Press, 2002.

Hodes, Martha, ed. *Sex, Love, Race: Crossing Boundaries in North American History.* New York: New York University Press, 1999.

Mandell, Daniel R. "Shifting Boundaries of Race and Ethnicity: Indian–Black Intermarriage in Southern New England, 1760–1880." *Journal of American History* 85 (1998): 466–501.

Rogers, J. A. *Sex and Race: A History of White, Negro and Indian Miscegenation in the Two Americas. Vol. 2: The New World* New York: Helga M. Rogers, 2000 [1942].

Sollers, Werner, ed. *Interracialism: Black White Intermarriage in American History, Literature, and Law.* New York: Oxford University Press, 2000.

Interracial Marriage and Sex (19th Century)

Northern Democrats coined the term *miscegenation* in 1863 as part of a campaign to discredit the Republican Party, claiming that President Lincoln and his supporters sought to promote the sexual mixing of the races. Although the word was new, efforts to portray race mixing as a threat to white supremacy had a long history in the United States even at that point. Laws prohibiting racial intermarriage and sexual relations first appeared on the books in the 1660s and lasted until the 1960s, making them among the most enduring of American racial restrictions.

The public attitude toward racial intermixture between whites and blacks in colonial North America was much more hostile than in the Caribbean and South America. Intermarriage between blacks and whites especially outraged English settlers in North America, and such unions were relatively infrequent. Interracial sex occurred more often, leading to a growing number of mulattos. Usually these sexual relations took place between white men and black women, but in areas such as the Chesapeake Bay, where there were large numbers of indentured single women from England in the 17th century, sexual intercourse between white servant women and enslaved black males was not uncommon. Miscegenation statutes sought primarily to prevent marriages between blacks and whites, but they also sought to discourage sexual relations between white women and black men.

The focus of these statutes was no accident. By largely ignoring sexual intercourse between male slaveholders and female slaves, the law provided southern masters with a significant economic opportunity. Contrary to English common law, most southern colonies adopted the legal doctrine that black and mulatto offspring inherited the mother's status. Thus any children born of sexual contacts between white men and enslaved black females added to the size of the slave labor force. The fact that mulatto children derived their status from their mother accounts in part for the anxiety of southern lawmakers about sexual relations between white women and black men. Unlike the biracial offspring of enslaved black females, mulatto children of white females could not be placed in bondage. Consequently, they contributed to the growth of the free mulatto class and threatened to blur the lines between slave and black, on the one hand, and free and white, on the other.

The majority of mulattos before the Civil War lived below the Mason–Dixon Line, and three-fifths of them were concentrated in the Upper South. The census of 1850 revealed that about 350,000 mulattos (about 85 percent of the mulatto population in the United States) lived in the slave states. Of this number only about 103,000 were free mulattos. The Lower South, revealing the influence of the West Indies, tended to treat free mulattos as an intermediate group between blacks and whites. Especially in Charleston and New Orleans, free mulattos achieved an elite status in African American communities. The growing hostility of southern whites during the 1850s, however, led to the collapse of this distinctive order, and mulattos found themselves pressed downward into the lower caste.

Some of the liaisons between white men and black women that resulted in mulatto children stemmed from mutual affection, but enslaved African American females clearly faced a limited choice in sexual matters involving their masters. The power differential between white men and black women ensured that psychological, if not physical, coercion was a significant element of any sexual encounter. Northern abolitionists charged that white slaveholders seduced or forced many of the enslaved black women on their plantations and farms into sexual relations with them. Although white southern men denied such accusations vehemently, there is no doubt that the sexual abuse of female slaves was widespread.

During the period between Independence and the Civil War, the American inclination to prohibit interracial marriage showed few signs of weakening. The new states that entered the Union, both slave and free, usually enacted legal bans on racial intermarriage. Some of the older states declared interracial unions not only punishable but also null and void, thus making any offspring illegitimate. In addition, several states imposed fines on clerks who issued licenses for mixed marriages and on officials who performed ceremonies for such unions. Massachusetts was one of the few states that went against the legislative tide, repealing the ban on interracial marriages in 1843. Iowa in 1851 and Kansas in 1857 passed similar repeals. By and large, however, laws forbidding racial intermarriage proliferated during the antebellum years. Those interracial couples who cohabited outside of wedlock did not escape the scrutiny of legislators either, and a number of states made such couples the target of special penalties.

Accompanying these efforts to strengthen the color barrier were legal attempts to set the limits of blackness and whiteness. Defining who belonged to which racial category was necessary in order to enforce miscegenation laws and other regulations discriminating against African Americans. The antebellum statutes generally applied one-fourth or one-eighth standards, meaning that anyone who had a black or mulatto ancestor within the previous two or three generations was defined as black. The usual rule of thumb, however, was that anyone who displayed the physical characteristics of African ancestry was deemed black.

Following the collapse of slavery at the end of the Civil War, American courts reexamined the legitimacy of the antebellum miscegenation bans. Southern whites, without slavery as a buttress to social order, became apprehensive about their ability to retain control over African Americans. Miscegenation quickly became one of the most volatile legal and social issues, and white anxiety over black male sexuality became particularly acute. Ironically, though, less miscegenation occurred than under slavery because emancipation ended the relationship of the white master and enslaved black female.

Playing upon white fears of miscegenation and black rape, those who rejected Republican efforts to ensure the legal rights of former slaves insisted that these policies would lead directly to race mixing. Despite Republican denials of any intention to legalize interracial marriages, critics of Reconstruction continued to make these charges. They recognized that the miscegenation issue was an effective way to split up white Republican support in the South and mobilize opposition to radical Reconstruction.

During the period of radical Republican ascendancy, several southern states dropped the ban on miscegenation. With the overthrow of radical Reconstruction, however, resurgent white supremacists in the South reenacted antebellum measures or put new statutes on the books outlawing miscegenation. In addition, seven southern states prohibited racial intermarriage by constitutional provision. As before the Civil War, these new laws usually pronounced interracial marriages void, making the parties to such marriages subject to prosecution for violation of the laws against fornication and cohabitation. Outside of the South, the hardening of the color line in the late 19th century led to a new wave of legislation against interracial marriage, mostly in western states that entered the Union after 1865. The most significant innovation of the West during these years was to include the growing number of Asians in the laws against miscegenation. In the North, most states continued to rely on customary rather than legal restraints to enforce racial separation in matrimony. Four northern states even abolished the prohibition: Rhode Island (1881), Maine (1883), Michigan (1883), and Ohio (1887). Between 1880 and 1920, however, 13 western states added laws against racial intermarriage to their books. By 1920, 30 of the 48 states had antimiscegenation statutes and four states—Alabama, Florida, Louisiana, and Nevada—also prohibited interracial cohabitation.

In the face of these legal barriers and rising racial violence, marriages between whites and blacks remained relatively infrequent throughout the United States during the early decades of the 20th century. The massive migration of African Americans to northern cities after World War I did not alter this pattern significantly. If anything, intermarriage in the North declined as African American communities became more cohesive and whites created more effective systems for restricting the social mobility of blacks. As before, the majority of interracial marriages in the North that did occur involved black men and white women.

A number of African American leaders such as W. E. B. Du Bois spoke out against laws that prohibited intermarriage, insisting that they were an affront to the dignity of black citizens. At the same time, however, most of these leaders discouraged the practice of interracial marriage.

Although black–white sexual relations and intermarriage preoccupied the minds of a society where race-based slavery existed, these were not the only interracial relationships at stake. Nineteenth-century government Indian policy focused, in large part, on the regulation of marriage between whites and Native Americans. As missionary and educational efforts increased, more whites came into contact with and sought to change traditional Native forms of family life, including the traditional roles of Native women. Native Americans had different notions of private property, marriage, and the sexual division of labor, as noted and condemned by white Europeans from the era of first contact well into the 19th century and beyond. As one official reported to the Office of Indian Affairs, "some of the Indians had several wives, who sometimes live in different towns, and at considerable distance from each other, [and] they are allowed by the Indian to own property not subject to their husbands."

White Americans held specific views about women's proper roles within the family, and, to the extent that Native Americans did not assume those same roles, marriage and the family were of particular concern to those seeking to incorporate Native Americans into the new nation. Encouraging Native peoples to assimilate so that "we shall all become Americans," President Thomas Jefferson suggested to tribal leaders in 1808 that Native men and women learn to adopt the Anglo American mode of farming as well as the white division of gender roles: "If the men will take the labor of the earth from the women they will learn to spin and weave and to clothe their families." The final part of Jefferson's vision was that "you will mix with us by marriage, your blood will run in our veins, and will spread with us over this great island."

Some Native groups responded to aggressive U.S. land policies by assimilating into Anglo American culture, including through intermarriage. Thomas Jefferson and many Indian agents in the first half of the century regularly promoted or sanctioned intermarriage, at least between white men and Indian women, as part of an overall policy toward instilling white gender conventions among Native peoples. The goal was to promote monogamy, discourage polygyny as practiced among some Native tribes, and privilege those couples agreeing to male land ownership and engaging in small family farming. Although in several early cases Cherokee women won their individual claims to their own property, in some cases these rulings facilitated the transfer of control of Cherokee lands and other property to white men through intermarriage. Such legal maneuvering seemed to have been on the mind of at least one potential suitor, a white man named Townsend who, intending to marry a Cherokee woman who had claims to her uncle's land, house, and other improvements, inquired of the courts, "on the eve of his marriage . . . to know whether he could have these improvements valued as his own property provided he married the girl."

Intermarriage served not only to facilitate economic goals, but it also served an important political function in Indian–white relations throughout the century, as Indian women, especially, could be useful as negotiators and interpreters between the two sides. In the late 1850s, a Modoc woman named Winema went against family and tradition by refusing the mate prearranged for her and marrying instead a white man, a Kentucky miner named Frank Riddle. She was not only going against her family's wishes, but as the Modocs were in constant conflict with white settlers, many saw her marriage as a betrayal. But when full-scale war broke out in the 1860s, both Winema and Frank became valuable peacemakers, and she served first as an interpreter and was later called upon by the U.S. government to help negotiate the terms of an 1864 treaty of peace.

Peter W. Bardaglio and Tiffany K. Wayne

See Also: Interracial Marriage and Sex (17th and 18th Centuries); Legal Status of Women (18th Century)

Further Reading

Bardaglio, Peter W. *Reconstructing the Household: Families, Sex, and the Law in the Nineteenth-Century South.* Chapel Hill: University of North Carolina Press, 1995.

Clinton, Catherine, and Michele Gillespie, eds. *The Devil's Lane: Sex and Race in the Early South.* New York: Oxford University Press, 1997.

Davis, Peggy Cooper. *Neglected Stories: The Constitution and Family Values.* New York: Hill and Wang, 1997.

Hodes, Martha, ed. *Sex, Love, Race: Crossing Boundaries in North American History.* New York: New York University Press, 1999.

Lemire, Elise. *"Miscegenation": Making Race in America.* Philadelphia: University of Pennsylvania Press, 2002.

Pascoe, Peggy. *What Comes Naturally: Miscegenation Law and the Making of Race in America.* New York: Oxford University Press, 2009.

Rogers, Joel A. *Sex and Race: A History of White, Negro, and Indian Miscegenation in the Two Americas. Vol. 2: The New World.* New York: Helga M. Rogers, 2000 [1942].

J

Jacobs, Harriet (1813–1897)

Harriet Jacobs escaped from slavery in 1842 and in 1861 she published her autobiography, *Incidents in the Life of a Slave Girl,* which detailed the horrors of slavery, especially those peculiar to enslaved women. The first fugitive slave narrative written by a woman, *Incidents* received praise from antislavery circles in the United States and Britain. It revealed the horrors of slavery from a woman's point of view and highlighted the sexual perversion of the South's peculiar institution. Abolitionists hoped the book would incite others, especially women, to oppose slavery based on its corrupting sexual aspects.

Harriet Ann Jacobs was born in 1813 in Edenton, North Carolina, to Delilah, a slave of Margaret Horniblow, and Elijah Jacobs, a slave of Andrew Knox. Like many young African Americans, Harriet did not realize she was someone's property until the age of six, when her mother died. When Harriet was a child, Horniblow taught her to read and sew, but Horniblow died in 1825, bequeathing Harriet to her three-year-old niece, Mary Matilda Norcom. Jacobs moved in with the Norcom family, where she was subjected to repeated sexual advances from Mary's father, physician James Norcom.

Jacobs's grandmother, a freed slave named Molly Horniblow, encouraged Jacobs to leave the Norcom residence and offered to help. Jacobs was frightened, however, and would not leave. Instead, in 1829, she began a relationship and had two children, Joseph and Louisa, with white attorney Samuel Tredwell Sawyer. Jacobs's behavior infuriated Norcom, who sent her to one of his plantations to work as a field hand. Terrified that her children would be forced to follow the same path, Jacobs ran away. After staying with various neighbors both black and white, she moved into a tiny crawlspace above a storeroom in her grandmother's house in 1835. She hoped that her absence would prompt Norcom to sell her children to their white father. Norcom, as expected, posted a reward for Jacobs's capture and return.

Jacobs remained in hiding in the crawl space for almost seven years. The space was nine feet long and seven feet wide, and had no light or ventilation. During those years, Jacobs emerged only for bief periods at night to exercise. She spent her time sewing, reading the Bible, and sending letters to Norcom to confuse him

as to her whereabouts. Sawyer purchased their children but did not emancipate either one of them. He moved them to a house nearby, and Jacobs could sometimes watch them through a peephole she had made as they played outside. When Sawyer won a seat in the United States House of Representatives in 1837, he moved to Washington, D.C., without the children. Instead he sent Louisa to Brooklyn to work as a house servant.

In 1842, Jacobs escaped by boat and headed to Brooklyn in search of Louisa. Although free from her life as a slave, she lived in constant fear of recapture. For the next 10 years, Norcom continued to search for her. Jacobs found a job as well as a place for her to live with both of her children. She worked as a nursemaid in Boston for Mary Stace and abolitionist poet Nathaniel Parker Willis. In 1849, Jacobs began 18 months living above the Rochester, New York offices of Frederick Douglass's antislavery newspaper, *The North Star.* In Rochester, she worked with her antislavery lecturer brother, John S. Jacobs, also a fugitive slave. She traveled frequently between Boston and New York, becoming an active member of a group of antislavery feminists, including Amy Post, who encouraged Jacobs to share her story with the public.

In 1852, the Willises purchased Jacobs and freed her. She then began working on her autobiography, *Incidents in the Life of a Slave Girl.* She wrote at the Willises' home, Idlewood, an isolated, 14-room writers' retreat on the shore of Moodna Creek. By day, Jacobs tended to the Willis children, and by night she worked on her memoirs in secret. Jacobs's letters to Post reveal a connection between her decision to tell her story and the recent death of her grandmother, Molly Horniblow. Jacobs felt that she could never share the sordid details of her life while her grandmother still lived; she feared that the sexual realities of her life as a slave would horrify her grandmother. In addition, Jacobs initially hoped that Harriet Beecher Stowe, author of the recently released *Uncle Tom's Cabin,* would make a good partner in the effort. Although this collaboration did not materialize, Jacobs's belief in the relationship between her own life's story and Stowe's fictional antislavery work indicates Jacobs's understanding of her potential contribution to the growing canon of slave literature.

Jacobs's work on her autobiography initially took the form of several anonymous letters to *New York Daily*

Tribune, where they were published in 1853. Her account of her sexual abuse shocked the American public and ultimately made it difficult for Jacobs to find a publisher. She enlisted the help of antislavery author Lydia Maria Child to get her story into print. *Incidents in the Life of a Slave Girl* was published in late 1860 by a Boston printer. It was published in London in 1861 as *The Deeper Wrong; Or, Incidents in the Life of a Slave Girl.* In both editions, Jacobs used a pseudonym, Linda Brent.

Jacobs maintained her dedication to African American causes throughout her life. Throughout the Civil War, Jacobs involved herself in relief efforts in the Washington, D.C., area. In particular, she aided the former slaves who had become wartime refugees, nursed African American troops, and taught the freedpeople. In 1863, she and her daughter founded the Jacobs Free School in Alexandria, Virginia, to train African American teachers for the freedpeople. When Jacobs and her daughter headed to Savannah, Georgia, in 1865, they moved the school with them. Jacobs returned to Edenton in 1867, where she promoted the welfare of former slaves.

In the postwar era, Jacobs continued her aid efforts. In 1868 she and Louisa raised money in London for an orphanage and home for the aged in Savannah, Georgia. Then the two returned to Massachusetts where, in 1870, they opened a boarding house in Cambridge. By the mid-1880s, Jacobs had settled in the District of Columbia with Louisa. In Washington, Jacobs worked at newly formed black schools and later at Howard University.

Soon before her death, she was involved in the organizing meetings of the National Association of Colored Women.

Harriet Jacobs died in Washington, D.C., on March 7, 1897, at the age of 84. She is buried next to her brother, John, at Mt. Auburn Cemetery in Cambridge, Massachusetts.

Eloise E. Scroggins

See Also: Abolitionism and the Antislavery Movement; Child, Lydia Maria; Douglass, Frederick; Slavery and the Civil War; Stowe, Harriet Beecher; Truth, Sojourner

Primary Document: 1861, *Incidents in the Life of a Slave Girl*

Further Reading

Carby, Hazel. *Reconstructing Womanhood: The Emergence of the Afro-American Woman Novelist.* Oxford: Oxford University Press, 1987.

Foster, Frances Smith. *Written by Herself: Literary Production by African-American Women, 1746–1892.* Bloomington: Indiana University Press, 1993.

Garfield, Deborah, and Rafia Zafar, eds. *Harriet Jacobs and 'Incidents in the Life of a Slave Girl': New Critical Essays.* New York: Cambridge University Press, 1996.

Jacobs, Harriet A. *Incidents in the Life of a Slave Girl,* edited by Jean Fagan Yellin. Cambridge, MA: Harvard University Press, 1987 [1861].

Yellin, Jean Fagan. *Harriet Jacobs: A Life.* New York: Basic Civitas Books, 2004.

K

Kemble, Fanny (1809–1893)

British-born actress and writer Fanny Kemble became an outspoken abolitionist after spending time on her husband's Georgia plantation. She achieved acclaim on the stage in her youth and later as a reader of Shakespeare, and she wrote plays, poetry, and other works. Her published journals of America, particularly her exposé of life under the slavery system, *Journal of a Residence on a Georgian Plantation,* reveal the horrors of life in the slave South and offer a window into 19th-century life.

Known familiarly as Fanny, she was born Frances Anne Kemble on November 27, 1809, into the famous Kemble family of actors; her uncle was John Philip Kemble, the leading authority on Shakespeare, and her aunt, Sarah Siddons, was the greatest actress of her time. Her father, Charles Kemble, himself a talented Shakespearean actor, assumed management of Covent Garden Theatre after John Philip's retirement. Fanny's sister, Adelaide, became an opera star.

The Kemble family was beset by financial difficulties, and creditors took possession of the theater. Fanny, having previously been deemed to have no acting talent, was given a strenuous crash course in the theatrical arts, and she made her debut as Juliet on October 5, 1825. She was a success with both her audience and her critics; the *Times* pronounced her debut the most triumphant they could remember. She was thrust into a whirlwind of performances and social engagements, and, although she enjoyed acting, she grew to hate the publicity the profession entailed.

Fanny Kemble's success on the London stage, however, proved to be not enough to rescue the theater, and her father decided to take her on a two-year professional tour of the United States. Fanny abhorred the idea, calling America a "dreadful" place, but consented to go. The two set sail on August 1, 1832. Fanny Kemble became a sensation in America, starting fashion trends, causing mobs at the box office, and attracting the attention of dignitaries. She received an audience with several prominent leaders, including President Andrew Jackson. On the whole, however, Kemble was unimpressed with the young republic, and she kept a journal of her observations, including comments on tobacco spitting and on servants who did not know their place.

Kemble also attracted male admirers, the most persistent of whom was Pierce Butler of Philadelphia. Butler came from a prominent Georgia family who owned two plantations on Butler and St. Simon's Islands, with the second largest slave population in the state. He and his brother (who died in 1848) were set to inherit the estates upon the death of their maiden aunt. Fanny Kemble married Pierce Butler in Philadelphia on June 7, 1834. The marriage proved to be a prolonged, bitter struggle, with cycles of feuds and reconciliations that ultimately led to heartbreak, divorce, and public scandal. Kemble expected to continue life the way she had lived it, free to attend the theater, participate in intellectual society, and express her views, whereas Butler and his family expected her to retire into what they believed to be a respectable life of quiet domesticity. Furthermore, each expected the other to come around to his or her own views on slavery.

To provide for her aunt's heirs, Kemble published her American journal against her husband's express command, because it contained material he thought embarrassing to his family. Her sharp and witty *Journal of America* (1835) was criticized by both the American and the British press, even as it became an instant bestseller. She gave birth to their first child, Sarah, that year, and to their second child, Frances ("Fan"), in 1838.

Kemble was deeply opposed to slavery even before she met Pierce Butler. When he inherited his estates in April of 1836, she pleaded with him to be allowed to accompany him to Georgia, and he consented. Fanny kept a travelogue of this experience from December 1838 to April 1839.

Although she admired the natural beauty of the land, especially on St. Simon's Island, Kemble was shocked by the primitive and poverty-stricken condition of the South, attributing it to the degrading influence of a slave economy. She criticized the aristocracy for its "ignorance," "sensuality," and "cruelty," and she regretted that Southern courtly manners could charm her native English countrymen far more than those of the egalitarian Yankees. But the greatest impact of her journal was in her observations of the wretched conditions and miserable complaints of the plantation slaves. She deeply sympathized with them, especially the women, who were put to hard work, violated sexually, and sometimes even

British-born actress Fanny Kemble later wrote about her experiences living on a Georgia slave plantation. (Library of Congress)

beaten while pregnant. Although she was in Georgia for only four months, Kemble established a slaves' hospital and nursery, rewarded cleanliness, and paid wages to her personal servants. She also appealed to her husband, although he inevitably refused to listen to her pleas and complaints. Back in Philadelphia, Kemble circulated her journal among her abolitionist friends, although her husband forbade her to do so.

On December 1, 1840, the couple sailed for London with their children after hearing that Charles Kemble had fallen ill. Fanny's father recovered, but Butler prolonged their stay, wasting money on gambling and extravagances. Kemble found letters in 1843 that contained evidence of Butler's infidelity, and she sought legal counsel. The following March, Butler was challenged to a duel for having an affair with a friend's wife. Pierce Butler presented her with a contract for a formal separation, and Fanny Kemble left for England in October of 1845. She once again took up acting when Butler reneged on his promise of support. Learning of her return to the stage, he began divorce proceedings; after two years he could claim desertion on her part.

Learning of Butler's actions to divorce her, Kemble returned to America in September 1848. She bought a house called The Perch, in Lenox, Massachusetts, and toured the country, performing. They were divorced September 22, 1849, with Kemble allowed to see her children for two months each year, but Butler did not honor his promise of support, due to financial difficulties. Kemble had to continue her readings for income, and Butler was forced to sell half of his slaves.

With the coming of the Civil War, Fanny Kemble predicted a Union victory and the end of slavery. Her two daughters held opposing views with one another. Sarah was supportive of the Union and against slavery, like her mother, and Fan showed sympathies more aligned with those of her father. During the war, Pierce Butler was imprisoned for a time by the federal government on suspicion of disloyalty, causing the girls much anxiety. Kemble published her Georgian journal in May 1863, braving yet more condemnation and possible estrangement from her daughters, particularly Fan.

After the war, Pierce Butler returned to his lands in Georgia to rebuild his estate, accompanied for a time by his daughter Fan, who wrote a journal of her experiences. Fanny Kemble remained in Europe, occasionally visiting the United States and keeping busy during her last decades with her readings, writing memoirs and other works, and receiving illustrious friends, like Henry James. In 1867, Pierce Butler died of malaria. Fan Butler married an Anglican minister, James Leigh, and moved to England with him after they had struggled unsuccessfully to manage the Butler Island plantation. Fanny Kemble lived with them in London until her death on January 15, 1893.

Gabrielle Bruns

See Also: Abolitionism and the Antislavery Movement; Slavery and the Civil War

Further Reading

Blainey, Ann. *Fanny and Adelaide: The Lives of the Remarkable Kemble Sisters.* Chicago, IL: Ivan R. Dee, 2001.

Clinton, Catherine. *Fanny Kemble's Civil Wars.* New York: Simon & Schuster, 2000.

Furnas, J. C. *Fanny Kemble: Leading Lady of the Nineteenth-Century Stage.* New York: Dial Press, 1982.

Simmons, James C. *Star Spangled Eden: 19th Century America through the Eyes of Dickens, Wilde, Frances Trollope, Frank Harris, and Other British Travelers.* New York: Carroll and Graf Publishers, 2000.

L

Labor Unions (19th Century)

The relationship between organized labor and women in the United States began with early industrialization in the Northeast. Many women worked as factory girls in textile mills in New England and even more worked at home for systems of outwork production in boots and shoes, garments, and hats throughout the northeastern states. The experiences of working for wages under the time discipline of factory life contrasted sharply with the female experience of unpaid household production for family subsistence before 1820. A dual model of appropriate work for women took shape in the early 19th century: the unmarried factory girl and the homebound wife who occasionally supplemented family income with paid work.

Women's involvement in labor protest started as early as the opening of the first factories. New England textile operatives conducted strikes against low wages in 1821, 1824, and 1827, while the turnouts in Lowell, Massachusetts, in the 1830s and 1840s marked the emergence of the first labor union organized and led by women workers. These early women's organizations cooperated with workingmen's associations that were active in the 1840s. Sarah Bagley of the Lowell Female Labor Reform Association edited *The Voice of Industry* and organized political activity among workingwomen in support of a 10-hour day. To justify their rebelliousness, New England textile operatives, like many protesting artisans and mechanics in the 1840s, identified with the rights won by their forebears in the American Revolution, specifically by evoking their status as "daughters of freemen." Labor protest and organization were more difficult for women outworkers who worked for low wages in their homes in isolation from other workers, although some shoe workers in Essex County, Massachusetts, and outworkers in New York City, Philadelphia, Newark, and other northeastern cities complained vociferously about working conditions and low wages and organized protests.

Most women's employment was in light industries that made cotton and woolen textiles, garments, shoes, hats, collars, paper, and carpets and printed books and newspapers. Their work was characterized by a sexual division of labor that for many of them meant low wages, low status, and poor working conditions. Patriarchal values in the family and the factory combined to direct working girls into temporary unskilled work with low wages and little future. Women seldom experienced formal apprenticeships and could not depend on the craft customs of male workers. Their status as temporary workers without skills seemed to threaten male jobs and resulted in the exclusion of women from trade union activity except when male unionists wished to control their presence in the industrial workplace. The family wage, one of the major goals of 19th-century trade unions, did not include the wages of workingwomen but rather applied to all male workers, whether married or unmarried.

In industries where the sexual division of labor prevented competition between men and women over work, cooperative relations often developed. In these situations, women workers in the textile, collar-making, parasol-making, bookbinding, shoemaking, and carpet-weaving industries developed and led their own organizations. The disruptive impact of Civil War casualties and westward migration on marriage forced many women reluctantly into the labor market and, after the war years, created a diverse female labor force that included self-supporting women and female heads of families as well as young, single factory girls and wives who returned to the workforce during times of depression. Balancing work, family responsibilities, ethnic ties, and gender expectations, some of these women fought to build their own unions, pursued power for female interests within the national labor movement, and developed connections with the women's rights movement.

In the National Labor Union of the late 1860s and the Knights of Labor in the 1880s, female members organized committees on women's work. They made common cause with women in different industries and regions and debated the importance of suffrage and temperance. As Knights of Labor, carpet weavers, textile workers, and shoe stitchers formed alliances on the community and national levels to gain power and representation for workingwomen. Within the Knights, however, two different and conflicting ideological positions on workingwomen limited the effectiveness of these efforts. The first was a moral critique of industrial capitalism based on the values of family life and domesticity. Some argued that a woman's natural sphere remained the home, not the workplace, and although women were welcome in the Knights' assemblies, they were expected to leave the workforce after marriage. The second position was a general commitment to equal rights for workingmen and workingwomen. Equality of rights was championed by women workers in the textile and shoe industries in the Northeast who fought for representation for women in the Knights and for autonomous female assemblies. In 1886 they persuaded the Knights to appoint Leonora Barry, a hosiery worker from New York, to investigate the conditions of workingwomen and encourage their organization. After 1886, however, many of these activists left the Knights for trade union organizations that later joined the American Federation of Labor.

Mary H. Blewett

See Also: Bagley, Sarah; *The Lowell Offering*; Lowell Textile Mills; Moral Reform; Working Women's Association; International Ladies' Garment Workers' Union (Vol. 2); Lawrence Textile Strike (Vol. 2)

Primary Document: 1845, Testimony of Female Factory Workers before Massachusetts State Legislature

Further Reading

Blewett, Mary H. *Men, Women, and Work: Class, Gender, and Protest in the New England Shoe Industry, 1780–1910.* Urbana: University of Illinois Press, 1990.

Blewett, Mary H. *Constant Turmoil: The Politics of Industrial Life in Nineteenth-Century New England.* Amherst: University of Massachusetts Press, 2000.

Dublin, Thomas. *Transforming Women's Work: New England Lives in the Industrial Revolution.* Ithaca, NY: Cornell University Press, 1994.

Murphy, Theresa Anne. *Ten Hours' Labor: Religion, Reform, and Gender in Early New England.* Ithaca, NY: Cornell Univeristy Press, 1992.

Zonderman, David A. *Uneasy Allies: Working for Labor Reform in Nineteenth-Century Boston.* Amherst: University of Massachusetts Press, 2011.

Lee, "Mother" Ann (1736–1784)

Ann Lee was born into a working-class family in Manchester, England. She had no schooling and from an early age worked in a mill preparing cotton for the looms. Despite her parents' traditional Anglican beliefs, Ann was attracted to a radical sect of Quakers led by Jane and James Wardley. This sect engaged in dancing, shouting, and speaking in tongues and became known as "shakers." Ann had little inclination to marry, but after sustained pressure from her parents, she reluctantly married Abraham Standerin in 1762. Standerin was a blacksmith who worked for Ann's father, and like Ann, he was illiterate. The couple had four children, but they all died at very young ages.

All of the deliveries were difficult, and Ann almost died giving birth to her last child. She became obsessed with seeking an explanation for her children's tragic deaths and her unhappy marriage. She concluded that relations with the opposite sex were at the root of her troubles and were contrary to the ways of Christ. Ann Lee returned to the Wardleys for spiritual comfort and gradually assumed spiritual leadership of the tiny religious group. Lee took her crusade to the streets, shouting exhortations at bystanders and disrupting services at local churches. She was arrested and imprisoned for disturbing the peace, destroying property, and assault. She eventually spent time in Bedlam, the notorious English insane asylum. Her visions intensified while she was confined, convincing her she was the female successor to Jesus Christ.

After her release from Bedlam, Lee's rowdy evangelization activities continued, but a vision told her to carry her mission to America. "Mother" Ann left England with eight followers in 1774, and immigrated to New York. There the tiny group disbanded in order to seek employment. It is likely Lee worked as a domestic servant for several years before her followers reunited and established a community at Niskayuna, near Albany. Lee was a committed pacifist, and the group's refusal to support the Revolutionary War caused suspicion among their neighbors. Lee was suspected of being a front for the British and was briefly imprisoned. Upon her release she garnered sympathy from other charismatic religious followers.

Independent religious revival groups flourished in New England, and Mother Ann's group of Shakers began attracting substantial followers for the first time. Celibacy and the public confession of sin were the cardinal principles of the group. Emulating the primitive church, Lee insisted that all things be held in common. She stressed neatness, economy, and charity toward the poor. Under her guidance, Shaker women enjoyed equal rights and responsibilities with men. Mother Ann's followers expressed themselves through unrestrained dancing, chanting, and foot stamping. Her insistence on egalitarian order, a communal lifestyle, and the rejection of marriage attracted many converts, but also roused the suspicion of traditionalists.

Mother Ann Lee's beliefs bordered on heresy for the generally conservative American colonists of the 18th century. When questions arose about a woman's ability to lead a church, Lee replied that she was acting in place of her absent husband, Jesus Christ. Her wild dancing was condemned as erotic displays. Her pacifism during a time of war appealed to some, but further stoked the fires of suspicion among many. She claimed to have the ability to speak in tongues and commune with the dead.

Ann Lee died in New York in 1784, following a deep depression caused by the death of her brother and most devoted follower, William Lee. She claimed that she wished to join him in death, and shortly before she passed, she claimed to have seen William coming toward her on a gold chariot. Ann Lee was illiterate and never committed any of her philosophy to print. Twenty-five years after her death, her followers set about interviewing the people who had known her, in an effort to record her life. *The Testimonies* were completed in 1816. Only 20 copies were printed and circulated to the leaders of Shaker communities. The book, commonly called "the Mother's sayings," was closely guarded, as they reveal a woman who was prone to bouts of weepiness, fluctuating moods, erratic behavior, and possibly alcoholism.

Despite the mystery that surrounded Ann Lee, the success of her charismatic religious movement is without question. The Shakers' rigid adherence to celibacy meant they could not sustain the group without a constant influx of converts. Within a few decades of Lee's death, the Shakers had more than 6,000 followers and were developing a unique style of artwork, architecture, and furniture that reflected Lee's philosophy of simplicity without adornment. Lee believed that skillful workmanship was in itself an act of prayer. An enormous amount of care and attention to detail went into the crafting and construction of Shaker products. They believed form must follow function, and each item should be carefully crafted to suit its intended purpose, but nothing else. All superfluous decoration, such as scrolls, inlays, and molding, were eliminated. Shaker furniture and products have a distinctive severe appearance and have had a lasting influence on American design.

Dorothy A. Mays

See Also: Quakers; Shakers; Utopian Communities

Further Reading

Francis, Richard. *Ann the Word: The Story of Ann Lee, Female Messiah, Mother of the Shakers, the Woman Clothed with the Sun.* New York: Penguin, 2001.

Stein, Stephen J. *The Shaker Experience in America: A History of the United Society of Believers.* New Haven, CT: Yale University Press, 1992.

Lee, Jarena (1783–?)

Jarena Lee, itinerant minister and author, was born in 1783 to a free African American family at Cape May, New Jersey. In 1804, at age 21, Lee attended a religious meeting of an itinerant Presbyterian missionary whose sermon, Lee claimed, challenged her to change from her sinful ways and seek a relationship with God. Shortly after her conversion to Christianity, Lee began attending the religious services of a Methodist Episcopal church in Philadelphia. In her quest to be used by God, Lee sought to attain sanctification, which she believed would help her end a lifelong struggle with selfish ambitions and set

Jarena Lee was the first female preacher in the African Methodist Episcopal (AME) Church. She published her autobiography, *Religious Experience and Journal of Mrs. Jarena Lee*, in 1836. (Library of Congress)

her apart as a Christian worker. Shortly thereafter, following an intense session in prayer, Lee recorded, "That very instant, as if lightning had darted through me, I sprang to my feet, and cried, 'The Lord has sanctified my soul!'"

In 1809, Lee heard a divine voice telling her to "Go preach the Gospel," which confirmed her "call" to ministry. Lee met with Richard Allen, a bishop in the African Methodist Episcopal (AME) Church, to discuss her desire to preach and serve as a licensed minister. Allen's response was less than enthusiastic declaring the Church *Discipline* "knew nothing at all about it—that it did not call for women preachers." Lee would not let the response of Bishop Allen deter her future work. In 1811, Lee married the minister of a small AME Church outside Philadelphia. Six years later, Lee returned to Philadelphia following the deaths of her husband and four of her six children. In 1818 or 1819, while in the presence of Bishop Allen at an AME service, Lee rose to her feet to offer an exhortation on the sermon. Upon hearing her words, Allen rescinded his earlier concerns, giving Lee permission to hold meetings in her home, to comment on public sermons, and to travel as an itinerant speaker.

Jarena Lee traveled thousands of miles throughout the United States and spoke in venues from Upstate New York to Maryland to Ohio. Lee's itinerancy took her into the camp meetings, homes, and churches of Quaker, Presbyterian, and Baptist adherents. During her preaching tours Lee spoke at a number of multiracial church gatherings, including religious meetings in Maryland with slaveholders in attendance. In 1836 Lee published her spiritual autobiography, *The Life and Religious Experience of Jarena Lee.* In 1849, she edited and published a second version of her autobiography, *Religious Experience and Journal of Mrs. Jarena Lee,* which included comments on the social and religious concerns of her day. No official documentation exists indicating the year or location of her death.

Jarena Lee sold copies of both versions of her spiritual autobiography at camp meetings, churches, and revivals. For Lee, the publications provided literary evidence of her "calling" by God and documented her religious experiences including her conversion to Christianity and subsequent spiritual empowerment through sanctification. An example of her work reveals a sense of relief following her conversion to Christianity: "Great was the ecstacy [*sic*] of my mind, for I felt that not only the sin of malice was pardoned, but all other sins were swept away together. That day was the first when my heart had believed, and my tongue had made confession unto salvation."

Lee's work shows how racism and sexism pervaded American religious culture as she dealt with inequity not only as an African American but also as a woman who desired authorization to speak for the African Methodist Episcopal Church. Lee believed God gave her authority to speak, to leave her children in the hands of others during her travels, and to write about her life and freedom found as a Christian African American woman. Lee cherished the community within the AME tradition yet branched out and held revivals for gatherings of men and women, both black and white. Her willingness to travel into Maryland, a slave state, demonstrated her social and religious convictions to preach to slave owners even at the possible expense of her own personal safety.

Christopher J. Anderson

See Also: Foote, Julia A. J.

Further Reading

Andrews, William, ed. *Sisters of the Spirit: Three Black Women's Autobiographies of the Nineteenth Century.* Bloomington: Indiana University Press, 1986.

Foster, Frances Smith. "Adding Color and Contour to Early American Self-Portraitures: Autobiographical Writings of Afro-American Women." In *Conjuring: Black Women, Fiction, and Literary Tradition*, edited by Marjorie Pryse and Hortense J. Spillers, 25–38. Bloomington: Indiana University Press, 1985.

Haywood, Chanta M. *Prophesying Daughters: Black Women Preachers and the Word, 1823–1913.* Columbia: University of Missouri Press, 2003.

Peterson, Carla L. *"Doers of the Word": African–American Women Speakers and Writers in the North.* New York: Oxford University Press, 1995.

Legal Status of Women (18th Century)

Most of the American colonies inherited English common law, a system of justice derived from tradition and custom rather than statutory law enacted by legislatures. English common law evolved from centuries of judicial decisions. The most important common-law principle relating to women was *coverture,* a doctrine that sublimated a woman's legal identity under that of her husband. A married woman could not buy, sell, earn, or possess property in her own name. She had no authority over how family money was spent, she could not enter into contracts, nor could she sue or be sued. Any legal action she wished to take needed to be brought to the court's attention via her husband's authorization.

Naturally, this presented a problem if a woman had a legal dispute with her husband, such as in the case of divorce, child custody, or control over her premarital assets. The law of coverture did not apply to women who were single or widows; these women retained their legal identities under *feme sole* status and had all the rights and privileges that men had, except for the right to vote and hold public office.

Equity law was a system aimed at addressing the inflexible nature of common law. A person who felt an injustice had been done in a common-law court could appeal to a chancery court. The judge at the chancery level was free to base his decisions on the spirit of the law, rather than on what was dictated by common law. Chancery courts used no juries. Many colonial settlers were highly distrustful of chancery courts, because such courts were often tools for the king's imperial dictates. Aside from the potential for arbitrary and tyrannical abuse, chancery courts offered women a place to take their grievances.

Divorces were difficult to obtain in colonial America, and many feuding couples opted to create a legal document outlining terms of a legal separation and financial support. Because the law of coverture virtually erased a wife's ability to have an independent legal identity, common law refused to recognize the validity of any legal document created between spouses. In such a case, the couple could appeal to a chancery court, which allowed for prenuptial agreements to be created and honored and for trusts and inheritances to be granted to married women without interference from their husbands.

Despite the protection afforded women by chancery courts, most colonial women lacked the sophistication and financial assets to bring a case before chancery courts. In some cases, the suit needed to be heard in a lower court before the chancery court could hear it. In other colonies, there might be only one chancery court located in the colony's capital city, an obvious barrier to a woman living in a remote area. Each colony developed its own rules regarding the extent that equity rulings could encroach on common-law tradition. Eventually, New England and the middle colonies eliminated separate chancery courts, opting instead to incorporate aspects of equity law into their common-law courts.

Dutch Colonies

Women in the Dutch colonies of New Netherlands had an unusually high level of legal autonomy. Holland's legal system was an amalgamation of Roman law and local Germanic customs. Dutch women preparing to marry had a right to select either a *manus* marriage or an *usus* marriage. A *manus* marriage meant a woman was subject to her husband, and her legal identity was sublimated under his authority. A woman who selected an *usus* marriage had substantial legal independence from her husband. She retained rights to all her premarital property; she could initiate and litigate contracts, establish and run a business, and retain her maiden name. A woman could renounce *manus* status after marriage and assume the legal responsibilities associated with an *usus* marriage if she chose.

Dutch inheritance custom was generally blind to gender. Whereas primogeniture was often the law of the land in English societies, sons and daughters tended to inherit equal amounts of property in Dutch colonies. A combination of legal freedom and the Dutch merchant tradition also afforded women the opportunity to participate in business to a high extent. Seventeenth-century records tell of Dutch women working as shopkeepers, brewers, shippers, fur traders, and tavern owners. It is possible that the women of New Netherlands did not participate in business at a markedly higher rate than women in the Anglo-American colonies, but because Dutch women were entitled to an independent legal status, they left traceable records to document their business involvement.

In 1664 the British took control of New Netherlands, renaming it New York. Property rights of Dutch settlers, including businesses owned by Dutch women, were respected. There was little dramatic change in Dutch women's status in the years immediately following British conquest, but as the decades passed, the colony became more English in character. Fewer women were business owners, and the option of an *usus* marriage dissolved. It appears that after English authorities assumed control over New York, English governors also typically respected Dutch tradition and continued to grant divorces.

Enslaved Women

Each colony established a series of "slave codes," which provided for the policing of slaves, the rights of slaves, the conduct of whites in dealing with slaves, and the rules for the manumission of slaves. Slaves were deprived of most basic human liberties the white population took for granted, but they were provided with a slim margin of protection by the law. Although there were variations among the colonies, the rules outlined below were generally applicable in all the southern colonies.

One of the first major legal cases regarding the laws of slavery was the decision to make slavery heritable through the mother. The common-law tradition of England granted children the legal status of their father, but this was unacceptable in the American South, where a high percentage of slave women bore the children of free white men. In 1655 Elizabeth Key successfully sued in a Virginia court for her freedom because she had a white father. Following this case, the law was changed to prevent children of enslaved women from becoming free based on their paternity.

Enslaved women were highly vulnerable to sexual exploitation from their owners, and the slave codes did nothing to protect them from such abuses. There were numerous antimiscegenation laws on the books throughout the colonies, but the laws were largely ignored unless a white person attempted to marry a black. Such a marriage would present a host of problems for the colonies, which were reluctant to recognize a black person's right to share the spousal benefits from marriage to a white. Although sexual exploitation of slaves was considered immoral among the white population, it was widespread and considered in poor taste to acknowledge the problem.

The isolation of women on plantations gave them virtually no ability to seek social or legal recourse for sexual harassment. Slave women could not physically defend themselves, because striking a white person was against the law, and punishment could be brutal. The first time a slave struck a white person, she was to be punished with a whipping. Second or third offenses could result in the death penalty.

No slave had the legal ability to enter a contract, making a binding marriage impossible. Slaves had ceremonial weddings, but they could be terminated if one partner was sold. Likewise, a woman could not be assured of her right to raise her own children. Because the children were the legal property of her master, he had the freedom to sell or relocate those children as he saw fit.

Protections for slaves were pitifully few and were often designed to benefit the local government. It was forbidden for owners to free their slaves unless the slave was able-bodied and capable of attaining self-sufficiency. Before this rule was established, cruel masters would free a slave when they were too old to work, and thus became a burden on the state. Masters were required to provide sufficient food, shelter, and clothing for a slave, although the standard of what was "sufficient" was sadly meager and subjective. South Carolina and Georgia insisted that slaves be allowed a day of rest on Sunday, but the working time for the other six days could be up to 16 hours.

Above all, it was important for slave owners to prevent anything that gave a slave the opportunity to escape or incite a rebellion. Slaves could not travel to neighboring plantations without a pass. Curfews required they be home before nightfall, and no one was to sell liquor to a slave. Limitations were placed on the number of slaves who could gather during off-work hours. Most colonies forbade slaves the ability to learn to write, although reading was acceptable in most areas. Reading and writing were taught as separate skills in colonial America, and many women were able to read without ever acquiring the subsequent skill of writing. Some masters even encouraged Christian slaves to learn to read the Bible, because doing so was believed to make them passive. Conversion to Christianity had no legal bearing on a slave's status, despite the claims of Quakers and other antislavery advocates that it was a sin to enslave a Christian.

Colonies assumed that all blacks were slaves unless they could prove their free status. Many women, especially those of mixed blood, attempted to pass for white after making a bid for freedom. Sumptuary laws that prohibited slaves from wearing elegant clothing were attempts to prevent women from acquiring the clothing that might aid in their escape.

Slaves could not testify against a white person in court, effectively closing the courts to them as a means of redress. Only two colonies, Georgia and South Carolina, permitted a slave to bring suit to question the legality of their enslavement.

Dorothy A. Mays

See Also: Bathsheba Spooner Case; Coverture; Divorce (before the Civil War); Elizabeth Freeman Case; *Feme Sole* and *Feme Sole* Trader Status

Further Reading

Biemer, Linda Briggs. *Women and Property in Colonial New York: The Transition from Dutch to English Law, 1643–1727*. Ann Arbor, MI: UMI Research Press, 1983.

Cleary, Patricia. *Elizabeth Murray: A Woman's Pursuit of Independence in Eighteenth-Century America*. Amherst: University of Massachusetts Press, 2000.

Dayton, Cornelia Hughes. *Women before the Bar: Gender, Law, and Society in Connecticut, 1639–1789*. Chapel Hill: University of North Carolina Press, 1995.

Salmon, Marylynn. *Women and the Law of Property in Early America*. Chapel Hill: University of North Carolina Press, 1986.

Sturtz, Linda L. *Within Her Power: Propertied Women in Colonial Virginia*. New York: Routledge, 2002.

Letters on the Equality of the Sexes (1838)

Letters on the Equality of the Sexes (published in 1837 and 1838) is the first in-depth philosophical discussion of women's rights by an American woman. In the *Letters,* Sarah Moore Grimké made a far-reaching examination into the conditions of the lives of women in the United States and around the world. She analyzed the laws affecting women; the inequities women faced in education and employment; the specific injuries suffered by female slaves; and the subjugation of women by men, especially in marriage. Most important, in the *Letters* Grimké provided a biblical justification for the liberty and equality of women as moral and autonomous beings.

Grimké and her sister, Angelina Grimké Weld, were prominent speakers on the abolitionist circuit at a time when it was considered inappropriate and immoral for women to speak in public. They were both acclaimed and condemned for their activism. The most vicious attack came in the form of a pastoral letter from the Council of Congregationalist Ministers of Massachusetts, which denounced their behavior as unwomanly and un-Christian. Sarah Grimké wrote the *Letters,* originally published as a series of articles in the *New England Spectator* in 1837, in direct response to the charges raised against her and her sister in the pastoral letter. She argued that God made no distinction between men and women as moral beings and that whatever was morally right for a man to do was also right for a woman.

The most significant contribution of the *Letters* to feminist thought is Grimké's demonstration of a scriptural basis for the equality of the sexes. Taking scriptural verses that for centuries had been used to demonstrate the *inequality* of the sexes, Grimké provided new interpretations that supported the essential equality of women and men. Specifically, she argued that the biblical account of creation showed (1) that both male and female are created in the image of God, and thus there can be no difference between them; (2) that God gave man and woman dominion over all other creatures, but not over each other; and (3) that woman was created to be a helpmate to man, *like unto himself.* She interpreted the story of Adam and Eve in the Garden of Eden as showing that since both ate the forbidden fruit, both sinned. Thus, though both women and men fell from innocence, they did not fall from equality. She also used notions from the New Testament, such as the idea that there is no male or female but only one in Christ, to demonstrate the equality of the sexes.

Grimké provided an important analysis of marriage in the *Letters.* She expressed concern that in marriage women were deprived of their moral autonomy. Women defined themselves before marriage solely in terms of attracting a future husband and after marriage in terms of fulfilling their husbands' needs. Moreover, the laws regarding married women, which deprived women of property and contract rights and of their very legal existence through the notion of coverture, assured women's moral dependence. Grimké argued as well that the functionalist attitude of husbands toward their wives—that wives were instruments of domestic comfort and physical pleasure rather than moral and intellectual companions—furthered the destruction of woman's autonomy and sense of self-worth.

In her analysis of woman's economic status and role, Grimké pioneered not only the notion that every vocational sphere should be open to women but also the notion of comparable worth—that a laundress who works as long and as hard as a wood sawyer should be paid equally with him. Atypical of many feminist tracts of this era, the issues addressed in the *Letters* were not confined to the concerns of white, middle-class women. Grimké was well aware of, and expressed concern for, the exceedingly hard labors of working-class women. Nevertheless, she was firmly entrenched in the 19th-century, middle-class cult of domesticity and consistently maintained that women must not abandon their special responsibilities in the home.

The *Letters* also contain many expressions of feminist sisterhood. Grimké paralleled the condition of degradation and subjugation of white, middle-class American women with those of female slaves and working-class women in the United States and with women in Europe, Asia, and Africa. In the *Letters,* though Grimké did not show a strong conception of the positive foundations of female solidarity, she did give clear expression to a notion of female bonding through common suffering.

Elizabeth Ann Bartlett

See Also: Grimké, Sarah Moore; Grimké Weld, Angelina

Primary Documents: 1837, Massachusetts Churches Respond to Grimké Sisters Speaking in Public; 1838, *Letters on the Equality of the Sexes*

Further Reading

Grimké, Sarah M. *Letters on the Equality of the Sexes and Other Essays,* edited and introduction by Elizabeth Ann Bartlett. New Haven, CT: Yale University Press, 1988.

Lerner, Gerda. *The Feminist Thought of Sarah Grimké.* New York: Oxford University Press, 1998.

Lerner, Gerda. *The Grimké Sisters from South Carolina: Pioneers for Women's Rights and Abolition.* New York: Oxford University Press, 1998.

The Liberator

Among the many antislavery and abolitionist newspapers of the mid-19th century, William Lloyd Garrison's *The Liberator* was unquestionably a leader. Although the paper never had more than 3,000 subscribers at any one time, it had an enormous impact on U.S. journalism and political culture while also inspiring and goading into action more than one generation of abolitionists. In *The Liberator*'s first issue, published on January 1, 1831, Garrison insisted on the immediate emancipation of the slaves, writing, "I am aware, that many object to the severity of my language; but is there not cause for severity; I will be as harsh as truth, and as uncompromising as justice. On this subject I do not wish to think, or speak, or write, with moderation."

For the next 35 years, Garrison's vehement and often scathing editorials guaranteed that the public would not only listen but react. The weekly also published national and regional news pertinent to the abolitionist movement, including horrifying accounts of slave torture, slaveowners' villainy, and slave escapes and captures as well as excerpts from both antislavery and proslavery books, speeches, and other literature. Garrison also published notices of upcoming antislavery meetings and conventions; letters from abolitionists in the field; and news of many other liberal social reform movements, including women's rights, temperature, the peace and nonresistance movements, and prison reform.

The Liberator also printed news of other reform activities, such as in the temperance and women's rights movements. Susan B. Anthony submitted letters to Garrison, with the understanding that he would publish them, just as she provided letters to Frederick Douglass's the *North Star,* Amelia Jenks Bloomer's *The Lily,* and Paulina Wright Davis's *The Una.* In one such letter published in *The Liberator* on February 8, 1861, Anthony described an evening lecture during the current "winter of mobs," when she, Stephen Symonds Foster, and Aaron M. Powell attempted to speak to their audience in Rome, New York. Her letter alerted *The Liberator*'s readers to the difficult conditions abolitionists faced in the field.

> At the evening session, I placed myself . . . to take the door fee. Some thirty passed up quietly, when there came, with heavy tramp, a compact gang of forty or fifty rowdies. . . . There they stamped, and howled, and whistled, and sang "the star spangled banner"—marched on to the platform, seated themselves at the table, pulled out a pack of cards,

and then took the table and threw it to the floor with a crash. Under the circumstances, we made no attempt to speak, and soon left the hall.

After the Emancipation Proclamation in 1863, Garrison became increasingly convinced that *The Liberator*'s mission had been fulfilled. In December 1865, as ratification of the Thirteenth Amendment guaranteeing the freedom of African Americans became a reality, he terminated publication of *The Liberator.*

Judith E. Harper

See Also: Abolitionism and the Antislavery Movement; Douglass, Frederick; Garrison, William Lloyd; *The Lily*; Slavery and the Civil War; *The Una*; Anthony, Susan B. (Vol. 2)

Further Reading

Cain, William E., ed. *William Lloyd Garrison and the Fight against Slavery.* New York: Bedford Press, 1995.

Mayer, Henry. *All on Fire: William Lloyd Garrison and the Abolition of Slavery.* New York: St. Martin's, 1998.

Streitmatter, Rodger. *Voices of Revolution: The Dissident Press in America.* New York: Columbia University Press, 2001.

The Lily

Inspired by the first women's rights convention in 1848, Amelia Bloomer and a group of Seneca Falls, New York women organized the Ladies' Temperance Society. The first issue of *The Lily* was published on January 1, 1849, as the official organ of the women's temperance movement. The magazine's flag announced that it was "published by a Committee of Ladies," but Amelia Bloomer was the driving force behind its publication. After starting out with a co-editor, Anna Mattison, who resigned after only the second issue of *The Lily,* Bloomer took sole responsibility for publishing the journal.

From the beginning, Bloomer boldly acknowledged the purpose of her journal was to advance the temperance movement and womankind:

> It is Woman that speaks through the *Lily.* It is upon an important subject, too, that she comes before the public to be heard. Intemperance is the great foe to her peace and happiness. Surely she has the right to wield the pen for its suppression.

The Lily contained opinions and ideas that had never before been publicly addressed by a woman in print, and some of these opinions proved upsetting to the public. It was also, Bloomer claimed, "the first paper devoted to the interests of women and, so far as I know, the first one owned, edited, and published by a woman." While other women, such as Jane Swisshelm, had worked as editors and publishers, Bloomer was the first to serve as owner, publisher, editor, writer, and business manager of a publication. With a meager circulation of only a few hundred for the first printing, *The Lily* drew a quick following, and the circulation rapidly grew into the thousands. Subscriptions cost 50 cents for each copy, with the journal published monthly.

The first columns of *The Lily* were a mixture of poetry, literature, and condemnation of intemperance. Bloomer often recounted stories she received from newspaper reports and even neighborhood gossip about men who lost their jobs and ended up being murdered in the streets for bottles of liquor and about women who turned to alcohol and left their families for the streets and prostitution. Bloomer emphasized the importance of women's becoming involved in the temperance movement:

> That woman has reason to feel deeply on the subject of Intemperance all must admit. It strikes directly at her happiness, and peace of mind. . . . She sees those whom she loves more than life itself, ruined in body and soul—their peace destroyed— their hopes blasted, and their bodies consigned to a drunkards grave. . . . We have long felt that woman was called upon to act, and act efficiently in the work of advancing the great temperance cause.

Soon, however, Bloomer began to publish articles that discussed more controversial topics than temperance, such as mental and physical education for women and girls, legal protection for women who were married to drunkards, and the expansion of women's employment opportunities. Despite the fact, however, that many of Bloomer's fellow women reformers had begun to speak out publicly in favor of women's right to legal representation, Bloomer herself had not quite accepted the idea, as she revealed in the following editorial, entitled "Woman's Rights":

> It is not our right to hold office or to rule our country, that we would now advocate. Much, very much, must be done to elevate and improve the character and minds of our sex, before we are capable of ruling our own households as we ought, to say nothing of holding in our hands the reins of government.

By the end of her first year as an editor, however, Bloomer began to be swayed by the more radical propositions of her sister reformers. Part of the reason for this was her budding relationship with Elizabeth Cady Stanton, who became a regular contributor to *The Lily* at the end of 1849 under the name Sun Flower. Stanton's columns on women's enfranchisement and the legal injustices against women caused Bloomer to rethink her position on woman suffrage, and *The Lily* saw changes in its second year. Gone was the majority of the poetry that had predominated during the first year. Also, the "Published by a Committee of Ladies" line was permanently eradicated, and Amelia Bloomer's name appeared alone at the top of each issue as editor and publisher. *The Lily* shifted from purely a temperance journal to one that espoused the ideas and opinions of the controversial women's rights movement.

In the first issue of the new year, Bloomer published an article by Stanton that said, "Among the many important questions of the day, there is none that more vitally affects the whole human family, than that which is technically termed woman rights." At the time, Bloomer was not an advocate for woman suffrage, but in February 1850, the Tennessee legislature, in debating women's right to own property, came to the conclusion that "women have no souls" and therefore "no right to hold property." This bold pronouncement invoked the wrath of many outspoken women reformers, but none more than Amelia Bloomer, who wrote a biting editorial:

> We have not deigned saying much ourself on the subject of "woman's rights," but we see and hear so much that is calculated to keep our sex down, and impress us with a conviction of our inferiority and helplessness, that we feel compelled to act on the defensive, and stand for what we consider our just rights. . . . We think it high time that women should open their eyes and look where they stand.

From this point on, Bloomer used the pages of *The Lily* to crusade for women's right to vote and even to run for political office if she so desired. Bloomer felt compelled to justify herself and refute her critics:

> *The Lily* is a woman's paper and one of its objects . . . is to open a medium through which woman's thoughts and aspirations might be developed. Gentlemen have no reason to complain if women avail themselves of this medium, and here dare utter aloud their thoughts, and protest against the wrongs and grievances which have been so long heaped upon their sex.

In 1851 Bloomer took up the cause of dress reform. She was introduced to a new mode of female dress by Elizabeth Smith Miller, the daughter of abolitionist Gerrit Smith, who was spending the winter in Seneca Falls. Miller had taken to wearing an outfit that consisted of full "Turkish" pants underneath a dress that fell below the knees. Bloomer became the outspoken champion of dress reform and began publicizing the new outfit through articles and illustrations in *The Lily*.

The topic of dress reform first graced the pages of *The Lily* in February 1851, when Bloomer included a written description of the outfit and suggested that for comfort and health's sake, women should throw aside their corsets and petticoats to adopt the new outfit. In addition to Bloomer and Miller, several other prominent leaders of the women's rights movement, such as Elizabeth Cady Stanton, Susan B. Anthony, Lucy Stone, and Sarah Grimké, adopted the new style, which was named the "bloomer costume" because, as one columnist put it, "Mrs. Bloomer, if not its inventor, has done more than any other to secure its adoption." Bloomer began including in *The Lily* engravings of herself and others wearing the outfit. Eventually, however, despite Bloomer's attempts, interest in the dress reform movement began to die, and many of the women who had once donned the offending garments returned to wearing the acceptable fashions of the day.

In 1854, Dexter Bloomer (formerly editor of the *Seneca County Courier* in New York) purchased a newspaper, *The Western Home Visitor*, located in Mount Vernon, Ohio. Amelia Bloomer not only continued her duties on *The Lily* but also assumed the role of her husband's assistant editor. In March 1854, she hired a woman typesetter to work in the paper's office and help with *The Lily*. The male employees did not find this situation to their liking and declared a strike. The walkout by the male printers prompted Amelia Bloomer to do something that she had always wanted to do and "resulted in the employment of women to set the type for the *Visitor*."

Soon after this incident took place, Dexter Bloomer sold his share in the newspaper and decided to relocate to Council Bluffs, Iowa. Realizing that with "no facilities for printing and mailing a paper with so large a circulation . . . except a hand press and a stagecoach," Amelia Bloomer decided "it was best . . . to part with the *Lily*." She made arrangements for Mary A. Birdsall of Richmond, Indiana, to take possession of the magazine for an undisclosed sum, in exchange for a promise that it would continue to "be published in the same form, and with the same general character." Bloomer also retained

the title of contributing editor and continued for a time to contribute columns on the progress of woman suffrage in the West. Without Bloomer's leadership, however, the journal took on a more literary style; the paper was discontinued after 1859.

Bloomer was a pioneer behind the development of a new genre of magazine, known as women's advocacy magazines. While for years before *The Lily* there were publications run by women, never before had one been so solely devoted to the unique concerns of the female sex. Her magazine showed the possibility of success for smaller, more specialized publications, which led to a proliferation of other women's rights magazines, such as *The Revolution, The Sibyl, The Una,* and others.

Barry Wise Smith

See Also: Bloomer, Amelia Jenks; Dress Reform; Seneca Falls Convention; *The Sibyl*; Temperance Movement*; The Una*; Stanton, Elizabeth Cady (Vol. 2); *The Revolution* (Vol. 2)

Further Reading

Hinck, Edward A. "The *Lily,* 1849–1856: From Temperance to Women's Rights." In *A Voice of Their Own: The Woman Suffrage Press, 1840–1910*, ed. Martha M. Solomon. Tuscaloosa: University of Alabama Press, 1991.

Hoffert, Sylvia D. *When Hens Crow: The Women's Rights Movement in Antebellum America*. Bloomington: Indiana University Press, 1995.

Russo, Ann, and Cheris Kramarae. *The Radical Women's Press of the 1850s*. New York: Routledge, 1991.

Livermore, Mary (1820–1905)

In addition to campaigning for suffrage and temperance, Mary Livermore was, with Dorothea Dix and Clara Barton, an important figure in the organization of medical and relief services during the Civil War in the United States. After long playing a prominent role in the Woman's Christian Temperance Union (WCTU), she espoused Christian socialism in her later years.

Born in Boston and brought up a Calvinist, Mary Ashton Rice converted to the Baptist faith when she was 14. She was educated at the Hancock Grammar School and at Martha Whiting's Female Seminary in Boston and stayed on at the seminary, teaching French, Latin, and Italian until 1838. In 1839 she took a post as private tutor to the children of a plantation owner in North Carolina, where she soon became repulsed by the ill treatment of slaves. After three years in the South, she returned

Mary Livermore organized medical relief services for the Union Army during the Civil War and was active in the women's rights and temperance movements. (Library of Congress)

to Massachusetts to teach at a coeducational school in Duxbury and married a Universalist minister and temperance leader, Daniel Parker Livermore, in 1845.

Although her time was primarily taken up with raising her three daughters, Livermore wrote articles to supplement the family's income and was active in the local temperance movement. In 1857 the Livermores moved to Chicago, where from 1857 to 1869, Mary and her husband edited the Universalist journal the *New Covenant;* she remained active in the abolitionist movement and worked for temperance as a member of the Washingtonians. She also gave time to charitable work for poor women and children through such bodies as the Home for Aged Women, the Hospital for Women and Children, and the Home for the Friendless.

During the Civil War, Livermore put her children in the care of her housekeeper and a governess, and after volunteering for the Chicago (later Northwestern) Sanitary Commission, spent the next four years undertaking a tour of military hospitals and assessing the supplies needed by them. Placed in charge of the Chicago branch of the Sanitary Commission in December 1862 and with

the help of a woman named Jane Hoge, Livermore organized 3,000 local relief groups in the Midwest to raise medical and food supplies for General Ulysses S. Grant's Union Army. She also raised $70,000 in funds to buy essential medical supplies by staging a Sanitary Fair in October 1863 that inspired numerous similar ventures across the North. Early in 1863, Livermore responded promptly to a threatened outbreak of scurvy among Grant's troops by haranguing farmers to send mountainous supplies of canned and dried fruit and fresh vegetables south by rail to Vicksburg. Livermore went to Vicksburg and sent back her account of her experiences to the *New Covenant.* In 1887 she published *My Story of the War: A Woman's Narrative of Four Years Personal Experience,* which became a best seller.

The experience of the Civil War heightened Livermore's growing sense of women's ability to play an important, reformist role in public life, and crucial to that role was their right to suffrage. When the war was over, she became an active supporter of the emergent suffrage movement in the United States, in 1868 calling a local convention of women suffragists and becoming president of the newly founded Illinois Woman Suffrage Association. A year later, she founded the association's journal, the *Agitator,* a forum for campaigning on temperance and women's suffrage, which she also edited. Responding to the call of Lucy Stone to establish an American Woman Suffrage Association (AWSA), Livermore became its vice president. In 1870 she merged the *Agitator* with the AWSA's official publication, the *Woman's Journal,* and moved back to Boston to take up its editorship. From 1875 to 1878, she was AWSA president.

In 1870 Livermore co-founded the Massachusetts Woman Suffrage Association, at a time when she was being increasingly drawn into a public career in lecturing; she was its president from 1893 to 1903. For the next 25 years, she toured on the lecture circuit as one of the most popular figures in the AWSA, noted for her passionate advocacy of women's education. She had been the first president, in 1873, of the Association for the Advancement of Women, and championed women's education in her much-called-for lecture, "What Shall We Do with Our Daughters?" (published in 1883). In 1872 Livermore gave up her editorship of the *Woman's Journal* because of her increased lecture commitments, which included speech making on behalf of the WCTU after she had been instrumental in founding its Massachusetts branch in 1874 (for which she served as president for 10 years). Livermore covered many topics in her lectures, including moral reform, religion, suffrage, marriage and divorce, immigration, women's need for physical exercise, and dress reform. In 1878 she was a delegate to the First International Congress on Women's Rights held in Paris, France, with Julia Ward Howe of the AWSA.

By the time she retired from public speaking in 1896, Livermore had acquired a high public profile as a leading voice in the temperance and suffrage movements in Massachusetts. She continued her good works through the Beneficent Society of New England and the Women's Education and Industrial Union of Boston and published her autobiography, *The Story of My Life,* in 1897–1899.

Helen Rappaport

See Also: Barton, Clara; Dix, Dorothea; Howe, Julia Ward; Stone, Lucy; Slavery and the Civil War; Temperance Movement; United States Sanitary Commission; American Woman Suffrage Association (Vol. 2); Woman's Christian Temperance Union (WCTU) (Vol. 2); *Woman's Journal* (Vol. 2); The Women's Suffrage Movement—International (Vol. 2)

Further Reading

Bordin, Ruth. *Woman and Temperance: The Quest for Power and Liberty, 1873–1900.* Philadelphia, PA: Temple University Press, 1981.

Ginzberg, Lori D. *Women and the Work of Benevolence: Morality, Politics, and Class in the Nineteenth-Century United States.* New Haven, CT: Yale University Press, 1990.

Tyrrell, Ian. *Woman's World/Woman's Empire: The Woman's Christian Temperance Union in International Perspective 1880–1930.* Chapel Hill: University of North Carolina Press, 1991.

Venet, Wendy Hamand. *A Strong-Minded Woman: The Life of Mary Livermore.* Amherst: University of Massachusetts Press, 2005.

The Lowell Offering

The Lowell Offering was a magazine of stories, poetry, sketches, recollections, and vignettes first published in October 1840. The journal ultimately attracted both national and international attention, not because of the magazine's contents, but rather the fact that the editors and contributors were female textile workers from the mills of Lowell, Massachusetts.

The Lowell Offering was initially an experimental product of the city's so-called improvement circles or literary clubs for factory women. The Reverend A. Charles Thomas, the pastor of Lowell's Second Universalist

The cover of the July 1845 edition of *The Lowell Offering,* a monthly periodical that showcased writings by women textile workers in Lowell, Massachusetts. (Courtesy Lowell Historical Society, Lowell, Massachusetts)

Church, served as *The Offering*'s editor for its first two years of publication. The first volume of four issues appeared irregularly between October 1840 and March 1841 but afterward began appearing monthly. Issues cost six and one-quarter cents per copy.

The small journal and Lowell's female operatives rose to international fame after English visitors marveled that factory operatives, particularly females, were not only highly literate but capable of producing works of fiction and nonfiction. Author Charles Dickens, in his *American Notes,* said, "Of the merits of *The Lowell Offering,* as a literary production, I will only observe—putting out of sight the fact of the articles having been written by these girls after the arduous hours of the day—that it will compare advantageously with a great many English annuals." A book of selections edited from the first two volumes was issued in London in 1844 and republished in Boston the following year, under the title *Mind among the Spindles.*

The Lowell Offering existed because so many of the city's female factory workers—mostly American-born farm women—were literate. Visitors marveled that female millworkers could usually be seen with books in hand. Some women, *Offering* contributor Harriet Robinson recalled, would write in their spare moments. "The literary girls among us would often be seen writing on scraps of paper which we hid between whiles in the waste-boxes upon which we sat while waiting for the looms or frames to need attention," Robinson said. *Lowell Offering* writer Lucy Larcom recalled: "We had all been fairly educated at public or private schools, and many of us were resolutely bent upon obtaining a better education. Very few were among us without some distinct plan for bettering the condition of themselves and those they loved."

The Lowell Offering provided more than just a literary outlet for factory women striving to improve themselves. It also served as a vehicle from which factory operatives could defend their work and station in life. A Boston magazine editor, Orestes Brownson, attacked factory women's virtue in his magazine, the *Boston Quarterly Review,* by stating that factory girls could not "ever return to their native places with reputations unimpaired. 'She has worked in a factory,' is sufficient to damn to infamy the most worthy and virtuous girl," he said. Similarly, other members of the public looked down upon female operatives, calling them "cotton bugs."

The Lowell Offering's writers used the pages of their magazine to set the record straight. Millworkers, according to the magazine, were virtuous, moral, literate, and almost always seeking to improve themselves intellectually. The *Offering*'s writers regularly presented and promoted factory work as a dignified means of making one's living. For example, an 1842 article noted:

To be able to earn one's own living by laboring with the hands, should be reckoned among female accomplishments; and I hope the time is not far distant when none of my countrywomen will be ashamed to have it known that they are better versed in useful, then they are in ornamental accomplishments.

The Lowell Offering was not a labor magazine, however, nor did it pretend to be. The magazine gave a rosy picture of factory life, calling millwork pleasurable and presenting Lowell as an extension of bucolic, pastoral life, rather than a humming company town. One article noted that it was a "great source of pleasure" for workers was to send money home to their parents, painting a far different picture from that seen by inspectors—humid factories filled with cotton dust because windows were nailed shut.

Both factory workers of the time and later scholars have criticized the journal for failing to support laborers' interests, particularly the fight for a 10-hour workday. A competing Lowell publication, *The Voice of Industry,* better represented laborers' needs and exposed the "model" mill system's shortcomings. This first generation of factory labor had many legitimate grievances—12-hour days, poor ventilation in mills and boardinghouses, short meal breaks, and wage reductions coupled with boardinghouse rent increases, to name but a few. Because *The Lowell Offering* was funded by Lowell textile magnate Amos Lawrence, the magazine was rarely critical of conditions in the city's mills and boardinghouses. What criticisms did appear were relatively mild in tone. For example, Harriet Farley stated in an October 1843 editorial that "it is much easier to instill a feeling of self-respect, of desire for excellence, among a well-paid, than an ill-paid class of operatives. There is a feeling of independence, a desire to form and retain a good character, a wish to do something for others." She did not take the argument any further, however, or blame any specific factory owners.

Sometimes *The Lowell Offering*'s editors told readers that factory work was actually better than other labor. "We are better and more regularly paid than most other female operatives. Our factory life is not often our all of life—it is but an episode in the grand drama and one which often has its attractions as well as its repulsions," Farley noted in an 1844 editorial.

When the magazine's editors placed blame, often operatives, not employers, were targets—particularly those workers who supported the emerging labor reform movements. For example, in the August 1843 issue, Harriet Farley wrote, "We do not think the employers perfect; neither do we think the operatives so. Both parties have their faults."

Later in the article Farley chastised workers who supported labor reform: "We could do nothing to regulate the price of wages if we would; we would not if we could—at least we would not make that a prominent subject in our pages, for we believe there are things of even more importance."

The editors expressed such views because they did not see themselves as permanent members of the working class. Many of the women spent only a few years in the mills, then were married, moved west, or pursued some other occupation, such as teaching.

The Lowell Offering ceased after five volumes in December 1845. Farley acknowledged that the magazine was ending because the very workers she wrote for failed to support *The Lowell Offering*. Despite its genteel and, some would say, incorrect presentation of factory life, *The Lowell Offering* is worthy of its place in history. Not only did it demonstrate that factory operatives could rise above society's expectations of them, but the magazine also spawned a host of other factory operative publications in New England in the 1840s, most of which did focus on inequalities, including a Lowell competitor, *The Operatives' Magazine*, *The Olive Leaf, Factory Girl's Repository* of Cabotville, Massachusetts, *The Wampanoag and Operatives' Journal* of Fall River, Massachusetts, the *New Market,* New Hampshire-based publication, *The Factory Girl, The Factory Girls' Garland* of Exeter, New Hampshire, and the *Factory Girl's Album and Operative's Advocate,* also of Exeter. Furthermore, a number of *The Lowell Offering*'s contributors went on to later fame as writers, editors, novelists, teachers, artists, and other creative professionals.

Harriet Farley reestablished the magazine under the title *The New England Offering* in September 1847and resumed publication again under the same name in April 1848. It lasted until March 1850.

Mary M. Cronin

See Also: Bagley, Sarah; Labor Unions (19th Century); Lowell Textile Mills

Primary Document: 1845, Testimony of Female Factory Workers before Massachusetts State Legislature

Further Reading

Bender, Thomas. *Toward an Urban Vision: Ideas and Institutions in Nineteenth Century America*. Baltimore, MD: Johns Hopkins University Press, 1975.

Eisler, Benita, ed. *The Lowell Offering: Writings by New England Mill Women (1840–1845)*. Philadelphia, PA: J. B. Lippincott, 1977.

Foner, Philip S., ed. *The Factory Girls: A Collection of Writings on Life and Struggle in the New England Factories of the 1840s*. Urbana: University of Illinois Press, 1977.

Robinson, Harriet H. *Loom and Spindle; or, Life among the Early Mill Girls*. Kailua, Hawaii: Pacifica Press, 1976 [1898].

Lowell Textile Mills

The Lowell textile mills are synonymous with the Industrial Revolution in America, and their practice of hiring large numbers of single women make them important to any history of American women. The early success of the Boston Manufacturing Company's textile mills led to their rapid expansion, and by 1826, the town of Lowell, named after the company's founder Francis Cabot Lowell, was a flourishing mill town. Raw cotton entered the mills and came out as cotton cloth; the mills completed the entire process. The Lowell mills were also revolutionary because of their advanced mechanization process and standardized business practices, requiring each mill to follow the same regulations. The location was also ideal, and for all these reasons, the business boomed during its heyday period, roughly between 1820 and 1860.

Less than 30 years after the first mill opened in 1813, more than 32 mills were operating in Lowell, and 8,000 people—nearly 40 percent of the town's population—were employed there. Women comprised three-quarters of the workforce in the mills, an unprecedented situation in America at that time. The majority of female mill workers were between the ages of 16 and 25, but some were as young as 10. Most worked at the mills for an average of four years. In the early years, they worked 13-hour days, six days a week, with a half hour break for dinner and one for supper.

Single women were purposefully recruited to satisfy the demand for workers, but in order to do so, owners had to ensure that the disreputable conditions of European factory life would not be an issue in Lowell. Workers had to agree to the rules, which included mandatory church attendance and strict curfews, set forth in the "Handbook to Lowell." They offered higher wages, at first, and guarded living conditions in boarding houses with older women serving as mentors and guardians. At various intervals, these boarding houses were partially subsidized by the company. Still, the remaining costs were deducted from weekly wages; a woman typically made $3.25 per week at the mill and paid $1.25 for boarding. Wages were paid in cash, rather than company scrip, and they were comparable with other job opportunities for women such as teaching or domestic service.

For some, the mill life was positive, and the restrictions put into place ensured a safe and reputable environment. Most "mill girls" were literate, and most were from rural areas outside of Lowell. They were self-sufficient and economically and socially independent, some for the first and only times in their lives. They had access to urban amenities such as reading rooms and circulating libraries, and they could participate in a variety of activities during their free time, such as evening lectures in the Lyceum and self-improvement clubs. The English writer Charles Dickens visited the mills in 1842 and wrote very favorably about the living and working conditions of the girls and their earnest attempts at self-improvement.

This opinion was frequently echoed in the *Lowell Offering,* a magazine of poems, essays, and stories written by mill workers. A. C. Thomas, a local minister, was the founder and editor from 1840 to 1842, until Harriet Farley, herself a mill worker, took over. The magazine was largely considered to be propaganda for the mill owners, and many new workers were drawn to the mills because of the *Offering.* The magazine gained an international readership, and launched the career of Lucy Larcom, a poet later included in Rufus W. Griswold's *Female Poets of America* (1874).

However, the magazine was also published in a time of unrest in the mills. Workers went on strike in 1834 petitioning for shorter days and increased wages, to little success. The influx of immigrants desperate for work and growth in the urban population due to the transformation of agriculture increased competition for jobs. Economic depressions during this period also caused financial difficulties for mill owners. But important steps were taken in the successful strike of 1836 against an increase in boarding costs; a woman spoke in public for the first time in Lowell, and the Factory Girls' Association was organized. Still, wages had not increased in years, but the women were made to work in more looms at once, thus increasing productivity at the expense of workers. In some cases, the number of looms assigned to a worker more than doubled, and the already arduous work day became even more difficult to endure.

The year 1845 was a particularly tumultuous time for the Lowell mills. In January, Sarah Bagley, a young mill worker, organized the Lowell Female Labor Reform Association (LFLRA), which was run entirely by women, and membership increased rapidly in Lowell, with chapters forming in other towns. The Reform Association advocated for a 10-hour workday, and 2,000 signatures were collected on a petition presented to the state legislature, which formed an investigative committee. Several mill workers, including Bagley, testified about difficult factory conditions and hours at public hearings in February 1845, but the committee declined to make changes. Although ultimately unsuccessful, the event marked the first investigation into labor disputes by a governing American body.

In July of that year, Bagley publicly claimed that the *Offering* was rejecting her articles that were critical of mill conditions, and she later accused Harriet Farley of acting as a management "mouth piece." Bitter disputes ended when the *Offering* suspended publication and Bagley brought the *Voice of Industry,* formerly published by the New England Workingmen's Association, to Lowell. The *Voice of Industry* was far more critical of factory conditions all over Massachusetts.

In January 1847, the LFLRA became the Lowell Female Industrial Reform and Mutual Aid Society, with Mary Emerson as president and Huldah Stone as secretary. That year, the workday was finally reduced to 11.5 hours. Although the society continued to advocate for reform, its activities were gradually limited to assisting members facing extreme hardship or illness. By 1853, the workweek was further reduced to 66 hours per week, for an average of 11 hours per day, although the number of looms assigned to each worker increased.

Continued disputes over conditions and lack of wage increases led many Yankee women to leave the mills by the 1850s, but owners replaced them with Irish immigrants. When the Civil War started and Southern cotton was no longer available, many of the mills permanently ceased operations.

Kari Miller

See Also: Bagley, Sarah; Labor Unions (19th Century); *The Lowell Offering*; Moral Reform

Primary Document: 1845, Testimony of Female Factory Workers before Massachusetts State Legislature

Further Reading

Dublin, Thomas. *Women at Work: The Transformation of Work and Community in Lowell, Massachusetts, 1826–1860.* New York: Columbia University Press, 1979.

Dublin, Thomas, ed. *Farm to Factory: Women's Letters, 1830–1860.* New York: Columbia University Press, 1981.

Eisler, Benita, ed. *The Lowell Offering: Writings by New England Mill Women (1840–1845).* Philadelphia, PA: J. B. Lippincott, 1977.

M

Martineau, Harriet (1802–1876)

Harriet Martineau was born in 1802 in Norwich, England, the sixth of eight children. Her father was a manufacturer of Huguenot decent and the family was Unitarian. Her relationship with her mother, who was not particularly nurturing, was especially strained and her mother's insistence that her daughters conform to very strictly feminine roles is often cited for influencing many of Martineau's strongly feminist views on the social role of women and mothers. The culture and era during which she was raised strongly discouraged women from writing and publishing.

Nonetheless, Martineau—who lost her sense of taste and much of her hearing as a child—became widely published as a social theorist, sociologist, and feminist thinker. Her initial writings were anonymous religious articles published beginning in 1823 in the Unitarian publication, *The Monthly Repository.* When her family fell on hard economic times in 1829, Martineau supported her family, in part, with proceeds from these articles. By 1832, Martineau had shifted her focus to strictly political writings and was commissioned to pen her first edited volume: *Illustrations of Political Economy.* More political writings followed. While she continued to write and win literary awards for *The Repository,* her most acclaimed work became a fictional tutorial in which she analyzed the work of such political, economic, and social theorists as contemporaries Thomas Malhaus, Jeremy Bentham, and David Ricardo.

In 1832, Martineau moved to London, where she was received in top intellectual company and became engaged in Whig politics—writing about reforms proposed to taxation by the political party. She also traveled to the United States in 1834 where she met with then-former president and American Founding Father, James Madison. She also spent significant time exploring the state of women's education in the United States and learning of the growing abolitionist movement. Upon returning to England, Martineau wrote several books about her observations in the United States. It has been suggested that two of these, *Society in America* (1837) and *How to Observe Morals and Manners* (1838), contributed to the birth of modern sociology. *How to Observe,* in particular, is noted for its contribution to sociological methods.

Martineau is also noted for her closeness to Charles Darwin and his brother, Erasmus. The brothers' father discouraged a romance between her and either of his sons because of her very vocal political views, but both brothers seem to have been enthralled by Martineau's intellect. Not long after her time spent with Erasmus, in particular, Martineau wrote several works of fiction, including *Deerbrook* (1838), an acclaimed romance novel.

Martineau was diagnosed with a uterine tumor that compelled her to travel throughout Europe seeking treatment and, for long spells, she remained confined due to her illness. She nonetheless wrote several books during her illness. The greatest of these, *Life in the Sickroom: Essays by an Invalid* (1844) was an autobiographical account of her struggle to maintain control of her life in the course of her illness and medical treatment. The religious community criticized this work, claiming it suggested too much self-reliance and not enough reliance on the divine. Though she recovered somewhat from the illness, it was believed that Martineau continued to suffer from hysteria—a common diagnosis for women during this period. She often turned to mersmerism for treatment of her symptoms, to which she attributed her cure from the affliction.

Despite her health problems, she became increasingly controversial in her writings and addressed issues such as the education of women (*Household Education,* 1848) and atheism (*Letters on the Laws of Man's Nature and Development,* 1851). The latter was influenced by the premise of evolution, about which she offered significant praise in 1859 when Darwin's *On the Origin of Species* was sent to her directly from Erasmus Darwin. A proponent of secularism, Martineau appreciated Darwin's work because it was not based on theology.

In her later years, Martineau often wrote for newspapers and took on significant women's political causes of the day. She supported the political activism of English feminist Barbara Bodichon in the 1850s and 1860s, signing petitions for both the Married Women's Property Bill of 1856 and the petition for women's suffrage in 1866. She also spoke out in support of changes to laws that punished prostitutes but which did little to acknowledge their customers.

Harriet Martineau was an English social theorist and writer who traveled to the United States in the 1830s and befriended many American reformers. (Perry-Castaneda Library)

While it was rare for women to write, let alone publish autobiographies at the time, Martineau spent many of her final years writing her own, which was published following her death in 1876.

Jennie Sweet-Cushman

See Also: Education of Women (before the Civil War); New York Married Women's Property Acts; Women's Suffrage Movement—International (Vol. 2)

Further Reading

David, Deirdre. *Intellectual Women and Victorian Patriarchy: Harriet Martineau, Elizabeth Barrett Browning, George Eliot.* Ithaca, NY: Cornell University Press, 1987.

Logan, Deborah A. *The Hour and the Woman: Harriet Martineau's "Somewhat Remarkable" Life.* DeKalb: Northern Illinois University Press, 2002.

Rees, Joan. *Women on the Nile: Writings of Harriet Martineau, Florence Nightingale, and Amelia Edwards.* London: Rubicon Press, 2008 [1995].

Sanders, Valerie. *Reason over Passion: Harriet Martineau and the Victorian Novel.* New York: St. Martin's Press, 1986.

May, Abigail Williams (1829–1888)

As the chairperson of the United States Sanitary Commission in 1862, Abigail Williams May distributed more than $1 million in supplies to Union and Confederate soldiers, and she traveled aboard a hospital transport ship to gain personal knowledge of wartime conditions to ameliorate the shortages and suffering of soldiers on the front. She directed the Sanitary Commission until it was disbanded in 1888 but was called Chair the rest of her life due to her leadership of the commission and her reform efforts in Boston, Massachusetts. May's leadership bridged the gap between women's political efforts at the local level and the growth of concerted efforts on behalf of women at the national level.

The product of two prominent New England families, the Mays and Goddards, Abigail May was born in Boston on May 21, 1829, as the third of Samuel J. and Mary (Goddard) May's seven children. Her parents were involved in the abolitionist movement. Their example served May well; she too found her life's work in reform efforts, including freedmen's aid, woman suffrage, and women's education.

Besides her parents' influence, May's lifework was informed by the ideas of several people. The preaching of several Unitarian ministers, including Theodore Parker, her brother Samuel J. May, Jr., and her first cousin Samuel Joseph May, also influenced her passion for philanthropic endeavors. May was first cousin to the social worker Abigail May Alcott and a close friend of Louisa May Alcott. Brought up believing that women should be educated and work outside the home to prevent future poverty and hardship, May attended Boston's private schools and the Boston School of Design, which she later shepherded as part of its governing committee.

Prior to her involvement with the United States Sanitary Commission, May founded and served as secretary of the Obstetrics Clinic of New England Female Medical College in 1859. Her Sanitary Commission efforts began in 1861 at the local level in Boston where she served as secretary of the New England Women's Auxiliary Association, a branch of the U.S. Sanitary Commission. She worked in this capacity until, at age 32, she coordinated the war relief efforts for the entire New England region. Then, in 1862, May became chairperson of the U.S. Sanitary Commision, the only civilian relief organization to receive official government sanction. Its women solicited supplies from localities for national distribution, offered battlefield support, and consulted with the Union army on medical matters. Given women's traditional role as nurses in the home, meeting the commission's objectives allowed women to expand their endeavors into public areas, prove their mettle as leaders, and address social and health needs. May strove to create a strong network of local relief organizations that would eventually meld into a larger, national movement.

May never married; her love of and dedication to public work and service outweighed any notions she had of being a man's helpmeet. Her family's financial support, coupled with the emotional support of her steadfast female friends, sustained her work. May died from an ovarian cyst at Massachusetts Homeopathic Hospital in Boston on November 30, 1888.

Rebecca Tolley-Stokes

See Also: Abolitionism and the Antislavery Movement; Alcott, Louisa May; Livermore, Mary; May, Samuel Joseph; Schuyler, Louisa Lee; United States Sanitary Commission

Further Reading

Giesberg, Judith Ann. *Civil War Sisterhood: The U.S. Sanitary Commission and Women's Politics in Transition.* Boston, MA: Northeastern University Press, 2000.

May, Samuel Joseph (1797–1871)

Unitarian minister, Garrisonian abolitionist, women's rights activist, and social reformer Samuel Joseph May was among the first of the American clergy to publicly support the franchise for women. Although May grew up, was educated, and received his ministerial training in the Boston area (he was uncle to Louisa May Alcott), he settled in Syracuse, New York, in 1845 and lived there until 1867.

May encouraged women to pursue equal opportunities in his congregation as early as 1823. As an abolitionist involved in the formation of the American Anti-Slavery Society (AASS) in 1833, he was committed to antislavery reform and agitation. In 1837, in the midst of a swirl of controversy and outrage about women speaking in public, May asked the abolitionists Angelina and Sarah Grimké to speak to his congregation in South Scituate, Massachusetts. Although at that time he was uncertain whether all women should have public roles, he strongly

opposed the efforts of the Massachusetts clergy to censor and silence abolitionists, particularly women antislavery activists.

As early as 1846, May wrote and published a tract entitled "The Rights and Condition of Women," which protested "this utter annihilation . . . of more than one half of the whole community." On the issue of woman suffrage, he declared:

This entire disfranchisement of females is as unjust as the disfranchisement of the males would be; for there is nothing in their [women's] moral mental or physical nature, that disqualifies them to understand correctly the true interests of the community, or to act wisely in reference to them.

May's experiences as an outspoken temperance activist led him to believe that temperance was an especially important issue for women to address. As Susan B. Anthony became increasingly involved in the women's rights movement in New York state, she frequently called upon May to speak at women's rights conventions and meetings. He soon recognized her considerable talents for reform. In August 1858, he wrote to her: "I wish there were thousands more in the world like you. Some foolish old conventionalisms would be utterly routed, and the legal and social disabilities of women would not long be what they are."

When Susan B. Anthony became New York agent for the AASS in 1856, Samuel May responded to her request that he join her corps of lecturers. In the winter of 1861, during the height of antiabolitionist mob violence, May was one of Anthony's loyal band of orators. Although forewarned of the probability of violence at their meeting in Syracuse in late January, the group decided to proceed with their lectures advocating abolitionism and disunionism. When both May and Anthony tried to speak, the screams of the mob obliterated their voices. The crowd then hauled effigies of May and Anthony through the streets of Syracuse and set them afire, yelling "Constitution and Union!"

Samuel May retained his commitment to universal suffrage after the Civil War, although he was persuaded of the need to temporarily postpone agitating for woman suffrage to gain the ballot for African American males. In spite of this concession, May never stopped working with Elizabeth Cady Stanton and Anthony for woman suffrage, forming a branch of the American Equal Rights Association (AERA) in Syracuse to gain more support for universal suffrage. He disdained his male abolitionist colleagues' abandonment of woman suffrage and was particularly incensed by Wendell Phillips's inflexible position, which prompted May to chastise him at an AERA meeting in 1867.

Although May remained in contact with Stanton and Anthony in the years immediately preceding his death in 1871, their association with George Francis Train, whom May labeled "a fool or a monomaniac," alienated him and prevented him from pursuing further close collaboration with them. Nevertheless, May spent his final years working to secure the ballot for both women and African American males.

Judith E. Harper

See Also: Abolitionism and the Antislavery Movement; Alcott, Louisa May; Fifteenth Amendment; Grimké, Sarah Moore; Grimké Weld, Angelina; May, Abigail Williams; Temperance; American Equal Rights Association (Vol. 2); Anthony, Susan B. (Vol. 2); Stanton, Elizabeth Cady (Vol. 2)

Further Reading

Kimmel, Michael S., and Thomas E. Mosmiller, eds. *Against the Tide: Pro-Feminist Men in the United States, 1776–1990: A Documentary History.* Boston, MA: Beacon Press, 1992.

Yacovone, Donald. *Samuel Joseph May and the Dilemmas of the Liberal Persuasion, 1797–1871.* Philadelphia, PA: Temple University Press, 1991.

Meriwether, Elizabeth Avery (1824–1916)

Novelist, playwright, journalist, public speaker, and crusader for temperance and woman suffrage, Elizabeth Avery Meriwether is best known for her memoir, *Recollections of 92 Years,* which offers an intimate and often frank look at the life of a white Southern woman struggling against female subordination.

Born and raised in West Tennessee, Elizabeth Avery was largely self-educated. She married civil engineer Minor Meriwether of Kentucky in 1852, and bore three sons. Before the outbreak of the Civil War, she participated pseudonymously in discussions of issues of the day in local newspapers, always from a feminist standpoint.

While her husband served as an engineer officer in the Confederate army, Meriwether sought to maintain her household of children and a few slaves, lending her voice to secession and Southern nationalism. Expelled from Memphis by Union commander William T. Sherman in late 1862, she gave birth to her third son, author and journalist (Minor) Lee Meriwether, while seeking

refuge in Mississippi. The family spent most of the war in Tuscaloosa, Alabama. To help support herself, she wrote "The Story of a Refugee," which received a monetary prize and in 1864 was serialized in the exiled newspaper, *The Sunday Mississippian.* Drawing on incidents in her life in Memphis under federal occupation, she hinted at some of the themes—the feminine nature of the South versus the masculine, militaristic North, and the injustice of the legal disabilities placed on women in both regions—that she would treat at greater length in postwar works.

The most notable of these, besides her memoir, is her novel, *The Master of Red Leaf.* Set on a Louisiana plantation during the Civil War, this work posits both the benignity of the slave system (in the proper hands) and the malignity of a social structure that subordinated women to men. A typical Victorian potboiler in many ways, replete with coincidence and disguise, some of the main female characters are much more than they seem.

After the war, the Meriwethers returned to Memphis, where Minor become a successful lawyer. Elizabeth herself became an expert on coverture, the legal subordination of wives to husbands, and became known as a public speaker, as well as the publisher and editor of a short-lived newspaper. In one famous incident, she insisted on casting a ballot (which was accepted but not counted) in the 1872 election. By the1880s the family had relocated to St. Louis. Elizabeth became an associate and ally of Elizabeth Cady Stanton and Susan B. Anthony, with whom she made a speaking tour.

Unlike many elite Southerners of the era, the Meriwethers were fairly openly skeptical of religion. Elizabeth Avery Meriwether died in late 1916, after the serialization of her *Recollections* in regional newspapers had begun.

Ed Frank

See Also: Slavery and the Civil War; Temperance Movement

Further Reading

Berkeley, Kathleen C. "Elizabeth Avery Meriwether, 'An Advocate for Her Sex': Feminism and Conservatism in the Post-Civil War South." *Tennessee Historical Quarterly* 43 (Winter 1984): 390–407.

Gardner, Sarah. *Blood and Irony: Southern White Women's Narratives of the Civil War, 1861–1937.* Chapel Hill: University of North Carolina Press, 2004.

Wheeler, Marjorie Spruill. *New Women of the New South: The Leaders of the Woman Suffrage Movement in the Southern States.* New York: Oxford University Press, 1993.

Missouri v. Celia, a Slave (1855)

In 1855, a slave named Celia was charged with murdering her master who had consistently raped her over a number of years. The murder trial of *Missouri v. Celia, a Slave,* demonstrated that black slave women in the United States in the pre–Civil War era had no protection under the law from sexual assault by their masters. Even though Missouri law supposedly protected all women from rape, a black woman raped by her slave owner could not defend herself because she was considered the property of her master. The *Celia* murder trial was conducted within the United States when the country was on the verge of a civil war over the issue of slavery.

In 1850, Robert Newsom purchased a 14-year-old slave girl named Celia. Because Newsom's wife had recently died, he decided that the slave girl could assist his daughters with some of the household chores. Newsom purchased Celia in Audrain County, Missouri, and raped Celia for the first time as he was transporting her back to his farm in Calloway County, Missouri. Newsom had Celia live in a small cabin near his farm, and he fathered two children with her over a five-year period.

Celia fell in love with a fellow slave named George and when she became pregnant again she was uncertain whether George or Newsom was the father of her unborn child. George then told Celia that he would no longer stay in a relationship with her if she continued to allow Newsom to have sexual relations with her. At this time, Celia asked Newsom's two daughters to talk to their father about leaving her alone.

On June 23, 1855, Celia asked Newsom to leave her alone but he stated that he would be visiting her in the cabin that evening. When Newsom arrived at the cabin and approached Celia, she hit him twice in the head with a heavy stick and he fell dead to the floor. Celia then spent the rest of the night burning Newsom's body in the fireplace and hiding the remaining bones under the floor of the cabin.

On the day after the murder, Newsom's family and friends questioned George, the slave involved in the relationship with Celia, about the whereabouts of Robert Newsom. George told them that Celia was involved in the disappearance of Newsom. Celia eventually signed a confession that she unintentionally committed the murder of Newsom when he made sexual advances toward her. Celia was arrested on June 25, 1855, and taken to the Calloway County jail.

When the murder trial of Celia began on October 9, 1855, she was represented by three court-appointed attorneys. Because slaves were not allowed to testify in criminal court in the 19th century, Celia's story was told to the court by persons who had interviewed Celia about her relationship with Robert Newsom. Celia's attorneys tried to convey to the jury that Celia had acted in self-defense in the murder of Newsom; however, the witnesses provided vague testimony about the relationship of Celia and Newsom, and prosecutors were fairly effective at preventing the motive of self-defense from being considered by the jury.

Under a Missouri statute of 1845, a woman had the right to defend herself if she was being sexually assaulted, even if she murdered her assailant. However, when one of Celia's attorneys attempted to have Judge William Hall inform the jury that a black slave woman should be treated equally as a free white woman under the Missouri law, Judge Hall refused to provide these instructions to the jury.

Under the Missouri Slave Code of 1804, there was no difference between a slave and personal property. Therefore, Judge Hall instructed the jury that Newsom could not have raped Celia because she was his property and the owner of property could not intrude upon his own property.

On October 10, 1855, the jury of 12 white men returned a verdict of guilty against Celia, and Judge Hall sentenced her to be hanged for the crime of murder. Under Missouri law, a pregnant woman could not be executed so the hanging was scheduled for November 16, 1855, when Celia would have already given birth to her child. The court records indicate that Celia gave birth to a stillborn child while awaiting her execution.

Celia's case was appealed to the Missouri Supreme Court based upon her attorneys' claims that Judge Hall had exercised prejudice in his rulings and also because he failed to instruct the jury about Celia's motive of self-defense. While the Missouri Supreme Court agreed to hear Celia's appeal, they refused to issue a stay of execution for Celia to prevent her hanging before the Missouri Supreme Court could actually hear her case. A number of citizens from Calloway County helped Celia escape temporarily from the jail in order to prevent her execution on November 16, 1855; however, she was later returned to authorities and a new execution date was scheduled. The Missouri Supreme Court finally ruled against the appeal of Celia, and she was hanged on December 21, 1855, at the age of 19.

The decision in the case of *Missouri v. Celia, a Slave,* was significant because, at the time, the entire country was forcefully engaged in a debate over the issue of slavery. Celia and her attorneys courageously challenged a system where the law had a limited effect over the behavior of paternalistic slave owners who routinely forced female slaves into sexual relationships. The Missouri Supreme Court also ruled in favor of slavery in the infamous *Dred Scott v. Sanford* (1857) case that was eventually appealed to the U.S. Supreme Court. The U.S. Supreme Court upheld the Missouri Supreme Court's decision in the *Dred Scott* case by holding that Congress could not force states to be "free states" and blacks could not sue for their freedom in federal court because they were not citizens under the U.S. Constitution. The *Dred Scott* decision has been cited by historians and legal scholars as one of the main causes of the Civil War.

Scott P. Johnson

See Also: Interracial Marriage and Sex (19th Century); Slavery and the Civil War

Primary Document: 1855, *Missouri v. Celia, a Slave*

Further Reading

Burke, Diane Mutti. *On Slavery's Border: Missouri's Small-Slaveholding Households, 1815–1865.* Athens: University of Georgia Press, 2010.

Frazier, Harriet C. *Slavery and Crime in Missouri, 1773–1865.* Jefferson, NC: McFarland & Company, 2001.

Gordon-Reed, Annette, ed. *Race on Trial: Law and Justice in American History.* New York: Oxford University Press, 2002.

Lubet, Steven. *Fugitive Justice: Runaways, Rescuers, and Slavery on Trial.* Cambridge, MA: Harvard University Press, 2010.

McLaurin, Melton A. *Celia, a Slave: A True Story of Violence and Retribution in Antebellum Missouri.* Athens: University of Georgia Press, 1991.

Maria Mitchell (seated), the first female professional astronomer, shown here with student Mary W. Whitney (standing) in the observatory at Vassar College. (Special Collections, Vassar College Libraries)

Mitchell, Maria (1818–1889)

Pre-eminent American astronomer and strong advocate for women's rights, Maria Mitchell grew up on Nantucket Island. She became famous in 1847 after discovering a comet. She was one of the first professors at Vassar College, the first post-secondary institute for women in the United States.

Mitchell credited her upbringing for much of her later success. Nantucket's isolation from the continent secluded the residents from many contemporary influences. People on the island prized learning, and Mitchell's Quaker upbringing stressed hard work, a quiet demeanor, and, in many respects, equal opportunities for women.

Mitchell was the first of 10 children in her family, nine of whom survived childhood. Her father was a banker and astronomer and her mother a librarian. From her early years, Mitchell loved to go up on the house's catwalk at night to practice astronomy with her father. By the time she was in her twenties, she led these expeditions to view the stars. In 1836 she assumed the position of librarian at the newly built Athenaeum. The job suited her well, because she could pursue her own studies when not helping someone.

In 1843, after much deliberation, Mitchell left the Quaker faith. She could not bear its distrust of color and beauty, and she disliked its harsh punishments for members whose infractions were, in her opinion, relatively mild. Nevertheless, she continued to hold onto Quaker attitudes, such as valuing simplicity and directness.

On October 1, 1847, Mitchell noticed the appearance of a strange fuzzy body through her telescope that she had never seen before. She called her father who identified it as a comet. He immediately reported the discovery, which turned out to be the first viewing ever of that particular comet. Maria Mitchell became an overnight sensation for her discovery. In 1848 she became the first female member of the American Academy of Arts and Sciences, the first of many honors. In 1849, Mitchell began working for the *American Euphemeris and Nautical Almanac.*

In 1857, a wealthy Chicago banker invited Mitchell to chaperone his young daughter through the South and then abroad to Europe. Mitchell saw this as a great opportunity to view the world and kept a journal of her experiences in the South. In her journal, Mitchell discussed the issue dominating the nation: slavery. She visited a slave market in New Orleans, heard white Southerners' defense of slavery, and observed related Southern attitudes about Northern "intrusions" into Southern affairs. As a result of her trip, Mitchell concluded that slavery was at least as great an evil for the master as for the slave.

One of Mitchell's brothers, Andrew, commanded a Union merchant ship in Mobile Bay during the Civil War. Another brother, Forster, went to the South to educate freedmen and later became a missionary.

After the war, Maria Mitchell took a position teaching astronomy at Vassar College in Poughkeepsie, New York. Throughout her 23-year tenure there, she was a strong supporter of and role model for women's rights. She died on June 28, 1889, in Lynn, Massachusetts.

Ellen H. Todras

See Also: Education of Women (before the Civil War); Quakers; Slavery and the Civil War

Further Reading

Albers, Henry, ed. *Maria Mitchell: A Life in Journals and Letters.* Clinton Corners, NY: College Avenue Press, 2001.

Bergland, Renee. *Maria Mitchell and the Sexing of Science: An Astronomer among the American Romantics.* Boston, MA: Beacon Press, 2008.

Wright, Helen. *Sweeper in the Sky: The Life of Maria Mitchell, First Woman Astronomer in America.* New York: College Avenue Press, 1997 [1949].

Molly Pitcher Legend

The name "Molly Pitcher" was a generic reference to women who provided artillery support during the American Revolution. Thousands of women lived among the army as camp followers and performed odd jobs such as mending, cooking, and nursing. Most camp followers were married to soldiers and stayed behind the lines during battle. Some courageous women stayed at the front, resupplying troops with ammunition, reloading guns, and serving on cannon teams. Each cannon needed at least three people to load, clean, and fire. Cannons needed to be kept cool and clean, lest remnants of smoldering gunpowder ignite while the cannon crew was reloading. Large amounts of water were needed to swab out the barrel of the cannon and relieve the thirst of the crew. No single woman can be credited with being the original Molly Pitcher, although two well-documented cases of female cannoneers are usually associated with the legend.

Margaret Corbin (1751–1800) lived most of her life in hardscrabble conditions, having been orphaned at the age of five when her father was killed by Indians and her mother taken captive, and never heard from again. Margaret Corbin married as a teenager and followed her husband, John, into the army at the outset of the American Revolution.

In November 1776 Margaret and her husband were defending Fort Washington along the banks of the Hudson River. The British frigate *Pearl* made its was up the river, firing on the fort at the same time Hessian troops assaulted the American position from below the ridge. Unable to lower their cannons to defend against the advancing Hessians, the American troops came under heavy fire. John Corbin was mortally wounded, and Margaret took his place swabbing and loading the cannon. She took three grapeshot wounds in her arm, almost severing it from her body. Totally disabled, she was taken prisoner after the fort fell to the British. Perhaps because of her gender, she was given over to the American hospital at Philadelphia, where she partially recovered.

Margaret Corbin never regained the use of her arm, but was willing to continue in service. She became part of the Corp of Invalids, composed of disabled veterans who could no longer fight but were able to perform guard duty and instruct new soldiers. She was transferred to the fort at West Point, where she served for the duration of the war. In 1779 Margaret Corbin was awarded with a lifetime annuity of one-half monthly pay in recognition of her service.

In her later years Margaret Corbin suffered lingering pain from her injuries and bitterness from not receiving the full pay of a soldier. She had always been a hard drinker, which worsened her already cantankerous temper. She was called "Captain Molly" by the locals, but

Stories of "Molly Pitcher" spread throughout the battlefields of the American Revolution. (National Archives and Records Administration)

"Dirty Kate" behind her back. The command at West Point sympathized with Corgin, knowing she was unable to care for herself, and tried to find families who would take her in. In 1786 an officer wrote: "I am at a loss what to do with Captain Molly. She is such an offensive person that people are unwilling to take her in charge." Margaret Corbin remained in the West Point area for the rest of her life. She was able to receive rations from the fort, but probably had little comfort in her final years. She is the only soldier of the Revolutionary War buried at the Military Academy at West Point.

Mary Ludwig (ca. 1754–1832) was working as a domestic servant when she married John Hayes, a barber. When John enlisted in the army at the beginning of the Revolution, Mary chose to continue working as a servant in Carlisle, Pennsylvania. After a few years, she decided to join her husband in the army as a camp follower. She was at his side during the Battle of Monmouth, where the temperatures soared to almost 100 degrees. She brought water to the thirsty troops, and when her husband collapsed from heat exhaustion, she took his place at the cannon. A private, Joseph Plumb Martin, later published his memoirs of the war. He recorded an incident at the Battle of Monmouth, which probably referred to Mary Hayes. He noted that a woman was helping her husband load a cannon when: "a cannon shot from the enemy passed directly between her legs without doing any other damage than carrying away all the lower part of her petticoat. Looking at it with apparent unconcern, she observed that it was lucky it did not pass a little higher, for in that case it might have carried away something else, and continued her occupation."

Both Mary Hays and her husband survived the war and returned to Carlisle, Pennsylvania. After her husband died, she married John McCauley, also a Revolutionary War veteran. Mary was never a person of comfortable financial means. She worked most of her life as a cleaning woman and received no pensions from the government until 1822, when she was awarded a modest annual annuity of $40.

Dorothy A. Mays

See Also: The American Revolution; Sampson, Deborah

Further Reading

Landis, John B. *A Short History of Molly Pitcher: The Heroine of the Battle of Monmouth.* Carlisle: Cornman Printing, 1905.

Teipe, Emily J. "Will the Real Molly Pitcher Please Stand Up?" *Prologue: Quarterly of the National Archives and Records Administration* 31 (1999): 118–126.

Ward, Harry M. "Two Mollies." In *Women in World History,* edited by Anne Commire. Waterford, CT: Yorkin Publications, 1999.

Moral Reform

In the 19th century, white women expanded upon their role as moral guardians of the home to reform themselves, women of other classes and locations, and eventually to address larger social problems, such as prostitution, alcoholism, poverty, crime, and disease. These social problems only a decade or so previous would have been less prominent features of American society, and they would certainly not have been appropriate concerns of America's wives and mothers.

With a religious motivation toward perfectionism (striving to be Christ-like), many of the earliest reform associations focused inward on improving the individual. For middle-class women, this meant improving themselves as mothers. The first "maternal association" was organized in Portland, Maine, in 1815, and numerous others were established in the coming decades throughout New England and New York. In maternal associations, women met together to discuss childrearing ideas, with older, or at least more experienced, women providing assistance to new mothers on "how best to train up our children." Such associations were usually church based, assisting mothers in the religious education of their children. The associations quickly became more like support groups on a range of parenting issues, with each member expected to "suggest to her sister members such hints as her own experience may furnish, or circumstances seem to render necessary."

Concern about the moral health of the family led to concern about other families and the community at large. Wives of merchants and lawyers gathered together under names like the Female Missionary Society, not to be missionaries themselves, but to raise funds to send young male missionaries into frontier areas where people might not be reached by the revivals then sweeping Northern cities. Middle-class white women concerned about the religious training of their own children and of the children of immigrants and workers as well were largely responsible for the emergence of a Sunday school movement in the early decades of the century, creating almost 50,000 Sunday schools in the United States by the 1820s.

Free black women also used the church as a springboard to female collectivity and activism. More so than the maternal associations of white women, the most popular self-help societies in Northern African American communities were the mutual relief societies or benevolent associations (characteristic of many urban immigrant communities as well). Both men and women of the working and middle classes organized such charitable organizations in the early 19th century. As precursors to the protections eventually offered by life or disability insurance policies, early benevolent or relief societies were established by churchwomen in order to collect and distribute food, clothing, and sometimes cash for the poor, sick, orphaned, or widowed. Between 1821 and 1829 the Philadelphia-based Daughters of Africa claimed some 200 women (themselves mostly poor and working class) as members, who raised money and channeled it back into the community in the form of payments to the sick who could not work or loans to families for funeral expenses. Other organizations had names such as the African Female Benevolent Society of Newport, Rhode Island, or the Colored Female Religious and Moral Society of Salem, Massachusetts.

In the 1830s, both black and white women focused on their own improvement by forming literary societies to educate themselves. Whereas white women focused on improving their education in order to more effectively perform their duties as wives and as mothers who must educate their children, black women perceived a different importance and justification for their own education, that of combating racism. As the Female Literary Association of Philadelphia described their mission in 1831: "As daughters of a despised race, it becomes a duty . . . to cultivate the talents entrusted to our keeping, that by so doing, we may break down the strong barrier of prejudice." These women reformers worked to combat racism, and therefore the philosophical justification for slavery, by proving themselves to be intelligent beings. One "Miss Jennings," speaking at an 1837 meeting of the Ladies' Literary Society in New York, emphasized that "the mind is the greatest" of black women's powers "and great care should be taken to improve it with diligence. Neglect will plunge us into deep degradation . . . while our enemies will rejoice and say, we do not believe (the colored people) have any minds; if they have, they are unsusceptible of improvement." Whether explicitly or implicitly, women's charitable and literary societies, both black and white, with their emphasis on women's moral authority, laid the foundations for women's prominent role in the emerging antislavery movement.

The religious and spiritual renewal of the era combined with women's expanded vision of their role in protecting the welfare of women and children throughout society. From maternal or literary associations of like-minded women from a specific community, reformers soon reached out to other women unlike themselves, such as widows, immigrants, and even prostitutes. The New York Female Moral Reform Society was founded in 1834 and the Boston Female Moral Reform Society the following year, in 1835. These organizations collectively claimed thousands of members and the moral reform movement quickly became national in scope, spawning the need for a national organization, the American Female Moral Reform Society, with its own publication, the *Advocate of Moral Reform*. By the 1840s, moral reform had moved from local church-based activities to a national movement involving women reformers in new types of political strategies and activism around issues such as abolitionism, prostitution reform, temperance, and women's rights.

Tiffany K. Wayne

See Also: Abolitionism and the Antislavery Movement; Beecher, Catharine; Education of Women (before the Civil War); Grimké, Sarah Moore; Grimké Weld, Angelina; Quakers; Temperance Movement

Further Reading

Abzug, Robert H. *Cosmos Crumbling: American Reform and the Religious Imagination*. New York: Oxford University Press, 1994.

Dixon, Chris. *Perfecting the Family: Antislavery Marriages in Nineteenth-Century America*. Amherst: University of Massachusetts Press, 1997.

Dorsey, Bruce. *Reforming Men and Women: Gender in the Antebellum City*. Ithaca, NY: Cornell University Press, 2002.

Ryan, Mary. *Cradle of the Middle Class: The Family in Oneida County, New York, 1790–1865*. New York: Cambridge University Press, 1981.

Sterling, Dorothy, ed. *We Are Your Sisters: Black Women in the Nineteenth Century*. New York: W. W. Norton, 1997.

Mott, Lucretia (1793–1880)

One of the pioneers of the women's movement in the United States, the Quaker abolitionist and feminist Lucretia Mott was the guiding light, with Elizabeth Cady

Quaker minister, abolitionist, and women's rights advocate Lucretia Mott played a major role in early 19th-century American reform movements. (Library of Congress)

Stanton, of the landmark 1848 Seneca Falls convention on women's rights. In her lifelong commitment to racial and women's equality, she defended women's right to a place in active public life. She also became a respected international figure, through whom ongoing links between feminists in the United States and Europe were firmly established.

Born in Nantucket, Massachusetts, where her father worked on the whaling ships of the Atlantic Ocean, Lucretia Coffin spent her early years under the influence of her mother and female neighbors during her father's long absences at sea, thus instilling in her an unshakable conviction in women's equality with men. The family moved inland in 1804, and from the age of 13, Lucretia was educated at the Society of Friends' Nine Partners boarding school near Poughkeepsie, New York. She stayed on there as an unpaid teacher to pay the tuition of her younger sister. After discovering that female teachers at the school were paid only half the salary of male teachers, she became an advocate of women's right to equal pay.

In 1811 Lucretia Coffin married James Mott, a fellow teacher, and moved to Philadelphia, where the couple reared six children. As members of the more liberally minded Hicksite Quaker faction, the couple were mutually supportive in shared causes, and James eventually gave up his commission business because it made money from slave-produced cotton. Having natural gifts as an orator, Lucretia Mott became a regular speaker at Quaker meetings from 1818 and in 1821 was ordained a minister. She began touring and lecturing on abolitionism, urging a boycott of slave-produced sugar and cotton and in 1829 speaking for the first time in black churches.

Mott attended the founding convention of the American Anti-Slavery Society (AASS), held by William Lloyd Garrison in 1833, but like all the other women present, she was not allowed to formally join. Later that year, the AASS changed its policy on women's exclusion, and Mott and several other women, seven of them free blacks, together founded a women's branch of the society in Philadelphia, with Mott as president. In May 1838 she and other women abolitionists had to run the gauntlet of mob violence, when they staged the first Anti-Slavery Convention of American Women, again held in Philadelphia. The baying crowds outside, accusing the convention's mixed audience of men and women, whites and blacks, of "promiscuity" for meeting together, only served to reinforce Mott's conviction that there were direct parallels between the slavery of blacks and the oppression of women. She would lay out her arguments on the subject in her 1840 pamphlet, "Slavery and 'The Woman Question.'"

When the American Anti-Slavery Society held its annual meeting in 1840, Mott was given a role in its administration by Garrison, along with Lydia Maria Child and Abby Kelly Foster. Several male members of the society walked out of the meeting in protest, and Mott would thereafter frequently be accused by conservatives in the Quaker movement of having "fanned the flames of dissension" and of demoralizing the antislavery ranks by raising the issue of women's public participation. In London later that year for the World Anti-Slavery Convention, Mott, Stanton, and five other women who had traveled from the United States again found themselves banned from taking part in the proceedings. Refused the right to sit on the main convention floor as delegates, they were obliged to secrete themselves in the balcony at the back of the hall, screened behind a curtain.

During the convention, Stanton was deeply impressed by Mott, who introduced her to the English feminist Mary Wollstonecraft's *A Vindication of the Rights of Woman,* long sections of which Mott knew by heart. The two women struck up a lifelong friendship, and Stanton would later describe Mott as being "an entirely new revelation of womanhood" to her. By the end of the convention, incensed by their segregation as women, Mott and Stanton returned to the United States determined to foster their own separate movement for women's rights and to set up a convention to discuss the subject.

Family and other commitments, however, prevented Mott and Stanton from bringing their plan to fruition until eight years later. In the intervening period, Mott was active in a range of causes: she spoke for the abolition of slavery in the legislatures of Delaware, New Jersey, and Pennsylvania; inspired the establishment of the Northern Association for the Relief of Poor Women; and also defended the rights of striking handloom workers. She even had the courage to criticize her own Quaker community, protesting its attempts to impose changes on the traditional life of the local Seneca peoples.

In 1848 Mott and Stanton finally organized a convention on women's rights at Seneca Falls, New York—the first of its kind to be held in the United States. Mott also helped to draft the convention's manifesto, the now-famous Declaration of Sentiments and Resolutions. On the final day of its discussion, Mott also spoke on the rights of women to take up the ministry and proposed "the overthrow of the monopoly of the pulpit." When the resolutions were finally voted on, Mott withheld her approval of resolution nine on women's suffrage for religious reasons. It was a fundamental Quaker principle at that time to boycott the vote until the U.S. government ended slavery. Like other Quaker women, Mott upheld this principle, although she would later modify her position on women's suffrage.

From Seneca Falls until her death, Mott remained a revered figure in the women's movement in the United States, as she traveled from one women's rights convention to another. In 1850 she published her "Discourse on Woman," in which she exposed the long-standing inequalities women had suffered legally and politically, most particularly in education and employment, and argued for their equality with husbands within marriage. During the 1850s, she traveled as a Quaker minister, and her advocacy of women's rights and equality in marriage was constantly reiterated in her sermons. Mott also made visits to prisons and mental asylums, throughout all of her campaigning being given unquestioning support by her husband, who joined her in her travels. Their harmonious life together became living confirmation of Mott's belief that "in the true relationship, the independence of the husband and wife is equal, their dependence mutual, and their obligations reciprocal."

The 1850s also marked Mott's increasing involvement with abolitionism in the lead-up to the Civil War. With the passing of the 1850 Fugitive Slave Act, the Motts' home was used as a staging post for the Underground Railroad, and during the war, as a pacifist, she continued to promote nonresistance and the rights of conscientious objectors, as well as organizing aid. Mott remained a powerful moral force during the war, in 1863 helping to found the National Women's Loyal League, which had as its objective passage of a constitutional amendment outlawing slavery. In the wake of the subsequent passage of the Thirteenth Amendment, Mott became caught up in the debate on black suffrage. She supported the awarding of the vote to male blacks and their access to better education through the Friends Association of Philadelphia for the Aid and Elevation of the Freedman. She joined the American Equal Rights Association in 1866 to campaign not just against racial intolerance but also for suffrage and civil rights for *all* Americans, including the right of women to divorce if their marriage was oppressive. Mott often took on the role of mediator between opposing factions in both the abolitionist and women's movements. In 1869, after presiding at the first convention of the National Woman Suffrage Association (NWSA), she attempted to prevent the suffrage movement from splitting into the two factions of NWSA and the American Woman Suffrage Association.

Similarly, she encouraged religious tolerance when, in 1867, she became a cofounder in Boston with other liberal Christians and Jews of the Free Religious Association. As a Quaker, Mott supported the Society of Friends' "Testimony of Peace," which repudiated all violence and war, as well as all forms of coercive government. In 1839 she had become a member of the New England Non-Resistance Society and stayed true to her belief in nonresistance when faced with hostility and mob violence during abolitionist conventions. During the Civil War, despite giving moral support to John Brown's militant abolitionism, she had abhorred the violence of his actions at Harper's Ferry. After the war, she and Alfred Love co-founded the Universal Peace Union and Pennsylvania Peace Society, with Mott serving the former as vice president from 1870 and the latter as president until her death.

Such was her reputation that even during her lifetime Mott would be heralded as the grandmother of the women's movement. Elizabeth Cady Stanton defined her as "a woman emancipated from all faith in man-made creeds, from all fear of his denunciations." Mott continued to attend Quaker, women's rights, and suffrage conventions until her death, making her last public appearance at a Quaker convention in 1880 at the age of 87.

In 1923, Alice Paul of the National Woman's Party named the proposed federal equal rights amendment the Lucretia Mott Amendment in Mott's honor, though it failed to be ratified.

Helen Rappaport

See Also: Aboltionism and the Antislavery Movement; Child, Lydia Maria; Foster, Abby Kelley; National Women's Loyal League; Quakers; Seneca Falls Convention; Wollstonecraft, Mary; American Equal Rights Association (Vol. 2); American Woman Suffrage Association (Vol. 2); Paul, Alice (Vol. 2); Stanton, Elizabeth Cady (Vol. 2)

Primary Document: 1848, Declaration of Sentiments

Further Reading

Bacon, Margaret Hope. *Valiant Friend: The Life of Lucretia Mott.* New York: Walker, 1980.

Faulkner, Carol. *Lucretia Mott's Heresy: Abolition and Women's Rights in Nineteenth-Century America.* Philadelphia: University of Pennsylvania Press, 2011.

McFadden, Margaret. *Golden Cables of Sympathy: The Transatlantic Sources of Nineteenth-Century Feminism.* Lexington: University Press of Kentucky, 1999.

McMillen, Sally G. *Seneca Falls and the Origins of the Women's Rights Movement.* New York: Oxford University Press, 2008.

Wellman, Judith. *The Road to Seneca Falls: Elizabeth Cady Stanton and the First Woman's Rights Convention.* Urbana: University of Illinois Press, 2004.

Mullaney, Kate (1845–1906)

Kate Mullaney (also Mullany) was the founder of the Collar Laundry Union (CLU) in 1864, which became a model for subsequent women's labor unions. Mullaney was also the first woman to be appointed to a national union office when, in 1868, she became assistant secretary and women's organizer for the National Labor Union (NLU).

Very little is known about Mullaney's early life or formal education. She was born in Ireland, and her family emigrated when she was a teen. Like many Irish Catholics, the Mullaneys were destined for a working-class life. Her family settled in Troy, New York, an industrial city that featured numerous iron foundries as well as commercial laundries that cleaned detachable shirt collars and cuffs. (These items were first developed in Troy in 1827, and the city manufactured about 90 percent of the nation's stock by the 1860s. In the 19th century, one usually laundered collars and cuffs far more frequently than entire shirts.) Her father died when Mullaney was 19, and her mother's delicate health required that Kate become the family breadwinner. More than 3,000 women toiled in Troy's 14 commercial laundries, often working up to 14 hours per day for as little as $3 per week. In addition, caustic chemicals, hot water, bleach, and the rapid pace of work exposed laundry workers to burns and other dangers. Newly developed starch machines were especially infamous for inducing horrifying burns.

Mullaney entered factory life in order to provide for her mother and four siblings. Troy was a strong union town, anchored by the Iron Molders Union (IMU) and its dynamic president and future NLU leader William Sylvis. Inspired by the molders and by unions like the Cigar Makers International Union which had begun to accept female members, Mullaney decided to organize Troy's laundresses into the CLU. Some sources credit this as the first women's labor union in the United States, though the Lowell Female Reform Association formed by Sarah Bagley in 1845 predates it.

On February 23, 1864, Mullaney, aided by the IMU, led a strike of about 300 women. In just a week's time, 14 Troy laundry establishments granted pay rises of over 20 percent and agreed to address safety concerns. In 1866, Mullaney led another successful strike that raised laundress wages to about $14 per week. In that same year, William Sylvis and other labor activists formed the NLU. Sylvis launched a rhetorical call to organize women based on the CLU's success. In 1868, Mullaney attended a New York City labor congress and was elected as second vice president of the NLU. Mullaney declined that honor, but Sylvis appointed her as an NLU assistant secretary and organizer for women's work.

Mullaney showed great acumen in building up the collar union's treasury, whose resources she occasionally used to show solidarity with other New York workers. In 1868, for example, the CLU donated $500 to striking New York City bricklayers. In March 1869, Mullaney helped CLU starchers win a strike. The CLU's phenomenal success ended later that year, however. When the CLU struck again in May, laundry owners decided to break the union. Workers received substantial financial assistance from the IMU and moral support from the NLU, but Troy laundry owners offered wage increases only to women who agreed to quit the CLU. Mullaney was briefly the president of the Union Line Collar and Cuff Manufactory, an attempt at a worker-owned cooperative. The co-op actually landed a major contract to supply A. T. Stewart, then New York City's largest department store, only to run afoul of technological change. The development of paper collars altered the equation, and both the CLU and Troy quickly faded as suppliers of collars, cuffs, and shirts.

The CLU was also damaged by the death of William Sylvis in July 1869. Sylvis was a champion of women's rights, and with his death, both financial support from the molders' union and the NLU's rhetorical commitment to working women declined. Both the CLU and the NLU disappeared shortly after Sylvis's death. In February 1870, Mullaney dissolved the CLU, and she and other women returned to work according to pre-May 1869 wage scales.

The CLU was an important forerunner and model for subsequent efforts at organizing women, especially those of the Knights of Labor. Not much is known about Mullaney's career after 1870. She eventually married John Fogarty and died in 1906. For many years her body lay in an unmarked grave in Troy. In the 1990s, Mullaney was belatedly recognized for her precocious accomplishments. Her Troy home became a National Historic Landmark in 1998, with Hilary Rodham Clinton adding her voice to those praising Mullaney. In 1999, local labor leaders and Irish cultural organizations adorned Mullaney's grave with a suitable monument.

Robert E. Weir

See Also: Bagley, Sarah; Labor Unions (19th Century); Lowell Textile Mills; Moral Reform

Further Reading

Kate Mullaney: A True Labor Pioneer. Albany: New York State Public Employees Federation, AFL-CIO, 1998.

"Kate Mullany National Historic Site." National Park Service, http://www.katemullanynhs.org/

Montgomery, David. "William Sylvis and the Search for Working-Class Citizenship." In *Labor Leaders in America*, edited by Melvyn Dubofsky and Warren Van Tine. Urbana: University of Illinois Press, 1987.

Sigillito, Gina. *Daughters of Maeve: 50 Irish Women Who Changed the World.* New York: Citadel Press, 2007.

Turbin, Carole. *Working Women of Collar City: Gender, Class, and Community in Troy, New York, 1864–86.* Urbana: University of Illinois Press, 1992.

Murray, Judith Sargent (1751–1820)

Judith Sargent Murray's voluminous writings can be credited with helping to define the role of women in the new United States and shaping the way they should be educated in the late 18th and early 19th centuries. Her father was a wealthy merchant, and Judith Sargent grew up in a financially privileged environment. After being raised in a home where she was envious of the fine education provided to only her brother, Judith railed against the sense of inadequacy she felt because of her inferior educational opportunities.

At age 18 Judith married John Stevens, a sea captain and merchant. The marriage was childless and appears to have been a disappointment to Judith. The couple struggled with finances throughout much of their marriage, causing Judith intense psychological anxiety. Her helplessness in the face of the family's mounting debts convinced her that women should be educated not only to be fit wives and mothers, but to provide them with the tools of economic self-sufficiency. In 1786 the family finances had sunk to such a state that her husband fled to the West Indies in order to avoid being sent to a debtors' prison. He died before he could repair his finances, leaving Judith to pay off the creditors. Although she was eventually able to do so, the experience gave her a lasting fear of financial insolvency.

In 1774 Judith had met and become intrigued by the Universalist minister John Murray. She cast aside her strict Congregationalist upbringing to embrace this optimistic doctrine, which stressed the beauty of human spirituality and God's benevolence toward mankind. Two years after she was widowed, Judith married John Murray and moved to Boston, where they established the first Universalist congregation in the city. Once again Murray was plagued by financial uncertainty, and she tried supplementing the family income through writing. Throughout her adulthood Murray had written poems and essays, but most of these had been privately circulated only among friends and family. She occasionally published under a pseudonym beginning in 1782, but by the 1790s she was turning out numerous poems and essays for publication under the pen name Constantia. In 1790 she published "On the Equality of the Sexes" in the *Massachusetts Magazine*. The provocative essay argued that women possessed essentially the same degree of reason, imagination, and intelligence as did men, but had been deprived of the education necessary to apply these talents toward worthy goals.

Many of Judith Murray's writings relate to education and the role of women. She is often credited with

Judith Sargent Murray was a Massachusetts essayist who wrote on many topics including religion, politics, and women's education in the 18th century. (Terra Foundation for American Art, Chicago/Art Resource, New York)

setting the stage for what is now called "Republican Motherhood," which stressed the importance of educated mothers. Well-educated women were most likely to be capable of raising children to become productive citizens in the new society. Although women had no formal role in the governance of the new republic, they were essential to instilling the virtues of honor and perseverance in their children. The survival of the republic depended on the quality of its citizens, and Judith Murray argued that it was women who were best positioned to convey these qualities to their children during their crucial, formative years. Her ideas were persuasive, and her writings were widely published in a number of journals throughout New England. It is ironic that as she succeeded in elevating the importance of motherhood, she helped create a cult of domesticity that kept women within the ever-narrowing realm of the home in the 19th century.

In 1798 Murray published a collection of her essays in the three-volume collection called *The Gleaner*, named after a male character she created, Mr. Virgillius, who was free to wander through the city, talking and observing various aspects of urban life. The fact that she chose to tell her stories through the male viewpoint of Mr. Virgillius speaks to Murray's belief that the thoughts of a man had a credibility that the average reader was unwilling to extend to a woman. She also delved into the world of the theater, writing two comedies, *The Medium* (1795) and *The Traveler Returned* (1796). Neither play was successful, and Murray blamed their failure on the unpopularity of her husband's Universalist religion.

Judith Murray was able to earn a modest living from her writing, but John Murray's health declined after a series of strokes. After his death in 1815 she moved to Mississippi to live with her daughter, who had married a wealthy planter.

Dorothy A. Mays

See Also: Adams, Abigail; Education of Women (before the Civil War); Republican Motherhood; Warren, Mercy Otis; Wollstonecraft, Mary

Primary Document: 1790, "On the Equality of the Sexes"

Further Reading

Harris, Sharon M. *Selected Writings of Judith Sargent Murray.* New York: Oxford University Press, 1995.

Judith Sargent Murray Society. Accessed January 31, 2010. http://www.jsmsociety.com/home.html

Skemp, Sheila L. *Judith Sargent Murray: A Brief Biography with Documents.* Boston, MA: Bedford/St. Martin's, 1998.

Skemp, Sheila L. *First Lady of Letters: Judith Sargent Murray and the Struggle for Female Independence.* Philadelphia: Pennsylvania University Press, 2009.

N

National Women's Loyal League

A group of reformers who wanted to play an active political role in the outcome of the American Civil War organized the National Women's Loyal League (NWLL) in 1863.

After President Abraham Lincoln issued the Emancipation Proclamation freeing slaves in the rebel states, effective January 1, 1863, abolitionists and women's rights activists Susan B. Anthony and Elizabeth Cady Stanton issued a "Call for a Meeting of the Loyal Women of the Nation" and organized women to urge Congress to pass a constitutional amendment permanently ending slavery everywhere. The resultant NWLL first met in New York on May 14, 1863, and its primary work over the next year and a half of its existence was to collect signatures in support of such an amendment. By August 1864, the league had approximately 5,000 members and had collected and presented to Radical Republican allies in Congress some 400,000 signatures. The Thirteenth Amendment to the Constitution, abolishing slavery throughout the United States, was ratified immediately after the war in 1865.

The founders and officers of the NWLL had been prominent women's rights leaders before the war. While the war temporarily slowed the efforts of the organized women's movement, many reformers from both the women's rights and the antislavery movements continued their efforts on behalf of the emancipation of slaves while emphasizing the need for an expanded role for women. At the first meeting of the NWLL, Stanton articulated women's desire to make a contribution to the war beyond sacrificing their sons, nursing, and supplying soldiers with clothes and food. Although society had given men the ability to act on the battlefield while women primarily remained on the home front, Stanton emphasized that women had a vital part to play in the war.

In their effort to include the concerns of women, Stanton and Anthony revived the issue of the vote—of women's right to equal citizenship—as one of the goals of the war. In a special resolution at the first meeting of the League, they declared that the peace and survival of the nation required equal rights and voting for all women and African Americans. Not all league members agreed with the demand for suffrage, however, with the opposition declaring the idea of giving the vote to women as well as blacks would endanger the League's larger goal of gathering support for immediate abolition. Newspapers reported on this debate and controversy within the NWLL by criticizing the fact that a group that had been created with exemplary patriotic motive to end slavery had instead transformed into a radical movement for women's rights. The women's suffrage resolution passed, but membership in the League declined after that point.

Although supportive of the Union cause, NWLL leaders such as Stanton and Ernestine Rose were publicly critical of President Abraham Lincoln for not demanding full emancipation as a stated goal of the war. For this political boldness, these women faced criticism by some newspapers, including the *New York Herald,* which cynically suggested that perhaps the women might take over national politics themselves. The NWLL met weekly in New York, even during the week of the July 1863 draft riots, and all of the major newspapers covered the proceedings of this "great uprising" of Northern women.

Thinking that their Republican congressional allies at least would agree with their aims, the women must have been disappointed when Charles Sumner thanked them for their work in collecting signatures but expressed dissatisfaction that women were engaged in the masculine field of politics. In the end, the relative success of the women's efforts in gathering and delivering their petitions was more a function of the public's perception of the wartime political participation of women as a function of extraordinary circumstances, not as a desirable model for women's continued political action. After the war, and especially after black men were granted the vote in 1870 with the Fifteenth Amendment, white women of the NWLL and their allies returned to a reorganized women's rights movement now focused exclusively on securing the vote for women.

Tiffany K. Wayne

See Also: Abolitionism and the Antislavery Movement; Fifteenth Amendment; Rose, Ernestine; Slavery and the Civil War; Anthony, Susan B. (Vol. 2); Stanton, Elizabeth Cady (Vol. 2)

Further Reading

Ryan, Mary. *Women in Public: Between Banners and Ballots, 1825–1880.* Baltimore, MD: Johns Hopkins University Press, 1990.

Venet, Wendy Hamand. *Neither Ballots nor Bullets: Women Abolitionists and the Civil War.* Charlottesville: University Press of Virginia, 1991.

New York Married Women's Property Acts

For six years, from 1854 to 1860, Susan B. Anthony waged a massive campaign to persuade legislators to amend the Married Women's Property Law in New York state. As a young woman, Anthony was only too aware of the problems that arose when married women had no rights to their inherited property. For the first half of the 19th century, a married woman's property belonged to her husband. When the New York state legislature enacted the original Married Women's Property Law in 1848, Anthony's mother, Lucy Read Anthony, at long last received the title to their Rochester farm, property that had been purchased in 1845 with money she had inherited from her parents. To protect the farm from being claimed by her husband Daniel Anthony's creditors, Read Anthony's brother, Joshua Read, had superintended her inheritance, made the actual purchase of the farm, managed its payments, and held its title in his name until the law was enacted.

Twelve years of activism preceded the passage of the 1848 property law. Both male and female reformers had been instrumental in the effort to secure its enactment. Ernestine Potowski Rose, Paulina Wright (Davis), and Elizabeth Cady Stanton, all of whom later became leaders in the women's rights movement and close colleagues of Anthony, were among the female activists who contributed to this campaign.

Although the 1848 law secured important legal rights for married women, they still did not have the right to ownership of their own wages and other income. When Anthony toured New York state in the summer and early fall of 1853 to check on temperance societies that she had helped form the previous summer, she was discouraged to discover that almost none had survived. In talking with the women she had helped organize, she found that they had disbanded because they did not possess the funds necessary to hire speakers, to engage a meeting hall, or to purchase or print their own literature. Upon reflecting on women's financial condition, particularly their lack of access to their own money, Anthony arrived at a conclusion that would transform her beliefs about women's most pressing needs:

> Thus as I passed from town to town was I made to feel the great evil of woman's entire dependency upon man, for the necessary means to aid on any & every reform movement. . . . Woman must have a *purse* of her own, & how can this be, so long as the *Wife* is denied the right to her *individual & joint* earnings. Reflections like these, caused me to see & really feel that there was no *true freedom* for woman without the possession of all her property rights, & that these rights could be obtained through *legislation* only, & so, the sooner the demand was made of the Legislature, the sooner would we be likely to obtain them.

In November 1853, Anthony persuaded Elizabeth Cady Stanton to write a speech on the subject of women's property rights. Anthony then organized 60 women to circulate petitions demanding an expanded married women's property law and woman suffrage. The women collected a total of 10,000 signatures in a matter of weeks. The women's rights convention held in Albany in February 1854 was enormously successful, and because of popular demand, the evening meetings were extended from a two-day engagement to two weeks. Stanton delivered her address to the Senate chamber of the New York state legislature as well as to the convention. Anthony had 50,000 copies of the speech printed for distribution and Ernestine Rose and William Henry Channing presented the petitions to the legislators. To the disappointment of every activist involved, the legislators failed to respond to the petitions by the end of the legislative session.

But Anthony knew that the increase in popular support and some serious press coverage had generated greater public awareness, a deeper understanding, and more discussion of the need for women's legal rights. In late 1854, she planned a one-woman canvass of 54 counties in New York state. In the afternoons, she met only with the women of a community, delivering half of the speech she would present in its entirety that evening. Anthony emphasized how the right to their own wages would help women with the economic problems they faced. She then closed the meeting by urging the women to return with their husbands for the evening meeting, where she charged 25 cents admission and exhorted them to sign the petition she circulated.

Male legislators were impervious to Anthony's proof of popular support for an amended law. In the spring of 1856, after Anthony had been campaigning for more than three years, the chair of the Senate Judiciary Committee finally responded. The committee's report completely sidestepped every issue Anthony and Stanton had presented, ignored the petitions signed by tens of thousands of their constituents, and dismissed the entire campaign with a sarcastic, demeaning humor. The chair's report stated:

> They [the legislators] have considered it [the petitions' demand] with . . . the experience married life has given them. Thus aided, they are enabled to state that the ladies always have the best place and choicest titbit at the table. They have the best seat in the cars, carriages and sleighs. . . . They have their choice on which side of the bed they will lie, front or back. . . . It has thus appeared . . . that if there is any inequality or oppression in the case, the gentlemen are the sufferers.

Over the next three years, Anthony continued to tour, lecture, and gather signatures, all culminating in her six-week lobbying of legislators in Albany in the winter of 1860. Her efforts were successful, and on March 20, the day following Elizabeth Cady Stanton's address to the legislature, the bill was enacted. The amended property rights law, officially named "An Act Concerning the Rights and Liabilities of Husband and Wife," ensured that women gained the following rights: to own property separately from their husbands, to engage in business transactions, to manage their wages and other income, to sue and be sued, and to be joint guardian of their children with their husbands.

The triumph was short-lived, however. In 1862, when women's rights activists were intentionally inactive because of the Civil War, the New York legislature reversed many provisions of the 1860 law. In spite of this setback, the six-year campaign demonstrated strong public support for an expansion of legal rights for women. The law's enactment also established an important precedent that could not be reversed—that women as citizens were entitled to legal equality with men. The bill, and the long campaign to achieve it, also positively influenced similar property rights campaigns in many other states.

Judith E. Harper

See Also: Davis, Paulina Kellogg Wright; Mott, Lucretia; Rose, Ernestine; Stone, Lucy; Anthony, Susan B. (Vol. 2); Blackwell, Antoinette Brown (Vol. 2); Stanton, Elizabeth Cady (Vol. 2)

Primary Document: 1848–1849, New York Married Women's Property Acts

Further Reading

Barry, Kathleen. *Susan B. Anthony: Biography of a Singular Feminist.* New York: New York University Press, 1988.

DuBois, Ellen Carol, ed. *The Elizabeth Cady Stanton–Susan B. Anthony Reader: Correspondence, Writings, Speeches.* Boston, MA: Northeastern University Press, 1992.

Nichols, Clarina Howard (1810–1885)

Clarina Howard Nichols was a prolific 19th-century writer and public speaker who devoted her adult life to improving the lives of women and their children. Born Clarina Howard in West Townshend, Vermont, in 1810, she was actively involved in the temperance and abolitionist movements, but it was through her efforts to win legal and economic gains for married women during the earliest years of the women's rights movement that she distinguished herself. Her career as an activist spanned nearly 40 years, and her thinking influenced legislators in many states as well as other women's rights activists, such as Susan B. Anthony.

Clarina Howard Nichols was afforded a rare opportunity when she took over the work of her second husband, George Nichols, as the editor and publisher of the *Windham County Democrat* in Vermont. She wrote a series of editorials that has been cited as ultimately persuading Vermont politicians to enact legislation liberalizing divorce laws and giving married women property rights, including the right to own, inherit, and bequeath property, and to insure their husbands' lives. Moreover, she was the first woman to address the Vermont Legislature and the only woman asked to speak at the Kansas Constitutional Convention.

Nichols's work at the Kansas Constitutional Convention has been hailed as her most significant and enduring contribution to the cause of women. She single handedly ensured that several women's rights provisions were incorporated into the state constitution, including property rights, equal guardianship of children, and the right to vote in school district elections. These provisions gave Kansas the distinction of entering the union in 1861 as the state with the most progressive women's rights laws at the time.

Joseph Gambone, the editor of her published papers, dubbed Nichols the "forgotten feminist of Kansas." The

Clarina Howard Nichols was an abolitionist and women's rights advocate in Kansas. (Stanton, Elizabeth Cady, Susan B. Anthony, and Matilda Joslyn Gage (eds.). *History of Woman Suffrage*, 1887)

paucity of scholarly attention is best accounted for by her decision in 1854, at the height of her career, to move from her home state of Vermont to Kansas as part of the New England Emigrant Aid Company in order to settle the territory and bring it into the Union as a free state. With her move came the increased demands of farming and a grueling pioneer existence. When her husband George Nichols died, she became sole support of their three children. These circumstances prevented her from continuing to speak at women's rights and temperance conventions or participating in national organizations, thus diminishing her presence in the historical record.

Although restricted geographically, Nichols's activism did not cease; she embarked on lecture tours in the new territory, speaking to scattered, small audiences on the frontier. In addition, she began relying more extensively on her skills as a writer to reach audiences outside her immediate area. For example, she edited the Kansas *Quindaro Chindowan* and served as a contributor and correspondent for a variety of newspapers, including papers across Kansas, on the East Coast, and

those focusing on women's rights. She chafed under the physical restrictions she faced. She wrote to Susan B. Anthony that she longed to "fight a *big* fight," saying, "I sometimes cry out at being hedged in by circumstances, from joining the triumphant march of womanhood. I seem almost to have dropped out by the way, unable to keep up. . . . But Oh, how I watch and pray! I do all I can with my pen."

Like other pioneers of the women's rights movement, she successfully contended with the double burden of justifying her right to speak as well as making a powerful case for women's rights. She accomplished this by making herself appear to be traditional, even though much about her life and experiences was atypical. Her ability to portray herself as a traditional, feminine woman is especially significant because, in her rhetoric, she most often took on the contradictory and combative persona of a lawyer. She stressed that women's rights would help women better fulfill their responsibilities as Christian wives and mothers, thus making the call for women's rights seem like a modest rather than a radical proposal.

Adrienne E. Christiansen

See Also: Stone, Lucy; Temperance Movement; Anthony, Susan B. (Vol. 2); Stanton, Elizabeth Cady (Vol. 2)

Further Reading

Blackwell, Marilyn S., and Kristen T. Oertel. *Frontier Feminist: Clarina Howard Nichols and the Politics of Motherhood.* Lawrence: University Press of Kansas, 2010.

Eickhoff, Diane. *Revolutionary Heart: The Life of Clarina Nichols and the Pioneering Crusade for Women's Rights.* Kansas City: Quindaro Press, 2006.

Nichols, Mary Gove (1810–1884)

Mary Gove Nichols was a 19th-century feminist, health reformer, and advocate of free love. She was well known as a lecturer on women's health and anatomy and as an advocate of the water cure, or hydropathy.

Born Mary Sargeant Neal in New Hampshire in 1810, she was married to Hiram Gove in 1831; she later divorced Gove and in 1848 married fellow reformer and free love advocate Thomas Low Nichols.

Mary Gove Nichols began her career as a physician and lecturer on women's health, hygiene, and anatomy. These were issues that greatly concerned other reformers of the 1840s and 1850s, including another well-known lecturer on women's health, Paulina Wright

Davis. Women like Davis and Nichols were not formally trained as physicians, as medical schools were not yet open to women. They were self-educated and motivated by a larger context of reform efforts for self-improvement, and moral and physical purity that included issues such as dress reform, vegetarianism, mesmerism, and hydropathy. Hydropathy was a philosophy that promoted water (cold baths, drinking pure water, enemas) as a cure for many illnesses and diseases. In the early 1850s she contributed articles to the widely circulated *Water-Cure Journal* and together with her husband, Thomas Nichols, published *Nichols' Journal of Health, Water-Cure, and Human Progress* and *Nichols' Monthly: A Magazine of Social Science, and Progressive Literature*. The couple founded the American Hydropathic Institute in 1851 for teaching the therapeutic methods. She also published an autobiographical reform novel, *Mary Lyndon,* in 1855.

Women's rights reformers of the 19th century sought women's autonomy over many aspects of their lives. Beginning with the writings of Mary Wollstonecraft, other prominent women's rights activists who spoke or wrote about women's abuse within marriage, or about marriage as an institution restricting women's self-development and "sovereignty," included Elizabeth Cady Stanton, Sarah Grimké, and Margaret Fuller. Many utopian communities of the 1830s and 1840s also promoted alternatives to monogamous marriage.

Mary Gove Nichols was critical of the institution of marriage as restrictive of both men and women's happiness and desires, but especially of men's ownership of women in marriage. In the mid-1800s, however, even radical women's rights reformers did not openly discuss women's right to control their own bodies or acknowledge women's sexuality as anything other than for reproduction. There was not yet a movement for birth control information, though some women's rights reformers began to speak in the mid-1800s of voluntary motherhood, or a woman's right to control the number and timing of pregnancies (and therefore control sexual intercourse within marriage). And they most certainly did not advocate divorce or extramarital sexual activity for women.

Mary Gove Nichols was controversial in that, first of all, she spoke and wrote about these issues publicly. Secondly, she and her husband advocated for free love, defined as an individual's right to experience affection and love without the social constraints of duty in marriage and childbearing. A century before the sexual revolution and women's liberation movement of the 1960s, Mary Gove Nichols and some of her more radical cohorts were arguing for the separation of sex from reproduction.

Though critical of marriage, Mary Gove Nichols was married twice, though she argued for divorce as a legitimate option for ending unhappy marriages. When she left her first husband, she lost custody of her daughter to him, an issue that many women's rights activists also addressed. Gove married again a few years later to Thomas Nichols, and together the couple wrote a book on *Marriage; Its History, Character and Results; Its Sanctities and Its Profanities; Its Science and Its Facts* (1854). The free love movement would become criticized and rejected by many public figures in the next generation when it became associated with notorious radicals such as Victoria Woodhull. The Nichols later rejected their previous free love ideology and became more conservative proponents of marriage after converting to Catholicism. Mary Gove Nichols died in London in 1884.

Tiffany K. Wayne

See Also: Birth Control (17th and 18th Centuries); Davis, Paulina Kellogg Wright; Divorce (before the Civil War); Grimké, Sarah Moore; Fuller, Margaret; Utopian Communities; Wollstonecraft, Mary; Free Love Movement (Vol. 2); Stanton, Elizabeth Cady (Vol. 2); Woodhull, Victoria (Vol. 2)

Further Reading

Horowitz, Helen. *Rereading Sex: Battles over Sexual Knowledge and Suppression in Nineteenth-Century America.* New York: Knopf, 2002.

Passet, Joan. *Sex Radicals and the Quest for Woman's Equality.* Urbana: University of Illinois, 2003.

Silver-Isenstadt, Jean L. *Shameless: The Visionary Life of Mary Gove Nichols.* Baltimore, MD: Johns Hopkins University Press, 2002.

Oberlin College

Founded in 1833, and still flourishing today as a prestigious academic institution, Oberlin College in northern Ohio was the first coeducational institution to grant undergraduate degrees to women. When the Oberlin Collegiate Institute was founded in 1833 by the Rev. John Shipherd and Philo Stewart, a Presbyterian minister and a missionary, women took classes alongside men. Then in 1837, women were allowed to enroll in degree programs in addition to what had been called the "Ladies Course." The first three female graduates—Caroline Mary Rudd, Elizabeth Prall, and Mary Hosford—earned their degrees in 1841. Oberlin's decision to educate women was based on the need for more missionaries as well as more educated women who would be worthy of becoming ministers' wives. Women took classes with men in all subjects, except theology. Women and men ate together but had separate libraries. Women were banned from speaking at commencement until 1859, and in 1870 a woman gave the commencement address at Oberlin for the first time.

As well as being the first consistently coeducational college, Oberlin, which became Oberlin College in 1850, also was a leader in the education of African Americans. Oberlin first admitted students of color in 1835. The campus was also a legendary station along the Underground Railroad for escaping slaves who were seeking freedom in the northern states and Canada before the end of the Civil War. Nineteenth-century abolitionists, women's rights activists, or other reformers who graduated from Oberlin College included Lucy Stone (1847), Antoinette Brown Blackwell (1847), Mary Church Terrell (1884), and Anna Julia Cooper (1884).

Located 35 miles southwest of Cleveland, the campus today is surrounded by farmland and suburbs. Its values of social consciousness persist and merge with the school's academic purpose. For example, in the late 1990s, the college leadership sought to build a new environmental studies center that would cultivate principles of stewardship. The building plans called for it to be able to evolve with advancing technology, discharge no water, use sunlight to the maximum ability, and limit the use of toxic materials in its construction. Controversial when it was ready for occupancy in 2000, the Adam Joseph Lewis Center won several awards for its design construction and energy efficiency, and spawned other "green" initiatives.

Today, in the 21st century, Oberlin College remains dedicated to recruiting students from diverse backgrounds to enroll in its liberal arts programs that reflect the college's commitment to progressive ideals and social justice.

Sandra Svoboda

See Also: Abolitionism and the Antislavery Movement; Education of Women (before the Civil War); Stone, Lucy; Underground Railroad; Young Ladies' Academy of Philadelphia; Blackwell, Antoinette Brown (Vol. 2); Cooper, Anna Julia (Vol. 2); Terrell, Mary Church (Vol. 2)

Further Reading

Bartlett, Peggy F., and Geoffrey W. Chase, eds. *Sustainability of Campus: Stories and Strategies for Change.* Cambridge, MA: MIT Press, 2004.

Blight, David W., ed. *Passages to Freedom: The Underground Railroad in History and Memory.* Washington, DC: Smithsonian Books, 2004.

Solomon, Barbara Miller. *In the Company of Educated Women: A Century of Women and Higher Education in America.* New Haven, CT: Yale University Press, 1985.

Oneida Community

Oneida was the most prominent of the American antebellum utopian communities. Founded by John Humphrey Noyes in 1848 near Kenwood, New York, Oneida practiced free sexual association, birth control, and eugenics while advocating abolition of the traditional family and private property. It lasted in this experimental form, under the charismatic domination of Noyes, from 1848 to 1879, when it was disbanded and reorganized into its present format of a joint stock company.

Noyes, influenced by Charles Fourier and the Shakers, developed his ideas from Christian perfectionism. Noyes' theology held that the kingdom of God had arrived, and traditional marriage was no longer valid.

Monogamy was seen as selfish and exclusive, to be replaced by "complex marriage" in which each member of the community would be married to all other members (pantagamy). Fundamental to the practice of "complex marriage" was Noyes' invention of "male continence," a method of birth control that required that males engage in sexual activity without achieving orgasm. Noyes advocated male continence to avoid involuntary procreation but also, in his words, to stop "the drain of life on the part of man." Sex was purified and glorified at Oneida. Women's sexuality was acknowledged, as was their right to sexual satisfaction. However, sexual intercourse was intended to transcend lust, and, therefore, male continence, which required transcendental control, was more noble and unselfish.

In practice, sexual relations were regulated by the community. Younger men, not yet adept at male continence, were not allowed sex with any but postmenopausal women. Noyes generally preempted the task of initiating virgins himself. While sexual activity might begin as young as 14 for a girl, she might not have a sexual partner her own age for 10 years. Males initiated all requests for sexual meetings through an intermediary, and women, theoretically, had the right to decline, although this right was subject to communal pressures. Vigilance was exercised to prevent exclusive affections. One discontented Oneida woman stated, "It was a man's plan, not a woman's."

The community embarked on an experiment in eugenics, termed "stirpiculture," during which 58 children were born. Noyes and a committee of elders approved couples for potential parenthood. Males were chosen on the basis of religious qualifications, and women under 20 years of age were excluded. In keeping with the community's attempts to enlarge the family unit, children were to be raised communally. After 15 months of age, the child was placed in a common nursery during the day. At age 4, the child moved to a separate children's quarters. Exclusive maternal love was condemned, as Oneidans regarded it as a deficiency in spiritual development, an example of the selfish and exclusive affections found in the larger society. In a ritual attempt to control the maternal instinct, the commune once held a ceremony in which the Oneida women and girls destroyed all their dolls in a fire.

Oneida endorsed the rhetoric of women's rights, openly espousing the cause in its publications and adopting dress reform based on the bloomer costume, but it did not believe in the innate equality of the sexes. Generally, spirituality was the basis for authority at Oneida, and the more advanced members were accorded the status of "ascending fellowship." While women could hold this status, Noyes believed males to be superior. However, attempts were made to widen the occupational roles of women, and contemporaries were struck by the roles women held in the Oneida businesses. Visitors also remarked on seeing an occasional Oneida man knitting. Generally, though, work was sexually stereotyped, and women were assigned to the tasks of housecleaning and cooking.

The end of the community came with the weakening of the elderly Noyes' authority. The stirpiculture experiment had left a legacy of patterns of familial affection, and younger members of Oneida wished greater control over sexual choices and a return to monogamy. Factions arose within the commune as attacks from the outside accelerated due to the increasing strength of the purity crusade. Noyes suggested the process whereby Oneida ended the practice of complex marriage in August 1879. Within a year, remaining members abandoned communal property as well.

Joan Iverson

See Also: Birth Control (17th and 18th Centuries); Dress Reform; Shakers; Utopian Communities; Free Love Movement (Vol. 2)

Further Reading

Fogarty, Robert S., ed. *Special Love/Special Sex: An Oneida Community Diary.* Syracuse, NY: Syracuse University Press, 1994.

Foster, Lawrence. *Women, Family, and Utopia, Communal Experiments of the Shakers, the Oneida Community, and the Mormons.* Syracuse, NY: Syracuse University Press, 1991.

Guarneri, Carl J. *The Utopian Alternative: Fourierism in Nineteenth-Century America.* Ithaca, NY: Cornell University Press, 1991.

Noyes, George Wallingford. *Free Love in Utopia: John Humphrey Noyes and the Origin of the Oneida Community,* edited by Lawrence Foster. Urbana: University of Illinois Press, 2001.

P

Peabody, Elizabeth (1804–1894)

The Transcendentalist educator Elizabeth Peabody contributed in no small way to the intellectual life of Boston during the 1840s and 1850s and was later a pioneer of kindergarten education in the United States. Born in Billerica, Massachusetts, Peabody was educated with her sisters Sophia and Mary at the private school run by their mother in Salem, where Elizabeth later worked as a teacher herself. When she was only 16, Elizabeth Peabody attempted to set up her own school at Lancaster in 1820, but when this venture failed, she worked as a governess in Maine for two years. In Boston, she came into contact with other intellectuals and, after setting up another school at Brookline in 1825, was invited to take the post of secretary and copyist to Unitarian theologian William Ellery Channing, who had enrolled his daughter at the school. As a religious leader involved in the New England Transcendentalist movement, Channing introduced Peabody to his liberal theological beliefs and wide knowledge of literature and philosophy during their close association until 1834. In 1837, largely through Channing's recommendation, Peabody became, along with Margaret Fuller, one of the few female members of the elite Transcendentalist Club.

In 1827, as a reflection of her frustration that higher education was still not open to women, Peabody began giving a series of readings and discussions in private homes that became known as her "Historical School," drawing on her own interests in theology, philosophy, and history. (She urged that the latter subject be included in the school curriculum and later, in 1856, provided her own text, *A Chronological History of the United States*.) By 1832, Peabody's school had closed, and in need of a means of financial support, she gave up private tutoring and published a textbook, *First Steps to the Study of History* (1832). Giving up her post with Channing, she became an assistant to the educator Bronson Alcott (father of the novelist Louisa May Alcott) who had set up his new, progressive Temple School in Boston in September 1834, in particular becoming a devotee of Alcott's penchant for Socratic debate. Peabody admired Alcott's intellect and his pioneering methods and in 1835 published an account of her experiences,

Records of a School, taken from her journal. Alcott became an increasingly controversial figure, however, and Peabody's involvement with the Temple School brought her renewed difficulties in finding other employment.

For all her love of intellectual discussion, Peabody feared being labeled as a bluestocking, yet she continued to yearn for a "serious pursuit" within the limitations of what was then socially acceptable for women. And so, in 1839, she moved with her family to a house at 13 West Street in a residential area of Boston, where she opened a modest bookshop. In itself, the move underlined Peabody's belief that women could go into business as the equals of men, and from the outset, she intended the bookshop to function as a venue for the interchange of ideas by providing access to foreign books and giving the shop the appearance of a comfortable family library. Soon Peabody's shop on West Street had become an unofficial club for literary gatherings, Transcendentalist meetings, and, most notably, Margaret Fuller's famous Wednesday afternoon series of "conversations." Members of Brook Farm, an experimental utopian community of Transcendentalists, also met here. Peabody also became one of the first female publishers in the United States, when she began publishing translations from German by Fuller as well as the early works of her brother-in-law, the writer Nathaniel Hawthorne (who married Sophia Peabody in 1842).

For a year, Peabody co-edited the Transcendentalist literary monthly the *Dial* with Fuller (1842–1843) and wrote articles for it and the journal *Aesthetic Papers*, her most notable being "A Glimpse of Christ's Idea of Society," an article that emphasized the importance of the education of young children and also promoted the work of the Brook Farm community in creating "the kingdom of God on earth." With the demise of the Transcendentalist movement by 1845, however, Peabody's bookshop went into decline, and after closing it in 1850 she returned to teaching, at the Eagleswood School in New Jersey. During the late 1850s, she was drawn into the abolitionist campaign while continuing to write and lecture on education.

In 1859 Peabody's life changed when she learned of the new kindergarten movement being introduced in Germany by Friedrich Froebel. She resolved to establish

Elizabeth Palmer Peabody was a writer, publisher, member of the Transcendentalist literary movement, and educator who founded the first kindergarten in the United States. (Library of Congress)

her own school based on its methods, which encouraged children to think and explore things for themselves rather than be taught everything by rote. With its emphasis too on nurture and the encouragement of the child's moral and intellectual capabilities, it appealed to Peabody as the perfect medium for her own strongly held beliefs about the spiritual aspects of education. She saw it as the conduit for inculcating Christian values and making a better society and believed that the presence of kindergartens would raise the moral tone of the environments around them, particularly in deprived and slum areas. In 1861 Peabody founded the first English-speaking kindergarten in the United States in Boston to provide a showcase for Froebel's pioneering methods, which she explained in her 1863 book, *Moral Culture of Infancy, and Kindergarten Guide*.

At home in the years of the Civil War (1861–1865), Peabody realized that at age 57 she was too old to join

Dorothea Dix's nurses in the U.S. Sanitary Commission and traveled to Washington to take up philanthropic work among lost and abandoned black children, who were living rough and begging on the streets of the capital. She set up an orphanage and engaged teachers for these children, organized fundraising fairs, and with the help of her nieces Ellen and Mary, raised enough money to build a school.

During 1867–1868, Peabody spent time in Germany studying kindergarten methods in greater detail and returned to the United States with several experienced German kindergarten teachers in order to spread the word and train others. Also in 1868, Peabody took up lecturing on education and inspired the creation of more private kindergartens, in St. Louis and San Francisco, and in 1870 the first public one, in Boston, which was supported by donations, until in 1877 a single benefactor took over its funding. She also fostered training schools for kindergarten teachers, such as that at New York City's Normal College, and edited a journal, the *Kindergarten Messenger* (1873–1876), in which she promoted Froebel's ideas. In 1877 Peabody was elected president of the American Froebel Union. She also succeeded in persuading the publishers Ernst Steiger and Milton Bradley to publish several of her education materials for children, such as *Kindergarten Culture* (1870), *The Kindergarten in Italy* (1872), and *Letters to Kindergarteners* (1886).

In the summer of 1882, Peabody was invited to lecture at Bronson Alcott's Concord Summer School of Philosophy, returning in subsequent years until the school closed in 1888. In her eighties, she became passionate about the women's suffrage movement and held meetings at her home. She also advocated improved access to education for Native Americans and made considerable donations from her own funds to Sarah Winnemucca's school for Paiute Indians. Shortly before her death, she took up yet another cause, the international peace movement. The Elizabeth Peabody House was opened in Boston in her memory in 1896, for use as a settlement house and kindergarten for the then-large immigrant community. In 1979 the house relocated to Somerville, Massachusetts.

Helen Rappaport

See Also: Alcott, Louisa May; Dall, Caroline Healey; Dix, Dorothea; Education of Women (before the Civil War); Fuller, Margaret; Utopian Communities; United States Sanitary Commission; Winnemucca, Sarah (Vol. 2)

Further Reading

Baylor, Ruth M. *Elizabeth Palmer Peabody: Kindergarten Pioneer*. Philadelphia, PA: University of Philadelphia Press, 1965.

Marshall, Megan. *The Peabody Sisters: Three Women Who Ignited American Romanticism.* Boston, MA: Houghton Mifflin Company, 2005.

Ronda, Bruce, ed. *Letters of Elizabeth Palmer Peabody, American Renaissance Woman.* Middletown, CT: Wesleyan University Press, 1984.

Ronda, Bruce. *Elizabeth Palmer Peabody: A Reformer on Her Own Terms.* Cambridge, MA: Harvard University Press, 1999.

Tharp, Louise Hall. *The Peabody Sisters of Salem.* Boston, MA: Little, Brown, 1950.

Phillips, Wendell (1811–1884)

Wendell Phillips was one of the few male reformers active in the antebellum women's rights movement. He attended many of the national, state, and local women's rights conventions throughout the 1850s and spoke frequently on women's rights on the social reform lecture circuit. At the second national women's rights convention held in Worcester, Massachusetts, in October 1851, he noted the significance of the women's rights movement: "I rejoice to see so large an audience gathered to consider this momentous subject, the most magnificent reform that has yet been launched upon the world. It is the first organized protest against the injustice which has brooded over the character and the destiny of one-half of the human race."

In May 1860, at the 10th national women's rights convention in New York City, Phillips stunned Susan B. Anthony and Elizabeth Cady Stanton when he strenuously objected to their resolutions concerning divorce reform. He insisted that their demands not only be rejected but that they be expunged from the record, a radical departure from normal convention proceedings. As he explained, a women's rights convention had no business discussing marriage and divorce because "this Convention, if I understand it, assembles to discuss the laws that rest unequally upon women, not those that rest equally upon men and women."

After expressing the wish that Phillips withdraw his motion to have the resolutions deleted, Anthony expressed her disagreement.

Marriage has ever been a one-sided matter, resting most unequally upon the sexes. By it, man gains all—woman loses all . . . the discussion is perfectly in order, since nearly all the wrongs of which we complain grow out of the inequality, the injustice of the marriage laws, that rob the wife of the right to herself and her children—that make her the slave of the man she marries.

The divorce resolutions remained on the record, but Phillips was far too important to their women's rights work for Anthony and Stanton to shrug off his rejection. As Stanton wrote later, Phillips's "words, tone, and manner came down on me like a clap of thunder." Since he had supported all of their previous claims to rights for women, there had been no reason to expect that that support would not continue.

After the convention, Phillips solidified his position on the divorce issue in a letter to Anthony: "of course it is no right & no wish of mine to dictate what shall be in our platform . . . . whenever it is understood that the platform will include these questions, I shall have nothing to do with the Convention." But despite his own convictions, he eventually recognized Anthony and Stanton's right to agitate the divorce issue. Three months after the convention, when Anthony wrote him to request money from the Hovey Fund to finance the publication of the divorce resolutions, he sent it with a genial letter.

It is clear that by 1860 both Wendell Phillips and William Lloyd Garrison were increasingly chafing at Anthony and Stanton's advancing radicalism and their growing power in the movement. The two men's censure of the divorce question and, seven months later, their heavy-handed attempts to curb Anthony's efforts to rescue a woman from an abusive husband indicate that their support of women's rights was not boundless. As several historians have suggested, the conflicts of 1860 foreshadowed the defection of men from the women's rights movement after the Civil War.

The outbreak of war and the cessation of all women's rights activities cooled the internal conflicts in the women's rights movement. By 1863, Anthony and Stanton had resumed positive, friendly working relations with Phillips. As Garrisonian abolitionists, they united with him to protest the projected postwar reconstruction policies of President Abraham Lincoln. Phillips strongly supported their National Women's Loyal League, and Anthony and Stanton stood firmly behind his campaign for 1864 presidential candidate John C. Frémont.

In 1865, at the end of the Civil War, Anthony and Stanton championed Phillips's move to assume the leadership of the AASS when Garrison stepped down. The two women entered the postwar years feeling assured of Phillips's support for women's rights, particularly woman suffrage. Yet in May 1865, he announced that his reform interests were now exclusively focused on achieving rights for African American men. "While I could continue, just as heretofore, arguing for woman's rights, just as I do for temperance every day, still I would not mix the movements. . . . I think such mixture would lose for the negro far more than we should gain for the woman." Adding to Stanton and Anthony's dismay, he continued, "I am now engaged in abolishing slavery in a land where abolition of slavery means conferring or recognizing citizenship, and where citizenship supposes the ballot for all men."

As Phillips aligned the AASS with Radical Republicans in Congress, women's rights and woman suffrage became marginal, expendable issues that could not be permitted to interfere with the mission to achieve full equality for African American males. Phillips never became actively involved in the American Equal Rights Association. He frustrated Anthony, Stanton, and Parker Pillsbury by refusing to continue publishing free of charge their notices and articles in the *National Anti-Slavery Standard,* by criticizing them for campaigning for woman suffrage in Kansas, and by refusing them AASS money for the woman suffrage cause.

At the national women's rights convention in May 1866, Phillips said that, despite his support of women's rights, he did not find woman suffrage important enough to be included on an amendment. He then shocked Anthony, Stanton, and Pillsbury by claiming that women already had significant power in society, particularly when compared with the absolutely powerless African Americans. After turning his back on their mission, he surprised them by being deeply hurt when they refused to support him in his all-out campaign for the Fifteenth Amendment. He retaliated by attacking them repeatedly in the *National Anti-Slavery Standard* in the summer of 1869: "The Women's Rights movement is essentially a selfish one; not disinterested as the Anti-Slavery cause was. It is women contending for their own rights; the Abolitionists toiled for the rights of others." Of course, Phillips's analysis neglected to consider Anthony and Stanton's years of commitment to abolitionism.

When the women's rights movement split in 1869, Phillips sided with the New England members who formed the American Woman Suffrage Association (AWSA). Following ratification of the Fifteenth Amendment and the disbanding of the AASS in 1870, Phillips turned his attention toward woman suffrage and other reforms. He died in February 1884.

Judith E. Harper

See Also*:* Abolitionism and the Antislavery Movement; Divorce (before the Civil War); Fifteenth Amendment; Garri-

son, William Lloyd; National Women's Loyal League; Pillsbury, Parker; American Equal Rights Association (Vol. 2); Anthony, Susan B. (Vol. 2); Stanton, Elizabeth Cady (Vol. 2)

Further Reading

Kimmel, Michael S., and Thomas E. Mosmiller, eds. *Against the Tide: Pro-Feminist Men in the United States, 1776–1990: A Documentary History.* Boston, MA: Beacon Press, 1992.

Stewart, James Brewer. *Wendell Phillips: Liberty's Hero.* Baton Rouge: Louisiana State University Press, 1986.

Pillsbury, Parker (1809–1898)

Parker Pillsbury was Susan B. Anthony's closest male colleague, friend, and kindred spirit. From the early 1850s until Pillsbury's death in 1898, they remained in close contact, inspiring and encouraging each other in the sometimes overwhelming struggles that they faced in abolitionist and women's rights reform. Like many of his fellow Garrisonian abolitionists, Pillsbury not only devoted himself to the antislavery cause but was also engrossed in the work of other reform movements, including women's rights, woman suffrage, temperance, peace, and political reform.

From 1840 until 1865, Pillsbury was consumed by his travels as lecture agent for the New Hampshire, Massachusetts, and American Anti-Slavery Societies (AASS). Pillsbury's radical antislavery doctrine and his ferocious, fire-breathing oratory regularly ignited controversy both inside and outside abolitionist circles, yet the AASS leadership trusted his reports from the field and always listened carefully to his views on the mood and mind-set of the public.

Despite Pillsbury's absorption in abolitionist reform, he was also devoted to the women's rights movement. In the 1850s, he attended women's rights conventions whenever his travel schedule permitted and wrote numerous articles supporting women's rights. Unlike many men involved in the movement, Pillsbury unstintingly and unreservedly supported complete gender equality in all areas of society. He was also unusual in that he practiced his views on women's equality in his daily life. He was known for regularly validating and publicizing the strengths of his fellow women reformers.

Pillsbury especially admired Susan B. Anthony's intensity and indefatigable commitment to reform, a respect he sometimes communicated to her by teasing her about her "idleness." When Anthony's father died in 1862, Pillsbury's letter of condolence indicates that he was one of the few people who fully understood all that her father had meant to her. "You must be stricken sore indeed in the loss of your constant helper in the great mission to which you are devoted, your counselor, your consoler, your all that man could be, besides the endearing relation of father. What or who can supply the loss?"

As coeditor of *The Revolution* from 1868 until the summer of 1869, Pillsbury also understood that Anthony's decision to terminate publication in 1870 was a huge loss, much greater than most people realized. His letter of consolation reveals that he had deep insight into the reasons for the newspaper's failure that troubled her most:

No one could do better than you have done. If any complain, ask them what they did to help you carry the paper. Suffrage is growing with the oaks. The whirling spheres will usher in the day of its triumph at just the right time, but your full meed of praise will have to be sung over your grave.

For her part, Anthony knew that she could depend on Pillsbury to back her completely and uncomplainingly, whenever humanly feasible. He braved the mobs with her in the late 1850s when she was the AASS agent for New York state. When Anthony planned a memorial for John Brown following his execution in 1859, Pillsbury was the only abolitionist who would agree to stand up and speak with her. But it was during the early years of Reconstruction (1865–1870) that Pillsbury proved his undivided, supreme loyalty to Anthony and to women's rights and became permanently estranged from many of his former abolitionist co-workers.

After he abandoned AASS president Wendell Phillips's campaigns for African American rights through the Fourteenth and Fifteenth Amendments, Pillsbury's ties with abolitionism were completely severed. Instead, he lectured incessantly for universal suffrage as part of the American Equal Rights Association's campaign to amend the New York state constitution. After 1870, however, Pillsbury remained loyal to the woman suffrage movement but also devoted time to other reforms. Anthony repeatedly entreated him to write a volume of his recollections of the Garrisonian abolitionist movement and "those times that tried men's & women's souls." Although she confided to William Lloyd Garrison, Jr., that she feared Pillsbury would never fulfill this wish, in 1883, Pillsbury published *Acts of the Antislavery Apostles,* his memoir of the Garrisonian movement.

Very late in life, Pillsbury developed a severe paralysis that limited him and that he found difficult to accept. In a letter to Anthony in 1895, he wrote, "I am very glad to have done my very best when at my best for Woman—her Wrongs, Rights and Responsibilities—and in so doing, I have had my sufficient reward. The approval of posterity, or the estimate of the world of such service, is to me, of small account."

Judith E. Harper

See Also: Abolitionism and the Antislavery Movement; Fifteenth Amendment; Garrison, William Lloyd; Phillips, Wendell; Reconstruction; American Equal Rights Association (Vol. 2); Anthony, Susan B. (Vol. 2); *The Revolution* (Vol. 2)

Further Reading

Robertson, Stacy M. *Parker Pillsbury: Radical Abolitionist, Male Feminist.* Ithaca, NY: Cornell University Press, 2000.

Pleasant, Mary Ellen (1814–1904)

Called the mother of civil rights in California, Mary Ellen Williams Smith Pleasant's legacy has been obscured by rumor and public scandal. A study in contradictions, Mammy Pleasant, as she was popularly known, is revered by many for her work as an abolitionist, activist, and feminist, but she was reviled by critics as a con artist, madam, and voodoo practitioner. She is reported to have donated $30,000 to aid John Brown's raid at Harper's Ferry in 1859, and, in 1866, she won a lawsuit that effectively desegregated San Francisco streetcars. Pleasant's life has been recreated and mythologized in plays, novels, magazine articles, and a silent film, most of whose content relies on rumor and legend.

Pleasant's biographical details are a subject of open debate. Her abolitionist activities demanded secrecy, and she neither confirmed nor denied the speculations surrounding her business and personal activities. She claimed she was born free to a black mother and Hawaiian father in Philadelphia, Pennsylvania, on August 19, 1814. However, her African American contemporaries believed she was born a slave in Augusta, Georgia, before being sent to Philadelphia and then to Nantucket, Massachusetts, where a Quaker family named Hussey raised her. In the 1830s, Pleasant moved to Boston, where she married abolitionist James Smith and befriended notable figures such as Frederick

Douglass and William Lloyd Garrison. Historians believe Pleasant inherited a large estate from Smith upon his death in the mid-1840s. Pleasant remarried in the late 1840s to John James Pleasants (the "s" was later dropped), another abolitionist. In 1852, they moved to San Francisco. A brilliant entrepreneur, Pleasant invested her wealth in banks, real estate, and mining, but she also worked as a cook for prominent wealthy families, owned a string of laundries, and ran several boardinghouses.

Pleasant offered refuge to fugitive slaves on the Underground Railroad and mobilized resources to aid in escaped slaves' court trials. She lived for a short time in Chatham, Ontario, a hotbed of abolitionist activity and the site of her meetings with John Brown, but she returned to San Francisco just before the Civil War. During the war years, Pleasant used litigation to fight for black voting rights and desegregation of schools and transportation.

In 1877, she built a 30-room mansion on San Francisco's Octavia Street, which she cohabited with her business partner, Thomas Bell, the Scottish vice president of the Bank of California. Locals were scandalized and dubbed the mansion the House of Mystery. Bell later married, but his family remained in the house with Pleasant. Seven years after Bell's 1892 death, his son Fred unsuccessfully accused Pleasant of murdering Bell by pushing him down the stairs. Bell's heirs engaged in a protracted legal battle to divest Pleasant of her wealth, claiming rightful ownership. Pleasant was also involved in the sensationalized divorce trial of United States Senator William Sharon in the 1880s; Sharon claimed the plaintiff, his alleged wife Sarah Althea Hill, was really a prostitute and Pleasant, her madam.

Pleasant died January 11, 1904, and she is buried in the Sherwood family cemetery in Napa, California. In 1965, the San Francisco Negro Historical and Cultural Society fulfilled a request Pleasant had made during her lifetime by marking her grave with a plaque reading, "She was a friend of John Brown." In 2005, the city of San Francisco declared February 10 Mary Ellen Pleasant Day in honor of her civil rights work.

Jennifer Jane Nichols

See Also: Abolitionism and the Antislavery Movement; Douglass, Frederick; Garrison, William Lloyd; Underground Railroad

Further Reading

Cliff, Michelle. *Free Enterprise: A Novel of Mary Ellen Pleasant*. New York: Dutton, 1993.

Holdredge, Helen. *Mammy Pleasant*. New York: G.P. Putnam's Sons, 1953.

Hudson, Lynn M. *The Making of "Mammy" Pleasant: A Black Entrepreneur in Nineteenth-Century San Francisco*. Urbana: University of Illinois Press, 2003.

Quakers

Quaker women, the most activist group of 19th-century American women, did much to propel the antislavery and women's movements forward.

In the 17th and 18th centuries, the Quakers, or Society of Friends, constituted a highly controversial sect of radical Protestants. The group's marginal position resulted from many of its positions, not the least of which was its view of women. The Society of Friends allowed women, as well as men, to be ministers. The Quaker belief system liberated women in other ways, too: women conducted affairs at their own meetings, took part in economic activity, gained education, and became politically active.

As Separatists, the Quakers kept themselves apart from other colonists in the nation's early years. Although few Quakers fought in the Revolutionary War—they believed in nonviolence—the war brought many of them into American everyday life. After witnessing the devastation of war on individuals, Quakers began to provide relief to needy civilians and soldiers. Historians see this activity as the beginning of the Quaker tradition of relief work, which often was women's work. The Revolutionary War also marked the beginning of Quakers' public opposition to slavery. As early as 1688, Friends in Germantown, Pennsylvania, urged other Quakers to free their slaves. By the 1770s and 1780s, various meetings began to disown Quakers who owned slaves.

As the Quaker faith grew in the early 1800s, a schism divided the Society. The split centered on Elias Hicks, a minister who opposed slavery and downplayed literal interpretations of the Bible in favor of the inner light, or the primacy of Christ inside the believer. Determined that theirs was the correct way, the Hicksites broke off from the Orthodox Quakers, who saw Hicks's preachings as heresy. The Hicksites' views on women differed from those of other Quakers as well. Hicksite women were more assertive than other women and did not ask the brethren for approval once they had decided on a course of action.

Quaker women's assertiveness allowed them to pursue reform, some focusing on the cause of antislavery and pursuing it diligently. In 1806, Alice Lewis, of the Philadelphia Women's Yearly Meeting, was the first to urge her Quaker sisters to boycott slave-produced goods such as sugar and cotton.

Other Quaker women focused on education. In 1833, Connecticut Quaker Prudence Crandall allowed a black girl to attend her Canterbury Female Boarding School. When the parents of other girls threatened to withdraw their daughters, Crandall closed the school but reopened it two months later with 20 black girls in attendance. Crandall was arrested and convicted but later freed. She closed the school after a mob attacked it.

In 1833, Philadelphia men formed the American Anti-Slavery Society. Four days later, Quaker Lucretia Mott and other women founded the Female American Anti-Slavery Society. They opened their society to Quakers and non-Quakers, as well as to blacks and whites. Female antislavery societies sprung up throughout the North, and women honed their organizational skills as they opposed the South's peculiar institution.

Two years later, South Carolina sisters Sarah and Angelina Grimké joined the Philadelphia Female Anti-Slavery Society and helped promote its goals. Despite their membership in the Orthodox Quaker sect, whose elders roundly criticized them for their public activities, the Grimké sisters took on prominent roles in the abolitionist movement. The American Anti-Slavery Society published a pamphlet by Angelina, in which she appealed to her Southern sisters to end slavery. The Grimké sisters' firsthand experiences with slavery gave them credence and made them authorities in the eyes of Northern antislavery activists. They began giving lectures to other women and then, as their fame spread, to men as well. Their public speaking engagements ended in 1838, but by then they had inspired another young Quaker woman, Abby Kelley, to continue their work.

Women's antislavery activities provoked controversy about women's roles. The debate over the realm of women in turn led to the formation of a women's rights movement. Quaker Lucretia Mott, along with Elizabeth Cady Stanton, organized the first women's rights convention in Seneca Falls, New York, in 1848. In addition to Mott, many other Quaker women—Susan B. Anthony among them—carried forward the battle for women's suffrage throughout the 19th century.

Quaker men and women worked together in the Pennsylvania Anti-Slavery Society, 1851 (Lucretia Mott is seated in front, in white). (Schlesinger Library, Radcliffe Institute, Harvard University/The Bridgeman Art Library)

During the Civil War, many Quaker women held to their nonviolent principles. For example, Mott supported young Quaker men who, as conscientious objectors, refused to enlist or fight when drafted. Other Quaker women, such as Cornelia Hancock and Amanda Way, nursed soldiers in the field and in city hospitals throughout the war. In addition, female Friends continued in their antislavery efforts, aiding the freedmen. As the war progressed, Laura Haviland, founder of the first antislavery society in Michigan and an effective conductor on the Underground Railroad, refocused her efforts. Haviland traveled in Mississippi and Louisiana, working for the Freedman's Aid Commission distributing relief supplies to former slaves. Abby Hopper Gibbons served as a nurse and aide to freed slaves in Washington, D.C., for more than three years.

Some Quaker women took their activism into the political spheres. Anna Dickinson began speaking on the cause of women's rights and abolitionism in 1860, at the age of 18. Her charisma and popularity as a speaker led the Republican Party to seek out Dickinson's services in 1863. Dickinson began stumping for Republican candidates across the North. She praised the Emancipation Proclamation and the use of African American soldiers in the fight against the Confederacy. Although Dickinson saw President Abraham Lincoln's antislavery stance as weak, she supported him in the 1864 presidential election.

Quaker women joined the Freedmen's Bureau's efforts to educate and aid the former slaves. Quaker Lucy McKim accompanied her father to the South Carolina Sea Islands during the war to prepare former slaves for freedom. McKim recorded the slave songs that she heard there and eventually published them in 1867 as *Slave Songs of the United States.*

Countless Quaker women worked for the passage of the Thirteenth, Fourteenth, and Fifteenth Amendments during the war and immediately afterward. Many continued this work even when it became clear that women would not get suffrage along with black men. They continued to come to the South to educate freed slaves too, many staying long after the war ended.

Ellen H. Todras

See Also: Abolitionism and the Antislavery Movement; Education of Women (before the Civil War); Fifteenth Amendment; Foster, Abby Kelley; Fourteenth Amendment; Freedmen's Bureau; Gibbons, Abigail Hopper; Grimké, Sarah Moore; Grimké Weld, Angelina; Moral Reform; Mott, Lucretia; Seneca Falls Convention; Slavery and the Civil War; Underground Railroad; Anthony, Susan B. (Vol. 2); Dickinson, Anna Elizabeth (Vol. 2); Stanton, Elizabeth Cady (Vol. 2)

Further Reading

Bacon, Margaret Hope. *Mothers of Feminism: The Story of Quaker Women in America.* New York: Harper & Row, 1986.

Brown, Elizabeth Potts, and Susan Mosher Stuard, eds. *Witnesses for Change: Quaker Women over Three Centuries.* New Brunswick, NJ: Rutgers University Press, 1989.

Larson, Rebecca. *Daughters of Light: Quaker Women Preaching and Prophesying in the Colonies and Abroad, 1700–1775.* New York: Alfred A. Knopf, 1999.

Silber, Nina. *Daughters of the Union: Northern Women Fight the Civil War.* Cambridge, MA: Harvard University Press, 2005.

Todras, Ellen. *Angelina Grimké: Voice of Abolition.* North Haven, CT: Linnet Books, 1999.

Wellman, Judith. *The Road to Seneca Falls: Elizabeth Cady Stanton and the First Woman's Rights Convention.* Urbana: University of Illinois Press, 2004.

R

Reconstruction (1865–1877)

Women of all regions, classes, and races played significant roles in the Reconstruction era. The federal government's quest to reform and reunite the nation after the destructive Civil War led to new policies and altered the course of the United States. Reconstruction was not only a political process, but also a cultural refashioning of the nation that had to take into account the four million newly freed slaves. Many women took an active role in the redefinition of citizenship, affecting the freedmen's transition from slavery.

The first postwar dilemma resulted from the struggle over whether the executive or legislative branch would control Reconstruction. The debate began even before the end of combat. During the war, President Abraham Lincoln and the United States Congress bantered back and forth about the control of Reconstruction. The end of the war and Lincoln's assassination spawned one of the greatest American political conflicts of the era. The newly inaugurated President Andrew Johnson and the Republican Congress split over how best to bring the Union back together. The Southern-born Johnson's plan of Reconstruction highlighted a policy of reconciliation to bring the seceded states back into the Union peacefully; he disagreed with plans that involved federal interference, African American rights, or punishing Confederates for treason. On the other side, Congress wanted to assure secession would never occur again and believed that the federal government had to punish Confederates for taking up arms against the nation as well as give political and civil rights to the freedmen.

Conflict arose over the role of the Bureau of Refugees, Freedmen, and Abandoned Lands. More commonly known as the Freedmen's Bureau, this military-run organization handled a wide variety of tasks associated with the newly freed African Americans. The Freedmen's Bureau dealt with land redistribution, setting up a court system, passing out Union pensions to former black soldiers, establishing hospitals and staffing them with nurses, many of whom were women, and negotiating labor contracts between the former slaves and their former owners. The Freedmen's Bureau also established schools and hired teachers to educate the freedpeople.

Northern women became involved in and aided this effort by becoming teachers and helping raise funds for the new schools.

Without white and black Northern women's efforts as teachers, missionaries, and social reformers, progress toward assimilating freedmen into society would have been greatly retarded. The Bureau provided the buildings for the schools, and Northern religious groups, such as the American Missionary Association, provided the teachers. The other large missionary organization, the American Freedmen's Union Commission (AFUC), also used many female teachers but excluded women from its leadership positions. Though denied positions in the AFUC leadership, women formed most of the Commission's aid societies. Women also created a few of their own missionary societies to aid the freedpeople. Founded by women, the National Freedmen's Relief Association began during the Civil War and remained active during Reconstruction.

By the end of 1865, the bureau employed 1,134 teachers, many of whom were women, to teach 90,589 students in 740 schools across the South and in the border states. Women filled most of the teaching positions in freedmen's schools, making up 75 percent of all Northern teachers in the schools. The primary goals of Reconstruction-era teachers went well beyond teaching reading, writing, and arithmetic. Their goals were also political and religious. The initial wave of missionary teachers consisted mostly of white middle-class women in their twenties who were unmarried, educated, and evangelical Christians. In addition, heading south as teachers liberated these women, however briefly, from their domestic roles. This experience exposed them to a different culture and made them actors in the fight for social justice—including their own.

Initially, only about 5 percent of Freedmen's Bureau teachers in the South were black and less than half were women. The lack of black teachers changed, however, largely due to the establishment of Freedmen's Bureau colleges that educated future teachers who would go south. The Freedmen's Bureau helped establish colleges such as Hampton, Howard, and Fisk, among others. All were coeducational, an uncommon occurrence in the 19th-century South. The curricula at these schools led to the growing number of black instructors in the South. By 1869 black teachers in the South outnumbered whites.

Female teachers, whether white or black, faced several obstacles. For example, Isabella Gibbons, a freedwoman in Virginia, had never taught before and had little idea of how to do so. She had students read the Bible and emphasized behaviors that she believed would gain the respect of others for her students. As an African American woman, she faced both race and gender prejudices.

Reconstruction allowed educational advances for black women who took advantage of the new opportunities. In 1872, African American Charlotte E. Ray became Howard University's first female law school graduate, as well as the first woman in the United States, white or black, to graduate from an accredited, nonprofit law school. That same year, the first female faculty member joined the Howard Medical School in defiance of the American Medical Association's code of ethics.

Like the colleges established by the Freedmen's Bureau, the Bureau's Southern schools included both men and women. When confronted in 1866 by a white North Carolinian who did not believe in educating freedwomen, General Oliver Otis Howard, commissioner of the Freedmen's Bureau and namesake of Howard University, responded that white Northern women had succeeded through education and so could African American women. Howard then took the man on a tour of a school full of black women. The man was "converted" according to Howard.

Freedmen's Bureau teachers faced violence and ostracism by white Southerners. Freedmen's teachers, white and black, were regularly intimidated, flogged, driven away, and murdered by white Southerners. After one teacher's murder, Howard urged others to stand strong, keep their faith, and continue to aid the freedmen. He advised them to be bold and take on a role he believed the government could not fulfill. As late as 1868, General J. J. Reynolds told Howard not to send women to Texas because he could not protect them against abuse there, where women made up 75 percent of Northern teachers. A Northern white female teacher readied herself for admission and baptism into a Baptist church in Louisville. However, when the white congregation discovered that she had taught in a freedmen's school and had lived at the home of a black pastor, she was denied admission to the church. Despite such treatment, African American students and teachers, as well as white teachers, persevered.

Reconstruction transformed freedwomen more than it did white Southern women. Freedom allowed African American women the opportunity to reunite their families, often divided by slavery, and to become full-time parents. As the war ended, black women sought to legitimize marriages and otherwise to take control of their lives. Like their male counterparts, freedwomen who worked outside the home faced discrimination and violence from white Southerners. The postwar changes in the black family, as well as the creation of Freedmen's schools, greatly disrupted the Southern labor force. African American children, who as slaves had been forced to work in the fields from sunup to sundown, now depended on their parents and went to school.

Freedwomen's rights did not advance as rapidly as did their educational opportunities. The Freedmen's Bureau and the Freedmen's Homestead Act designated the man as the head of the family, making it difficult, if not impossible, for female heads of household to claim land. In addition, the Fifteenth Amendment did not include women in the granting of suffrage to citizens, regardless of race. As a result, African American women, like their white counterparts, did not gain many of the new civil rights, such as serving on juries, which black men had recently attained. Despite these roadblocks, black women, like their white counterparts, refused to exclude themselves from political activity. For example, when they went to their jobs in white homes, many black maids wore presidential campaign buttons supporting Ulysses S. Grant.

Taking political activity further, former slave Sojourner Truth worked tirelessly for women's suffrage and had waged a campaign for it even before emancipation. In 1870, Truth gained an introduction to President Grant to discuss suffrage. She, like prominent suffragist Susan B. Anthony, would not live to vote. African American women, including Truth, traveled the country raising money to aid freedmen. Truth gave speeches to raise money, petitioned Congress for support, and traveled to Kansas in December 1870 to encourage westward settlement. Two other women, Emily Howland of Virginia and Cornelia Hancock of South Carolina, bought land to sell and rent to former slaves.

The Civil War and Reconstruction led to changes that would ultimately alter the lives of all Southerners, including white women. During this period, more women went to school than had in the antebellum years. In addition, poverty forced many women to venture into the public sphere to do tasks that servants had previously performed as well as to find employment for themselves. White women also had to perform their own domestic service, or they had to compete with freedwomen for scarce job opportunities. Elite white Southern women continued to hold antebellum ideals in high esteem while becoming more publicly visible, better educated, and more politically active.

Reconstruction activity intersected with the women's reform movement. Women's inability to hold key positions in the freedmen's aid movement demonstrated society's fear of the expansion of women's power outside the home. Nevertheless, Northern women's activity in aiding freedpeople through charity and utilizing federal power was revolutionary. As a result, white Northern women, freedwomen, white Southern women, and America were impacted by women's roles in Reconstruction.

Scott L. Stabler

See Also: Fifteenth Amendment; Fourteenth Amendment; Freedmen's Bureau; Grimké, Charlotte L. Forten; Slavery and the Civil War; Truth, Sojourner

Further Reading

Butchart, Ronald E. *Northern Schools, Southern Blacks, and Reconstruction: Freedmen's Education, 1862–1875*. Westport, CT: Greenwood Press, 1980.

Censer, Jane Turner. *The Reconstruction of White Southern Womanhood, 1865–1895*. Baton Rouge: Louisiana State University Press, 2003.

Edwards, Laura F. *Gendered Strife and Confusion: The Political Culture of Reconstruction*. Urbana: University of Illinois Press, 1997.

Faulkner, Carol. *Women's Radical Reconstruction: The Freedmen's Aid Movement*. Philadelphia: University of Pennsylvania Press, 2004.

Foner, Eric. *Reconstruction: America's Unfinished Revolution, 1863–1877*. New York: Harper & Row, 1988.

Jones, Jacqueline. *Soldiers of Light and Love: Northern Teachers and Georgia Blacks, 1865–1873*. Chapel Hill: University of North Carolina Press, 1992.

Whites, LeeAnn. *Gender Matters: Civil War, Reconstruction, and the Making of the New South*. New York: Macmillan, 2005.

Remond, Sarah Parker (1826–1894)

African American antislavery activist Sarah Parker Remond promoted abolitionism in the Civil War era and better conditions for the freedpeople after the war. Remond raised money and lectured in both the United States and Great Britain, publishing many of her speeches, as well as some of her other writings. Remond's life clearly reflected her commitment to social activism and, more important, to self-determination, which she exhibited throughout her life.

Born in Massachusetts to successful and affluent free black parents who valued education, Sarah Remond attended public schools in Salem while young, but she was primarily self-educated. Her parents were members of the social and financial black elite of New England, and they participated extensively in the Massachusetts antislavery society, the Underground Railroad, and other national abolitionist organizations. Sarah's mother also taught her to pursue liberty legally and that being African American was not a crime. Sarah's brother, Charles, was one of the first African American speakers on the antislavery circuit.

Charles first encouraged Sarah's entry into antislavery activities and then helped shape her performance on the speakers' platform. For about a decade starting in 1859, Sarah Remond intermittently gave lecture tours in England, Ireland, and Scotland, sponsored by British antislavery societies. Remond's speeches focused on raising money for American Anti-Slavery Society activities and on raising English consciousness about attitudes toward blacks in their Caribbean colonies. Remond believed that African Americans should speak out on their own behalf against slavery, especially since the American press had done such a poor job of it. She relied on facts and statistics to provide an arena in which her listeners were rationally convinced to see the injustices of slavery, rather than emotionally moved. The manner and substance of her work won her continued respect in Europe, where she lectured after the war against the discrimination and ill treatment of the freedpeople and raised money in England for their relief.

Her family background made Remond well aware of the horrors of slavery and the efforts to end the institution. It also affected Remond's reaction when she personally experienced racial discrimination. After purchasing a ticket to the opera in New York City and being seated with friends, Remond was injured while being forcibly removed from her seat. She sued the theater managers and won her case in the mid-1850s. While touring for the American Anti-Slavery Society, Sarah and Charles encountered insults and discrimination in accommodations. When in England in the mid-1860s, Sarah Remond applied for a visa to visit France and was turned down by an American embassy agent asserting that African Americans were not citizens of the United States. The British Foreign Secretary later approved her request.

On her extended stays in England, Remond attended college classes in London and visited not only the countries of the British Isles, but France and Italy. Her move to Florence, Italy, became permanent in 1866 when she entered medical school at the Santa Maria Nuova Hospital; she received a diploma in 1871 and practiced medicine in Florence for 20 years. She married a Sardinian man and resided in Italy until her death in 1894. She is buried in Rome.

Donna Cooper Graves

See Also: Abolitionism and the Antislavery Movement; Education of Women (before the Civil War); Underground Railroad

Further Reading

Foner, Philip S., and Robert James Branham, eds. *Lift Every Voice: African American Oratory, 1787–1900.* Tuscaloosa: University of Alabama Press, 1998.

Peterson, Carla L. *"Doers of the Word": African-American Women Speakers and Writers in the North (1830–1880).* New Brunswick, NJ: Rutgers University Press, 1995.

Sterling, Dorothy. *We Are Your Sisters: Black Women in the Nineteenth Century.* New York: W. W. Norton, 1984.

Republican Motherhood

"Republican Motherhood" is the name historians have given to an ideology that gave American women a political function after the Revolution, that of raising children to be moral, virtuous citizens of the new republic, without their engaging in political activity outside the domestic realm.

During the American Revolution many women of all classes became politically active and participated in various ways for the cause. Women took part in boycotts and riots, served as "Daughters of Liberty," raised money, and spun and wove cloth in their own homes. Camp followers performed necessary services for their husbands, fathers, and other relatives in the army, and some women acted as spies and couriers; a few fought, disguised as men, in the army.

After the Revolution, although regarded as citizens of the new republic, women were not given a larger place in political life or allowed the franchise (except, briefly, in New Jersey). In the late 18th century, public and private spheres of activity were more sharply defined than ever before, and women's role was defined as wholly within the private sphere, even though such a separation would be possible only for the minority of women who were above the lower middle class.

Since the male thinkers who worked out the new relationship between individuals and the republican state paid very little attention to the role of women, it was left to the women themselves to discover their function and place in the great new experiment. Denied a part in political life, they invested their domestic sphere with political importance. The Great Awakening (the religious revival that swept the Atlantic Coast in the 1730s and 1740s) and the literary sentimentalism of the late 18th century gave woman the role of upholder and reformer of society's manners and morals. As a morally superior being she nurtured virtue within the home through her influence on her husband and as teacher of her children. Therefore, even if women did not take part in public life, through their role in the home they could raise their sons to become the upholders of the virtues needed by freemen in a free society. The role of Republican Motherhood, then, recognized the reality of restrictions on women but also gave them a vital role—ensuring the success of the republic by instilling in its future generations the moral and political values necessary for good citizenship.

Although the ideology restricted women to a narrow political role and may have delayed the legal recognition of married women as persons at law, it had a positive effect on women's education. Advocates of female education in the late 18th and early 19th centuries, such as Benjamin Rush, were able to argue that girls must be educated in order for them to properly perform their domestic function of instructing their sons in the duties and virtues they would need to maintain the liberty and self-government won for them by their fathers.

Gertrude McKay

See Also: The American Revolution; The Constitution and Women; Education of Women (before the Civil War); Murray, Judith Sargent; Republican Motherhood; Young Ladies' Academy of Philadelphia

Primary Documents: 1774, "An Occasional Letter on the Female Sex"; 1780, "The Sentiments of an American Woman"; 1787, "Thoughts upon Female Education"; 1790, "On the Equality of the Sexes"

Further Reading

Gunderson, Joan R. *To Be Useful to the World: Women in Revolutionary America, 1740–1790.* New York: Twayne Publishers, 1996.

Kerber, Linda K. *Women of the Republic: Intellect and Ideology in Revolutionary America.* Chapel Hill: University of North Carolina Press, 1980.

Ulrich, Laurel Thatcher. *Good Wives: Image and Reality in the Lives of Women in Northern New England, 1650–1750.* New York: Random House, 1980.

Restell, Madame [Anna Trow Lohman] (1812–1878)

"Madame Restell" was the name by which "New York's most notorious abortionist" was known. She was born Anna Trow in 1812 in Painswick, England, into a farm family. Anna married her first husband, Henry Sommers, before she was 20. The couple left England for the United States and arrived in New York City in 1831. Sommers died two years later. Anna seems then to have taken up midwifery in order to support herself, and may have begun her practice of assisting women with birth control and abortion during this period. She continued her work after she remarried, to Charles Lohman, a printer. Anna advertised in the New York papers in the early 1830s, under the name "Madame Restell." The origin of the name is a mystery; it may have simply sounded more exotic than her legal name, and she may have wanted to use an alias in order to safeguard her privacy.

Madame Restell provided birth control and abortion services to women in New York in the mid-1800s. (Walling, George W. *Recollections of a New York City Chief of Police*, 1887)

Madame Restell offered the very services in demand among many American women of the period: abortion, birth control, and the placement of illegitimate children. The first two of these were illegal at the time; the third was illegal in the way that Restell was accused of practicing it. Early in Restell's career, Mary Applegate, an unhappy young mother, accused Restell of having given her infant to unknown persons without her consent. Restell was charged with numerous offenses, but eventually the charges were all mysteriously dropped. During her lifetime, several other women charged her with the same offense; in each case the charges were either dropped or not filed. In 1847, Restell was charged with aborting the child of Maria Bodine. Amid a media circus, Restell's attorney attacked Bodine's credibility and reputation, obtaining his client's conviction on a misdemeanor instead of the felony with which she was originally charged. Restell spent 12 months in prison, while her activities remained front page news. She continued to be the object of public derision for the rest of her life.

Anthony Comstock, the well-known crusader against "obscenity," brought Restell's career to an end in 1878 by representing himself as an impoverished man whose wife needed assistance with an abortion. When she agreed to help, he had her arrested and charged with the illegal possession of certain medical instruments. On April 1, 1878 she committed suicide, apparently unwilling or unable to face the prospect of yet another trial.

Restell was a pioneer in the struggle for women's reproductive freedom. She and individuals like her represented a source of assistance for both rich and poor women who found themselves faced with unwanted children at a time when neither public nor private services were available to address the problem. She risked her life and liberty by providing desperately needed but illegal services. Her motivations seem not to have been solely the desire for money, since she seems always to have assisted those who could not pay her. She is certainly among the victims of Comstock's exaggerated sense of morality which dominated the United States during the last quarter of the 19th century.

Christine A. Corcos

See Also: Abortion (17th and 18th Centuries); Birth Control (17th and 18th Centuries); The Comstock Act (Vol. 2); Sanger, Margaret (Vol. 2)

Further Reading

Brodie, Janet Farrell. *Abortion and Contraception in 19th Century America.* Ithaca, NY: Cornell University Press, 1994.

Keller, Allan. *Scandalous Lady: The Life and Times of Madame Restell, New York's Most Notorious Abortionist.* New York: Atheneum, 1981.

Mohr, James C. *Abortion in America: The Origins and Evolution of National Policy, 1800–1900.* New York: Oxford University Press, 1978.

Ropes, Hannah (1809–1863)

Nurse, supervisor, author, feminist, abolitionist, free soiler, and reformer, Hannah Ropes lost her life in the service of her country and for a cause about which she was unusually passionate.

Hannah Anderson Chandler was born June 13, 1809, in New Gloucester, Maine, to Peleg and Esther Parsons Chandler. She had nine siblings. Her father and two brothers were lawyers involved in Massachusetts politics. Through family and acquaintances, she became friends with politically powerful people like Charles Sumner and Nathaniel P. Banks. In 1834, she married William Henry Ropes, a teacher and farmer. The couple had four children, only two of whom survived childhood. William abandoned Hannah and the children some time between 1847 and 1855. They never divorced but apparently never saw each other again.

As a single mother, Hannah reveled in her newfound freedom and joined the abolitionist movement. In 1855 she challenged proslavery sentiments with her son, Edward Elson Ropes, in the tumultuous Kansas territory. In Lawrence, Kansas, she nursed the sick until 1856 when she returned to Massachusetts as the violence in Kansas escalated. That same year, she wrote a book detailing her experiences in Kansas called *Six Months in Kansas: By a Lady.* She remained involved in political issues and benevolent works, publishing a second book in 1859 entitled *Cranston House: A Novel,* a fictional work loosely based on events in her own life.

In June 1862, following her son's enlistment in the Second Massachusetts Volunteer Infantry Regiment, Hannah signed on as a nurse under the supervision of Dorothea Dix, superintendent of the United States army nurses. Hannah wanted a part in the war effort and turned to one of the few arenas open to women and for which she had talent: nursing. She had been strongly influenced by Florence Nightingale's *Notes on Nursing: What It Is, and What It Is Not,* and Nightingale's philosophy motivated her to fight for better conditions for wounded soldiers. She embraced the belief that it was her duty and honor to mother "her boys." She arrived in Georgetown, Washington, D.C., in June 1862 and began her work as matron of nurses at the Union Hotel Hospital.

In her 1863 novel, *Hospital Sketches,* Louisa May Alcott, one of the nurses working under Ropes, nicknamed the hospital the "Hurly-burly House," given the chaotic and poor conditions. It was an old building, poorly ventilated, damp, and cold. Ropes oversaw 10 nurses and 400 patients. She immediately worked to improve the conditions, sanitation, and patient treatment. As a part of that work, she reported two officers—a chief surgeon and a steward—for malfeasance. She accused them of depriving patients of food, stealing from patients, selling supplies meant for patients, and treating patients cruelly. When the surgeon general ignored her complaints, she appealed to Secretary of War Edwin Stanton. The two men were arrested and imprisoned, and Stanton reassigned the administrators.

Tragically, in January 1863, both Ropes and Alcott fell ill with typhoid pneumonia at the hospital. Alcott survived, but Ropes died. She is buried in New Gloucester, Maine.

Paula Katherine Hinton

See Also: Abolitionism and the Antislavery Movement; Alcott, Louisa May; Dix, Dorothea; Slavery and the Civil War

Further Reading

Brumgardt, John R., ed. *Civil War Nurse: The Diary and Letters of Hannah Ropes.* Knoxville: University of Tennessee Press, 1980.

Schultz, Jane E. *Women at the Front: Hospital Workers in Civil War America.* Chapel Hill: University of North Carolina Press, 2004.

Rose, Ernestine (1810–1892)

The Polish-born freethinker, secularist, and feminist Ernestine Rose was an outstanding intellectual. Her contribution to the early women's movement in the United States, for many years as its first and only Jewish woman activist, has yet to be properly acknowledged. Yet it is she, along with another immigrant, the Scottish-born Frances Wright, whom women such as Elizabeth Cady Stanton and Susan B. Anthony acknowledged as being among the pioneer advocates of women's suffrage in the United States.

A rabbi's daughter, Ernestine Rose was born in Piotrków Trybunalski, Poland, in what was then part of the Jewish Pale of Settlement of the Russian Empire; her

Ernestine Rose, Jewish American advocate of women's rights. (Library of Congress)

family name was Potowski. A natural-born rebel who had been taught the Torah and Talmud and brought up in a strict Orthodox home, she rejected the constraints of her religion at the age of 14, in particular its subordination of women. At 16 she went to the secular courts to fight for her dead mother's inheritance, when her father was about to make it over as a dowry on her marriage to an older man. Soon after, giving up her inheritance to her father of her own free will, she left for Germany, where she lived alone in Berlin for two years and supported herself by selling her own invention, a deodorizing perfumed paper. After that, Rose spent time in the Netherlands and France before arriving in England in 1831, having survived a shipwreck where she had lost all her possessions. There she mixed with reformers such as Elizabeth Fry and the radical leader Robert Owen, with him cofounding a utopian-socialist group, the Association of All Classes of All Nations, in 1835.

In 1836 Ernestine married the jeweler and silversmith William Rose, also a follower of Robert Owen, and at age 26 emigrated with him to the United States, where they opened their own shop selling silver goods and a brand of toilet water concocted by Ernestine. As an admirer of another rebel and individualist, Frances Wright, who had been an early advocate of women's rights in the United States, Rose joined other émigré intellectuals in the Society for Moral Philanthropists. She demonstrated a flair for public speaking (becoming known as the "Queen of the Platform") and began lecturing at the society, speaking out on "the evils of the social system, the formation of human character, slavery, the rights of woman, and other reform questions."

During her first winter in the United States, Rose began petitioning the New York state legislature in support of a bill for reform of women's property rights. She toured almost every major city in the state and over the course of the next 11 years assaulted the state legislature with regular petitions, addressing it on five occasions. In April 1848, the New York legislature passed the Married Women's Property Act, which allowed divorced women to retain some of their possessions. Rose was supported in her campaigning on marriage reform by Anthony, Stanton, and Lucretia Mott. In 1843, together with other utopian socialists of both sexes, Rose founded an Owenite colony in Skaneateles, New York, a venture that lasted until 1846.

During the 1850s, in addition to working for women's rights, Rose supported the causes of temperance and abolitionism. She spoke at the first national convention for women's rights, held in Worcester, Massachusetts, in 1850, where she called for a resolution on women's political, social, and legal equality with men. At the third national women's rights convention, held in Syracuse in 1852, she engaged in a forceful debate over the Bible's position on women's rights. Freethinker Rose challenged the need for any "written authority," biblical or otherwise, to pontificate on the basic human rights to which she believed women were entitled. At the 10th national women's rights convention in New York in 1860, Rose paid tribute to the pioneering work of Frances Wright and joined in another intensive debate, this time on marriage reform. Here she challenged her detractors, who had accused her of supporting "free love." She argued that it was immoral for society to oppose divorce and expect two people to remain together in what amounted to a relationship of legalized prostitution, where "there are only discord and misery to themselves, and vice and crime to society."

During the Civil War, Rose joined Stanton and Anthony in working for the abolition of slavery through the National Women's Loyal League. In 1867 she spoke at the first annual meeting of the American Equal Rights Association, held in New York, to resume the fight for women's suffrage, which had been sidelined by the war. Like many other suffragists, Rose was dismayed at the award of suffrage to black men ahead of women under the Fourteenth and Fifteenth Amendments and joined Anthony and Stanton in founding the National Woman Suffrage Association.

Rose returned to Europe in 1869 for a rest cure, only days after finally taking U.S. citizenship. She settled in England, where she took an interest in the suffrage movement as well as the work of the Universal Peace Union, and returned to the United States to sell her possessions there and attend the 1873 convention of the National Woman Suffrage Association. In December 1882, Elizabeth Cady Stanton visited a sad and dispirited Rose in London, finding her still "as bright, witty, and sarcastic as ever" but remarking with compassion on Rose's isolation, "with not one soul with a drop of her blood in their veins living, not one life-long friend at hand on whom to call." Rose died in 1892 and is buried at that famous resting place of many pioneering freethinkers, writers, and socialists, Highgate Cemetery in London, not far from the grave of Karl Marx.

Helen Rappaport

See Also: Abolitionism and the Antislavery Movement; Divorce (before the Civil War); Mott, Lucretia; National Women's Loyal League; New York Married Women's Property Acts; Utopian Communities; Wright, Frances; Anthony, Susan B. (Vol. 2); Blackwell, Antoinette Brown (Vol. 2); Free Love Movement (Vol. 2); National Woman Suffrage Association (Vol. 2); Stanton, Elizabeth Cady (Vol. 2)

Primary Documents: 1848–1849, New York Married Women's Property Acts; 1861, Address on Behalf of the New York Divorce Bill

Further Reading

Bolt, Christine. *The Women's Movements in the United States and Britain from the 1790s to the 1920s.* London: Harvester Wheatsheaf, 1993.

Ceniza, Sherry. *Walt Whitman and Nineteenth-Century Women Reformers.* Tuscaloosa: University of Alabama Press, 1998.

Jacoby, Susan. *Freethinkers: A History of American Secularism.* New York: Henry Holt and Company, 2005.

Kolmerton, Carol A. *The American Life of Ernestine L. Rose.* Syracuse, NY: Syracuse University Press, 1999.

Suhl, Yuri. *Ernestine Rose and the Battle for Human Rights.* New York: Biblio Press, 1990 [1959].

Ross, Araminta. See Tubman, Harriet

S

Sampson, Deborah (1760–1827)

Deborah Sampson's (or Samson) life began in a conventional manner, having been born into a rural farming family in Plympton, Massachusetts. Her father died when she was young, and the family sank into severe poverty. As was the custom for very poor children who had been orphaned, Deborah was bound out to become a servant in a neighboring farm. She was treated well at the prosperous farm of Jeremiah Thomas, learning to spin, sew, and care for animals.

Deborah Sampson stayed with the Thomas family even after her indenture ended in 1778, but the drudgery of life on a farm seemed too mundane and she was tempted to see the world by joining the army. In 1782 she made her first attempt to join the army by binding her breasts with a strip of cloth, tying her hair back, and dressing in boy's clothing. She successfully enrolled under the name Timothy Thayer and pocketed the substantial bounty the army was awarding men who agreed to enlist for a three-year term. That evening Sampson went to a tavern where she became drunk and boisterous, but she never reported to duty the next morning. An elderly woman from the neighborhood had recognized Sampson/Thayer when she enlisted and reported her to authorities. Sampson was forced to return the money she had not already consumed in drink, and her reputation in her small town was ruined.

In May 1782 Sampson traveled to Uxbridge, Massachusetts, where she once again disguised herself as a young man and successfully enrolled in the Fourth Massachusetts Regiment under the assumed name of Robert Shurtliff. This time her disguise would not be discovered for years. Her family suspected that Sampson had absconded to the army and made a few attempts to locate her. Seeking to allay her mother's fears, Deborah wrote a letter home, saying she had "found agreeable work" among a "large but well-regulated family."

Over the coming months Sampson/Shurtliff partook in a series of raids, battles, and sieges. She went on campaigns to hunt down raiding parties of Tories. She fought against Indians in western New York. She lived in tents with men, using the latrine and bathing under cover of darkness. She wore a tight vest to bind her breasts throughout her service in the military. In one skirmish she took a bullet in the thigh and had to be treated at a hospital. A French doctor cut away her pant leg and treated the wound, but her secret remained safe.

In 1783 her regiment was sent to Philadelphia to help suppress a group of American soldiers who were threatening to mutiny. She was assigned to be an orderly for Major General John Patterson, who was in charge of court-martial proceedings. Shortly after arriving in Philadelphia, Sampson/Shurtliff became infected with a debilitating fever and was hospitalized. She drifted in and out of consciousness. During one of her lucid moments, she recalled overhearing fellow soldiers discussing who would inherit her clothing after she died. At the worst of her illness, she was examined by Dr. Barnabas Binney, who discovered her secret while feeling for a heartbeat. The doctor did not immediately reveal her secret, but ordered her to be transferred to his home where she was cared for in private.

Sampson maintained her male disguise while recovering and was eventually sent home to West Point at the close of the war, still dressed as a man. With her she carried a sealed letter from Dr. Binney addressed to her commanding officer, Major General Patterson. The letter revealed Sampson's sex, which was met with disbelief by the officers until Deborah verified its truth. They accepted the situation with good humor and provided Sampson with a private apartment and clothes of either sex. She generally preferred to continue wearing men's clothing, claiming she suffered less harassment from the soldiers when she was so dressed.

In October 1783 Sampson was granted an honorable discharge from the army. She headed to a small town in Massachusetts, where she took work on her uncle's farm. Initially, she continued to live as a man, using the name Ephraim Sampson, although her uncle certainly knew the truth. In 1784 she began living as a woman again and married Benjamin Gannett the following year. They moved into a two-story farmhouse, where they raised three children.

The Gannetts always suffered from poverty. Deborah later claimed her war injuries prevented her from fully helping on the farm. In 1797 she became acquainted

Deborah Sampson disguised herself as a man and fought in several battles of the American Revolution. (Library of Congress)

with Herman Mann, who set upon a plan to capitalize on Sampson's unusual story. He helped her write her memoirs and wrote a prepared speech for her to deliver at public gatherings. The memoirs were highly exaggerated, which Sampson later acknowledged and wished to correct. Her speaking engagements were popular and earned her a decent living. She began the lecture dressed in female clothing and explained her motives for wishing to serve in the military. She then changed into uniform and performed the "manual of arms" with a regulation musket. She lectured throughout New England and is believed to have been the first paid female lecturer in America.

Despite her speaking tour, Deborah Sampson Gannett died in poverty at the age of 66. Her husband appealed for a widower's pension, claiming that Deborah's war wounds had contributed to her death. By the time the pension was granted, Benjamin had died. The generous pension award was divided equally among their three children.

Dorothy A. Mays

See Also: The American Revolution

Primary Document: 1804, Paul Revere Defends Deborah Sampson Gannett, a Female Soldier

Further Reading

Berkin, Carol. *Revolutionary Mothers: Women in the Struggle for America's Independence.* New York: Knopf, 2005.

Young, Alfred F. *Masquerade: The Life and Times of Deborah Sampson, Continental Soldier.* New York: Knopf, 2004.

Schuyler, Louisa Lee (1837–1926)

Social reformer Louisa Lee Schuyler helped lead the United States Sanitary Commission during the Civil War. She was born in New York City to a socially prominent and affluent family. Her great-grandfathers were Revolutionary War Generals Phillip Schuyler and Alexander Hamilton. Despite her privileged background, she dedicated her life to public service, which had long been a tradition in her family. As a young woman, Schuyler was active in the Children's Aid Society of New York.

Shortly after the Civil War erupted, Harry Raymond, founder of the *New York Times,* placed an advertisement in his newspaper asking for women to join his wife in compiling and preparing supplies for wounded soldiers. Women throughout the North responded by gathering in private homes and churches to produce the necessary items for Union soldiers. On April 26, 1861, Schuyler organized a meeting of 4,000 women in New York City and founded the Women's Central Association of Relief for the Sick and Wounded of the Army. She wanted her organization, which was modeled after the British Sanitary Commission created during the Crimean War to combat the unsanitary conditions that caused disease, to be national in scope.

Schuyler attempted to get the federal government to recognize her organization, but initially there was little interest. President Abraham Lincoln believed that the organization would be difficult to administer. However, on June 13, 1861, he reluctantly signed an order officially establishing the United States Sanitary Commission. By 1863, there were over 7,000 local commissions throughout the North. Schuyler served as chairman of the Committee on Correspondence and Publicity for the Commission. She wrote reports and letters, spoke to the local commissions, and gave public lectures on the Sanitary Commission's work. Schuyler, along with other members of the U.S. Sanitary Commission, inspected

Union army camps and prison camps operated by the Confederate army, and she wrote detailed reports for the government on the unsanitary conditions she found there.

Thousands of women volunteered with the Sanitary Commission. Under Schuyler's leadership, the women collected food, clothing items, and medical supplies for Union soldiers. Over 25,000 packages were sent to Union troops, and amazingly only one package was lost. The women served as nurses in army hospitals and camps. They used their homes to provide sleeping quarters and meals for soldiers traveling to and from the war-front. The Commission supplied and operated steamships, provided by the government, that were used as floating hospitals, and it pioneered the use of trains as mobile hospitals and a field ambulance corps. Schuyler helped to organize sanitary fairs in many large cities. The fairs were operated by the women volunteers and attracted the public by selling baked goods and hand-made crafts, among other items. Over the course of the Civil War, the U.S. Sanitary Commission collected and distributed nearly $6 million.

After the war, Schuyler devoted the rest of her life to promoting social welfare. She founded the New York State Charities Aid Association in 1872. This organization inspected homeless shelters and made recommendations to improve the standards of care. Louisa Lee Schuyler died in 1926.

Gene C. Gerard

See Also: Slavery and the Civil War; United States Sanitary Commission

Further Reading

Attie, Jeanie. *Patriotic Toil: Northern Women and the American Civil War.* Ithaca, NY: Cornell University Press, 1998.

Giesberg, Judith Ann. *Civil War Sisterhood: The U.S. Sanitary Commission and Women's Politics in Transition.* Boston, MA: Northeastern University Press, 2000.

Seneca Falls Convention (1848)

Although the Nineteenth Amendment prohibiting discrimination against women in voting was not ratified until 1920, scholars often trace the start of the U.S.

Cartoon representation of the first American women's rights convention, held at Seneca Falls, New York, in July 1848. (Library of Congress)

women's suffrage movement to the first organized women's rights convention, which met at the Wesleyan Chapel (now a national historic site) in Seneca Falls, New York, on July 19 and 20, 1848. Elizabeth Cady Stanton and Lucretia Mott, who called the meeting just days before it was held, largely organized the convention, which about 300 men and women attended.

The women's rights convention adopted a Declaration of Sentiments. Patterned after the U.S. Declaration of Independence, it declared that "all men and women are created equal," and listed numerous deprivations that women faced. These included the denial of the right to vote, the requirement that women submit to laws that they had no part in making, the moribund legal status of married women, the subjection of women to physical punishment by their husbands, the denial of the guardianship of children to women who were divorced, the exclusion of women from key professions, and the like. In one highly controversial passage, the declaration noted that "He [mankind] has withheld from her rights which are given to the most ignorant and degraded men—both natives and foreigners."

Although the convention was the brainchild of Stanton and Mott, Mott's husband, as well as the husband of another participant, presided over the meeting to prevent undue offense to public sensibilities at a time when women did not speak in public unless it was to a group of other women. One hundred delegates, both men and women, subsequently signed a set of resolutions designed to provide for women's equality. Although the Nineteenth Amendment (as well as future calls for an Equal Rights Amendment) can be traced to these resolutions, the 1848 convention did not specifically call for a constitutional amendment or set of amendments. Interestingly, the provision for "the elective franchise" was considered to be the most controversial; so much so, that it was the only provision not to be adopted unanimously, and many who signed the resolutions later renounced them. It probably would not have been included but for the insistence of Elizabeth Cady Stanton and Frederick Douglass that the right to vote was the key to other rights and privileges. Stanton's own husband absented himself from the convention; her father reportedly "rushed to Seneca Falls fearing for his daughter's sanity"; and her older sister "wept over . . . her involvement in such a radical cause." Not surprisingly, the resolution for women's suffrage was long the subject of journalistic ridicule, and the task of obtaining suffrage proved to be far more extended than many probably would have anticipated.

Only one young woman who was present at the Seneca Falls convention, Charlotte Woodward, survived long enough to cast her vote in a presidential election 72 years later. In the meantime, the Seneca Falls convention sparked other conventions, including one that was held two weeks later in Rochester, New York, and the first of many subsequent national women's rights conventions, which was held in Worcester, Massachusetts, in 1850. During the next seven decades, Carrie Chapman Catt noted that women participated in a total of 56 campaigns of state referenda, 480 campaigns to convince state legislatures to submit suffrage amendments to voters, 47 campaigns attempting to get state constitutional conventions to write woman suffrage into state constitutions, and 19 campaigns with 19 successive Congresses.

John R. Vile

See Also: Douglass, Frederick; Mott, Lucretia; Suffrage in Early America; Equal Rights Amendment (Vol. 3); Nineteenth Amendment (Vol. 2); Stanton, Elizabeth Cady (Vol. 2);

Primary Document: 1848, Declaration of Sentiments

Further Reading

Bernhard, Virginia, and Elizabeth Fox-Genovese, eds. *The Birth of American Feminism: The Seneca Falls Woman's Convention of 1848.* St. James, NY: Brandywine Press, 1995.

McMillen, Sally G. *Seneca Falls and the Origins of the Women's Rights Movement.* New York: Oxford University Press, 2008.

Palmer, Kris E. *Constitutional Amendments: 1789 to the Present.* Detroit, MI: Gale Group, 2000.

Wellman, Judith. *The Road to Seneca Falls: Elizabeth Cady Stanton and the First Woman's Rights Convention.* Urbana: University of Illinois Press, 2004.

Wheeler, Marjorie S., ed. *One Woman, One Vote: Rediscovering the Woman Suffrage Movement.* Troutdale, OR: New Sage, 1995.

Seton, Elizabeth (1774–1821)

Founder of the first American order of Catholic women and a canonized saint, Elizabeth Ann Bayley was the second of three daughters born to Dr. Richard Bayley, a compassionate physician committed to public health. She grew up in a privileged environment in New York City, where she received an adequate education, undertook a busy social calendar, and led a life of leisure. At age 19 she married William Seton, a young merchant on

Elizabeth Seton was the first American to be canonized and was committed to the causes of charity and education. (Hulton Archive/Getty Images)

Wall Street. It was a love match, and the couple's first years of marriage were idyllic, save for the concern over William's health. Shortly after their marriage it became apparent he had consumption, a condition that was usually fatal.

Despite her husband's gradual decline, Elizabeth gave birth to three daughters and two sons. She engaged in activities typical of prosperous ladies, such as hosting afternoon teas and attending balls and theatrical shows. Perhaps as a balance to her affluent life, Elizabeth Seton took a sincere interest in charitable works. Her father's occupation as New York's first health commissioner exposed her to the plight of the poor and the sick. She witnessed malnourished Irish immigrants disembarking at the port of Staten Island and experienced frustration with her inability to change their dilemma. In 1797 she joined forces with Isabella Marshall Graham to establish one of the first organized charities for the relief of the poor.

Nearing the end of the 1790s Elizabeth Seton began to experience the gnawing fear of poverty herself. Her husband's business suffered a series of downturns and went into bankruptcy in 1800. Her father died of yellow fever, contracted during his duties as a quarantine officer. Her husband's health became so critical she was advised to take him to the Mediterranean in an attempt to save his life by exposure to a new climate. Seton sold most of her remaining household goods to fund the voyage, but William died less than two months after arriving in Italy.

In a state of profound spiritual depression, Elizabeth Seton was cared for by the Filicchi family, associates of her husband's business. She attended Catholic mass and was counseled by members of the Catholic clergy. By the time she returned to New York, she was ready to convert to Catholicism, but faced severe pressure from family, friends, and her Episcopal minister to refrain from conversion. Catholics were considered by many in high society to be poor, uneducated, and unenlightened. Lingering prejudice against Catholicism was alive and well among the elite society in which Seton lived, and pressure against conversion was strong. In addition to her spiritual uncertainty, Seton was confronted with earning a living to support herself and her five children. She accepted charity from her in-laws and established a boardinghouse for boys who were attending private school in New York. She formally converted to Catholicism in 1805.

Seton was barely able to make ends meet, but her relationship with her husband's sisters grew closer as they too became attracted to Catholicism. When Cecilia Seton converted to Catholicism, much of Elizabeth's financial support from her in-laws evaporated. In 1808 she accepted a position teaching in a Catholic girls' school in Baltimore. The following year she began working toward a long-cherished dream, the establishment of a convent for a charitable order of nuns. Her sisters-in-law, Cecilia and Harriet Seton, joined the order along with four other young women. Called the Sisters of Charity, the order began in a small farmhouse in Emmitsburg, Maryland. On formal occasions they wore black habits with white bonnets, but for daily work they dressed in ordinary clothing of the day. They established St. Joseph's School for the education of Catholic girls. Some of the wealthiest families in Maryland were Catholic, and many sent their daughters to be educated at Seton's private school. Using the generous tuition payments, Seton was able to fund charitable work, including free schooling for poor girls, nursing for the sick, and relief for the hungry.

The Sisters of Charity flourished. Within a few years they were able to build a more substantial home for the order, and additional communities were founded in Philadelphia (1814) and New York (1817). Despite her professional success, Elizabeth Seton's personal life continued to be marred by tragedy. The consumptive disease that killed her husband had spread to many members of her family. Seton's three daughters were being raised at the convent, and two daughters died of the disease while they were teenagers. Both of Seton's sisters-in-law died of the disease, and by her forties, Elizabeth herself was suffering from consumption. She did not let her health impede her charitable work. She vowed to a sister, "I will be wild Betsy to the last." She died at age 46. Her daughter Catherine became a Sister of Mercy and carried out charitable works until she died at age 91. Seton's son William was a disappointment to her. He had a reputation for living a self-centered life; he had squandered much of the money his mother saved for him. Despite her disappointment in William, Elizabeth would have been pleased to know that his son Robert Seton would one day become an archbishop. Seton Hall College was named in her honor in 1856.

Efforts to seek canonization for Mother Elizabeth Seton began in the 1880s. In 1963 she was beatified, and in 1975 she became the first American saint of the Catholic Church. Her order of the Sisters of Charity has expanded to include more than 11,000 women.

Dorothy A. Mays

See Also: Education of Women (before the Civil War)

Further Reading

Dirvin, Joseph I. *Mrs. Seton: Foundress of the American Sisters of Charity.* New York: Farrar, Straus and Giroux, 1975.

Emmitsburg Area Historical Society. "St. Elizabeth Ann Seton." Accessed February 14, 2012. http://www.emmitsburg.net/setonshrine/

Spalding, Thomas. "Elizabeth Ann Bayley Seton." In *American National Biography,* edited by John A. Garraty. New York: Oxford University Press, 1999.

Shakers

The Shaker religion began with the visions of Ann Lee, an illiterate Englishwoman born to working-class parents in Manchester, England, in 1736. Very little is known of her early life, but she was apparently greatly troubled by religious questions and by the nature of human sexuality. In 1758 Lee joined a small Quaker-inspired sect and found a degree of comfort in their ritualistic dances, or shaking, as this was called. In spite of her fears of sexuality she married a blacksmith and became pregnant eight

Separation of the sexes during meals in a Shaker dining room. (*Frank Leslie's Popular Monthly.* Vol. XX, July to December 1885, p. 668)

times. Four of those pregnancies ended in miscarriage, and her four children died in infancy; her experiences with sex, pregnancy, and childbirth confirmed her antipathy to the sexual side of human nature. During her marriage Lee suffered great mental and physical anguish, which culminated in 1770 in a series of visions and the conviction that she was the female Christ and that sexual relations were at the heart of human depravity. After this point her sect of "Shaking Quakers" demanded celibacy; membership thus remained small.

In 1774 "Mother" Ann Lee and eight followers sailed to the American colonies. The exigencies of earning a living caused them to scatter temporarily, but in 1776 they reunited in Niskayuna, New York, and began building their order. Aided by the strong revival spirit sweeping the new American nation in the late 18th century, the Shaker sect began to grow. Missionary efforts led to the founding of 10 Shaker communities. After Ann Lee died in 1784, a follower, Joseph Meacham, took charge of the group (1786) and gathered it into an ordered union with a published set of principles. The Meacham system became the Shaker way. At their peak in the mid-19th century, 6,000 Shakers resided in 18 communities in eight states, in New York, Massachusetts, New Hampshire, Connecticut, Maine, Kentucky, Ohio, and Indiana. Fewer than a dozen members remain today.

Shaker society was communal. Members gave up private property to the group when they entered the sect and, in turn, received material support from the group. The Shakers believed in manual labor for all and took pride in their productivity, their husbandry, and their craftsmanship. The group was organized into "families" of 25–150 persons (50 was the optimal number) that became the center of religious and economic life. A Shaker community might include several families. Men and women of the family occupied the same dwelling under the dual leadership of two elders and two elderesses. Although its members were strictly regulated because of the Shaker commitment to celibacy, the family worked together as an economic unit to provide subsistence for itself and surpluses for sale. Shakers divided the burden of labor quite traditionally; women performed domestic "female" tasks, while males did the heavier outdoor labor. The Shakers were not economic separatists. They gladly traded with the world and took pride in the high quality of the goods they manufactured or produced for sale.

Shaker theological beliefs and the practice of celibacy made the group quite controversial, and the controversy continues today as scholars try to determine whether Shaker beliefs and practices liberated or confined its women members. The Shakers believed that Ann Lee was the female Christ, and they incorporated the idea of the equality of women into their governmental structure. Women controlled their own sectors of the Shaker family, for example, and were equals in respect to visions and revelations. Shaker theology, however, emphasized the radical differences between men and women; men were active and positive in nature, while women were passive and negative. Shaker doctrine also defined women as more sexual and animalistic than men; women and their sexuality must be controlled if the Shakers were to achieve perfection. Because men and women were so different, a female Christ was necessary to act as intercessor for the female half of the human race. Mother Ann Lee had come to save women. She was also necessary for the salvation of men, however, because until women reached a position of dignity and self-control, society would be unable to create a new order and attain perfection.

Scholars who argue the liberating aspects of Shakerism for women point to the female Christ figure; to the leadership roles that included elderesses as the equals of elders; and to the replacement of the patriarchal family, childbirth, and motherhood with celibate communalism. Those who see Shakerism as less than liberating for women stress the theology that emphasized biological differences and the economic division of labor, which was very traditional. These scholars do concede, however, that the opportunity for religious leadership among the Shakers was empowering for Shaker women.

One active Shaker community remains. Seven women maintain the colony at Sabbathday Lake, Maine, where they continue their faith's rich musical and cultural practices. Historic Shaker designs in architecture, furniture, fabrics, and furnishings as well as their unique musical heritage are widely celebrated as vital influences on the American artistic and folk traditions.

Paula M. Nelson

See Also: Lee, "Mother" Ann; Quakers; Utopian Communities

Further Reading

Foster Lawrence. *Women, Family, and Utopia: Communal Experiments of the Shakers, the Oneida Community, and the Mormons.* Syracuse, NY: Syracuse University Press, 1991.

Skees, Suzanne. *God among the Shakers: A Search for Stillness and Faith at Sabbathday Lake.* New York: Hyperion, 1998.

Stein, Stephen J. *The Shaker Experience in America: A History of the United Society of Believers.* New Haven, CT: Yale University Press, 1992.

Wergland, Glendyne R. *Sisters in the Faith: Shaker Women and Equality of the Sexes.* Amherst: University of Massachusetts Press, 2011.

The Sibyl

Lydia Sayer Hasbrouck launched her reform publication, *The Sibyl: A Review of the Tastes, Errors and Fashions of Society* on July 1, 1856. The biweekly opposed a number of ills—from tobacco to liquor—but clearly its major push was for women's rights. Like many other reformers of the day, Hasbrouck saw abolitionism and women's rights as vitally linked, as she explained in 1856,

> We [*The Sibyl*] have another mission. It is with white slaves both of the north and south. The mass are as servilely bound as are the black slaves of the south. Many are content with their bonds; yet, as maybe seen by our columns, others are writhing beneath the burthen, and would fain cast them off. For these and all others we labor; for every slave bound on this broad earth we toil; yet wholly and solely refuse to devote all our energies to one particular branch of slavery. Our mission . . . is too broad for this.

Hasbrouck believed in the immediate abolition of slavery without compensation. Her vision with regard to the emancipation of women was more complex. Women should dress to free themselves from the bondage of society. They should wear the lighter weight bloomer garb, which allowed them freedom from the constriction of the corset and 19th-century fashion. When others in the women's rights organizations abandoned the reform, Hasbrouck labeled them "conservatives." Short dresses were, in their estimation, "too weighty a question to sustain."

In her women's rights vision, married women should be given full rights to property. In the antebellum period, few states accorded such rights. Women should also have the vote. Neither Hasbrouck nor readers would accept the argument that the husband represented the wife at the ballot box. Moreover, women should be paid the same amount as the men. One subscriber complained about the money paid female clerks compared to men doing the same job. Women made only 600 dollars a

year, compared to 1,200–1,800 dollars a year for men. The writer asked, "Is that justice?"

That subscriber illustrated an important function that *The Sibyl* played within the women's rights movement, especially during the Civil War. Like other reform publications, *The Sibyl* welcomed letters from readers. In so doing, Hasbrouck and her *Sibyl* accomplished two things: first, the news coverage expanded, and, second, feminist editorial comment increased. *The Sibyl* was one of the few forums for such "radical" thoughts. Women from Wisconsin, Illinois, and Indiana, especially, shared their perspectives on dress reform, equal pay for equal work, and national politics and policies. Hasbrouck had no objection to publishing critical comments on the president, the personalities, and the policies during the Civil War. Women had a special role to play in the conflict, Hasbrouck argued in *The Sibyl*. They should turn their back on fashion, wear the bloomer garb, and do their part on farms and in businesses. Women should also work in the hospitals, caring for the sick and wounded, one reader suggested. However, Hasbrouck was ill at ease with Dorothea Dix's handling of women nurses during the war, especially after Mrs. F. R. Harris Reid of Berlin, Wisconsin, reported that female nurses had been instructed to leave their bloomer outfits at home. Reid wrote, "If men cannot be nursed by women in comfortable but unfashionable attire, they may die for all my going in long skirts to nurse them." Soon Hasbrouck was editorially questioning Dix's other rulings. She wrote that Dix "seems to be particularly *hard* on young women, pretty women, and we were about to add women of common sense."

Although the war increasingly dominated the editorial columns of *The Sibyl,* Hasbrouck never gave up the women's rights cause. She was dismayed that the established women's rights groups languished during the Civil War.

> They have money at their disposal, and should combat these wrongs to women when they are accruing, instead of waiting until they become laws and fixtures, harder to set aside than now.

Although established women's rights activities languished, Hasbrouck and her *Sibyl* did not. She frequently editorially supported dress reform. (In 1863–1864, she also served as president of the National Dress Reform Association.) Even though the nation was at war, she urged women not to pay taxes until they had the vote.

The war did take a toll on both Hasbrouck and *The Sibyl*. At the start of the war, the frequency of the newspaper had to be cut, from biweekly to monthly, and its subscription price slashed from four dollars to fifty cents a year. While her husband published the newspaper at his shop, Hasbrouck did all the writing and editing of *The Sibyl*. Although the newspaper's editorial quality never slipped, its popularity did begin to wane. The women of the nation had to wait decades before gaining the right to vote, and *The Sibyl* was never again revived. The June 1864 issue was its last.

The Sibyl never had a large, national circulation. Yet, it is still played an important role, especially during the Civil War, when most women's rights voices were silenced.

Kathleen L. Endres

See Also: Abolitionism and the Antislavery Movement; Dix, Dorothea; Dress Reform; Hasbrouck, Lydia Sayer; Slavery and the Civil War

Further Reading

Cunningham, Patricia A. *Reforming Women's Fashion, 1850–1920: Politics, Health, and Art.* Kent, OH: Kent State University Press, 2003.

Fischer, Gayle V. *Pantaloons and Power: A Nineteenth-Century Dress Reform in the United States.* Kent, OH: Kent State University Press, 2001.

Solomon, Martha M., ed. *A Voice of Their Own: The Woman Suffrage Press, 1840–1910.* Tuscaloosa: University of Alabama Press, 1991.

Slavery and the Civil War

In perhaps the best-known female slave narrative of the 19th century, *Incidents in the Life of a Slave Girl* (published in 1861), former slave Harriet Jacobs lamented, "Slavery is terrible for men; but it is far more terrible for women. Superadded to the burden common to all, they have wrongs, and sufferings, and mortifications peculiarly their own." The very purpose of Jacobs's story was to emphasize what those "peculiar" burdens of women were: namely, that slave women were not only expected to perform many of the same tasks as men in the field and in white households but were also subjected to sexual exploitation by white masters, including the expectation that they would reproduce the slave workforce.

Although slavery existed in all the American colonies before the Revolution, the Southern colonies in particular were founded for the purpose of profit making through slave agricultural labor, a system propelled in the 19th century by the geographical expansion of the new United States as well as technological advances, such as the invention of the cotton gin in 1793. The North did not need slavery in the same way, for its family farms and merchants were not engaged in large-scale commercial agriculture. However, well into the 19th century, profitable Northern industries such as the textile mills, which employed large numbers of young white women, were dependent upon and fueled by the cotton boom in the slave South. By 1804, all of the Northern states had abolished slavery, although some were in the process of doing so only through gradual emancipation so that there were still some legal slaves in the North. In 1808, the international slave trade was abolished, but the United States continued to see heavy growth in the domestic slave population, primarily because of the reproductive work of slave women. The spread of the cotton economy into new territories and states after 1800 brought new opportunities for white pioneers but often had a disastrous effect on the slave community, separating spouses and families, as children and young male laborers were sold farther west.

African and African American men and women had been enslaved for 200 years and had, from the beginning, resisted their enslavement. But it was not until the early 19th century that an organized movement of free blacks as well as whites arose to begin the public fight to end slavery. Both black and white women took a prominent role in the abolitionist movement, which helped propel the nation toward civil war and ultimately secured the freedom of nearly four million African Americans. After the war women continued to work as reformers and as teachers committed to helping the newly freed people.

The war itself affected women, both North and South, black and white, as individuals and as members of families. Both Northern and Southern women responded as patriots, lending their support and assistance to their side's cause by weaving blankets for soldiers, feeding and clothing troops, economizing at home with scarce resources, volunteering as nurses, and managing farms and businesses while men were away. For Southern white women this meant the added responsibility of overseeing slaves and plantations in the absence of men. And in some cases, white women both North and South played unofficial roles with the military as spies and even as soldiers disguised as men. As one Southern woman put it, the onset of war was "an entire disruption of our domestic relations."

Slave Women

In the colonial period there were generally more African men than women imported as slaves and by the mid-18th century there were still more men in the overall American slave population. But by 1800 the sex ratio was more evenly balanced because of the natural increase of the slave population. Neither male nor female slaves had any control over the most basic aspects of their lives. Both were subject to harsh physical labor, malnourishment, cruel punishments, and separation from their families. But there were many gendered differences to the slave experience as well.

One of the earliest laws regulating slavery spoke of the particular circumstances of slave women. A 1662 Virginia statute established that, unlike the English common law upon which most of the colonial legal system depended, the status of Africans in colonial America, whether slave or free, would be determined by the status of the mother:

> Whereas some doubts have arisen whether children got by any Englishman upon a Negro woman should be slave or free, Be it therefore enacted and declared by this present grand assembly, that all children borne in this country shall be held bond or free only according to the condition of the mother.

This statute guaranteed that any slave children born on a particular farm or plantation automatically increased the property value of the owner. More devastating, it legally sanctioned the rape and sexual exploitation of black women and institutionalized their status as breeders. Defining the "children got by an Englishman upon a Negro woman" as slaves also allowed one of the most unfathomable cruelties of the system, in that many white men made the decision to sell their own children as slaves, a story repeated over and over throughout the history of slavery.

Young slave girls began their lives in a world where tasks and family life itself were separated by age and sex. Their mothers were often sent right back to the fields or the white households immediately after giving birth and most slave babies were taken care of by elderly slave women. In turn, young slave girls and boys might spend some time helping take care of infants, running errands, or tending animals before themselves being turned into field laborers and assistants. After reaching a certain age, most slave girls and women were integrated into networks of other women from whom they learned to negotiate the demands of daily life. From these other women, young girls learned not only to perform the specific tasks assigned to them on the plantation but also to cook, spin, sew, and take care of each other when they were sick.

Once a girl became a teenager she might be able to choose a mate, if she was lucky. More likely she had little say in determining her own sexual life and could be subject to rape and exploitation by the master or be forced to "marry" another slave. Texas slave Laura Smalley recounted stories she had heard: "You know, jus' like a big fine looking woman, big fine looking man, you know, old boss wants, you know, children from them, you know. They just fasten them up in the house or somewhere, you know, and go off and leave them in there. Wan' to breed them like they was hogs or horses something like that I say." A woman who did not bear children could be forced by her master to have sexual relations with different men, and, if she still did not conceive, she might be sold off to perform other work. Although some masters approved of slaves choosing their own marriage partners, primarily as a way of keeping their workers happy, whites also had an economic interest in producing slave children. It was for all of these reasons that former slave Harriet Jacobs lamented giving birth to a daughter: "When they told me my newborn babe was a girl, my heart was heavier than it had ever been before."

All slaves were important investments, but an attractive woman could garner sometimes twice as much as even the most robust male laborer on the slave auction block. Any slave woman of childbearing age could be valued and sold for her reproductive abilities or potential, and any woman was at all times at risk of sexual exploitation by white men, but "fancy girls" constituted a separate market in the slave trade. These were women, young and often lighter-skinned, who were valued not as laborers or even potential breeders, but as prostitutes for their sexual services to the wealthiest white men, with reports of such women sold for as much as $5,000 at auction.

Owners had different expectations in assigning responsibilities based on age, ability, and sex. At cotton-picking time everyone, including children and the elderly, worked in the fields. A male slave from South Carolina remembered: "Women worked in de field same as de men. Some of dem plowed jes' like de men and boys. Couldn't tell'em apart in de field, as dey wore pantalets or breeches." Besides working in the field, women might be used as housekeepers, nannies for white children, laundresses, cooks, personal servants, caregivers for slave children (usually elderly women), or sexual mistresses for the master. In addition, slave women often had the added responsibility for their own families or for other slaves on the same plantation, which meant spending their evenings preparing food, tending children, mending clothes, and trying to maintain clean living quarters.

Most Southern women, black or white, were aided in childbirth by rural midwives, and many white women were attended as well by black midwives. Enslaved midwives enjoyed a more privileged status than possible for other slaves and possessed a skill that they could pass on to younger slave women. A skilled midwife served not only her own plantation but was frequently called upon and hired out to other plantations, and so she was an especially valuable addition to a slaveholder's income.

Although older children or elderly slaves were sometimes assigned to care for babies and toddlers, many slave mothers had no choice but to take their young children right along with them into the fields or the kitchen. Serving as a cook or housekeeper was also a more privileged position for slave women in that it at least potentially gave them some independence and control over their work and also gave them greater access to food on a regular basis. The importance of household slaves to the white family did not necessarily protect them from physical abuse. Indeed, that proximity sometimes increased their vulnerability, especially to the sexual advances of white men, and, subsequently, the humiliation, jealousy, and sometimes violence of the white mistress.

Slave Women's Resistance

In many instances female slaves resisted and outright refused both sexual exploitation and demands for their labor by running away, responding with violence, feigning illness, or sabotaging both white efforts to control them and white economic interests. From the beginning, slave men and women actively resisted their enslavement, but sometimes in different ways. On the earliest slave ships, through what became known as the middle passage or journey across the Atlantic, Africans were often separated by sex, and, according to a 1789 report on slave transport, females were not always shackled as were the men. One trader noted that "we couple the sturdy Men together with Irons; but we suffer the Women and children to go freely about." Of course, going "freely about" was not quite the case, as there were many documented instances of women being abused, physically

and sexually, by the ship's European crew members, and, shackled or not, all slaves were given little or no food or water on the long journey. In 1785, the captain of a slave ship was attacked by a group of women who tried to throw him overboard. The captain was rescued by his crew but some of the women, rather than risk punishment or an uncertain future as slaves, further resisted by starving themselves to death.

There was also daily resistance on many levels to plantation slavery in the United States. According to newspaper ads for runaway slaves, there were consistently more male than female runaways. One reason offered for this fact is that slave women were more likely to stay on the plantations if they had children, as they did not want to leave them behind and it was too difficult and dangerous to attempt to run away or revolt with children in tow. In some cases entire families attempted to run away together, but in others only the father or other men escaped alone, planning to return or send for the others at a later date. In some cases women only ran away temporarily to visit family on other plantations. In *Incidents in the Life of a Slave Girl,* Harriet Jacobs recounted her experience of escaping slavery by going only as far as her nearby grandmother's house, where she hid out in a crawl space above the kitchen for seven years before finally escaping to the North.

In 1850, the U.S. Congress passed the Fugitive Slave Act, making it more difficult for slaves to find refuge in the Northern states by requiring law enforcement, the courts, and citizens to assist in the return of fugitive slaves to the South. Harriet Tubman, herself an escaped slave from Maryland, was probably the best-known "conductor" on the Underground Railroad, a network of individuals and safe houses that guided thousands of enslaved African Americans through the now-dangerous Northern states to the freedom of Canada. Tubman was personally responsible for helping several hundred slaves, including her own siblings and parents, reach freedom. As a result of her actions, she was wanted in Southern states where officials offered as much as $40,000 for her capture.

Other women played silent but vital roles in the Underground Railroad, sometimes assisting fugitive slaves without leaving their homes. Women created elaborate quilts that communicated clues and instructions for slaves escaping to the North. Patterns and colors on the quilts might indicate which direction to travel or highlight specific landmarks to reach, such as the "Crossroads" pattern, which usually referred to Cleveland, Ohio, as a meeting place. The spacing of the stitching or the size of the squares could be counted to indicate how many miles between safe houses. Black women would hang their quilts in their windows to be aired out, as was often done, and in this manner, the fugitive slaves could easily view them. In the case of quilts along the Underground Railroad, women's traditional domestic work took on a more subversive political role or meaning.

One of the most extraordinary stories of exploitation, violence, and resistance in the 19th century was that of a Missouri slave named Celia, who was raped by her master on the very day he purchased her in 1850 when she was only 14 years old. Over the next few years Celia was repeatedly sexually abused by her master. She gave birth to several children by him. Her master provided her with her own separate cabin on his property, undoubtedly so that he could have access to her away from the eyes of his own grown children, but the private cabin ultimately allowed her to exact her own revenge. The only reason Celia's story is recorded in history is because she resisted her conditions by killing her white master, dismembering him, and burning parts of the body in her fireplace, acts for which she was ultimately put on trial and executed.

One of the ways slave women resisted rape and forced breeding was by refusing to bear children for white masters or refusing to allow their own children to become enslaved. The use of birth control, including abortion, was one way that women attempted to maintain some control over their bodies. Slave women did not necessarily act alone in these forms of resistance, but were often aided by other women with knowledge of medicines or herbs as well as instructions on specific methods. It is difficult for historians to ascertain precise numbers on how many slave women engaged in such practices, just as it was difficult for white owners to prove that such methods of sabotage had been used by their own slaves. But reports abounded of slave women who failed to produce any children during years of bondage but who went on to have several children after they were freed.

Access to the white household allowed for very particular types of resistance. White families knew that they were vulnerable because of the trust they instilled in cooks, housekeepers, and nannies of their own children. A house servant named Delia later almost humorously recalled, "How many times I spit in the biscuits and peed in the coffee just to get back at them mean white folks." White masters were afraid of being poisoned by slaves in the kitchen and of kitchen slaves who sabotaged their masters by stealing or simply destroying food and other provisions. Women resisted slavery in

a variety of ways, but despite the cruelties and indignities of slavery, African American women endured and survived the roles imposed upon them as slaves and as women.

Plantation Mistresses

Before the Civil War, Southern white women occupied a precarious and paradoxical position in the American slave system. On the one hand, they were not slaves, and the gender ideology of the 19th-century plantation South meant that white women were seen as frail, feminine, and morally superior. On the other hand, they were members of the slaveholding class and the reality of most Southern white women's lives of the 19th century was defined by violence as much as by hard work. Southern white women of all classes managed farms, homes, children, and sometimes slaves. Like their Northern counterparts, they were responsible for tasks such as organizing the household, food production, attending to the medical needs of their families, and educating their own children.

Women of the slaveholding class had little choice in the matter of slavery as it existed in their own households, although they certainly could choose how to respond to individual slaves. Many white women were privately critical of slavery, and, in particular, of its effect on white women, who were often tormented over illicit relationships between their own husbands and female slaves. Numberless white women endured this indignity quietly, while others took their anger and humiliation out on the slaves themselves. One of the most famous Civil War-era diarists, Mary Chesnut of South Carolina, criticized the activities of white men and the blindness of white women to what was going on in their own homes. Chesnut reflected on the shame that pervaded white Southern society so that "the mulattoes one sees in every family partly resemble the white children. Any lady is ready to tell you who the father is of all the mulatto children in everybody's household but her own."

Given such isolation from other white families and friends, many white women depended upon the friendship and company of their female slaves and certainly many formed lifelong bonds with their servants, cooks, and nannies. Others, however, lived in fear of the slaves in their midst. Mary Chesnut's cousin was smothered by a slave, leading Chesnut's sister, Kate, to be wary of her own house servant: "Does she mean to take care of me—or to murder me?" White women were also capable of inflicting physical punishment on their slaves, and, in some cases, such actions were demanded of them in their role as slave managers when their husbands were away.

Civil War

Once war broke out, women were called upon to support the war, either from afar or within their own backyards, in addition to continuing to carry out their duties in their own households. For many women throughout the South, as well as some women in the North, the war hit too close to home when their towns and neighborhoods became the battlefield. Women and children could be caught in the crossfire, with soldiers demanding food, stealing horses, and supplies, and injured soldiers needing help. Many women were willing to give assistance where needed. One plantation mistress in Louisiana was so wearied by not only troops, but also poor white families going from town to town looking for food and shelter, that she set up two rooms in her house specifically for the use of strangers. Other women were forced into service; in some instances, they were literally brought onto the battlefield to nurse the sick or to provide other assistance to troops coming through town.

Although local women with no formal medical or volunteer experience attended many soldiers, throughout the North women began to organize hospitals and relief societies to officially support the war effort. The Civil War resulted in the shift in nursing, in particular, from a formerly male to a predominantly female occupation, with as many as 2,000 Northern women serving the Union cause during the war. Women were now in a role that took them out of the home and onto the front lines of the sick and dying as well as into new executive roles. For many volunteers, such as Louisa May Alcott, who worked as a nurse in Washington, D.C., and published a fictional account of her experiences, *Hospital Sketches,* in 1863, wartime service was an extraordinary and temporary experience, but other women made new careers out of nursing. Dorothea Dix, a former teacher and prison and asylum reformer, emerged as a leader of this new army of female nurses in her role as Union Superintendent of Nurses. Concerned about the propriety of women working so closely with male soldiers, Dix set up strict regulations for recruiting volunteers, requiring that nurses be more than 30 years old and "plain looking women." The government eventually paid female nurses under Dix $12 per month at a time when male nurses were paid three times that amount.

The women of one of the largest relief organizations, the United States Sanitary Commission, founded in 1861 to attend to the health needs of soldiers on the battlefield, took pride in their "executive talents" put to use in organizing food and medical supplies to be sent to troops in the field. Mary Livermore used her wartime experience to launch a public service and reform career after the war, as did Clara Barton, a nurse and organizer of relief efforts for the Union army during the war who later founded the American Red Cross in 1881 to carry on her mission of bringing assistance and supplies to those in need.

Many Northern abolitionists as well as women's rights activists simply expanded their already established public roles as reformers to lend their support to the Union cause. Susan B. Anthony and Elizabeth Cady Stanton established the National Women's Loyal League in 1863 to push for a constitutional amendment to end slavery. The league specifically sought to provide a role for activist women interested in supporting and contributing to the war effort beyond the typical women's roles of "nursing the sick and wounded, knitting socks, and making jellies." Stanton emphasized that the war concerned women just as much as men, and the group created some controversy when Stanton and other members were publicly critical of President Lincoln's hesitance in pursuing emancipation. The newspapers reported on this "great uprising of the women of the North," who, by the end of the war, had collected nearly 400,000 signatures that they presented to Congress.

For African American women the war brought the promise of freedom. After the Emancipation Proclamation of January 1, 1863, African American men could enlist in the Union army as soldiers, but many formerly enslaved women also joined Union camps, working as cooks, laundresses, seamstresses, and nurses. Susie King Taylor was one such woman who worked in a variety of roles with the Union's first black regiment and later recounted her story in *Reminiscences of My Life in Camp with the 33rd U.S. Colored Troops, Late 1st South Carolina Volunteers.* King Taylor had been born a slave, but had received an education and was freed early in the war. She worked for the Union army, first as a laundress and then as a nurse and a teacher for escaped slaves living behind Union lines during the war. She even taught several soldiers enlisted with the black regiments to read and write. King Taylor realized what an important role she had taken on and wrote her autobiography precisely because, years after the war, she realized that, "There are many people who did not know what some of the colored women did during the war."

Even before the war ended, Northern women, white and black, followed closely behind the armies to provide relief to devastated and poverty-stricken Southern black communities and to assist in the transition from slavery to freedom. Women rushed in as missionaries and teachers to teach reading and writing as preparation for freedom. Approximately 4,000 women were responsible for establishing and running schools for freedpeople in the South throughout the 1860s and early 1870s. Charlotte Forten (later Grimké) was a free black from Philadelphia who worked as an abolitionist and a teacher before the war. Many of these female teachers continued with their educational and reform work in the South through the end of the century.

Working closely with the military as nurses, teachers, and in other positions led some women to make themselves available as spies during the war. One of the Confederacy's most famous female spies, Maria Isabella "Belle" Boyd, began her work as a nurse in Virginia but was employed because of her skills on horseback to travel and spy on the Union army and to carry information between Confederate officials. She was only 17 years old when the Union newspapers called her "the Siren of the Shenandoah" for her aid to Stonewall Jackson. She hid messages back and forth in her shoes, baked into bread, or hidden inside fruit, and was captured, imprisoned, and released on several occasions. Her account of her exploits, *Belle Boyd in Camp and Prison,* was published in 1865 at the end of the war.

It is estimated that as many as 400 women dressed as men and served as soldiers. Some employed this strategy in order to accompany husbands and spouses into battle, while others enlisted and fought on their own out of a desire to serve. Such women used male names and many were successful at keeping their disguises for long periods of time before being discovered because of injury or death. Female spies and soldiers were celebrated by the press both during and after the war, and many subsequently published accounts of their wartime experiences. Sarah Emma Edmonds was one of the few women, however, who, having served as a nurse, spy, and soldier by the name of "Frank Thompson," was ultimately officially recognized by the Union army, and, in 1884, began to receive a military pension.

The end of the Civil War brought freedom for some four million African American men and women, but it left a generation of people struggling to rebuild their lives, economically and socially, including reconnecting with families separated by slavery and by war. As one Freedmen's Bureau official noted of what was often described as the "wandering" of black people after the war, "Every mother's son seemed to be in search of his mother; every mother in search of her children."

A Mississippi woman was moved to ask after the war, "Is I free? Hasn't I got to get up before daylight and go into the field to work?" Another who had stayed on with her former owners bitterly realized, "dere wusn't no difference in freedom cause I went right on working for Miss."

Nevertheless, sharecropping allowed black women, in particular, to have some control over their work lives, and, more important, over their own homes. Despite the hardships and the economic inequalities, sharecropping meant that families worked together, and the opportunity of tending to her own children in her own home was one that no former slave woman took for granted. Many preferred fieldwork to working in white households whenever possible, escaping the potential for sexual exploitation by white men that had prevailed under the slave system. Years after the Civil War, one black woman vowed, "There is no sacrifice I would not make . . . rather than allow my daughters to go in service where they would be thrown constantly in contact with Southern white men, for they consider the colored girl their special prey." Many black women were eventually forced by economic necessity to do domestic work for white families but, even then, they preferred day work to living in so that they could return to their own homes and families at the end of the day.

Southern white women were also economically devastated by the war. They had disproportionately lost their husbands and sons to the war, as well as their farms, and, in many cases, their slaves. Gertrude Thomas recalled that with the end of the war, "We were reduced from a state of affluence to comparative poverty, so far as I am individually concerned to utter beggary for the thirty thousand dollars Pa gave me when I was married was invested in Negroes alone." Widows had to depend only on themselves to rebuild their farms and livelihoods. One Virginia woman resorted to driving the plow herself, pulled by her two young daughters, as the family no longer owned any livestock.

Black and white middle-class women were inspired by the war to continue their reform efforts into the Reconstruction era and to fulfill the promise of true "freedom" begun by the abolition of slavery. Women, including many former abolitionists, were central to the work of the Freedmen's Bureau. In 1872 the Freedmen's Bureau was closed as an office of the federal government and funding to such projects was ended. By that time, however, it had enlisted nearly 9,000 volunteer teachers, half of them women and many of whom continued on in their work, even without government assistance. By the end of the century, black women reformers, in particular, organized a national "club movement" to address issues from black civil rights and antilynching to public health and education reform.

Tiffany K. Wayne

See Also: Abolitionism and the Antislavery Movement; Alcott, Louisa May; Barton, Clara; Bread Riots; Dix, Dorothea; Douglass, Frederick; Edmonds, Sarah Emma; Elizabeth Freeman Case; Fifteenth Amendment; Fourteenth Amendment; Freedmen's Bureau; Grimké, Charlotte L. Forten; Grimké, Sarah Moore; Grimké Weld, Angelina; Higginson, Thomas Wentworth; Jacobs, Harriet; Kemble, Fanny; *Missouri v. Celia, a Slave*; National Women's Loyal League; Reconstruction; Stowe, Harriet Beecher; Taylor, Susie Baker King; Truth, Sojourner; Tubman, Harriet; Underground Railroad; United States Sanitary Commission; Wakeman, Sarah Rosetta; Walker, Mary Edwards; "Woman Order"

Primary Documents: 1852, *Uncle Tom's Cabin*; 1861, *Incidents in the Life of a Slave Girl*; 1861, Female Soldiers Discovered during the Civil War; 1862, A Northern Newspaper Supports Butler's Woman Order; 1863, Women in Richmond Participate in Bread Riot; 1863, National Women's Loyal League Petitions to End Slavery

Further Reading

Burgess, Laura, ed., *An Uncommon Soldier: The Civil War Letters of Sarah Rosetta Wakeman, alias Private Lyons Wakeman, 153rd New York State Volunteers.* New York: Oxford University Press, 1995.

Clinton, Catherine. *The Plantation Mistress: Woman's World in the Old South.* New York: Pantheon Books, 1982.

Clinton, Catherine, and Nina Silber, eds., *Divided Houses: Gender and the Civil War.* New York: Oxford University Press, 1992.

Creighton, Margaret S. *The Colors of Courage: Gettysburg's Forgotten History: Immigrants, Women, and African Americans in the Civil War's Defining Battle.* New York: Perseus Books, 2005.

Eggleston, Larry G. *Women in the Civil War: Extraordinary Stories of Soldiers, Spies, Nurses, Doctors, Crusaders, and Others.* Jefferson, NC: McFarland, 2003.

Faust, Drew Gilpin. *Mothers of Invention: Women of the Slaveholding South in the American Civil War.* Chapel Hill: University of North Carolina Press, 1996.

Fox-Genovese, Elizabeth. *Within the Plantation Household: Black and White Women in the Old South.* Chapel Hill: University of North Carolina Press, 1988.

Frankel, Noralee. *Freedom's Women: Black Women and Families in Civil War Era Mississippi.* Bloomington: Indiana University Press, 1999.

Gaspar, David Barry, and Darlene Clark Hine, eds. *More than Chattel: Black Women and Slavery in the Americas.* Bloomington: Indiana University Press, 1996.

Leonard, Elizabeth D. *Yankee Women: Gender Battles in the Civil War.* New York: W. W. Norton, 1994.

Leonard, Elizabeth D. *All the Daring of the Soldier: Women of the Civil War Armies.* New York: W. W. Norton, 1999.

Schultz, Jane E. *Women at the Front: Hospital Workers in Civil War America.* Chapel Hill: University of North Carolina Press, 2004.

White, Deborah Gray. *Ar'n't I a Woman?: Female Slaves in the Plantation South.* New York: W. W. Norton, 1985.

Smith, Gerrit (1797–1874)

Wealthy philanthropist; politician and member of Congress; social reformer; abolitionist; advocate of women's rights, temperance, and prison reform; and accomplice to John Brown in his raid on the federal arsenal at Harpers Ferry, Virginia, Gerrit Smith funded and was actively engaged in a dizzying array of social reform causes. Eccentric and unpredictable, Smith was as generous in broadcasting his often unorthodox opinions as he was in making donations to his favorite causes. Despite his far-flung interests and idiosyncrasies, Smith's views on social and political issues were sought after and respected.

Gerrit Smith had a profound early influence on his young cousin, Elizabeth Cady. As a young adult, she frequently visited Smith and his family at their home in Peterboro, New York. There she was swept up in the whirlwind of Smith's reform interests, particularly abolitionism. As a staunch believer in the necessity of finding political solutions to slavery, Smith was closely involved in the formation of the Liberty Party when it split off from the American Anti-Slavery Society (AASS) in 1840. Elizabeth Cady learned and absorbed much in this political environment, and it was through Smith that she met her husband-to-be, the abolitionist Henry Brewster Stanton.

Smith strongly supported the women's rights movement and attended local, state, and national conventions until 1856, when he refused further participation and donations because the women's rights movement had stopped agitating for dress reform, an issue that he believed was the key to women's emancipation. By this time women's rights activists had long since abandoned the dress reform issue and were concentrating on efforts to achieve legal and civil equality. Despite Smith's stated position, Anthony appealed to him for donations regularly throughout the late 1850s, and he usually responded, although not as generously as she knew he did to other causes.

Elizabeth Cady Stanton and Susan B. Anthony clashed with Smith during Reconstruction, when he, a loyal Republican, sided with Wendell Phillips and agreed with the Radical Republicans that women must postpone their quest for suffrage until after the enfranchisement of African American men. Despite this position, he claimed he was never against enfranchising women, and after the ratification of the Fifteenth Amendment he again backed woman suffrage. He also publicly supported Anthony when she voted in the presidential election of 1872 and when she was arrested and put on trial in 1873.

Judith E. Harper

See Also: Abolitionism and Antislavery Movement; Dress Reform; Fifteenth Amendment; Phillips, Wendell; Reconstruction; Slavery and the Civil War; Anthony, Susan B. (Vol. 2); Stanton, Elizabeth Cady (Vol. 2)

Further Reading

Griffith, Elisabeth. *In Her Own Right: The Life of Elizabeth Cady Stanton.* New York: Oxford University Press, 1984.

Renehan, Edward. *The Secret Six: The True Tale of the Men Who Conspired with John Brown.* New York: Crown, 1995.

Stauffer, John. *The Black Hearts of Men: Radical Abolitionists and the Transformation of Race.* Cambridge, MA: Harvard University Press, 2001.

Southworth, E.D.E.N. (1819–1899)

E.D.E.N. Southworth, probably the most widely read female author of the 19th century, was described by a contemporary as a Southern woman with Northern principles. Through stories set in the plantation South, Southworth exposed slavery as damaging to all whites who condoned it. Her melodramatic novels often featured unconventional and independent heroines and a sharp critique of men's power over women's lives. Serialized in mass circulation weekly newspapers, her work enjoyed tremendous popular success from the early 1850s to the late 1880s in both the North and the South.

Emma Dorothy Eliza Nevitte was born December 26, 1819, in Alexandria, Virginia. Her mother, Maria McIntosh, came from generations of landed Southern gentry and married Charles Lecompte Nevitte, an importer who owned a fleet of ships. Emma adored her father, who died when she was four, having never fully recovered from a wound received in the War of 1812. Emma remembered herself as a shy, awkward, unattractive child, with a pretty younger sister who was the family favorite. She grew increasingly isolated and withdrawn, and much of her lonely childhood was spent in the kitchen listening to the servants' ghost stories, legends, and tales of the family's bygone wealth. The Nevittes faced constant financial problems, but summers with her extended family in Maryland exposed Emma to the plantation life often depicted in her novels.

Emma's mother remarried to a schoolmaster in Washington, D.C. After being educated in his school, Emma taught there for five years. In 1840 she married Frederick Southworth, a New York inventor, and they moved to the Wisconsin frontier. After they returned to Washington, he abandoned Emma and their two children in 1844. She returned to teaching to support the children and began writing fiction to supplement her inadequate salary. Her first story appeared in the *Baltimore Saturday Visiter* in 1846, and others the next year in the *National Era,* the capital's abolitionist newspaper. Ill and despairing, with 80 pupils, a bedridden child, and editors to satisfy, she wrote her first novel, *Retribution.*

Retribution, serialized in the *National Era,* launched Southworth's prolific career as a writer of popular fiction. It ran for 14 installments in 1849 and was so well received that Harper's published it in book form the same year. Drawn from her own abandonment and her firm antislavery convictions, it is the story of a heroine, working to free her slaves, with an unfaithful husband. Suddenly, people offered Southworth friendship and sympathy. She had found independence, respect, and a career. The *National Era* continued to feature her work, and she went on writing abolitionist fiction despite criticism from her family and the Southern press. The *National Era*'s editor wanted an even more damning and attention-getting portrayal of slavery and began installments of Harriett Beecher Stowe's *Uncle Tom's Cabin* in 1851. Southworth continued to write for the *National Era* and sold some pieces to the *Saturday Evening Post.* Throughout her long career, she produced about two novels a year.

Hard work brought financial success. She moved into Prospect Cottage on the Potomac Heights in Georgetown in 1853. Among the many guests she entertained there were her friends John Greenleaf Whittier and Harriet Beecher Stowe.

In 1857, Robert Bonner of the *New York Ledger,* the most widely read paper in America, signed Southworth to an exclusive contract, securing the right to serialize all her novels before they were published in book form. Southworth's novels were its chief selling point, dominating the front page and often continuing for six months. Each week's episode, eagerly awaited by readers, was accompanied by a dramatic woodcut illustration. *The Hidden Hand* first appeared in 1859 and was her most popular tale. It was serialized again in 1868 and 1883 before being released as a book in 1888. Some 19th-century critics found fault with her overblown language, extravagant and improbable plot contrivances, imperfectly drawn characters, and sensational treatment of race and sex, but the reading public could not get enough. Her work was widely translated and reprinted abroad.

Southworth sailed for England in 1859, remaining there until 1862. On her return, she firmly supported the Union despite her Southern roots. Her letters to Robert Bonner of the *Ledger* clearly express her anti-Confederate sentiments. She nursed wounded soldiers, and her cottage was several times used as an auxiliary hospital.

Because her work was serialized and issued as books with a variety of titles and publishers, estimates of the number of novels she produced between 1849 and 1886 vary from 40 to 60. Literary scholars initially categorized her with the sentimental literary domestic tradition because she spun melodramatic tales that often ended in a happy marriage. More recently, scholars interpret Southworth's fondness for heroines who are rewarded for their independence and rebellion against Victorian female passivity as providing a subversive outlet for the fantasies of repressed female readers. Because she adapted the romantic Southern genre of the plantation novel to her storytelling style and because her most successful novel, *The Hidden Hand,* was not as explicitly abolitionist as her earlier works, 20th-century critical consensus accused her of abandoning her antislavery principles. However, in the years before the Civil War, the *National Ledger*'s editorial policy stressed neutrality in the interest of circulation. Southern readers had grown increasingly sensitive to Northern attacks on slavery, and Bonner allowed nothing that would offend them. Southworth, practiced in lampooning gender conventions, applied the same subversive literary techniques to race in *The Hidden Hand.* Beginning with the sale of its white heroine into slavery as an infant, the novel is full of episodes demonstrating that race had looser boundaries and less significance than many whites believed.

E.D.E.N. Southworth died at Prospect Cottage on June 30, 1899.

Nancy Gray Schoonmaker

See Also: Abolitionism and the Antislavery Movement; Slavery and the Civil War; Stowe, Harriet Beecher

Further Reading

Homestead, Melissa J., and Pamela T. Washington, eds. *E.D.E.N. Southworth: Recovering a Nineteenth-Century Popular Novelist.* Knoxville: University of Tennessee Press, 2012.

Sizer, Lyde Cullen. *The Political Work of Northern Women Writers and the Civil War, 1850–1872.* Chapel Hill: University of North Carolina Press, 2000.

Southworth, Emma Dorothy Eliza Nevitte. *The Hidden Hand,* with Introduction by Nina Baym. New York: Oxford University Press, 1997.

Swisshelm, Jane Grey Cannon. *Half a Century.* New York: Source Book Press, 1970 [1880].

Stewart, Maria W. (1803–1879)

Essayist and lecturer Maria W. Stewart was born Maria Miller to free African American parents in Hartford, Connecticut, in 1803. When she was five years old, her parents died, and she was "bound out" as a servant for a clergyman's household for the next 10 years. She subsequently worked as a domestic servant while educating herself by attending Sabbath School classes and studying the Bible. In the 1820s, she moved to Boston. There she met James W. Stewart, a veteran of the War of 1812 and successful shipping agent who outfitted whaling and fishing vessels, whom she married on August 10, 1826, and settled into the activist-minded free African American community.

After only three years of marriage, Maria Stewart's husband became ill and died, plunging her into grief and destitution. James Stewart had amply provided for his wife in his will, but his white business associates defrauded her of her inheritance. Maria Stewart's sorrow deepened when her close friend David Walker, author of the radical *Appeal,* died in 1830, and then Thomas Paul, founder of the First African Baptist Church that she attended and the minister who officiated at her wedding, died in 1831. The young widow sought solace in Christianity and experienced religious conversion. She believed God called her to address the spiritual and political issues facing the African American community. In 1832, Stewart became the first American woman to deliver a speech to a "promiscuous" audience composed of African American and white males and females. During her three-year public career, she published a political pamphlet, spiritual meditations, and antislavery writings, and she delivered four lectures. William Lloyd Garrison advertised and published her work in the *Liberator,* a weekly abolitionist newspaper.

In 1833 Maria Stewart ended her controversial public-speaking career and began moving south in search of a place where she could continue her community activism and support herself. She first settled in New York and worked in the abolitionist movement and women's literary societies and began a teaching career. In 1835, she published a collection of meditations and lectures she had presented in Boston. Stewart moved on to Baltimore and continued teaching before relocating to Washington, D.C., in 1861 where she founded a school before accepting a position as the Matron of the Freedmen's Hospital. Near the end of her life, Stewart petitioned the U.S. government and received a pension as a veteran's widow. She secured her legacy by investing the money in a new edition of her work. Stewart died in December 1879.

Stewart's writings and speeches reflect her belief that God called her to embark on a public career to rouse African Americans to fight for freedom and equality. She revealed the spiritual nature of her calling in her *Lecture Delivered at the Franklin Hall* (1832): "Methinks I heard a spiritual interrogation—'Who shall go forward, and take off the reproach that is cast upon the people of color? Shall it be a woman?' And my heart made this reply—'If it is thy will, be it even so, Lord Jesus!'" Stewart realized the danger she faced by stepping into the public arena but expressed a willingness to die for God's cause and her people. She relied on the Bible as the chief source for her work. Her speeches and essays also reflected David Walker's revolutionary ideas regarding racial uplift and her knowledge of history and current events.

In her work, Stewart focused her attention on the free African American community, whom she considered only slightly better off than slaves did because they refused to challenge restrictions on their liberty. She expressed concern for African Americans' temporal affairs and eternal salvation and urged them to develop their talents and intellect, live moral lives, and devote themselves to racial activism. Stewart challenged her audience to emulate the valor of the pilgrims and

American revolutionaries in demanding freedom, and advised them to establish institutions such as grocery stores and churches to support their community. She was particularly concerned with the plight of African American women whom she encouraged to be virtuous mothers and use their influence in the home to affect change in their communities. Stewart directed most of her ire at African American men, however, whom she chided for not fulfilling their role as community leaders.

Stewart also included admonitions to white members of her audience. She scolded white women for failing to acknowledge their privileged position and ignoring the needs of African American children. Stewart demanded white Americans' support for African American freedom as they had backed other nations, such as Poland, in their fight for liberty. She particularly decried colonization. In *An Address Delivered at the African Masonic Hall,* Stewart declared, "They would drive us to a strange land. But before I go, the bayonet shall pierce me through." Stewart reminded white Americans that African blood had enriched America's soil and warned them that God would repay them for wrongs done to African Americans.

Scholars have described Stewart in a variety of ways, including abolitionist, evangelist, feminist, journalist, and prophet. Stewart helped to create a literary tradition for African American women by giving speeches and publishing her writings that advocated militant Christianity as the means by which African Americans could transform their lives during a time when women were unwelcome in the public sphere. Stewart's writings and speeches, characterized by one scholar as "political sermonizing," reflect the inner struggles that led her to engage in social activism, while her other work exemplifies the depth of her commitment to racial uplift.

Rhondda Robinson Thomas

See Also: Abolitionism and the Antislavery Movement; Cary, Mary Ann Shadd; Garrison, William Lloyd; *The Liberator*

Further Reading

Foster, Frances Smith. *Written by Herself: Literary Production by African American Women, 1746–1892.* Bloomingdale: Indiana University Press, 1993.

Logan, Shirley Wilson, ed. "African Origins/American Appropriations: Maria Stewart and 'Ethiopia Rising.'" In *We Are Coming: The Persuasive Discourse of Nineteenth Century Black Women,* 23–43. Carbondale: Southern Illinois University Press, 1999.

Moody, Joycelyn. *Sentimental Confessions: Spiritual Narratives of Nineteenth-Century African American Women*. Athens: University of Georgia Press, 2001.

Peterson, Carla L. *Doers of the Word: African-American Women Speakers and Writers in the North, 1830–1880*. New Brunswick, NJ: Rutgers University Press, 1998.

Royster, Jacqueline. *Traces of a Stream: Literacy and Social Change among African American Women*. Pittsburgh, PA: University of Pittsburgh Press, 2000.

Stone, Lucy (1818–1893)

Lucy Stone was a dignified campaigner for women's equality and a fine orator, like her sister-in-law Antoinette Brown Blackwell. She led the moderate suffrage group the American Woman Suffrage Association (AWSA), formed in reaction to the establishment of the National Woman Suffrage Association (NWSA) by Susan B. Anthony and Elizabeth Cady Stanton in 1869. Stone retained her own name after marriage to reformer Henry Blackwell and, although recognizing the benefits of having an enlightened partner, was nevertheless

Lucy Stone was one of the leading figures of the 19th-century women's rights movement. (Library of Congress)

unequivocal in her belief that "marriage is to woman a state of slavery."

Stone grew up on a farm in West Brookfield, Massachusetts, where she helped herd the cows at the age of eight and developed a sense of the injustice of women's inferior position to men. She was forced to undertake her own education when her strict father refused to give her funds to attend college as he had her brothers. Objecting to her belittlement as a woman, she took work as a schoolteacher from the age of 16 for $1 a week, using the money to study at various schools, including Mount Holyoke Female Seminary.

After working and saving for nine years, Stone had enough money only to study for one term at the first coeducational, mixed-race establishment in the United States, Oberlin College in Ohio. During her time there from 1843 to 1847, Stone worked to pay her way, teaching for two hours a day and doing domestic chores. There she found a friend and fellow advocate of women's rights in Antoinette Brown Blackwell, who joined the school in 1845 and encouraged Stone's interest in debate. However, as soon as the two women joined in debates with male students, they were banned from doing so again.

After her graduation in 1847, Stone gave her first speech on women's rights, from the pulpit of her brother's church. She had been an admirer of the abolitionist work of the Grimké sisters (Angelina Grimké and Sarah Grimké) since her childhood, and in 1848 she became an agent of the Massachusetts Anti-Slavery Society. As a touring lecturer, traveling alone across many states, Stone fought to be allowed to devote some of her time lecturing to speaking on women's issues, arguing: "I was a woman before I was an abolitionist. I must speak for the women." Stone's physical demeanor on the podium belied her toughness as a gifted speaker. This she demonstrated in memorable speeches such as "The Social and Industrial Disabilities of Woman," "Legal and Political Disabilities," and "Moral and Religious Disabilities," all containing subject matter guaranteed to provoke an antagonistic and often aggressive response in audiences.

The passion of Stone's belief in women's rights came across particularly strongly in "Disappointment Is the Lot of Women" (1855), in which she averred that since women were forever being disappointed in their attempts to take their equal place "in education, in marriage, in religion," she had resolved that "it shall be the business of my life to deepen this disappointment in every woman's heart until she bows down to it no longer." Beginning in 1853, Stone was courted by the abolitionist

Henry Blackwell, whom she married in 1855 after making a private agreement with him to hold their property separately. Stone was also adamant that she retain her maiden name, an act that soon became widespread public knowledge and caused her much difficulty over the years, including unwarranted accusations that Stone also advocated free love.

Stone lived in New Jersey and continued lecturing until after the birth of her only child, Alice Stone Blackwell, in 1857. Although no longer lecturing, Stone continued to give moral support to women's fight for economic independence and their right to pursue a professional career. In 1858, in an act of defiance similar to that made by Abby Kelley Foster, Stone made a feminist stand on "no taxation without representation" when she refused, as an unenfranchised woman, to pay her property tax. Her household possessions were confiscated and sold but were soon after bought back and restored to her by a sympathetic neighbor.

In the belief that women would achieve equality with men earlier if given greater access to coeducation, she sent her own daughter to the progressive, coeducational Chauncy Hall School in Boston. Stone also supported the protection of women's health through birth control, although this belief was largely negated by her later support for the Comstock Act of 1873 (which prohibited the sending of literature on birth control and sex education through the post) as part of the gathering social purity campaign. Similarly, in 1860, when Stone attended a national women's rights convention during which the issue of marriage was vigorously debated at the instigation of Elizabeth Cady Stanton, Stone felt it was inappropriate to discuss such a topic so publicly, preferring that Stanton discuss marriage at a separate convention. Yet on the issue of her use of her maiden name, Stone retained a radically adamant but dignified tone, frequently finding herself obliged to sign documents as "Lucy Stone, wife of Henry Blackwell," determined not to jeopardize the cause of suffrage by taking a public stand against her critics.

During the Civil War, Stone, like many other women activists, joined the National Women's Loyal League in lobbying for the Thirteenth Amendment, which would abolish slavery. In 1866 she became a member of the American Equal Rights Association, which was dedicated to the emancipation of both women and blacks. Resuming her work for women's suffrage through the New Jersey Woman Suffrage Association, in 1868 Stone also became an executive member of the New England Woman Suffrage Association. In 1869 Stone joined the American Woman Suffrage Association, a moderate group that differed on fundamental aspects of policy with the NWSA and favored the gradualist approach of working almost exclusively for the award of women's suffrage on a state-by-state basis. In January 1870, with Mary Livermore, she raised the money to found what would be the most influential women's rights publication in the United States, the *Woman's Journal,* which Stone edited until 1893.

Becoming increasingly conservative in later life, Stone kept out of the political limelight and avoided controversy, chairing the executive committee of the newly amalgamated National American Woman Suffrage Association when the two rival suffrage organizations united in 1890. Stone gave her final public lecture to the World's Columbian Exposition at Chicago in 1893. Although a huge crowd turned out for her funeral, Stone was later eclipsed in the histories of women's suffrage by the more forceful and high-profile figures of Stanton and Anthony (who minimized mention of Stone in their own *History of Woman Suffrage*). Many of Stone's speeches, given extemporaneously, did not survive, although her ideas speak loud and strong in her numerous articles and editorials for the *Woman's Journal.* After Stone's death, her daughter Alice edited the journal and also published a biography of her mother.

Helen Rappaport

See Also: Abolitionism and the Antislavery Movement; Foster, Abby Kelley; Grimké, Sarah Moore; Grimké Weld, Angelina; Livermore, Mary; National Women's Loyal League; American Equal Rights Association (Vol. 2); American Woman Suffrage Association (Vol. 2); Anthony, Susan B. (Vol. 2); Blackwell, Alice Stone (Vol. 2); Blackwell, Antoinette Brown (Vol. 2); Blackwell, Henry Brown (Vol. 2); The Comstock Act (Vol. 2); National American Woman Suffrage Association (Vol. 2); Stanton, Elizabeth Cady (Vol. 2); *The Woman's Journal* (Vol. 2)

Primary Document: 1855, Marriage Protest of Lucy Stone and Henry Blackwell

Further Reading

Kerr, Andrea Moore. *Lucy Stone: Speaking Out for Equality.* New Brunswick, NJ: Rutgers University Press, 1992.

Lasser, Carol, and Marlene Deahl Miller, eds. *Friends and Sisters: Letters between Lucy Stone and Antoinette Brown Blackwell, 1846–93.* Urbana: University of Illinois Press, 1987.

McMillen, Sally G. *Seneca Falls and the Origins of the Women's Rights Movement.* New York: Oxford University Press, 2008.

Rodier, Katharine. "Lucy Stone and the *Woman's Journal.*" In *Blue Pencils and Hidden Hands: Women*

Editing Periodicals, 1830–1910, edited by Sharon M. Harris, 99–122. Boston, MA: Northeastern University Press, 2004.

Wheeler, Leslie. *Loving Warriors: Selected Letters of Lucy Stone and Henry B. Blackwell, 1853–1893.* New York: Dial Press, 1981.

Stowe, Harriet Beecher (1811–1896)

Abolitionist and author Harriet Beecher Stowe stirred up antislavery sentiment with her novel *Uncle Tom's Cabin; Or, Life among the Lowly.* The novel, first published in serial form beginning in 1851, railed against slavery as the cornerstone of the Southern plantation economy and guaranteed Stowe a place in the historical and literary canon.

Harriet Beecher Stowe's best-selling 1852 novel, *Uncle Tom's Cabin,* so aroused Northern feeling against slavery in the United States that it is considered one of the causes of the American Civil War. (National Archives)

Born in Litchfield, Connecticut, on June 14, 1811, Harriet Elizabeth Beecher was the daughter of prominent Congregationalist minister Lyman Beecher and his first wife, Roxana Foote. Like her older sisters, she attended the Litchfield Female Academy, a progressive school for girls. At the age of 13, she enrolled at the Hartford Female Seminary, a school founded by her older sister Catharine Beecher. Harriet later taught there. In 1832, she began teaching at Catharine Beecher's Western Female Institute in Ohio. In 1836, Harriet Beecher married Calvin Stowe, a biblical scholar and theologian who taught at Lane Theological Seminary in Cincinnati.

Harriet Beecher Stowe began writing early in her life. In April 1834, "A New England Sketch" was published in *Western Monthly Magazine,* a literature periodical. *The Mayflower* (1843), a collection of stories and sketches, launched her career as an antislavery writer. Her earliest writing was modeled after Joseph Addison's *The Spectator,* utilizing Enlightenment rhetoric to inculcate moral lessons.

By the time she wrote *Uncle Tom's Cabin* at her kitchen table in Maine, Stowe was the mother of seven children. She drew partly on her experiences in Ohio and her contact with escaped slaves there to create the characters and situations in the book. The novel first appeared in serial form in the *National Era,* a Washington-based abolitionist newspaper, from June 5, 1851, to April 1, 1852. The 40-installment novel captured public attention. Its popularity in the papers led to its publication as a book and provided publicity for the book's release on March 20, 1852. The novel would spawn plays, songs, and games.

Like many women of her time, Stowe took up her pen as a weapon to fight injustices that she perceived to threaten the American family. Inspired by the fiends and giants in John Bunyan's *Pilgrim's Progress* (1678), Stowe's landmark narrative against slavery was driven by chiaroscuro, the interplay of light and dark or good and evil. The character of Marie St. Clare, a selfish and self-centered invalid who lived in luxury and used her ailment to avoid taking action, was for Stowe the personification of feminine evil. Her inaction prevents St. Clare from caring for weaker and more ignorant individuals in her household and fulfilling her role as a mother. In this and other situations, *Uncle Tom's Cabin* spotlighted the conflict between slavery and motherhood as a result of literary devices that Stowe employed to prompt sympathetic imitation among American women. For example, at one point Stowe's narrator asks readers if they have ever felt the loss of a child, hoping to direct them to imitate a sequence of emotions as if the characters were neighbors or friends.

Stowe was idolized for her novel in England and in the North, but vehemently criticized for it across the slaveholding Southern states. She had never traveled south of northern Kentucky and received criticism from Southerners who said she knew nothing about their peculiar institution. To counter this criticism and to add credence to her critique of Southern society, Stowe published *A Key to Uncle Tom's Cabin* (1853). This follow-up contained documentary evidence about slavery culled from graphic anecdotes in Southern newspapers. Her sources for these stories, gathered by Southern abolitionists Sarah and Angelina Grimké, were originally published in *American Slavery as It Is: Testimony of a Thousand Witnesses* (1839) by Sarah Grimké and her brother-in-law Theodore Weld. The documents illuminate the basis for many of Stowe's characters and storylines. For example, the character of Lucy may have been styled after Margaret Garner, a slave who escaped with four children, only to be returned to the South on a ship that went down. Garner, who had killed her three-year-old child in prison, drowned her infant and then refused to let herself be saved.

In all of her work, Stowe used real-life experience to explore common themes. She understood the emotional conflicts that arose in parenting and infused this ordinary, everyday drama into her writing. During a cholera epidemic in 1849, she lost her youngest child Charlie when he was 18 months old. During his life, Charlie presented Stowe with challenges that contradicted the angelic fictional children presented in Victorian children's literature. She wrote *Our Charley, and, What to Do with Him* (1858), a children's book of short stories, that seemed to convey the simple sentimentalism of a grieving mother even as it presented a realistic and lovable boy character who vacillated between good and bad behavior without having the opportunity of full character development.

Charlie's death had a tremendous impact on Stowe's writing. She told friends that her loss of him helped her understand the horrors that slave mothers faced in the South. She, too, knew what it was like to have a child torn from her. Perhaps Stowe's mourning for her lastborn, as well as her rage over changes in the Fugitive Slave Act, shaped her creation of the fictional character of Little Eva, a child redeemer endowed with an intuitive spiritual sensibility in *Uncle Tom's Cabin*.

In subsequent works, Stowe continued to write about what she considered her society's biggest problems.

In 1856, Stowe published another antislavery novel, *Dred: A Tale of the Dismal Swamp*. In this book, she presented black characters who she thought would evoke the sympathy of her white middle-class readers. In this work, Stowe showed herself as a radical abolitionist who called for emancipation. However, she stopped short of integration and instead supported the colonization of freed slaves. In *The Minister's Wooing* (1859), she satirized Calvinism and demonstrated her frustration with married women's limitations under the law. However, Stowe, like her sister Catharine Beecher, tapped into the powerful ideology of female labor as a woman's duty, particularly in one passage suggesting that housework should be completed in the morning to leave the rest of the day free for social obligations, familial repose, and intellectual development.

Embedded in *Uncle Tom's Cabin* was the benevolent female influence that Catharine Beecher promoted in her *Essay on Slavery and Abolition with Reference to the Duty of American Females* (1837) that encouraged women to appropriately assert their power of persuasion in the domestic sphere. This essay, a reproach on the radical abolitionism practiced by Sarah and Angelina Grimké, ignited a debate among American women. Angelina Grimké responded to the essay with her *Letters to Catharine Beecher in Reply to "An Essay on Slavery and Abolitionism," Addressed to A.E. Grimké* (1838).

After Abraham Lincoln announced the drafting of an Emancipation Proclamation in late September 1862, Stowe called on First Lady Mary Todd Lincoln in New York City to request an invitation to the White House. Stowe was granted an invitation for tea on December 2, 1862, but she was not impressed by the First Lady. When she and her children arrived in Washington, D.C., they visited hospitals and tourist destinations in the area. When Stowe met President Lincoln, he supposedly greeted her with the apocryphal comment, "So you're the little woman who wrote the book that made this great war." When news of the Emancipation Proclamation arrived on January 1, 1863, Stowe was attending a New Year's Jubilee celebration at the Boston Music Hall. Recognizing her book as a major influence in pushing the nation toward abolition, the crowd gave Stowe a standing ovation, repeatedly calling out her name.

During the Civil War, Stowe's son Fred enlisted in the Union army, as did many of her husband's students. The war took a toll on the Beecher and Stowe families, as it did on nearly every family, North and South. Many of the men of Harriet's family who served were wounded, and some of the women came down with tuberculosis. In addition, Stowe's health had been compromised by closely spaced pregnancies and by the death of her father in 1863. Harriet Beecher Stowe helped support her family during these difficult times.

The Pearl of Orr's Island (1862) was the only book Stowe published during the Civil War. As it had prior to the war, much of her work centered on domestic themes and women's issues. In *The Pearl,* Stowe embedded feminine logic in ordinary domestic experiences, creating an innovative gender schema. She subtly intertwined gender roles so that her female characters baked, sewed, and navigated boats while the male characters practiced the law and hung curtains, redefining gender.

During the war, Stowe also submitted articles that were serialized in *The Atlantic Monthly* and published in a bound volume as *Household Papers and Stories* (1865). She started working for *Hearth and Home Magazine* during the same year. After the Civil War, she captured the social life and customs of post-Revolutionary New England in *Old Town Folks,* published in 1869. *Uncle Tom's Cabin,* an all-time best seller, made Stowe a literary success, but that success came without copyright protection. Stowe had received $10,000 for the first three months of sales for the work, but she felt that she was owed much more. Not having reaped the monetary benefits of a best seller, Stowe was forced to continue writing to support her retired husband, unmarried daughters, and a son who was driven to drink by his experiences during the Civil War. In 1866, she began to publish articles and books under the pseudonym Christopher Crowfield to give herself the freedom to write without bias for her past work or her gender. Under the name Crowfield, her *House and Home Papers* was published in 1869.

Stowe collaborated with her sister Catharine Beecher, who could no longer afford a home of her own, on *American Woman's Home* in 1869. Stowe contributed ideas for practical design elements for the household while Catharine promoted the idea of female-headed households. *American Woman's Home* defined the American household as a Christian institution combining home, school, and church complete with illustrated designs for multifunctional spaces.

Late in life, Stowe divided her time between Hartford and Florida, where she wrote children's stories and hymns. Harriet Beecher Stowe died in Hartford, Connecticut, on July 1, 1896.

Meredith Eliassen

See Also: Abolitionism and the Antislavery Movement; Beecher, Catharine; Grimké, Sarah Moore; Grimké Weld, Angelina; Slavery and the Civil War

Primary Documents: 1852, *Uncle Tom's Cabin*; 1869, "Why Women Should Not Seek the Vote" (Vol. 2)

Further Reading

Boydston, Jeanne, Anne Margolis, and Mary Kelley. *The Limits of Sisterhood: The Beecher Sisters on Women's Rights and Woman's Sphere.* Chapel Hill: University of North Carolina Press, 1988.

Hedrick, Joan. *Harriet Beecher Stowe: A Life.* New York: Oxford University Press, 1994.

McFarland, Philip. *Loves of Harriet Beecher Stowe.* New York: Grove Press, 2007.

Sizer, Lyde Cullen. *The Political Work of Northern Women Writers and the Civil War, 1850–1872.* Chapel Hill: University of North Carolina Press, 2000.

White, Barbara A. *The Beecher Sisters.* New Haven, CT: Yale University Press, 2003.

Suffrage in Early America

Women rarely had the opportunity to vote in early America, but this made them little different from other disenfranchised people, including racial minorities, the poor, and recent immigrants. There were a few isolated instances of women who protested their disenfranchisement. In 1648, Margaret Brent requested the right to vote based on her status as a major landholder in Maryland. Her request was dismissed with little discussion.

Early America was governed primarily by English common law, which extended the vote only to men who possessed substantial property. Although there are no reliable statistics for what percentage of the population met the property qualifications in England, the number was roughly 10 percent of adult males. The colonies of early America tended to be slightly more egalitarian, but they retained their concern for limiting the vote to men of property. It was believed that poor people who were dependent on others for employment were not stakeholders in society, and their votes could be bought.

At the time of the American Revolution, each colony drafted its own state constitution. Most states included language that excluded women from the right to vote. Various exclusionary phrases were used. Pennsylvania, Maryland, Delaware, and North Carolina extended the vote to all *freemen.* Other terms used included *white male inhabitant* (Georgia), *free white man* (South Carolina), *male inhabitant* (New York), *male person* (Massachusetts), and simply *man* (Vermont). The only state that did not exclude women from the franchise was New Jersey, whose constitution extended the vote to adult inhabitants "worth £50."

Because New Jersey did not exclude women from voting, any single woman with at least £50 of property was entitled to vote. Married women, because they could own no property exclusive of their husbands, did not qualify to vote. It has been suggested that the ability of women to vote in New Jersey was the result of sloppy wording in the state constitution, but there was no outcry against the female vote once it became apparent that some women intended to exercise their right to participate in elections.

Between 1776 and 1807 single women of property took an active part in New Jersey elections. The liberal election law in New Jersey also extended the vote to any blacks or immigrants who could meet the property requirement. In the late 1780s when the two-party system began developing, both the Federalist and Republican Parties courted women voters in New Jersey, although there was no emergence of a "women's issues" platform.

In the years prior to the 1808 presidential election, New Jersey reformed its election law to exclude blacks, women, and immigrants. The amendment passed without controversy or outcry from women. Their disenfranchisement was justified as protecting women from the crude world of politics, and there is little to reflect that women complained of the action.

The case of New Jersey was an anomaly. Most women in the early republic never aspired to the vote. Disenfranchisement did not mean a disinterest in public life. Women took an active part in community affairs through church and charity involvement. During times of political unrest they took part in boycotts and petition campaigns. The most common belief about the proper role of women in the political sphere was in their role in raising intelligent, virtuous sons who would safeguard the republic. Not until the abolitionist movement of the mid-19th century would a feminist consciousness emerge in which women drew a parallel between their disenfranchised and dependent status and that of enslaved blacks.

Dorothy A. Mays

See Also: The American Revolution; Boycotts; The Constitution and Women; Legal Status of Women (18th Century); New York Married Women's Property Acts; Republican Motherhood; Seneca Falls Convention

Further Reading

Baker, Paula. "The Domestication of Politics: Women and American Political Society, 1780–1920." In *Unequal Sisters,* edited by Ellen Carol DuBois and Vicki L. Ruiz, 71–73. New York: Routledge, 1990.

Keyssar, Alexander. *The Right to Vote: The Contested History of Democracy in the United States.* New York: Basic Books, 2000.

Klinghoffer, Judith Apter, and Lois Elkins. "The Petticoat Electors: Women's Suffrage in New Jersey, 1776–1807." *Journal of the Early Republic* 12 (1992): 159–193.

Zagarri, Rosemarie. *Revolutionary Backlash: Women and Politics in the Early American Republic.* Philadelphia: University of Pennsylvania Press, 2007.

Swisshelm, Jane Grey (1815–1884)

Jane Grey Swisshelm was a journalist, feminist, and abolitionist. Born Jane Grey Cannon on December 6, 1815, she worked and lived in Pennsylvania, Minnesota, Chicago, and Washington, D.C., over the course of her life. Swisshelm was highly influential during her lifetime, especially before and during the Civil War, and her writings touched people across the country.

Swisshelm's religious background as a member of the Covenanter (Presbyterian) Church, which opposed slavery and encouraged its members to take abolitionist action, was instrumental in her commitment to abolitionism. In her twenties, Swisshelm began to write, at first anonymously but soon under her own name, poetry and prose for newspapers and other periodicals. Her themes included the rights of women as well as the abolition of slavery. An inheritance from her mother enabled her to begin publishing the *Pittsburgh Saturday Visiter* in 1847, making her one of the first women to publish and edit her own paper and certainly the first to focus primarily on politics rather than on literature and domestic life. The paper was not a financial success, but its articles were often cited or reprinted by other editors, and Swisshelm's views on slavery and women's rights became well known. She hired female compositors for the paper on an equal basis with men, extending her theoretical beliefs into her practical life.

In 1857, after the failure of the *Pittsburgh Saturday Visiter* and her marriage to James Swisshelm, Jane Swisshelm moved with her daughter to St. Cloud, Minnesota, where she started a new paper, the *St. Cloud Visiter.* Minnesota politics were far from genteel, and

Swisshelm's disagreements with local Democrats ended with the destruction of her presses by vigilantes. Undeterred, she soon reopened, and, when a libel suit connected to the earlier problems forced her to close the *Visiter,* she started the *St. Cloud Democrat.* In these papers she continued to make the abolitionist argument and to work for political parties that pursued abolitionism. Swisshelm supported Abraham Lincoln.

Horrified by the 1863 Dakota War, Swisshelm moved to Washington, D.C., hoping unsuccessfully to influence governmental attitudes on frontier issues. She took a position as one of the first women in the War Department's quartermaster general's office. During her employment, Swisshelm wrote many private and public letters on women as civil service workers and continued to write general political articles for newspapers nationwide. She also became interested in the war hospitals, striving to improve the health of the wounded and the nursing practices of women volunteers. She devoted many pages in her autobiography to "an inside history of the hospitals during the war of the Rebellion."

After the war, Swisshelm began the *Reconstructionist,* a paper published in Washington, D.C., from 1865 to 1866. She then left to live with her daughter in Chicago. Later she moved back to Pennsylvania, where she continued to write for many publications and to give public lectures.

Jane Grey Swisshelm died on July 21, 1884.

JoAnn E. Castagna

See Also: Abolitionism and the Antislavery Movement; Slavery and the Civil War

Further Reading

Hoffert, Sylvia D. *Jane Grey Swisshelm: An Unconventional Life, 1815–1884.* Chapel Hill: University of North Carolina Press, 2004.

Larsen, Arthur J., ed. *Crusader and Feminist: Letters of Jane Grey Swisshelm 1858–1865.* Saint Paul: Minnesota Historical Society Press, 1934.

T

Taylor, Susie Baker King (1848–1912)

A Georgia slave when the war began, Susie Baker King Taylor gained her freedom in 1862. She worked as a laundress for a Union army regiment, nursed soldiers, and taught other freed slaves to read and write. As the only written recollection of a black woman who served during the Civil War, her memoir is unique in Civil War literature.

Susan Baker grew up in Savannah, Georgia, in the care of her enslaved grandmother, who lived much like a freed black. Despite laws against literacy for slaves, Susie Baker learned to read. Her first lessons came from a freed black woman who ran a secret school. Other teachers included a white girl and the son of her grandmother's landlord.

When the Union army attacked Fort Pulaski in Savannah Harbor in 1862, Baker fled behind Union lines with her uncle and his family. Such slaves were considered freed, although this predated the Emancipation Proclamation by more than eight months. Amazed at her ability to read and write, Union officers asked Baker to teach other contrabands in their care, which she did for about a month. When some of the former slaves formed the First South Carolina Volunteer Infantry to fight for the Union, Baker became a laundress for the troops. She also continued to teach soldiers to read and write, and she nursed them through injury and illness. She later nursed soldiers for the Massachusetts Fifty-fourth Infantry Regiment, a colored unit.

Susie Baker married Edward King, a sergeant from the South Carolina regiment, in 1862. He died suddenly in 1866. She married Russell Taylor 13 years later.

After the war, Susie King taught school in rural Georgia and then in Savannah. She later worked as a laundress and a cook. She moved North in the 1880s, where she worked for the Women's Relief Corps, a branch of the Grand Army of the Republic.

In 1902, Taylor published her memoir, *Reminiscences of My Life in Camp: With the 33rd United States Colored Troops, late 1st S.C. Volunteers.* It provides insight into the feelings of African Americans in the South during and after the Civil War. Particularly poignant is her discussion of the excitement among the slaves on the day the Emancipation Proclamation went into effect. She also detailed the unequal treatment of the races and the vast disrespect for blacks she experienced when she returned South for a visit in 1898. Taylor's memoir concluded with her faith that justice for African Americans would ultimately prevail.

Susie Baker King Taylor died in 1912.

Ellen H. Todras

See Also: Slavery and the Civil War

Further Reading

Schultz, Jane E. *Women at the Front: Hospital Workers in Civil War America.* Chapel Hill: University of North Carolina Press, 2004.

Taylor, Susie King. *A Black Woman's Civil War Memoirs,* edited by Patricia W. Romero and Willie Lee Rose. Princeton, NJ: Markus Weiner Publisher, 1988.

Susie Baker King Taylor, an escaped slave from South Carolina, joined the 33rd U.S. Colored Troops as a laundress, teacher, and nurse during the Civil War. (Library of Congress)

Temperance Movement

Spanning the entire 19th century, and into the 20th century, the American temperance movement used varying strategies at different times in its history. The motivations and tactics of reformers in the pre-Civil War decades differed from their late 19th-century and early 20th-century counterparts, even when they identified the problems as the same. Temperance activity began in the antebellum period in the larger context of other reform movements, where it was linked explicitly with ideas about the moral superiority of women and the religious enthusiasm of the 1820s and 1830s.

The American Society for the Promotion of Temperance was founded in 1826 and in 1833 the first national temperance convention was held. Focusing on the perceived sinfulness and loss of self-control caused by a rapidly changing society, temperance advocates saw alcohol use and abuse as one of several problems introduced into American society by urbanization and industrialization, along with prostitution, poverty, and an increase in crime. Indeed, alcohol abuse was often

This 1874 Currier and Ives lithograph, "Woman's Holy War," illustrates the aggressive mission of crusaders against the sale and consumption of alcoholic beverages. (Library of Congress)

portrayed as at the root of these other problems, and, therefore, as a foundational reform. It was a problem that affected not only drinkers, but the family and community as well by threatening the safety and morality of women and children.

With stories of abusive or deserting husbands and financially ruined households, groups such as the Female Total Abstinence Society in 1838 urged that all women stand "united in a holy phalanx to arrest an evil which has poured its bitterest causes upon the head of women." Women made up half or more of temperance society membership throughout the century. They relied heavily on a message of self-control, mandatory abstinence among their own members, and on "moral suasion" as a strategy, that is, attempting to convince individuals of the immorality of their actions. Married women formed associations and threatened to withhold sexual services if their husbands did not give up the drink, and, drawing on an emerging women's rights discourse, demanding the "right" of every woman to have a sober husband.

Temperance reform was not limited to middle-class women's groups only, as a working-class organization, the Washingtonians, brought former alcohol abusers into the crusade to tell their stories of degradation, despair, and redemption. Washingtonian members included many men from the artisan and lower classes and inspired parallel female Martha Washington societies. Presenting themselves as concerned with woman's legitimate interests in religion, charity, and the health of the family, female reformers slowly expanded their sphere of influence into the public realm outside their own families, concerning themselves with the activities and habits of other men besides their husbands.

The temperance movement grew to become perhaps the largest reform movement of the century with hundreds of thousands of supporters and members. In 1874, the Woman's Christian Temperance Union (WCTU) was formed to bring together reformers in various states. The WCTU clearly and forcefully presented temperance as a women's issue because, as stated at one of their national conventions, "women are among the greatest sufferers from the liquor traffic." With the goal of the WCTU nothing less than the elimination of the national liquor industry, they targeted not only users of alcohol, but producers, retailers (saloons and bars), and, most importantly, legislators. Although Maine had established a state-level prohibition in 1851, the work of women reformers through the WCTU was responsible for propelling the alcohol issue into the 20th century and eventually achieving national prohibition in 1919 with the Eighteenth Amendment to the U.S. Constitution (subsequently repealed in 1933).

From the temperance movement emerged one of the most active and dynamic reformers of the century, Frances Willard, president of the Woman's Christian Temperance Union from 1879 until her death in 1898. Willard was a former teacher and president of a women's college who, even before her work with the WCTU, advocated a wide range of political and social reforms related to women. She brought to the WCTU a policy of "Do Everything," establishing WCTU departments committed not only to temperance, but also marriage equality, dress reform, child labor reform, education reform, and woman suffrage. She explained the wide-reaching scope of the temperance movement in terms of an overarching view of women's roles as reformers in society: "Were I to define in a sentence, the thought and purpose of the Woman's Christian Temperance Union, I would reply: *It is to make the whole world HOMELIKE.*" Under Frances Willard's direction, the late 19th-century suffrage and temperance campaigns were often linked because, like many other female reform leaders, Willard soon recognized women's need for political power in order to accomplish their reform goals.

Tiffany K. Wayne

See Also: Bloomer, Amelia Jenks; Moral Reform; Eighteenth Amendment (Vol. 2); Willard, Frances (Vol. 2); Wittenmyer, Annie (Vol. 2); Woman's Christian Temperance Union (Vol. 2)

Further Reading

Dorsey, Bruce. *Reforming Men and Women: Gender in the Antebellum City.* Ithaca, NY: Cornell University Press, 2002.

Martin, Scott C. *Devil of the Domestic Sphere: Temperance, Gender, and Middle-Class Ideology, 1800–1860.* DeKalb: Northern Illinois University Press, 2008.

Mattingly, Carol. *Well-Tempered Women: Nineteenth-Century Temperance Rhetoric.* Carbondale: Southern Illinois University Press, 1998.

Rorabaugh, W.J. *The Alcoholic Republic, an American Tradition.* New York: Oxford University Press, 1979.

Tyrrell, Ian. *Sobering Up: From Temperance to Prohibition in Antebellum America, 1800–1860.* Westport, CT: Greenwood Press, 1979.

Tilton, Theodore (1835–1907)

Influential editor and abolitionist Theodore Tilton had a powerful impact on the women's rights and woman suffrage movements from 1866 through the early 1870s. His career in journalism began at the *New York Tribune* in the early 1850s and was followed by a stint at the *New York Observer,* a Presbyterian newspaper. While at the *Observer,* Tilton regularly recorded the sermons of the nationally renowned liberal Congregational minister Henry Ward Beecher. Tilton quickly became a disciple of Beecher and a devotee of Beecher's "Gospel of Love." In 1856, Tilton was named managing editor of the liberal Congregational newspaper the *Independent.* His journalistic prowess and his penchant for attracting celebrity literary talent to the *Independent* were instrumental in making it a leading national journal with an extensive circulation. In 1861, when Beecher became editor-in-chief of the *Independent,* Tilton, who had been Beecher's ghostwriter from 1856 to 1860, assumed the post of assistant editor and became Beecher's closest friend. Through Beecher, Tilton gained access to the world of social reformers, particularly Garrisonian abolitionists and women's rights activists.

During the Civil War years, Tilton became good friends with Susan B. Anthony and Elizabeth Cady Stanton and was a strong supporter of the National Women's Loyal League. In 1866, Tilton suggested that the women's rights cause and the American Anti-Slavery Society (AASS) merge to form one powerful organization dedicated to obtaining the franchise for all women and African American men. Although this idea did not materialize, Tilton joined Anthony, Stanton, Parker Pillsbury, Lucy Stone, and other women's rights reformers in pursuing the American Equal Rights Association's (AERA) mission to obtain universal suffrage. Although Tilton strongly supported woman suffrage, by 1869 he had discontinued promoting the ballot for women and had aligned himself with Wendell Phillips, Lucy Stone, Henry Blackwell, Henry Ward Beecher, and New England Republican AERA members to work solely to secure the ballot for African American males through the Fifteenth Amendment. Unlike Anthony and Stanton, Tilton did not consider this move an abandonment of women's rights.

After the May 1869 AERA convention caused the women's rights movement to split, Tilton became increasingly distressed that the suffrage movement was weakening itself by dividing its forces, thereby needlessly delaying the attainment of national woman suffrage. In 1870, he developed an ambitious plan to unite Anthony and Stanton's National Woman Suffrage Association (NWSA) and Stone and Blackwell's American Woman Suffrage Association (AWSA). He called a meeting for April 1870 and invited three delegates each from the NWSA, the AWSA, and the Union Woman Suffrage Association—the latter a newly proposed group that he had created to bring about the unification. Anthony and Stanton assured him of their support for the merger. In spite of their personal misgivings about a reconciliation with Stone and Blackwell, they wanted to demonstrate to their rivals and to the public that NWSA leaders were not the divisive element in the rupture. At the May 1870 NWSA convention, with Anthony and Stanton's approval, members were persuaded to vote to accept the merger and Tilton as president. In the end, however, the AWSA rejected Tilton's plan, and the UWSA dissolved.

In the midst of the 1870 unification effort, a crisis erupted in Tilton's personal life that ultimately exploded into the Beecher–Tilton Scandal, a debacle that had long-lasting repercussions for the woman suffrage movement, 19th-century social reform, and the lives of many social reformers, including Anthony and Stanton. The crisis erupted when Tilton's wife Elizabeth Richards Tilton confessed to her husband that she had been engaged in an extramarital relationship with Henry Ward Beecher. Not only were Tilton's two most important relationships destroyed, but the scandal and the subsequent courtroom trial wrecked Tilton's reputation, ruined his career, and consumed his financial resources. In 1883, he emigrated to Europe, eventually settling in Paris, where he eked out a poor livelihood selling his prose and poetry.

Judith E. Harper

See Also: Abolitionism and the Antislavery Movement; Fifteenth Amendment; Garrison, William Lloyd; National Women's Loyal League; Phillips, Wendell; Pillsbury, Parker; Stone, Lucy; American Equal Rights Association (Vol. 2); American Woman Suffrage Association (Vol. 2); Anthony, Susan B. (Vol. 2); Blackwell, Henry Brown (Vol. 2); Free Love Movement (Vol. 2); National Woman Suffrage Association (Vol. 2); Stanton, Elizabeth Cady (Vol. 2); Woodhull, Victoria (Vol. 2)

Further Reading

Applegate, Debby. *The Most Famous Man in America: The Biography of Henry Ward Beecher*. New York: Doubleday, 2006.

Fox, Richard Wightman. *Trials of Intimacy: Love and Loss in the Beecher–Tilton Scandal*. Chicago, IL: University of Chicago Press, 1999.

McMillen, Sally G. *Seneca Falls and the Origins of the Women's Rights Movement*. New York: Oxford University Press, 2008.

Towne, Laura Matilda (1825–1901)

Laura M. Towne dedicated her life to the abolitionist cause and to educating former slaves in the South Carolina Sea Islands.

Laura Towne was born in Pittsburgh, Pennsylvania, on May 3, 1825. She was the fourth child of John and Sarah Robinson Towne. Soon after Laura's birth, her mother died and John took the family to Boston, where the Towne family became exposed to the abolitionist movement. It was not until moving to Philadelphia and attending the First Unitarian Church, however, that Laura Towne actively engaged in abolitionist activities. During this time, she also studied at the Woman's Medical College.

At the beginning of the Civil War, Laura Towne was living in Newport, Rhode Island. Immediately, she began assisting soldiers in their preparations for war by sewing clothing and performing other necessary duties. Towne, however, wanted to do more to help the Union war effort. In 1862, she volunteered to assist the federal government with the education of former slaves living on the South Carolina Sea Islands. Through her associations in Philadelphia, Towne was selected to act as an agent of the Freedmen's Aid Society of Pennsylvania. On April 9, 1862, Towne boarded the steamer *Oriental* and sailed from New York to Port Royal, South Carolina. She was soon joined in the Sea Islands by her friend, Ellen Murray.

Towne and Murray settled on Saint Helena Island, where they assisted the local freedmen population. The training that Towne received at the Women's Medical College in Philadelphia assisted her in providing medical aid to the former slaves. In September 1862, Towne received funding to open a school in the Brick Church on Saint Helena Island. The school proved successful, but it became overcrowded with 80 students enrolled for lessons. The Pennsylvania Freedmen's Association provided for the construction of a new schoolhouse, the Penn School, across from the Brick Church. The new schoolhouse provided the basis for the promotion of the educational, political, and economic advancement of freedmen in the Sea Islands. Towne also utilized her medical knowledge to assist the freedmen during outbreaks of disease.

After the Civil War, Towne and Murray remained dedicated to their work in the Sea Islands. Eventually, they purchased a home and estate, Frogmore, on Saint Helena Island and made it their permanent home. Their Northern sponsors, however, became increasingly less concerned with the plight of the freedmen. When the

Freedmen's Relief Association dissolved, it caused the near financial collapse of the Penn School. Dedicated to the school's mission, Towne paid teacher salaries and other school expenses out of her pocket until she finally secured permanent Northern charitable funding. Laura Towne died in 1901, but her spirit remained evident in the buildings and advancements made by the Penn School on Saint Helena Island.

Kristina K. Dunn

See Also: Abolitionism and the Antislavery Movement; Freedmen's Bureau; Reconstruction

Further Reading

Faulkner, Carol. *Women's Radical Reconstruction: The Freedmen's Aid Movement.* Philadelphia: University of Pennsylvania Press, 2004.

Holland, Rupert Sargent, ed. *Letters and Diary of Laura M. Towne: Written from the Sea Islands of South Carolina, 1862–1884.* New York: Negro University Press, 1969.

Rose, Willie Lee. *Rehearsal for Reconstruction: The Port Royal Experiment.* Athens: University of Georgia Press, 1999 [1964].

Truth, Sojourner (1797–1883)

The only female former slave to mount the podium to speak against the injustices of slavery and for the rights of women, Sojourner Truth stands alone in the history of the women's rights movement. She was, perhaps, the most celebrated African American woman of the 19th century and, unlike many of her contemporaries on the lecture circuit, she was listened to and admired by both men and women of the period.

Born in 1797, in Hurley, New York, in Ulster County, Sojourner Truth was first named Isabella and was the youngest of 13 children born to James and Betsey, who were the property of Colonel Johannes Hardenbergh. As a child, her first language was Dutch due to the community in which they lived, but she had no formal education and never learned to read or write. Although she came from a large family, Isabella did not know her brothers and sisters since most of them were sold to other slavers while she was still in infancy. At nine years old, she too was sold for 100 dollars. She passed through multiple owners before being bought by John Dumont of New Paltz, New York. When she turned 14, Dumont insisted that she marry an older slave, Thomas, by whom she had five children.

Sojourner Truth, a former slave, spoke out for the abolition of slavery and for women's rights in America. (Library of Congress)

As the date which had been set for liberating the slaves living in New York (July 4, 1827) neared, Isabella learned that Dumont did not intend to grant her freedom. Taking her infant daughter, Sophia, she ran away in 1826, seeking refuge with a Quaker family, the Van Wagenens, whose last name she adopted. She had to leave her other children with their father because they were not legally free until they reached their 20th birthday. Isabella spent several months with the Van Wagenens, doing light housework for the family, as well as working among the city's poor and acquiring a step toward literacy. During the period, she learned that Dumont had illegally sold her son, Peter, to an Alabama plantation owner. At that time, New York State law forbade the selling of slaves to anyone who lived outside of the state. Isabella successfully sued Dumont to have her son returned to her.

In 1829, Isabella, Peter, and Sophia moved to New York City. She worked briefly with the Magdalene Society, a Methodist mission to reform prostitutes, before joining Robert Matthews' Zion Hill commune. When

Matthews was arrested for murder, however, the group disbanded. Shortly after, her son Peter took a berth on a whaling ship and, with the exception of five hurried letters to his mother, he was not heard of again.

Inspired by the Millerites, a religious group that predicted the Second Coming of Christ in 1843, Isabella Van Wagenen changed her name to Sojourner Truth, selected as a pseudonym that implied a wandering evangelist who spoke honestly. A self-proclaimed Pentecostal minister, she walked through Long Island and Connecticut, preaching to anyone who would listen. Following the dissolution of the Millerites after the Great Disappointment, when Jesus did not appear as predicted, Truth moved to Massachusetts and joined the Northampton Association, a utopian community organized around a communally owned and operated mill. The Northampton group was led by George Benson, brother-in-law of William Lloyd Garrison, editor of the antislavery newspaper, *The Liberator.* Through her association with this group, Truth met leaders, such as Frederick Douglass, William Lloyd Garrison, and feminist Olive Gilbert, and was exposed to radical new ideas like emancipation and women's rights. After the group was dissolved in 1846, she continued to work as a housekeeper for Benson, maintained her association with the abolitionists, and earned extra income by creating and selling portraits with the tagline, "I sell the Shadow to support the Substance."

In 1850, after being persuaded by Garrison, Truth dictated her life story to Olive Gilbert. The work was published as the *Narrative of Sojourner Truth, a Northern Slave, Emancipated from Bodily Servitude by the State of New York, in 1828.* Sales were immediate and impressive, enabling her to purchase a home and giving the abolitionists a powerful tool in their quest for liberation. Based on the name recognition generated by her published work, she was invited to join the abolitionist speakers' bureau through which, using her personal narrative as a presentation tool, she gained a reputation for unsentimental straight talk. Early in her travels, she noted that women, herself included, were considered part of the abolitionist movement but were discouraged from taking part in the proceedings. She attended her first women's rights convention in Worcester, Massachusetts.

Truth then attended the national convention that took place in Akron, Ohio, in 1851. On the second day of the convention, a group of ministers joined the gathering and began their usual protests concerning the superiority of men, backing up their arguments with select quotes from scripture, and lamenting the sins of the "first mother," Eve. Whether she had planned it or not, Truth rose from her seat and ascended the podium. A hushed silence permeated the room; the audience was awed by the fact that any woman, much less a black woman, was being allowed to speak to the group. She countered each of the arguments made by the ministers. Starting almost every point with "Ain't I A Woman," Truth rallied the audience to her side by asserting that women deserved equal rights because they were equal in capability to men. She ended her presentation by asserting that, although Jesus was a man, a comment introduced by one of the preachers, he was the offspring of a woman. The discourse assured her place in the women's movement as well as in the abolitionist movement and in history. She advocated direct action, urging the women to take the rights they wanted and demanding that the group also consider the needs of black women. In this, she was one of the first to make the connection between abolitionism and women's rights, stating that not all slaves were men and not all women were white.

Between 1851 and 1853, Truth was in demand as a speaker; her tour covered most of the East and areas of the West and when she was not traveling, she dictated pieces for inclusion in the *Anti-Slavery Bugle.* In 1855, a second printing of the *Narrative* was offered for sale and did so well that it enabled her purchase of a larger home in Harmonia, near Battle Creek, Michigan. Her speaking tours continued, almost without interruption, until after the Civil War.

In 1864, she met Abraham Lincoln and reported to him on the plight of the former slaves. When the Civil War ended, Truth went to Washington, D.C., to offer aid to freed blacks through the Freedmen's Bureau. While in Washington, Truth took the city's streetcar companies to task by lobbying against segregation and thanks, in part, to her efforts, a congressional ban was issued against the streetcar companies in 1865 that prohibited them from separating black and white patrons on their conveyances.

While touring in upstate New York, Truth met Elizabeth Cady Stanton in 1867. After meeting with some of Stanton's colleagues, Truth initiated a job placement program to match poor black freedmen with employers in the region. She clearly saw the economic and educational gap between blacks and whites and was one of the first to discuss reparation, federal payment due to blacks for their enslavement. In 1870, she submitted an unsuccessful petition to Congress to give free parcels of land in the West to former slaves. Although the petition failed to gain congressional approval, she did enable the movement of many blacks to lands in Kansas.

Having met Ulysses Grant, Truth attempted to vote for him in 1872 but was turned away from the polls. She died in her home in Battle Creek, Michigan, on November 26, 1883 after a long battle with skin ulcers. Over a thousand people attended her funeral.

A U.S. postage stamp was issued in honor of Sojourner Truth in February 1986, and the Mars Pathfinder Microrover was named in her honor. In 2004, Senator Hillary Rodham Clinton introduced legislation to add Truth's likeness to the statue of Lucretia Mott, Elizabeth Cady Stanton, and Susan B. Anthony that sits in the Capitol Rotunda in Washington, D.C. In 2009, a new bust of Truth was dedicated by First Lady Michelle Obama.

Joyce D. Duncan

See Also: Abolitionism and the Antislavery Movement; Cary, Mary Ann Shadd; Douglass, Frederick; Freedmen's Bureau; Garrison, William Lloyd; *The Liberator*; Mott, Lucretia; Slavery and the Civil War; Stewart, Maria W.; Tubman, Harriet; Anthony, Susan B. (Vol. 2); Stanton, Elizabeth Cady (Vol. 2)

Primary Document: 1851, "Aren't I a Woman?"

Further Reading

Logan, Shirley Wilson, ed. *With Pen and Voice: A Critical Anthology of Nineteenth Century African-American Women.* Carbondale: Southern Illinois University Press, 1993.

Painter, Nell Irvin. *Sojourner Truth: A Life, A Symbol.* New York: W. W. Norton, 1997.

Stetson, Erlene, and Linda David. *Glorying in Tribulation: The Lifework of Sojourner Truth.* East Lansing: Michigan State University Press, 1994.

Walker, Robbie Jean, ed. *The Rhetoric of Struggle: Public Address by African American Women.* New York: Garland, 1992.

Washington, Margaret. *Sojourner Truth's America.* Chicago: University of Illinois Press, 2009.

Yee, Shirley J. *Black Women Abolitionists: A Study in Activism 1828–1860.* Knoxville: University of Tennessee Press, 1992.

Tubman, Harriet (1822–1913)

Born into slavery on the Eastern Shore of Maryland, Harriet Tubman gained fame as an Underground Railroad operator, abolitionist, Civil War spy and nurse, suffragist, and humanitarian. After escaping from enslavement in 1849, Tubman defied legal restraints to battle slavery and oppression, earning her the biblical

Harriet Tubman was hailed as "the Moses of her people" because of her efforts in helping hundreds of African Americans escape from slavery on the Underground Railroad. (Library of Congress)

name Moses and a place among the nation's most famous historical figures.

Harriet Tubman was born Araminta Harriet Ross in early 1822 on the plantation of Anthony Thompson, in Dorchester County, Maryland. Tubman was the fifth of nine children of Harriet "Rit" Green and Benjamin Ross, both slaves. Edward Brodess, the stepson of Anthony Thompson, owned Rit and her offspring through his mother. Ben Ross, the legal property of Anthony Thompson, was a highly valued timber inspector who supervised and managed a large timbering operation on Thompson's land. Tubman's relatively stable family life was shattered around 1824 when Edward Brodess took Rit and her children to his own farm in Bucktown, Maryland. Brodess often hired young Harriet out to temporary masters, some of whom were cruel and brutal in their treatment of slaves. He also illegally sold other members of her family to out-of-state buyers, permanently fracturing her family.

During the late 1830s and early 1840s, she worked for John T. Stewart, a Madison merchant and shipbuilder, bringing her back to the familial and social community near where her father lived and where she had been born. Around 1844 she married a local free black named John Tubman, and she shed her childhood name Araminta in favor of Harriet.

On March 7, 1849, Edward Brodess died on his farm at Bucktown, leaving Tubman and her family at risk of being sold to settle his large debts. In the late fall of 1849, Tubman took her own liberty, tapping into an Underground Railroad that was already functioning well on the Eastern Shore. She found her way to Philadelphia where she found work as a domestic, and saved her money to help the rest of her family escape. From 1850 to 1860, Tubman conducted about 13 escape missions, bringing away approximately 70 individuals, including her brothers, parents, and other family and friends, while also giving instructions to roughly 60 more who found their way to freedom independently. The Fugitive Slave Act of 1850 left most refugee slaves vulnerable to recapture, and many fled to the safety and protection of Canada. Tubman brought many of her charges to St. Catharines, Ontario, where they settled into a growing community of freedom seekers.

Her dangerous missions won the admiration of black and white abolitionists throughout the North, who provided her with funds to continue her activities. In 1858, Tubman met with the legendary abolitionist John Brown in her home in St. Catharines. Impressed by his passion for ending slavery, she committed herself to helping him recruit former slaves into his army for his planned raid at Harper's Ferry, Virginia, in 1859. That same year, Tubman purchased a home in Auburn, New York, from William Henry Seward, Lincoln's future secretary of state, where she eventually settled her aged parents and other family members. On her way to Boston in April 1860, Tubman helped incite a riot to rescue a fugitive slave, Charles Nalle, from the custody of United States marshals charged with returning him to his Virginia master.

At the urging of Massachusetts governor John Andrew, Tubman joined Northern abolitionists in support of Union activities at Port Royal, in the Hilton Head district of South Carolina in early 1862. On June 2, 1863, Tubman became the first American woman to plan and execute an armed expedition during wartime. Acting as an advisor to Colonel James Montgomery, Tubman led a raid from Port Royal 25 miles up the nearby Combahee River. Using communication networks that were the provenance of black mariners, Tubman's spy missions provided crucial details about rebel enforcements and heavily mined waters. Under the cover of darkness, Tubman and a local scout, directed three gunboats loaded with men from Montgomery's Second South Carolina Volunteer Infantry Regiment, a black unit, along the heavily mined river.

Montgomery and his men effectively dispersed Confederate gunners, set fire to several plantations, and confiscated thousands of dollars worth of rice, corn, and cotton. In addition, Montgomery sent small boats to the riverbanks to retrieve the hundreds of slaves fleeing their homes, but the boats were soon swamped by the frantic and desperate freedom seekers. Using her extraordinary voice, Tubman began to sing, encouraging the crowds to stay calm. People on the riverbanks started singing, shouting, and clapping, easing the pressure on the small boats and the evacuation continued safely. The expedition successfully freed about 750 former slaves. A reporter from the *Wisconsin State Journal,* who witnessed the victorious return, wrote a lengthy article crediting Tubman with planning and directing the raid, calling her the Black She Moses.

Her services as a scout and spy were highly valued by Union officers, who recognized her great ability to extract intelligence from the local population of former slaves who had fled their Confederate masters. Tubman received about $200 from the government for her scouting services, but much of it was used to pay other scouts and spies for information, and some was used to build a wash house to train local women to earn wages by providing laundry services to Union officials. Her expenditures made it difficult for Tubman to support herself and to save money to send back to her ailing parents in Auburn, New York. She was not a soldier, officially, and her on-again, off-again role as a scout and a spy precluded any formal pay arrangement with the army. She never received any pay for her nursing services either; so she struggled to support herself by making and selling pies and root beer and by washing and sewing for the local Union officers.

Granted a furlough in June 1864, Tubman stopped in Boston where she met Sojourner Truth, an antislavery and women's rights activist. Born a slave and deeply religious, Truth had much in common with Tubman. They differed, however, in their assessment of Abraham Lincoln. Truth had campaigned for Lincoln and believed he had done much for the betterment of African Americans, but identifying herself with the thousands of black troops during the Civil War who were paid less than half of white soldiers were paid for the same service,

Tubman also resented that Lincoln had been at first hesitant to enlist black men for military service.

During late spring 1865, Tubman was recruited by the United States Sanitary Commission to work in Union hospitals, where the need for her services was great. By early fall 1865, Tubman headed back to Auburn to care for her elderly parents. While riding on a train from Philadelphia to New York on a government pass, she was ordered to the smoking car, where other African Americans were forcibly segregated. She refused and was violently thrown from the train by four white men, breaking her arm and several ribs. It would take her months to recuperate. Unable to work, Tubman and her family suffered greatly from hunger and cold that winter.

Committed to woman suffrage, Tubman was also a lifelong community activist and humanitarian, feeding, clothing, and housing anyone in need who came to her door. Illiterate her entire life, Tubman dictated part of her life story to Sarah Bradford, a local central New York author. Published in 1869, this short biography, *Scenes in the Life of Harriet Tubman,* brought brief fame and financial relief to Tubman and her family. She married veteran Nelson Davis that same year; her husband John Tubman had been killed in 1867 in Maryland. Though she and Davis operated a brick-making business and sold produce from their small farm, Tubman battled poverty for the rest of her life. Denied her own military pension, she eventually received an $8 widow's pension as the wife of Nelson Davis and later a $12 Civil War nurse's pension.

Her humanitarian work triumphed with the opening of the Harriet Tubman Home for the Aged, located on land abutting her own property in Auburn, which she transferred to the African Methodist Episcopal Zion Church in 1903. Tubman continued to appear at local and national suffrage conventions until the early 1900s. She died at the age of 91 on March 10, 1913, in Auburn, New York.

Kate Clifford Larson

See Also: Abolitionism and the Antislavery Movement; Slavery and the Civil War; Truth, Sojourner; Underground Railroad; United States Sanitary Commission

Further Reading

Clinton, Catherine. *Harriet Tubman: The Road to Freedom.* New York: Little, Brown, and Company, 2004.

Humez, Jean M. *Harriet Tubman: The Life and the Life Stories.* Madison: University of Wisconsin Press, 2003.

Larson, Kate Clifford. *Bound for the Promised Land: Harriet Tubman, Portrait of an American Hero.* New York: Ballantine Books, 2004.

Lowry, Beverly. *Harriet Tubman, a Biography.* New York: Doubleday, 2007.

U

The Una

When wealthy feminist Paulina Wright Davis introduced *The Una* in 1853, it was by no means clear that public interest would be piqued by a publication with such a narrow focus. Devoted mainly to suffrage and "the elevation of Woman," *The Una* (a mystical character from Spenser's *The Faerie Queen* who symbolized truth) challenged prevailing publishing wisdom that dictated that magazines for women needed to present a broad spectrum of literature, fashion, and domestic concerns related to woman's sphere. While Amelia Bloomer's *The Lily* had appeared a few years prior to promote temperance, *The Una* was the first publication to promote the broader goals of the women's rights movement.

Although *The Una* survived only two years and ten months, it is a landmark in suffrage history because its appearance signaled a professional approach to the battle for women's rights and because it served as a prototype on which later suffrage publications were based. As Davis herself saw it, a journal was "the most powerful engine for the change of public sentiment." At the time it first circulated, however, *The Una*'s singularly focused feminist approach as a magazine met criticism and cynicism.

When Davis published the inaugural monthly issue of *The Una* on February 1, 1853, she offered her journal as an alternative to the "Ladies' Books, Ladies' Magazines, and Miscellanies," arguing that American women needed "stronger nourishment; and with a work so peculiarly their own, they need at least one paper which will give a correct history of its progress and be a faithful exponent of its principles." She promised that her journal would "discuss with candor and earnestness, the Rights, Relations, Duties, Destiny and Sphere of Woman. Her Education—Literary, Scientific, and Artistic.—Her Avocation—Industrial, Commercial, and Professional. Her Interests—Pecuniary, Civil and Political."

When Davis delved into publishing, she already was one of the leaders of the women's rights movement and a primary organizer of the first national women's rights convention, which was held in October 1850 in Worcester, Massachusetts. Like many of the early feminists, Davis came to the women's rights movement by way of antislavery activism.

Her journal published the writing of noted female authors of the day, including Sara Clarke Lippincott ("Grace Greenwood"), Sara Payson Willis ("Fanny Fern"), and Elizabeth Cady Stanton. She also provided space for published "calls" to women's rights conventions that were held around the nation and then reported on the meetings after they occurred. The back pages of her magazine included notices for women physicians and publicity for medical colleges that accepted women and other schools that also would accept women.

Although specific circulation figures were never published, Davis noted that she had exhausted the supply of copies of the first issue. During the year 1853, she also published the names of subscribers who contributed the one dollar annual fee, including many of the prominent names in the women's rights movement. By the end of the first year, about 600 people had been named as subscribers. Not surprisingly, the list included Susan B. Anthony, Lucy Stone, Elizabeth Cady Stanton, and Lucretia Mott.

By December 1854, Davis was exhausted from the strenuous burden of publishing the 16-page monthly journal. Davis lamented in print that she had tried "in vain to convince women that they needed an organ which could give to the future a correct history of this revolution." She called upon Caroline Healey Dall to assist her as coeditor, while Davis herself temporarily moved her editorial base to Washington, D.C., for several months.

Throughout its short life (the final issue was printed in October 1855), *The Una* advocated a firm and steady course toward equal rights for women and saw full woman suffrage as the most important symbol of that goal. Even after Dall joined Davis as editor, they reiterated their original editorial philosophy. *The Una* was politically independent and officially represented no one organization. The paper promoted the full range of women's rights, including civil and religious freedom, education for women, equal compensation, and the right of women to work in any employment they wanted.

After *The Una* folded, Paulina Wright Davis continued her activism for suffrage. She wrote occasionally for the subsequent suffrage publication, *The Revolution,* and helped found the New England Woman Suffrage

Association. Davis's coeditor, Caroline Dall, spoke and wrote extensively on the subject of women's rights until 1867 and then turned her attention to preaching, writing biographical and historical works related to women and Transcendentalism, and writing her own memoirs.

Agnes Hooper Gottlieb

See Also: Bloomer, Amelia; Dall, Caroline Healey; Davis, Paulina Kellogg Wright; Fern, Fanny; *The Lily*; Mott, Lucretia; Stone, Lucy; Anthony, Susan B. (Vol. 2); *The Revolution* (Vol. 2); Stanton, Elizabeth Cady (Vol. 2)

Further Reading

Russo, Ann, and Cheris Kramarae. *The Radical Women's Press of the 1850s.* New York: Routledge, 1991.

Tonn, Mari Boor. "*The Una*, 1853–1855: The Premiere of the Woman's Rights Press." In *A Voice of Their Own: The Woman Suffrage Press, 1840–1910,* edited by Martha M. Solomon. Tuscaloosa: University of Alabama Press, 1991.

Wayne, Tiffany K. *Woman Thinking: Feminism and Transcendentalism in 19th-Century America.* Lanham, MD: Lexington Books, 2005.

Underground Railroad

The Underground Railroad is the metaphorical name given to the routes, safe houses, and river and border crossings that escaped slaves used to reach the northern United States, where they could try to live freely, and also Canada, where slavery was abolished three decades before it was outlawed in the United States. The first American Fugitive Slave Act, adopted by Congress in 1793, made aiding escapees a crime, and the railroad became even more dangerous for its "riders" and "conductors" after the 1850 Fugitive Slave Act which made the federal government (instead of states) responsible for its enforcement. The change meant escaped slaves living in the North could now be captured and returned to their owners, and anyone who interfered or aided their escapes was breaking the new law.

In the years leading up to the Civil War, support for abolitionism increased, with many women involved in the antislavery efforts. In 1852, Harriet Beecher Stowe published *Uncle Tom's Cabin,* a novel she said was

An informal network of abolitionists, the Underground Railroad helped guide fugitive slaves to safety across the Canadian border or into free states during the years prior to the American Civil War. (Library of Congress)

inspired by witnessing slavery during her early years living in Cincinnati and events following passage of the 1850 Act. Historians credit the book as one of the forces galvanizing American and international opposition to slavery in the southern United States and contributing to the Underground Railroad's successes.

The most famous person associated with the Underground Railroad is an escaped slave named Harriet Tubman. She is credited with leading hundreds of escaped slaves to their freedom. Nicknamed "Moses," Tubman became an icon of the abolitionist movement. Born on a plantation in eastern Maryland—the exact year is not known but has been reported as 1815 and 1825—she was hired out as a domestic slave as a child and bore scars from several beatings. Sometime around 1844 she married a freeman named John Tubman, and five years later fled Maryland. She took the name "Harriet" in the North, shedding her birth name of "Araminta." In 1850, she got word that her niece and her niece's two children were to be sold further south and Tubman returned to Maryland to smuggle out her family members. Her life as a "conductor" had begun.

Throughout the next decade Tubman made an estimated 20 trips into the South and is credited with leading 200 slaves to freedom on the Underground Railroad. She was well known for leading mass escapes and her notoriety reached epic proportions in the mid-19th century. She was considered a hero in the North and was vilified in the South. She was known for her disguises, once reportedly using a sunbonnet and some chickens to trick a former master. Another time she dressed as a stooping old woman to fool authorities in New York. Eventually Tubman made her home in Upstate New York's Finger Lakes region where she lived permanently after the Civil War. Today she is memorialized for her work on the Underground Railroad in both the United States and Canada with schools, parks, statues, and public artwork.

Other women contributed to the Underground Railroad's successes from Canada. Mary Ann Shadd Cary, for example, is credited with promoting Canada as a safe destination for both escaped slaves and free blacks. Born in Delaware in 1823, her family was free but suffered the discrimination and fear that came with her race during the era. She moved to Canada in 1851, establishing a school for refugee children and urging black migration to the U.S. neighbor to the north. Two years after her arrival, she founded the *Provincial Freeman* newspaper which she used as her voice to encourage self-reliance and rights for blacks and women. Her circle of associates include many of the leading abolitionists of the time, and she famously edited and published the account of John Brown's raid at Harper's Ferry as told by Osborne Perry Anderson, the only black man to survive the event. One of Shadd Cary's contemporaries, Laura Haviland, also worked along the Michigan–Canada border and made Underground Railroad "journeys" to the South, where she aided fugitive slaves traveling North. Haviland, a Canadian-born Quaker, became one of Michigan's most notable "conductors." Like Harriet Tubman, she found inspiration for her abolitionist work through her religion and spirituality. The town of Haviland, Kansas, is named after her, and a statue is erected in her honor in Adrian, Michigan.

Sandra Svoboda

See Also: Abolitionism and the Antislavery Movement; Cary, Mary Ann Shadd; Quakers; Slavery and the Civil War; Stowe, Harriet Beecher; Tubman, Harriet

Further Reading

Blight, David W., ed. *Passages to Freedom: The Underground Railroad Project in History and Memory*. Washington, DC: Smithsonian Books, 2004.

Tobin, Jacqueline L., and Raymond G. Dobard. *Hidden in Plain View: A Secret Story of Quilts and the Underground Railroad*. New York: Doubleday, 1999.

Tobin, Jacqueline L., and Hettie Jones. *From Midnight to Dawn: The Last Tracks of the Underground Railroad*. New York: Doubleday, 2007.

United States Sanitary Commission

The United States Sanitary Commission (USSC) was a privately run philanthropic organization established during the American Civil War to collect and distribute supplies, to assist the federal government in the management of military hospitals, and to make inquiries and give advice on issues of sanitation and medicine. The USSC was the only civilian-run organization to receive official recognition from the federal government. Middle- and upper-class men, who sought to reassert their social and political status after the expansion of the franchise and the advent of machine politics, comprised the executive board of the USSC. Northern women of various socioeconomic backgrounds comprised the leadership of the commission branches and the bulk of the volunteers. The wartime relationship between these men and women provided much needed battlefield assistance, along with conflict over the place and value of women's work.

The USSC emerged from the Women's Central Association of Relief (WCAR) in response to the U.S. Army's failure to maintain adequate sanitation and supply sufficient medicine in the aftermath of the Battle of Bull Run in the spring of 1861. Elizabeth Blackwell, the first female doctor in the United States, founded the WCAR in the spring of 1861 to manage relief work, communicate directly with the U.S. Army Medical Department, and select and train women nurses. WCAR Vice President Henry W. Bellows traveled to Washington, D.C., to establish political connections, but he shifted his thinking regarding the nature of a wartime relief organization after visiting army camps and military hospitals. Rather then presenting the proposal laid out by the WCAR, Bellows informed Secretary of War Simon Cameron that a wartime relief agency, based in the capital, would improve and maintain the physical and mental health of the army, manage the organization of military hospitals and camps, and advise the transportation of the wounded. The USSC received executive approval in June 1861.

In September 1862, the USSC recognized the WCAR as an auxiliary branch, but it continued to function independently from the parent organization. The establishment of female associate managers, who communicated supply requests to the homefront and provided reports on the conditions of the homefront and battlefront, provided branch managers with more time for recruitment activities. Local soldiers' aid societies provided the bulk of the support for the USSC coming from the Northern homefront. By late fall 1862, over 1,400 soldiers' aid societies were associated with the USSC, and, over the course of the war, nearly 7,000 aid societies were created. Both the regional branch offices of the USSC and the local soldiers' aid societies were managed, worked, and sustained primarily by women.

The course of the war and Northern sympathy toward the war influenced the amount of money and supplies held by the USSC at any given moment. Inspectors thoroughly investigated and reported the conditions of camps and troops, including sewage disposal, cleanliness, clothing, cooking, and diets, and advisors made recommendations to the War Department. The USSC advised the War Department to improve the diets of soldiers to include greater nutritional variety, to reorganize the Medical Bureau to better care for the sick and wounded in hospitals, and to allow the commission to participate in the transportation of supplies and of the wounded and sick to hospitals.

Women on the Northern homefront provided over $15 million worth of supplies over the course of the war, including ice, bandages, lint, pens, paper, clothing, and food. When the USSC was unable to obtain supplies from local aid societies, they bought goods on the market. To keep the Northern homefront abreast of its supply and distribution activities, the USSC began publishing *The Sanitary Commission Bulletin* in November 1863, along with lecture tours in USSC regions. Both attempts at improved communication with the homefront were suggestions of female branch managers. The *Bulletin* was published twice a month and circulated to local aid societies and troops.

Due to wartime cooperation with the federal government and the Northern homefront, the USSC experienced conflict and controversy. Advice offered by the USSC to the federal government was not always welcome. While the USSC criticized the Medical Bureau for failing in its duties to the troops, the bureau believed the Sanitary Commission exaggerated its concerns about sickness and sanitation. The women of the Northern homefront proved to be the commission's most formidable foe during the course of the war. At the beginning of the war, the executive board believed that they could easily gain the support and participation of women and that women would naturally and dutifully carry out benevolent activity, while the structure and centralized organization of the USSC would bring direction and efficiency to their activities. But women questioned why the federal government was unable to provide the necessary supplies for war, particularly in light of rising taxes. They indicated their anger over supposed corrupt and fraudulent practices on the part of the USSC. Specifically, women feared that the supplies they provided were not getting to the battlefront or were being sold. Some women sent supplies directly to the battlefront, rather than to the USSC, as instructed. Sanitary fairs, which were successful fundraising activities for local branches, were seen by the USSC to be violations of its emphasis on centralization.

The USSC chose not to involve itself directly in the process of demobilization, although commission women sought to continue their activities by assisting returning soldiers and families. At the conclusion of the war, the USSC informed branches to continue operating until July 4, 1865, after which they needed to forward remaining supplies and money to the Sanitary Commission. The last official act of the USSC came with the publication of its official history in 1866, entitled *History of the United States Sanitary Commission*.

Sarah K. Nytroe

See Also: Barton, Clara; Blackwell, Elizabeth; Dix, Dorothea; Livermore, Mary; May, Abigail Williams; Slavery and the Civil War; Wormeley, Katharine Prescott

Further Reading

Attie, Jeanie. *Patriotic Toil: Northern Women and the American Civil War*. Ithaca, NY: Cornell University Press, 1998.

Giesberg, Judith Ann. *Civil War Sisterhood: The U.S. Sanitary Commission and Women's Politics in Transition*. Boston, MA: Northeastern University Press, 2000.

Leonard, Elizabeth D. *Yankee Women: Gender Battles in the Civil War*. New York: W.W. Norton & Company, 1994.

Utopian Communities

Utopian communities are typically formed out of a collective desire for a better lifestyle than that offered by mainstream society, and they have been popular throughout America's history. Some of these communities, such as the Shakers in New York (1774 to early 1900s), were founded on religious values, whereas others, such as Brook Farm in Roxbury, Massachusetts (1841–1847), were founded on social principles. While many communities eventually disbanded, some have continued even into the present day.

Within the various types of communities over the centuries, the status of women has varied greatly. In general, utopian communities provide women with higher status and value than they find in the outside world and are therefore progressive from a feminist viewpoint. However, in a small number of communities, women are accorded lower status than men and are given a greater burden of the workload.

While issues of gender equality vary amongst the many utopian communities in America, these differences are not consistent based on the religious or economic ideologies of the communities. Some communities, such as the Rugby community in Tennessee (1880–1900), simply preserved the standard gender roles of mainstream society. Socialist communities, such as Harmony in Pennsylvania (1805–1905) and Ruskin in Tennessee (1894–1901), granted equal status to men and women, who were able to vote, share wealth, and make decisions about the community. The Shaker community, founded by Mother Ann Lee, also accorded equal status to men and women in all areas of community life. In other communities, women and men were treated very differently but with equal status. For example, in many of the Moravian communities in Georgia in the 18th and 19th centuries, women and men were separated and encouraged to work only with their own sex. In still other communities, such as the Amana colonies of Iowa (1843–1932), women were considered equal to men but were not allowed to hold leadership positions and were relegated to jobs such as child care and domestic chores traditionally considered "women's work." In the Fruitlands community (1843–1844), founded by Louisa May Alcott's father Bronson Alcott in Concord, Massachusetts, women provided nearly all of the labor needed to sustain the small group, a factor that led to its early demise, as Louisa May Alcott explored in her later short story "Transcendental Wild Oats" (1873) about the experiment.

However, the majority of utopian communities place an equal value on all kinds of work completed to sustain the community, so there is less differentiation between the types of jobs completed and the rewards for completed work. Domestic work, therefore, is as equally valued as any other work performed in the community. In the Ruskin community and in Brook Farm, men and women were paid equally no matter what type of work they completed. As well, in many communities, residents have the ability to choose the type of work they prefer. In Twin Oaks in Louisa, Virginia (1967–present), residents must work 42 hours per week at one of the community's income-generating projects in addition to tasks such as child care, cleaning, lawn maintenance, and so on. Residents have the freedom to choose a variety of tasks each week.

The role of women in marriage and their status as mothers also varied widely amongst the various types of communities. A few communities, such as the Zoar Society in Zoar, Ohio (1817–1898), advocated for celibacy amongst its members, and others, such as Harmony, enforced it during periods of difficulty in the community. The majority of utopian communities place a high value on monogamous marriages, even if those marriages are not sanctioned by the church or government but are rather formed in the community.

But other groups, such as the anarchist Home Colony in Washington (1896–1921), saw marriage as limiting a woman's freedom and control. The Home Colony not only supported "free love," but also welcomed single mothers and unmarried, cohabiting couples. The Farm (1971–present), located near Summerstown in Tennessee, places few limits on sexual practices within and without marriage, and they have especially focused on natural childbirth. Some communities encouraged childbirth as a way to propagate the community, but others discouraged it as an unnecessary burden. Perhaps the most extreme example of this is the Oneida community of Oneida, New York (1848–1878), which purposefully paired older men with younger women and older women with younger men as sexual partners to avoid high rates of conception.

In many utopian communities, especially in those founded on social principles, child care was typically a communal service rather than an individual responsibility. Other communities only offered communal child care after a child reached a certain age. The Amana colonies offered a two-year maternity leave to women, during which they were exempt from community work but still full-fledged members; similarly, in the Icarian movement (1848–1898), new mothers were exempt from other community work until their children turned five and entered kindergarten. In the Moravian communities, men were responsible for the care of male children, while women cared for females.

There are many reasons due to which women chose to join utopian communities, either because they wanted to transform society or because they simply wanted a better life for themselves. Scholars have also suggested that some women were escaping abusive or harmful relationships. Women of all backgrounds and classes came together in these communities, and for many, the effects of communal living lasted throughout their lives, even if they left the communities. Although the majority of these utopian communities ultimately failed, they showed the possibilities of reconceiving the roles of women, focusing especially on domestic duties, spiritual commitments, and social activism.

Kari Miller

See Also: Alcott, Louisa May; Lee, "Mother" Ann; Nicholas, Mary Gove; Oneida Community; Shakers; Truth, Sojourner; Wright, Frances; Free Love Movement (Vol. 2); Mormons and Polygamy (Vol. 2)

Further Reading

Chmielewski, Wendy, Louis J. Kern, and Marlyn Klee-Hartzell, eds. *Women in Spiritual and Communitarian Societies in the United States.* Syracuse, NY: Syracuse University Press, 1993.

Foster, Lawrence. *Women, Family, and Utopia: Communal Experiments of the Shakers, the Oneida Community, and the Mormons.* Syracuse, NY: Syracuse University Press, 1991.

Francis, Richard. *Fruitlands: The Alcott Family and Their Search for Utopia.* New Haven, CT: Yale University Press, 2010.

Guarneri, Carl J. *The Utopian Alternative: Fourierism in Nineteenth-Century America.* Ithaca, NY: Cornell University Press, 1991.

Sreenivasan, Jyotsna. *Utopias in American History.* Santa Barbara, CA: ABC-CLIO, 2008.

Van Lew, Elizabeth (1818–1900)

A native Virginian who served as a Union spy in the Confederate capital of Richmond, Virginia, Elizabeth Van Lew was often referred to as Crazy Bet. Van Lew's efforts on behalf of the Union during the Civil War led to the escape of dozens of Union prisoners from Libby Prison in Richmond, the collection of vital intelligence on Confederate military positions in and around the city, and other successful activities of the Union underground throughout the war.

Elizabeth Van Lew was born October 15, 1818, in Richmond, Virginia, the first child of John and Eliza Louise Baker Van Lew. In the 1830s her parents sent her to Philadelphia to live with relatives while she received her education. Although the Van Lews owned slaves, Elizabeth developed a strong abolitionist stance that provided a foundation for her actions during the Civil War. She not only believed that slavery had corrupted Southern society but also that its immoral nature made it a national sin.

As the war began, Confederate women in their Church Hill neighborhood asked Van Lew and her mother to join them in providing sustenance and supplies to the growing Confederate armies that flocked to Richmond. The Van Lew women refused the requests, creating suspicion about the family's loyalty that would follow them throughout the conflict. In an effort to deflect the criticism, occasionally Van Lew would minister to the Confederate wounded and encamped soldiers. She also became an accomplished hostess, entertaining Confederate officers and government officials in the family's home, as well as boarding a Confederate captain and his family for a time. She even explained her desire to visit Union prisoners as a reflection of a proper Confederate woman's Christian duty to minister to those deemed most unworthy. This public persona was simply a way for Van Lew to gain access to people and information that would further the Union cause while raising the least suspicion.

The public perception of her as crazy may have developed from the odd clothing she wore and nonsensical mutterings she uttered as she walked through the streets of the city during the war. However, the most recent biography contends that factual evidence does not exist to support such contentions; instead, resentment for her Unionism, her radical stance on slavery, and her lifelong spinsterhood and reclusive lifestyle may be more the cause of the nickname of "Crazy Bet."

The majority of Van Lew's early war work related to providing for and assisting in the escape of Union prisoners held in Richmond. Both personally and with the aid of free blacks, slaves, and other Unionists, Van Lew sent prisoners messages that were hidden in the spines of books, in the false bottoms of food platters, in the soles of her servants' shoes, or in a hollow egg in a basket of eggs. She had her own encryption code, composed of letters and numbers, which she kept secure in the back of her watch, and she used the family property around the city as relay stations to pass on information to Union officials. She also used much of her family's finances to bribe Confederate guards and clerks.

Van Lew supervised an extensive spy network that may have included Mary Elizabeth Bowser, believed to be Van Lew's former black servant who gained a maid position in the Confederate White House and sent information back to Van Lew. Some doubt exists about her identity and relationship to Van Lew, but the extent and success of the Union underground led by Van Lew, including the 1864 escape of 103 prisoners from Libby Prison, makes the story plausible.

By 1864, Van Lew began to work as chief correspondent of the Unionist spy network, sending information to Generals George H. Sharpe (chief of the Secret Service), Benjamin F. Butler (Army of the James), George G. Meade (Army of the Potomac), and Ulysses S. Grant (overall Union commander). The information coming from Unionists in Richmond led to a failed raid by General Judson Kilpatrick and Colonel Ulrich Dahlgren to free more prisoners and to the successful final Union assault by Grant's forces on Richmond. Gratitude for her services during the war eventually led to a government payment of $5,000 in 1867 and her appointment as postmaster of Richmond by President Ulysses Grant in 1869, a post she held for eight years. Community

Elizabeth Van Lew was a Union spy during the Civil War. (*Harper's Monthly Magazine.* Vol. CXXIII, 1911)

resentment toward Van Lew continued for the remainder of her life due to her Republican politics, her advocacy for African American equality, and her perpetual association with Southern disloyalty and the conquering Union.

Elizabeth Van Lew died September 25, 1900, in Richmond, Virginia.

Kristen L. Streater

See Also: Slavery and the Civil War

Further Reading

Leonard, Elizabeth D. *All the Daring of the Soldier: Women of the Civil War Armies.* New York: W. W. Norton & Company, 1999.

Ryan, David, ed. *A Yankee Spy in Richmond: The Civil War Diary of "Crazy Bet" Van Lew.* Mechanicsburg, PA: Stackpole Books, 1996.

Varon, Elizabeth R. *Southern Lady, Yankee Spy: The True Story of Elizabeth Van Lew, a Union Agent in the Heart of the Confederacy.* New York: Oxford University Press, 2003.

Wakeman, Sarah Rosetta [Lyons Wakeman] (1843–1864)

Sarah Rosetta Wakeman was one of the several hundred women who fought in the American Civil War disguised as men. Enlisting in a regiment of New York volunteers on August 30, 1862, under the name Lyons Wakeman, she fought undetected for nearly two years until her death from dysentery on June 19, 1864. The collection of letters to her family she left behind provides unusual insight into the experience of a disguised woman soldier. Unlike narratives prepared for publication by other women soldiers, including Sarah Emma Edmonds and Loretta Janeta Velazquez, Wakeman's letters present a simple and unembellished account of her experience.

Born on January 16, 1843, in Afton, New York, Wakeman was the oldest of Harvey Anable and Emily Hale Wakeman's nine children. After some schooling and work as a domestic, she left home in early August 1862. Masquerading as a man under the name Lyons Wakeman, she became a boatman on the Chenango Canal, but enlisted in the One hundred Fifty-third Regiment of New York State volunteers on August 30, 1862. Although Wakeman's letters do not indicate clear motivations behind her decision to take on the role of a man, the motivations of women soldiers could include patriotism, a search for adventure, the desire to stay close to a loved one, or economic pressures. Her letters, however, attest to her enjoyment of the soldier's life. She wrote, "I like to be a soldier very much." She also clearly appreciated the independence gained through army life, writing, "I am as independent as a hog on ice."

Mustered into the Union army in October 1862, Wakeman's regiment served guard duty in Alexandria, Virginia, and in Washington, D.C. The One Hundred and Fifty-third Regiment joined Major General Nathaniel P. Bank's Red River campaign in Louisiana in February 1864, and in April Wakeman had her first engagement with the enemy. Falling ill with dysentery during the retreat to Alexandria after the failure of the campaign, Wakeman was admitted to the regimental hospital on May 3, 1864. By May 22, 1864, she had been sent to a larger hospital in New Orleans, Louisiana. Although she lingered for nearly a month before her death on June 19,

1864, medical personnel never recorded the secret of her sex on her records, and her headstone in the Chalmette National Cemetery of New Orleans reads simply "Lyons Wakeman."

Juliana Kuipers

See Also: Edmonds, Sarah Emma; Slavery and the Civil War; Van Lew, Elizabeth

Primary Document: 1861, Female Soldiers Discovered during the Civil War

Further Reading

Blanton, DeAnne, and Lauren M. Cook. *They Fought Like Demons: Women Soldiers in the American Civil War.* Baton Rouge, LA: Louisiana State University Press, 2002.

Burgess, Lauren Cook, ed. *An Uncommon Soldier: The Civil War Letters of Sarah Rosetta Wakeman, Alias Private Lyons Wakeman, 153rd Regiment, New York State Volunteers.* New York: Oxford University Press, 1995.

Leonard, Elizabeth D. *All the Daring of the Soldier: Women of the Civil War Armies.* New York: W. W. Norton & Company, 1999.

Walker, Mary Edwards (1832–1919)

Mary Edwards Walker was a Civil War surgeon, prisoner of war, and the only woman ever awarded a United States Medal of Honor for military service.

Born in New York on November 26, 1832, as the child of free thinking abolitionists, Mary Walker had an unconventional childhood. Her parents raised her and her sisters to be as independent as their only son. The intellectual atmosphere surrounding Mary during her youth became heightened as a result of the Seneca Falls convention on women's rights in 1848, the establishment of utopian reform communities, and the dress reform movement, as well as spiritualism, temperance, and abolitionism.

Mary attended Falley Seminary and taught at the Muretto Village a short distance from her home. Throughout his life, her father voraciously read medical books in search of a cure for his recurring illness.

Dr. Mary Edwards Walker was a surgeon during the Civil War and remains the only woman to receive a U.S. Medal of Honor for military service. Committed to women's rights and dress reform, she often wore male attire. (National Library of Medicine)

Years later, those same books prompted Walker to seriously consider medical school. Her parents prohibited the fashionable tight clothing, such as corsets, that restricted movement and circulation. They agreed with some medical professionals who believed that snug-fitting dress caused permanent and irreversible damage to women's bodies, sentiments Walker advocated her entire life. After acceptance to Syracuse Medical College in December 1853, Walker experimented with clothing design, permanently deciding on a uniform of shortened skirt with trousers underneath. Due to her choice of garments, Walker endured a life of ridicule, police arrests, and taunting by the press. She graduated with her medical degree in June 1855 and a few months later married classmate Dr. Albert Miller.

The marriage had a rocky start. Ignoring traditional wedding attire at the ceremony, Walker donned her usual uniform, had the word "obey" stricken from the vows, and preferred to hyphenate her last name, never acknowledging the title of Mrs. Miller. After a few years of marriage and a shared medical practice, rumors of Albert's infidelities reached Mary; he confessed after she confronted him. Although she left him and set up her own medical practice, she could not secure a divorce until after the Civil War.

Caught up in the dress reform movement in 1857, Walker published articles in *The Sibyl,* a fashion reform magazine. Additionally, she lectured about temperance and women's suffrage. Throughout her life she remained dedicated to women's rights, serving on boards, speaking, and confronting the U.S. Congress on an array of issues including pensions for Civil War nurses. Walker authored two books: *Hit* and *Unmasked, or the Science of Immortality.* Both covered a variety of topics including marriage, social diseases, and women's health issues. She headed to Washington, D.C., a few months after the war began to answer the Union call for physicians in October 1861.

Holding her MD degree, Mary Walker sought a formal commission as a military surgeon when the Civil War broke out. When the federal government agreed to hire her as a nurse, Walker volunteered her services as a doctor instead. She initially served voluntarily as assistant surgeon for Dr. J. N. Green while she worked to secure a paid commission from the Union army. As assistant surgeon, she met ambulances, prescribed medications, made diagnoses, and administered treatment. Walker left Washington in January 1862 to attend medical classes, but in November she raced to Virginia to help General Ambrose Burnside and his troops. After escorting sick soldiers by rail to Washington, she headed for Fredericksburg to help in the field. In Washington, she established free lodging for women looking for wounded loved ones, escorted mortally wounded soldiers to their homes, searched for missing soldiers, and advocated against amputation when she deemed it unnecessary.

In January 1864, Walker received an official appointment to the Fifty-second Ohio Volunteer Infantry under General George H. Thomas at Gordon's Mills. On April 10, 1864, she was taken prisoner of war and incarcerated in Castle Thunder Prison for four months. Then, in October 1864, she obtained an official contract as acting assistant surgeon, U.S. Army. She served the rest of the war in a female military prison in Louisville. On January 24, 1866, Mary received the Congressional Medal of Honor from President Andrew Johnson for merito-rious service, but the decoration was later rescinded by the United States Congress. Walker unsuccessfully petitioned Congress for reinstatement of the medal but failed. Refusing to return the award as requested, she defiantly wore the medal until her death on February 21, 1919. Congress reinstated Walker's medal posthumously on June 10, 1950.

Adriana G. Schroeder

See Also: Barton, Clara; Dress Reform; Hasbrouck, Lydia Sayer; Seneca Falls Convention; *The Sibyl*; Slavery and the Civil War

Primary Document: 1867, Support for Female Physicians

Further Reading

Graf, Mercedes. *A Woman of Honor: Dr. Mary E. Walker and the Civil War.* Gettysburg, PA: Thomas Publica-tions, 2001.

Harrison, Sharon M. *Dr. Mary Walker: An American Radi-cal, 1832–1919.* New Brunswick, NJ: Rutgers Univer-sity Press, 2009.

Mattingly, Carol. *Appropriate[ing] Dress: Women's Rhe-torical Style Women's in Nineteenth-Century America.* Carbondale: Southern Illinois University Press, 2002.

Mikaelian, Allen, and Mike Wallace. *Medal of Honor: Profiles of America's Military Heroes from the Civil War to the Present.* New York: Hyperion, 2003.

Walker, Dale L. *Mary Edwards Walker: Above and Be-yond.* New York: Macmillan, 2005.

Ward, Nancy (ca. 1738–1822)

Nancy Ward was named Nanye'hi at birth, and she be-came one of the most influential Cherokee women in early America. She was raised in eastern Tennessee, where her early life was like that of any other Cherokee girl. In her late teens she married Kingfisher, a Cherokee warrior with whom she had two children. The action that first brought her renown occurred when she accompa-nied Kingfisher to the 1755 Battle of Taliwa against the Creek Indians, long-standing enemies of the Cherokee. Nanye'hi took cover behind a log and helped Kingfisher reload his rifle. When he was killed beside her, she took up his rifle and rallied other warriors to help rout the Creek. The Cherokees won the battle, and Nanye'hi was given the title "Beloved Woman," a position of great honor reserved for heroic women.

In her capacity as Beloved Woman, Nanye'hi was al-lowed to sit with and vote as part of the General Council of Chiefs. It was believed that the Great Spirit used Be-loved Women to communicate his message. Nanye'hi was given the authority to speak at council, even though her messages were not always heeded.

In the late 1750s Nanye'hi married a white trader named Bryant Ward and Anglicized her name to Nancy Ward. They had one child, Elizabeth, before Bryant re-turned to live in white society. The Wards had a cu-rious relationship. Their marriage endured only a few years, but they remained friendly for the rest of their lives. Even after Bryant Ward remarried, this time to a white woman, Nancy was known to spend extended pe-riods of time visiting the couple in South Carolina. She maintained friendships within the white community in both Tennessee and South Carolina, which had impor-tant implications during the Revolutionary War.

The Cherokees, in tandem with most other Native American tribes, sided with the British during the Rev-olution, but Nancy Ward sided with the patriots. In 1776 she passed information to John Sevier, a leader of the Tennessee militia, warning of an impending Cherokee–British attack. Sevier was able to head off the brunt of the attack, but Mrs. Lydia Bean was taken captive by the Cherokees. When Mrs. Bean refused to reveal condi-tions within the settlers' fort, she was tied to a stake and condemned to be burned alive. Ward, in her capacity of Beloved Woman, had been given power of life or death over prisoners of war. She arrived in camp just as the flames had been lit and rescued Mrs. Bean from the fire. In gratitude, Lydia Bean taught Ward the art of making cheese and butter. Ward later became the first Cherokee person to own a herd of cattle, and she profited greatly from this skill.

Over the years Nancy Ward passed other messages to the patriots regarding British and Indian raids. Vari-ous theories have been proposed for her actions. Most likely, Ward believed the patriots would be victorious and the Cherokee people would benefit from her alli-ance. Her intelligence work was not common knowl-edge, and if the patriots' cause failed, Ward would not be punished. If the British won, the Cherokees would reap the rewards for their British alliance. When the tide turned in favor of the patriots, Colonel William Chris-tian led a series of retaliatory raids against Cherokee villages. Out of respect for Ward, her home village of Chote was left untouched.

Following the Revolution, Nancy Ward retained her position of prestige within the Cherokee community. She was a spokeswoman for peace at a 1781 meeting between Cherokee and U.S. representatives. She pre-sented the diplomats with a string of beads, which she called a "chain of friendship." Ward eventually opened an inn alongside the Ocoee River and became a semilegendary figure during her own lifetime. She died in 1822, and witnesses at her death swore they saw a light rise from her body and flutter toward her ancestral home of Chote.

The Nancy Ward legend was memorialized in books, including Theodore Roosevelt's *The Winning of the West* (1891) and E. Sterling King's highly romantic novel *The Wild Rose of the Cherokee* (1895).

Dorothy A. Mays

See Also: The American Revolution; Interracial Marriage and Sex (18th Century)

Primary Documents: 1781–1821, Letters and Petitions on Cherokee Removal; 1830, Ohio Women Petition against Indian Removal

Further Reading

Carney, Virginia Moore. *Cherokee Women: Cultural Persistence in Their Letters and Speeches.* Knoxville: University of Tennessee, 2005.

Perdue, Theda. *Cherokee Women: Gender and Culture Change, 1700–1835.* Lincoln: University of Nebraska, 1998.

Perdue, Theda. "Nancy Ward (1738?–1822)." In *Portraits of American Women: from Settlement to the Present,* edited by G. J. Barker-Benfield and Catherine Clinton, 83–100. New York: Oxford University Press, 1998.

Mercy Otis Warren wrote about politics and history during the American Revolutionary period. (Museum of Fine Arts, Boston, Massachusetts, USA/Bequest of Winslow Warren/The Bridgeman Art Library)

Warren, Mercy Otis (1728–1814)

Mercy Otis Warren lived amidst the leaders and opinion shapers of the American Revolution. To a large extent, her own writing helped compel fence-sitters to take a stand during the turbulent years of revolution.

Mercy Otis was born into a prosperous farming family in Barnstable, Massachusetts. Although she had no formal education, she was surrounded by highly intellectual friends and neighbors and had access to her father's excellent library. A college education for a woman was unheard of at the time, but as her brothers prepared for entrance into Harvard, Mercy read the same classical texts as though she herself were preparing to enter school. In 1754, the 26-year-old Mercy Otis married James Warren, a wealthy farmer and aspiring politician who shared her family's radical Whig political beliefs. The Warren marriage was a love match, as evidenced by the affectionate letters written throughout their 54-year marriage.

Mercy and James Warren were passionately interested in politics. They loathed the concept of a monarchy and a privileged class. They eagerly embraced revolutionary doctrines and were at the forefront of radical Boston political action. Mercy's eldest brother, James Otis, coined the famous phrase, "Taxation without representation is tyranny." Her neighbors were John and Abigail Adams. She counted Alexander Hamilton among her close personal friends. In this environment, it is not surprising that Mercy Otis Warren drank deeply from the well of revolutionary propaganda. By the early 1770s, she had become one of the Revolution's most articulate public voices.

The Adulateur: A Tragedy As It Is Now Acted in Upper Servia (1773) was Warren's first publication to skewer royalist policies. It was published anonymously in serial form in the radical newspaper the *Massachusetts Spy.* The publication was so popular she released it in an expanded version in pamphlet form. The piece was written in the form of a play, and the lead character, Rapatio, is a clear personification of Massachusetts's hated governor, Thomas Hutchinson. Rapatio is depicted as a corrupt force eager to bleed the colony white in order to enrich himself. The outraged patriots Brutus (modeled after Mercy's brother James) and Cassius (Sam Adams) urge their fellow citizens to "force a way to freedom." The play was wordy and clearly never intended for public performance, but as propaganda, it had value. A sequel, *The Defeat,* was published the following year, featuring many of the same characters.

Following the Boston Tea Party in December 1773, Warren acted on John Adams's advice and memorialized the event in the poem "The Squabble of the Sea Nymphs." Other political poems followed, such as one appearing in the *Royal American Magazine,* in which she castigated ladies who refused to forgo imported luxuries. Her criticism of loyalist women grew harsher in her 1779 play, *The Motley Assembly.* Characters such as Mrs. Flourish and Miss Turncoat flirt with British officers, exposing themselves as provincial Anglophiles who are easily dazzled by fancy uniforms and effeminate manners.

The fervor of revolution gave Mercy Warren entrée into the highest political circles of the patriots' cause. Following the successful conclusion of the war, her radical beliefs were no longer as popular. Warren and her husband were accused of supporting Shays Rebellion (1786–1787), an uprising in Massachusetts when rural farmers complained of high taxes. More serious was the Warrens' opposition to the ratification of the U.S. Constitution. The Warrens believed government should remain as small and local as possible, and the proposed Constitution smacked too much of an all-powerful distant government that had little concern for the common man. The long friendship between the Warrens and the Adamses cracked under the pressure of political differences. Whereas John and Abigail Adams were revolted by the excesses of the French Revolution, the Warrens believed it was an expression of true democracy.

The conclusion of the American Revolution gave Warren an opportunity for a new style of writing. She immediately embarked on writing a history of both the war and the creation of the new government. Although the work was not published until 1805, the three-volume *History of the Rise, Progress, and Termination of the American Revolution* was a remarkable work because of the insight Warren provides into the leading figures of the patriotic cause, many of whom she counted as personal friends. The book furthered her rift with John Adams, who had recently completed his term as president. Warren makes it clear she disapproved of Adams's Federalist tendencies, believing him to have lost faith in genuine democracy. She wrote that she was reluctant to criticize her old friend, but felt it was her moral obligation to alert the public to the danger of encroaching federalism.

James Warren died in 1808, leaving Mercy an 80-year-old widow. Remarkably, it was not too late for her to repair her friendship with the Adamses. James had been the most zealous in his condemnation of John Adams, and without him, Mercy was able to extend the hand of reconciliation and friendship.

Not all of Mercy Warren's writings were political. Some of her poems were deeply personal reflections on her family and religion. Aspects of Puritanical guilt sometimes underlay her writing. She struggled to maintain her faith in God and feared that she placed her love of her husband and children before her devotion to God.

A notable writer, opinion maker, and mother, Mercy Warren's life was remarkably full, but marred with tragedy. Prior to the Revolution, her adored brother, James, had been savagely beaten for his political views and never fully recovered. His head injuries resulted in prolonged periods of insanity, through which Warren nursed him until his death in 1783. Three of her five sons died in early adulthood, and her son James suffered severe physical and emotional problems. Her writing on the history of the Revolution was repeatedly delayed as she wrestled with bouts of blindness and sank into depression following the death of her sons—Winslow in 1791 and George in 1800.

Dorothy A. Mays

See Also: The American Revolution; The Constitution and Women; Murray, Judith Sargent

Further Reading

Davies, Kate. *Catharine Macaulay and Mercy Otis Warren: The Revolutionary Atlantic and the Politics of Gender.* New York: Oxford University Press, 2005.

Richards, Jeffrey H. *Mercy Otis Warren.* New York: Twayne, 1995.

Stuart, Nancy Rubin. *The Muse of the Revolution: The Secret Pen of Mercy Otis Warren and the Founding of a Nation.* Boston, MA: Beacon Press, 2009.

Zagarri, Rosemarie. *A Woman's Dilemma: Mercy Otis Warren and the American Revolution.* Wheeling, IL: Harlan Davidson, 1995.

Weld, Angelina Grimké. See Grimké Weld, Angelina

Wheatley, Phillis (1753–1784)

Phillis Wheatley was one of America's first African American female poets. She was born in Senegal, Africa. At the age of seven, she was sold in a slave market. John and Susannah Wheatley of Boston bought her as a household servant and as an attendant for Susannah. They treated her as a member of the family, and she was raised with the Wheatleys' other two children. Mary, the Wheatleys' daughter, took it upon herself to teach Phillis how to read and write English. Phillis surprised everyone by her quick and sharp intellect. By the time she was 12, Phillis was reading Greek and Latin classics, and passages from the Bible. By 14, she had become a poet. She had some minor household duties, but was free to write whenever inspiration struck.

The Wheatleys introduced Phillis to the Boston Literary Circle and she soon became a literary sensation.

Phillis Wheatley, born in Africa and brought to America as a slave, became an accomplished poet in Boston and travelled to London to publish her work. (Library of Congress)

Through this literary and theological circle, Wheatley was exposed to a wide variety of books and religious texts. Her poetry is clearly influenced by the Scriptures. Major English poets, Milton, Pope, and Gray also exerted a strong influence on her verse. Although she was free to write anything that she wanted, Wheatley was frequently called upon to write poems for special occasions. Many of her elegiac poems were borne out of such requests. Her first poem was published in the *Newport Mercury* newspaper in 1767. In 1770, she wrote a poetic elegy for the popular Rev. George Whitefield. Although this elegy made her an overnight sensation in Boston, Phillis and the Wheatleys were unable to get her poems published in Boston. About the same time, Countess Selina of Huntington invited Wheatley to London to assist her in the publication of her poems.

In 1773, thirty-nine of Wheatley's poems were published as *Poems on Various Subjects, Religious and Moral*. The governor of Massachusetts, her master John Wheatley, and dozens of other clergymen and dignitaries from Boston wrote a signed letter to the public vouching the text as Wheatley's original work. In addition to the Wheatleys and Countess Selina, Obour Tanner, a former slave who made it through the middle passage journey with Wheatley, was also one of the strong supporters of her poetry.

Eventually, Wheatley returned to America to take care of ailing Mrs. Wheatley. Back in America, she was rewarded—perhaps her greatest gift, with freedom from slavery. Mrs. Wheatley died in 1774. The Revolutionary War changed Wheatley's life quite dramatically. Mr. Wheatley and his daughter Mary died in 1778. Soon afterward Wheatley married John Peters, a free man from Boston. Due to either a lack of personal qualities, or racial prejudices and the lack of opportunities, John Peters was unsuccessful as businessman and was unable to support his wife and their children. They moved briefly to Wilmington, Massachusetts. Two of their children died during this period. Wheatley was able to publish a few poems during this period; a few were published as pamphlets.

In 1776, while her owner was still alive, Wheatley wrote a poem to George Washington, praising his appointment as commander of the Continental Army, and it was well received. After her marriage, she addressed several other poems to George Washington. She sent them to him, but he never responded again. Wheatley was a strong supporter of independence during the Revolutionary War. She felt that the issue of slavery separated whites from true heroism. Eventually John Peters deserted Wheatley, and, to support herself and her surviving child, she took a job as a maid in a boardinghouse. She died on December 5, 1784; just hours later, her surviving child also died.

Phillis Wheatley displays a classical quality and restrained emotion in her poetry. Christianity was a very important theme in Wheatley's poetry. Her first published poem, about two soldiers who barely escaped drowning, demonstrates Wheatley's Christian spirituality. The poem states that the soldiers were saved by the grace of God alone. Most of her poems are occasional pieces, written on the death of some notable person or on some special occasion. Wheatley uses classical mythology and ancient history as allusive devices. She maintains that people of all races need salvation.

One example of this is Wheatley's most anthologized poem: "On Being Brought from Africa." On the surface, this poem seems like an enthusiastic response of a sincere convert. But later in the poem Wheatley expresses that, according to the Christian message, God makes no distinctions between blacks and whites, and that all believers are promised redemption. This was a subtle but powerful message against prevailing racism. She comments on her being brought from her *pagan* land to the *Saviour* and to *redemption* by *mercy*. She thus turns her kidnapping and enslavement into a positive experience, an act of mercy, an act willed by God. She thus denies any power to the people who kidnapped and sold her. The choice of the word *benighted* is also an interesting one: it means, "overtaken by night or darkness." Metaphorically, it means "being in a state of moral or intellectual darkness."

Thus, Wheatley equates her skin color with her original state of ignorance of Christian redemption. She describes her race as *sable*. Sable is very valuable and desirable. This word is directly in contradiction with the phrase *diabolic die* used in the next line. Here she is able to make the readers question their belief that slaves are an inferior race. She uses the verb *remember* in the form of a direct command, thus, assuming the role of a teacher or a preacher.

The first poem in Wheatley's published collection is "To Mæcenas." She invokes the male muse to grant her permission to speak. Wheatley addresses her muse as *sire*. Mæcenas lived in 70 bc and was a friend of the emperor Augustus. The fact that Wheatley chooses to invoke the wealthy, white male Roman as her muse is important. She sees herself as helpless without the white male master and muse. Only after obtaining permission, can she speak her mind. She thus gains power by subjugating herself to the forces stronger than hers.

The historical significance of Phillis Wheatley as one of the first African American woman poets sometimes overshadows her poetical achievements. From the beginning, Wheatley had a bifurcated audience. The signatories of her first volume of poetry assured the readers that *Poems on Various Subjects* was indeed "written by Phillis, a young Negro Girl, who was but a few years since, brought an uncultivated Barbarian from Africa." When Wheatley arrived in Boston after the publication of her book, the *Boston Gazette,* the newspaper of revolutionary, lauded the young slave woman as "the extraordinary Poetical Genius."

Regarding the quality of her poetry, two respected people of the time had two entirely opposite opinions. Voltaire announced that her poetry is the proof of the facts that: the genius exists in all parts of the world, and the *perfectibility of the Negroes*. Thomas Jefferson on the other hand declared that her poetry proved that the Negroes lacked imagination and her poetry was "dull, tasteless, and anomalous."

Pratibha Kelapure

See Also: The American Revolution; Jacobs, Harriet

Further Reading

Erkkila, Betsy. *Mixed Bloods and Other Crosses: Rethinking American Literature from the Revolution to the Culture Wars.* Philadelphia: University of Pennsylvania Press, 2004.

Gates, Henry Louis, Jr. *The Trials of Phillis Wheatley: America's First Black Poet and Encounters with the Founding Fathers.* New York: Basic Civitas Books, 2003.

Robinson, William H. *Critical Essays on Phillis Wheatley.* Boston, MA: G. K. Hall, 1982.

Shields, John C., ed. "Phillis Wheatley's Struggle for Freedom in Her Poetry and Prose." In *The Collected Works of Phillis Wheatley.* New York: Oxford University Press, 1988.

Widowhood

Beyond the psychological stress associated with losing a spouse, early American women often faced the possibility of severe economic crisis upon the death of the family breadwinner. Most of the income in early America was generated through manual labor. Whether through farming, building, or manufacture, work usually depended on the physical strength of the head of the household. If a man in the prime of his life died, it is possible his widow would be unable to carry on his work. Law dictated that a widow was entitled to at least one-third of her husband's estate, although in practice husbands often gave more than the law required. Known as a dower right, or a "widow's thirds," this was to protect a widow from becoming a public charge or allowing greedy children means of getting control of the entire estate.

The severity of the economic consequences of widowhood was often dictated by the age at which a woman was widowed. If she was under age 30, her likelihood of remarriage was high. Older women often had sons mature enough to fill the deceased father's shoes. Women in their middle years were most likely to find themselves in a difficult position. They were too young to have accumulated a substantial estate, too old to easily attract a new husband, and with children not yet ready to assume gainful employment. Most widowed women had four options for supporting themselves and children: gainful employment, remarriage, dependence on kin, or reliance on charitable assistance.

Gainful employment was difficult, though not impossible, for a woman. In the 17th and early 18th centuries, division of labor between the sexes was not as pronounced as it would come to be in later times. Women hoed fields, tended crops and farm animals, and assisted with harvesting and preserving produce. They supplemented the family income by selling products such as cheese, candles, soap, or spun wool. Such ventures were merely supplemental to the family income and would never have been sufficient to support a household. Although virtually all women in colonial America worked, they were rarely paid wages that were sufficient to support a family. Studies indicate that women who received wages for work performed outside of the home were generally paid between 30 and 40 percent of a man's average wage.

Although it is unlikely that a sole woman would have been able to operate a farm without the assistance of an adult male, the widows of shopkeepers, printers, and craftsmen were often able to maintain the family business. Such women were usually middle class and living in an urban area. Widows became gunsmiths, leather tanners, shopkeepers, upholsterers, printers, and shoemakers. Skilled labor such as this would have taken years to learn and could not have been suddenly initiated upon the death of a husband. It is likely these women spent years closely associated with the daily operations of the shop. Women who inherited and were capable of operating such businesses were in the minority. Because most families were supported by agriculture, most widows were in working-class, rural communities. Such women would have to depend on the manual labor of sons, brothers, or extended kin to keep the farms operational.

Dependence on kin usually meant dependence on children. Because so much of a husband's estate was typically bound up in a family farm or business, it was often difficult to separate a portion for the support of the widow. Although the farm might be left to an oldest son, a certain number of rooms or a percentage of the annual harvest were typically set aside for the maintenance of the widow. In cases where children were not old enough to assume responsibility for the family business, a woman would either have to serve as a steward until her children came of age or turn to a trusted neighbor or relative for assistance.

Many women were confronted with the complex chore of serving as executor of their husband's will. This involved supervising the inventory of the estate, settling debts, and distributing property. Mary Willing Byrd (1740–1814) suffered an especially heavy burden. Her husband, William Byrd III, had committed suicide in the face of a mountain of debt. Byrd's plantations and investments had been immense, but his financial obligations were threatening to obliterate the fortune of one of Virginia's leading families. While caring for her eight young children, Mary Byrd took careful inventory of what could be sold or made more profitable. It took three years and the sale of most of the outlying property, but she was able to save the famous Byrd estate.

Remarriage was surprisingly rare for widows. The exception to this rule was in the early decades of settlement or in frontier areas where women were scarce. After the sex ratio came into balance in the 18th century, only about one-third of widowed women remarried. Those who did remarry spent an average of five years in widowhood before finding another husband. The age at which a woman was widowed played a large role in her likelihood of remarriage. Eighty percent of those widowed before age 30 remarried, whereas about half of the women widowed between 30 and 39 eventually remarried. Those widowed at later ages almost never remarried.

Re-establishing a family unit was often necessary for the survival of the family, and there was little stigma associated with women who remarried within a few months of their widowhood. Regardless, statistics reveal that widows with no children were more likely to remarry than those who had children. This could be interpreted two ways: Either the presence of children made them less desirable to single men, or women who had children on the verge of becoming economically productive had no need of a new husband. Both scenarios were doubtlessly major factor determining choices and varied widely depending on the unique circumstances of each case.

By far the least desirable option for a woman was to depend on the charity of the colony or church. Not until the 20th century did the welfare state develop to the point at which it was a reliable safety net for women. A handful of widely scattered charitable institutions developed in the urban areas of colonial America. Reliance on charity was considered a shameful condition, believed to indicate laziness and moral weakness. Conditions at workhouses were made deliberately bleak in order to discourage the poor from taking advantage of charity. Poorhouses were intended only for adults, with separate facilities for destitute children and orphans. The lack of resources for women who wished to live with their children further discouraged widows from turning to public help.

Dorothy A. Mays

See Also: The American Revolution; Coverture; Divorce (before the Civil War); *Feme Sole* and *Feme Sole* Trader Status; Legal Status of Women (18th Century)

Further Reading

Conger, Vivian Bruce. *The Widow's Might: Widowhood and Gender in Early British America.* New York: New York University Press, 2009.

Smith, Daniel Scott. "Inheritance and Social History of Early American Women." In *Women in the Age of the American Revolution,* edited by Ronald Hoffman and Peter J. Albert. Charlottesville: University Press of Virginia, 1989.

Wilson, Lisa. *Life after Death: Widows in Pennsylvania, 1750–1850.* Philadelphia, PA: Temple University Press, 1992.

Wulf, Karin. *Not All Wives: Women of Colonial Philadelphia.* Ithaca, NY: Cornell University Press, 2000.

Willard, Emma Hart (1787–1870)

In the history of women's education in the United States, Emma Willard was one of the first to advocate for the establishment of high schools for girls and women's colleges. She also promoted the idea of coeducational colleges and universities in a wider vision of women's improved social responsibilities through education, although she saw these as being confined primarily to the separate domestic sphere.

Emma Willard was a pioneer in women's education and founded the highly successful Troy Female Seminary in 1821. (Cirker, Hayward and Blanche Cirker, eds., *Dictionary of American Portraits,* 1967)

Willard was one of 17 children born on a farm in Berlin, Connecticut. In 1802–1803 Emma Hart studied at the nearby Berlin Academy and began teaching local children while continuing with her own program of self-study. In 1807 she secured an appointment as principal of a girls' academy at Middlebury, Vermont, but left in 1809 upon her marriage to Dr. John Willard.

In 1814 Willard opened a boarding school, Middlebury Female Seminary, in her own home in an attempt to supplement her husband's financial losses. She boldly offered a curriculum that included subjects never taught girls in school, such as philosophy, geometry, mathematics, and even anatomy—all intended to better prepare them for a college education. But she encountered difficulty in obtaining funding for the school and petitioned the state legislature for support in the form of "An Address to the Public, Particularly to the Members of the Legislature of New York, Proposing a Plan for Improving Female Education" (published in 1819 at her own expense), which was read on her behalf (it was socially unacceptable for Willard to read it herself). In the address, she argued that a nation's prosperity rested in part on the good character of its citizens, especially its mothers. She therefore criticized the exclusivity of private education and called for funding from the state to establish public girls' schools and promote higher standards in women's education, which would in turn enable women to contribute to the moral reform of society. Although her proposal was rejected, Willard's ideals impressed Governor De Witt Clinton, who suggested she transfer her school to Waterford, New York. She did so in 1819 but was unable to raise funding there either. Eventually, in 1821, thanks to taxes raised by local residents of Troy and donations from patrons, Willard was able to build Troy Female Seminary (which in 1895 became the Emma Willard School and survives to this day). In 1825, John Willard, Emma Hart Willard's husband, died.

As the first women's high school in the United States, with 300 students by 1831, Troy became the prototype for other women's establishments, such as Mary Lyon's Holyoke Seminary in Massachusetts, and a training ground for many influential teachers. Willard introduced progressive subjects such as gymnastics, improved the methodology of teaching geography and history, and wrote numerous textbooks, including the popular *Last Leaves of American History* (1849), which ran into several editions.

In 1830 Willard went to Europe. At this time, she published poetry, including her famous poem "Rocked in the Cradle of the Deep," and her *Journal and Letters from France and Great Britain* (1833). She used some of her royalties to found a training school for teachers in Athens, Greece, in 1833. Back in the United States, she established the Willard Association for the Mutual Improvement of Female Teachers to encourage further recruitment of women to the profession.

In 1838 Willard retired from Troy, leaving her son and daughter-in-law to run the seminary. A brief second marriage in 1838 to the spendthrift Christopher Yates ended in divorce in 1843. She continued to travel and lecture on equal opportunities for women teachers and joined educator Henry Barnard in calling for improvements to public schools. During 1845–1847, Willard is said to have traveled 8,000 miles in the South and West of the United States in her crusade to encourage improvements to standards of education, school buildings, and the salaries of women teachers. In 1854 she was one of only two delegates representing the United States at the World's Educational Convention in London.

Never a suffragist and having otherwise conservative views, Willard nevertheless supported women's right to their own property and to financial independence. But for her the essential building blocks of social progress for women lay in their education, thus ensuring they would be suitably equipped to be the moral guardians of better generations of children.

Helen Rappaport

See Also: Beecher, Catharine; Education of Women (before the Civil War); Oberlin College; Republican Motherhood

Primary Documents: 1815, The Risks of Marrying; 1819, "A Plan for Improving Female Education"; 1856–1857, Writings on Women's Education

Further Reading

Edwards, June. *Women in American Education, 1820–1955: The Female Force and Education Reform.* Wesport, CT: Greenwood, 2002.

Goodsell, Willystine, ed. *Pioneers of Women's Education in the United States.* New York: AMS, 1970.

Solomon, Barbara Miller. *In the Company of Educated Women: A History of Women and Higher Education in America.* New Haven, CT: Yale University Press, 1985.

Wittenmyer, Annie Turner (1827–1900)

Involved in temperance, education reform, and benevolent work, Annie Turner Wittenmyer also served as a tireless advocate for soldiers' aid and relief during and after the Civil War. Utilizing her political, administrative, and organizational skills, she fought sexism and local politicians to improve the situations of innumerable Americans.

Sarah Ann Turner was born August 26, 1827, in Sandy Springs, Ohio, to John G. and Elizabeth Smith Turner. In 1847, she married merchant William Wittenmyer and three years later moved to Keokuk, Iowa. Of the couple's four children, only one, Charles Albert, survived childhood. In March 1853, Wittenmyer began her life of benevolence, founding the first tuition-free school for underprivileged children. Because her parents had ensured that she received an education, she adamantly insisted other children should have the opportunity. Her husband William's death in 1860 left Annie a single mother.

When the Civil War began, Wittenmyer joined the Union war effort as a nurse in the Estes House, a hotel converted to a hospital. The unsanitary conditions, inadequate food, and psychological turmoil the soldiers suffered horrified her. In 1861 the Keokuk Ladies' Soldiers' Aid Society (KLSAS) elected her corresponding secretary. In that capacity she visited the hospitals in her region to determine their needs, gathered and distributed supplies, secured transportation for the wounded, and helped organize a coalition of women's groups. Her work was often impeded by the Iowa branch of the United States Sanitary Commission (USSC), run by local men with connections to state politicians. Tensions rose between the KLSAS and the USSC as both fought for relationships with women's groups in Iowa. To circumvent these problems, Wittenmyer eventually accepted a salaried position as one of the Iowa State sanitary agents. Once the state legislature approved her position in September 1862, she and the KLSAS gained official status. As a sanitary agent, she continued collecting and distributing food, medicine, bandages, clothing, and beds.

Despite working together, the KLSAS and the USSC continued to spar. Wittenmyer and the other women of the KLSAS argued that as women they were morally and emotionally better equipped for the work and far better organized than the USSC men. The KLSAS publicly challenged the Iowa Sanitary Commission, characterizing it as incompetent at best. The two groups eventually combined into the Iowa Sanitary Commission. Wittenmyer remained a sanitary agent for about six months but resigned in May 1864 to devote her energies elsewhere.

Wittenmyer gained nationwide fame through her establishment of over 100 Special Diet Kitchens in Union army hospitals. A visit to her brother, a patient in one of the hospitals, revealed to Wittenmyer the inedible and inappropriate food fed to patients. She hoped to reorganize kitchens so that each patient would receive individualized doctor-prescribed menus, suitable for that patient's circumstances. Wittenmyer's model helped save countless lives as the wounded and ill began receiving healthier, more nutritious, and better tasting food. At her request, the United States Christian Commission agreed to help fund and organize these revolutionary kitchens, still utilized today. Wittenmyer hired the staff, appointed managers, and supervised the 200 paid women working in the kitchens.

Wittenmyer had other concerns as well. She began organizing orphanages in Iowa for Union soldiers' children in the fall of 1863, with the first one opening in 1864. In 1865 she applied to Congress for and received barracks in Davenport, Iowa, where the Iowa Soldiers' Orphans' Home was built later that year. (It remained in existence until 1975, by which time it had become a residential facility for troubled youth with special needs.)

During the next three decades, Wittenmyer published several books and articles, and she served as editor for *Home and Country*.

Wittenmyer is perhaps best known as the founder and first president of the Woman's Christian Temperance Union, organized in 1874. In 1889 she moved to Pennsylvania and was elected president of the Woman's Relief Work of the Grand Army of the Republic, a national organization dedicated to helping former Union hospital workers obtain homes and pensions. She helped ensure the passage of the Army Nurses Pension Law in 1892.

Annie Wittenmyer died on February 2, 1900. She was buried in Edgewood Cemetery in Sanatogo, Pennsylvania.

Paula Katherine Hinton

See Also: Temperance Movement; United States Sanitary Commission; Woman's Christian Temperance Union (Vol. 2); Willard, Frances (Vol. 2)

Further Reading

Holland, Mary Gardner. *Our Army Nurses: Stories from Women in the Civil War*. Roseville, MN: Edinborough Press, 1998.

Leonard, Elizabeth D. *Yankee Women: Gender Battles in the Civil War*. New York: W. W. Norton & Company, 1994.

Murdock, Catherine Gilbert. *Domesticating Drink: Women, Men, and Alcohol in America, 1870–1940*. Baltimore, MD: Johns Hopkins University Press, 1998.

Schultz, Jane E. *Women at the Front: Hospital Workers in Civil War America*. Chapel Hill: University of North Carolina Press, 2004.

Wollstonecraft, Mary (1759–1797)

Educator, writer, social critic, and political activist, Mary Wollstonecraft was born on April 27, 1759, in London, England. While still a young woman, Wollstonecraft, two of her sisters, and Wollstonecraft's childhood friend, Fanny, opened their own school for the education of young women in Newington, England. It was there she met famous Dissenter, the Reverend Richard Price, and through him, her patron and future publisher, Joseph Johnson. Johnson provided Wollstonecraft with an advance on her first book, *Thoughts on the Education of Daughters* (1787) and offered her employment as a reviewer and editorial assistant for the *Analytic Review*. The next year she was able to write *Mary, a Fiction* (1788) and *Original Stories from Real Life* (1788), which would

English writer Mary Wollstonecraft promoted women's education and equality in her highly influential 1792 work, *A Vindication of the Rights of Woman*. (Library of Congress)

later be republished in 1796 with illustrations done by William Blake. Wollstonecraft's translation of Jacques Necker's *Of the Importance of Religious Opinions* from French was also published that same year (1788).

The year 1789 saw the publication of Wollstonecraft's first attempt at an anthology of writing specifically for women called *The Female Reader: Miscellaneous Pieces in Prose and Verse Selected from the Best Writers and Disposed under Proper Heads for the Improvement of Young Women*. A turning point in Wollstonecraft's career, she turned her pen toward political writing to defend the works of the Reverend Richard Price in response to the work of Edmund Burke, and in 1791 began work on what would be her most famous and lasting literary accomplishment, *A Vindication of the Rights of Woman with Strictures on Political and Moral Subjects*.

Thoroughly enmeshed in the political and literary activism of the day, in 1792, Mary Wollstonecraft traveled to France in the midst of the French Revolution during which a French King would be executed and the monarchy, the aristocracy, and the church overthrown. She

also fell in love with Gilbert Imlay, a Kentucky land speculator later employed by the U.S. embassy who became her lover as the two traveled through France.

At 35, she gave birth to a child she named Fanny in tribute to her friend Fanny who had died from childbirth. Her relationship with Imlay failed, and a distraught Wollstonecraft attempted suicide in both May and October 1775. A year later, Mary Wollstonecraft and William Godwin began their relationship. They were married in March 1797. Mary was four months pregnant with her second child, Mary Shelley, who would grow up to be the author of *Frankenstein* (1818) and the wife of Romantic poet, Percy Shelley. Wollstonecraft died from the complications of childbirth.

Wollstonecraft's influence on American women and the pursuit of women's rights in the United States was profound. From the time of its first publication in America (1792) to the point when American women were allowed to vote (1920), no fewer than eight editions of Wollstonecraft's book, *A Vindication of the Rights of Woman*, were published in the United States. American women's rights activists such as Quakers Lucretia Mott and Sarah Grimké encouraged later activists Elizabeth Cady Stanton and Susan B. Anthony to use Wollstonecraft's work to help articulate demands for the equality of women as part and parcel of their work for the abolitionist movement. Also influenced by Wollstonecraft's work was Margaret Fuller, contemporary of Henry David Thoreau and Ralph Waldo Emerson. Fuller discussed Wollstonecraft as part of her own call for civil rights in "The Great Lawsuit. Man *versus* Men. Woman *versus* Women" (1843).

In addition to her influence on the pursuit of civil and political rights for women in the United States, Wollstonecraft's influence remains strong in the field of 19th- and 20th-century feminist literary studies as well. Literary critics have examined the influence of Wollstonecraft's fiction; her cautionary tales depicting the plight of women and the potential dangers of both passion and motherhood in a world that denies women the right to control their own bodies. These themes and Wollstonecraft's death had an impact on the literary work of her youngest daughter, Mary Shelley, and on later feminist theories and writings about women, creativity, motherhood, and the body.

Darcy Zabel

See also: The American Revolution; Education of Women (before the Civil War); Fuller, Margaret; Grimké, Sarah; Mott, Lucretia; Murray, Judith Sargent; Republican Motherhood; Anthony, Susan B. (Vol. 2); Stanton, Elizabeth Cady (Vol. 2)

Further Reading

Botting, Eileen Hunt, and Christine Cary. "Wollstonecraft's Philosophical Impact on Nineteenth-Century American Women's Right Advocates." *American Journal of Political Science* 48.4 (2004): 707–722.

Mandell, Laura. "The First Women (Psycho)analysts, or The Friends of Feminist History." *Modern Language Quarterly* 65.1 (2004): 69–92.

Todd, Janet. *Mary Wollstonecraft: A Revolutionary Life.* London: Weidenfeld and Nicolson, 2000.

Tomaselli, Sylvana. "Mary Wollstonecraft." *Stanford Encyclopedia of Philosophy* (Winter 2012 Edition), edited by Edward N. Zalta. http://plato.stanford.edu/archives/win2012/entries/wollstonecraft. Accessed April 30, 2014.

Woman in the Nineteenth Century (1845)

Margaret Fuller's *Woman in the Nineteenth Century* was published in 1845, making it one of the earliest feminist treatises in the United States. Fuller began the work even earlier, however, as an 1843 essay entitled "The Great Lawsuit. Man *versus* Men. Woman *versus* Women."

"The Great Lawsuit" was published in the *Dial* magazine, a Transcendentalist literary journal which Fuller coedited with Ralph Waldo Emerson and to which she regularly contributed. Between 1843 and 1845 Fuller worked as a literary reviewer for the *New York Tribune* and expanded "The Great Lawsuit" into a longer and more reform-minded text as *Woman in the Nineteenth Century,* thus reaching a larger audience and helping lay the intellectual foundation for the emerging American women's rights movement.

In *Woman in the Nineteenth Century,* Fuller focused on the female struggle for self-development. Semiautobiographical at times, the text explored the cultural expectations for women, namely their duties in marriage, with women's own desire for a more public role. Fuller focused, in particular, on a woman's right to education and to pursuit of a vocation. These issues would be taken up by the women's rights movement at large, but Fuller's work was infused with more literary and philosophical themes and influences, and she drew her examples and arguments not from contemporary political or legal contexts but rather from mythology, religion, poetry, and philosophy. She was particularly influenced in her writings on ideal womanhood by contemporary thinkers such as German poet and philosopher Johann Wolfgang von Goethe and the Swedish mystic Emanuel Swedenborg. For example, she argued for equality in marriage, but she did so through the idealist–Transcendentalist view of harmony between the sexes as a goal for the betterment of humanity, rather than simply for legal rights. Likewise, her famous exhortation on women's employment—"I do not care what case you put; let them be sea-captains, if you will"—was more a vision of each individual's right to self-realization than a call for opening up of specific professions to women. These goals were not contradictory and Fuller's feminist theory arose from her own frustrations as a woman in the 19th century attempting to balance private expectations and a public identity and career; it was simply that Fuller's language and purpose were toward a broader philosophical ideal of equality rather than promoting a specific reform cause.

Indeed, Fuller's work predated the beginnings of an organized women's rights movement in the United States, which is generally dated to the convention organized by Elizabeth Cady Stanton and Lucretia Mott at Seneca Falls, New York, in 1848. What role Fuller might have taken in that movement will never be known since, by 1848, she had moved to Italy as a foreign correspondent for the *Tribune* and died in 1850 on her return home to the United States. The example of her own life, as much as her published writings, continued to influence and inspire the next generation of feminists. Women's rights leaders such as Stanton, Paulina Wright Davis, Caroline Dall, and Julia Ward Howe explicitly acknowledged Fuller's role in arguing for a woman's "right to think." Dall and Davis, especially, memorialized Fuller in the pages of their own women's rights paper, *The Una,* and in later histories of the Transcendentalist movement.

Tiffany K. Wayne

See Also: Dall, Caroline Healey; Davis, Paulina Kellogg Wright; Education of Women (before the Civil War); Farnham, Eliza; Fuller, Margaret; Howe, Julia Ward; *The Una*; Stanton, Elizabeth Cady (Vol. 2)

Further Reading

Bailey, Brigitte, Katheryn P. Viens, and Conrad Edick Wright, eds. *Margaret Fuller and Her Circles.* Lebanon: University of New Hampshire Press, 2012.

Capper, Charles. *Margaret Fuller: An American Romantic Life, vol. 2, The Public Years.* New York: Oxford University Press, 2007.

Urbanski, Marie Mitchell Olesen. *Margaret Fuller's Woman in the Nineteenth Century: A Literary Study of*

Form and Content, of Sources and Influences. Westport, CT: Greenwood Press, 1980.

Wayne, Tiffany K. *Woman Thinking: Feminism and Transcendentalism in Nineteenth-Century America.* Lanham, MD: Lexington Books, 2005.

"Woman Order" (General Order No. 28) (1862)

Union General Benjamin Franklin Butler issued General Order Number 28, his infamous "Woman Order," on May 15, 1862, in New Orleans, two weeks after Admiral David Farragut had taken the city and turned it over to Butler's administrative control. The order generated immediate controversy and threatened to topple respectable Southern ladies from their pedestal of protection and reduce their status to that of prostitutes if they continued to behave disrespectfully toward Union soldiers and officers. The threat implied by the order inflamed Confederate passions, garnered criticism from elsewhere in the Union and abroad, and earned the general lasting infamy throughout the South. In recent decades feminist authors have forged new interpretations of the Woman Order that suggest how the gender and class politics of the time made Butler's order effective and why it has achieved such lasting significance.

New Orleans's unrepentant and unruly rebel residents initially proved unwilling to submit to federal authority when troops occupied the city in late April 1862. Butler soon took matters in hand and later recalled that he quickly had the men of New Orleans completely under control. He was dismayed, however, to find that the city's women, especially those of the upper class, continued to abuse and disrespect his men. The behaviors that Butler and his troops found so galling included ladies exiting streetcars and leaving churches when officers or soldiers entered, teaching and encouraging children to sing Confederate songs, displaying or pinning small Confederate flags to their clothing, and choosing to walk in the middle of the streets or turning their backs to avoid acknowledging their occupiers. In a small number of cases, ladies also reportedly spat on officers or allowed their children to do so, and, in one outrageous incident, Butler reported that one of them dumped a "vessel" of "not very clean water" (possibly a chamber pot) on the head of Admiral David Farragut as he passed below her balcony.

To stem the tide of the females' disrespect, Butler created an order that brilliantly manipulated the South's existing gender and class ideologies while also taking advantage of the city's well-known reputation for harboring and tolerating large numbers of prostitutes. General Order Number 28 stated that, despite their courteous treatment of civilians, "the officers and soldiers of the United States have been subject to repeated insults from the women (calling themselves ladies) of New Orleans." As a result, "it is ordered that hereafter when any female shall, by word, gesture or movement, insult or show contempt for any officer or soldier of the United States, she shall be regarded and held liable to be treated as a woman of the town plying her avocation."

Butler's order cut right to the heart of both the class privilege accorded to and the gender expectations demanded from upright, respectable Southern ladies. Confederates outside New Orleans howled with indignation about the sexual threat they perceived in the Woman Order. Southern political leaders, ranging from Louisiana's exiled governor to President Jefferson Davis, took exception to the order in formal statements. Davis also placed a bounty on Butler's head and ordered his summary execution if he was ever captured. The predictable outrage in Confederate circles also spread to newspapers in France and England, where Butler's order was condemned on the floor of Parliament.

Butler denied that his order contained an implicit sexual threat and defended it in his autobiography, claiming that it was necessary in response to the treatment received by soldiers. He also claimed that the order did not lead to any arrests, but historical records indicate that at least two women were imprisoned for infractions covered by the order, most notably prominent Confederate sympathizer and diarist Eugenia Levy Phillips.

Butler continued to upset gender conventions throughout his occupation of New Orleans. He kept women in his figurative line of fire when he demanded that they, like male Confederates, sign loyalty oaths to stay in the city. Butler's offensiveness was not limited to ladies, nor was his administrative brilliance a match for his abrasiveness, inflexibility, and financial opportunism. Foreign consuls bristled at his insensitive treatment and complained to Washington. These complaints, accompanied by rumors that Butler was using his position to gain personal financial advantage, led to his dismissal and replacement by Nathaniel Banks in December 1862.

Alecia P. Long

See Also: Bread Riots; Slavery and the Civil War

Primary Document: 1862, A Northern Newspaper Supports Butler's Woman Order

Further Reading

Faust, Drew Gilpin. *Mothers of Invention: Women of the Slaveholding South in the American Civil War.* Chapel Hill: University of North Carolina Press, 1996.

Hearn, Chester. *When the Devil Came Down to Dixie: Ben Butler in New Orleans.* Baton Rouge: Louisiana State University Press, 1997.

Rable, George. " 'Missing in Action': Women of the Confederacy." In *Divided Houses: Gender and the Civil War,* edited by Catherine Clinton and Nina Silber, 134–146. New York: Oxford University Press, 1992.

Ryan, Mary P. *Civic Wars: Democracy and Public Life in the American City during the Nineteenth Century.* Berkeley: University of California Press, 1997.

Women's Magazines (18th and Early 19th Centuries)

The first American magazine for women, *The Lady's Magazine and Repository of Entertaining Knowledge* (1792–1793), was a novel venture in a volatile age. Even after the political and ideological changes of the American Revolution, women were not expected to engage in the public sphere as speakers. Yet restrictions on women's self-representation faced the incursions of a democratic culture: Liberalizing standards for public speech were rousing and inflecting public debate, and the literary marketplace was also diversifying, expanding public access to a widening range of discourse.

The over 100 "ladies' magazines" that were launched in America between 1790 and 1830 meant that women were anything but silent in the public realm. Print culture promised virtually revolutionary possibilities. Its democratic openness and participatory dynamics promised to subvert and to redress women's silence in the public sphere. Contributors made use of the early women's magazine, helping to raise the "woman question" and to put forward strategic possibilities for women's self-representation in the new American nation.

Three of the most successful early American women's periodicals were *The Lady's Magazine and Repository of Entertaining Knowledge* (Philadelphia, 1792–1793); the long-lived *Weekly Visitor or Ladies' Miscellany* (New York, 1802–1812); and the *American Ladies' Magazine* (Boston, 1828–1836), the periodical in which Sarah Josepha Hale, the trendsetting editor of the best-selling 19th-century women's magazine, *Godey's Lady's Book* (1830–1898), got her start in the business.

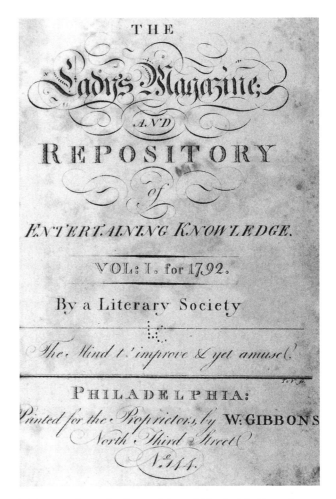

Title page from the first edition of *The Lady's Magazine, and Repository of Entertaining Knowledge*, December 1792. (Library of Congress)

Ironically, although early American women's magazines wanted women's words, their very democratic openness limited women's presence in their pages. The earliest women's magazines were often monopolized by male voices. The early American women's magazines, however, still operated as a female forum, providing a site of collaboration and group support for women writers and readers. And, they made available a space for experimental self-representation, constructing new possibilities for argumentation, authorial subjectivity, language, narrative and reader response.

Themes

Many apparently female-authored contributions discuss "feminine" interests such as matrimony and its ominously autonomous opposite, "spinsterhood"; seduction and its consequences; and female virtue, rightly defined. But these seemingly traditional themes sometimes raised radical questions about women's unequal status, about obedience, subservience and their limits. In the July 1792 issue of the *Ladies Magazine,* for example, the female author of "On Matrimonial Obedience" talks in public, legalistic terms about the ostensibly "private" matter of marriage, pursuing the argument that the partners in marriage ought to be equals: "The word obey, in the promise or vow to be made by the woman [is] very improper," she writes, "and ought not to be." Continuing, she explains why: "Obliging a woman to make a vow to obey their husbands [is] . . . obliging them to perjure themselves." The promise cannot be made by anyone, she asserts, without "reservations." Balancing a "feminine" language of self-restraint with the judicial concept of "perjury," the contributor repositions "masculine" and "feminine" values from the perspective of justice. The issue of "spinsterhood" in the magazines raised questions about the status of women from another angle: the lady as autonomous individual.

Gendered Genres

The understanding of the magazine as a nexus for the exchange of information largely controlled by participating readers explains why letters were so central to early American publications. Historically, the letter is a gendered genre, carrying particular meanings for women and men writers respectively. While women's letters might be dismissed as private, nonliterary, and emotional, prohibitions against women's writing and reading never included letters. The letter was perhaps the one genre that had always been available for women's use.

The "natural" affiliation of women and letter writing is affirmed in early American ladies magazines. Gibbons' *Ladies Magazine and Repository,* for example, highlighted the publication of readers' letters as "Specimens of Female Literature." Several magazines published letters as "models of female comportment." Over time, the letters section became a shorthand in some women's magazines for articles about culturally constituted "women's issues"; subjects such as virtue, marriage, motherhood, and "female character" are collected across monthly editions under the generic editorial earmark "Letters On . . ." The letter form allowed an allegedly private female author to present her "unladylike" outrage in a public forum for all the journal's readers to see.

For example, "From A Young Lady To Her Seducer," published in White's *Weekly Visitor* in April 1807, uses the intimacy of a letter to make angry accusations against "masculine" characteristics and cultural privileges: "Was it not sufficient that you added my name to the list of your infamous triumphs? . . . that you had ranked me among the daughters of wretchedness and ignomy?" she asks. "Were not these things sufficient," she presses, "without adding to them the baseness of publicly speaking of me in the streets, in language that a gentleman would not have used to the vilest wanton that ever breathed." The writer's list of grievances constitutes a public attack on a man who has violated her in public. "Weak, unhappy man! I am not ashamed of defeat," she declares.

This letter writer's righteous anger about male mistreatment sets up an important reversal that represents at least a rhetorical victory for the female point of view. The seducer may have "ruined" his abandoned mistress by male-authored public standards, but, in the context of the woman's letter, the seducer, rather than the person seduced, is seen to be weak, miserable, debased, and defeated. Such treatments of the issue of seduction set up critical authorial reversals that would have enormous ramifications for women's narratives in magazines and outside them in the decades to come. What's more, in the present, the abandoned lady is not alone. Eliza writes to the implied audience, readers of the *Visitor,* as much as to the intended addressee.

Gender, Genre, and the New Democratic Nation

Using the democratic openness and audience participation of the early American women's magazine, contributors explored strategies of self-representation amidst and against the silencing idioms of male authority and authorship. By revealing previously invisible angles, writing new subject positions and collaborating in the creation and critique of gender discourse, communities of women's magazine readers and writers began to envision new cultural positions and elaborate new stories for themselves. As women's magazine contributors began to write "Woman" from a position of dutiful silence into a discourse of virtuous presence moving into the 19th century, women began to constitute themselves as a distinct public in American life and letters.

Amy Beth Aronson

See Also: *Godey's Lady's Book*; Hale, Sarah Josepha

Further Reading

Cmeil, Kenneth. *Democratic Eloquence: The Fight over Popular Speech in Nineteenth Century America.* New York: William Morrow and Company, 1990.

Douglas, Ann. *The Feminization of American Culture.* New York: Anchor Press, 1988.

Goldsmith, Elizabeth C., ed. *Writing the Female Voice: Essays on Epistolary Literature.* Boston, MA: Northeastern University Press, 1989.

Okker, Patricia. *Our Sister Editors: Sarah J. Hale and the Tradition of Nineteenth-Century American Women Editors.* Athens: University of Georgia Press, 1995.

Shevelow, Kathryn. *Women and Print Culture: The Construction of Femininity in the Early Periodical.* New York: Routledge, 1989.

Tebbel, John, and Mary Ellen Zuckerman,. *The Magazine in America 1741–1990.* New York: Oxford University Press, 1991.

Tompkins, Jane. *Sensational Designs: The Culture Work of American Fiction 1790–1860.* New York: Oxford University Press, 1985.

Warner, Michael. *Letters of the Republic.* Cambridge, MA: Harvard University Press, 1990.

Working Women's Association

When Susan B. Anthony established the Working Women's Association (WWA) in September 1868, she hoped to encourage women to explore ways to increase their wages and to expand their opportunities for advancement in the trades. Equally important, she wanted working women to realize that obtaining the ballot was the key to achieving equality with men. Anthony was also eager to form the WWA so that she and other women could participate in the National Labor Union (NLU) Congress in September 1868. Both she and Elizabeth Cady Stanton were optimistic that a strong alliance with the NLU would eventually add the political power that the suffrage movement needed to secure the franchise.

Most of the original WWA members were typesetters in the printing trade. Women typesetters were vastly outnumbered by men and faced universal discrimination. Because the all-male unions denied women union membership, women were also prevented from participation in union apprenticeship programs. Without the training they needed to obtain the best jobs, women typesetters were relegated to low-paying printing jobs that required less skill. Women typesetters and other working women who joined the WWA were mostly interested in improving their economic condition. They were resistant to Anthony's emphasis on the importance of securing the ballot as the best means to achieve their economic

objectives. In 1869, WWA member Aurora S. Phelps articulated the perspective of many WWA members.

The poor working-women do not, most of them, want the ballot. . . . I say we want bread and clothes and *homes* first, and after we caught as good pay for our work as the men do for theirs . . . it will be time enough for you to talk to us about wanting the ballot.

Although Phelps and other women kept trying to communicate to Anthony their most pressing concerns, Anthony was not swayed from her agenda. She continued to try to persuade them of the preeminence of the ballot. This conflict intensified until many working women abandoned the WWA because they believed the leadership was not serious about addressing their needs.

In spite of this conflict, WWA members managed to collaborate on their goals for a number of months. Encouraged by Anthony, Augusta Lewis organized the Women's Typographical Union (WTU) to overcome the discriminatory practices that the all-male National Typographical Union (NTU) used to keep women typesetters out of the trade. The NTU leadership immediately responded. Because NTU members feared the potential of a women's union to undercut men's wages and the NTU's power as a bargaining unit, they invited the WTU membership to join them as equal members in the NTU, as long as the WTU did not accept any new members. The NTU also vowed to secure equal pay for WTU members. This was an immense victory, and as Anthony told WTU members in 1868, "you have taken a great, a momentous step forward in the path to success."

Anthony also formed a second chapter of the WWA, which comprised women working in the sewing trade. With the addition of new middle-class members, the WWA investigated the deplorable working conditions of ragpickers in New York City and also provided assistance to Hester Vaughan, an immigrant and domestic servant unjustly charged with infanticide. But when, during a strike, Anthony managed to persuade an association of book printing employers to establish a typesetting school for unskilled women, she deeply alienated many WWA members and trade unionists in the NTU and the NLU. Her efforts, which were interpreted as strikebreaking, harmed the NTU's bargaining position as it attempted to reach a favorable settlement during the strike.

This event caused Anthony to be unseated at the 1869 NLU Congress and contributed to the demise of the WWA. The WTU struggled to carry on under the leadership of Augusta Lewis. But by 1871, the NTU no longer made efforts to eliminate discrimination, and women typesetters eventually lost the few gains they had achieved. Because Anthony and Stanton's alliance with organized labor and their attempts to organize working women did not produce the suffrage constituency they were seeking, they abandoned these efforts and focused instead on developing stronger connections with middle-class women.

Judith E. Harper

See Also: Labor Unions (19th Century); Anthony, Susan B. (Vol. 2); Stanton, Elizabeth Cady (Vol. 2)

Further Reading

DuBois, Ellen Carol. *Feminism and Suffrage: The Emergence of an Independent Women's Movement in America 1848–1869*. Ithaca, NY: Cornell University Press, 1978.

Kugler, Israel. *From Ladies to Women: The Organized Struggle for Woman's Rights in the Reconstruction Era*. Westport, CN: Greenwood Press, 1987.

Wormeley, Katharine Prescott (1830–1908)

Wealthy Rhode Islander Katharine Wormeley volunteered as a nurse and hospital administrator for the Union army in 1862 and 1863. She later wrote a history of the United States Sanitary Commission (USSC), as well as a memoir of her Civil War nursing experiences.

Wormeley was born in England in 1830 to a wealthy family. Her father had roots in Virginia, and the family moved to the United States after his 1852 death. They settled in Newport, Rhode Island, and wintered in both Boston and Washington.

When the Civil War began, the formation of the Women's Central Association of Relief inspired Wormeley to found a similar organization in Newport, the Woman's Union Aid Society. Wormeley also became the assistant manager of the New England women's branch of the Sanitary Commission. In 1861, recognizing the soldiers' need for clothing, Wormeley used donations to the society to hire unemployed seamstresses to make the necessary supplies. Her group generated 50,000 army shirts in this manner from 1861 to 1862. In May 1862 the secretary of the USSC, Frederick Law Olmsted, invited Wormeley to volunteer on the first hospital transport ship, which supported wounded Union forces during the Peninsular campaign. She oversaw the linens, bedding, feeding of patients, and general conditions of the hospital wards until that summer.

In September 1862, Wormeley became the superintendent of the Women's Department of the Lowell General Hospital for convalescing soldiers in Portsmouth Grove, Rhode Island. Serving with her were women Wormeley had worked with on the hospital transport ships, including sisters Georgeanna and Jane Woolsey, their cousin Sarah Woolsey, and Harriet D. Whetten. Their positions at the Lowell General Hospital marked the first time that women served in such capacities in a general hospital. A year later, Wormeley returned to private life in Newport, Rhode Island. Her history of the USSC, *The United States Sanitary Commission: A Sketch of Its Purpose and Work* (1863), was sold at sanitary fairs to raise money for the organization.

In 1889 Wormeley published a memoir of her experiences on the hospital transport ships. *The Other Side of War: With the Army of the Potomac* describes female nurses' experiences and reveals the class distinctions between women during the war. It also describes how some Civil War nurses lost their interest in politics, instead focusing only on the wounded in their care. After the war, in addition to continuing her volunteer work, Wormeley became an expert translator of French authors such as Balzac and Molière.

Ellen H. Todras

See Also: Slavery and the Civil War; United States Sanitary Commission

Further Reading

Austin, Anne. *The Woolsey Sisters of New York: A Family's Involvement in the Civil War and a New Profession (1860–1900)*. Philadelphia, PA: American Philosophical Society, 1971.

Giesberg, Judith Ann. *Civil War Sisterhood: The U.S. Sanitary Commission and Women's Politics in Transition*. Boston, MA: Northeastern University Press, 2000.

Schultz, Jane E. *Women at the Front: Hospital Workers in Civil War America*. Chapel Hill: University of North Carolina Press, 2004.

Silber, Nina. *Daughters of the Union: Northern Women Fight the Civil War*. Cambridge, MA: Harvard University Press, 2005.

Wright, Frances (1795–1852)

Born into a prosperous Scottish family in Dundee, Fanny Wright was a woman ahead of her times who suffered for her freethinking and her radicalism. Like many feminists who dared to speak out on sexual

Fanny Wright was an early-19th-century freethinker, whose ideas on slavery, the relations between the sexes, and a national public education system were too radical for most of her contemporaries but had a profound influence on later generations of American reformers. (Cirker, Hayward and Blanche Cirker, eds. *Dictionary of American Portraits*, 1967)

equality when prevailing attitudes sought to keep women firmly confined to the domestic sphere, she had to brave constant criticism and vilification. In her advocacy of a "national, rational and republican system of education for all," dress reform, birth control, and other issues of sexual nonconformity, she paid no heed to social convention and went on the lecture circuit to become one of the most talked-about female radicals in the United States. Wright also experimented with a utopian scheme to liberate slaves through their own labor on land she purchased for the purpose in Nashoba, Tennessee.

Fanny Wright was brought up by progressive relatives in England after her father and mother died within months of each other when she was two. Privileged to have been left a large fortune, she began pursuing a literary career. Wright visited the United States in 1818–1820 with her sister Camilla. In 1819 her play *Altdorf,* about the struggle for independence in Switzerland, was staged in New York but closed after three performances. On her return to England, she published her travel memoirs of the United States, *Views of Society and Manners in America* (1821), a largely uncritical panegyric full of admiration for the spirit of Republicanism and American democracy that nevertheless criticized the "pestilence" of slavery. Although published 11 years before Frances Trollope's *Domestic Manners of the Americans* (1832; a sanguine view of U.S. society by the mother of the English novelist Anthony Trollope), Wright's work was subsequently totally eclipsed by Trollope's and largely forgotten. Influenced by the romanticism of Lord Byron, Wright published a utopian discourse, *A Few Days in Athens,* in 1822.

In 1821 Wright met and developed a romantic crush on the Marquis de Lafayette (a hero of the American Revolution who refused her proposal of marriage) and returned to the United States on a tour with him in 1824. During their travels, they visited Robert Owen's utopian community in New Harmony, Indiana, where she adopted short hair as well as the pantaloons worn by female members of the community (well ahead of Amelia Bloomer's well-publicized advocacy of them in the 1850s).

After a trip up the Mississippi in 1825, Wright published *A Plan for the Gradual Abolition of Slavery in the United States without Danger of Loss to the Citizens of the South* (1825), in which she advocated her own bold social experiment, whereby the U.S. government should buy large tracts of land on which to settle and ultimately emancipate slaves. Determined to put her ideas into practice, Wright bought 640 acres of land for the purpose at Chicasaw Bluffs in western Tennessee, naming it Nashoba. After purchasing 18 slaves, she set them up in a cooperative colony there along the lines of Owen's at New Harmony. Wright and various friends and supporters also joined the project, with the objective that the slaves, through their own hard work, would earn their own freedom after five years. The sexual code Wright established at Nashoba was also libertarian, focused on the rights and responsibilities of both male and female members and stated: "No woman can forfeit her individual rights or independent existence, and no man assert over her any rights of power whatsoever beyond what he may exercise over her free and voluntary affection."

But the community did not prosper. The labor was arduous, the climate was debilitating, the crop returns were poor, and its leadership was disrupted by Wright's frequent absences on visits to New Harmony or trips to

Europe. Eventually, Nashoba's notoriety was its downfall, when in 1827 a scandal-mongering article appeared, accusing Wright of practicing free love and mixed-race breeding at Nashoba. This, combined with other attacks made on her for her feminism and public lecturing against organized religion, forced Wright to abandon the project, having invested and lost a good half of her fortune in it. The 30 slaves were later sent to Haiti at Wright's expense, where they were set free and helped with finding homes and jobs.

Wright took to the lecture circuit during a period of revivalism that followed, speaking out against organized religion. In 1828 she spent time at New Harmony helping Robert Owen's son edit the *New Harmony Gazette,* and in 1829 settled on a farm in New York City. She bought a disused old church in New York's Bowery and converted it into a Hall of Science, where she could hold lectures for workers and hoped to set about educating them through a network of free state schools supported by public funds, where she could offer them a secular education as well as vocational training. With these goals in mind, she cofounded the Association for the Protection of Industry and for the Promotion of National Education. In her other lectures, Wright continued to raise the issues of women's emancipation, their rights to education and birth control (supporting Owen's 1830 tract "Moral Physiology"), and liberalization of the divorce laws. While publishing the radical newspaper the *Free Enquirer* with Owen during 1829–1830, Wright criticized the practice of imprisonment for debt and continued to argue for socialism, universal suffrage for both blacks and whites, and secular education. She once more set out on the lecture circuit along the East Coast, speaking to mixed audiences on slavery and the influence of established religion on political affairs. Some of these talks were collected in 1829 as the *Course of Popular Lectures* (expanded in 1836).

In the summer of 1830, Wright returned to Europe. Her prolonged absence saw the demise of her Hall of Science and the collapse of her national education movement. In Paris she had an affair with a fellow Owenite, the French doctor Guillaume D'Arusmont. Discovering she was pregnant in 1831, Wright kowtowed to convention and married D'Arusmont. The marriage was a disaster and led to a long legal wrangle over Wright's property and royalties, which lasted until their divorce in 1850 and beyond. Not all the issues had been resolved by the time of her death.

In 1833 Wright was back in the United States, where she took up lecturing on the evils of modern society,

this time turning against banking monopolies and favoring a state banking system; she also wrote articles for the Boston *Investigator.* She campaigned for Andrew Jackson and the Democrats during the elections of 1836 and 1838, but with public interest in her arguments waning, she returned to Europe in 1839. Her existence was a restless one over the next 10 years, with Wright traveling back and forth between the United States and the Continent before she finally settled in Cincinnati, where she died two years later, in 1852. Her *Biography, Notes and Political Letters* was published in Boston in 1849.

Wright found herself duly consigned by the moral majority to the fires of hell and damnation for her unfeminine ways. But she insisted, "I am not one who speaks my thoughts in whispers, nor who do [*sic*] things in corners." The U.S. press fanned public hostility with its denunciations of Wright as the "whore of Babylon" and the "Red Harlot of Infidelity," and her only support was among fellow male and female Owenites and radicals. Thanks to her courage and vision and those of other socialist thinkers of Wright's day, such as Anna Doyle Wheeler, a tradition of women's social criticism was established in the 1820s and 1830s that would lay the theoretical foundations of the women's movements that developed from the 1850s.

Helen Rappaport

See Also: Abolitionism and the Antislavery Movement; Bloomer, Amelia Jenks; Dress Reform; Education of Women (before the Civil War); Utopian Communities; Wollstonecraft, Mary; Free Love Movement (Vol. 2)

Further Reading

Bartlett, Elizabeth Ann. *Liberty, Equality, Sorority: The Origins and Interpretation of American Feminist Thought: Frances Wright, Sarah Grimké, and Margaret Fuller.* Brooklyn, NY: Carlson Publishing, 1994.

Eckhardt, Celia Morris. *Fanny Wright: Rebel in America.* Cambridge, MA: Harvard University Press, 1984.

Horowitz, Helen. *Rereading Sex: Battles over Sexual Knowledge and Suppression in Nineteenth-Century America.* New York: Knopf, 2002.

Kissel, Susan S. *In Common Cause: The "Conservative" Frances Trollope and the "Radical" Frances Wright.* Bowling Green, OH: Bowling Green State University Press, 1993.

Lane, Margaret. *Frances Wright and the 'Great Experiment.'* Manchester, UK: Manchester University Press, 1972.

Young Ladies' Academy of Philadelphia

Founded in 1787, the Young Ladies' Academy of Philadelphia was the first chartered institution of higher learning for girls in America. The school was founded and administered by men, mostly from the ranks of Philadelphia's elite social class. These men believed that educated women made better wives and mothers. They were aware that their school was a grand experiment in providing a practical education for young women. Subjects included reading, writing, arithmetic, and geography. Noticeably neglected in the curriculum were "ornamental" subjects, such as music, art, and foreign languages. In the words of cofounder Benjamin Rush, mastery of such subjects was admirable, but too time-consuming to achieve. The number of hours needed to become truly fluent in a musical instrument or a foreign language would detract from the hours that could have been used to explore history, philosophy, or the practical arts.

Writing was considered the foremost skill the students should develop. Good writing reflected a well-rounded education, and the writer needed to possess a large vocabulary, a mastery of classical allusions, excellent penmanship, and the ability to express one's thoughts with clarity. Eloquent writing was considered a hallmark of social status, but the trustees of the school also considered mathematics important as a practical measure. A good wife should be able to assist her husband in his business endeavors, which often involved keeping accounts. Understanding arithmetic was also necessary for a housewife to practice thrift, a quality admired even among the wealthy. Finally, it was acknowledged that a widow would need a good head for numbers when she assumed responsibilities for her deceased husband's affairs.

The Young Ladies' Academy was an immediate success. In the first year of operation it attracted more than 100 pupils. Most were drawn from the ranks of Philadelphia's elite families, but a few came from Georgia, the Carolinas, Virginia, Maryland, and Massachusetts. The local girls resided at home, and the out-of-state students lived with friends or family members.

Six-hour examinations were given to the pupils at least twice per year. The girls read, spelled, answered questions, and submitted writing samples to a panel consisting of members of the board of trustees. A series of classes had to be successfully completed before a pupil could be awarded a diploma. A diploma from the Young Ladies' Academy was considered a mark of high distinction and was awarded in an elaborate and formal ceremony. A large audience of trustees, parents, and townspeople attended the events, and the valedictorian and salutatorian delivered orations. This commencement ceremony was one of the few times women outside of the theater delivered formal speeches to large crowds in early America.

The Young Ladies' Academy was a rare phenomenon. Educating women was an expensive luxury, and only a tiny fraction of Philadelphia's population could aspire to send their daughters to such a school. Most young women needed to be profitably employed in household chores or had already embarked on marriage. The school was not designed to prepare women for employment anywhere except as a mother or high-society hostess.

Dorothy A. Mays

See Also: Education of Women (before the Civil War); Murray, Judith Sargent; Republican Motherhood; Warren, Mercy Otis

Primary Documents: 1787, "Thoughts upon Female Education"; 1790, "On the Equality of the Sexes"

Further Reading

Gordon, Ann D. "The Young Ladies' Academy of Philadelphia." In *Women of America: A History,* edited by Carol Ruth Berkin and Mary Beth Norton. Boston, MA: Houghton Mifflin, 1979.

Gundersen, Joan R. *To Be Useful to the World: Women in Revolutionary America, 1740–1790.* New York: Twayne, 1996.

Kerber, Linda. *Toward an Intellectual History of Women: New Feminist Essays.* Chapel Hill: University of North Carolina Press, 1997.

Nash, Margaret. *Women's Education in the United States, 1780–1840.* New York: Palgrave Macmillan, 2005.

Z

Zakrzewska, Marie (1829–1902)

Born in Berlin to Polish parents, medical practitioner Marie Zakrzewska worked with Elizabeth Blackwell in the forefront of women's medical training and the establishment of women's hospitals in the United States. Zakrzewska was educated to the age of 14 and began assisting her mother in her work as a midwife at the Royal Charité Hospital in Berlin. When she was 18, she applied to train at a midwives' school, and during her studies worked for Dr. Joseph Schmidt, who made her his teaching assistant. After qualifying in 1851, Zakrzewska began training other midwives a year later and was promoted to principal midwife at the Royal Charité Hospital in 1852.

Suffering criticism for being promoted to such a senior position at the age of only 22, Zakrzewska decided to go to the United States. There, she was convinced, she would find greater opportunities for training in a medical career, particularly as she knew she would not be allowed to train as a doctor in Germany. Her father was dismayed at Zakrzewska's determination to become a doctor and, after she emigrated to New York with her sister in 1853, wrote to her: "If you were a young man, I could not find words in which to express my satisfaction and pride . . . but you are a woman, a weak woman; and all that I can do for you now is to grieve and to weep. O my daughter! Return from this unhappy path."

After a year of making a subsistence living as a seamstress, Zakrzewska approached Elizabeth Blackwell for work at her dispensary. With Blackwell's help and despite the fact that she spoke very little English, Zakrzewska obtained a place at Cleveland Medical College in Ohio in 1854 and, after graduating in 1856, set up a small private practice at Blackwell's home in New York. Together the women raised funds to open the New York Infirmary for Women and Children in 1857, the first hospital in the United States to be staffed by women, where they were joined by Blackwell's sister Emily. Zakrzewska served as the hospital's first resident physician and also as its general manager, in which capacity she set up a system of record keeping for patient histories.

In 1859 Zakrzewska set out on a fundraising trip for the infirmary, during which time she also helped set up canteens for working women and community projects for Jewish immigrants as well as lending her support to the women's suffrage and antislavery movements. She did not return to the infirmary; instead, she accepted the post of professor of obstetrics and diseases of women at the New England Female Medical College in Boston, which had been established in 1848. There and at the college's adjacent Hospital for Women and Children, she struggled to introduce new medical practices and the use of microscopes, but finding it impossible to improve academic standards, she resigned in 1862, and the college's hospital was closed almost immediately. Zakrzewska reopened it as her own clinical hospital, the New England Hospital for Women and Children, beginning with only 10 beds and an all-female staff, which she directed for the next 30 years.

With the support of many nonmedical patrons and feminists such as Ednah Dow Cheney, Zakrzewska established her own school to train nurses and give valuable hospital experience to women doctors. As the hospital grew, eventually relocating in 1872, it attracted many women pioneers in nursing and medicine, including Susan Dimock, one of the first female surgeons in the United States. Zakrzewska undertook free medical care among Boston's underprivileged, as well as running a private practice. By 1881, such were the high standards at the New England Hospital that the women training there as doctors were graduating with full credentials.

Zakrzewska's role became an increasingly administrative one as the hospital expanded, and by 1887 her role as a doctor there was only advisory. She also ran a social service program based at the hospital. In 1878 she founded the New England Hospital Medical Society and was its first president. She retired in 1899. The New England Female Medical College was eventually absorbed into the Boston University School of Medicine, but the original building of the New England Hospital for Women and Children survives as the Dimock Community Health Center in Boston.

Helen Rappaport

See Also: Blackwell, Elizabeth

Primary Document: 1867, Support for Female Physicians

Further Reading

Blake, Catriona. *The Charge of the Parasols: Women's Entry to the Medical Profession.* London: Women's Press, 1990.

Bonner, Thomas Neville. *To the Ends of the Earth: Women's Search for Education in Medicine.* Cambridge, MA: Harvard University Press, 1992.

Morantz-Sanchez, Regina. *Sympathy and Science: Women Physicians in American Medicine.* New York: Oxford University Press, 1985.

Walsh, Mary Roth. *"Doctors Wanted: No Women Need Apply": Sexual Barriers in the Medical Profession, 1835–1975.* New Haven, CT: Yale University Press, 1977.

Primary Documents

"An Occasional Letter on the Female Sex" (1774), Thomas Paine

Thomas Paine, the English-American author, revolutionary, and political theorist and activist, explored the injustices that women faced in marriage and domestic life with sympathy and insight in his "An Occasional Letter on the Female Sex."

> O Woman! lovely Woman!
> Nature made thee to temper man,
> We had been Brutes without you.
> OTWAY.

IF we take a survey of ages and of countries, we shall find the women, almost-without exception-at all times and in all places, adored and oppressed. Man, who has never neglected an opportunity of exerting his power, in paying homage to their beauty, has always availed himself of their weakness. He has been at once their tyrant and their slave.

Nature herself, in forming beings so susceptible and tender, appears to have been more attentive to their charms than to their happiness. Continually surrounded with griefs and fears, the women more than share all our miseries, and are besides subjected to ills which are peculiarly their own. They cannot be the means of life without exposing themselves to the loss of it; every revolution which they undergo, alters their health, and threatens their existence. Cruel distempers attack their beauty—and the hour which confirms their release from those is perhaps the most melancholy of their lives. It robs them of the most essential characteristic of their sex. They can then only hope for protection from the humiliating claims of pity, or the feeble voice of gratitude. Society, instead of alleviating their condition, is to them the source of new miseries. More than one half of the globe is covered with savages; and among all these people women are completely wretched. Man, in a state of barbarity, equally cruel and indolent, active by necessity, but naturally inclined to repose, is acquainted with little more than the physical effects of love; and, having none of those moral ideas which only can soften the empire of force, he is led to consider it as his supreme law, subjecting to his despotism those whom reason had made his equal, but whose imbecility betrayed them to his strength. "Nothing" (says Professor Miller, speaking of the women of barbarous nations) "can exceed the dependence and subjection in which they are kept, or the toil and drudgery which they are obliged to undergo. The husband, when he is not engaged in some warlike exercise, indulges himself in idleness, and devolves upon his wife the whole burden of his domestic affairs. He disdains to assist her in any of those servile employments. She sleeps in a different bed, and is seldom permitted to have any conversation or correspondence with him."

The women among the Indians of America are what the Helots were among the Spartans, a vanquished people, obliged to toil for their conquerors. Hence on the banks of the Oroonoko, we have seen mothers slaying their daughters out of compassion, and smothering them in the hour of their birth. They consider this barbarous pity as a virtue.

"The men," says Commodore Byron, in his account of the inhabitants of South-America, "exercise a most despotic authority over their wives, whom they consider in the same view they do any other part of their property, and dispose of them accordingly. Even their common treatment of them is cruel; for though the toil and hazard of procuring food lies entirely on the women, yet they are not suffered to touch any part of it till the husband is satisfied; and then he assigns them their portion, which is generally very scanty, and such as he has not a stomach for himself."

Among the nations of the East we find another kind of despotism and dominion prevail—the Seraglio and the domestic servitude of woman, authorized by the manners and established by the laws. In Turkey, in Persia, in India, in Japan, and over the vast empire of China, one half of the human species is oppressed by the other.

The excess of oppression in those countries springs from the excess of love.

All Asia is covered with prisoners, where beauty in bondage awaits the caprices of a master. The multitude of women there assembled have no will, no inclinations but his. Their triumphs are only for a moment; and their rivalry, their hate, and their animosities continue till death. There the lovely sex are obliged to repay even their servitude with the most tender affections; or, what is still more mortifying, with the counterfeit of an affection, which they do not feel. There the most gloomy tyranny has subjected them to creatures, who, being of neither sex, are a dishonor to both. There, in short, their education tends only to debase them; their virtues are forced; their very pleasures are involuntary and joyless; and after an existence of a few years—till the bloom of youth is over—their period of neglect commences, which is long and dreadful. In the temperate latitude where the climates, giving less ardor to passion, leave more confidence in virtue, the women have not been deprived of their liberty, but a severe legislation has, at all times, kept them in a state of dependence. One while they were confined to their own apartments, and debarred at once from business and amusement; at other times, a tedious guardianship defrauded their hearts, and insulted their understandings. Affronted in one country by polygamy, which gives them their rivals for their inseparable companions; enslaved in another by in dissoluble ties, which often join the gentle to the rude, and sensibility to brutality. Even in countries where they may be esteemed most happy, constrained in their desires in the disposal of their goods, robbed of freedom of will by the laws, the slaves of opinion, which rules them with absolute sway, and construes the slightest appearances into guilt; surrounded on all sides by judges, who are at once tyrants and their seducers, and who, after having prepared their faults, punish every lapse with dishonor—nay, usurp the right of degrading them on suspicion! Who does not feel for the tender sex? Yet such, I am sorry to say, is the lot of women over the whole earth. Man with regard to them, in all climates, and in all ages, has been either an insensible husband or an oppressor; but they have sometimes experienced the cold and deliberate oppression of pride, and sometimes the violent and terrible tyranny of jealousy. When they are not beloved they are nothing;

and, when they are, they are tormented. They have almost equal cause to be afraid of indifference and of love. Over three-quarters of the globe nature has placed them between contempt and misery.

"The melting desires, or the fiery passions," says Professor Ferguson, "which in one climate take place between the sexes, are, in another, changed into a sober consideration, or a patience of mutual disgust. This change is remarked in crossing the Mediterranean, in following the course of the Mississippi, in ascending the mountains of Caucasus, and in passing from the Alps and the Pyrenees to the shores of the Baltic.

The burning ardors and torturing jealousies of the seraglio and harem, which have reigned so long in Asia and Africa, and which, in the southern parts of Europe, have scarcely given way to the differences of religion and civil establishments, are found, however, with an abatement of heat in the climate, to be more easily changed, in one latitude, into a temporary passion, which engrosses the mind without enfeebling it, and which excites to romantic achievements. By a farther progress to the north it is changed into a spirit of gallantry, which employs the wit and fancy more than the heart, which prefers intrigue to enjoyment, and substitutes affection and vanity where sentiment and desire have failed. As it departs from the sun, the same passion is further composed into a habit of domestic connection, or frozen into a state of insensibility, under which the sexes at freedom scarcely choose to unite their society."

Even among people where beauty received the highest homage we find men who would deprive the sex of every kind of reputation. "The most virtuous woman," says a celebrated Greek, "is she who is least talked of." That morose man, while he imposes duties upon women, would deprive them of the sweets of public esteem, and in exacting virtues from them, would make it a crime to aspire at honor.

If a woman were to defend the cause of her sex, she might address him in the following manner:

"How great is your injustice? If we have an equal right with you to virtue, why should we not have an equal right to praise? The public esteem ought to wait upon merit. Our duties are different from yours, but they are not therefore less difficult to fulfil, or of less consequence to society: They are the fountains of your felicity, and the sweetness of life. We are wives and mothers. 'Tis we who form the union and the cordiality of families. 'Tis we who soften that savage rudeness which considers everything as due to force, and which would involve man with man in eternal war. We cultivate in you that humanity which makes you feel for the misfortunes of others, and our tears forewarn you of your own danger. Nay, you cannot be ignorant that we have need of courage not less than you. More feeble in ourselves, we have perhaps more trials to encounter. Nature assails us with sorrow, law and custom press us with constraint, and sensibility and virtue alarm us with their continual conflict. Sometimes also the name of citizen demands from us the tribute of fortitude—When you offer your blood to the State think that it is ours. In giving it our sons and our husbands we give more than ourselves. You can only die on the field of battle, but we have the misfortune to survive those whom we love most. Alas! while your ambitious vanity is unceasingly laboring to cover the earth with statues, with monuments, and with inscriptions to eternize, if possible, your names, and give yourselves an existence, when this body is no more, why must we be condemned to live and to die unknown? Would that the grave and eternal forgetfulness should be our lot. Be not our tyrants in all: Permit our names to be sometimes pronounced beyond the narrow circle in which we live. Permit friendship, or at least love, to inscribe its emblem on the tomb where our ashes repose; and deny us not that public esteem which, after the esteem of one's self, is the sweetest reward of well doing."

All men, however, it must be owned, have not been equally unjust to their fair companions. In some countries public honors have been paid to women. Art has erected them monuments. Eloquence has celebrated their virtues, and history has collected whatever could adorn their character.

Source: The Writings of Thomas Paine, Vol. 1. Collected and Edited by Moncure Daniel Conway. New York: G. P. Putnam's Sons, 1894.

"The Sentiments of an American Woman" (1780), Anonymous [Esther DeBerdt Reed]

In May of 1780, George Washington reported that his troops were facing serious shortages of supplies, and immediate relief was needed. A group of women in Philadelphia, led by Esther DeBerdt Reed and Sarah Bache Franklin, formed the Ladies Association of Philadelphia, and went from house to house soliciting support. This was one of the first times American women organized to raise money on behalf of a public cause. They were immensely successful; according to a letter from Reed to Washington, they raised more than $300,000 in paper currency.

This broadside, published anonymously but attributed to Reed, explains, defends, and encourages women's fundraising efforts for the patriotic cause. It sets out examples of women's patriotic deeds in the near and distant past to justify women's involvement in political action and encourage women to make sacrifices to serve the public good.

On the commencement of actual war, the Women of America manifested a firm resolution to contribute as much as could depend on them, to the deliverance of their country. Animated by the purest patriotism, they are sensible of sorrow at this day, in not offering more than barren wishes for the success of so glorious a Revolution. They aspire to render themselves more really useful; and this sentiment is universal from the north to the south of the Thirteen United States. Our ambition is kindled by the fame of those heroines of antiquity, who have rendered their sex illustrious, and have proved to the universe, that, if the weakness of our Constitution, if opinion and manners did not forbid us to march to glory by the same paths as the Men, we should at least equal, and sometimes surpass them in our love for the public good. I glory in all that which my sex has done great and commendable. I call to mind with enthusiasm and with admiration, all those acts of courage, of constancy and patriotism, which history has transmitted to us: The people favored by Heaven, preserved from destruction by the virtues, the zeal and the revolution of Deborah, of Judith, of Esther! The fortitude of the mother of the Macchabees, in giving up her sons to die before her eyes: Rome saved from the fury of a victorious efforts of Volumnia, and other Roman ladies: So many famous sieges where the Women have been seen forgetting the weakness of their sex, building new walls, digging trenches with their feeble hands, furnishing arms to their defenders, they themselves darting the missile weapons on the enemy, resigning the ornaments of their apparel, and their fortune, to fill the public treasury, and to hasten the deliverance of their country; burying themselves under its ruins; throwing themselves into the flames rather than submit to the disgrace of humiliation before a proud enemy.

Born for liberty, disdaining to bear the irons of a tyrannic Government, we associate ourselves to the grandeur of those Sovereigns, cherished and revered, who have held with so much splendor the scepter of the greatest States, the Batildas, the Elizabeths, the Marys, the Catherines, who have extended the empire of liberty, and contended to reign by sweetness and justice, have broken the chains of slavery, forged by tyrants in the times of ignorance and barbarity. The Spanish Women, do they not make, at this moment, the most patriotic sacrifices, to increase the means of victory at the hands of their Sovereign. He is a friend to the French Nation. They are our allies. We call to mind, doubly interested, that it was a French Maid who kindled up amongst our fellow-citizens, the flame of patriotism buried under long misfortunes: It was the Maid of Orleans who drove from the kingdom of France the ancestors of those same British, whose odious yoke we have just shaken off; and whom it is necessary that we drive from this Continent.

But I must limit myself to the recollection of this small number of achievements. Who knows if the persons disposed to censure, and sometimes too severely with regard to us, may not disapprove our appearing acquainted even with the actions of which our sex boasts? We are at least certain, that he cannot be a good citizen who will not applaud our efforts for the relief of the armies which defend our lives, our possessions, our liberty? The situation of our soldiery has been represented to me; the evils inseparable from war, and the firm and generous spirit which has enabled them to support these. But it has been said, that they may apprehend, that in the course of a long war, the view of their distresses may be lost, and their services be forgotten. Forgotten! Never; I can answer in the name of all my sex. Brave Americans, your disinterestedness, your courage, and your constancy will always be dear to America, as long as she shall preserve her virtue.

We know that at a distance from the theater of war, if we enjoy any tranquility, it is the fruit of your watchings, your labors, your dangers. If I live happy in the midst of my family; if my husband cultivates his field, and reaps his harvest in peace; if, surrounded with my children, I myself nourish the youngest, and press it to my bosom, without being afraid of seeing myself separated from it, by a ferocious enemy; if the house in which we dwell; if our barns, our orchards are safe at the present time from the hands of those incendiaries, it is to you that we owe it. And shall we hesitate to evidence to you our gratitude? Shall we hesitate to wear a clothing more simple, hair dressed less elegant, while at the price of this small privation, we shall deserve your benedictions. Who amongst us, will not renounce with the highest pleasure, those vain ornaments, that she shall consider that the valiant defenders of America will be able to draw some advantage from the money which she may have laid out in these; that they will be better defended from the rigours of the seasons, that after their painful toils, they will receive some extraordinary and unexpected relief; that these presents will perhaps be valued by them at a greater price, when they will have it in their power to say: *This is the offering of the Ladies.* The time is arrived to display the same sentiments which animated us at the beginning of the Revolution, when we renounced the use of teas, however agreeable to our taste, rather than receive them from our persecutors; when we made it appear to them that we placed former necessaries in the rank of superfluities, when our liberty was interested; when our republican and laborious hands spun the flax, prepared the linen intended for the use of our soldiers; when exiles and fugitives we supported with courage all the evils which are the concomitants of war. Let us not lose a moment; let us be engaged to offer the homage of our gratitude at the alter of military valor, and you, our brave deliverers, while mercenary slave combat to cause you to share with them, the irons with which they are loaded, and receive with a free hand our offering, the purest which can be presented to your virtue.

By an AMERICAN WOMAN.

Source: "An American Time Capsule: Three Centuries of Broadsides and Other Printed Ephemera," American Memory, Library of Congress, http://hdl.loc.gov/loc.rbc/rbpe.14600300. Introduction in Crista DeLuzio, Women's Rights: People and Perspectives. Santa Barbara, CA: ABC-CLIO, 2009.

Letters and Petitions on Cherokee Removal (1781–1821), Cherokee Women and Nancy Ward

Before the European colonization, Cherokee society was matriarchal. As part of their adaptation to Western practice, and influenced by Christianity, the Cherokee altered their social and government systems to be more male-focused. Much of the debate about Indian removal involved male political and cultural leaders, although women continued to pay an important role in Cherokee everyday life. Nancy Ward rallied the Cherokee into battle in 1755, earning the title Cherokee Beloved Woman. In a series of speeches, letters, and petitions over several years, Ward and other Cherokee women expressed their anxieties about Cherokee removal.

Speech to the US Treaty Commissioners, by Nancy Ward, 1781

You know that women are always looked down upon as nothing; but we are your mothers; you are our sons. Our cry is all for peace; let it continue. This peace must last forever. Let your women's sons be ours; our sons be yours. Let your women hear our words.
Letter to President Franklin [Benjamin Franklin, Governor of Pennsylvania], 1787

[. . .]

Brother,

I am in hopes if you Rightly consider it that woman is the mother of All – and that woman Does not pull Children out of Trees or Stumps nor out of old Logs, but out of their Bodies, so that they ought to mind what a woman says, and look upon her as a mother – and I have Taken the privelage to Speak to you as my own Children, & the same as if you had sucked my Breast – and I am in hopes you have a beloved woman amongst you who will help to put her Children Right if they do wrong, as I shall do the same – the great men have all promised to Keep the path clear & straight, as my Children shall Keep the path clear & white so that the Messenger shall go & come in safety Between us – the old people is never done Talking to their Children – which makes me say so much as I do. The Talk you sent to me was to talk to my Children, which I have done this day, and they all liked my Talk well, which I am in hopes you will heare from me Every now & then that I keep my Children in piece—tho' I am a woman giving you this Talk, I am in hopes that you and all the Beloved men in Congress will pay particular Attention to it, as I am Delivering it to you from the Bottom of my heart, that they will Lay this on the white stool in Congress, wishing them all well & success in all their undertakings – I hold fast the good Talk I Received from you my Brother, & thanks you kindly for your good Talks, & your presents, & the kind usage you gave to my son.

From KATTEUHA, The Beloved woman of Chota.
Petition to the Cherokee National Council, May 2, 1817

The Cherokee Ladys now being present at the meeting of the chiefs and warriors in council have thought it their duty as mothers to address their beloved chiefs and warriors now assembled.

Our beloved children and head men of the Cherokee Nation, we address you warriors in council. We have raised all of you on the land which we now have, which God gave us to inhabit and raise provisions. We know that our country has once been extensive, but by repeated sales has become circumscribed to a small track, and [we] never have thought it our duty to interfere in the disposition of it till now. If a father or mother was to sell all their lands which they had to depend on, which

their children had to raise their living on, [it] would be indeed bad & [so would it be] to be removed to another country. We do not wish to go to an unknown country which we have understood some of our children wish to go [to] over the Mississippi, but this act of our children would be like destroying your mothers.

Your mothers, your sisters ask and beg of you not to part with any more of our lands. We say ours. You are our descendants; take pity on our request. But keep it for our growing children, for it was the good will of our creator to place us here, and you know our father, the great president, will not allow his white children to take our country away. Only keep your hands off of paper talks for it is our own country. For [if] it was not, they would not ask you to put your hands to paper, for it would be impossible to remove us all. For as soon as one child is raised, we have others in our arms, for such is our situation & [they] will consider our circumstances.

Therefore, children, don't part with any more of our lands but continue on it & enlarge your farms & cultivate and raise corn & cotton and your mothers and sisters will make clothing for you which our father the president has recommended to us all. We don't charge any body for selling any lands, but we have heard such intentions of our children. But your talks become true at last & it was our desire to forwarn you all not to part with our lands.

Nancy Ward to her children: Warriors to take pity and listen to the talks of your sisters. Although I am very old yet [I] cannot but pity the situation in which you will here of their minds. I have great many grand children which I wish them to do well on our land.
Petition to the Cherokee National Council, June 30, 1818

Beloved Children,

We have called a meeting among ourselves to consult on the different points now before the council, relating to our national affairs. We have heard with painful feelings that the bounds of the land we now possess are to be drawn into very narrow limits. The land was given to us by the Great Spirit above as our common right, to raise our children upon, & to make support for our rising generations. We therefore humbly petition our beloved children, the head men & warriors, to hold out to the last in support of our common rights, as the Cherokee nation have been the first settlers of this land; we therefore claim the right of the soil.

We well remember that our country was formerly very extensive, but by repeated sales it has become circumscribed to the very narrow limits we have at present. Our Father the President advised us to become farmers, to manufacture our own clothes, & to have our children instructed. To this advice we have attended in every thing as far as we were able. Now the thought of us being compelled to remove [to] the other side of the Mississippi is dreadful to us, because it appears to us that we, by this removal, shall be brought to a savage state again, for we have, by the endeavor of our Father the President, become too much enlightened to throw aside the privileges of a civilized life.

We therefore unanimously join in our meeting to hold our country in common as hitherto.

Some of our children have become Christians. We have missionary schools among us. We have heard the gospel in our nation. We have become civilized and enlightened, & are in hopes that in a few years our nation will be prepared for instruction in other branches of sciences & arts, which are both useful and necessary in civilized society.

There are some white men among us who have been raised in this country from their youth, are connected with us by marriage, & have considerable families, who are very active in encouraging the emigration of our nation. These ought to be our truest friends but prove our worst enemies. They seem to be only concerned how to increase their riches, but do not care what becomes of our Nation, nor even of their own wives and children.

Petition to the Cherokee National Council, October 1821 [printed in *Cherokee Phoenix,* 1831]

To the Committee and Council,

We the females, residing in Salequoree and Pine Log, believing that the present difficulties and embarrassments under which this nation is placed demands a full expression of the mind of every individual, on the subject of emigrating to Arkansas, would take upon ourselves to address you. Although it is not common for our sex to take part in public measures, we nevertheless feel justified in expressing our sentiments on any subject where our interest is as much at stake as any other part of the community.

We believe the present plan of the General Government to effect our removal West of the Mississippi, and thus obtain our lands for the use of the State of Georgia, to be highly oppressive, cruel and unjust. And we sincerely hope there is no consideration which can induce our citizens to forsake the land of our fathers of which they have been in possession from time immemorial, and thus compel us, against our will, to undergo the toils and difficulties of removing with our helpless families hundreds of miles to unhealthy and unproductive country. We hope therefore the Committee and Council will take into deep consideration our deplorable situation, and do everything in their power to avert such a state of things. And we trust by a prudent course their transactions with the General Government will enlist in our behalf the sympathies of the good people of the United States.

———————

Source: Kilcup, Karen, ed. *Native American Women's Writings.* Cambridge, MA: Blackwell, 2000.

"Thoughts upon Female Education" (1787), Benjamin Rush

Benjamin Rush (1746–1813) was a physician and social reformer whose progressive writing on social reform did much to shape attitudes in the late 18th century. He was an ardent opponent of slavery and capital punishment. He was one of the first physicians to recognize the development of physical dependence on alcohol and tobacco. Recognizing the importance of education, he was nevertheless critical of the education traditionally afforded the daughters of the elite. He believed that "ornamental arts," such as painting, foreign languages, and mastery of musical instruments, had little practical value. Rush helped found the Young Ladies' Academy of Philadelphia, a school that provided a rigorous education for women.

Addressed to the Visitors of the Young Ladies' Academy of Philadelphia

There are several circumstances in the situation, employments, and duties of women in America which require a peculiar mode of education.

I. The early marriages of our women, by contracting the time allowed for education, renders it necessary to contract its plan, and to confine it chiefly to the more useful branches of literature.

II. The state of property, in America, renders it necessary for the greatest part of our citizens to employ themselves, in different occupation, for the advancement of their fortunes. This cannot be done without the assistance of the female members of the community. They must be the stewards, and guardians of their husbands' property. That education, therefore, will be most proper for our women, which teaches them to discharge the duties of those offices with the most success and reputation.

III. From the numerous avocations to which a professional life exposes gentlemen in America from their families, a principal share of the instruction of children naturally devolves upon the women. It becomes us therefore to prepare them by a suitable education, for the discharge of this most important duty of mothers.

IV. The equal share that every citizen has in the liberty, and the possible share he may have in the government of our country, make it necessary that our ladies should be qualified to a certain degree by a peculiar and suitable education, to concur in instructing their sons in the principles of liberty and government.

V. In Great Britain the business of servants is a regular occupation; but in America this humble station is the usual retreat of unexpected indigence; hence the servants in this country possess less knowledge and subordination than are required from them; and hence, our ladies are obliged to attend more to the private affairs of their families, than ladies generally do, of the same rank in Great Britain.

The branches of literature most essential for a young lady in this country, appear to be,

I. A knowledge of the English language. She should not only read, but speak and spell it correctly. And to enable her to do this, she should be taught the English grammar, and be frequently examined in applying its rules in common conversation.

II. Pleasure and interest conspire to make the writing of a fair and legible hand, a necessary branch of female education. For this purpose she should be taught not only to shape every letter properly, but to pay the strictest regard to points and capitals.

III. Some knowledge of figures and bookkeeping is absolutely necessary to qualify a young lady for the duties which await her in this country. There are certain occupations in which she may assist her husband with this knowledge; and should she survive him, and agreeably to the custom of our country be the executrix of his will, she cannot fail of deriving immense advantages from it.

IV. An acquaintance with geography and some instruction in chronology will enable a young lady to read history, biography, and travels, with advantage; and thereby qualify her not only for general intercourse with the world, but, to be an agreeable companion for a sensible man. To these branches of knowledge may be added, in some instances, a general acquaintance with the first principles of astronomy, and natural philosophy, particularly with such parts of them as are calculated to prevent superstition, by explaining the causes, or obviating the effects of natural evil.

V. Vocal music should never be neglected, in the education of a young lady, in this country. Besides preparing her to join in that part of public worship which consists in psalmody, it will enable her to soothe the cares of domestic life. The distress and vexation of a husband—the noise of a nursery, and, even, the sorrows that will sometimes intrude into her own bosom, may all be relieved by a song, where sound and sentiment unite to act upon the mind. I hope it will not be thought foreign to this part of our subject to introduce a fact here, which has been suggested to me by my profession, and that is, that the exercise of the organs of the breast, by singing, contributes very much to defend them from those diseases to which our climate, and other causes, have of late exposed them.

VI. Dancing is by no means an improper branch of education for an American lady. It promotes health, and renders the figure and motions of the body easy and agreeable. I anticipate the time when the resources of conversation shall be so far multiplied, that the amusement of dancing shall be wholly confined to children. But in our present state of society and knowledge, I conceive it to be an agreeable substitute for the ignoble pleasures of drinking and gaming, in our assemblies of grown people.

VII. The attention of our young ladies should be directed, as soon as they are prepared for it, to the reading of history, travels, poetry, and moral essays. These studies are accommodated, in a peculiar manner, to the present state of society in America, and when a relish is excited for them, in early life, they subdue that passion for reading novels, which so generally prevails among the fair sex.

VIII. It will be necessary to connect all these branches of education with regular instruction in the Christian religion. For this purpose the principles of the different sects of Christians should be taught and explained, and our pupils should early be furnished with some of the most simple arguments in favor of the truth of Christianity. A portion of the bible (of late improperly banished from our school) should be read by them every day, and such questions should be asked, after reading it, as are calculated to imprint upon their minds the interesting stories contained in it.

IX. If the measures that have been recommended for inspiring our pupils with a sense of religious and moral obligation be adopted, the government of them will be easy and agreeable. I shall only remark under this head, that strictness of discipline will always render severity unnecessary, and that there will be the most instruction in that school, where there is the most order.

I have said nothing in favor of instrumental music as a branch of female education, because I conceive it is by no mean accommodated to the present state of society and manners in America. The price of musical instruments, and the extravagant fees demanded by the teachers of instrumental music, form but a small part of my objections to it.

To perform well, upon a musical instrument, requires much time and long practice. From two to four hours in a day, for three or four years, appropriated to music, are an immense deduction from that short period of time which is allowed by the peculiar circumstances of our country for the acquisition of the useful branches of literature that have been mentioned. How many useful ideas might be picked up in these hours from history, philosophy, poetry, and the numerous moral essays with which our language abounds, and how much more would the knowledge acquired upon these subjects add to the consequence of a lady, with her husband and with society, than the best performed pieces of music upon a harpsichord or a guitar!

I beg leave further to bear a testimony against the practice of making the French language a part of female education in America. In Britain, where company and pleasure are the principal business of ladies, where the nursery and the kitchen form no part of their care, and where a daily intercourse is maintained with Frenchmen and other foreigners who speak the French language, a knowledge of it is absolutely necessary. But the case is widely different in this country. Of the many ladies who have applied to this language, how great a proportion of them have been hurried into the cares and duties of a family before they had acquired it; of those who have acquired it, how few have retained it after they were married; and of the few who have retained it, how seldom have they had occasion to speak it in the course of their lives! It certainly comports more with female delicacy, as well as the natural politeness of the French nation, to make it necessary for Frenchmen to learn to speak our language in order to converse with our ladies than for our ladies to learn their language in order to converse with them.

Let it not be said in defense of a knowledge of the French language that many elegant books are written in it. Those of them that are truly valuable are generally translated, but, if this were not the case, the English language certainly contains many more books of real utility and useful information than can be read without neglecting other duties by the daughter or wife of an American citizen.

It is with reluctance that I object to drawing as a branch of education for an American lady. To be the mistress of a family is one of the great ends of a woman's being, and while the peculiar state of society in America imposes this station so early and renders the duties of it so numerous and difficult, I conceive that little time can be spared for the acquisition of this elegant accomplishment.

I am not enthusiastical upon the subject of education. In the ordinary course of human affairs, we shall probably too soon follow the footsteps of the nations of Europe in manners and vices. The first marks we shall perceive of our declension will appear among our women. Their idleness, ignorance and profligacy will be the harbingers of our ruin. Then will the performance of a buffoon on the theatre be the subject of more conversation and praise than the patriot or the minister of the gospel. Then will our language and pronunciation be enfeebled and corrupted by a flood of French and Italian words. Then will the history of romantic amours be preferred to the immortal writings of Addison, Hawkesworth and Johnson. Then will our churches be neglected, and the name of the supreme being never called upon, but in profane exclamations. Then will our Sundays be appropriated, only to feasts and concerts. And then will begin all that train of domestic and political calamities. But I forbear. The prospect is so painful, that I cannot help, silently, imploring the great arbiter of human affairs, to interpose his almighty goodness, and to deliver us from these evils, that at least one spot on Earth may be reserved as a monument of the effects of good education, in order to show in some degree what our species was before the fall, and what it shall be, after its restoration.

I cannot dismiss the subject of female education without remarking that the city of Philadelphia first saw a number of gentlemen associated for the purpose of directing the education of young ladies. By means of this plan, the power of teachers is regulated and restrained, and the objects of education are extended. By the separation of the sexes in the unformed state of their manners, female delicacy is cherished and preserved. Here the young ladies may enjoy all the literary advantages of a boarding-school, and at the same time live under the protection of their parents. Here emulation may be excited without jealousy, ambition without envy, and competition without strife. The attempt to establish this new mode of education for young ladies, was an experiment, and the success of it hath answered our expectations. Too much praise cannot be given into execution. The proficiency which the young ladies have discovered in reading, writing, spelling, arithmetic, grammar, geography, music, and their different catechisms, since the last examination, is a less equivocal mark of the merit of our teacher, than any thing I am able to express in their favour.

To you, therefore, YOUNG LADIES, an important problem is committed for a solution; and that is, whether our present plan of education be a wise one, and whether it be calculated to prepare you for the duties of social and domestic life. I know that the elevation of the female mind, by means of moral, physical and religious truth, is considered by some men as unfriendly to the domestic character of a woman. But this is the prejudice of little minds, and springs from the same spirit which opposes the general diffusion of knowledge among the citizens of our republics. If men believe that ignorance is favorable to the government of the female sex, they are certainly deceived; for a weak and ignorant woman will always be governed with the greatest difficulty. I have sometimes been led to ascribe the invention of ridiculous and expensive fashions in female dress, entirely to the gentlemen, in order to divert the ladies from improving their minds, and thereby secure a more arbitrary and unlimited authority over them. It will be in your power, LADIES, to correct the mistakes and practice of our sex upon these subjects, by demonstrating, that the female temper can only be governed by reason, and that the cultivation of reason in women, is alike friendly to the order of nature, and to private as well as public happiness.

Source: "Thoughts upon Female Education, accommodated to the present state of Society, Manners, and Government, in the United States of America. Addressed to the Visitors of the Young Ladies Academy in Philadelphia, 28th July, 1787, at the close of the quarterly examination, by Benjamin Rush, M.D." _The Universal Asylum_ and _The Columbian Magazine._ Philadelphia: April, 1790, 209–213; May, 1790, 288–292. Introduction in Dorothy A. Mays, _Women in Early America: Struggle, Survival, and Freedom in a New World._ Santa Barbara, CA: ABC-CLIO, 2004.

"On the Equality of the Sexes" (1790), Judith Sargent Murray

Judith Sargent Murray was one of the strongest voices championing the equality of all human beings during and after the Revolutionary War period in the United States. Her essay "On the Equality of the Sexes" challenges male dominion in no uncertain terms. The key to woman's raising herself to true humanity is a liberal education, broadly defined. Murray's impact on her contemporaries was limited. Her plays were denounced by Thomas Paine, probably out of jealousy, and Paine even publicly stated that the plays were written by her husband, John Murray. While her defense of women was unparalleled in its time, it had little immediate effect on American society and a backlash against women's equality manifested itself after 1800.

TO THE EDITORS OF THE MASSACHUSETTS MAGAZINE,
GENTLEMEN,

The following ESSAY is yielded to the patronage of Candour.—If it hath been anticipated, the testimony of many respectable persons, who saw it in manuscripts as early as the year 1779, can obviate the imputation of plagiarism.

THAT minds are not alike, full well I know,
This truth each day's experience will show;
To heights surprising some great spirits soar,
With inborn strength mysterious depths explore;
Their eager gaze surveys the path of light,
Confest it stood to Newton's piercing sight.
　Deep science, like a bashful maid retires,
And but the _ardent_ breast her worth inspires;
By perseverance the coy fair is won.
And Genius, led by Study, wears the crown.
　But some there are who wish not to improve
Who never can the path of knowledge love,
Whose souls almost with the dull body one,
With anxious care each mental pleasure shun;
Weak is the level'd, enervated mind,
And but while here to vegetate design'd.
The torpid spirit mingling with its clod,
Can scarcely boast its origin from God;

Stupidly dull—they move progressing on—
They eat, and drink, and all their work is done.
While others, emulous of sweet applause,
Industrious seek for each event a cause,
Tracing the hidden springs whence knowledge
flows,
Which nature all in beauteous order shows.
  Yet cannot I their sentiments imbibe,
Who this distinction to the sex ascribe,
As if a woman's form must needs enrol,
A weak, a servile, an inferiour soul;
And that the guise of man must still proclaim,
Greatness of mind, and him, to be the same:
Yet as the hours revolve fair proofs arise,
Which the bright wreath of growing fame supplies;
And in past times some men have *sunk* so *low,*
That female records nothing *less* can show.
But imbecility is still confin'd,
And by the lordly sex to us consign'd;
They rob us of the power t'improve,
And then declare we only trifles love;
Yet haste the era, when the world shall know,
That such distinctions only dwell below;
The soul unfetter'd, to no sex confin'd,
Was for the abodes of cloudless day design'd.
  Mean time we emulate their manly fires,
Though erudition all their thoughts inspires,
Yet nature with *equality* imparts
And *noble passions,* swell e'en *female hearts.*

Is it upon mature consideration we adopt the idea, that nature is thus partial in her distributions? Is it indeed a fact, that she hath yielded to one half of the human species so unquestionable a mental superiority? I know that to both sexes elevated understandings, and the reverse, are common. But, suffer me to ask, in what the minds of females are so notoriously deficient, or unequal. May not the intellectual powers be ranged under these four heads—imagination, reason, memory and judgment. The province of imagination hath long since been surrendered to us, and we have been crowned and undoubted sovereigns of the regions of fancy. Invention is perhaps the most arduous effort of the mind; this branch of imagination hath been particularly ceded to us, and we have been time out of mind invested with that creative faculty. Observe the variety of fashions (here I bar the contemptuous smile) which distinguish and adorn the female world: how continually are they changing, insomuch that they almost render the wise man's assertion problematical, and we are ready to say, *there is something new under the sun.* Now what a playfulness, what an exuberance of fancy, what strength of inventine imagination, doth this continual variation discover? Again, it hath been observed, that if the turpitude of the conduct of our sex, hath been ever so enormous, so extremely ready are we, that the very first thought presents us with an apology, so plausible, as to produce our actions even in an amiable light. Another instance of our creative powers, is our talent for slander; how ingenious are we at inventive scandal? what a formidable story can we in a moment fabricate merely from the force of a prolifick imagination? how many reputations, in the fertile brain of a female, have been utterly despoiled? how industrious are we at improving a hint? suspicion how easily do we convert into conviction, and conviction, embellished by the power of eloquence, stalks abroad to the surprise and confusion of unsuspecting innocence. Perhaps it will be asked if I furnish these facts as instances of excellency in our sex. Certainly not; but as proofs of a creative faculty, of a lively imagination. Assuredly great activity of mind is thereby discovered, and was this activity properly directed, what beneficial effects would follow. Is the needle and kitchen sufficient to employ the operations of a soul thus organized? I should conceive not, Nay, it is a truth that those very departments leave the intelligent principle vacant, and at liberty for speculation. Are we deficient in reason? we can only reason from what we know, and if an opportunity of acquiring knowledge hath been denied us, the inferiority of our sex cannot fairly be deduced from thence. Memory, I believe, will be allowed us in common, since everyone's experience must testify, that a loquacious old woman is as frequently met with, as a communicative man; their subjects are alike drawn from the fund of other times, and the transactions of their youth, or of maturer life, entertain, or perhaps fatigue you, in the evening of their lives.

"But our judgment is not so strong—we do not distinguish so well."—Yet it may be questioned, from what doth this superiority, in this determining faculty of the soul, proceed. May we not trace its source in the difference of education, and continued advantages? Will it be said that the judgment of a male of two years old, is more sage than that of a female's of the same age? I believe the reverse is generally observed to be true. But from that period what partiality! how is the one exalted, and the other depressed, by the contrary modes of education which are adopted! the one is taught to aspire, and the other is early confined and limitted. As their years increase, the sister must be wholly domesticated, while the brother is led by the hand through all the flowery paths of science. Grant that their minds are by nature equal, yet who shall wonder at the *apparent* superiority, if indeed custom becomes *second nature;* nay if it taketh place of nature, and that it doth the experience of each day will evince. At length arrived at womanhood, the uncultivated fair one feels a void, which the employments allotted her are by no means capable of filling. What can she do? to books she may not apply; or if she doth, *to those only of the novel kind,* lest she merit the appellation of a *learned lady;* and what ideas have been affixed to this term, the observation of many can testify. Fashion, scandal, and sometimes what is still more reprehensible, are then called in to her relief; and who can say to what lengths the liberties she takes may proceed. Meantimes she herself is most unhappy; she feels the want of a cultivated mind. Is she single, she in vain seeks to fill up time from sexual employments or amusements. Is she united to a person whose soul nature made equal to her own, education hath set him so far above her, that in those entertainments which are productive of such rational felicity, she is not qualified to accompany him. She experiences a mortifying consciousness of inferiority, which embitters every enjoyment. Doth the person to whom her adverse fate hath consigned her, possess a mind incapable of improvement, she is equally wretched, in being so closely connected with an individual whom she cannot but despise. Now, was she permitted the same instructors as her brother, (with an eye however to their particular departments) for the employment of a rational mind an ample field would be opened. In astronomy she might catch a glimpse of the immensity of the Deity, and thence she would form amazing conceptions of the august and supreme Intelligence. In geography she would admire Jehovah in the midst of his benevolence; thus adapting this globe to the various wants and amusements of its inhabitants. In natural philosophy she would adore the infinite majesty of heaven, clothed in condescension; and as she traversed the reptile world, she would hail the goodness of a creating God. A mind, thus filled, would have little room for the trifles with which our sex are, with too much justice, accused of amusing themselves, and they would thus be rendered fit companions for those, who should one day wear them as their crown. Fashions, in their variety, would then give place to conjectures, which might perhaps conduce to the improvements of the literary world; and there would be no leisure for slander or detraction. Reputation

would not then be blasted, but serious speculations would occupy the lively imaginations of the sex. Unnecessary visits would only be indulged by way of relaxation, or to answer the demands of consanguinity and friendship. Females would become discreet, their judgments would be invigorated, and their partners for life being circumspectly chosen, an unhappy Hymen would then be as rare, as is now the reverse.

Will it be urged that those acquirements would supersede our domestick duties. I answer that every requisite in female economy is easily attained; and, with truth I can add, that when once attained, they require no further *mental attention.* Nay, while we are pursuing the needle, or the superintendency of the family, I repeat, that our minds are at full liberty for reflection; that imagination may exert itself in full vigor; and that if a just foundation is early laid, our ideas will then be worthy of rational beings. If we were industrious we might easily find time to arrange them upon paper, or should avocations press too hard for such an indulgence, the hours allotted for conversation would at least become more refined and rational. Should it still be vociferated, "Your domestick employments are sufficient"—I would calmly ask, is it reasonable, that a candidate for immortality, for the joys of heaven, an intelligent being, who is to spend an eternity in contemplating the works of the Deity, should at present be so degraded, as to be allowed no other ideas, than those which are suggested by the mechanism of a pudding, or the sewing the seams of a garment? Pity that all such censurers of female improvement do not go one step further, and deny their future existence; to be consistent they surely ought.

Yes, ye lordly, ye haughty sex, our souls are by nature *equal* to yours; the same breath of God animates, enlivens, and invigorates us; and that we are not fallen lower than yourselves, let those witness who have greatly towered above the various discouragements by which they have been so heavily oppressed; and though I am unacquainted with the list of celebrated characters on either side, yet from the observations I have made in the contracted circle in which I have moved, I dare confidently believe, that from the commencement of time to the present day, there hath been as many females, as males, who, by the *mere force of natural powers,* have merited the crown of applause; who, *thus unassisted,* have seized the wreath of fame. I know there are who assert, that as the animal power of the one sex are superiour, of course their mental faculties also must be stronger; thus attributing strength of mind to the transient organization of this earth born tenement. But if this reasoning is just, man must be content to yield the palm to many of the brute creation, since by not a few of his brethren of the field, he is far surpassed in bodily strength. Moreover, was this argument admitted, it would prove too much, for occular demonstration evinceth, that there are many robust masculine ladies, and effeminate gentlemen. Yet I fancy that Mr. Pope, though clogged with an enervated body, and distinguished by a diminutive stature, could nevertheless lay claim to greatness of soul; and perhaps there are many other instances which might be adduced to combat so unphilosophical an opinion. Do we not often see, that when the clay built tabernacle is well nigh dissolved, when it is just ready to mingle with the parent soil, the immortal inhabitant aspires to, and even attaineth heights the most sublime, and which were before wholly unexplored. Besides, were we to grant that animal strength proved any thing, taking into consideration the accustomed impartiality of nature, we should be induced to imagine, that she had invested the female mind with superiour strength as an equivalent for the bodily powers of man. But waving this however palpable advantage, for *equality only,* we wish to contend.

I AM aware that there are many passages in the sacred oracles which seem to give the advantage to the other sex; but I consider all these as wholly metaphorical. Thus David was a man after God's own heart, yet see him enervated by his licentious passions! behold him following Uriah to the death, and shew me wherein could consist the immaculate Being's complacency. Listen to the curses which Job bestoweth upon the day of his nativity, and tell me where is his perfection, where his patience–*literally* it existed not. David and Job were types of him who was to come; and the superiority of man, as exhibited in scripture, being also emblematical, all arguments deduced from thence, of course fall to the ground. The exquisite delicacy of the female mind proclaimeth the exactness of its texture, while its nice sense of honour announceth its innate, its native grandeur. And indeed, in one respect, the preeminence seems to be tacitly allowed us; for after an education which limits and confines, and employments and recreations which naturally tend to enervate the body, and debilitate the mind; after we have from early youth been adorned with ribbons, and other gewgaws, dressed out like the ancient victims previous to a sacrifice, being taught by the care of our parents in collecting the most showy materials that the ornamenting our exterior ought to be the principal object of our attention; after, I say, fifteen years thus spent, we are introduced into the world, amid the united adulation of every beholder. Praise is sweet to the soul; we are immediately intoxicated by large draughts of flattery, which being plentifully administered, is to the pride of our hearts, the most acceptable incense. It is expected that with the other sex we should commence immediate war, and that we should triumph over the machinations of the most artful. We must be constantly upon our guard; prudence and discretion must be our characteristicks; and we must rise superiour to, and obtain a complete victory over those who have been long adding to the native strength of their minds, by an unremitted study of men and books, and who have, moreover, conceived from the loose characters which they have seen portrayed in the extensive variety of their reading, a most contemptible opinion of the sex. Thus unequal, we are, notwithstanding, forced to the combat, and the infamy which is consequent upon the smallest deviation in our conduct, proclaims the high idea which was formed of our native strength; and thus, indirectly at least, is the preference acknowledged to be our due. And if we are allowed an equality of acquirements, let serious studies equally employ our minds, and we will bid our souls arise to equal strengths. We will meet upon even ground, the despot man; we will rush with alacrity to the combat, and, crowned by success, we shall then answer the exalted expectations, which are formed. Though sensibility, soft compassion, and gentle commiseration, are inmates in the female bosom, yet against every deep laid art, altogether fearless of the event, we will set them in array; for assuredly the wreath of victory will encircle the spotless brow. If we meet an equal, a sensible friend, we will reward him with the hand of amity, and through life we will be assiduous to promote his happiness; but from every deep laid scheme, for our ruin, retiring into ourselves, amid the flowery paths of science, we will indulge in all the refined and sentimental pleasures of contemplation: And should it still be urged, that the studies thus insisted upon would interfere with our more peculiar department, I must further reply, that *early hours,* and close application, will do wonders; and to her who is from the first dawn of reason taught to fill up time rationally, both the requisites will be easy. I grant that niggard fortune is too generally unfriendly to the mind; and that much of that valuable treasure, time, is necessarily expended upon the wants of the body; but it should be remembered;

that in embarrassed circumstances our companions have as little leisure for literary improvements, as is afforded to us; for most certainly their provident care is at least as requisite as our exertions. Nay, we have even more leisure for sedentary pleasures, as our avocations are more retired, much less laborious, and, as hath been observed, by no means require that avidity of attention which is proper to the employments of the other sex. In high life, or, in other words, where the parties are in possession of affluence, the objection respecting time is wholly obviated, and of course falls to the ground; and it may also be repeated, that many of those hours which are at present swallowed up in fashion and scandal, might be redeemed, were we habituated to useful reflections. But in one respect, O ye arbiters of our fate! we confess that the superiority is indubitably yours; you are by nature formed for our protectors; we pretend not to vie with you in bodily strength; upon this point we will never contend for victory. Shield us then, we beseech you, from external evils, and in return we will transact *your* domestick affairs. Yes, *your,* for are you not equally interested in those matters with ourselves? Is not the elegancy of neatness as agreeable to your sight as to ours; is not the well favoured viand equally delightful to your taste; and doth not your sense of hearing suffer as much, from the discordant sounds prevalent in an ill regulated family, produced by the voices of children and many *et ceteras*?

CONSTANTIA.

By way of supplement to the foregoing pages, I subjoin the following extract from a letter, wrote to a friend in the December of 1780

AND now assist me, O thou genius of my sex, while I undertake the arduous task of endeavouring to combat that vulgar, that almost universal errour, which hath, it seems, enlisted even Mr. P—under its banners. The superiority of your sex hath, I grant, been time out of mind esteemed a truth incontrovertible; in consequence of which persuasion, every plan of education hath been calculated to establish this favourite tenet. Not long since, weak and presuming as I was, I amused myself with selecting some arguments from nature, reason, and experience; against this so generally received idea, I confess that to sacred testimonies I had not recourse. I held them to be merely metaphorical, and thus regarding them, I could not persuade myself that there was any propriety in bringing them to decide in this *very important debate.* However, as you, sir, confine yourself entirely

to the sacred oracles, I mean to bend the whole of my artillery against those supposed proofs, which you have from thence provided, and from which you have formed an intrenchment *apparently* so invulnerable. And first, to begin with our great progenitors; but here, suffer me to premise, that it is for mental strength I mean to contend, for with respect to animal powers, I yield them undisputed to that sex, which enjoys them in common with the lion, the tyger, and many other beasts of prey; therefore your observations respecting the *rib under the arm, at a distance from the head,* &c.&c. in no sort militate against my view. Well, but the woman was first in the transgression. Strange how blind *self love* renders you men; were you not wholly absorbed in a partial admiration of your own abilities, you would long since have acknowledged the force of what I am now going to urge. It is true some ignoramuses have absurdly enough informed us, that the beauteous fair of paradise, was seduced from her obedience, by a malignant demon, *in the guise of a baleful serpent;* but we, who are better informed, know that the fallen spirit presented himself to her view, *a shining angel still;* for thus, saith the criticks in the Hebrew tongue, ought the word to be rendered. Let us examine her motive—Hark! the seraph declares that she shall attain a perfection of knowledge; for is there aught which is not comprehended under one or other of the terms *good* and *evil.* It doth not appear that she was governed by any one sensual appetite; but merely by a desire of adorning her mind; a laudable ambition fired her soul, and a thirst for knowledge impelled the predilection so fatal in its consequences. Adam could not plead the same deception; assuredly he was not deceived; nor ought we to admire his superiour strength, or wonder at his sagacity, when we so often confess that example is much more influential than precept. His gentle partner stood before him, a melancholy instance of the direful effects of disobedience; he saw her not possessed of that wisdom which she had fondly hoped to obtain, but he beheld the once blooming female, disrobed of that innocence, which had heretofore rendered her so lovely. To him then deception became impossible, as he had proof positive of the fallacy of the argument, which the deceiver had suggested. What then could be his inducement to burst the barriers, and to fly directly in the face of that command, which *immediately* from the mouth of deity *he* had received, since, I say, he could not plead that fascinating stimulous, the accumulation of knowledge, as indisputable conviction was so visibly portrayed before him. What mighty cause impelled him to sacrifice myriads of beings yet unborn, and by one impious act, which *he saw* would be productive of such fatal effects, entail undistinguished ruin upon a race of beings, which he was yet to produce. Blush, ye vaunters of fortitude; ye boasters of resolution; ye haughty lords of the creation; blush when ye remember, that he was influenced by no other motive than a bare pusilianimous attachment to a woman! by sentiments so exquisitely soft, that all his sons have, from that period, when they have designed to degrade them, described as highly feminine. Thus it should seem, that all the arts of the grand deceiver (since means adequate to the purpose are, I conceive, invariably pursued) were requisite to mislead our general mother, while the father of mankind forfeited his own, and relinquished the happiness of posterity, merely in compliance with the blandishments of a female. The subsequent subjection the apostle Paul explains as a figure; after enlarging upon the subject, he adds, *"This is a great mystery; but I speak concerning Christ and the church."* Now we know with what consummate wisdom the unerring father of eternity hath formed his plans; all the types which he hath displayed, he hath permitted *materially* to fail, in the very virtue for which *they* were famed. The reason for this is obvious, we might otherwise mistake his economy, and render that honour to the creature, which is due only to the creator. I know that Adam was a figure of him who was to come. The grace contained in this figure, is the reason of my rejoicing, and while I am very far from prostrating before the shadow, I yield joyfully in all things the preeminence to the second federal head. Confiding faith is prefigured by Abraham, yet he exhibits a contrast to affiance, when he says of his fair companion, she is my sister. Gentleness was the characteristick of Moses, yet he hesitated not to reply to Jehovah himself, with unsaintlike tongue he murmured at the waters of strife, and with rash hands he break the tables, which were inscribed by the finger of divinity. David, dignified with the title of the man after God's own heart, and yet how stained was his life. Solomon was celebrated for wisdom, but folly is write in legible characters upon his almost every action. Lastly, let us turn our eyes to man in the aggregate. He is manifested as the figure of strength, but that we may not regard him as any thing more than a figure, his soul is formed in no sort superiour, but every way equal to the mind of her who is the emblem of weakness and whom he hails the gentle companion of his better days.

Source: The Massachusetts Magazine, or, Monthly Museum Concerning the Literature, History, Politics, Arts, Manners, Amusements of the Age, Vol. II. Boston, MA: I. Thomas and E. T. Andrews, 1790. Introduction in Sara

E. Schueneman-Ayala, "Judith Sargent Murray. "'On the Equality of the Sexes'" and other writings (c. 1790)." In *Feminist Writings from Ancient Times to the Modern World: A Global Sourcebook and History.* Ed. Tiffany K. Wayne. Santa Barbara, CA: Greenwood, 2011.

Paul Revere Defends Deborah Sampson Gannett, a Female Soldier (1804)

In Paul Revere's letter to William Eustis, a member of Congress from Massachusetts, Revere argues for a military pension for Deborah Sampson Gannett, who served in the Continental Army during the American Revolution disguised as a man.

William Eustis, Esq
Member of Congress
Washington

Sir

Mrs. Deborah Gannett of Sharon informes me, that she has inclosed to your Care a petition to Congress in favour of Her. My works for manufactureing of Copper, being a Canton, but a short distance from the Neighbourhood where She lives; I have been induced to enquire her situation, and Character, since she quitted the Male habit, and Soldiers uniform; for the more decent apparel of her own Sex; & Since she has been married and become a Mother.— Humanity, & Justice obliges me to say, that every person with whom I have conversed about Her, and it is not a few, speak of Her as a woman of handsom talents, good Morals, a dutifull Wife and an affectionate parent.—She is now much out of health; She has several Children; her Husband is a good sort of a man, 'tho of small force in business; they have a few acres of poor land which they cultivate, but they are really poor.

She told me, she had no doubt that her ill health is in consequence of her being exposed when She did a Soldiers duty; and that while in the Army, She was wounded.

We commonly form our Idea of the person whom we hear spoken off, whom we have never seen; according as their actions are described, when I heard her spoken off as a Soldier, I formed the Idea of a tall, Masculine female, who had a small share of understandg, without education, & one of the meanest of her Sex.—When I saw and discoursed with I was agreeably surprised to find a small, effeminate, and converseable Woman, whose education entitled her to a better situation in life.

I have no doubt your humanity will prompt you to do all in Your power to git her some releif; I think her case much more deserving than hundreds to whom Congress have been generous.

I am sir with esteem & respect your humble servant

Paul Revere

Source: Letter from Paul Revere to William Eustis, 20 February 1804. Miscellaneous Bound Manuscripts, Massachusetts Historical Society. http://www.masshist.org

The Risks of Marrying (1815), Emma Hart Willard

As marriage changed from being an arrangement negotiated by parents for reasons of money, position, or conformity within a particular religion to being a love match between individuals, advice on marriage became more important. A literature of advice books and advice columns in women's magazines developed during the 19th century to speak to matters of marriage, childbearing, raising children, family and household management, and related concerns. In this letter, Emma Willard, who ran a female academy in Middlebury, Vermont, and who had married a physician much older than herself, provides advice to her younger sister, Almira Hart, about the possible pitfalls of marriage. She suggests that a woman now responsible for her own happiness needs to inquire into the character and circumstances of her suitor and be realistic about the prospects for happiness. In a word, the woman needs to consider her own interests.

Middlebury, July 30, 1815.

Dear Sister:

You think it strange that I should consider a period of happiness as more likely than any other to produce future misery. I know I did not sufficiently explain myself. Those tender and delicious sensations which accompany successful love, while they soothe and soften the mind, diminish its strength to bear or to conquer difficulties. It is the luxury of the soul; and luxury always enervates. A degree of cold that would but brace the nerves of the hardy peasant, would bring distress or death to him who had been pampered by ease and indulgence. This life is a life of vicissitude. A period of happiness, by softening and enervating the soul, by raising a thousand blissful images of the future, naturally prepares the mind for a greater or less degree of disappointment, and unfits us to bear it; while, on the contrary, a period of adversity often strengthens

the mind, and, by destroying inordinate anticipation of the future, gives a relish to whatever pleasures may be thrown in our way. This, perhaps you may acknowledge, is generally true; but you cannot think it applies to your case—otherwise than that you acknowledge yourself liable to disappointment by death. But we will pass over that, and we will likewise pass of over the possibility of your lover's seeing some object that he will consider more interesting than you, and likewise that you may hereafter discover some imperfection in his character. We will pass this over, and suppose that the sanction of the law has been passed upon your connection, and you are secured to each other for life. It will be natural that, at first, he should be much devoted to you; but, after a while, his business must occupy his attention. While absorbed in that he will perhaps neglect some of those little tokens of affection which have become necessary to your happiness. His affairs will sometimes go wrong, and perhaps he will not think proper to tell you the cause; he will appear to you reserved and gloomy, and it [will] be very natural in such a case for you to imagine that he is displeased with you, or is less attached than formerly. Possibly you may not in every instance manage a family as he has been accustomed to think was right, and he may sometimes hastily give you a harsh word or a frown. But where is the use, say you, of diminishing my present enjoyment by such gloomy apprehensions? Its use is this, that, if you enter the marriage state believing such things to be absolutely impossible, if you should meet them, they would come upon you with double force. We should endeavor to make a just estimate of our future prospects, and consider what evils, peculiar situations in which we may be placed, are most likely to beset us, and endeavor to avert them if we can; or, if we must suffer them, to do it with fortitude, and not magnify them by imagination, and think that, because we cannot enjoy all that a glowing fancy can paint, there is no enjoyment left. I hope I shall see Mr. L—. I shall be very glad to have you come and spend the winter with me, and, if he could with propriety accompany you, I should be glad to see him. I am involved in care. There [are] forty in our family and seventy in the school. I have, however, an excellent house-keeper and a very good assistant in my school. You seem to have some wise conjectures floating in your brain, but, unfortunately for your skill in guessing, they have no foundation in truth. . . .

Yours affectionately,

Emma Willard

Source: Emma Willard to Almira Hart, July 30, 1815, in Lord, John. *The Life of Emma Willard.* New York: Appleton, 1873, 44–45; Reprinted and Introduction in Zeman, Theodore J., et al., eds. *Daily Life through American History in Primary Documents.* Santa Barbara, CA: Greenwood, 2011.

"A Plan for Improving Female Education" (1819), Emma Hart Willard

In Willard's pamphlet, she shares her ideas for improving female education. She firmly believed that women's education could be more than just finishing school and that women can excel in subjects like math and philosophy. Her passion pushed her to fight for women's higher education.

The object of this Address, is to convince the public, that a reform with respect to female education is necessary; that it cannot be effected by individual exertion, but that it requires the aid of the legislature; and further, by shewing the justice, the policy, and the magnanimity of such an undertaking, to persuade that body to endow a seminary for females, as the commencement of such reformation. . . .

Defects in the Present Mode of Female Education, and Their Causes

Civilized nations have long since been convinced that education, as it respects males, will not, like trade, regulate itself; and hence, they have made it a prime object to provide that sex with everything requisite to facilitate their progress in learning: but female education has been left to the mercy of private adventurers; and the consequence has been to our sex, the same, as it would have been to the other, had legislatures left their accommodations, and means of instruction, to chance also.

. . . Male education flourishes, because, from the guardian care of legislatures, the presidencies and professorships of our colleges are some of the highest objects to which the eye of ambition is directed. Not so with female institutions. Preceptresses of these, are dependent on their pupils for support, and are consequently liable to become the victims of their caprice. In such a situation, it is not more desirable to be a preceptress, than it would be to be a parent, invested with the care of children, and responsible for their behavior, but yet depending on them for subsistence, and destitute of power to enforce their obedience.

Feminine delicacy requires, that girls should be educated chiefly by their own sex. . . . Boarding schools, therefore, whatever may be their defects, furnish the best mode of education provided for females. [. . .]

Of the Principles by Which Education Should Be Regulated

. . . Education should seek to bring its subjects to the perfection of their moral, intellectual and physical nature: in order, that they may be of the greatest possible use to themselves and others: or, to use a different expression, that they may be the means of the greatest possible happiness of which they are capable, both as to what they enjoy, and what they communicate. . . .

Studies and employments should, therefore, be selected from one or both of the following considerations; either, because they are peculiarly fitted to improve the faculties; or, because they are such, as the pupil will most probably have occasion to practice in future life.

These are the principles, on which systems of male education are founded; but female education has not yet been systematized. Chance and confusion reign here. Not even is youth considered in our sex, as in the other, a season, which should be wholly devoted to improvement. Among families, so rich as to be above labour, the daughters are hurried through the routine of boarding school instruction, and at an early period introduced into the gay world; and, thenceforth, their only object is amusement.—Mark the different treatment, which the sons of these families receive. While their sisters are gliding through the mazes of the midnight dance, they employ the lamp, to treasure up for future use the riches of ancient wisdom; or to gather strength and expansions of the mind, in exploring the wonderful paths of philosophy. When the youth of two sexes has been so spent so differently, is it strange . . . that our sex have been considered by the other, as the pampered, wayward babies of society. . . .

It is the duty of a government, to do all in its power to promote the present and future prosperity of the nation . . . This prosperity will depend on the character of its citizens. The characters of these will be formed by their mothers . . . If this is the case, then it is the duty of our present legislators to begin now, to form the characters of the next generation, by controlling that of the females, who are to be their mothers. . . .

But should the conclusion be almost admitted, that our sex too are the legitimate children of the legislature; and that it is their duty to afford us a share of their paternal bounty; the phantom of a college-learned lady would be ready to rise up, and destroy every good resolution, which the admission of this truth would naturally produce in our favour.

To shew that it is not a masculine education which is here recommended, and to afford a definite view of the manner in which a female institution might possess the respectability, permanency, and uniformity of operation of those appropriated to males; and yet differ from them, so as to be adapted to that difference of character and duties, to which the softer sex should be formed, is the object of the following imperfect

Sketch of a Female Seminary

    I. . . . There would be needed a building, with commodious rooms for lodging and recitation, apartments for the reception of apparatus, and for the accommodation of the domestic department.

    II. A library, containing books on the various subjects in which the pupils were to receive instruction; musical instruments, some good paintings, to form the taste and serve as models for the execution of those who were to be instructed in that art; maps, globes, and a small collection of philosophical apparatus.

    III. A judicious board of trust, competent and desirous to promote its interests, would in a female, as in a male literary institution, be the corner stone of its prosperity. On this board it would depend to provide,

    IV. Suitable instruction . . . 1. Religious and moral. 2. Literary. 3. Domestic. 4. Ornamental. . . .

    V. There would be needed, for a female, as well as for a male seminary, a system of laws and regulations, so arranged, that both the instructors and pupils would know their duty; and thus, the whole business move with regularity and uniformity . . .

Perhaps the term allotted for the routine of study at the seminary, might be three years. The pupils, probably, would not be fitted to enter, till about the age of fourteen.

Benefits of Female Seminaries

. . . They would constitute a grade of public education, superior to any yet known in the history of our sex; and through them, the lower grades of female instruction might be controlled. The influence of public seminaries, over these, would operate in two ways; first, by requiring certain qualifications for entrance; and secondly, by furnishing instructresses, initiated in their modes of teaching, and imbued with their maxims.

    Female seminaries might be expected to have important and happy effects on common schools in general;

and in the manner of operating on these, would probably place the business of teaching children in hands now nearly useless to society; and take it from these, whose services the state wants in many other ways. . . .

    1. Females, by having their understandings cultivated, their reasoning powers developed and strengthened, may be expected to act more from the dictates of reason, and less from those of fashion and caprice.

    2. With minds thus strengthened . . . they might be expected to acquire juster and more enlarged views of their duty, and stronger and higher motives to its performance.

    3. This plan of education, offers all that can be done to preserve female youth from a contempt of useful labour. The pupils would become accustomed to it . . . and it is to be hoped that both from habit and association, they might in future life regard it as respectable.

        To this it may be added, that if housewifery could be raised to a regular art, and taught upon philosophical principles, it would become a higher and more interesting occupation . . .

    4. The pupils might be expected to acquire a taste for moral and intellectual pleasures, which would buoy them above a passion for show and parade . . .

    5. By being enlightened in moral philosophy, and in that, which teaches the operations of the mind, females would be enabled to perceive the nature and extent of that influence, which they possess over their children, and the obligations, which this lays them under, to watch the formulations of their characters with unceasing vigilance, to become their instructors, to devise plans for their improvement, to weed out the vices from their minds, and to implant and foster the virtues . . .

In calling my patriotic countrymen, to effect so noble an object, the consideration of national glory, should not be overlooked. . . . Where is that wise and heroic country, which has considered, that our rights are sacred, though we cannot defend them? that tho' a weaker, we are an essential part of the body politic, whose corruption or improvement must affect the whole? . . . History shows not that country . . . Yet though history lifts not her finger to such an one, anticipation does. She points to a nation, which, having thrown off the shackles of authority and precedent, shrinks not from schemes of improvement, because other nations have never attempted them; but which, in its pride of independence, would rather lead than follow in the march of human improvement . . . Does not every American exult that this country is his own? And who knows how great and good a race of men may yet arise from the forming hand of mothers, enlightened by the bounty of that beloved country,–to defend her liberties,–to plan her future improvement,–and to raise her to unparalleled glory?

Source: Willard, Emma. "An Address to the Public; Particularly to the Members of the Legislature of New York, Proposing A Plan for Improving Female Education." Middlebury: J.W. Copeland, 1819. Reprinted in: Lerner, Gerda, ed. *The Female Experience: An American Documentary.* New York: Oxford, 1977; 1992, 215–223.

Ohio Women Petition against Indian Removal (1830)

Negotiating treaties between white American settlers and Native Americans was a strategy to easy conflicts and tensions. The women of Steubenville, Ohio, exercised their only political right—to petition—to protest Cherokee removal.

MEMORIAL OF THE LADIES OF STEUBEN-VILLE, OHIO,
Against the Forcible removal of the Indians without the limits of the United States
FEBRUARY 15, 1830
Read:– ordered that it lie upon the table.
To the Honorable the Senate and House of Representatives of the United States.

The memorial of the undersigned, residents of the state of Ohio, and town of Steubenville,

RESPECTFULLY SHEWETH:

That your memorialists are deeply impressed with the belief, that the present crisis in the affairs of the Indian nations, calls loudly on *all* who can feel for the woes of humanity, to solicit, with earnestness, your honorable body to bestow on this subject, involving, as it does, the prosperity and happiness of more than fifty thousand of our fellow Christians, the immediate consideration demanded by its interesting nature and pressing importance.

It is readily acknowledged, that the wise and venerated founders of our country's free institutions have committed the powers of Government to those whom nature and reason declare the best fitted to exercise them; and your memorialists would sincerely deprecate any presumptuous interference on the part of their own sex with the ordinary political affairs of the country, as wholly unbecoming the character of the American females. Even in private life, we may not presume to direct the general conduct, or control the acts of those who stand in the near and guardian relations of husbands and brothers; yet all admit that *there are times* when duty and affection call on us to *advise* and *persuade,* as well as to cheer or console. And if we approach the public Representatives of our husbands and brothers, only in the humble character of suppliants in the cause of mercy and humanity, may we not hope that even the small voice of *female* sympathy will be heard?

Compared with the estimate placed on woman, and the attention paid to her on other nations, the generous and defined deference shown by all ranks and classes of men, in this country, to our sex, forms a striking contrast; and as an honorable and distinguishing trait in the American Character, has often excited the admiration of intelligent foreigners. Nor is this general kindness lightly regarded or coldly appreciated; but, with warm feelings of affection and pride, and hearts swelling with gratitude, the mothers and daughters of America bear testimony to the generous nature of their countrymen.

When, therefore, injury and oppression threaten to crush a hapless people within our borders, we, the feeblest of the feeble, appeal with confidence to those who should be representatives of national virtues as they are the depositaries of national powers, and implore them to succor the weak and unfortunate. In despite of the *undoubted national right* which the Indians have to the land of their forefathers, and in the face of solemn treaties, pledging the faith of the nation for their secure possession of those lands, it is intended, we are told, to force them from their native soil, to compel them to seek new homes in a distant and dreary wilderness. To you, then, as the constitutional protectors of the Indians within our territory, and as the peculiar guardians of our national character, and our counter's welfare, we solemnly and honestly appeal, to save this remnant of a much injured people from annihilation, to shield our country from the curses denounced on the cruel and ungrateful, and to shelter the American character from lasting dishonor.

And your petitioners will ever pray.

Frances Norton, Catharine Norton, Mary A. Norton, M.J. Hodge, Emily N. Page, Rachel Mason, E. Anderson, S. Ashburn, A. Wilson, S.J. Walker, E.J. Porter, A. Cushener, M.J. Kelly, Frances P. Wilson, Eliza M. Rogers, Ann Eliza Wilson, Sarah Moodey, Mary Jenkinson, Jane Wilson, Editha Veirs, Mary Veirs, Nancy Fuston, Sarah Hoghland,

Nancy Laremore, Nancy Wilson, Elizabeth Sheppard, Mary C. Green, Anna Woods, Anna Dike, Margaretta Woods, Margaret Larimore, Maria E. Larimore, Sarah S. Larimore, Martha E. Leslie, Catharine Slacke, W. D. Andrews, P. Lord, Eliza S. Wilson, Sarah Wells, Rebecca R. Morse, Hetty E. Beatty, Caroline S. Craig, Elizabeth Steenrod, Elloisa Lefflen, Lucy Whipple, N. Kilgore, C. Colwell, E. Brown, M. Patterson, R. Craig, J. M. Millan, Betsey Tappan, Margaret M. Andrews, Sarah Spencer, Mary Buchannan, do., Rebecca J. Buchannan, do., Hetty Collier, Eunice Collier, Elizabeth Beatty, Jane Beatty, Sarah Means, Elizabeth Sage.

Source: "Memorial of the Ladies of Steubenville, Ohio, Against the forcible removal of the Indians without the limits of the United States." Probable Date: February 15, 1830. United States House of Representatives, Bills and Resolutions, 21st Congress, 1st Session, Report no. 209. A Century of Lawmaking for a New Nation: U.S. Congressional Documents and Debates, American Memory, Library of Congress.

Letter to Catherine Beecher (1836), from Angelina Grimké

The letter below is addressed to Catherine Beecher, a prominent reformer on behalf of women's education. Beecher promoted teaching as a career for women, claiming that it utilized women's "natural" nurturing talent. Unlike Angelina Grimké, Beecher rejected the notion that the sexes should have equal rights, advocating instead that women pursue careers within their own sphere. Grimké starkly and eloquently protested that when it came to rights, the only consideration was being human, and that differences in sex or race were irrelevant.

The investigation of the rights of the slave has led me to a better understanding of my own. I have found the Anti-Slavery cause to be the high school of morals in our land—the school in which *human rights* are more fully investigated, and better understood and taught, than in any other. Here a great fundamental principle is uplifted and illuminated, and from this central light, rays innumerable stream all around. Human beings have *rights,* because they are *moral* beings: the rights of *all* men grow out of their moral nature; and as all men have the same moral nature, they have essentially the same rights. These rights may be wrested from the slave, but

they cannot be alienated: his title to himself is as perfect *now,* as is that of Lyman Beecher: it is stamped on his moral being, and is, like it, imperishable. Now if rights are founded in the nature of our moral being, then the *mere circumstance of sex* does not give to man higher rights and responsibilities, than to woman. To suppose that it does, would be to deny the self-evident truth, that the "physical constitution is the mere instrument of the moral nature." To suppose that it does, would be to break up utterly the relations, of the two natures, and to reverse their functions, exalting the animal nature into a monarch, and humbling the moral into a slave; making the former a proprietor, and the latter its property. When human beings are regarded as *moral beings, sex,* instead of being enthroned upon the summit, administering upon rights and responsibilities, sinks into insignificance and nothingness . . .

This regulation of duty by the mere circumstance of sex, rather than by the fundamental principle of moral being, has led to all that multifarious train of evils flowing out of the anti-Christian doctrine of masculine and feminine virtues. By this doctrine, man has been converted into the warrior, and clothed with sternness, and those other kindred qualities, which in common estimation belong to his character as a *man;* whilst woman has been taught to lean upon an arm of flesh, to sit as a doll arrayed in "gold, and pearls, and costly array," to be admired for her personal charms, and caressed and humored like a spoiled child, or converted into a mere drudge to suit the convenience of her lord and master . . .

. . . I recognize no rights but *human* rights—I know nothing of men's rights and women's rights; for in Christ Jesus, there is neither male nor female. It is my solemn conviction, that, until this principle of equality is recognised and embodied in practice, the church can do nothing effectual for the permanent reformation of the world. Woman was the first transgressor, and the first victim of power. In all heathen nations, she has been the slave of man, and Christian nations have never acknowledged her rights. Nay more, no Christian denomination or Society has ever acknowledged them on the broad basis of humanity. I know that in some denominations, she is permitted to preach the gospel; not from a conviction of her rights, nor upon the ground of her equality as a *human being,* but of her equality in spiritual gifts—for we find that woman, even in these Societies, is allowed no voice in framing the Discipline by which she is to be governed.

Now, I believe it is woman's right to have a voice in all the laws and regulations by which she is to be *governed,* whether in Church or State; and that the present arrangements of society, on these points, are *a violation of human rights, a rank usurpation of power,* a violent seizure and confiscation of what is sacredly and inalienably hers—thus inflicting upon woman outrageous wrongs, working mischief incalculable in the social circle, and in its influence on the world producing only evil, and that continually. *If* Ecclesiastical and Civil governments are ordained of God, *then* I contend that woman has just as much right to sit in solemn counsel in Conventions, Conferences, Associations and General Assemblies, as man—just as much right to sit upon the throne of England, or in the Presidential chair of the United States.

Source: Grimké, Angelina Emily. *Letters to Catherine Beecher: In Reply to an Essay on Slavery and Abolitionism, Addressed to A. E. Grimké, Revised by the Author.* Boston, MA: I. Knapp, 1838, 103–121. Reprinted and Introduction in Langley, Winston E., and Vivian C. Fox, eds. *Women's Rights in the United States: A Documentary History.* Santa Barbara, CA: Greenwood, 1994.

Massachusetts Churches Respond to Grimké Sisters Speaking in Public (1837)

The following letter was written by the Congregational Church leaders in Massachusetts in response to the public antislavery addresses of Angelina and Sarah Grimké in that state. Strongly condemnatory, it referred to the Grimké speeches as "promiscuous conversation" since men were also present, and warned that should this activity persist and scriptural injunction continue to be trespassed, the female character would suffer "permanent injury." The letter only fueled the women's rights commitment of the Grimké sisters and others.

. . . We invite your attention to the dangers which at present seem to threaten the female character with widespread and permanent injury.

The appropriate duties and influence of woman are clearly stated in the New Testament. Those duties and that influence are unobtrusive and private, but the source of mighty power. When the mild, dependent, softening influence of woman upon the sternness of man's opinions is fully exercised, society feels the effects of it in a thousand forms. The power of woman is in her dependence, flowing from the consciousness of that weakness which God has given her for her protection, and which keeps her in those departments of life that form

the character of individuals and of the nation. There are social influences which females use in promoting piety and the great objects of Christian benevolence which we cannot too highly commend. We appreciate the unostentatious prayers and efforts of woman in advancing the cause of religion at home and abroad; in Sabbath-schools; in leading religious inquirers to the pastors for instruction; and in all such associated effort as becomes the modesty of her sex; and earnestly hope that she may abound more and more in these labors of piety and love.

But when she assumes the place and tone of man as a public reformer, our care and protection of her seem unnecessary; we put ourselves in self-defence against her; she yields the power which God has given her for protection, and her character becomes unnatural. If the vine, whose strength and beauty is to lean upon the trellis-work and half conceal its clusters, thinks to assume the independence and the overshadowing nature of the elm, it will not only cease to bear fruit, but fall in shame and dishonor into the dust. We cannot, therefore, but regret the mistaken conduct of those who encourage females, to bear an obtrusive and ostentatious part in measures of reform, and countenance any of that sex who so far forget themselves as to itinerate in the character of public lecturers and teachers.—We especially deplore the intimate acquaintance and promiscuous conversation of females with regard to things "which ought not to be named"; by which that modesty and delicacy which is the charm of domestic life, and which constitutes the true influence of woman in society, is consumed, and the way opened, as we apprehend, for degeneracy and ruin.

We say these things not to discourage proper influences against sin, but to secure such reformation (!) as we believe is Scriptural, and will be permanent.

Source: "Pastoral Letter of the General Association of Massachusetts (Orthodox) to the Churches under Their Care (1837)." Reprinted and Introduction in Langley, Winston E., and Vivian C. Fox, eds. *Women's Rights in the United States: A Documentary History.* Santa Barbara, CA: Greenwood, 1994.

Letters on the Equality of the Sexes (1838), Sarah Grimké

In the following letters, Sarah Grimké depicts the condition of women in America during the 1830s as limited and superficial, immoral, and unequal. She rests the blame for this deplorable state on society's belief that there are basic differences between the sexes. As a result, women are used—willingly in the fashionable world—as men's play objects, and—unwillingly in the world of slavery—to satisfy the lust of masters.

In addition, this stress on sexual differences has relegated females almost solely to domestic affairs and precluded equal education with men. While church officials forbid women to preach, they hypocritically allow women to teach Sunday school. Grimké finds that these false, socially constructed distinctions harm society.

Letter VIII

. . . I shall now proceed to make a few remarks on the condition of women in my own country. . . .

They seldom think that men will be allured by intellectual acquirements, because they find, that where any mental superiority exists, a woman is generally shunned and regarded as stepping out of her "appropriate sphere," which, in their view, is to dress, to dance, to set out to the best possible advantage her person, to read the novels which inundate the press, and which do more to destroy her character as a rational creature, than any thing else. Fashionable women regard themselves, and are regarded by men, as pretty toys or as mere instruments of pleasure; and the vacuity of mind, the heartlessness, the frivolity which is the necessary result of this false and debasing estimate of women, can only be fully understood by those who have mingled in the folly and wickedness of fashionable life.

Letter XV

To perform our duties, we must comprehend our rights and responsibilities; and it is because we do not understand, that we now fall so far short in the discharge of our obligations.

Unaccustomed to think for ourselves, and to search the sacred volume, to see how far we are living up to the design of Jehovah in our creation, we have rested satisfied with the sphere marked out for us by man, never detecting the fallacy of that reasoning which forbids women to exercise some of her noblest faculties, and stamps with the reproach of indelicacy those actions by which women were formerly dignified and exalted in the church.

I should not mention this subject again, if it were not to point out to my sisters what seems to me an irresistible conclusion from the literal interpretation of St. Paul, without reference to the context, and the peculiar circumstances and abuses which drew forth the expressions,

"I suffer not a woman to teach"—"Let your women keep silence in the church," i.e. congregation. It is manifest, that if the apostle meant what his words imply, when taken in the strictest sense, then women have no right to *teach* Sabbath or day schools, or to open their lips to sing in the assemblies of the people; yet young and delicate women are engaged in all these offices; they are expressly trained to exhibit themselves, and raise their voices to a high pitch in the choirs of our places of worship. I do not intend to sit in judgment on my sisters for doing these things; I only want them to see, that they are as really infringing a *supposed* divine command, by instructing their pupils in the Sabbath or day schools, and by singing in the congregation, as if they were engaged in preaching the unsearchable riches of Christ to a lost and perishing world. Why, then, are we permitted to break this injunction in some points, and so sedu[l]ously warned not to overstep the bounds set for us by our *brethren* in another? Simply, as I believe, because in the one case we subserve *their* views and *their* interests, and act *in subordination to them;* whilst in the other, we come in contact with their interests, and claim to be on an equality with them in the highest and most important trust ever committed to man, namely, the ministry of the word. It is manifest, that if women were permitted to be ministers of the gospel, as they unquestionably were in the primitive ages of the Christian church, it would interfere materially with the present organized system of spiritual power and ecclesiastical authority, which is now vested solely in the hands of men. It would either show that all the paraphernalia of theological seminaries, &c. &c. to prepare men to become evangelists, is wholly unnecessary, or it would create a necessity for similar institutions in order to prepare women for the same office; and this would be an encroachment on that learning, which our kind brethren have so ungenerously monopolized. I do not ask any one to believe *my* statements, or adopt my conclusions, because they are mine; but I do earnestly entreat my sisters to lay aside their prejudices, and examine these subjects *for themselves,* regardless of the "traditions of men," because they are intimately connected with their duty and their usefulness in the present important crisis.

All who know any thing of the present system of benevolent and religious operations, know that women are performing an important part in them, in *subserviency to men,* who guide our labors, and are often the recipients of those benefits of education we toil to confer, and which we rejoice they can enjoy, although it is their mandate which deprives us of the same advantages. Now, whether our brethren have defrauded us intentionally, or unintentionally, the wrong we suffer is equally the same . . .

There is another and much more numerous class in this country, who are withdrawn by education or circumstances from the circle of fashionable amusements, but who are brought up with the dangerous and absurd idea, that *marriage* is a kind of preferment; and that to be able to keep their husband's house, and render his situation comfortable, is the end of her being. Much that she does and says and thinks is done in reference to this situation; and to be married is too often held up to the view of girls as the sine qua non of human happiness and human existence. For this purpose more than for any other, I verily believe the majority of girls are trained. This is demonstrated by the imperfect education which is bestowed upon them, and the little pains taken to cultivate their minds, after they leave school, by the little time allowed them for reading, and by the idea being constantly inculcated, that although all household concerns should be attended to with scrupulous punctuality at particular seasons, the improvement of their intellectual capacities is only a secondary consideration, and may serve as an occupation to fill up the odds and ends of time. In most families, it is considered a matter of far more consequence to call a girl off from making a pie, or a pudding, than to interrupt her whilst engaged in her studies. This mode of training necessarily exalts, in their view, the animal above the intellectual and spiritual nature, and teaches women to regard themselves as a kind of machinery, necessary to keep the domestic engine in order, but of little value as the *intelligent* companions of men.

Let no one think, from these remarks, that I regard a knowledge of housewifery as beneath the acquisition of women. Far from it: I believe that a complete knowledge of household affairs is an indispensable requisite in a woman's education,—that by the mistress of a family, whether married or single, doing her duty thoroughly and *under standingly,* the happiness of the family is increased to an incalculable degree, as well as a vast amount of time and money saved. All I complain of is, that our education consists so almost exclusively in culinary and other manual operations. I do long to see the time, when it will no longer be necessary for women to expend so many precious hours in furnishing "a well spread table," but that their husbands will forego some of their accustomed indulgences in this way, and encourage their wives to devote some portion of their time to mental cultivation, even at the expense of having to dine sometimes on baked potatoes, or bread and butter . . .

There is another way in which the general opinion, that women are inferior to men, is manifested, that bears with tremendous effect on the laboring class, and indeed on almost all who are obliged to earn a subsistence, whether it be by mental or physical exertion—I allude to the disproportionate value set on the time and labor of men and of women. A man who is engaged in teaching, can always, I believe, command a higher price for tuition than a woman—even when he teaches the same branches, and is not in any respect superior to the woman. This I know is the case in boarding and other schools with which I have been acquainted, and it is so in every occupation in which the sexes engage indiscriminately.

Source: Grimké, Sarah. *Letters on the Equality of the Sexes and the Condition of Women Addressed to Mary S. Parker.* Boston, MA: I. Knapp, 1838, 46–55,115–128. Reprinted and Introduction in Langley, Winston E., and Vivian C. Fox, eds. *Women's Rights in the United States: A Documentary History.* Santa Barbara, CA: Greenwood, 1994.

The Right of the People, Men and Women, to Petition (1838), John Quincy Adams

This document concerns some of the discussion in the House of Representatives regarding the question of women's right to petition. Since women could not vote, the petition was one of the few means open to them by which to influence public policy. They used this instrument over and over again to protest against slavery and to enlarge their rights in the public sphere.

Women from the Massachusetts district represented by John Quincy Adams, ex-President and now member of the House, wrote petitions against the extension of slavery in Texas. Mr. Howard, chairman of the Committee of Foreign Affairs, maintained that even the petition should be declared out of bounds for women; their proper sphere was the domestic one. Adams, however, believed otherwise. In his refutation of Howard, he brought to bear evidence from the Bible, from history, and from the Constitution, which supported women's right to petition.

. . . When I last addressed the House I was engaged in discussing the principle asserted by the chairman of the Committee on Foreign Affairs; the practical effect of which must be to deprive one half the population of these United States of the right of petition before this House. I say it goes to deprive the entire female sex of all right of petition here. The principle was not an abstract principle. It is stated abstractedly, in the report of his remarks, which I have once read to the House. I will read it again; it is highly important, and well deserving of the attention of this House, and its solemn decision. It referred to all petitions on the subject of the annexation of Texas to this Union which come from women.

"Many of these petitions were signed by women. He always felt regret when petitions thus signed were presented to the House relating to political matters. He thought that these females could have a sufficient field for the exercise of their influence in the discharge of their duties to their fathers, their husbands, or their children, cheering the domestic circle, and shedding over it the mild radiance of the social virtues, instead of rushing into the fierce struggles of political life. He felt sorrow at this departure from their proper sphere, in which there was abundant room for the practice of the most extensive benevolence and philanthropy, because he considered it discreditable, not only to their own particular section of the country, but also to the national character, and thus giving him a right to express this opinion."

Now, I say, in the first place, that this principle is erroneous, vicious. As a moral principle it is vicious; and in its application the chairman of the committee made it the ground of a reproach to the females of my district; thousands of whom, besides those 238 who signed the first petition I presented here, have signed similar petitions.

Why does it follow that women are fitted for nothing but the cares of domestic life? for bearing children, and cooking the food of a family? devoting all their time to the domestic circle—to promoting the immediate personal comfort of their husbands, brothers, and sons? Observe, sir, the point of departure between the chairman of the committee and myself. I admit that it is their duty to attend to these things. I subscribe, fully, to the elegant compliment passed by him upon those members of the female sex who devote their time to these duties. But I say that the correct principle is, that women are not only justified, but exhibit the most exalted virtue when they do depart from the domestic circle, and enter on the concerns of their country, of humanity, and of their God. The mere departure of woman from the duties of the domestic circle, far from being a reproach to her, is a virtue of the highest order, when it is done from purity of motive, by appropriate means, and towards a virtuous purpose. [. . .]

Now, I aver, further, that in the instance to which his observation refers, viz: in the act of petitioning against the annexation of Texas to this Union, the motive was

pure, the means appropriate, and the purpose virtuous, in the highest degree. As an evident proof of this I recur to the particular petition from which this debate took its rise, viz: to the first petition I presented here against the annexation—a petition consisting of three lines, and signed by 238 women of Plymouth, a principal town in my own district. Their words are:

"The undersigned, women of Plymouth (Mass.), thoroughly aware of the sinfulness of slavery, and the consequent impolicy and disastrous tendency of its extension in our country, do most respectfully remonstrate, with all our souls, against the annexation of Texas to the United States, as a slaveholding territory."

Those are the words of their memorial. And I say that, in presenting it here, their motive was pure, and of the highest order of purity. They petitioned under a conviction that the consequence of the annexation would be the advancement of that which is sin in the sight of God, viz: slavery. I say, further, that the means were appropriate, because it is Congress who must decide on the question; and, therefore, it is proper that they should petition Congress if they wish to prevent the annexation. And I say, in the third place, that the end was virtuous, pure, and of the most exalted character, viz: to prevent the perpetuation and spread of slavery through America. I say, moreover, that I subscribe, in my own person, to every word the petition contains.

Source: Adams, John Quincy. *The Right of the People, Men and Women, to Petition: On the Freedom of Speech and Debate.* Washington, D.C.: Gales and Seaton, 1838, pp. 67–68. Reprinted and Introduction in Langley, Winston E., and Vivian C. Fox, eds. *Women's Rights in the United States: A Documentary History.* Westport, CT: Praeger, 1994, 1998.

Mississippi Married Women's Property Act (1839)

Prior to the Married Women's Property Act, American women could not own property, earn a salary, or enter into contracts. Over several decades, statutes were passed that allowed women to participate more fully. The Mississippi Married Women's Property Law allowed women to own property, including slaves.

AN ACT for the protection and preservation of the rights and property of Married Women.

Section 1. *Be it enacted, by the Legislature of the State of Mississippi,* That any married woman may become seized or possessed of any property, real or personal, by direct bequest, demise, gift, purchase, or distribution, in her own name, and as of her own property: *Provided,* the same does not come from her husband after coverture.

Section 2. *And be it further enacted,* That hereafter when any woman possessed of a property in slaves, shall marry, her property in such slaves and their natural increase shall continue to her, notwithstanding her coverture; and she shall have, hold, and possess the same, as her separate property, exempt from any liability for the debts or contracts of the husband.

Section 3. *And be it further enacted,* That when any woman, during coverture, shall become entitled to, or possessed of, slaves by conveyance, gift, inheritance, distribution, or otherwise, such slaves, together with their natural increase, shall enure and belong to the wife, in like manner as is above provided as to slaves which she may possess at the time of marriage.

Section 4. *And be it further enacted,* That the control and management of all such slaves, the direction of their labor, and the receipt of the productions thereof, shall remain to the husband, agreeably to the laws heretofore in force. All suits to recover the property or possession of such slaves, shall be prosecuted or defended, as the case may be, in the joint names of the husband and wife. In the case of the death of the wife, such slaves descend and go to the children of her and her said husband, jointly begotten, and in case there shall be no child born to the wife during such her coverture, then such slaves shall descend and go to the husband and to his heirs.

Section 5. *And be it further enacted,* That the slaves owned by a feme covert under the provisions of this act, may be sold by the joint deed of husband and wife, executed, proved, and recorded, agreeably to the laws now in force in regard to the conveyance of the real estate of feme coverts, and not otherwise.

Approved, February 15, 1839.

Source: Alden, T.J. Fox, and J.A. Van Hoesen. *A Digest of the Laws of Mississippi, Comprising All the Laws of a General Nature, Including the Acts of the Session of 1839.* New York: Alexander S. Gould, 1839, 920–921.

A Treatise on Domestic Economy (1841), Catharine Beecher

In 1841 Catharine Beecher wrote a book that attempted to explain the duties that American women should perform at home. Rather than looking outside the home to contribute to American society, Beecher spelled out ways that the chores carried out by the wife at home were important in the development of America. She believed that women should be educated so that they could teach their children, were more needed at home, and the involvement of women in politics would corrupt them.

There are some reasons, why American women should feel an interest in the support of the democratic institutions of their Country, which it is important that they should consider which is the basis of all our civil and political institutions, is, that "all men are created equal," and that they are equally entitled to "life, liberty, and the pursuit of happiness."

But it can readily be seen, that this is only another mode of expressing the fundamental principle which the Great Ruler of the Universe has established, as the law of His eternal government.

"Thou shalt love thy neighbor as thyself;" and "Whatsoever ye would that men should do to you, do ye even so to them," are the Scripture forms, by which the Supreme lawgiver requires that each individual of our race shall regard the happiness of others, as of the same value as his own; and which forbid any institution, in private or civil life, which secures advantages to one class, by sacrificing the interests of another.

The principles of democracy, then, are identical with the principles of Christianity.

But, in order that each individual may pursue and secure the highest degree of happiness within his reach, unimpeded by the selfish interests of others, a system of laws must be established, which sustain certain relations and dependencies in social and civil life. What these relations and their attending obligations shall be, are to be determined, not with reference to the wishes and interests of a few, but solely with reference to the general good of all; so that each individual shall have his own interest, as well as the public benefit, secured by them.

For this purposes it is needful that certain relations be sustained, which involve the duties of subordination. There must be the magistrate and the subject, one of whom is the superior, and the other the inferior. There must be the relations of husband and wife, parent and child, teacher and pupil, employer and employed, each involving the relative duties of subordination. The superior, in certain particulars, is to direct, and the inferior is to yield obedience. Society could never go forward, harmoniously, nor could any craft or profession be successfully pursued, unless these superior and subordinate relations be instituted and sustained.

But who shall take the higher, and who the subordinate, stations in social and civil life? This matter, in the ease [case] of parents and children, is decided by the Creator. He has given children to the control of parents as their superiors, and to them they remain subordinate, to a certain age, or so long as they are members of their household. And parents can delegate such a portion of their authority to teachers and employers as the interests of their children require.

In most other cases, in a truly Democratic State, each individual is allowed to choose for himself who shall take the position of his superior. No woman is forced to obey any husband but the one she chooses for herself; nor is she obliged to take a husband, if she prefers to remain single. So every domestic, and every artisan or laborer, after passing from parental control, can choose the employer to whom he is to accord obedience, or if he prefers to relinquish certain advantages, he can remain without taking a subordinate place to any employer.

Each subject, also has equal power with every other to decide who shall be his superior as a ruler. The weakest, the poorest, the most illiterate has the same opportunity to determine this question, as the richest, the most learned, and the most exalted.

And the various privileges that wealth secures, are equally open to all classes. Every man may aim at riches, unimpeded by any law or institution which secures peculiar privileges to a favored class, at the expense of another. Every law, and every institution, is tested by examining whether it secures equal advantages to all; and, if the people become convinced that any regulation sacrifices the good of the majority to the interests of the smaller number, they have power to abolish it.

The institutions of monarchical and aristocratic nations are based on precisely opposite principles. They secure, to certain small and favored classes, advantages, which can be maintained, only by sacrificing the interests of the great mass of the people. Thus, the throne and aristocracy of England are supported by laws and customs, which burden the lower classes with taxes, so enormous as to deprive them of all the luxuries, and of most of the comforts, of life. Poor dwellings, scanty food, unhealthy employments, excessive labor; and entire destitution of the means and time for education, are, appointed for the lower classes, that a few may live in palaces, and riot in every indulgence.

The tendencies of democratic institutions in reference to the rights and interests of the female sex, have been fully developed in the United States; and it is in this aspect, that the subject is one of peculiar interest to American women. In this Country, it is established, both by opinion and by practice, that woman has an equal interest in all social and civil concerns; and that no domestic, civil, or political, institution, is right, which sacrifices her interest to promote that of the other sex. But in order to secure her the more firmly in all these privileges, it is decided, that, in the domestic relation she take a subordinate station, and that, in civil and political concerns, her interests be intrusted to the other sex, without her taking any part in voting, or in making and administering laws. The result of this order of things has been fairly tested, and is thus portrayed by M. De Tocqueville, a writer, who for intelligence, fidelity, and ability, ranks second to none.

"There are people in Europe, who, confounding together the different characteristics of the sexes, would make of man and woman beings not only equal, but alike. They would give to both the same functions, impose on both the same duties, and grant to both the same rights. They would mix them in all things,—their business, their occupations, their pleasures. It may readily be conceived, that, by *thus* attempting to make one sex equal to the other, both are degraded; and, from so preposterous a medley of the works of Nature, nothing could ever result, but weak men and disorderly women.

"It is not thus that the Americans understand the species of democratic equality, which may be established between the sexes. They admit, that, as Nature has appointed such wide differences between the physical and moral constitutions of man and woman, her manifest design was to give a distinct employment to their various faculties; and they hold that improvement does not consist in making beings so dissimilar do pretty nearly the same things, but in getting each of them to fulfil their respective tasks in the best possible manner. The Americans have applied to the sexes the great principle of political economy, which governs the manufacturing of our age, by carefully dividing the duties of man from those of woman, in order that the great work of Society may be the better carried on.

"In no country has such constant care been taken, as in America, to trace two clearly distinct lines of action for the two sexes, and to make them keep pace one with the other, but in two pathways which are always different. American women never manage the outward concerns of the family, or conduct a business, or take a part in political life; nor are they, on the other hand, ever compelled to perform the rough labor of the fields, or to make any of those laborious exertions, which demand the exertion of physical strength. No families are so poor, as to form an exception to this rule.

"If, on the one hand, an American woman cannot escape from the quiet circle of domestic employments, on the other hand, she is never forced to go beyond it. Hence it is, that the women of America, who often exhibit a masculine strength of understanding, and a manly energy, generally preserve great delicacy of personal appearance, and always retain the manners of women, although they sometimes show that they have the hearts and minds of men.

"Nor have the Americans ever supposed, that one consequence of democratic principles, is, the subversion of marital power, or the confusion of the natural authorities in families. They hold, that every association must have a head, in order to accomplish its object; and that the natural head of the conjugal association is man. They do not, therefore, deny him the right of directing his partner; and they maintain, that, in the smaller association of husband and wife, as well as in the great social community, the object of democracy is, to regulate and legalize the powers which are necessary, not to subvert all power.

"This opinion is not peculiar to one sex, and contested by the other. I never observed, that the women of America considered conjugal authority as a fortunate usurpation of their rights, nor that they though themselves degraded by submitting to it. It appears to me, on the contrary, that they attach a sort of pride to the voluntary surrender of their own will, and make it their boast to bend themselves to the yoke, not to shake it off. Such, at least, is the feeling expressed by the most virtuous of their sex; the others are silent; and in the United States it is not the practice for a guilty wife to clamor for the rights of woman, while she is trampling on her holiest duties.

[. . .]

It is true, that the Americans rarely lavish upon women those eager attentions which are commonly paid them in Europe. But their conduct to women always implies, that they suppose them to be virtuous and refined; and such is the respect entertained for the moral freedom of the sex, that, in the presence of a woman, the most guarded language is used, lest her ear should be offended by an expression. In America, a young unmarried woman may, alone, and without fear, undertake a long journey.

Thus the Americans do not think that man and woman have either the duty, or the right, to perform the same offices, but they show; an equal regard for both their respective parts; and though their lot is different they consider both of them, as being of equal value. They do not give to the courage of woman the same form, or the same direction, as to that of a man; but they never doubt her courage and if they hold that man and his partner ought not always to exercise their intellect and understanding in the same manner, they at least believe the understanding of one to be as sound as that of the other, and her intellect to be as clear. Thus, then, while they have allowed the social inferiority of woman to subsist they have done all they could to raise her, morally and intellectually, to the level of man; and, in this respect, they appear to me to have excellently understood the true principle of democratic improvement.

As for myself, I do not hesitate to avow, that, although the women of the United States are confined within the narrow circle of domestic life, and their situation is, in some respects, one of extreme dependence, I have nowhere seen women occupying a loftier position; and if I were asked, now I am drawing to the close of this work, in which I have spoken of so many important things done by the Americans, to what the singular prosperity and growing strength of that people ought mainly to be attributed, I should reply,—*to the superiority of their women.*"

[. . .]

It appears, then, that it is in America, alone, that women are raised to an equality with the other sex; and that, both in theory and practice, their interests are regarded as of equal value. They are made subordinate in station, only where a regard to their best interests demands it, while, as if in compensation for this, by custom and courtesy, they are always treated as superiors. Universally in this country, through every class of society, precedence is given to woman, in all the comforts, conveniences, and courtesies, of life.

In civil and political affairs, American women take no interest or concern, except so far as they sympathize with their family and personal friends; but in all cases, in which they do feel a concern, their opinions and feelings have a consideration, equal, or even superior, to that of the other sex.

In matters pertaining to the education of their children, in the selection and support of a clergyman, in all benevolent enterprises, and in all questions relating to morals or manners, they have a superior influence. In such concerns, it would be impossible to carry a point, contrary to their judgement and feelings; while an enterprise, sustained by them, will seldom fail of success.

If those who are bewailing themselves over the fancied wrongs and injuries of woman in this Nation, could only see things as they are, they would know, that, whatever remnants of a barbarous or aristocratic age may remain in our civil institutions, in reference to the interests of women, it is only because they are ignorant of them, or do not use their influence to have them rectified; for it is very certain that there is nothing reasonable, which American women would unite in asking, that would not readily be bestowed.

The preceding remarks, then, illustrate the position, that the democratic institutions of this Country are in reality no other than the principles of Christianity carried into operation, and that they tend to place woman in her true position in society, as having equal rights with the other sex; and that, in fact they have secured to American women a lofty and fortunate position, which, as yet, has been attained by the women of no other nation.

There is another topic, presented in the work of the above author, which demands the profound attention of American women.

The following is taken from that part of the Introduction to the work, illustrating the position, that, for ages, there has been a constant progress, in all civilized nations, towards the democratic equality attained in this Country.

"The various occurrences of national existence have every where turned to the advantage of democracy; all men have aided it by their exertions; those who have intentionally labored in its cause, and those who have served it unwittingly; those who have fought for it, and those who have declared themselves its opponents, have all been driven along in the same track, have al labored to one end; 'all have been blind instruments in the hands of God.'

"The gradual developement of the equality of conditions, is, therefore, a Providential fact; and it possesses all the characteristics of a Divine decree: it is universal, it is durable, it constantly eludes all human interference, and all events, as well as all men, contribute to its progress.

"The whole book, which is here offered to the public, has been written under the impression of a kind of religious dread, produced in the author's mind, by the contemplation of so

irresistible a revolution, which has advanced for centuries, in spite of such amazing obstacles, and which is still proceeding in the midst of the ruins it has made.

"It is not necessary that God Himself should speak, in order to disclose to us the unquestionable signs of His will. We can discern them in the habitual course of Nature, and in the invariable tendency of events.

"If the men of our time were led, by attentive observation, and by sincere reflection, to acknowledge that the gradual and progressive developement of social equality is at once the past and future of their history, this solitary truth would confer the sacred character of a Divine decree upon the change. To attempt to check democracy, would be, in that case, to resist the will of God; and the nations would then be constrained to make the best of the social lot awarded to them by Providence."

[. . .]

But the part to be enacted by American women, in this great moral enterprise, is the point to which special attention should here be directed.

The success of democratic institutions, as is conceded by all, depends upon the intellectual and moral character of the mass of the people. If they are intelligent and virtuous, democracy is a blessing; but if they are ignorant and wicked, it is only a curse, and as much more dreadful than any other form of civil government, as a thousand tyrants are more to be dreaded than one. It is equally conceded, that the formation of the moral and intellectual character of the young is committed mainly to the female hand. The mother forms the character of the future man; the sister bends the fibres that are hereafter to be the forest tree; the wife sways the heart, whose energies may turn for good or for evil the destinies of a nation. Let the women of a country be made virtuous and intelligent, and the men will certainly be the same. The proper education of a man decides the welfare of an individual; but educate a woman, and the interests of a whole family are secured.

If this be so, as none will deny, then to American women, more than to any others on earth, is committed the exalted privilege of extending over the world those blessed influences, which are to renovate degraded man, and "clothe all climes with beauty."

No American woman, then, has any occasion for feeling that hers is; an humble or insignificant lot. The value of what an individual accomplishes, is to be estimated by the importance of the enterprise achieved, and not by the particular position of the laborer. The drops of heaven which freshen the earth, are each of equal value, whether they fall in the low-land meadow, or the princely parterre. The builders of a temple are of equal importance, whether they labor on the foundations, or toil upon the dome.

Thus, also, with those labors which are to be made effectual in the regeneration of the Earth. And it is by forming a habit of regarding the apparently insignificant efforts of each isolated laborer, in a comprehensive manner, as indispensable portions of a grand result, that the minds of all, however humble their sphere of service, can be invigorated and cheered. The woman, who is rearing a family of children; the woman, who labors in the schoolroom; the woman, who, in her retired chamber, earns, with her needle, the mite, which contributes to the intellectual and moral elevation of her Country; even the humble domestic, whose example and influence may be moulding [and] forming young minds, while her faithful services sustain a prosperous domestic state;—each and all may be animated by the consciousness that they are agents in accomplishing the greatest work that ever was committed to human responsibility. It is the building of a glorious temple whose base shall be coextensive with the bounds of the earth, whose summit shall pierce the skies, whose splendor shall beam on all lands, and those who hew the lowliest stone, as much as those who carve the highest capital, will be equally honored, when its top-stone shall be laid, with new rejoicings of the morning stars, and shoutings of the sons of God.

Source: Beecher, Catharine E. *A Treatise on Domestic Economy, for the Use of Young Ladies at Home, and at School, rev. ed.* Boston, MA: T. H. Webb, 1842. Reprinted and Introduction in Zeman, Theodore J., and Jolyon P. Girard, et al., eds. *Daily Life through American History in Primary Documents.* Santa Barbara, CA: Greenwood, 2011.

Shaw v. Shaw (1845)

The state of Connecticut recognized "intolerable cruelty" as grounds for divorce. The case of Shaw v. Shaw *gives a fairly standard example of the terrifying circumstances women had to face in order to satisfy the requirement of intolerable cruelty. In this case the requirement was not satisfied. In the face of what two judges of the lower court found to be "torture inflicted upon" Mrs. Shaw, the supreme court of the state rejected her plea for divorce and upheld what it considered the authority of the husband in the home.*

A decree of divorce, on the ground of intolerable cruelty, will not be granted, unless the acts complained of are in fact intolerable, and as cruel at least as those for which, under the head of extreme cruelty, the courts in Great Britain and elsewhere divorce a mensa et thoro.

Vulgar, obscene and harsh language, with epithets suited deeply to wound the feelings and excite the passions, but not accompanied with any act or menace indicating violence to the person, does not constitute such cruelty. The unreasonable exercise of the husband's authority in regard to his wife's social intercourse with her relatives and friends, excluding them from his house and forbidding her to visit them, does not constitute such cruelty.

Where it was found, that the husband repeatedly compelled his wife, against her wishes and remonstrances, to occupy the same bed with himself, when, in consequence of her ill health, it was indelicate, improper, unreasonable and injurious to her health so to do, and was calculated to endanger, and did in fact endanger her health; though this effect was not in fact intended or forseen by him; it was held, that such conduct of the husband did not constitute intolerable cruelty, within the statutes.

And where it was further found, that though she had no reason to fear from him personal violence of any other character; yet she had just reason to fear, that he would again compel her to occupy the same bed with him, regardless of the consequences to her health; it was held, that this fact, neither by itself, nor in connection with the other facts in the case, entitled her to a decree of divorce. [One judge dissenting]

Source: Shaw v. Shaw, 17 Conn. 189 (1845). Reprinted and Introduction in Langley, Winston E., and Vivian C. Fox, eds. *Women's Rights in the United States: A Documentary History.* Santa Barbara, CA: Greenwood, 1994.

Testimony of Female Factory Workers before Massachusetts State Legislature (1845)

Labor leader, reformer, and entrepreneur, Sarah Bagley, along with others, petitioned and gathered signatures demanding a 10-hour day. She testified before the Massachusetts State Legislature, giving evidence of unhealthy conditions and long hours working in the mills.

Massachusetts House Document, no. 50, March, 1845.

The Special Committee to which was referred sundry petitions relating to the hours of labor, have considered the same and submit the following Report:

{ . . .}

The whole number of names on the several petitions is 2,139, of which 1,151 are from Lowell. A very large proportion of the Lowell petitioners are females. Nearly one half of the Andover petitioners are females. The petition from Fall River is signed exclusively by males.

In view of the number and respectability of the petitioners who had brought their grievances before the Legislature, the Committee asked for and obtained leave of the House to send for "persons and papers," in order that they might enter into an examination of the matter, and report the result of their examination to the Legislature as a basis for legislative action, should any be deemed necessary.

On the 13th of February, the Committee held a session to hear the petitioners from the city of Lowell. Six of the female and three of the male petitioners were present, and gave in their testimony.

The first petitioner who testified was *Eliza R. Hemmingway*. She had worked 2 years and 9 months in the Lowell Factories; 2 years in the Middlesex, and 9 months in the Hamilton Corporations. Her employment is weaving-works by the piece . . . Her wages average from $16 to $23 a month exclusive of board. She complained of the hours for labor being too many, and the time for meals too limited. In the summer season, the work is commenced at 5 o'clock, A.M., and continued till 7 o'clock, P.M., with half an hour for breakfast and three quarters of an hour for dinner. During eight months of the year, but half an hour is allowed for dinner. The air in the room she considered not to be wholesome. There were 293 small lamps and 61 large lamps lighted in the room in which she worked, when evening work is required. These lamps are also lighted sometimes in the morning. About 130 females, 11 men, and 12 children (between the ages of 11 and 14) work in the room with her. She thought the children enjoyed about as good health as children generally do. The children work but 9 months out of 12. The other 3 months they must attend school. Thinks that there is no day when there are less than six of the females out of the mill from sickness. Has known as many as thirty. She, herself, is out quite often, on account of sickness. There was more sickness in the Summer than in the Winter months; though in the Summer, lamps are not lighted. She thought there was a general desire among the females to work but ten hours, regardless of pay.

[. . .] A large number come to Lowell to make money to aid their parents who are poor. She knew of many cases where married women came to Lowell and worked in the mills to assist their husbands to pay for their farms. The moral character of the operatives is good. There was only one American female in the room with her who could not write her name.

Miss Sarah G. Bagley said she had worked in the Lowell Mills eight years and a half, six years and a half on the Hamilton Corporation, and two years on the Middlesex. She is a weaver, and works by the piece. She worked in the mills three years before her health began to fail. She is a native of New Hampshire, and went home six weeks during the summer. Last year she was out of the mill a third of the time. She thinks the health of the operatives is not so good as the health of females who do house-work or millinery business. The chief evil, so far as health is concerned, is the shortness of time allowed for meals. The next evil is the length of time employed—not giving them time to cultivate their minds. She spoke of the high moral and intellectual character of the girls. That many were engaged as teachers in the Sunday schools. That many attended the lectures of the Lowell Institute; and she thought, if more time was allowed, that more lectures would be given and more girls attend. She thought that the girls generally were favorable to the ten hour system. She had presented a petition, same as the one before the Committee, to 132 girls, most of whom said that they would prefer to work but ten hours. In a pecuniary point of view, it would be better, as their health would be improved. They would have more time for sewing. Their intellectual, moral and religious habits would also be benefited by the change. Miss Bagley said, in addition to her labor in the mills, she had kept evening school during the winter months, for four years, and thought that this extra labor must have injured her health.

Miss Judith Payne testified that she came to Lowell 16 years ago, and worked a year and a half in the Merrimack Cotton Mills, left there on account of ill health, and remained out over seven years. She was sick most of the time she was out. Seven years ago she went to work in the Boott Mills, and has remained there ever since; works by the piece. She has lost, during the last seven years, about one year from ill health. She is a weaver, and attends three looms. Last pay-day she drew $14.66 for five weeks work; this was exclusive of board. She was absent during the five weeks but half a day. She says there is a very general feeling in favor of the ten hour system among the operatives. She attributes her ill health to the long hours of labor, the shortness of time for meals, and the bad air of the mills. She had never spoken to Mr. French, the agent, or to the overseer of her room, in relation to these matters. She could not say that more operatives died in Lowell than other people.

Miss Olive J. Clark is employed on the Lawrence Corporation; has been there five years; makes about $1.62 1/2 per week, exclusive of board. She has been home to New Hampshire to school. Her health never was good. The work is not laborious; can sit down about a quarter of the time. About fifty girls work in the spinning room with her, three of whom signed the petition. She is in favor of the ten hour system, and thinks that the long hours had an effect upon her health. She is kindly treated by her employers. There is hardly a week in which there is not some one out on account of sickness. Thinks the air is bad, on account of the small particles of cotton which fly about. She has never spoken with the agent or overseer about working only ten hours.

Miss Cecilia Phillips has worked four years in Lowell. Her testimony was similar to that given by Miss Clark.

Miss Elizabeth Rowe has worked in Lowell 16 months, all the time on the Lawrence Corporation, came from Maine, she is a weaver, works by the piece, runs four looms. "My health," she says, "has been very good indeed since I worked there, averaged three dollars a week since I have been there besides my board; have heard very little about the hours of labor being too long." She consented to have her name put on the petition because Miss Phillips asked her to. She would prefer to work only ten hours. Between 50 and 60 work in the room with her. Her room is better ventilated and more healthy than most others. Girls who wish to attend lectures can go out before the bell rings; my overseer lets them go, also Saturdays they go out before the bell rings. It was her wish to attend four looms. She has a sister who has worked in the mill seven years. Her health is very good. Don't know that she has ever been out on account of sickness. The general health of the operatives is good. Have never spoken to my employers about the work being too hard, or the hours too long. Don't know any one who has been hastened to a premature grave by factory labor. I never attended any of the lectures in Lowell on the ten hour system. Nearly all the female operatives in Lowell work by the piece; and of the petitioners who appeared before the Committee, Miss Hemmingway, Miss Bagley, Miss Payne and Miss Rowe work by the piece, and Miss Clark and Miss Phillips by the week. {. . .}

Source: Massachusetts House Document, no. 50, March, 1845. *Documents Printed by Order of the House of Representatives of the Commonwealth of Massachusetts, During the Session of the General Court, A.D. 1845.* Boston, MA: Dutton and Wentworth, 1845.

Declaration of Sentiments (1848)

Principally drafted by Elizabeth Cady Stanton and approved by the delegates at the first women's rights convention, held in Seneca Falls, New York, in July of 1848, the Declaration of Sentiments became the foundational document in the organized movement for women's rights in the United States. Stanton and the delegates purposely modeled their manifesto on the Declaration of Independence. The first part of the Declaration, excerpted below, outlined women's civil, social, legal, religious, and political grievances. This was followed by a series of Resolutions, which proclaimed for women the same rights and responsibilities men enjoyed as citizens of a democracy.

Reaction to the Declaration of Sentiments was decidedly mixed, even among supporters of women's rights. Many feared that the document's emphasis on woman suffrage might impede the fight for other rights for women, including married women's property rights. Other, far more critical, observers chastised the female convention participants for dangerously overstepping the bounds of woman's sphere. Women's rights advocates fully expected that their bold statement would be summarily mocked and dismissed. They nonetheless continued to rely on the Declaration of Sentiments as a source of inspiration and direction as they bravely forged ahead in the struggle for gender equality in the decades to come.

When, in the course of human events, it becomes necessary for one portion of the family of man to assume among the people of the earth a position different from that which they have hitherto occupied, but one to which the laws of nature and of nature's God entitle them, a decent respect to the opinions of mankind requires that they should declare the causes that impel them to such a course.

We hold these truths to be self-evident: that all men and women are created equal; that they are endowed by their Creator with certain inalienable rights; that among these are life, liberty, and the pursuit of happiness; that to secure these rights governments are instituted, deriving their just powers from the consent of the governed. Whenever any form of government becomes destructive of these ends, it is the right of those who suffer from it to refuse allegiance to it, and to insist upon the institution of a new government, laying its foundation on such principles, and organizing its powers in such form, as to them shall seem most likely to effect their safety and happiness. Prudence, indeed, will dictate that governments long established should not be changed for light and transient causes; and accordingly all experience hath shown that mankind are more disposed to suffer, while evils are sufferable, than to right themselves by abolishing the forms to which they were accustomed. But when a long train of abuses and usurpations, pursuing invariably the same object, evinces a design to reduce them under absolute despotism, it is their duty to throw off such government, and to provide new guards for their future security. Such has been the patient sufferance of the women under this government, and such is now the necessity which constrains them to demand the equal station to which they are entitled.

The history of mankind is a history of repeated injuries and usurpations on the part of man toward woman, having in direct object the establishment of an absolute tyranny over her. To prove this, let facts be submitted to a candid world.

He has never permitted her to exercise her inalienable right to the elective franchise.

He has compelled her to submit to laws, in the formation of which she had no voice.

He has withheld from her rights which are given to the most ignorant and degraded men—both natives and foreigners.

Having deprived her of this first right of a citizen, the elective franchise, thereby leaving her without representation in the halls of legislation, he has oppressed her on all sides.

He has made her, if married, in the eye of the law, civilly dead.

He has taken from her all right in property, even to the wages she earns.

He has made her morally, an irresponsible being, as she can commit many crimes with impunity, provided they be done in the presence of her husband. In the covenant of marriage, she is compelled to promise obedience to her husband, he becoming, to all intents and purposes, her master—the law giving him power to deprive her of her liberty, and to administer chastisement.

He has so framed the laws of divorce, as to what shall be the proper causes, and in case of separation, to whom the guardianship of the children shall be given, as to be wholly regardless of the happiness of the women—the law, in all cases, going upon a false supposition of the supremacy of man, and giving all power into his hands.

After depriving her of all rights as a married woman, if single, and the owner of property, he has taxed her to support a government which recognizes her only when her property can be made profitable to it.

He has monopolized nearly all the profitable employments, and from those she is permitted to follow, she receives but a scanty remuneration. He closes against her all the avenues to wealth and distinction, which he considers most honorable to himself. As a teacher of theology, medicine, or law, she is not known.

He has denied her the facilities for obtaining a thorough education, all colleges being closed against her.

He allows her in Church, as well as State, but a subordinate position, claiming Apostolic authority for her exclusion from the ministry, and, with some exceptions, from any public participation in the affairs of the Church.

He has created a false public sentiment by giving to the world a different code of morals for men and women, by which moral delinquencies which exclude women from society, are not only tolerated but deemed of little account in man.

He has usurped the prerogative of Jehovah himself, claiming it as his right to assign for her a sphere of action, when that belongs to her conscience and to her God.

He has endeavored, in every way that he could, to destroy her confidence in her own powers, to lessen her self-respect, and to make her willing to lead a dependent and abject life.

Now, in view of this entire disfranchisement of one-half the people of this country, their social and religious degradation—in view of the unjust laws above mentioned, and because women do feel themselves aggrieved, oppressed, and fraudulently deprived of their most sacred rights, we insist that they have immediate admission to all the rights and privileges which belong to them as citizens of the United States.

In entering upon the great work before us, we anticipate no small amount of misconception, misrepresentation, and ridicule; but we shall use every instrumentality within our power to effect our object. We shall employ agents, circulate tracts, petition the State and National legislatures, and endeavor to enlist the pulpit and the press in our behalf. We hope this Convention will be followed by a series of Conventions embracing every part of the country.

———————

Source: Stanton, Elizabeth Cady, Susan B. Anthony, and Matilda Joslyn Gage, eds. *History of Woman Suffrage, Vol. 1.* Rochester, NY: Charles Mann, 1881–1887, 70–71. Reprinted and Introduction in DeLuzio, Crista. *Women's Rights: People and Perspectives.* Santa Barbara, CA: ABC-CLIO, 2009.

New York Married Women's Property Acts (1848–1849)

Colonization and revolution in America did not fundamentally alter the English common law tradition of the legal identity of a husband and wife, a legal concept known as coverture. Although each colony, then state, enacted its own laws on property and inheritance rights, in principle the position of married women fit Blackstone's description that "husband and wife are one in law."

This meant that a wife could not enter into a contract, be sued or sue, or make a will. All her personal property belonged to her husband, including clothes, jewels, furniture, and wages, which he could dispense with as he saw fit. He was constrained by having to obtain his wife's permission to sell her real property, but he had the right to manage it and to derive the benefits from it. Finally, coverture allowed the husband to chastise his wife and to appoint guardians other than her for their children in the case of his death.

By the 1830s and 1840s the legal fiction of marital unity began to undergo modification through the enactment of married women's property acts, which allowed married women to keep their property in their own name. The married women's property acts, passed by New York State, became a model for other states. By the end of the Civil War period some 29 states had passed such acts.

AN ACT for the effectual protection of the property of married women.

Passed April 7, 1848.

The People of the State of New York, represented in Senate and Assembly do enact as follows:

Sec. 1. The real and personal property of any female who may hereafter marry, and which she shall own at the time of marriage, and the rents issues and profits thereof shall not be subject to the disposal of her husband, nor be liable for his debts, and shall continue her sole and separate property, as if she were a single female.

Sec. 2. The real and personal property, and the rents issues and profits thereof of any female now married shall not be subject to the disposal of her husband; but shall be her sole and separate property as if she were a single female except so far as the same may be liable for the debts of her husband heretofore contracted.

Sec. 3. It shall be lawful for any married female to receive, by gift, grant devise or bequest, from any person other than her husband and hold to her sole and separate use, as if she were a single female, real and personal property, and the rents, issues and profits thereof, and the same shall not be subject to the disposal of her husband, nor be liable for his debts.

Sec. 4. All contracts made between persons in contemplation of marriage shall remain in full force after such marriage takes place.

AN ACT to amend an act entitled "An act for the more effectual protection of the property of married women," passed April 7, 1848.

Passed April 11, 1849.

The People of the State of New York, represented in Senate and Assembly, do enact as follows:

Sec. 1. The third section of the act entitled "An act for the more effectual protection of the property of married women," is hereby amended so as to read as follows:

Sec. 3. Any married female may take by inheritance or gift, grant, devise or bequest, from any person other than her husband and hold to her sole and separate use and convey and devise real and personal property, and any interest of estate therein, and the rents, issues and profits thereof in the same manner and with like effect as if she were unmarried, and the same shall not be subject to the disposal of her husband nor be liable for his debts.

Sec. 2. Any person who may hold or who may hereafter hold as trustee for any married woman, any real or personal estate or other property under any deed of conveyance or otherwise, on the written request of such married woman accompanied by a certificate of a justice of the supreme court that he has examined the condition and situation of the property, and made due enquiry into the capacity of such married woman to manage and control the same, may convey such married woman by deed or otherwise, all or any portion of such property or the rents issues or profits thereof, for her sole and separate use and benefit.

Sec. 3. All contracts made between persons in contemplation of marriage shall remain in full force after such marriage takes place.

Source: New York Married Women's Property Act (1848–1849). Chapter 200 of the Laws of 1848, Series 13036, Enrolled acts of the State Legislature, 1778–2005, New York State Department of State Bureau of Miscellaneous Record. Reprinted and Introduction in Langley, Winston E., and Vivian C. Fox, eds. *Women's Rights in the United States: A Documentary History.* Santa Barbara, CA: Greenwood, 1994.

"Aren't I a Woman?" (1851), Sojourner Truth

Much of what we know about the life of Sojourner Truth (c. 1797–1883) comes second hand, from the pen of her biographers, Olive Gilbert and Frances Titus, abolitionists who worked with William Lloyd Garrison and Truth. The Narrative of Sojourner Truth was published in 1850 by Gilbert and revised by Titus in 1870. What we know of her public work is second hand as well. Sojourner Truth was illiterate, and her speeches were recorded by listeners. Because knowledge about her depends on the abilities and ethics of the recorders, contemporary scholars have called into question both certain biographical details related to her life and the language of her speeches. Yet without that record, readers today would know nothing of Sojourner Truth's remarkable life and work.

Her speech making was enhanced by her participation in an antislavery association whose members included abolitionists William Lloyd Garrison, Frederick Douglass, and Wendell Phillips, and she began attracting sizable audiences at her talks. Her autobiography became popular at antislavery and women's right's meetings, including the Women's Rights Convention in Akron, Ohio, where she delivered her famous "Aren't I a Woman?" speech in 1851.

[As recorded by Frances Gage, who presided at the convention.]

Well, children, where there is so much racket there must be something out o' kilter. I think that 'twixt the Negroes of the South and the women of the North all a-talking about rights, the white men will be in a fix pretty soon.

But what's all this here talking about? That man over there says that women need to be helped into carriages, and lifted over ditches, and to have the best place everywhere. Nobody ever helps me into carriages, or over mud puddles or gives me any best place and aren't I a woman? Look at me! Look at my arm! (*And she bared her right arm to her shoulder, showing her tremendous muscular power.*) I have plowed, and I have planted, and gathered into barns, and no man could head me— and aren't I a woman? I could work as much and eat as much as a man (when I could get it), and bear the lash as well—and aren't I woman? I have borne thirteen children and seen them almost all sold off into slavery, and when I cried out with a mother's grief, none but Jesus heard—and aren't I a woman? Then they talk about this thing in the head—what's this they call it? (*"Intellect,"* whispered someone near.) That's it, honey. What's that got to do with women's rights or Negroes' rights? If my cup won't hold but a pint and yours holds a quart, wouldn't you be mean not to let me have my little half-measure full?

Then that little man in black there, he says women can't have as much rights as man, 'cause Christ wasn't a woman. Where did your Christ come from? Where did your Christ come from? From God and a woman. Man had nothing to do with him.

If the first woman God ever made was strong enough to turn the world upside down, all alone, these together ought to be able to turn it back and get it right side up again; and now they are asking to do it, the men better let them.

'Bliged to you for hearing on me, and now old Sojourner hasn't got anything more to say.

———

Source: Truth, Sojourner. "Speech at the Women's Rights Convention, Akron, Ohio, 1851." In Campbell, Karlyn Kohrs, ed. *Man Cannot Speak for Her: Key Texts of the Early Feminists, Vol. 2.* Westport, CT: Greenwood Press, 1989, 99–102. Note on source: Campbell's version removes the dialect spelling used in the Gage transcription of Truth's speech, including changing "Ain't I a woman?" to "Aren't I a woman?" Gage's parenthetical commentary is also removed in this version. Introduction in Hephzibah Roskelly, "Sojourner Truth: 'Aren't I a Woman?' (1851)." In *Feminist Writing from Ancient Times to the Modern World: A Global Sourcebook and History.* Ed. Tiffany K. Wayne. Santa Barbara, CA: Greenwood, 2011.

"Reflections on Woman's Dress" (1851), Elizabeth Smith Miller

In 1892, Elizabeth Smith Miller looked back on the dress reform movement of the mid-19th century of which she was a part. The early women's rights movement had embraced changes in women's apparel that lifted both physical and social restrictions on women's movement and emphasized more utilitarian and functional options.

The subjections of woman to the fashion that demands tight waists and heavy, trailing skirts, is a matter of grave importance, involving not only her own well-being, but that of generations of men and women who shall succeed her. It is universally admitted that compressing the waist forces breathing into the upper part of the lungs and causes displacement and disease in the pelvic region. The skirt is hazardous from its weight; and when bedraggled with wet and mud, and the usual concomitants of street sweepings, it is often the case of colds to which the poor abused lungs readily succumb. It is said, too, that in brushing these scavenger skirts, the system may be poisoned by inhaling the dried germs which float from them. The arguments against these fashions are countless, and none can be offered in their favor; and yet the mass of women cling to them, even at the sacrifice of comfort, cleanliness, and health. The Paris dressmaker, who is the standard for the dressmakers of all civilized nations, says, as she adjusts the tight waist: "*Il faut souffrir pir être belle.*" Women say: "We might as well be out of the world as out of the fashion." The Chinese woman of noble birth has the same opinion in regard to the fashion which cramps and distorts her feet. She justly remarks, however, on examining American fashion plates: "China woman pinch foot. You say China woman velly bad. Melican woman pinch here (laying her hand on her waist). Life here; life not in foot. Melican woman much more bad than China woman."

[. . .]

In the spring of 1851, while spending many hours at work in the garden, I became so thoroughly disgusted with the long skirt, that the dissatisfaction, the growth of years, suddenly ripened into the decision that this shackle should no longer be endured. The resolution was at once put into practice. Turkish trousers to the ankle, with a skirt reaching some four inches below the knee, were substituted for the heavy, untidy, exasperating old garment.

[. . .]

I wore the short dress and trousers for many years, my husband being at all times and in all places my staunch supporter. My father gave the dress his full approval, and I was also blessed by the tonic of Mrs. Stanton's inspiring words: "The question is no longer, *rags*, how do you look? But *woman*, how do you feel?"

[. . .]

All hail to the day when we shall have a reasonable and beautiful dress, that shall encourage exercise on the road and in the field; that shall leave us the free use of our limbs; that shall help and not hinder our perfect development.

ELIZABETH SMITH MILLER.

Source: Miller, Elizabeth Smith. "Reflections on Woman's Dress, and the Record of a Personal Experience." *Arena* (September 1892), 491–95.

Uncle Tom's Cabin (1852), Harriet Beecher Stowe

Harriet Beecher Stowe's best-selling, antislavery novel, Uncle Tom's Cabin, *was written in 1852. The novel depicts the realities of slavery and Christian values. The following excerpt from Chapter VII—The Mother's Struggle demonstrates a mother's love that drives her to escape so that her child won't be sold to the slave trader. Stowe pleads with readers to sympathize with Eliza and her plight, asking if any mother wouldn't do the same?*

It is impossible to conceive of a human creature more wholly desolate and forlorn than Eliza, when she turned her footsteps from Uncle Tom's cabin.

Her husband's suffering and dangers, and the danger of her child, all blended in her mind, with a confused and stunning sense of the risk she was running, in leaving the only home she had ever known, and cutting loose from the protection of a friend whom she loved and revered. Then there was the parting from every familiar object,—the place where she had grown up, the trees under which she had played, the groves where she had walked many an evening in happier days, by the side of her young husband,—everything, as it lay in the clear, frosty starlight, seemed to speak reproachfully to her, and ask her whither could she go from a home like that?

But stronger than all was maternal love, wrought into a paroxysm of frenzy by the near approach of a fearful danger. Her boy was old enough to have walked by her side, and, in an indifferent case, she would only have led him by the hand; but now the bare thought of putting him out of her arms made her shudder, and she strained him to her bosom with a convulsive grasp, as she went rapidly forward.

The frosty ground creaked beneath her feet, and she trembled at the sound; every quaking leaf and fluttering shadow sent the blood backward to her heart, and quickened her footsteps. She wondered within herself at the strength that seemed to be come upon her; for she felt the weight of her boy as if it had been a feather, and every flutter of fear seemed to increase the supernatural power that bore her on, while from her pale lips burst forth, in frequent ejaculations, the prayer to a Friend above— "Lord, help! Lord, save me!"

If it were your Harry, mother, or your Willie, that were going to be torn from you by a brutal trader, tomorrow morning,—if you had seen the man, and heard that the papers were signed and delivered, and you had only from twelve o'clock till morning to make good your escape,—how fast could you walk? How many miles could you make in those few brief hours, with the darling at your bosom,—the little sleepy head on your shoulder,—the small, soft arms trustingly holding on to your neck?

For the child slept. At first, the novelty and alarm kept him waking; but his mother so hurriedly repressed every breath or sound, and so assured him that if he were only still she would certainly save him, that he clung quietly round her neck, only asking, as he found himself sinking to sleep,

"Mother, I don't need to keep awake, do I?"

"No, my darling; sleep, if you want to."

"But, mother, if I do get asleep, you won't let him get me?"

"No! so may God help me!" said his mother, with a paler cheek, and a brighter light in her large dark eyes.

"'You're *sure*, ain't you, mother?"

"Yes, *sure!*" said the mother, in a voice that startled herself; for it seemed to her to come from a spirit within, that was no part of her; and the boy dropped his little weary head on her shoulder, and was soon asleep. How the touch of those warm arms, the gentle breathings that came in her neck, seemed to add fire and spirit to her movements! It seemed to her as if strength poured into her in electric streams, from every gentle touch and movement of the sleeping, confiding child. Sublime is the dominion of the mind over the body, that, for a time, can make flesh and nerve impregnable, and string the sinews like steel, so that the weak become so mighty.

The boundaries of the farm, the grove, the wood-lot, passed by her dizzily, as she walked on; and still she went, leaving one familiar object after another, slacking not, pausing not, till reddening daylight found her many a long mile from all traces of any familiar objects upon the open highway.

She had often been, with her mistress, to visit some connections, in the little village of T—, not far from the Ohio river, and knew the road well. To go thither, to escape across the Ohio river, were the first hurried outlines of her plan of escape; beyond that, she could only hope in God.

When horses and vehicles began to move along the highway, with that alert perception peculiar to a state of excitement, and which seems to be a sort of inspiration, she became aware that her headlong pace and distracted air might bring on her remark and suspicion. She therefore put the boy on the ground, and, adjusting her dress and bonnet, she walked on at as rapid a pace as she thought consistent with the preservation of appearances. In her little bundle she had provided a store of cakes and apples, which she used as expedients for quickening the speed of the child, rolling the apple some yards before them, when the boy would run with all his might after it; and this ruse, often repeated, carried them over many a half-mile.

After a while, they came to a thick patch of woodland, through which murmured a clear brook. As the child complained of hunger and thirst, she climbed over the fence with him; and, sitting down behind a large rock which concealed them from the road, she gave him a breakfast out of her little package. The boy wondered and grieved that she could not eat; and when, putting his arms round her neck, he tried to wedge some of his cake into her mouth, it seemed to her that the rising in her throat would choke her.

"No, no, Harry darling! mother can't eat till you are safe! We must go on—on—till we come to the river!" And she hurried again into the road, and again constrained herself to walk regularly and composedly forward.

She was many miles past any neighborhood where she was personally known. If she should chance to meet any who knew her, she reflected that the well-known kindness of the family would be of itself a blind to suspicion, as making it an unlikely supposition that she could be a fugitive. As she was also so white as not to be known as of colored lineage, without a critical survey, and her child was white also, it was much easier for her to pass on unsuspected.

On this presumption, she stopped at noon at a neat farmhouse, to rest herself, and buy some dinner for her child and self; for, as the danger decreased with the distance, the supernatural tension of the nervous system lessened, and she found herself both weary and hungry.

The good woman, kindly and gossiping, seemed rather pleased than otherwise with having somebody come in to talk with; and accepted, without examination, Eliza's statement, that she "was going on a little piece, to spend a week with her friends,"—all which she hoped in her heart might prove strictly true.

An hour before sunset, she entered the village of T—, by the Ohio river, weary and foot-sore, but still strong in heart. Her first glance was at the river, which lay, like Jordan, between her and the Canaan of liberty on the other side.

It was now early spring, and the river was swollen and turbulent; great cakes of floating ice were swinging heavily to and fro in the turbid waters. Owing to the peculiar form of the shore on the Kentucky side, the land bending far out into the water, the ice had been lodged and detained in great quantities, and the narrow channel which swept round the bend was full of ice, piled one cake over another, thus forming a temporary barrier to the descending ice, which lodged, and formed a great, undulating raft, filling up the whole river, and extending almost to the Kentucky shore.

Eliza stood, for a moment, contemplating this unfavorable aspect of things, which she saw at once must prevent the usual ferry-boat from running, and then turned into a small public house on the bank, to make a few inquiries.

The hostess, who was busy in various fizzing and stewing operations over the fire, preparatory to the evening meal, stopped, with a fork in her hand, as Eliza's sweet and plaintive voice arrested her.

"What is it?" she said.

"Isn't there any ferry or boat, that takes people over to B—, now?" she said.

"No, indeed!" said the woman; "the boats has stopped running."

Eliza's look of dismay and disappointment struck the woman, and she said, inquiringly,

"May be you're wanting to get over?—anybody sick? Ye seem mighty anxious?"

"I've got a child that's very dangerous," said Eliza. "I never heard of it till last night, and I've walked quite a piece today, in hopes to get to the ferry."

"Well, now, that's onlucky," said the woman, whose motherly sympathies were much aroused; "I'm re'lly consarned for ye. Solomon!" she called, from the window, towards a small back building. A man, in leather apron and very dirty hands, appeared at the door.

"I say, Sol," said the woman, "is that ar man going to tote them bar'ls over tonight?"

"He said he should try, if 't was any way prudent," said the man.

"There's a man a piece down here, that's going over with some truck this evening, if he durs' to; he'll be in here to supper tonight, so you'd better set down and wait. That's a sweet little fellow," added the woman, offering him a cake.

But the child, wholly exhausted, cried with weariness. "Poor fellow! he isn't used to walking, and I've hurried him on so," said Eliza.

"Well, take him into this room," said the woman, opening into a small bed-room, where stood a comfortable bed. Eliza laid the weary boy upon it, and held his hands in hers till he was fast asleep. For her there was no rest. As a fire in her bones, the thought of the pursuer urged her on; and she gazed with longing eyes on the sullen, surging waters that lay between her and liberty.

Here we must take our leave of her for the present, to follow the course of her pursuers.

Though Mrs. Shelby had promised that the dinner should be hurried on table, yet it was soon seen, as the thing has often been seen before, that it required more than one to make a bargain. So, although the order was fairly given out in Haley's hearing, and carried to Aunt Chloe by at least half a dozen juvenile messengers, that dignitary only gave certain very gruff snorts, and tosses

of her head, and went on with every operation in an unusually leisurely and circumstantial manner.

For some singular reason, an impression seemed to reign among the servants generally that Missis would not be particularly disobliged by delay; and it was wonderful what a number of counter accidents occurred constantly, to retard the course of things. One luckless wight contrived to upset the gravy; and then gravy had to be got up *de novo,* with due care and formality, Aunt Chloe watching and stirring with dogged precision, answering shortly, to all suggestions of haste, that she "warn't a going to have raw gravy on the table, to help nobody's catchings." One tumbled down with the water, and had to go to the spring for more; and another precipitated the butter into the path of events; and there was from time to time giggling news brought into the kitchen that "Mas'r Haley was mighty oneasy, and that he couldn't sit in his cheer no ways, but was a walkin' and stalkin' to the winders and through the porch."

"Sarves him right!" said Aunt Chloe, indignantly. "He'll get wus nor oneasy, one of these days, if he don't mend his ways. *His* master'll be sending for him, and then see how he'll look!"

"He'll go to torment, and no mistake," said little Jake.

"He desarves it!" said Aunt Chloe, grimly, "he's broke a many, many, many hearts,—I tell ye all!" she said, stopping, with a fork uplifted in her hands, "it's like what Mas'r George reads in Ravelations,—souls a callin' under the altar! and a callin' on the Lord for vengeance on sich!—and by and by the Lord he'll hear 'em—so he will!"

Aunt Chloe, who was much revered in the kitchen, was listened to with open mouth; and, the dinner being now fairly sent in, the whole kitchen was at leisure to gossip with her, and to listen to her remarks.

"Sich'll be burnt up forever, and no mistake, won't ther?" said Andy.

"I'd be glad to see it, I'll be boun'," said little Jake.

"Chil'en!" said a voice, that made them all start. It was Uncle Tom, who had come in, and stood listening to the conversation at the door.

"Chil'en!" he said, "I'm afeard you don't know what ye're sayin'. Forever is a *dre'ful* word, chil'en; it's awful to think on 't. You oughtenter wish that ar to any human crittur."

"We wouldn't to anybody but the soul-drivers," said Andy; "nobody can help wishing it to them, they's so awful wicked."

"Don't natur herself kinder cry out on 'em?" said Aunt Chloe. "Don't dey tear der suckin' baby right off his mother's breast, and sell him, and der little children as is crying and holding on by her clothes,—don't dey pull 'em off and sells 'em? Don't dey tear wife and husband apart?" said Aunt Chloe, beginning to cry, "when it's jest takin' the very life on 'em?—and all the while does they feel one bit, don't dey drink and smoke, and take it oncommon easy? Lor, if the devil don't get them, what's he good for?" And Aunt Chloe covered her face with her checked apron, and began to sob in good earnest.

"Pray for them that spitefully use you, the good book says," says Tom.

"Pray for 'em!" said Aunt Chloe; "Lor, it's too tough! I can't pray for 'em."

"It's natur, Chloe, and natur 's strong," said Tom, "but the Lord's grace is stronger; besides, you ougher think what an awful state a poor crittur's soul 's in that'll do them ar things,—you oughter thank God that you 'an't *like* him, Chloe. I'm sure I'd rather be sold, ten thousand times over, than to have all that ar poor crittur's got to answer for."

"So 'd I, a heap," said Jake. "Lor, *shouldn't* we cotch it, Andy?"

Andy shrugged his shoulders, and gave an acquiescent whistle.

"I'm glad Mas'r didn't go off this morning, as he looked to," said Tom; "that ar hurt me more than sellin', it did. Mebbe it might have been natural for him, but 't would have come desp't hard on me, as has known him from a baby; but I've seen Mas'r, and I begin ter feel sort o' reconciled to the Lord's will now. Mas'r couldn't help hisself; he did right, but I'm feared things will be kinder goin' to rack, when I'm gone Mas'r can't be spected to be a pryin' round everywhar, as I've done, a keepin' up all the ends. The boys all means well, but they's powerful car'less. That ar troubles me."

The bell here rang, and Tom was summoned to the parlor.

"Tom," said his master, kindly, "I want you to notice that I give this gentleman bonds to forfeit a thousand dollars if you are not on the spot when he wants you; he's going today to look after his other business, and you can have the day to yourself. Go anywhere you like, boy."

"Thank you, Mas'r," said Tom.

"And mind yourself," said the trader, "and don't come it over your master with any o' yer nigger tricks; for I'll take every cent out of him, if you an't thar. If he'd hear to me, he wouldn't trust any on ye—slippery as eels!"

"Mas'r," said Tom,—and he stood very straight,—"I was jist eight years old when ole Missis put you into my arms, and you wasn't a year old. 'Thar,' says she, 'Tom, that's to be your young Mas'r; take good care on

him,' says she. And now I jist ask you, Mas'r, have I ever broke word to you, or gone contrary to you, 'specially since I was a Christian?"

Mr. Shelby was fairly overcome, and the tears rose to his eyes.

"My good boy," said he, "the Lord knows you say but the truth; and if I was able to help it, all the world shouldn't buy you."

"And sure as I am a Christian woman," said Mrs. Shelby, "you shall be redeemed as soon as I can any bring together means. Sir," she said to Haley, "take good account of who you sell him to, and let me know."

"Lor, yes, for that matter," said the trader, "I may bring him up in a year, not much the wuss for wear, and trade him back."

"I'll trade with you then, and make it for your advantage," said Mrs. Shelby.

"Of course," said the trader, "all's equal with me; li'ves trade 'em up as down, so I does a good business. All I want is a livin', you know, ma'am; that's all any of us wants, I, s'pose."

Mr. and Mrs. Shelby both felt annoyed and degraded by the familiar impudence of the trader, and yet both saw the absolute necessity of putting a constraint on their feelings. The more hopelessly sordid and insensible he appeared, the greater became Mrs. Shelby's dread of his succeeding in recapturing Eliza and her child, and of course the greater her motive for detaining him by every female artifice. She therefore graciously smiled, assented, chatted familiarly, and did all she could to make time pass imperceptibly.

At two o'clock Sam and Andy brought the horses up to the posts, apparently greatly refreshed and invigorated by the scamper of the morning.

Sam was there new oiled from dinner, with an abundance of zealous and ready officiousness. As Haley approached, he was boasting, in flourishing style, to Andy, of the evident and eminent success of the operation, now that he had "farly come to it."

"Your master, I s'pose, don't keep no dogs," said Haley, thoughtfully, as he prepared to mount.

"Heaps on 'em," said Sam, triumphantly; "thar's Bruno—he's a roarer! and, besides that, 'bout every nigger of us keeps a pup of some natur or uther."

"Poh!" said Haley,—and he said something else, too, with regard to the said dogs, at which Sam muttered,

"I don't see no use cussin' on 'em, no way."

"But your master don't keep no dogs (I pretty much know he don't) for trackin' out niggers."

Sam knew exactly what he meant, but he kept on a look of earnest and desperate simplicity.

"Our dogs all smells round considable sharp. I spect they's the kind, though they han't never had no practice. They's *far* dogs, though, at most anything, if you'd get 'em started. Here, Bruno," he called, whistling to the lumbering Newfoundland, who came pitching tumultuously toward them.

"You go hang!" said Haley, getting up. "Come, tumble up now."

Sam tumbled up accordingly, dexterously contriving to tickle Andy as he did so, which occasioned Andy to split out into a laugh, greatly to Haley's indignation, who made a cut at him with his riding-whip.

"I's 'stonished at yer, Andy," said Sam, with awful gravity. "This yer's a seris bisness, Andy. Yer mustn't be a makin' game. This yer an't no way to help Mas'r."

"I shall take the straight road to the river," said Haley, decidedly, after they had come to the boundaries of the estate. "I know the way of all of 'em,—they makes tracks for the underground."

"Sartin," said Sam, "dat's de idee. Mas'r Haley hits de thing right in de middle. Now, der's two roads to de river,—de dirt road and der pike,—which Mas'r mean to take?"

Andy looked up innocently at Sam, surprised at hearing this new geographical fact, but instantly confirmed what he said, by a vehement reiteration.

"Course," said Sam, "I'd rather be 'clined to 'magine that Lizy 'd take de dirt road, bein' it's the least travelled."

Haley, notwithstanding that he was a very old bird, and naturally inclined to be suspicious of chaff, was rather brought up by this view of the case.

"If yer warn't both on yer such cussed liars, now!" he said, contemplatively as he pondered a moment.

The pensive, reflective tone in which this was spoken appeared to amuse Andy prodigiously, and he drew a little behind, and shook so as apparently to run a great risk of failing off his horse, while Sam's face was immovably composed into the most doleful gravity.

"Course," said Sam, "Mas'r can do as he'd ruther, go de straight road, if Mas'r thinks best,—it's all one to us. Now, when I study 'pon it, I think de straight road de best, deridedly."

"She would naturally go a lonesome way," said Haley, thinking aloud, and not minding Sam's remark.

"Dar an't no sayin'," said Sam; "gals is pecular; they never does nothin' ye thinks they will; mose gen'lly the contrary. Gals is nat'lly made contrary; and so, if you thinks they've gone one road, it is sartin you'd better go t' other, and then you'll be sure to find 'em. Now, my private 'pinion is, Lizy took der road; so I think we'd better take de straight one."

This profound generic view of the female sex did not seem to dispose Haley particularly to the straight road, and he announced decidedly that he should go the other, and asked Sam when they should come to it.

"A little piece ahead," said Sam, giving a wink to Andy with the eye which was on Andy's side of the head; and he added, gravely, "but I've studded on de matter, and I'm quite clar we ought not to go dat ar way. I nebber been over it no way. It's despit lonesome, and we might lose our way,—whar we'd come to, de Lord only knows."

"Nevertheless," said Haley, "I shall go that way."

"Now I think on 't, I think I hearn 'em tell that dat ar road was all fenced up and down by der creek, and thar, an't it, Andy?"

Andy wasn't certain; he'd only "hearn tell" about that road, but never been over it. In short, he was strictly noncommittal.

Haley, accustomed to strike the balance of probabilities between lies of greater or lesser magnitude, thought that it lay in favor of the dirt road aforesaid. The mention of the thing he thought he perceived was involuntary on Sam's part at first, and his confused attempts to dissuade him he set down to a desperate lying on second thoughts, as being unwilling to implicate Liza.

When, therefore, Sam indicated the road, Haley plunged briskly into it, followed by Sam and Andy.

Now, the road, in fact, was an old one, that had formerly been a thoroughfare to the river, but abandoned for many years after the laying of the new pike. It was open for about an hour's ride, and after that it was cut across by various farms and fences. Sam knew this fact perfectly well,—indeed, the road had been so long closed up, that Andy had never heard of it. He therefore rode along with an air of dutiful submission, only groaning and vociferating occasionally that 'twas "desp't rough, and bad for Jerry's foot."

"Now, I jest give yer warning," said Haley, "I know yer; yer won't get me to turn off this road, with all yer fussin'—so you shet up!"

"Mas'r will go his own way!" said Sam, with rueful submission, at the same time winking most portentously to Andy, whose delight was now very near the explosive point.

Sam was in wonderful spirits,—professed to keep a very brisk lookout,—at one time exclaiming that he saw "a gal's bonnet" on the top of some distant eminence, or calling to Andy "if that thar wasn't 'Lizy' down in the hollow;" always making these exclamations in some rough or craggy part of the road, where the sudden quickening of speed was a special inconvenience to all parties concerned, and thus keeping Haley in a state of constant commotion.

After riding about an hour in this way, the whole party made a precipitate and tumultuous descent into a barn-yard belonging to a large farming establishment. Not a soul was in sight, all the hands being employed in the fields; but, as the barn stood conspicuously and plainly square across the road, it was evident that their journey in that direction had reached a decided finale.

"Wan't dat ar what I telled Mas'r?" said Sam, with an air of injured innocence. "How does strange gentleman spect to know more about a country dan de natives born and raised?"

"You rascal!" said Haley, "you knew all about this."

"Didn't I tell yer I *know'd*, and yer wouldn't believe me? I told Mas'r 't was all shet up, and fenced up, and I didn't spect we could get through,—Andy heard me."

It was all too true to be disputed, and the unlucky man had to pocket his wrath with the best grace he was able, and all three faced to the right about, and took up their line of march for the highway.

In consequence of all the various delays, it was about three-quarters of an hour after Eliza had laid her child to sleep in the village tavern that the party came riding into the same place. Eliza was standing by the window, looking out in another direction, when Sam's quick eye caught a glimpse of her. Haley and Andy were two yards behind. At this crisis, Sam contrived to have his hat blown off, and uttered a loud and characteristic ejaculation, which startled her at once; she drew suddenly back; the whole train swept by the window, round to the front door.

A thousand lives seemed to be concentrated in that one moment to Eliza. Her room opened by a side door to the river. She caught her child, and sprang down the steps towards it. The trader caught a full glimpse of her just as she was disappearing down the bank; and throwing himself from his horse, and calling loudly on Sam and Andy, he was after her like a hound after a deer. In that dizzy moment her feet to her scarce seemed to touch the ground, and a moment brought her to the water's edge. Right on behind they came; and, nerved with strength such as God gives only to the desperate, with one wild cry and flying leap, she vaulted sheer over the turbid current by the shore, on to the raft of ice beyond. It was a desperate leap—impossible to anything but madness and despair; and Haley, Sam, and Andy, instinctively cried out, and lifted up their hands, as she did it.

The huge green fragment of ice on which she alighted pitched and creaked as her weight came on it, but she staid there not a moment. With wild cries and desperate energy she leaped to another and still another cake; stumbling—leaping—slipping—springing upwards again! Her shoes are gone—her stockings cut from her feet—while blood marked every step; but she saw nothing, felt nothing, till dimly, as in a dream, she saw the Ohio side, and a man helping her up the bank.

"Yer a brave gal, now, whoever ye ar!" said the man, with an oath.

Eliza recognized the voice and face for a man who owned a farm not far from her old home.

"O, Mr. Symmes!—save me—do save me—do hide me!" said Elia.

"Why, what's this?" said the man. "Why, if 'tan't Shelby's gal!"

"My child!—this boy!—he'd sold him! There is his Mas'r," said she, pointing to the Kentucky shore. "O, Mr. Symmes, you've got a little boy!"

"So I have," said the man, as he roughly, but kindly, drew her up the steep bank. "Besides, you're a right brave gal. I like grit, wherever I see it."

When they had gained the top of the bank, the man paused.

"I'd be glad to do something for ye," said he; "but then there's nowhar I could take ye. The best I can do is to tell ye to go thar," said he, pointing to a large white house which stood by itself, off the main street of the village. "Go thar; they're kind folks. Thar's no kind o' danger but they'll help you,—they're up to all that sort o' thing."

"The Lord bless you!" said Eliza, earnestly.

"No 'casion, no 'casion in the world," said the man. "What I've done's of no 'count."

"And, oh, surely, sir, you won't tell any one!"

"Go to thunder, gal! What do you take a feller for? In course not," said the man. "Come, now, go along like a likely, sensible gal, as you are. You've arnt your liberty, and you shall have it, for all me."

The woman folded her child to her bosom, and walked firmly and swiftly away. The man stood and looked after her.

"Shelby, now, mebbe won't think this yer the most neighborly thing in the world; but what's a feller to do? If he catches one of my gals in the same fix, he's welcome to pay back. Somehow I never could see no kind o' critter a strivin' and pantin', and trying to clar theirselves, with the dogs arter 'em and go agin 'em. Besides, I don't see no kind of 'casion for me to be hunter and catcher for other folks, neither."

So spoke this poor, heathenish Kentuckian, who had not been instructed in his constitutional relations, and consequently was betrayed into acting in a sort of Christianized manner, which, if he had been better situated and more enlightened, he would not have been left to do.

Haley had stood a perfectly amazed spectator of the scene, till Eliza had disappeared up the bank, when he turned a blank, inquiring look on Sam and Andy.

"That ar was a tolable fair stroke of business," said Sam.

"The gal 's got seven devils in her, I believe!" said Haley. "How like a wildcat she jumped!"

"Wal, now," said Sam, scratching his head, "I hope Mas'r'll 'scuse us trying dat ar road. Don't think I feel spry enough for dat ar, no way!" and Sam gave a hoarse chuckle.

"You laugh!" said the trader, with a growl.

"Lord bless you, Mas'r, I couldn't help it now," said Sam, giving way to the long pent-up delight of his soul. "She looked so curi's, a leapin' and springin'—ice a crackin'—and only to hear her,—plump! ker chunk! ker splash! Spring! Lord! how she goes it!" and Sam and Andy laughed till the tears rolled down their cheeks.

"I'll make ye laugh t' other side yer mouths!" said the trader, laying about their heads with his riding-whip.

Both ducked, and ran shouting up the bank, and were on their horses before he was up.

"Good-evening, Mas'r!" said Sam, with much gravity. "I berry much spect Missis be anxious 'bout Jerry. Mas'r Haley won't want us no longer. Missis wouldn't hear of our ridin' the critters over Lizy's bridge tonight;" and, with a facetious poke into Andy's ribs, he started off, followed by the latter, at full speed,—their shouts of laughter coming faintly on the wind.

———

Source: Stowe, Harriet Beecher. *Uncle Tom's Cabin; or, Life Among the Lowly.* London: George Routledge & Co., 1852, 59–73.

Address to the Legislature of New York (1854), Elizabeth Cady Stanton

This address by reformer Elizabeth Cady Stanton to the New York legislature, which was adopted by the Women's Rights Convention in Albany on February 14 and 15, 1854, gives an overview of the issues in the lives of women that Stanton believed needed to be addressed, with an emphasis on the right to participate in the political process in order to effect change.

To the Legislature of the State of New York:

"The thinking minds of all nations call for change. There is a deep-lying struggle in the whole fabric of society; a boundless, grinding collision of the New with the Old."

The tyrant, Custom, has been summoned before the bar of Common Sense. His Majesty no longer awes the multitude—his sceptre [*sic*] is broken—his crown is trampled in the dust—the sentence of death is pronounced upon him. All nations, ranks and classes have, in turn, questioned and repudiated his authority; and now, that the monster is chained and caged, timid woman, on tiptoe, comes to look him in the face, and to demand of her brave sires and sons, who have struck stout blows for liberty, if, in this change of dynasty, she, too, shall find relief.

Yes, gentlemen, in republican America, in the 19th century, we, the daughters of the revolutionary heroes of '76, demand at your hands the redness [redress] of our grievances—a revision of your state constitution—a new code of laws. Permit us then, as briefly as possible, to call your attention to the legal disabilities under which we labor.

1st, Look at the position of woman as woman. It is not enough for us that by your laws we are permitted to live and breathe, to claim the necessaries of life from our legal protectors—to pay the penalty of our crimes; we demand the full recognition of all our rights as citizens of the Empire State. We are persons; native, free-born citizens; property-holders, tax-payers; yet are we denied the exercise of our right to the elective franchise. We support ourselves, and, in part, your schools, colleges, churches, your poor-houses, jails, prisons, the army, the navy, the whole machinery of government, and yet we have no voice in your councils. We have every qualification required by the constitution, necessary to the legal voter, but the one of sex. We are moral, virtuous and intelligent, and in all respects quite equal to the proud white man himself, and yet by your laws we are classed with idiots, lunatics and negroes; and though we do not feel honored by the place assigned us, yet, in fact, our legal position is lower than that of either; for the negro can be raised to the dignity of a voter if he possess himself of $250; the lunatic can vote in his moments of sanity, and the idiot, too, if he be a male one, and not more than nine-tenths a fool; but we, who have guided great movements of charity, established missions, edited journals, published works on history, economy and statistics; who have governed nations, led armies, filled the professor's chair, taught philosophy and mathematics to the *savans* of our age, discovered planets, piloted ships across the sea, are denied the most sacred rights of citizens, because, forsooth, we came not into this republic crowned with the dignity of manhood! Woman is theoretically absolved from all allegiance to the laws of the state. Sec. 1, Bill of Rights, 2 R.S., 301, says that no authority can, on any pretence whatever, be exercised over the citizens of this state but such as is or shall be derived from, and *granted by, the people of this state.*

Source: Address to the Legislature of New York, Adopted by the Women's Rights Convention Held at Albany, Tuesday and Wednesday, February 14 and 15, 1854. Albany, NY: Weed, Parsons and Company, 1854. Introduction in Theodore J. Zeman, Jolyon P. Girard, et al., eds. *Daily Life through American History in Primary Documents.* Santa Barbara, CA: Greenwood, 2011.

Missouri v. Celia, a Slave (1855)

The following excerpts from Missouri v. Celia *provide details about the murder trial of the slave Celia, who fatally clubbed her master after years of rape and abuse. During the inquest, Celia confessed to the crime and provided evidence of his burned remains. At the trial, family members and others testified before an all-male jury. Celia was found guilty, and despite defense efforts to save her from the gallows, she was hanged in 1855.*

Celia, a slave, duly sworn, belonging to Robert Newsom says that she killed her master on the night of the 23rd day of June 1855—about two hours after dark by striking him twice on the head with a stick, and then put his body on the fire and burnt it nearly up, then took up the ashes on the morning after daylight. After breakfast, the bones were not entirely burnt up. I took up the ashes and bones out of the fireplace in my cabin where I burnt the body and emptied them on the right hand side of the path leading from my cabin to the stable.

Sworn to & Subscribed before us
this 25th day of June 1855

D M Whyte J.P.

     her

Celia   X

     mark

We hereby certify that the foregoing is the testimony taken in the inquest held over the remains of Robert Newsom at his late residence in Callaway County on the 25th day of June AD 1855 –

D M Whyte J.P.
Isaac P Howe J.P.

Celia a slave the defendant being examined says that on the night of the 23rd day of June 1855 she killed

Mr. Robert Newsom her master by striking him on the head twice with a stick about two hours after dark. After she found she had killed him she put his body on the fire in her cabin to burn it up. The bones were not entirely consumed by morning and after daylight in the morning she took the ashes and pieces of bones up out of the fireplace and emptied them on the path leading from her cabin to the stable. She stated she did not intend to kill him when she struck him but only wanted to hurt him.

We hereby certify that the above is the testimony of Celia a slave taken before us on the trial of a case wherein the State of Missouri is Plaintiff and the said Celia is defendant on the 25th day of June A.D. 1855.

D.M. Whyte J.P.
Isaac P. Howe J.P.

Source: Missouri v. Celia, a slave *(1855). Records from Callaway County Circuit Court. Celia File No. 4496.*

Marriage Protest of Lucy Stone and Henry Blackwell (1855)

Lucy Stone, a graduate of Oberlin College, abolitionist, and women's rights reformer met Henry Brown Blackwell, of the prominent Blackwell family, who shared her views on slavery and women's rights. Blackwell, seven years her junior, courted Stone, who was reluctant to give up her independence, for five years, promising her "perfect equality" in a marriage he believed would follow the principle of progression and improve over time. In their marriage vows, printed below, Stone and Blackwell joined a number of other feminist couples who protested against the institution of marriage as it then existed and who strove for a spiritual marriage informed by justice and love.

While acknowledging our mutual affection by publicly assuming the relationship of husband and wife, yet in justice to ourselves and a great principle, we deem it a duty to declare that this act on our part implies no sanction of, nor promise of voluntary obedience to such of the present laws of marriage, as refuse to recognize the wife as an independent, rational being, while they confer upon the husband an injurious and unnatural superiority, investing him with legal powers which no honorable man would exercise, and which no man should possess. We protest especially against the laws which give to the husband:

1. The custody of the wife's person.

2. The exclusive control and guardianship of their children.
3. The sole ownership of her personal, and use of her real estate, unless previously settled upon her, or placed in the hands of trustees, as in the case of minors, lunatics, and idiots.
4. The absolute right to the product of her industry.
5. Also against laws which give to the widower so much larger and more permanent an interest in the property of his deceased wife, than they give to the widow in that of the deceased husband.
6. Finally, against the whole system by which "the legal existence of the wife is suspended during marriage," so that in most States, she neither has a legal part in the choice of her residence, nor can she make a will, nor sue or be sued in her own name, nor inherit property.

We believe that personal independence and equal human rights can never be forfeited, except for crime; that marriage should be an equal and permanent partnership, and so recognized by law; that until it is so recognized, married partners should provide against the radical injustice of present laws, by every means in their power.

We believe that where domestic difficulties arise, no appeal should be made to legal tribunals under existing laws, but that all difficulties should be submitted to the equitable adjustment of arbitrators mutually chosen.

Thus reverencing law, we enter our protest against rules and customs which are unworthy of the name, since they violate justice, the essence of law.

HENRY B. BLACKWELL,
LUCY STONE

Source: "A Marriage under Protest," *New York Times,* May 4, 1855. Reprinted and Introduction in Langley, Winston E., and Vivian C. Fox, eds. *Women's Rights in the United States: A Documentary History.* Santa Barbara, CA: Greenwood, 1994.

Writings on Women's Education (1856–1857), Sarah Josepha Hale

Sarah Josepha Hale edited and wrote for the popular women's magazine Godey's Ladies Journal *in the early 19th century, later supporting herself and her five children by writing and becoming the editor of* Godey's Lady's Book. *The following statements give insight into her arguments for improved female education.*

What Is Needed in America

Thanks to the spirit of Christian freedom, women in our land are favored above the sex in any other nation. The absurd and degrading customs or usages of the common law, and the partial and, therefore, unjust statutes of kings, brought by our forefathers from England, are fast passing away, or being rendered nugatory by new enactments, more in accordance with reason and righteousness. The Homestead laws, and the security given that the property of a married woman shall remain in her own possession, are great safeguards of domestic comfort. The efforts made to open new channels of industry and profitable professions for those women who have to support themselves are deserving of much praise; but one great act of public justice yet remains undone. Government, national or State, has never yet provided suitably for the education of women. Girls, as well as boys, have the advantages of the free school system; but no public provision has been made, no college or university endowed where young women may have similar advantages of instruction now open to young men in every State of the Union. True, there are very many private institutions devoted to female education; but these are defective for the want of a higher model than private enterprise has yet given. Of course, the better woman is educated the higher she will be estimated, and the more careful will legislators be to frame laws just and equitable which are to guard her happiness and protect her rights; men will thus improve their own *hearts* and elevate their views. The standard of woman is the moral thermometer of the nation.

Holding these sentiments, our "Book" has never swerved from its straight forward course of aiding women to improve themselves, while it has aimed to arouse public sentiment to help onward this improvement. For this, we give patterns and directions for feminine employment, we show the benefits of female education, and for this we have *twice* brought before congress our petition for aid; and now we come a *third* time, intending to persevere till some noble champion arises to advocate the cause and win the victory:—

Source: Hale, Sarah J. "Editor's Table." *Godey's Lady's Book.* January, 1855.

Memorial

To the Honourable Senate and House of Representatives in Congress assembled.

Whereas, there are now more than two millions of children in our country destitute of the opportunity of education, demanding sixty thousand *teachers* to supply them at the same ratio as is common in our best educated sections, your memorialists beg to call your attention to these considerations:—

1. That, while the great West, California, and the wide ocean invite young men to wealth and adventure, and while the labors of the school-room offer so little recompense or honor, the sixty thousand teachers needed cannot be obtained from their ranks; and, therefore, the young women of our country must become teachers of the common schools, or these must be given up.

2. That the reports of common school education show that women are the *best* teachers, and that in those States where education is most prosperous the average of female teachers to that of the other sex is as *five* to *one*.

3. That while, as a general rule, women are not expected to support families, nor to pay from their earnings to support the State, they can afford to teach for a smaller compensation than men; and, therefore, funds bestowed to educate female teachers gratuitously will in the end prove a measure of *economy*, and at the same time will tend to render education more universal and more elevated by securing the best class of teachers at a moderate expense.

4. That those most willing to teach are chiefly found in the industrial class, which as yet has received few favors from National or State Legislatures.

5. That providing for such gratuitous advantages for women to act as educators will secure a vast number of well-educated teachers, not by instituting a class of *celibates*, but by employing the unoccupied energies of thousands of young women from their school-days to the period of marriage, while, at the same time, they will thus be qualifying themselves for the most arduous duties of their future domestic relations.

In view of these considerations, your memorialists petition that THREE OR FOUR MILLIONS OF ACRES OF THE PUBLIC NATIONAL DOMAINS be set apart to endow at least one *Normal School* in every State for the gratuitous educations of female teachers.

These institutions could be modelled and managed in each State to suit the wishes of its inhabitants; and young ladies of every section would be trained as instructors for children in their own vicinity; this would be found of immense advantage in the States where schools have hitherto been neglected.

While such vast portions of the national domains are devoted to national aggrandizements or physical advantages, we humbly petition that a moderate share may be conferred to benefit the daughters of our Republic, and thus at the same time to provide educators for two millions of its most neglected children.

Source: Sarah J. "Editor's Table." *Godey's Lady's Book.* July, 1855.

On Women and Medical Knowledge

TWELVE REASONS why more attention should be given to the more general diffusion of physiological and hygienic knowledge among the present and prospective mothers of our country; and why ladies should be educated for the practice of medicine among their own sex and children:—

1. Because to the mother is consigned the physical, as well as the moral training of infancy, childhood, and youth; hence she becomes the natural guardian of the health of the household.

2. Because the education of woman is not generally conducted with regard to her natural position as wife and mother.

3. Because to a want of correct information in reference to the laws of life and health may much the greater part of infantile suffering and early mortality be attributed.

4. Because the mother, when properly instructed, may early detect the approach of serious or perhaps fatal diseases and, by a judicious interference, avert, or so modify the threatened attack, as to render it harmless, and shorten its duration.

5. Because, by the observance of the laws of health, of which mothers, unfortunately, seldom have an expansive and philosophical comprehension, a corresponding degree of health and physical development would be attained by their offspring.

6. Because nowhere so the beauty and excellence of the feminine character stand out more prominently than in the sick-room.

7. Because to those philanthropic, Christian ladies, whose sense of duty calls them to labor in the cause of foreign missions, a medical education will be of inestimable value. As healers of the sick, they can be admitted to the harems of the east, which are inaccessible to the Christian *man;* and, while they administer to the physical necessities of the sick, a most fitting opportunity will be afforded for administering the consolations of our

holy religion; and through their own women can the light of Gospel truths be made to shine upon the benighted minds of the other sex. A missionary woman, thus qualified, combines two essential elements of usefulness and success; she goes forth both a moral and religious instructor, and a scientific physician.

8. Because, from her quickness of perception, activity of mind, readiness to receive instructions, and the facility with which she applies what she learns to the practical purposes of life, woman is preeminently qualified to study the healing art to advantage and effect.

9. Because, from the very intuitions of her sex, her natural kindness and sympathy, her peculiar adaptation to the necessities of the sick, her patience, perseverance, and endurance in scenes of affliction, she is admirably suited to the *practice* of medicine, particularly in its more delicate departments.

10. Because she has already *demonstrated,* by her eminent success in practicing the healing-art in these departments, her peculiar fitness for this highly important vocation.

11. Because it opens an appropriate avenue for employment both honorable and profitable for women.

12. Because thoroughly educated female physicians can relieve and remove sufferings of a vast and increasing number of the most delicate and refined of their own sex, many of whom, from an instinctive sense of propriety, too often endure their tortures even unto death, rather than submit to the necessary treatment by the male physician.

Source: Hale, Sara J. "Editor's Table." *Godey's Lady's Book.* February, 1857.

Commonwealth v. Fogerty (1857)

The law has attempted to reinforce the right to one's own body as a right by making unconsented sexual intercourse a crime—the crime of rape. However, in early American law, a husband, even if he engaged in sexual intercourse with his wife "against her will," could not be held guilty of rape. The case that follows represents an attempt to exploit that exception in an indictment (a written statement formally charging one with a crime). Although the court disagreed with the complaining party, it did affirm that during a trial (as distinct from a

mere statement charging one with a crime), a man would have a valid defense to the charge of rape by proving that he was the husband of the victim.

G. *M. Stearns,* for the defendants.

1. In order to constitute this offence, the carnal knowledge must be had "by force" as well as "against the will" of the woman . . .

It is therefore necessary to allege the act in the words of the statute, or in equivalent words . . .

The words "with force and arms" in the indictment, if they could be applied to the allegation of ravishment (which they cannot, as it is a separate traversable allegation), would only show that force was a concomitant, not that it was the means of accomplishment of the act. An act may be done "violently," and yet not accomplished "by force."

2. A man cannot commit a rape on his own wife. . . . It is therefore necessary to allege, as in the case of adultery, that the woman was not the wife of the defendant; because the facts alleged may be true, and yet no crime committed . . .

Bigelow, J. The indictment in the present case is in conformity with well established precedents. It sufficiently sets forth all the elements necessary to constitute the offence of rape. It alleges that the carnal knowledge was had "violently," which means by violence, and was against the consent of the prosecutrix. The word "ravished"—*rapuit*—of itself imports the use of force, and, when coupled with the allegation that the act was done against the consent of the woman, technically charges the crime of rape, which is the carnal knowledge of a woman by force and against her will . . .

Of course, it would always be competent for a party indicted to show, in defence of a charge of rape alleged to be actually committed by himself, that the woman on whom it was charged to have been committed was his wife. But it is not necessary to negative the fact in the indictment.

Exceptions overruled.

Source: Commonwealth v. Fogerty, 74 Mass. 489 (1857). Introduction in Winston Langley and Vivian C. Fox, eds. *Women's Rights in the United States: A Documentary History.* Santa Barbara, CA: Greenwood, 1994.

Hair v. Hair (1858)

One area of discrimination faced by married women concerned the right to determine where they would live. The husband had the right to decide the domicile of the family, and the wife was obliged to comply with his decision. Even where the husband and wife had made an explicit agreement to the contrary, as in Hair v. Hair, *the court ruled that such an agreement bore no weight in face of the superior right of the husband.*

The plaintiff charges in her bill that her husband, the defendant . . . before the solemnization of their nuptials, entered into a solemn engagement, that if she would marry him, he would never remove her, without her consent, from the neighborhood of her mother, or to a place where she could not enjoy her mother's society, and that of her friends. On this condition she married him, as she says. Her mother (Mrs. Matheney) also obtained from him (as it is charged) a similar promise, as the condition of her assent to the marriage. The marriage was celebrated on the 13th October, 1853. From that time the young pair lived with the plaintiff's mother until the 9th December, 1854, during which period, the plaintiff bore to her husband a daughter, who is the only issue of the marriage. At the last mentioned date, the defendant, with his wife and child, went to live at a place which he had bought, about a half mile distant from that of his mother-in-law, where, as the plaintiff herself says, they "lived in comfort, peace, and harmony, up to the twenty-seventh day of September, 1857."

This statement appears to be in strict conformity with the truth, except as relates to some immoralities on his part which had come to her knowledge, and which were condoned on her part by their subsequent cohabitation. After the plaintiff and defendant had gone to live at their own home, he became restless and dissatisfied, and anxious to remove to Louisiana, to which State some of his near relatives had emigrated. His land was poor, and he wished, as he says in his answer, to better his condition, by moving to a country where lands were fertile and cheap. But his wife was unwilling to go, positively refused, and pleaded his solemn engagement and promise made previous to their marriage . . .

They had frequent and intemperate altercations on the subject, he insisting that she should accompany him in his move to the west, and she pertinaciously refusing and declaring that she never would leave the place near her mother's, where she then lived. Perceiving that he could make no impression upon her mind, nor effect any change of her will, he announced to her his determination to go without her, unless she should choose to accompany him. She said he might go and leave her, provided he would leave her the negroes (three in number, the only ones he had, which he had acquired by his marriage with her.) She says in her bill that he consented

to this arrangement about leaving the negroes. In his answer he denies it, and there is no further proof. Under these circumstances, and at this stage of the controversy, he commenced making preparations for his departure. He rented his land, sold his crop in the field, some hogs, & c., with the view of raising the necessary funds.

Whether his preparations were made secretly, as charged in the bill, or not, he did not communicate to her the fact that he was making his preparation, nor his design then to go. She had no reason to believe that he was going at that particular time. It took her by surprise. In fact, it would seem that she did not believe that he would go at all, unless she consented to accompany him. Having completed his preparations, on Sunday, the 27th September, 1857, about the hour of midnight, he called his two negro women to the field, under the pretence of driving out the hogs, but, in fact, with the view of securing and carrying them off. He seized them both. They made a great outcry, which reached the ear of the plaintiff at the house. The negroes were unwilling to go; one of them (Hager) made her escape, the other one (Ann) he tied, went to the house and got her young child. He put them both in a conveyance which he had ready, carried them to Black-ville, where he put them on the cars that same night, and carried them off to Louisiana, where they yet remain. The plaintiff continued to reside, and still resides, at the same house . . .

On the eleventh day after the defendant's departure, the plaintiff filed this bill, setting forth the facts that have been recited, and praying an injunction to restrain him from disturbing her in the possession of the property in her possession, or from selling or disposing of the same, until some adequate provision shall be made by the defendant, under the order of this Court, for the support of the plaintiff and her child.

The defendant, on learning that his wife had filed a bill against him for alimony, immediately returned to South Carolina, filed his answer, and has submitted himself to the judgment of the Court. On his return the defendant visited his wife, and made earnest overtures to her to accompany him to his new home in the Parish of Bienville, in Louisiana, promising to treat her with the kindness and affection due to her as his wife. These overtures were rejected by her with firmness and with passionate disdain . . . She intimated that she would live with him if he would come back to the place which he had left. She said she would not go with him to the west to save his life, and that she intended to live and die where she was. The defendant, in his answer, iterates his proposals to take his wife and child with him to his home in the west, and to provide for them to the best of his ability.

These are the undisputed facts of the case, and the question for the court to decide is, whether under these circumstances, the plaintiff is entitled to a decree for alimony. The circuit decree allowed her claim for alimony, and ordered a reference. But we are of opinion, that the decree cannot be sustained upon the principles which prevail in this Court on the subject . . .

. . . In . . . South Carolina, alimony is granted for bodily injury inflicted or threatened and impending . . . Alimony is also granted in South Carolina for the desertion of the wife by the husband. To these may be added a third class of cases, in which, though the husband has inflicted or threatened no bodily injury upon the wife, yet practices such obscene and revolting indecencies in the family circle, and so outrages all the sentiments of delicacy and refinement characteristic of the sex, that a modest and pure minded woman would find these grievances more dreadful and intolerable to be borne, than the most cruel inflictions upon her person, she would be held justifiable in fleeing from the polluting presence of that monster, with whom in an evil hour she had united her destinies . . .

Except in cases embraced within the three classes above commented on, I am not aware that a suit for alimony has been sustained in South Carolina. The plaintiff has sought to bring her case within the principles of the second class. She charges desertion . . .

The question is, whether the plaintiff has made out a case of desertion. That the defendant left her and removed to another State, is beyond controversy, and not denied. But did he leave her in an unjustifiable manner? Her own declarations in her bill shew that he most earnestly solicited her for years, to accompany him. His solicitations amounted to importunity. At length, upon her persistent, I may well say, obstinate refusal, he went alone—without his wife and child. Certainly the husband, by our laws, is lord of his own household, and sole arbiter on the question as to where himself and family shall reside. But she complains that before the marriage he entered into a solemn engagement, without which, the marriage would never have been solemnized, that he would not take her away from the immediate neighborhood of her mother without her consent.

This promise, she says, was also made to her mother, without which, her assent would have been withheld. The defendant, in his answer, denies these allegations. But the evidence brings the charges home to him. My opinion is that he made the promises in the manner charged in the bill. But they created a moral obligation only . . . The contract of matrimony has its well understood and its well defined legal duties, relations and obligations, and it is not competent for the parties to interpolate into the marriage compact any condition in abridgment of the husband's lawful authority over her person, or his claim to her obedience . . .

Stripped of all extraneous matters, the simple question is, did the defendant desert his wife, the plaintiff? It must be a legal desertion. It is not every withdrawal of himself by the husband from the society of the wife that constitutes desertion in legal contemplation. The conduct of the wife must be blameless. If she elopes, or commits adultery, or violates or omits to discharge any of the important hymeneal obligations which she has assumed upon herself, the husband may abandon her without providing for her support; and this Court would sustain him in such a course of conduct.

The husband has the right, without the consent of the wife, to establish his domicile in any part of the world, and it is the legal duty of the wife to follow his fortunes, wheresoever he may go. The defendant, in the exercise of his undoubted prerogative, had determined to make his domicile in the Parish of Bienville, in the State of Louisiana, and wished his wife to accompany him. She, preferring the society of her mother and her relatives, refused to go—in opposition to his wishes, his importunate solicitations, his earnest entreaties. Considering the relative duties and obligations of husband and wife, as defined by the law, who, under these circumstances, is guilty of desertion? The wife, assuredly.

What I have said would constitute a sufficient ground for refusing the prayer of the bill. Yet, there is another additional and sufficient ground of defence on the part of the husband. Within a very short period after the filing of the bill, he returned to the State, for the purpose, I must believe of inviting his wife to his new home, which he had established in the west. He twice visited her for this purpose. To these invitations, she gave a stern, angry, and insulting refusal.

To the Court, in his answer, he renews these overtures, and offers to receive his wife in his new home, and to treat her with conjugal affection and tenderness. Under these circumstances the Court could not give alimony, even if he was wrong in the beginning. Though alimony has been decreed, if the husband makes a bona fide offer to take back the wife whom he has deserted, and to treat her with conjugal kindness and affection, and the wife refuses, on application by the husband, the Court will, if satisfied of the sincerity of the husband's offers, rescind the decree for alimony . . .

It is ordered and decreed, that the Circuit decree be reversed, and that the bill [for alimony] be dismissed.

Source: Hair v. Hair, 10 Rich. 172 (1858). Introduction in Winston Langley and Vivian C. Fox, eds. *Women's Rights in the United States: A Documentary History*. Santa Barbara, CA: Greenwood, 1994.

Incidents in the Life of a Slave Girl (1861), Harriet Jacobs

This slave narrative, published by Harriet Jacobs in 1861, gives readers insight into the life of a slave, her experiences, and her decisions as she struggled to gain freedom for herself and her family. The work highlights the brutal existence of female slaves, in particular, as they faced sexual abuse, harsh treatment from masters and mistresses, and the taking away and sale of their children.

I had entered my sixteenth year, and every day it became more apparent that my presence was intolerable to Mrs. Flint. Angry words frequently passed between her and her husband. He had never punished me himself, and he would not allow any body else to punish me. In that respect, she was never satisfied; but, in her angry moods, no terms were too vile for her to bestow upon me. Yet I, whom she detested so bitterly, had far more pity for her than he had, whose duty it was to make her life happy. I never wronged her, or wished to wrong her; and one word of kindness from her would have brought me to her feet.

After repeated quarrels between the doctor and his wife, he announced his intention to take his youngest daughter, then four years old, to sleep in his apartment. It was necessary that a servant should sleep in the same room, to be on hand if the child stirred. I was selected for that office, and informed for what purpose that arrangement had been made. By managing to keep within sight of people, as much as possible during the day time, I had hitherto succeeded in eluding my master, though a razor was often held to my throat to force me to change this line of policy. At night I slept by the side of my great aunt, where I felt safe. He was too prudent to come into her room. She was an old woman, and had been in the family many years. Moreover, as a married man, and a professional man, he deemed it necessary to save appearances in some degree. But he resolved to remove the obstacle in the way of his scheme; and he thought he had planned it so that he should evade suspicion. He was well aware how much I prized my refuge by the side of my old aunt, and he determined to dispossess me of it. The first night the doctor had the little child in his room alone. The next morning, I was ordered to take my station as nurse the following night. A kind Providence interposed in my favor. During the day Mrs. Flint heard of this new arrangement, and a storm followed. I rejoiced to hear it rage.

After a while my mistress sent for me to come to her room. Her first question was, "Did you know you were to sleep in the doctor's room?"

"Yes, ma'am."

"Who told you?"

"My master."

"Will you answer truly all the questions I ask?"

"Yes, ma'am."

"Tell me, then, as you hope to be forgiven, are you innocent of what I have accused you?"

"I am."

She handed me a Bible, and said, "Lay your hand on your heart, kiss this holy book, and swear before God that you tell me the truth."

I took the oath she required, and I did it with a clear conscience.

"You have taken God's holy word to testify your innocence," said she. "If you have deceived me, beware! Now take this stool, sit down, look me directly in the face, and tell me all that has passed between your master and you."

I did as she ordered. As I went on with my account her color changed frequently, she wept, and sometimes groaned. She spoke in tones so sad, that I was touched by her grief. The tears came to my eyes; but I was soon convinced that her emotions arose from anger and wounded pride. She felt that her marriage vows were desecrated, her dignity insulted, but she had no compassion for the poor victim of her husband's perfidy. She pitied herself as a martyr; but she was incapable of feeling for the condition of shame and misery in which her unfortunate, helpless slave was placed.

Yet perhaps she had some touch of feeling for me; for when the conference was ended, she spoke kindly, and promised to protect me. I should have been much comforted by this assurance if I could have had confidence in it; but my experiences in slavery had filled me with distrust. She was not a very refined woman, and had not much control over her passions. I was an object of her jealousy, and, consequently, of her hatred; and I knew I could not expect kindness or confidence from her under the circumstances in which I was placed. I could not blame her. Slave-holders' wives feel as other women would under similar circumstances. The fire of her temper kindled from small sparks, and now the flame became so intense that the doctor was obliged to give up his intended arrangement.

I knew I had ignited the torch, and I expected to suffer for it afterwards; but I felt too thankful to my mistress for the timely aid she rendered me to care much about that. She now took me to sleep in a room adjoining her own. There I was an object of her especial care, though not of her especial comfort, for she spent many a sleepless night to watch over me. Sometimes I woke up, and found her bending over me. At other times she whispered in my ear, as though it was her husband who was speaking to me, and listened to hear what I would answer. If she startled me, on such occasions, she would glide stealthily away; and the next morning she would tell me I had been talking in my sleep, and ask who I was talking to. At last, I began to be fearful for my life. It had been often threatened; and you can imagine, better than I can describe, what an unpleasant sensation it must produce to wake up in the dead of night and find a jealous woman bending over you. Terrible as this experience was, I had fears that it would give place to one more terrible.

My mistress grew weary of her vigils; they did not prove satisfactory. She changed her tactics. She now tried the trick of accusing my master of crime, in my presence, and gave my name as the author of the accusation. To my utter astonishment, he replied, "I don't believe it; but if she did acknowledge it, you tortured her into exposing me." Tortured into exposing him! Truly, Satan had no difficulty in distinguishing the color of his soul! I understood his object in making this false representation. It was to show me that I gained nothing by seeking the protection of my mistress; that the power was still all in his own hands. I pitied Mrs. Flint. She was a second wife, many years the junior of her husband; and the hoary-headed miscreant was enough to try the patience of a wiser and better woman. She was completely foiled, and knew not how to proceed. She would gladly have had me flogged for my supposed false oath; but, as I have already stated, the doctor never allowed any one to whip me. The old sinner was politic. The application of the lash might have led to remarks that would have exposed him in the eyes of his children and grandchildren. How often did I rejoice that I lived in a town where all the inhabitants knew each other! If I had been on a remote plantation, or lost among the multitude of a crowded city, I should not be a living woman at this day.

The secrets of slavery are concealed like those of the Inquisition. My master was, to my knowledge, the father of eleven slaves. But did the mothers dare to tell who was the father of their children? Did the other slaves dare to allude to it, except in whispers among themselves? No, indeed! They knew too well the terrible consequences.

___

Source: Jacobs, Harriet A. *Incidents in the Life of a Slave Girl. Written by Herself.* Ed. Lydia Maria Francis Child. Boston, MA: Author, 1861.

Address on Behalf of the New York Divorce Bill (1861), Elizabeth Cady Stanton

Beginning in the early 1850s, feminists such as Elizabeth Cady Stanton, Susan B. Anthony, and Lucy Stone argued that marriages that degrade women should be allowed to end. But antebellum America was scandalized by divorce, believing that it would ruin family life, promote free love, and encourage social chaos. In particular, Stanton recognized the inconsistency between a wife's elevated social status and the humiliation she experienced in marriage. When New York State introduced a divorce bill in 1860 similar to the one passed in Indiana in 1859, which expanded the grounds for divorce to include habitual drunkenness, Stanton spoke on its behalf, addressing her remarks to the Judiciary Committee of the New York Senate on February 8, 1861.

Gentlemen of the Judiciary—In speaking to you, gentlemen, on such delicate subjects as marriage and divorce, in the revision of laws which are found in your statute books, I must use the language I find there.

May I not, without the charge of indelicacy, speak in a mixed assembly of Christian men and women, of wrongs which my daughter may tomorrow suffer in your courts, where there is no woman's heart to pity, and no woman's presence to protect?

I come not before you, gentlemen, at this time, to plead simply the importance of divorce in cases specified in your bill, but the justice of an entire revision of your whole code of laws on marriage and divorce. . . . If civilly and politically man must stand supreme, let us at least be equals in our nearest and most sacred relations . . .

The contract of marriage is by no means equal. From Coke down to Kent, who can cite one law under the marriage contract where woman has the advantage? The law permits the girl to marry at twelve years of age, while it requires several more years of experience on the part of the boy. In entering this compact, the *man* gives up nothing that he before possessed; he is a *man* still: while the legal existence of the woman is suspended during marriage and is known but in and through the husband.

She is nameless, purseless, childless; though a woman, an heiress, and a mother . . .

The laws on divorce are quite as unequal as those on marriage; yes, far more so. The advantages seem to be all on one side, and the penalties on the other. In case of divorce, if the husband be the guilty party he still retains a greater part of the property! If the wife be the guilty party she goes out of the partnership penniless . . . In New York and some other states the wife of the guilty husband can now sue for a divorce in her own name, and the costs come out of the husband's estate; but in a majority of the states she is still compelled to sue in the name of another, as she has no means of paying costs, even though she may have brought her thousands into the partnership . . . Many jurists, . . . "are of opinion that the adultery of the husband ought not be noticed or made subject to the same animadversions as that of the wife, because it is not evidence of such entire depravity, nor equally injurious in its effects upon the morals and good order and happiness of domestic life." . . .

There can be no heaven without love; and nothing is sacred in the family and home, but just so far as it is built up and anchored in purity and peace. Our newspapers teem with startling accounts of husbands and wives having shot or poisoned each other, or committed suicide, choosing death rather than the indissoluble tie, and still worse, the living death of faithless men and women, from the first families in the land, dragged from the privacy of home into the public prints and courts, with all the painful details of sad, false lives.

Now, do you believe, honorable gentlemen, that all these wretched matches were made in heaven? That all these sad, miserable people are bound together by God? But, say you, does not separation cover all these difficulties? No one objects to separation, when parties are so disposed.

. . . Now, if a noble girl of seventeen marries, and is unfortunate in her choice, because the cruelty of her husband compels separation, in her dreary isolation, would you drive her to a nunnery, and shall she be a nun indeed? She, innocent child, perchance the victim of a father's pride, or a mother's ambition . . . Henceforth, do you doom this fair young being . . . to a joyless, loveless, solitude? By your present laws you say, though separated, she is married still; indissolubly bound to one she never loved; by whom she was never wooed or won; but by false guardians sold. And now, no matter though in the coming time her soul should for the first time wake to love, and one of God's own noblemen should echo back her choice, the gushing fountains of her young affections must be stayed. Because some man still lives who once called her wife, no other man may give her his love; and

if she love not the tyrant to whom she is legally bound, she shall not love at all . . .

What do our present divorce laws amount to? Those who wish to evade them have only to go into another state to accomplish what they desire. If any of our innocent children trembling with fear fly to the corners and dark places of the house, to hide from the wrath of drunken, brutal fathers, but forgetting their past sufferings rush out again at their mother's frantic screams, "Help! oh, help!" Beyond the agonies of those young hearts as they see the only being on earth they love, dragged about the room by the hair of her head, kicked and pounded and left half dead and bleeding on the floor! Call that sacred, where fathers like these have the power and legal right to hand down their natures to other beings, to curse other generations with such moral deformity and death! . . .

Fathers! do you say, let your daughters pay a life-long penalty for one unfortunate step? How could they, on the threshold of life, full of joy and hope, believing all things to be as they seemed on the surface, judge of the dark windings of the human soul? How could they foresee that the young man, today so noble, so generous, would in a few short years be transformed into a cowardly, mean tyrant or a foul-mouthed, bloated drunkard? What father could rest at his home by night, knowing that his lovely daughter was at the mercy of a strong man, drunk with wine and passion, and that, do what he might, he was backed up by law and public sentiment? The best interests of the individual, the family, the state, the nation, cry out against these legalized marriages of force and endurance.

Say you, these are but the opinions of men? On what else, I ask, are the hundreds of women depending who this hour demand in our courts a release from burdensome contracts? Are not these delicate matters left wholly to the discretion of the courts? Are not young women, from our first families, dragged into your public courts—into assemblies of men exclusively? The judges all men, the jurors all men! No true woman there to shield them by her presence from gross and impertinent questionings, to pity their misfortunes or to protect against their wrongs! The administration of justice depends far more on the opinions of eminent jurists than on law alone, for law is powerless when at variance with public sentiments . . .

If marriage is a human institution, about which man may legislate, it seems but just that he should treat this branch of his legislation with the same common sense that he applies to all others. If it is a mere legal contract, then it should be subject to the restraints and privileges of all other contracts. A contract, to be valid in law, must be formed between parties of mature age, with an honest intention in said parties to do what they agree. The least concealment, fraud or intention to deceive, if proved, annuls the contract . . . But in marriage, no matter how much fraud and deception are practiced, nor how cruelly one or both parties have been misled; no matter how young or inexperienced or thoughtless the parties, nor how unequal their condition and position in life, the contract cannot be annulled. Think of a husband telling a young and trusting girl, but one short month his wife, that he married her for her money; that those letters, so precious to her, that she read and re-read, and kissed and cherished, were written by another; that their splendid home, of which, on their wedding day, her father gave to him the deed, is already in the hands of his creditors; that she must give up the elegance and luxury that now surround her, unless she can draw fresh supplies of money to meet their wants . . .

Thus far, we have had the man-marriage, and nothing more. From the beginning, man has had the whole and sole regulation of the matter. He has spoken in Scripture, and he has spoken in law. As an individual, he has decided the time and cause for putting away a wife; and as a judge and legislator he still holds the entire control.

Source: Address of Elizabeth Cady Stanton on the Divorce Bill Before the Judiciary Committee of the New York State Senate in the Assembly Chamber, February 8, 1861 (Albany, 1861). Introduction in Winston Langley and Vivian C. Fox, eds. *Women's Rights in the United States: A Documentary History.* Santa Barbara, CA: Greenwood, 1994.

Female Soldiers Discovered during the Civil War (1861)

At least several hundred women dressed as men to fight as members of the Union or Confederate army. In many instances, women were able to shield their sex by binding breasts, smoking tobacco, dressing appropriately, and otherwise acting masculine. For many women, their ability to pass for men ended when medics and soldiers had to tend to their war wounds. Early in the war, before the creation of the so-called colored units, some African Americans tried to pass for white to enlist in the Union army. The following article discusses the discovery of a black woman passing for a white man and reveals 19th-century attitudes about race and gender.

The Female Sold-Uier

Our readers may remember the case of Jasper, a correspondent of the Daily *Times*, driven from Charleston awhile ago; and his wonderful escape, under many disguises, may not be quite forgotten yet. If Jasper's story was true—and we sincerely hope that it was—he is certainly one of the seven wonders of the world; but alas for human fame! He has been thrown completely in the shade by a more recent discovery.

An exchange, published somewhere in the country, fills of a column with this sublime statement:

A slave woman has been discovered in one of the Ohio regiments. She was discharged.

That is all. Clear, quiet, and simple in language, thrilling in meaning, and totally incomprehensible of understanding, we present it to our readers just as we find it. Our eyes do not deceive us.

A black woman has passed herself off as a white soldier. Shade of Jasper! What a metamorphosis. Was she whitewashed? Did she "paint an inch thick" to come "to that complexion?" How did she pass the medical examination unsuspected? What was her object? Did she wear a beard? The more questions we ask, the more profound our mystification grows. Is it an enigma, a conundrum? What-Is-It? We give it up. But, if this sort of thing is prevalent, what regiment is safe from these female Ethiopian Jaspers? How do we know that our army, which we have loved and esteemed so much, is not largely composed of negro wenches! Can anybody swear that Brigadier-General Pierce is not a colored maiden in disguise? If he is, let him also be discharged and speedily.

Seriously, it doesn't seem likely that this can be a very common case. Jasper's was not, and Munchausen's adventures were unique. Let us hope that the Ohio regiment is the only one in whose ranks a Chloe or a Phyllis has found even a temporary asylum, and let us rejoice that in that case "she was discharged." It is probable that McAron's army alone boasts of an organization of "light quadroons;" and that we can put down a rebellion better than by Putting it Down in Black and White.

Source: Vanity Fair 4, no. 81 (July 13, 1861): 16. Reprinted and Introduction in Frank, Lisa Tendrich. *Women in the American Civil War.* Santa Barbara, CA: ABC-CLIO, 2007.

A Northern Newspaper Supports Butler's Woman Order (1862)

Major General Benjamin F. Butler's Woman Order shocked many Southerners for its willingness to treat defiant Confederate women not only as the enemy, but also as prostitutes. The policy seemed to betray the standards of treatment typically reserved for female civilians under occupation. As a result, many Southerners began to refer to the Union leader as Beast Butler. The Woman Order surprised some Northerners as well. In the following article, Vanity Fair *declares its support for the order and for Butler.*

Our Chief Butler

The bottled spirits of New Orleans are finding themselves in a tight place now that the BUTLER has taken to looking after them himself. Neither the Crescent nor the Cross have found the slightest favor from that stern chief, who has promptly suppressed both of them—the one represented by a newspaper, the other by the "ladies" of the city, if not of the town. BUTLER is not the man to stand any nonsense; and it is now well understood at New Orleans that ladies who contort their faces in defiance of Union soldiers, must serve out a term of imprisonment in a place called the "Calaboose." This may be considered by some as an aboose of the authority vested in General BUTLER's hands, but that depends upon what you call aboose. It may be remarked that as there are no cellars at New Orleans, our BUTLER must find himself rather astray there; but people will do well to remember that the Port of that city was never in better order than it has been since it came into his keeping.

Source: Vanity Fair *5, no. 128 (June 7, 1862): 272; Reprinted and Introduction in Frank, Lisa Tendrich.* Women in the American Civil War. *Santa Barbara, CA: ABC-CLIO, 2007.*

Women in Richmond Participate in Bread Riot (1863)

In the spring of 1863, hundreds of women across the South took to the streets to protest the price of bread and other necessities. These rioters were primarily poor white women who were frustrated that they were making sacrifices for the Confederacy while their government ignored their immediate needs. Rather than expressions of disloyalty or Unionism, the riots were in fact public statements that called on the Confederate government for assistance and an end to policies that magnified their economic troubles. In the following excerpt, the New York Herald *details the upheaval in Richmond, the largest of the bread riots. Similar uprisings took place in North Carolina, Georgia, Alabama, and elsewhere across the South.*

A refugee from Richmond, who left that city on Tuesday, gives an interesting account of the riot of the 2d inst [April 2].

Considerable excitement had prevailed for some time in consequence of the exorbitant prices, and rumors of a popular movement had been in circulation for several days. Females had begged in the streets and at the stores until begging did no good, and many had been driven to robbery to sustain life. On the morning of the 2d inst a large meeting, composed principally of the wives and daughters of the working classes, was held in the African church, and a committee appointed to wait upon the Governor to request that articles of food should be sold at government rates. After the passage of sundry resolutions the meeting adjourned, and the committee proceeded to wait upon Governor Letcher. The functionary declined to take any steps in the matter, and upon urging the case the ladies were peremptorily ordered to withdraw. The result of the interview was soon made public, when a body of females, numbering about three hundred, collected together and commenced helping themselves to bread, flour, meat, articles of clothing, &c. The entire city was at once thrown into consternation.

Stores were closed, the windows barred, doors bolted, and every precaution taken against forcible entries; but hatchets and axes in the hands of women rendered desperate by hunger made quick work, and building after building was rapidly broken open. The destruction commenced on Carey street, above Fifteenth street, and was becoming general in that section of the city, when the City Guard, with fixed bayonets, arrived at the scene of operations. A few individuals attempted to resist the women, but without success. One man who struck a female was wounded in the shoulder by a shot from a revolver, and the threatening attitude of those armed with hatchets, &c. intimidated others from attempting force. The Mayor soon appeared, and, mounting a stool on the sidewalk, proceeded to read the Riot Act. During the reading of that document a portion of the crowd suspended operations; but no soon had the Mayor concluded than the seizure of provisions commence again more vigorously than before. At this juncture an attempt was made to arrest the more violent; but the party immediately scattered, and, entering Main street, resumed operations.

Gov. Letcher then appeared, and, mounting a vehicle in the centre of the street, addressed the throng, characterizing the demonstration as a disgrace and a stigma upon the city, and announcing that but five minutes would be given them in which to disperse. If in that time the order was not complied with, the troops would be called upon to act. Again the crowd broke up, and in a few moments burst into the stores of Franklin street, But little damage was done here, however, and the riot finally subsided; but not until after the arrest of about forty of the women, and the promise of the Governor to relieve the wants of the destitute. A large amount of bread and bacon was carried off, and all engaged in the riot succeeded in getting a good supply of provisions. Steps have been taken to provide for the immediate wants of some of the families; but great suffering still prevails and is daily increasing. Another uprising is feared, and precautionary measures for its suppression have been instituted; but great uneasiness is felt throughout the city, and merchants are adding to the strength of doors and shutters in every possible manner.

The effect of this riot upon the troops about Richmond was very demoralizing. The authorities are much exercised over it, and the greatest vigilance is enjoined upon the police force. The leading men of the city attempted to circulate the report that the women were "Irish and Yankee hags," endeavoring to mislead the public concerning the amount of loyal sentiment in the city, miserably failed. The fact of their destitution and respectability was too palpable, and the authorities are forced to admit the conclusion that starvation alone incited the movement.

Troops are being hurried up from Richmond to Fredericksburg. There is still a large force in the vicinity of Richmond; but these, it is believed, are about to leave for the Rappahannock.

Fortifications are being thrown up on the Rapidan river, and the force in that section is being augmented. No work is going on upon the defenses about Richmond. Two gunboats (iron clads) are afloat in James river. The Virginia Vessel has been trying to get below the obstructions, and now lies near Drury Bluff. The third is unfinished, but is rapidly approaching completion. The iron works are worked to their utmost in the manufacture of munitions of war; but the iron is of miserable quality, and many of their projectiles contain pieces of stone.

The railroads have almost entirely given out, and no material is to be had for their repair. Great despondency prevails, and the events of the next three months are awaited with most absorbing anxiety.

Source: New York Herald (April 2, 1863). Reprinted and Introduction in: Frank, Lisa Tendrich. Women in the American Civil War. Santa Barbara, CA: ABC-CLIO, 2007.

National Women's Loyal League Petitions to End Slavery (1863)

In 1863, Elizabeth Cady Stanton and Susan B. Anthony called for a constitutional amendment to end slavery in the United States. The amendment would extend the recent Emancipation Proclamation to include slaves living within the Union as well as preclude future slavery in the United States. The National Women's Loyal League organized the petition drive and called on local affiliates to gather a million signatures and support for the cause. The group disbanded with the passage of the Thirteenth Amendment. The following article from The Liberator *explains the rationale and importance of the movement and petition.*

A Noble Enterprise

We have been remiss in not earlier calling the attention of our readers to the great work undertaken by the Women's Loyal League of New York, at their meeting last May. They then formed an organization, of which Mrs. E. C. Stanton is President, and Miss Susan B. Anthony Secretary, for the purpose, first, of procuring a *million signatures* to a petition to Congress, for the emancipation by law of all the slaves in the country. This petition; drawn up by Hon. Robert Dale Owen, and already signed by thousands of men and women in all parts of the land, is printed to-day at the head of our columns, and will remain there until the meeting of Congress, for the convenience of our readers who may wish to sign or circulate it. It is a petition that few of the loyal people of the North can refuse to sign; for if it be objected that Congress has no power to pass such an act, and if this objection be well founded (which we deny), then of course "the earliest practicable day" will be after such changes have been made in the Constitution as will allow such a law to be passed.

Certainly, there can be few *loyal* men in the North, who do not earnestly pray for the emancipation of the slaves at the "earliest practicable day," since Reverdy Johnson, the Maryland lawyer, has just declared that to be his prayer. This petition, then, if Congress decide the matter to be out of its jurisdiction, will serve as an indication of the popular wish for such action in other ways as shall bring about the same result. Therefore all who honestly prefer Freedom to Slavery can and ought to sign it.

Miss Anthony, the efficient Secretary of the League, which is extending itself over the whole North and West, is now in Boston, making arrangements for the circulation of the petition throughout New England, where, as yet, few signatures have been procured. We commend her and her enterprise to the assistance of our readers, and of all friends of the Union and of Freedom. It will be seen by the following pledge, adopted by the League last May, how broad is the basis of principles on which it is proposed to operate:—

We, the Undersigned, Women of the United States, agree to become members of the Women's Loyal National League; hereby pledging our most earnest influence in support of the Government, in its prosecution of the War for Freedom, and for the restoration of the National Unity.

God speed these patriotic women in their labor of love!—*Commonwealth*

The Loyal Women's Petition

Subscription papers were sometime since sent to several ladies in this city, with the request that they would interest themselves in procuring signatures. We do not know what has been done in the matter, but presume not much, as we have heard of no plan of systematic action being adopted; and without some systematic method, such a work cannot be properly accomplished.

Mr. Willits, of Mercer County, has lately undertaken to set the ball in motion in this and adjoining counties, and is devoting himself to the cause. In some places, he calls public meetings, at which the people are stirred up to the importance of the subject, and committees appointed to canvass towns and neighborhoods for the signatures of all women who wish to hasten the day of universal emancipation for our slavery-cursed country—and there are few women who do not. In other places, he finds individuals who volunteer to go out independently, and canvass for signatures.

There is another petition, similar to the foregoing, for subscription by men. They will generally be circulated together, and it is hoped the men will not fall behind the women in the number of their signatures, but that a full million at least of them will be sent into Congress, to plead for the regeneration of our country.

This is the most important petition that was ever circulated for signatures, and we hope the means will be adopted to insure its presentation to every woman in the North. We have no doubt but a million of names, and more, will be obtained if proper exertions are made; and we have very little doubt but Congress will pass the act thus petitioned for before its adjournment next summer. We hope Mr. Willits will find ready co-operators here, and wherever he goes in the good work of making

arrangements for the circulation of the petition.—*Galesburg Free Democrat*

Source: "A Noble Enterprise," *The Liberator* 33, no. 42 (October 16, 1863): 167. Reprinted and Introduction in Frank, Lisa Tendrich. *Women in the American Civil War.* Santa Barbara, CA: ABC-CLIO, 2007.

Support for Female Physicians (1867), Ann Preston

This letter from Ann Preston, a doctor, Quaker, antislavery and women's rights supporter, pioneer in women's medical education, and the first dean of the Female Medical College, makes a plea for supporting female physicians.

[To] *Editor,* Medical and Surgical Reporter:
I have read with surprise the preamble and resolution adopted by the Philadelphia County Medical Society, and published in the *Medical and Surgical Reporter* of the 6th ult., in reference to the status of women-physicians; and as a subscriber to the *Reporter,* and one personally interested in the bearing of that decision, I trust I may be permitted, through the same channel, to examine the arguments which support the resolution . . .

The "very grave objections to women taking on themselves the heavy duties and responsibilities of the profession" appear to be based, in the *first* place, upon the assumption that they do not possess the "ability to bear up under the bodily and mental strain to which they would be unceasingly subjected in this new vocation;" in the *second,* upon the presumed incompatibility of professional practice with the best home influence of the woman and the duties of the mother; in the *third* place, upon the collision and practical difficulties that might arise if different members of the same family should two physician—a man and a woman; and *lastly,* the objections are made upon the ground of the equivocal effect of medical consultations upon the modesty and delicacy of feeling of those who may thus meet; and also upon the fact, that "in no other country but our own is a body of women authorized to engage in the general practice of medicine."

In regard to the *first* difficulty, few words need be expended. Pausing merely to allude to the fact, that in barbarous communities woman is pre-eminently the laborious drudge, and that in civilized society she is the *nurse,* keeping her unceasing vigils not only by the cradle of infancy, but by every bed of sickness and suffering, with a power of sustained endurance that man does not claim to possess; that her life is as long, and her power of surmounting its painful vicissitudes not inferior to his, we come to the open, undeniable fact, that women *do* practice medicine, that they *are* able to "bear up under the bodily and mental strain" that this practice imposes, and that "natural obstacles" have not obstructed their way.

There are in this city women who have been engaged in the practice of medicine a dozen years, who to-day have more vigor and power of endurance than they possessed in the beginning of their career; and the fact of "their delicate organization and predominance of the nervous system," combined with their "trained self-command," is the very reason that in some cases their counsel has been preferred to that of the more robust man.

The *second* objection, bearing upon the home influence of woman, has certainly another side.

Probably more than half the women of this city and country are under the stern necessity of supporting themselves by their own exertions. Some mothers leave their young children day by day and go out to labor, in order to be able to bring them bread at night; others sew away their strength for the pittance which barely keeps famine from their doors, and, exhausted with their labors, they are indeed not in "a fit frame of mind to interchange endearment with their beloved little ones;" nor can they, even with the price of life itself, surround them with the home influence and comforts needful to their healthful and harmonious development.

If the woman who has studied medicine should be surrounded by a family of young children, we should surely regard it as a misfortune if the same overpowering necessity should compel her to follow an active practice during the period that these heavy maternal claims were pressing upon her; although even then, her duties would be less exhausting, and her time less continuously occupied than are hers who supports her family by sewing or washing . . .

The *third* objection, in regard to collisions and "heartburnings," could scarcely apply to high-toned physicians who know what belongs to the properties of their position. The danger would seem to be equally imminent if the medical advisers were both of the same sex, and yet we all know it is quite common in this city for more than one practitioner to attend the different members of the same family—one

being preferred for his supposed skill in one class of cases, another for his superior reputation in another class; and we have yet to learn that injurious results follow this proximity of practitioners.

The natural tendency would seem to be, to foster care and research; and if mutual observation of the results of treatment should occasionally suggest improved methods and break up old, sluggish routine in either party, the profession and the community will surely be gainers by this mutual stimulus.

The objection upon the ground of the invasion of delicacy in examining questions of disease and treatment is indeed an astonishing one, to come from a body of scientific and right-minded physicians. Who are the patients treated by these men? Often women—the sensitive and refined. The whole nature of the malady must be investigated and the means of recovery enforced. If, as frequently happens, to save the shrinking sensitiveness of the young woman, some tender experienced mother or elder friend informs the physician of the symptoms and conveys to the patient his conclusions, she, for the time, performs the part of the attending physician in reference to the consulting one; yet who will dare assert that her womanly modesty is compromised, or that "the delicate reserve with which" a man "is accustomed to address woman in the sick-room" is injuriously affected by this necessary and humane intervention?

. . . But leaving these special points, there are broad, general grounds upon which, as physicians and as women, we stand, and appeal from the resolution of the Philadelphia County Society to the better judgment of true-hearted professional men.

When once it is admitted that women have souls, and that they are accountable to God for the uses of the powers which He has given them, then the exercise of their own judgment and conscience in reference to these uses, becomes a thing which they cannot, rightfully, yield to any human tribunal.

As responsible beings, who must abide by the consequences of our course for time and for eternity, we have decided for ourselves that the study and practice of medicine are proper, womanly, and adapted to our mental, moral, and physical constitution.

We will scarcely be charged with presumption in supposing that our instincts may be as pure, our intuitions as clear, our sense of what is right and fitting for ourselves as reliable, as are those of the men who condemn our course . . .

That we have not had the facilities for acquiring medical information is a charge that, it seem to us, should hardly come from those who have systematically closed hospitals and colleges against our applications for admission, and who have endeavored to prevent the members of their fraternity from assisting us in our struggle for knowledge.

That we have stemmed this tide of opposition, and found opportunities for obtaining medical instruction—some in other cities and across the ocean, some by persevering and long-continued efforts in various sways at home; that we have found noble men in the profession to assist us, and that we have been able to found hospitals and open various channels for practical education—*is due to the inherent vitality of our cause,* and its strong hold upon the sympathies and convictions of the community.

That we have not yet all the facilities for instruction that are needed, we are fully aware.

That "there are female graduates who are a disgrace to the medical profession," we also know too well; for the sake of humanity we would that we could truly add, that the graduates who disgrace the profession are found *only* among women!

From the nature of the relation of physicians to society, not more than one man in hundreds follows medicine as a profession, and the proportion of women, under the most favoring circumstances, will probably not be greater; but the systematic training, and the knowledge of physiological functions and hygienic conditions involved in a thorough medical education for the few, will, we believe, be reflected in many homes, and be one of the means of radically changing that mistaken plan of education, and those destructive social customs and habits, which are now undermining the health, and darkening the lives of so many of the women of this country . . .

But on behalf of a little band of true-hearted young women who are just entering the profession, and from whose pathway we fain would see annoyances and impediments removed, we must protest, in the sacred name of our common humanity, against the injustice which places difficulties in our way,—not because we are ignorant, or pretentious, or incompetent, or unmindful of the code of medical or Christian ethics, but because we are women.

Philadelphia, April 22, 1867

ANN PRESTON, M.D.

Source: "Preamble and Resolution of the Philadelphia County Medical Society upon the Status of Women Physicians with a Reply by a Woman." Philadelphia: Stuchey, 1867, pamphlet.